An Introduction to
MICROECONOMICS
SECOND EDITION

Paul Wonnacott
University of Maryland

Ronald Wonnacott
University of Western Ontario

McGraw-Hill Book Company

New York St. Louis San Francisco Auckland Bogotá Hamburg
Johannesburg London Madrid Mexico Montreal New Delhi
Panama Paris São Paulo Singapore Sydney Tokyo Toronto

Library of Congress Cataloging in Publication Data

Wonnacott, Paul.
    An introduction to microeconomics.

    "This book includes chapters 1 to 6 and 19 to 37
of Economics"—Verso of t.p.
    Includes index.
    1. Microeconomics.   I. Wonnacott, Ronald J.
II. Title.
HB172.W692   1982   338.5   81-20909
ISBN 0-07-071583-1   AACR2

AN INTRODUCTION TO MICROECONOMICS

    4 5 6 7 8 9 0   DODO   8 9 8 7 6 5 4 3

ISBN 0-07-071583-1

See Photo Credits on pages 543-544.
Copyrights included on this page by reference.

This book was set in Souvenir Light by Black Dot, Inc. (ECU).
The editors were Bonnie E. Lieberman, Michael Elia, and Edwin Hanson;
the designer was Anne Canevari Green;
the production supervisor was Dominick Petrellese.
New technical drawings were done by J & R Services, Inc.;
part opening drawings were done by Anne Canevari Green.
The cover was designed by Merrill Haber;
the cover illustration was done by Bob Shein.
R. R. Donnelley & Sons Company was printer and binder.

To the memory of
Jacob Viner and Alvin Hansen
teachers and scholars extraordinary

Contents

MICROECONOMICS

9 Costs and Perfectly Competitive Supply 162

10 Perfect Competition and Economic Efficiency 191

PART THREE
MICROECONOMICS: HOW INCOME IS DISTRIBUTED

21 Natural Resources, Conservation, and Growth 434

22 Energy 447

Preface

Economics is like the music of Mozart. On one level, it holds great simplicity: Its basic ideas can be quickly grasped by those who first encounter it. On the other hand, below the surface there are fascinating subtleties that remain a challenge even to those who spend a lifetime in its study. We therefore hold out this promise. In this introductory study, you will learn a great deal about how the economy works—the simple principles governing economic life that must be recognized by those in government and business who make policy decisions. At the same time, we can also guarantee that you won't be able to master it all. You should be left with an appreciation of the difficult and challenging problems of economics that remain unsolved.

Perhaps some day you will contribute to their solution.

HOW TO USE THIS BOOK

We have tried to design this book to make the basic propositions of economics as easy as possible to grasp. Key steps in the argument are emphasized with boldface type, and definitions are printed in red. These highlights should be studied carefully during the first reading, and during later review. (A glossary is provided at the back of the book, containing a list of definitions of terms used in this book plus other common economics terms that you may encounter in class or in readings.) The basic arguments of each chapter are summarized in the Key Points at the end of the chapter, and the new concepts introduced in the chapter are also listed.

When you read a chapter for the first time, don't worry about what is in the boxes. This material is optional; it is set aside from the text to keep the main argument as simple and straightforward as possible. (Several types of material are presented in the boxes. Some boxes provide levity or color—for example, Kurt Vonnegut's tale in Box 23-3 of the Handicapper-General whose aim is to ensure that people will not only start out equal but also finish that way. Other boxes present detailed theoretical explanations; they are not needed to grasp the main argument.) If you want to glance at the boxes that are fun and easy to read, fine. But when you first read a chapter, don't worry about those that contain more difficult material. On the first reading, you may also skip starred (*) sections of the text, along with the footnotes and appendixes; these also tend to be more difficult. Come back to them later, after you have mastered the basic ideas. And listen to your instructor, who will tell you which of the boxes and starred sections are most important for your course.

Economics is not a spectator sport. You can't learn just from observation; you must work at it. When you have finished reading a chapter, work on the problems listed at the end; they are designed to reinforce your understanding of important concepts. [The starred (*) problems are either based on material in a box, or are more difficult questions designed to provide a challenge to students who want to do more advanced work.] Because each chapter builds on preceding ones, and because the solution to some of the problems depends on those that come before, remember this important rule: Don't fall behind in a problem-solving course. To help you keep up, we recommend Peter Howitt's *Study Guide* (second edition), which is designed specially to assist you in working through each chapter. It should be available in your bookstore.

TO THE INSTRUCTOR

In the second edition, there are two new chapters:

Chapter 13, on regulation. When is regulation in the interests of the firms being regulated, and when is it not? Was there too much regulation during the 1970s? Is there a risk of an overreaction? May there be too little regulation during the 1980s?

Chapter 22, on energy. This chapter studies energy policy, in the light of the conflict between efficiency and equity. In the face of the rapid escalation of international oil prices, similar rises in the prices of domestic oil and its products were desirable from the viewpoint of efficiency. But it was generally considered unfair to allow domestic oil prices to skyrocket, and thus provide oil producers with a bonanza at the expense of consumers. Consequently, a complex price control system was used during the 1970s. And the decontrol of oil prices was accompanied by a windfall profits tax. This chapter also discusses alternative sources of energy, including the environmental problems with some sources. (Oil prices appear not only in this chapter, but are also a recurring topic in this second edition.)

As we have added new material, we have continued to aim at the three major objectives we set in the first edition. The first two objectives grew out of questions that arose in our teaching—and out of our uneasiness regarding the answers.

For macroeconomics, covered in a companion volume, *An Introduction to Macroeconomics,* the principal question was this: After studying introductory economics, are students able to understand public controversies over such topics as the level of government spending and taxation, the desirability of wage and price controls, and monetary policies? Are we training our students to understand the front pages of the newspaper? For many years, the introductory course was aimed at teaching students how policy should be run; that is, at providing a cookbook of "right" answers. While many books express more doubts and qualifications than was the case a decade ago, our course is focused even more strongly in this direction, as we build up to the seven controversial questions dealt with in the chapters of Part 3: Is fiscal or monetary policy the key to aggregate demand? How can inflation exist at the same time as a high rate of unemployment? How does the economy adjust to inflation, and what are the temporary and the lasting effects of inflation? To what extent should we attempt to "fine tune" the economy? Why is the economy unstable? Why have productivity and growth been so disappointing in recent years? Should exchange rates be fixed or flexible?

While there are no simple, indisputably "correct" answers to these questions, we believe that the major issues can be presented clearly to beginning economics students, thereby providing them with an understanding of important, recurring public debates over macroeconomic policy.

For microeconomics—in this volume—the question was this: Does the introductory study of microeconomics lack coherence? To the student, does microeconomics tend to become just one thing after another—a guided tour through the economist's workshop, introducing as many polished pieces of analytic machinery as possible for later use in more advanced courses? Most students do not continue to advanced economics courses. For them, there is little point in concentrating on analytic techniques for their own sake, when time could be spent studying interesting policy issues instead. Even for those who do continue in economics, we doubt that it is useful to focus so heavily on analytic techniques. True, such a focus gives students some head start in their later courses; but it also increases the risk that they will be bored by repetition, and will miss some of the forest while concentrating on the trees. Therefore, we follow a simple rule of thumb: In introducing analytical concepts, we focus on those most useful in studying policy questions.

At the same time, we have been able to go some distance in accommodating users' requests for additional analytic material. For example, we now introduce the chapter on costs and supply with the production function, showing how a firm uses it to calculate its costs curves as a step in finding its profit-maximizing output (Chapter 9). We believe that the economist's distinction between the long run and the short run is clarified by the presentation of the long-run production function (Table 9-5), and the short-run production function as a row within this table. (A discussion of production isoquants is provided in the Appendix to Chapter 9.) A new box in Chapter 9 describes the equilibrium of the firm using total cost and total revenue curves; but the emphasis in this chapter remains on marginal cost and marginal revenue. In addition, we now emphasize the importance of entry in determining the long-run supply curve, and the long-run response of a competitive market to changes in demand. (We now also emphasize the importance of labor mobility in Chapter 18.)

In the second edition, as in the first, we have attempted to make microeconomics more interesting by organizing our discussion around two continuing themes: **efficiency** and **equity**. In Part 2, our focus is on efficiency, and we accordingly emphasize marginal curves: For efficiency, equating marginal cost and marginal benefit is the key. And the study of marginal curves leads naturally to consumer surplus and producer surplus, which are building blocks for the study of income distribution and equity in Part 3.

In recent years, the topic of equity has increased in importance. At least until the beginning of the Reagan administration, the government has been redistributing an increasing percentage of income as our national income has grown. The discussion of income redistribution leads us to one of the most interesting—but discouraging—recent developments in microeconomics. For years, many economists regarded the negative income tax as a way of resolving the equity/efficiency conflict. However, extensive experimental evidence from Seattle and Denver has led observers to be far less optimistic—as we explain in Chapter 24.

The second edition also describes developments in the theory of public choice (Chapter 15). We consider the problem of the oppressive majority; logrolling (when it is in conflict with the public interest, and when it may actually promote it); and the theory of bureaus—why, in a world in which private monopolies may employ too few resources, public monopolies may employ too many.

Other new or greatly expanded topics in the second edition include Robert Coase's theory of property rights; the many roles of a union in addition to bargaining for higher wages; a more subtle and extensive discussion of the labor bargaining process and the reasons that strikes occur; and an expanded discussion of rent. (In Chapter 20, we now explicitly consider two reasons for rent: First, there may be differences in the productivity and incomes of factors in their present occupations; second, there may be differences in their productivity and incomes in their best alternative occupations—that is, there may be differences in their opportunity costs. Other introductory books typically examine one or the other source of rent, but not both.)

LOOKING AHEAD

Because we have attempted to make the discussion build up in orderly steps, we recommend that teachers look ahead to later passages before introducing certain subjects. Specifically:

We recommend that instructors who wish to teach indifference curves read not only the first indifference curve appendix (in Chapter 8), but also the second (in Chapter 10) before introducing this topic to their classes. In the second appendix, we consider a topic not found frequently in elementary tests; namely, how indifference curves can be used to illustrate the way in which a perfectly competitive economy results in an efficient allocation of resources. Students find this an interesting topic. And this use of indifference curves fits directly into our emphasis on efficiency throughout Part 2 of this book.

The central theme of Part 2—economic efficiency—is laid out in Chapter 10. In order to prepare the groundwork for this chapter, we would recommend that instructors read it before beginning to teach Chapters 7, 8, and 9.

OTHER POINTS OF INTEREST

Finally, we draw your attention to a number of ways in which our treatment differs from that of many competing books.

● In emphasizing efficiency and the gains from specialization, we have given greater attention to economies of scale than is frequently the case. In Chapters 3 and 16, economies of scale are given billing almost equal to comparative advantage. In our opinion, economies of scale are an important source of gain from specialization, and they should not be avoided because of the difficult analytic prob-

lems to which they lead. (Most of the analytic problems can be avoided in an introductory text.)

● We place more than usual emphasis on externalities—both negative (Chapter 14) and positive (Chapter 15).

● Because of our emphasis on major themes and problems, our discussion of international economics is organized differently than in most books. The gains from trade and the effects of protection fit into the topic of efficiency, and therefore they are included in Part 2 (Chapters 16 and 17). But exchange rate arrangements are most closely related to such issues as inflation and unemployment, and they are therefore included in the macroeconomic volume. By keeping international topics next to related domestic topics, we hope to counteract the neglect of international economics in many introductory courses.

● Students are introduced to the important idea of dynamic efficiency. Any detailed analysis of dynamic efficiency has traditionally been regarded as too difficult for an elementary course. Initially we sympathized with this view, until we discovered that most beginning students *can* handle a problem like the most efficient pattern of resource use over time (optional Box 21-3).

● We show how conflicts can exist not only between objectives (such as equity and efficiency), but also between groups of people in the economy. For example: The theory of comparative advantage illustrates how foreign trade can increase a nation's real income. We go one step further, to emphasize how trade affects various groups differently. Low-cost imports benefit consumers, but they hurt competing domestic producers. It is easy for students to identify such winners and losers. They thereby can appreciate the irony of complaints about agricultural price supports from business executives who benefit from tariffs that prop up the prices of the goods *they* produce. Moreover, this identification of different groups (and the differences in their political power) helps the student to answer one of the basic questions raised by the theory of public choice: Why is there a difference between what the government *should* do, and what it *does* do?

We wish to thank. . .

In developing this second edition, we have shamelessly accumulated intellectual debts to our colleagues and coworkers. Special thanks go to the editing and production staffs of McGraw-Hill. In particular we should like to thank our editor, Mike Elia. We remain in debt to those who helped in the development of the first edition, particularly Lloyd C. Atkinson of the Congressional Budget Office, Heidemarie C. Sherman and Allen R. Thompson of the University of New Hampshire, and Frank D. Tinari of Seton Hall University. The great many suggestions we received during the preparation of the second edition are acknowledged on the following pages. To all, we express our deepest thanks.

Paul Wonnacott
Ronald Wonnacott

Acknowledgments

Carol Adams
University of California, Santa Cruz

Clopper Almon
University of Maryland

Richard Anderson
Texas A&M University

Martin Bailey
University of Maryland

Anthony Barkume
California State University

Robert Barry
College of William & Mary

Peter Barth
University of Connecticut

Ray Battalio
Texas A&M University

Marion Beaumont
California State University, Long Beach

Deepak Bhattasali
Boston University

John Bishop
University of Wisconsin

Vin Blankenship
U.S. Department of Agriculture

Ake Blomqvist
University of Western Ontario

Ed Corcoran
Community College of Philadelphia

Richard Du Boff
Bryn Mawr College

Stanley Duobinis
Shippensburg State College

Mark Frankena
University of Western Ontario

K. K. Fung
Memphis State University

Marshall Goldman
Harvard University

Timothy Greening
Tulane University

R. J. Gunderson
Northern Arizona State University

Knick Harley
University of Western Ontario

Curtis Harvey
University of Kentucky

P. J. Hill
University of Alaska

Catherine Hoffman
University of Idaho

Peter Howitt
University of Western Ontario

Harry Hutchinson
University of Delaware

Phyllis Iseley
Norwich University

John Kagel
Texas A&M University

Robert Kirk
Purdue University at Indianapolis

Marvin Kosters
American Enterprise Institute for Public Policy

Joseph Kreitzer
College of St. Thomas

Ulrich Lachler
University of Maryland

David Laidler
University of Western Ontario

James Mak
University of Hawaii

John George Marcis
Kansas State University

Arthur Martel
Indiana University of Pennsylvania

Forrest McCluer
Bates College

Tapan Monroe
University of Pacific

William Moscoff
San Gamon State University

Dennis Mueller
University of Maryland

Peter Murrell
University of Maryland

John Palmer
University of Western Ontario

Michael Parkin
University of Western Ontario

Jerry Pelovsky
College of the Sequoias

Barry Pfitzner
North Virginia Community College

Bette Polkinghorn
California State University

Thomas Robinson
Clinton County Community College

Samuel Schrager
Villanova University

Michael Shields
Southern Illinois University

Norman Taylor
Franklin and Marshall College

Roswell G. Townsend
Chatham College

Richard Tyson
University of Wisconsin, Stout

Joseph Walker
University of Montevallo

Paul Weinstein
University of Maryland

Arthur Wright
University of Connecticut

Biography

Biography briefs
of four influential economists
Adam Smith
Alfred Marshall
Karl Marx
Lord John Maynard Keynes

Two of the great traditional economists, and . . .

Adam Smith (1723–1790)

Modern economics is often dated from 1776, the year that Adam Smith published his *Inquiry into the Nature and Causes of the Wealth of Nations*. In the same year, the Declaration of Independence was signed in Philadephia. The timing was not entirely a coincidence. The Declaration of Independence proclaimed the freedom of the American colonies from British rule. The *Wealth of Nations* put forth the doctrine of economic freedom.

In his book, Smith argued for economic liberalism—that is, free enterprise within a country and free trade among countries. The government should interfere less in the market place; it should leave people alone to pursue their own self-interest. Smith believed that there is an "invisible hand" that causes the producer to promote the interests of society. Indeed, "by pursuing his own interest he frequently promotes that of society more effectually than when he really intends to promote it." [In advocating laissez faire (French for "leave it alone"), Smith did however recognize that government inter-vention might be desirable in some circumstances; for example, when the nation's defense is at stake.]

Smith was born in 1723, soon after his father died, in the small Scottish seaport of Kirkaldy, where some of the townsfolk still used nails as money. It is said that when he was 4, he was carried off by gypsies, who later abandoned him. One biographer comments: "He would have made, I fear, a poor gypsy."

He remained a bachelor throughout his life. "I am a beau in nothing but my books" was the way he described his lack of appeal for the opposite sex. He suffered from severe absent-mindedness. One biographer describes how Smith, the most illustrious citizen of Edinburgh, would stroll its streets "with his eyes fixed on infinity and his lips moving in silent discourse. Every pace or two he would hesitate as if to change his direction, or even reverse it." In his mannerisms he may have been awkward, but when he picked up a pen, he became a giant; he was one of the foremost philosophers of his age.

His writing caught the eye of Charles Townshend, an amateur economist of great wit but little common sense. (As British Chancellor of the Exchequer, he was responsible for the tea tax that brought on the American Revolution.) When Townshend offered Smith the lucrative job of tutoring his ward, Smith accepted and spent 4 years in Switzerland and France, where he met Voltaire and other leading French philosophers. When the brother of his ward was murdered on a French street, Smith returned to Britain. There, thanks to a pension provided by Townshend, he completed *The Wealth of Nations*.

This was his second and last book. He went into semiretirement, occasionally revising his books and beginning two new ones. But he wrote that "the indolence of old age, tho' I struggle violently against it, I feel coming fast upon me, and whether I shall ever be able to finish either is extremely uncertain." He lost the struggle, dying at the age of 67—but not before he had his two unfinished works burned.

By blending themes developed by other economists and by adding his own contributions, Alfred Marshall became the father of modern microeconomics (the detailed study of how individual goods are produced and priced).

Marshall was born in 1842 in Clapham, then a green suburb of London. His father, a cashier in the Bank of England, was a man of tyrannical disposition who wrote a book called *Man's Rights and Woman's Duties*. As a good Victorian, he exercised strong parental control: He overworked his son, insisted that he prepare himself for the Ministry, and even made him promise not to play chess—"a waste of time." This childhood repression may have left lasting scars: For the rest of his life, Marshall remained fearful of idleness, hypercritical of his own writing, and nervous about his health almost to the point of hypochondria.

Young Marshall did eventually rebel against the father, rejecting the Oxford scholarship he had won to study classics and theology and turning to mathematics instead. This was important to him later in economics: He used diagrams to illustrate economic theory (for which, it is said, some students have never forgiven him). Marshall eventually became a professor at Cambridge, where he reigned over the British economics profession for almost 25 years until his retirement in 1908. He was everyone's idea of a professor—white hair, white mustache, and bright eyes.

Although a man of overflowing ideas, Marshall—like Adam Smith—was in no hurry to rush into print. Just as Smith had burnt his unfinished writing, Marshall threw much of his into the wastebasket. He kept back printed proofs of one book for 15 years before allowing it to be published. Such long delays meant that many of the ideas he had developed and taught years before had become common knowledge by the time they reached the printed page. (Indeed, this makes it difficult for historians to

Alfred Marshall (1842–1924)

sort out exactly what he discovered and what he did not.)

Marshall's masterpiece was his *Principles of Economics*, first published in 1890. One of his concerns was the problem of poverty: "The study of the causes of poverty is the study of the causes of the degradation of a large part of mankind."

The many dimensions of Marshall's genius are perhaps best summarized by this tribute:

> The master-economist must possess a rare combination of gifts. He must be mathematician, historian, statesman, philosopher. . . . He must be purposeful and disinterested . . . ; as aloof and incorruptible as an artist; yet sometimes as near the earth as a politician.

This tribute was written by Marshall's most illustrious student, John Maynard Keynes, who himself achieved such fame that he is described on the following right page.

... two critics who established traditions of their own

Karl Marx (1818–1883)

"Workers of the world unite; you have nothing to lose but your chains." This popular paraphrase of Marx's most famous quote illustrates his passionately held views. In his writings, passages of dry economics are punctuated by emotional outbursts against the existing economic system. Marx is most eloquent when he describes the misery of the working class in England over a century ago. On the other hand, he is least convincing when he predicts that this misery will increase.

Whereas Smith and Marshall believed in free enterprise—with the government intervening only in special circumstances—Karl Marx believed the free enterprise system should, and inevitably would, be replaced by a wholly different system: communism. Under communism the nation's wealth (capital) would be held, not individually, but instead by everyone collectively. *Das Kapital* (or *Capital*, in its English translation) was Marx's most important book; and the *Communist Manifesto* (written with Friederick Engels in 1848, the year when revolutionary fires swept across Europe) is still the most celebrated pamphlet in the history of communism.

Marx was born in 1818 in the city of Trier in the Prussian Rhineland, now part of West Germany. As an undergraduate at the University of Bonn and as a graduate student in Berlin, he became increasingly associated with radical groups; his best friend was jailed for radical activity. (Although Marx in later life had periodic difficulties with the authorities, the only day he ever spent in jail was when he was a student—on a charge of being drunk and disorderly.)

Marx was a man of great contradictions. He remained something of an intellectual recluse, avoiding other economists and sociologists, with whom he might have had much to discuss. Despite his broad intellectual attainments, he was the victim of strange obsessions. (He believed that Lord Palmerston, the British foreign minister, was an agent of the Russians.) He was determined not to let a capitalist society turn him into a "money-making" machine, yet he was willing to live off gifts from Engels, himself a capitalist. Marx was an affectionate father, yet he sacrificed the health of his children because he could seldom bring himself to seek paid employment. (His one steady source of earned income was writing articles for the *New York Herald Tribune*.) Before Engels was able to afford sizable gifts, Marx lived with his family in poverty; once they were evicted and their possessions seized. Several of his children died, "a sacrifice to [capitalist] misery." In one case his wife had to borrow to buy a coffin.

In 1883, broken by the death of his wife and eldest daughter, and having made the remarkable statement that has bewildered his disciples ever since ("I am not a Marxist"), Marx died. He could little realize the influence he would have on history. Today about one-third of the world lives in a communist system, where Marx is revered. In much of the other two-thirds of the world, he is viewed as the most controversial economist who ever lived.

Just as Marshall fathered modern microeconomics, so Keynes became the father of modern macroeconomics (the broad-brush study of the economy "in the large," focusing on overall employment and production). Keynes' great contribution to economics is *The General Theory of Employment, Interest and Money*, published in 1936. This book was eagerly anticipated: Keynes was already famous for his views on a variety of topics, from the gold standard to the 1919 peace treaty imposed on Germany. Moreover, it was widely known that he was writing on the economic problem that concerned people most in the 30s: the worldwide depression, when there were 14 million unemployed in the United States alone.

The General Theory turned out to be a blistering attack on traditional (classical) economists who believed that, with time, unemployment would cure itself. Not so, said Keynes. Unemployment could persist. In such circumstances, the government should step in and increase its spending. Then more goods would be produced, and more people put to work.

In the 19th century, Karl Marx had prophesied the doom of the existing economic system. Keynes recognized that the system had serious flaws, but he believed that it could be reformed. Thus, his views lay somewhere between those of a laissez faire economist like Adam Smith and those of a revolutionary like Karl Marx.

Keynes was born in 1883, the year that Karl Marx died. Keynes' father was an eminent logician and political economist and his mother was a justice of the peace and mayor of Cambridge, England. The intellectual gifts of their son were almost immediately evident; by age 6, young Keynes was trying to figure out how his brain worked. On scholarship at Eton, Keynes blossomed. He grew a mustache, bought a lavender waistcoat, and developed his life-long taste for champagne. Then he went to undergraduate studies at Cambridge, where his brilliance was quickly evident to his teachers, including Alfred Marshall.

Keynes went from success to success. Biog-

John Maynard Keynes (1883–1946)

raphers have speculated that, just as Marx's prophecy of economic doom reflected the privation that marked his personal life, so Keynes's optimistic promotion of solutions reflected a life of accomplishment. At only 28, he became editor of the most prestigious British economic journal, a post he held for most of the rest of his life. He became a teacher at King's College, Cambridge, and a shrewd investor. Under his financial guidance, a small £30,000 King's College fund was expanded by more than ten times. And by applying himself for only half an hour each morning—before he got out of bed—he was able to earn a personal fortune of more than $2 million through speculation on the foreign currency and commodity markets. (But his own personal success did not soften his harsh judgment of the costs to society when the public becomes caught up in a whirlpool of speculation: "When the capital development of a country becomes a by-product of the activities of a casino, the job is likely to be ill-done.")

PART ONE

BASIC ECONOMIC CONCEPTS

CHAPTER 1
Economic Problems and Economic Goals

Economy is the art of making the most out of life.
George Bernard Shaw

Some years ago, a Japanese mass-circulation newspaper, the *Mainichi,* conducted a survey of 4,000 people, asking them what they thought of first when they heard the word *takai* (high). Twelve percent responded, "Mount Fuji." The overwhelming majority—88 percent—said: "Prices." In the United States, an elected president has been defeated at the polls only twice since 1912. In 1932, Herbert Hoover lost by a landslide; the economy was approaching the low point of the Great Depression, with more than one worker in five out of a job. In 1980, Jimmy Carter also lost by a landslide. In that year, the average level of prices paid by American families rose by 12.4 percent. Clearly, we care very much about the problems of unemployment and inflation. And, with the rare exception of the individual who inherits great wealth, most of us spend a large part of our energy in the struggle to make a living.

Economics **is the study of how people make their living, how they acquire the food, shelter, clothing, and other material necessities and comforts of this world. It is a study of the problems they encounter, and of the ways in which these problems can be reduced.**

Under this broad definition, economics addresses a great number of specific questions. To list but a few:

- How are goods produced and exchanged? How do we choose which goods to produce?
- What jobs are available? What do they pay? What skills are needed to get a good job?
- Does it pay to go to college? Why are jobs hard to get at some times, and easy at other times?
- Why are taxes so high?
- Why did we produce so much more in 1981 than our parents produced in 1948?

Economics is a study of success, and it is a study of failure.

ECONOMIC PROGRESS . . .

From the vantage point of our comfortable homes of the late twentieth century, it is easy for us to forget how many people, through history, have been losers in the struggle to make a living. Unvarnished economic history is the story of deprivation, of 80-hour weeks, of child labor—and of starvation. But also, it is the story of the slow climb of civilization toward the goal of relative affluence, where the general public as well as the fortunate few can have a degree of material well-being and leisure.

One of the most notable features of the United States economy has been its growth. Although there have been interruptions and setbacks, economic progress has been remarkable. Figure 1-1 shows one of the standard

3

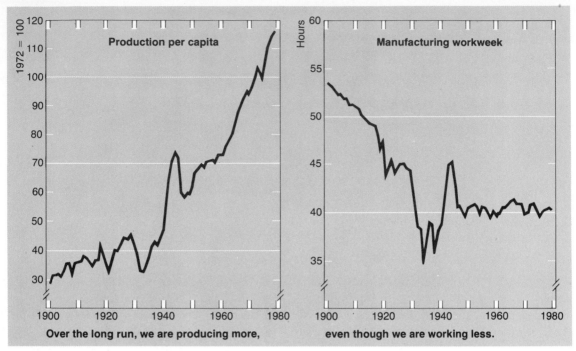

Figure 1-1
Production per person and hours worked
Source: Board of Governors of the Federal Reserve, *1980 Historical Chart Book.*

measures of success—the increase in total production per person. (The precise measure of production in this diagram is *gross national product,* GNP for short, a concept explained in Chapter 7 of our companion volume.) The average American now produces almost twice as much as the average American of 1945, and four times as much as the average American at the turn of the century. And the higher output is produced with less effort: The average workweek has declined about 25 percent during this century. Thus, economic progress in the United States has been reflected both in an increase in the goods and services that we produce and enjoy, and in a greater amount of leisure time.

A similar tale of success has occurred in many other countries, as illustrated in Figure 1-2. Between 1963 and 1979, output grew at an average annual rate of 4.5 percent in France, 3.7 percent in Germany, 4.1 percent in Italy, and 4.7 percent in Canada. Nor has growth been confined to the countries of Europe and North

America. Particularly notable has been the growth of the Japanese economy. From the ashes of the Second World War, Japan has emerged as one of the leading success stories, with output per person that is now greater than Britain.[1] Other tales of success have come from such diverse countries as Brazil and Korea.

[1]The success of the Japanese economy has made that country the subject of good-natured humor. In a speech at Miami University (Ohio), Paul McCracken of the University of Michigan—who served as chairman of the President's Council of Economic Advisers from 1969 to 1971—recalled that on his first trip to Japan in the fifties, he had gone to offer the Japanese advice on growth policy. Added McCracken, "I've been trying to remember ever since what we told them."

There are substantial problems in comparing output per person in various countries. However, careful work indicates that Japan passed Britain about 1970. See Irving B. Kravis and others, *A System of International Comparisons of Gross Product and Purchasing Power,* United Nations International Comparison Project: Phase One (Baltimore: Johns Hopkins University Press, 1975), p. 231.

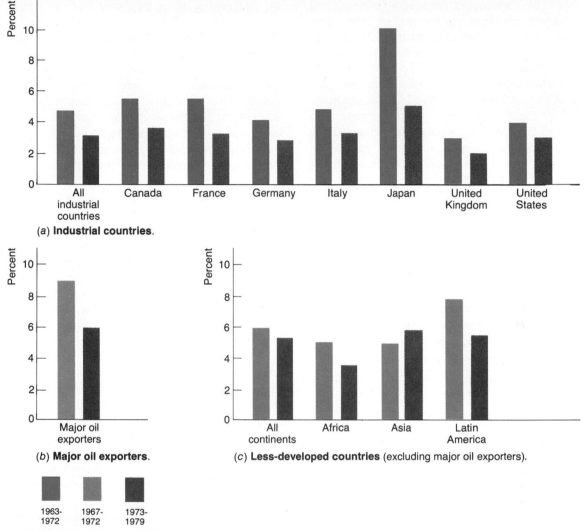

(a) **Industrial countries**.

(b) **Major oil exporters**.

(c) **Less-developed countries** (excluding major oil exporters).

1963-1972   1967-1972   1973-1979

Figure 1-2
Annual rates of increase in output, 1963–1979
Rapid rates of growth have occurred in many countries. Growth was particularly
fast in Japan between 1963 and 1972, when output increased at an average
annual rate of 10 1/2 percent. Note that for most countries, growth has been
much slower since 1973 than during the previous decade (with the less developed
economies of Asia being an exception). This slower growth may be traced in part
to the disruptions caused by the rapid increase in the price of oil.
Source: International Monetary Fund, *Annual Report, 1980,* pp. 8–12.

. . . AND ECONOMIC PROBLEMS

But successful growth, though widespread, has
been neither universal nor automatic. In a number of countries, with India being the most

conspicuous example, the standard of living
remains abysmally low. True, even India has
enjoyed some growth; over the past two decades, output per person has increased by 1.4
percent per year. But progress remains uncer-

tain. The increase in population continuously threatens to outrun the increase in production. The streets of Indian cities such as Calcutta are clogged with the homeless and the destitute.

Furthermore, such very poor countries are doing less well than the less developed countries (LDCs) as a whole.[2] The World Bank (an international institution whose major purpose is to lend to the LDCs) estimates that, between 1970 and 1980, real output per person rose at an average annual rate of only 1.7 percent in the poorest countries, compared to 3.1 percent for the middle-income countries (and a very impressive 5.7 percent for the middle-income countries of East Asia).[3]

Even in the relatively affluent countries, substantial economic problems remain. (See Box 1-1.)[4] For example, we may wonder:

● Why are so many unable to find work, when so much needs to be done?

● Why have prices spiraled upward—to the discomfort of Japanese and U.S. citizens alike?

● Why does the average black in America have a lower income than the average white?

● Are we really going to run out of oil? What will happen if we do?

● Are we really producing the right things? Should we produce more housing and fewer cars? Or more medical services and fewer sports spectaculars?

● Why is pollution such a problem? And what should be done about it?

---

[2]The term "less developed country" is often used to describe countries with substantially lower per capita incomes than the United States, Canada, Japan, and the countries of Western Europe. A common alternative term—"developing countries"—is more diplomatic, but less accurate. (Some of the LDCs are developing rapidly, but some are not. Singapore and Taiwan are growing rapidly. But over the past two decades, output per person has declined in Bangladesh.)

[3]The World Bank, *World Development Report, 1980* (Washington, 1980), pp. 99, 110.

[4]Throughout this book, the boxes present illustrative and supplementary materials. They can be disregarded without losing the main thread of the discussion.

ECONOMICS IS A POLICY STUDY

Why? and *What should be done?* are the two key questions in economics. The ultimate objective of economics is to *develop policies to deal with our problems.* But, before we can formulate policies, we must first make every effort to understand how the economy has worked in the past, and how it works today. Otherwise, well-intentioned policies may go astray and lead to unforeseen and unfortunate consequences.

When economic policies are studied, the center of attention tends to be the policies of the government—policies such as taxation, government spending programs, and the regulation of particular industries, such as electric power and the railroads. But the policies of private businesses are also important. How should they organize production in order to make their goods at the lowest possible cost? What prices should a business charge? When should a supermarket increase the stocks of goods in its warehouse?

The controversial role of government

For more than 200 years, economics has been dominated by a controversy over the proper role of government. In what circumstances should the government take an active role? And when is it best for governments to leave decisions to the private participants in the economy? On this topic, the giants of economics have repeatedly met to do battle.

In 1776, Scottish scholar **Adam Smith** published his pathbreaking book, *An Inquiry into the Nature and Causes of the Wealth of Nations.*[5] Modern economics may be dated from that historic year, which was also notable for the Declaration of Independence. Smith's message was clear. Private markets should be liberated from the tyranny of government control. In pursuit of their private interests, individual producers would make the goods that consumers want. It is not, said Smith, "from the benevolence of the butcher, the brewer, or the baker

---

[5]Available in Modern Library edition (New York: Random House, 1937). Smith's book is commonly referred to as *The Wealth of Nations.*

BOX 1-1

WANTED: INTELLIGENT ECONOMIST, FOR IMMEDIATE SERVICE

EDWARD HEATH (BRITISH PRIME MINISTER, 1970–1974)[†]

LONDON—The world is confronted by five economic factors that it has never before had to face at the same time: high inflation, high unemployment, high interest rates, stagnant production and the continuous increase in the price of the raw material on which all industry is based, namely oil. . . . Never before have we encountered the present combination of factors at the same time. What is to be done about them?

The price of oil has increased from $1.80 a barrel in 1970 to $26 a barrel today,[‡] an escalation of 1,350 percent in 10 years. As a result, this year at least $120 billion are being diverted to members of the Organization of Petroleum Exporting Countries, largely from the developed countries, though the impact on the more fragile economies of the developing countries is more damaging. . . .

In the last five years, many of the developing countries have found themselves unable to cover the increased price of oil by means of larger exports, especially with the industrialized countries in a permanent state of recession and becoming increasingly protectionist. They have been faced with a dilemma: to cut back on other imports or pay for them through incurring more indebtedness. If they chose the former, industrialized countries would have suffered still further,

and their unemployment today would have been three million higher. But developing countries chose the latter—more debt. With what result?

No one in the developing world expected interest rates to rise to such extraordinarily high levels. The combined burden of high oil prices and high interest rates has put in jeopardy the ability of some countries to service their debt. [That is, they find it difficult to pay interest, and to repay the debt as it comes due.] The combined deficit of the developing world for 1980 is now estimated at $72 billion. Where is that amount of money to come from?

The commercial banks . . . have now concluded that in most cases they have reached the limit of the investment in developing countries that they can justify. But if any of the latter were forced to default on their interest payments or loan repayments, it would rebound onto the whole of the Western world's banking system. A collapse would certainly trigger a domino chain of events. There is no time for delay.

To sum up, the industrialized countries have 18 million unemployed; the figure may well be 20 million by this winter. They have $250 billion to $450 billion worth of unused industrial capacity. The developing countries have an incalculable need for our products but their demands are ineffective because they cannot finance them. How can these factors be reconciled?

Intelligent economist desperately needed. He will earn every bit of his keep. ■

†Excerpted from his guest column in *The New York Times,* May 14, 1980, with permission.
‡By early 1981, the price had risen to almost $35.

that we expect our dinner, but from their regard to their own interest." There is an "invisible hand," he wrote, that causes the producer to promote the interests of society. Indeed, "by pursuing his own interest he frequently promotes that of the society more effectually than when he really intends to promote it." In general, said Smith, the government should be cautious in interfering with the operations of the private market. According to Smith, the best policy is **laissez faire**—leave it alone. Government intervention usually makes things worse. For example, government imposition of a tariff is generally harmful. (A **tariff** or **duty** is a tax on a foreign-produced good as it enters the country.) Even though domestic producers may well benefit from a tariff (because it gives them an advantage over the foreign producer), the country as a whole loses. Specifically, a tariff increases the cost of goods available to consumers, and this cost to consumers outweighs the benefits to producers. Smith's work has been refined and modified during the past 200 years, but many of his laissez faire conclusions have stood up remarkably well. For example, there is still a very strong economic argument against high tariffs on imported goods. In recent decades, one of the principal areas of international cooperation has been the negotiation of lower tariffs.

A century and a half after the appearance of Smith's *Wealth of Nations* (that is, during the Great Depression of the 1930s), **John Maynard Keynes** wrote his *General Theory of Employment, Interest and Money* (also known, more simply, as the *General Theory*).[6] In this book, Keynes (which rhymes with Danes) attacked the laissez faire tradition of economics. The government, said Keynes, has the duty to put the unemployed back to work. Of the several ways in which this could be done, one stood out in its simplicity. By building public works, such as roads, post offices, and dams, the government could directly provide jobs, and thus provide a cure for the Depression.

With his proposals for a more active government, Keynes drew the ire of many business executives. They feared that as a result of his recommendations, the government would become larger and larger and private enterprise would gradually be pushed out of the picture. But Keynes did not see this result; in his own way, he was fundamentally conservative. By providing jobs, the government could remove the explosive frustrations caused by the mass unemployment of the 1930s, and could make it possible for Western political and economic institutions to survive. And certainly, when compared with Marx, Keynes was very conservative indeed. (For a brief introduction to Marx and his views, see Box 1-2.)

Thus, Smith and Keynes took apparently contradictory positions—Smith arguing for less government, and Keynes for more.[7] It is possible, of course, that each was right: Perhaps the government should do more in some respects, and less in others. Economic analysis does not lead inevitably either to an activist or a passive position on the part of the government. The economist's rallying cry should not be, "Do something." Rather, it should be, "Think first."

ECONOMIC GOALS

We have already noted that the ultimate goal of economics is to develop better policies to minimize our problems and to maximize the benefits we get from our daily toil. More specifically, there is widespread agreement that we should strive for the following goals:

1 A high level of employment. People willing to work should be able to find jobs reason-

[6](London: Macmillan, 1936.)

[7]Conflicting views over the proper role of government may be found in the works of two retired professors: the University of Chicago's Milton Friedman (for laissez faire) and Harvard's John Kenneth Galbraith (who argues for more government). See John Kenneth Galbraith, *The Affluent Society* (Boston: Houghton-Mifflin, 1958), and Milton Friedman and Rose Friedman, *Free to Choose* (New York: Harcourt Brace Jovanovich, 1980). (We strongly recommend that if you read one of these books, you read them both. Each of the books puts forth a convincing case. But they are flatly contradictory.)

BOX 1-2

Karl Marx

The main text refers to two towering economists—Adam Smith and John Maynard Keynes. In the formation of the intellectual heritage of most American economists, Smith and Keynes have played leading roles. But, if we consider the intellectual heritage of the world as a whole, Karl Marx is probably the most influential economist of all. In the Soviet Union and the People's Republic of China, Marx is more than the source of economic "truth"; he is the Messiah of the state religion.

Many business executives viewed Keynes as a revolutionary because he openly attacked accepted economic opinion and proposed fundamental changes in economic policy. But, by revolutionary standards, Keynes pales beside Marx. No parlor intellectual was Marx. The Marxist call to revolution was shrill and direct: "Workers of the world, unite! You have nothing to lose but your chains."

Why did they have nothing to lose? Because, said Marx, workers are responsible for the production of all goods. Labor is the sole source of value. But workers get only part of the fruits of their labor. A large—and in Marx's view, unearned—share goes to the exploiting class of capitalists. (Capitalists are the owners of factories, machinery, and other equipment.) Marx believed that, by taking up arms and overthrowing capitalism, workers could end exploitation and obtain their rightful rewards.

On our main topic—the role of government—Marx was strangely ambivalent. Who would own the factories and machines once the communist revolution had eliminated the capital-

ist class? Ownership by the state—by all the workers as a group—was the obvious solution. And, in fact, this has been the path taken by countries such as the Soviet Union: The revolution has led to state ownership of the means of production. Yet, Marx also believed that the revolution would eventually lead to the "withering away" of the state. There has been no perceptible sign of this withering away in Marxist societies. ■

ably quickly. Widespread unemployment is demoralizing, and it represents an economic waste: Society forgoes the goods and services that the unemployed could have produced.

2 Price stability. Rapid increases (or decreases) in the average price level should be avoided.

3 Efficiency. When we work, we want to get as much as we reasonably can out of our productive efforts.

4 An equitable distribution of income. When many live in affluence, no group of citizens should suffer stark poverty.

5 Growth. As Figure 1-1 illustrates, the United States economy has grown substantially during the twentieth century. Continuing growth, which would make possible an even higher standard of living in the future, is generally considered an important objective (although this objective has become more controversial during the past decade).

The list is far from complete. Not only do we want to produce more, but we want to do so without the degradation of our environment; the **reduction of pollution** is important. **Economic freedom**—the right of people to choose their own occupations, to enter contracts, and to spend their incomes as they please—is a desirable goal. So, too, is **economic security**—freedom from the fear that chronic illness or other catastrophe will place an individual or a family in a desperate financial situation.

The achievement of our economic goals provides the principal focus of this book. As a background for later chapters, we now look at the major goals in more detail.

1 A high level of employment

The importance of the objective of full employment was illustrated most clearly during the Great Depression of the 1930s, when the United States (and many other countries) conspicuously failed to achieve it. During the sharp contraction of the economy from 1929 to 1933, total output in the United States fell by 30 percent, and spending for new buildings, machinery, and equipment decreased by almost 80 percent. As the economy slid downward, more and more workers were thrown out of jobs; by 1933, one quarter of the labor force was unemployed. (See Figure 1-3.) Long lines of the jobless gathered at factory gates in the hope of work; disappointment was their common fate. Nor was the problem quickly solved. The downward slide into the depths of the Depression went on for a period of 4 years, and the road back to a high level of employment was even longer. It was not until the beginning of the 1940s, when American industry began working around the clock to produce weapons, that many of the unemployed were able to find jobs. There was not a single year during the whole decade 1931–1940 that unemployment averaged less than 14 percent of the labor force.

A *depression* exists when there is a very high rate of unemployment over a long period of time.

Something had clearly gone wrong with the economy—disastrously wrong. Large-scale unemployment involves tremendous waste; time lost in involuntary idleness is gone forever. The costs of unemployment go beyond the loss of output; unemployment involves the dashing of hopes. Those unable to find work suffer frustration and a sense of worthlessness, and their skills are lost as they remain idle.

The term **unemployed** is reserved for those who are willing and able to work, but are unable to find jobs. Thus, those of you who are full-time college students are not included among the unemployed: Your immediate task is to get an education, not a job. Similarly, the 70-year-old retiree is not included in the statistics of the unemployed. Nor are inhabitants in prisons or mental institutions, since they are not available for jobs.

A person is *unemployed* if he or she is available and looking for work, but has not found it.

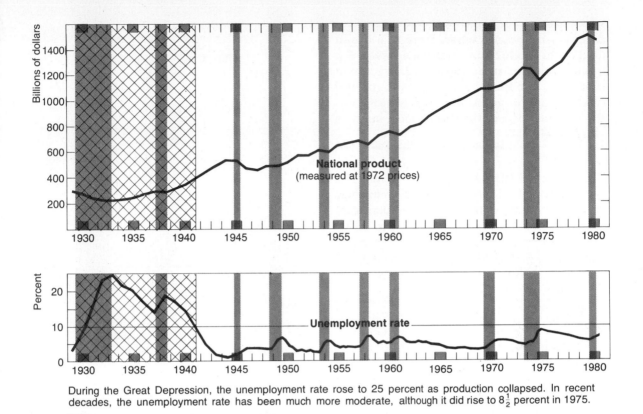

During the Great Depression, the unemployment rate rose to 25 percent as production collapsed. In recent decades, the unemployment rate has been much more moderate, although it did rise to $8\frac{1}{2}$ percent in 1975.

■ Recessions   ◇◇◇ The Great Depression

Figure 1-3
Output and unemployment in the United States, 1929–1981

The unemployment rate is calculated as a percentage of the total labor force—the labor force being the sum of those who are actually employed, plus those who are unemployed. (Labor force and employment statistics are tied to the traditional definition of "jobs." Thus, for example, the mother who stays at home to raise her children is neither "in the labor force" nor "employed," although she certainly *works*.)

At the end of the Second World War, the Great Depression was still a fresh memory. The public, the politician, and the economist shared a common determination that a repeat of the 1930s could not be permitted. This determination was reflected in the ***Employment Act of 1946,*** which stated that:

It is the continuing responsibility of the Federal Government to use all practical means . . . to promote

maximum employment, production, and purchasing power.

Since the end of the Second World War, we have been successful in our determination to prevent a repetition of the unemployment of the 1930s. But the postwar period has not been an unbroken story of success. From time to time, there have been downturns in the economy—much more moderate, it is true, than the slide of 1929 to 1933, but downward movements nonetheless. These more moderate declines, or ***recessions,*** have been accompanied by an increase in the unemployment rate. In 1975, during the worst recession of the past four decades, the unemployment rate averaged 8½ percent. While we have been successful in preventing big depressions, the problem of periodic recessions has not been solved.

A *recession* occurs when there is a broad decline in production, causing a rise in the unemployment rate. (By broad, we mean that the decline involves a substantial fraction of the economy, and is not confined to just one or two industries, such as steel or aircraft.)

2 Stability of the average price level

Unemployment caused the downfall of Herbert Hoover in 1932. *Inflation* was a significant reason for the defeat of Jimmy Carter in 1980.

Inflation is an increase in the average level of prices. (Deflation is a fall in the average level of prices.)

We can see in Figure 1-4 how the average of prices paid by consumers has risen with increasing speed in recent years. In this diagram, note that a *ratio* (or *logarithmic*) scale is used on the vertical axis. On such a scale, equal *percentage* changes show up as equal distances. For example, the distance from 50 to 100 (an increase of 100 percent) is the same as the distance from 100 to 200 (also an increase of 100 percent). In such a diagram, if something grows at a *constant rate* (for example, by 5 percent per year), it shows up as a *straight line.* Thus, by looking for the steepest sections of the curve in Figure 1-4, we can identify the periods when inflation has been most rapid: Prices rose at the most rapid rate after World War I, and for a brief period after World War II. Since 1973, inflation has been unusually severe for peacetime periods. (More detail on how diagrams are drawn is included in the Appendix to Chapter 1 of the Study Guide which accompanies this text.)

While unemployment represents sheer waste—society loses the goods which might have been produced by those out of work—the problem with inflation is less obvious. When a price rises, there is both a gainer and a loser. The loser is the buyer who has to pay more. But there is a gain to the seller, who gets more. On balance, it is not clear whether the society is better or worse off.

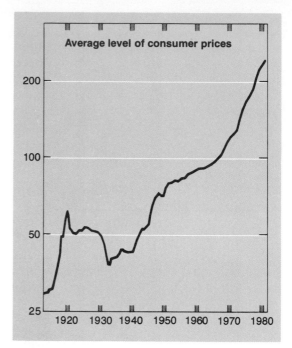

Figure 1-4
Consumer prices
Occasionally prices have fallen—for example, during the early 1930s. In recent decades, however, the trend of prices has been clearly upward. In 1974, and again in 1979 and 1980, the United States suffered from "double-digit" inflation—a rise in the average level of prices by more than 10 percent per year.

It is true, of course, that there is much resentment against inflation. But perhaps at least some of this resentment reflects a peculiarity of human nature. When people find the goods they sell rising in price, they see the increase as perfectly right, normal, and justified. But when they find the goods they *buy* rising in price, they often view the increase as evidence of the seller's greed. When the price of wheat rises, farmers see themselves at last getting a reasonable return from their toil. When the price of oil increases, the oil companies argue that they are getting no more than the return necessary to finance the search for more oil. When the price of books rises, authors feel that they are getting no more than a "just" return for their creative efforts, and book publishers insist that they are no more than adequately compensated for their risks. But when the farmer, the oil company, the author, and the book publisher find that the prices of the goods they *buy* have increased, they believe they have been cheated by inflation. We may all be the victims of an illusion—the illusion that each of us can and should have a rise in the price of what we sell, but that the price of what we buy should remain stable. For the economy as a whole, this is not possible.

This two-sided nature of price increases—a gain to the seller but a loss to the buyer—makes it difficult to evaluate the dangers of inflation. And, indeed, there has been considerable controversy as to whether a low rate of inflation (say, 1 or 2 percent per annum) is dangerous, or whether, on the contrary, it may actually be beneficial to society. (Some say that a small rate of inflation makes it easier for the economy to adjust to changes, and makes it easier to maintain a high level of employment.)

But, when inflation gets beyond a moderate rate, there is widespread agreement that it becomes a menace. It becomes more than a mere transfer of money from the buyer to the seller; it interferes with the production and exchange of goods. This has most clearly been the situation during very rapid inflations, when economic activity was severely disrupted.

Hyperinflation—that is, a skyrocketing of prices at annual rates of 100 percent, 1000 percent, or even more—occurred in the South during our Civil War, in Germany during the early 1920s, and in China during its Civil War in the late 1940s. (Hyperinflations most commonly occur during or soon after a military conflict, when government spending shoots upward.) A hyperinflation means that money rapidly loses its ability to buy goods; people are anxious to spend money as quickly as possible while they can still get something for it.

Clearly, hyperinflation of 100 percent or more per year is an extreme example. But lower rates of inflation, amounting to 10 percent or less per year, can also have serious consequences:

1 Inflation hurts people living on fixed incomes and people who have saved fixed amounts of money for their retirement or for a rainy day (future illness or accident). The couple who put aside $1,000 in 1960 for their retirement have suffered a rude shock: In 1980, $1,000 bought no more than $360 bought in 1960.

2 Inflation can cause business mistakes. For good decisions, businesses need an accurate picture of what is going on. When prices are rising rapidly, the picture becomes obscured and out of focus. Decision-makers cannot see clearly. (For example, business accounting is done in dollar terms. When there is rapid inflation, some businesses may report profits when, on a more accurate calculation, they might actually be suffering losses. Consequently, inflation can temporarily hide problems.) Our economy is complex, and it depends on a continuous flow of accurate information. *Prices are an important link in the information chain.* For example, a high price should provide a signal to producers that consumers are especially anxious to get more of a particular product. But in a severe inflation, producers find it difficult to know whether this is the message, or whether the price of their product is rising simply because all prices are rising. In brief, *a severe inflation obscures the message carried by prices.*

Here, it is important to distinguish between a rise in the **average level of prices** (inflation) and a change in **relative** prices. Even if the average level of prices were perfectly stable (that is, no inflation existed), not all individual prices would be constant. In an ever-changing economy, conditions in specific markets change. For example, new inventions have cut the cost of producing computers, and computer companies have as a result been able to cut prices sharply. At the same time, U.S. energy prices (for oil, gasoline, electricity, etc.) have risen rapidly, in response to the rise in the price of oil we import. The resulting fall in the price of computers relative to the price of oil has performed a useful function: It has encouraged businesses to use more of the relatively cheap computers in their operations, and to conserve on the relatively expensive oil. (This is not, of course, to deny that the rise in the price of oil has been painful, particularly to those living in the colder areas of the country.)

3 Efficiency

This illustration—of how businesses use more computers when they become cheaper—is one example of economic efficiency.

In an economy, both the unemployment rate and the inflation rate may be very low, but performance may still be poor. For example, fully employed workers may be engaged in a lot of wasted motion, and the goods being produced may not be those which are most needed. Obviously, this is not a satisfactory state of affairs.

Efficiency is the goal of getting the most out of our productive efforts.

Under this broad definition, two types of efficiency can be distinguished: **allocative efficiency** and **technical efficiency.**

To illustrate *technical efficiency,* let us consider two bicycle manufacturers. One uses a large number of workers and many machines to produce 1,000 bicycles. The other uses fewer workers and fewer machines to produce the same number of bicycles. The second manufacturer is not a magician; he is simply a better manager. He is technically efficient, whereas the first manufacturer is technically inefficient. [Technical inefficiency exists when the same output could be produced with fewer machines and fewer workers, working at a reasonable pace. (Technical efficiency does not require a sweatshop.) Technical inefficiency involves wasted motion and sloppy management; better management is the solution.]

Allocative efficiency, on the other hand, involves the production of the *best combination of goods,* using the *best combination of inputs.* How much food should we produce, and how many houses? Suppose we produce only food, and do so in a technically efficient way, with no wasted motion. We will still not have achieved the goal of allocative efficiency, because consumers want both food and housing.

Thus, allocative efficiency involves the choice of the right combination of outputs. And it also involves using the right combination of inputs. Consider our earlier illustration: The cost of computers is coming down, while the cost of imported oil is rising. If businesses fail to adjust—and fail to conserve oil and to use computers more—then there is allocative inefficiency.

Relative prices perform a key role in encouraging allocative efficiency: As we have noted, the decrease in the price of computers encourages businesses to use more computers, and less of the other, relatively more expensive inputs.

4 An equitable distribution of income

Ours is an affluent society. Yet many people remain so poor that they have difficulty in buying the basic necessities of life, such as food, clothing, and shelter. In the midst of plenty, some live in dire need. The moral question must then be faced: Should some have so much, while others have so little?

Put this way, the compelling answer must surely be no. Our sense of justice is offended by extreme differences, and compassion requires that assistance be given to those crushed by illness and to those born and raised in cruel deprivation. In the view of the large majority, society has a responsibility to help those at the bottom of the economic ladder.

Our sense of equity, or justice, is offended by extreme differences. Thus, most people think of "equity" as a move toward "equality." But not all the way. The two words are far from synonymous. While there is widespread agreement that the least fortunate should be helped, there is no consensus that the objective of society should be an equal income for all. Some individuals are willing to work overtime; it is generally recognized as both just and desirable for them to have a higher income as a consequence. Otherwise, why should they work longer hours? Similarly, it is generally considered "right" for the hardworking to have a larger share of the pie; after all, they have greatly contributed to the production of the pie in the first place. On the other side, some are loafers. If they were automatically given the same income as everyone else, our sense of equity would be offended: They don't deserve an equal share. (And if incomes were guaranteed equal, how many people would work?)

There is no agreement that we should aim toward complete equality of incomes; the "best" division (or distribution) of income is ill-defined. Much of the discussion of income distribution therefore attempts to answer a relatively narrow question: What is happening to those at the bottom of the ladder? What is happening to the families who live in poverty?

Poverty is hard to define in precise dollar terms. For one thing, everyone's needs are not the same. The sickly have the greatest need for medical care; large families have the most compelling need for food and clothing. Those who live in the city, where the costs of food and shelter are high, need more money for basic necessities than do those who live on the farm, where families can grow some of their own food. There is no simple, single measure of the "poverty line," below which families may be judged to be poor. Reasonable standards may, however, be established by taking into consideration such obvious complications as the number of individuals in a family. The poverty standards defined by the U.S. government are shown in Table 1-1.

Table 1-1
Poverty Standards, 1981
(rounded to nearest $100)

Size of family	Poverty standard	
	Nonfarm	Farm
One person	$4,300	$3,700
Two persons	5,700	4,900
Three persons	7,100	6,000
Four persons	8,500	7,200
Five persons	9,800	8,400
Six persons	11,200	9,500

According to U.S. government standards, families were considered poor in 1981 if their incomes fell below these figures. For example, a three-member family was poor if it lived in a city and its income was less than $7,100.

Source: Department of Labor.

Over the past two decades, the number of poor families has declined—although not at a steady rate. During the long economic expansion of the 1960s, a particularly large number escaped from poverty. During recessions, on the other hand, people tended to slip back into poverty. Thus, a general increase in production may be one of the most effective ways of fighting poverty. In the words of President John Kennedy, "A rising tide lifts all boats." As the general level of income rises throughout the economy, the incomes of those at the lower end will also rise.

But increasing the size of the pie is only one of the ways of dealing with poverty. Another way is to increase the share of the pie going to people with the lowest incomes. Thus, poverty may be combatted by a ***redistribution of income.*** For example, the well-to-do may be taxed in order to finance government programs aimed at helping the poor. An important government objective (particularly in the Great Society programs of President Johnson) has been to raise the share of the nation's income going to the poorest families.

During the fifties and sixties, some progress was made toward that goal. Between 1950 and 1960, the share of the poorest 20 percent of families rose from 4.5 to 4.8 percent of the total "pie" of society. By 1969, it had risen to 5.6 percent. Furthermore, between 1950 and 1969, a "rising tide was lifting all boats." Average family income was rising by about 40 percent (even after adjusting for inflation). The "rising tide" and the changing shares combined to raise the incomes of the poorest fifth of the families by more than 70 percent (again, after adjusting for inflation). Thus, the poorest of 1969 were much better off than the poorest of 1950. Nevertheless, they were still very poor by the overall standards of society.

Since 1969, large government expenditures on antipoverty programs have reduced the numbers living in poverty, but the problem is still far from cured. Why is it so difficult to eliminate poverty? One explanation of why progress has not been more rapid is unemployment: The unemployment rate has been much higher in the

1970s (averaging 7.0 percent from 1975 to 1980) than it was in 1968 and 1969 (3.6 percent). Unemployment adds to the miseries of the poor, and it tends to make incomes less equal. Other possible explanations include the tendency for workers to retire early (at which time they tend to drop into the low-income group), and the tendency for families to divide into more than one group: Young people move out of the parental home more readily than they used to, old people are less likely to live with their children, and more marriages are splitting up. In other words, families tend to split into several smaller units, some of which have very low incomes. Thus, the general rise in income may have enabled Americans to achieve "the luxury of living apart from their relatives."[8]

5 Growth

In an economy with large-scale unemployment, output can be increased by putting the unemployed back to work. But once this is done, there is a limit to the amount that can be produced with the available labor force and the available land, factories, and equipment. To increase output beyond this limit requires either an addition to the available resources (for example, an increase in the number of factories and machines) or an improvement in technology (that is, the invention of new, more productive types of machines or new ways of organizing production). When economists speak of growth, they typically mean an increase in output that results from technological improvement and additional factories, machines, or other resources.

The advantages of growth are obvious. If the economy grows, our incomes will be bigger in the future; we and our children will have higher standards of material comfort. Moreover, as the economy grows, some of the rising production of the economy can be used to benefit the poor. We will be able to provide income to the poorer sections of the population without taking it from the rich. During the early 1960s, growth became a prominent national goal, both because of its economic advantages, and in order to "keep ahead of the Russians."

During the late 1960s and early 1970s, doubts began to develop about the importance of growth as an objective of economic policy. While its advantages are obvious, growth comes at a cost. If we are to grow more rapidly, more of our current efforts will have to be directed toward the production of machines, and away from the production of consumption goods. In the future, of course, as the new machines begin operating, they will turn out more consumption goods—more clothing, radios, or canned food. Thus, current policies to stimulate growth will make possible higher consumption in the future. But, for the moment, consumption will be less. Thus, to evaluate a high-growth policy, we have to compare the advantage of higher *future* consumption with the sacrifice of lower *current* consumption.

Seen in this light, it is not clear that the faster the rate of growth, the better. Why, for example, should I live modestly, just so my children may at some future date live in luxury? The future generations should be considered; but so should the present one.

And, even if we were concerned solely with the welfare of coming generations, it would not be so clear that the more growth, the better. Increasing levels of production use increasing quantities of raw materials. A moderate rate of growth, by making possible a conservation of scarce raw materials, may be in the best interests of future generations.

Furthermore, very rapid rates of growth may harm the environment. If our primary objective is to produce more and more steel and automobiles, we may pay too little heed to the belching smoke of the steel mills, or to the effect of the automobile on the quality of the air which we breathe. Thus, during the 1970s, there was

[8]Alice M. Rivlin, "Income Distribution—Can Economists Help?" *American Economic Review,* May 1975, p. 5. The definition of the family unit makes it difficult to interpret the statistics on income distribution. Yet it is not clear how this problem can be avoided. It makes no sense to look at individuals singly. The 3-month-old baby has zero income, yet it is scarcely poverty-stricken if it lives in the average family. To study poverty, one must look at families—defined somehow.

less emphasis on growth than there had been during the early 1960s, and more emphasis on goals such as preservation of the environment.

During the early Reagan administration, the pendulum swung back toward growth as an objective. In part, this was a reaction to what some thought was excessive attention to the environment; in part, it reflected a similar view to that of the Kennedy administration, that vigorous growth was a way of dealing with many economic problems, including poverty. And Kennedy's phrase—that a "rising tide lifts all boats"—again became popular in Washington. (In rebuttal, Herbert Stein observed: "Unfortunately, that is not true. A rising tide does not lift the boats that are under water. . . . Many kinds of poverty will not be significantly relieved by faster growth.")[9]

INTERRELATIONSHIPS AMONG THE GOALS

The achievement of one goal may help in the achievement of others. As we have noted, growth may make it easier to solve the poverty problem: More income may be provided to the poor out of the growth in total income, without reducing the income of those at the top. Thus, social conflicts over the share of the pie may be reduced if the size of the pie is increasing.

Similarly, the poverty problem is easier to solve if the unemployment rate is kept low, so that large numbers of unemployed do not swell the ranks of the poor. When goals are **complementary** like this (that is, when achieving one helps to achieve the other), economic policy-making is relatively easy. By attacking on a broad front and striving for several goals, we can increase our chances of achieving each.

Unfortunately, however, economic goals are not always complementary; in many cases, they are in conflict. For example, when the unem-

ployment problem is reduced, the inflation problem tends to get worse. There is a reason for this. Heavy purchasing by the public tends to reduce unemployment, but it also tends to increase inflation. It reduces unemployment because, as the public buys more cars, unemployed workers get jobs again in the auto factories; and when families buy more homes, construction workers find it easier to locate jobs. But, at the same time, heavy purchasing tends to increase inflation because producers are more likely to raise their prices if buyers are clamoring for their products. Such conflicts among goals test the wisdom of policy makers; they feel torn in deciding which objective to pursue.

A PREVIEW

These, then, are the five major objectives of economic policy: *high employment, price stability, efficiency, an equitable distribution of income,* and *growth.* The first two goals are related to the stability of the economy. If the economy is unstable, moving along like a roller coaster, its performance will be very unsatisfactory. As it heads downhill into recession, large numbers of people will be thrown out of work. And, as it heads upward into a runaway boom, prices will soar as the public scrambles to buy the available goods. The first two goals may therefore be looked on as two aspects of a single objective: That of achieving an **equilibrium** with stable prices and a low unemployment rate. This is the major topic of our companion volume, *An Introduction to Macroeconomics.*

Equilibrium is the first of three main "E's" of economics. The second E—*efficiency*—will be studied in Part 2 (Chapters 7 through 17). Are we getting the most out of our productive efforts? When does the free market—where buyers and sellers come together without government interference—encourage efficiency? And where the free market does not encourage efficiency, what should be done?

Part 3 (Chapters 18 through 25) deals primarily with the third E—**equity.** If the government takes a laissez faire attitude, how much

[9]Herbert Stein, "Economic Policy, Conservatively Speaking," *Public Opinion,* February 1981, p. 4. (Stein was Chairman of the Council of Economic Advisers from 1972 to 1974.)

income will go to workers? To the owners of land? To others? How do labor unions affect the incomes of their members? How can the government improve the lot of the poor?

The final major objective—growth—cuts across a number of other major topics, and thus appears periodically throughout the book. But first, before we get into the meat of policy issues, we must set the stage with some of the basic concepts and tools of economics. To that task we now turn (in Chapters 2 through 6).

Key Points

1 Economics is the study of how people make their living, how they acquire food, shelter, clothing, and other material necessities and comforts. It is a study of the problems they encounter, and of the ways in which these problems can be reduced.

2 During the twentieth century, substantial economic progress has been made in the United States and many other countries. We are producing much more, even though we spend less time at work than did our grandparents.

3 Nevertheless, substantial economic problems remain: problems such as poverty, high rates of unemployment, and inflation.

4 One of the things we study in economics is how we can deal with our problems, either through private action or through government policies.

5 In the history of economic thought, the role of government has been controversial. Adam Smith in 1776 called for the liberation of markets from the tyranny of government control. By 1936, John Maynard Keynes was appealing to the government to accept its responsibilities and to undertake public works in order to get the economy out of the Depression.

6 Important economic goals include the following:

(a) An equilibrium with high employment and price stability.

(b) Efficiency. *Allocative efficiency* involves the production of the right combination of goods, using the right combination of inputs. *Technical efficiency* involves producing the most with the smallest quantity of inputs feasible (while working at a reasonable pace).

(c) Equity in the distribution of income.

(d) A satisfactory rate of growth.

Key Concepts

economics	ratio (or logarithmic) scale	equal distribution of income
laissez faire	the average level of prices	equitable distribution of income
depression	relative prices	growth
recession	allocative efficiency	complementary goals
unemployment	technical efficiency	conflicting goals
inflation	poverty	
hyperinflation		

Problems

1-1 According to Smith's "invisible hand," we are able to obtain meat, not because of the butcher's benevolence, but because of his self-interest. Why is it in the butcher's self-interest to provide us with meat? What does the butcher get in return?

1-2 Suppose another depression occurs like the Depression of the 1930s. How would it affect you? (Thinking about this question provided a major motivation for a generation of economists. They were appalled at the prospect, and determined to play a role in preventing a repeat of the Great Depression.)

1-3 The section on an equitable distribution of income reflects two views regarding the proper approach to poverty:

(a) The important thing is to meet the basic needs of the poor; that is, to provide at least a minimum income for the purchase of food, shelter and other necessities.

(b) The important thing is to reduce inequality; that is, to reduce the gap between the rich and the poor.

These two views are not the same. For example, if there is rapid growth in the economy, objective (a) may be accomplished without any progress being made toward (b). Which is the more important objective? Why? Do you feel strongly about your choice? Why?

1-4 In Figure 1-1, observe that the downward trend in the length of the workweek ended about 1950. Prior to that date, part of the gains of the average worker came in the form of shorter hours. But, since 1950, practically all the gains have consisted of higher wages and fringe benefits. Do you see any reason why the workweek leveled out in 1950?

1-5 Explain how an upswing in purchases by the public will affect (a) unemployment and (b) inflation. Does this result illustrate economic goals that are complementary, or in conflict?

CHAPTER 2
Scarcity:

The Economizing Problem

Economize: manage with care or frugality; to be careful in outlay.

Webster's Dictionary

In Chapter 1, economics was defined as the study of how people make their living. Such a broad definition was needed to encompass the wide range of issues that economists study—problems such as inflation and unemployment, and objectives such as efficiency and equity.

The objective of this chapter will be to become more specific, to present a fundamental economic concept: *scarcity*. Reconsider, for a moment, the broad-brush economic history of the United States in the twentieth century. The average worker now produces about four times as much as the worker at the turn of the century—and does so with less effort, in a shorter workweek. If the average worker can now produce so much, why don't we relax? If, with relatively little effort, we can have higher incomes than our grandparents, why should we worry about economic problems at all? Why do we continue to struggle to make a living?

There are two fundamental reasons:

1 Our material *wants* are virtually unlimited or insatiable.
2 Economic *resources* are limited or scarce.

Because of these two basic facts, we cannot have everything we want. We are therefore faced with the necessity of *making choices*.

UNLIMITED WANTS . . .

Consider, first, our wants. If the one-horse shay was good enough for great-grandpa, why isn't it good enough for us?

Material wants arise for two reasons. First, each of us has basic biological needs: The need for food, the need for shelter, and the need for clothing (particularly in cold climates). But there is also a second reason. Clearly, we are prepared to work more than is required just to meet our minimum needs. We want more than the basic diet of vegetables and water needed to sustain life. We want more than a lean-to shelter which will provide minimal protection from the elements. And we want more than the minimum wardrobe needed to protect us from the cold. In other words, we want the goods and services which can make life more pleasant. Of course, the two basic reasons for material wants cannot be sharply separated. When we sit down to a gourmet meal at a restaurant, we are satisfying our biological need to eat. But we are also doing more. We are savoring exotic foods, in a stylish atmosphere. We are getting both the basics and the frills. These frills are sufficiently pleasant that we are willing to work to obtain them.

The range of consumer wants is exceedingly wide. We want **goods,** such as houses, cars, shoes, shirts, and tennis rackets. Similarly, we want **services:** medical care, haircuts, and laundry services. And, when we get what we want, it may whet our appetites for something more. If we own a Chevrolet, perhaps we will want an Oldsmobile next time. Or, after we buy our house, we may wish to replace the carpets and drapes. Furthermore, as new products are introduced, we want them too. We want TV sets, tape recorders, air conditioners, and a host of other products that our great-grandparents never even heard of. Even though it is conceivable that, some day, we will say, "Enough," that day seems far away. Our wants show no sign of being completely satisfied.

. . . AND SCARCE RESOURCES

Wants cannot all be satisfied because of the second fundamental fact. While our productive capacity is large, it is not without limit. There are only so many workers in the labor force; and we have only a certain number of machines and factories. In other words, our resources are limited.

Resources are the basic inputs used in the production of goods and services. Therefore, they are also frequently known as **factors of production**. They can be categorized under three main headings: land, capital, and labor.

Economists use the term **land** in a broad sense, to include not only the arable land used by the farmer and the city land used as building lots, but also the other gifts of nature that come with the land. Thus, the minerals which are found under the soil, and the water and sunlight which fall upon the soil, are all part of the land resource.

Capital refers to the buildings, equipment, and other materials used in the productive process. An automobile assembly plant is "capital," and so are the machines in the plant and the steel with which automobiles will be built. In contrast to land, which has been *given* to us by nature, capital has been *produced* at some time in the past. This may have been the distant past; the factory may have been built 15 years ago. Or it may have been the recent past; the steel may have been manufactured last month. The process of producing and accumulating capital is known as **investment**.

Unlike *consumer goods* (such as shoes, shirts, or food), *capital goods* or "investment goods" (such as tractors, factories, or machinery in the factories) are not designed to satisfy human wants directly. Rather, they are intended for use in the production of other goods. Capital produced now will satisfy wants only indirectly, and at a later time, when it is used in the production of a consumer good. The production of capital therefore involves the willingness of someone to wait. When a machine is produced, rather, say, than a car, someone is willing to forgo the car now in order to produce the machine and thus be able to produce more cars (or other goods) in the future. Thus, capital formation involves a choice between consumption **now** and more consumption **in the future.**

One point of terminology should be emphasized. Unless otherwise specified, when economists use the term "capital" they mean **real capital** (buildings, machines) and not financial capital, such as common stocks or money. While an individual might consider 100 shares of General Motors stock as part of his or her "capital," they are not capital in the economic sense. They are not a resource with which goods and services can be produced. Similarly, when economists talk of investment, they generally mean *real* investment—the accumulation of machines and other real capital—and not financial investment (such as the purchase of a government bond).

Labor involves the physical and mental talents of human beings, applied to the production of goods and services. The ditchdigger provides labor, and so does the college professor or the physician. (The professor produces educational services, and the doctor produces medical services.)[1]

Special emphasis should be given to one particular human resource: **entrepreneurial ability**. The French word *entrepreneur* means, literally, someone who undertakes or attempts to do a task. In economics, the entrepreneur is a person who:

1 undertakes to put together the factors of production—land, labor, and capital—to produce goods and services.

2 is responsible for business decisions.

3 is a risk taker. (There is no guarantee that business decisions will turn out to be correct.)

4 is an innovator, introducing new products, new technology, and new ways of organizing business.

Thus, the entrepreneur plays a key role in the economy: The ability of the entrepreneur helps to determine the dynamism and the growth of the economy.

SCARCITY AND CHOICE: THE PRODUCTION POSSIBILITIES CURVE

With unlimited wants and limited resources, we face the fundamental economic problem of **scarcity**. We cannot have everything we want; we must make choices.

The problem of scarcity—and the need to make choices—can be illustrated with a **pro-**

duction possibilities curve (PPC). This curve shows what can be produced with the existing quantity of land, labor, and capital at our disposal, and with our existing technology. Although our resources are limited and our capacity to produce is likewise limited, we have an option as to what sorts of goods and services we produce. We may decide to produce fewer cars and more bicycles and aircraft, or less wheat and more corn.

In an economy with thousands of products, the choices before us are complex. In order to reduce the problem to its simplest form, we consider the most basic economy, one in which only two goods (cotton clothing and wheat) can be produced. If we decide to produce more food (wheat), and redirect our efforts in that direction, then we will be able to produce less clothing.

The options open to us are shown in the production possibilities table (Table 2-1) and the corresponding production possibilities curve (Figure 2-1). Consider first an extreme example, where all our resources are directed toward the production of food. In this case, illustrated by option *A,* we would produce 20 million tons of food. But no clothing would be produced. This clearly does not represent a desirable composition of production; we would be well fed, but we would be running around naked. The production possibilities curve is intended to illustrate what is *possible;* the points on it need not be *desirable.* And point *A* is a possibility.

At the other extreme, if we produced nothing but clothing, we would make 5 billion yards, as illustrated by point *F.* Again, this is a possible outcome, but not a desirable one; we would be well dressed as we faced starvation.

The shape of the production possibilities curve: Increasing opportunity costs

More interesting cases, and more reasonable ones, are those in which we produce some of both goods. Consider how the economy might move from point *A* toward point *F.* At point *A,* nothing is produced but food; it is grown on all types of arable land throughout the United States. In order to begin the production of clothing, we would plant cotton on the lands

---

[1]The preceding paragraphs have presented the traditional division of the factors of production into the categories of land, labor, and capital. While still popular, this traditional division is not universally used by present-day economists. In particular, economists now sometimes talk of "human capital"; that is, education and training which add to the productivity of labor. This human capital has two of the important characteristics of physical capital discussed above. During the training period, waiting occurs; the individual does not produce goods or services while occupied in learning. Second, human capital, like physical capital, can increase the productive capacity of the economy, since a trained worker can produce more than an untrained one.

Table 2-1
Production Possibilities

Option	Clothing (billions of yards)	Food (millions of tons)	Units of food that must be given up to produce one more unit of clothing (opportunity cost)
A	0	20	
			1
B	1	19	
			2
C	2	17	
			4
D	3	13	
			5
E	4	8	
			8
F	5	0	

which are comparatively best suited for cotton production—those in Alabama and Mississippi. From these lands, we would get a lot of cotton, while giving up just a small amount of food that might have been grown there. This is illustrated as we move from point A to point B: Only 1 unit of food is given up in order to produce the first unit of clothing.

As we decide to produce more cotton, however, we must move to land which is somewhat less suited to cotton production. Thus, in order to get the second unit of clothing, we must give up 2 units of food: Food production falls from 19 to 17 units as we move from point B to point C. The **opportunity cost** of the second unit of clothing—the food we have to give up to acquire it—is thus greater than the opportunity cost of the first unit.

Figure 2-1
The production possibilities curve
The curve illustrates the options open to society, given its limited resources of land, labor, and capital.

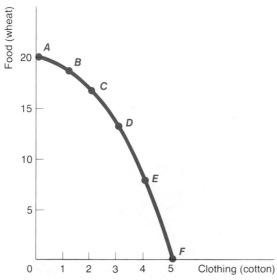

The **opportunity cost** of a product is the alternative which must be given up to produce that product. (In this illustration, the opportunity cost of a unit of clothing is the wheat which must be given up when that unit of clothing is produced.)

Further increases in the production of clothing come at higher and higher opportunity costs. As we move to the third unit of clothing, we must start planting cotton in the corn belt of Iowa; a lot of food must be given up to produce that third unit of clothing. Finally, as we move from point E to point F, we are switching all our resources into the production of clothing. This comes at an extremely high opportunity cost in terms of lost output of food. Wheat production is stopped on the farms of North Dakota and Minnesota, which are no good at all for producing cotton. The wheat lands remain idle, and the farmers of North Dakota and Minnesota migrate further south, where they can make only minor contributions to cotton production. Thus, the last unit of clothing (moving from point E to F) comes at an astronomical cost of 8 units of food.

Thus, the *increasing opportunity cost of cotton is a reflection of the specialized characteristics of our resources.* Our resources are not completely adaptable to alternative uses. The lands of Minnesota and Mississippi are not equally well suited to the production of cotton and wheat. Thus, the opportunity cost of cotton rises as its production is increased. The production possibilities curve is *concave to the origin;* that is, it bows outward, as shown in Figure 2-1.

THE PRODUCTION POSSIBILITIES CURVE IS A "FRONTIER"

The production possibilities curve illustrates what an economy is capable of producing. It shows the maximum possible combined output of the two goods. In practice, actual production can fall short of our capabilities. Obviously, if there is large-scale unemployment, we are wasting some of our labor resources. Such a situation is shown by point *U,* inside the production possibilities curve in Figure 2-2. Beginning at such a point, we could produce more food *and* more clothing (and more to point *D*) by putting our labor force back to work. (With full employment, we alternatively could choose any other point on the production possibilities curve, such as *B, C,* or *E.*)

Thus, while the production possibilities curve represents options open to the society, it does not include all conceivable options. Specifically, it does not include options like point *U,* which involve large-scale unemployment and which therefore lie *inside* the curve. Thus, the production possibilities curve traces out a "frontier" of the options open to us. We can pick a

point on the frontier if we manage our affairs well and maintain a high level of employment. Or we can end up inside the curve if we mismanage the economy into a depression. But we cannot produce at points (such as *T*) outside the curve with our present quantities of land, labor, and capital, and with our present technology.

GROWTH: THE OUTWARD SHIFT OF THE PRODUCTION POSSIBILITIES CURVE

As time passes, however, a point such as *T* may come within our grasp as our productive capacity increases and the economy grows. There are three main sources of growth:

1 Technological improvement, involving new and better ways of producing goods

Figure 2-2
Unemployment and the production possibilities curve
Point *U* represents a position of large-scale unemployment. If people are put back to work, the economy can be moved to point *D,* with more food and more clothing. (Alternatively, the economy can be moved to any other point on the curve, such as *B, C,* or *E.*)

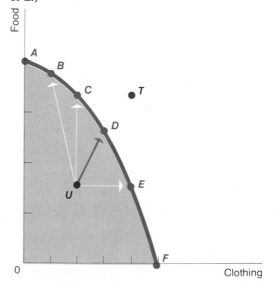

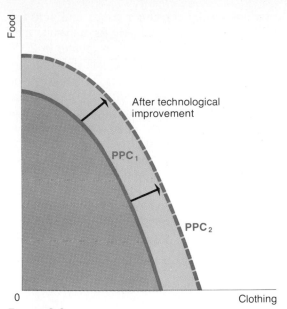

Figure 2-3
Technological improvement
As a result of the development of a new fertilizer, our productive capabilities increase. (The production possibilities curve moves outward.)

2 An increase in the quantity of capital[2]
3 An increase in the labor force

Consider a change in technology. Suppose a new type of fertilizer is discovered that substantially increases the output of our land, whether cotton or wheat is being grown. Then we will be able to produce more wheat and more cotton. The production possibilities curve will shift out to the new curve (PPC₂) shown in Figure 2-3.

[2]Including "human" capital, which makes an important contribution to growth. Indeed, in his study of the sources of growth in the United States economy, Edward F. Denison found that education was almost as important as physical capital. (According to Denison's estimates, physical capital accounted for growth of 0.50 percent per annum, while education accounted for 0.41 percent.) Edward F. Denison, *Accounting for United States Economic Growth, 1929–1969* (Washington: The Brookings Institution, 1974), p. 127.

Growth **is defined as an outward movement of the production possibilities curve.**

The effect of the new fertilizer illustrated in Figure 2-3 is to increase our capabilities in the production of both wheat and cotton. Alternatively, it is possible that technological improvement might affect our capabilities in only one of the goods—for example, the development of a new disease-resistant strain of wheat will increase our ability to produce wheat but not cotton. In this case, illustrated in Figure 2-4, nothing will happen to the place where the production possibilities curve meets the axis for cotton: If we direct all our resources to the production of cotton, we can still produce no more than shown by point *F*. But the increase in wheat-producing capabilities will cause an upward movement in the point where the curve meets the food axis, from *A* to *B*. Thus, the development of the new wheat causes an outward movement of the production possibilities curve to PPC₃.

Figure 2-4
Technological improvement in a single good
When a new, improved strain of wheat is developed, the production possibilities curve moves out to PPC₃.

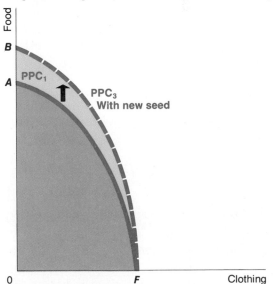

GROWTH: THE CHOICE BETWEEN CONSUMER GOODS AND CAPITAL GOODS

As an alternative to technological change, consider the second source of growth listed above: an increase in the quantity of capital. The capital which we have today is limited. But capital itself can be produced. The quantity of capital in the year 2000 will in large part be determined by how much capital we choose to produce this year and in coming years.

In order to study this choice, we must look at a different production possibilities curve—not one showing food and clothing, but rather, one that shows the choice between the production of *capital goods* (such as machines and factories) and the production of *consumer goods* (such as food, clothing, and TV sets).

In Figure 2-5, two hypothetical economies are compared. Starting in 1980, these two countries face the same initial production possibilities curve (PPC$_{1980}$). The citizens of Extravagania (on the left) believe in living for the moment. They produce mostly consumer goods and very few capital goods (at point A). As a result, their capital stock will be not much greater in 2000 than it is today, so their PPC will shift out very little. In contrast, the citizens of Thriftiana (on the right) keep down the production of consumer goods in order to build more capital goods (at point B). By the year 2000, their productive capacity will be greatly increased, as shown by the large outward movement of the PPC. Because they have given up so much consumption now, their income (and ability to consume) will be much greater in the future. Thus, any society faces a choice: How much consumption should it sacrifice now in order to be able to consume more in the future?

Economic development: The problem of takeoff

For some countries, the question of growth may be approached in a relatively relaxed manner. For the United States, the issue is not a matter of life or death. Even if we consume most of our

Figure 2-5
Capital formation now helps to determine future productive capacity

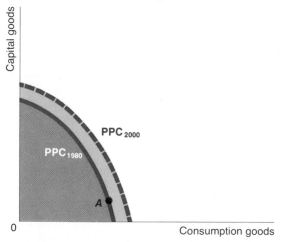

(a) **Extravagania**. Most productive capacity is directed toward the satisfaction of current wants (point **A**). Little investment takes place. The result is slow growth.

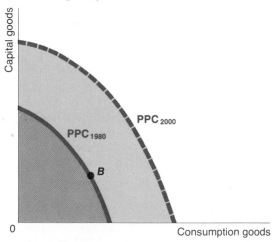

(b) **Thriftiana**. Much of current (1980) capacity is used to produce capital goods (point **B**). The result is rapid growth (that is, a large outward movement of the production possibilities curve by the year 2000).

current output and grow relatively slowly, we will still be relatively comfortable in the year 2000. The same is true for Japan and for the countries of Western Europe. (However, Japan conspicuously has not taken a relaxed approach to the growth question. Japan has been "Thriftiana" *par excellence*, investing a large share of national output and growing very rapidly.)

Some other countries, however, face a much more critical situation. They are so poor that they can scarcely take a relaxed view either of the present or of the future. They face a cruel dilemma (illustrated in Figure 2-6). If they consume all their current output (at point A), then they will remain stuck on PPC_1. Their future will be just as bleak as the present.[3] On the other hand, if they want to grow, they will have to produce capital, and this means cutting back on their production of consumer goods. (If they choose the growth strategy and move initially to point B_1, then the production of consumer goods will fall from A to B.) Since the already low level of consumption is depressed further, more people may starve.

But in the long run, the growth strategy pays off. Because capital is produced at B_1, productive capacity grows. The production possibilities curve shifts out to PPC_2. Now the nation can pick point B_2, where it not only produces capital goods, but also as many consumer goods as it originally did at A. (B_2 is directly above point A.) The economy has achieved a **takeoff**. Because it is now producing capital goods, its PPC is continuously moving out. Consequently, the nation can produce *ever increasing* amounts of both consumer and capital goods.

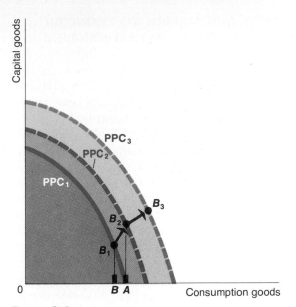

Figure 2-6
"Takeoff" into economic growth
If point B_1 is initially chosen (on PPC_1), then growth will occur. The economy can move progressively to B_2, B_3, and beyond. The problem is: What short-term miseries will be caused by the initial choice of B_1 rather than A?

But the long-run process does not solve the painful problem of the present: Should consumption be depressed, at the possible risk of starvation, in order to initiate the growth process? How can the economy take off without the danger of a crack-up halfway down the runway? (The danger may be political as well as economic. If a government chooses point B_1, the population may be unimpressed with promises of a brighter long-run future; they may vote the government out, or rebel.)

One possible solution to this crucial problem lies with other countries. Richer countries can provide the resources for the early stages of growth, either by granting aid or through private investment. (For example, a Western European tractor manufacturer might build a plant in the developing country.) In this way, economic takeoff might occur without the sacrifices that capital formation normally requires.

---

[3]In this simplified example, it is assumed that only capital changes, and that technology and population remain constant. But, in fact, all three major determinants of growth (capital, labor, and technology) may change.

If technology improves, growth may occur even in the absence of investment; the outlook is not as bleak as suggested above. On the other hand, population pressures may make the outlook even worse. As population grows, output must grow if the already low standard of living is not to fall even lower. Thus, just to maintain the present standard, some capital formation may be required.

AN INTRODUCTION TO ECONOMIC THEORY: THE NEED TO SIMPLIFY

The production possibilities curve is the first piece of theoretical equipment which the beginning economics student typically encounters. There will be many more. At this early stage, it is appropriate to address directly a problem which often bothers both the beginning and the advanced student of economics. The production possibilities curve, and many other theoretical concepts that will be introduced in later chapters, represent gross simplifications of the real world. When the PPC is drawn, it is assumed that only two types of goods can be produced—food and clothing, or consumer goods and capital goods. (Diagrams are limited to two alternatives because the printed page has only two dimensions.) Yet, obviously, there are thousands of goods produced in the modern economy. This raises a question: With our simple approach, can we say anything of relevance to the real world?

Since we have already used the production possibilities curve, it is not surprising that our answer to this question will be yes. To see why, let us briefly consider the role of theory in economics. Economics is a study of such questions as how consumers behave; why cars are produced in Detroit and steel in Pittsburgh; why prices are sometimes stable and sometimes volatile. To study economics, we must consider *cause* and *effect*.

Theory necessarily involves simplification
If we wished to describe the real world in detail, we could go on without end. But a complete description would be useless as a guide to private behavior or public policy; it would be too complex. In a sense, theory is like a map. A road map is necessarily incomplete; in many ways, it is not very accurate, and, indeed, downright wrong. Towns and villages are not round circles. Roads of various qualities do not really come in different colors. If a road map were more realistic, it would be less useful for its intended purpose; if it tried to show every house and every tree, it would be an incomprehensible

jumble of detail. A road map is useful precisely because it is a simplification that shows in stark outline the various roads which may be traveled. The objective of economic theory is similarly to draw in stark outline the important relationships among producers and consumers.

A map is useful in part because it involves simplification. When a road map is drawn, with details left out, it gains clarity for its intended purpose as a guide to the auto traveler. But, at the same time, it loses value for other purposes. A road map is a poor guide for airplane pilots. They need a map with the height of mountains clearly marked. A road map is a poor guide for sales managers, who need a map which indicates population density. The way in which a map is constructed depends upon its intended use. Various maps are "true," but they do not represent the "whole truth." An important question for a map user thus becomes: Do I have the best map for my purpose?

The same generalization holds for economic theory. If we wish to study long-run growth, we may use quite different theoretical tools from those we would use to study short-term fluctuations. If we want to study the consequences of price controls on the housing market, we may use different tools from those we would choose to investigate the economic consequences of a cut in the defense budget. Just as in the case of the map, the "best" theory cannot be identified unless we know the purposes for which it is to be used.

The purpose of the production possibilities curve is to illustrate the concept of scarcity. If our resources are fully utilized to begin with, and if we decide to produce more of one good, then its production must come at the cost of less production of some other good or service. This is a significant point. But the first "if" clause is important. It tells us the assumption behind the production possibilities frontier, and thus it tells us when this theoretical road map is relevant. (When the initial "if" clause is violated—when the economy begins with large-scale unemployment—then quite a different conclusion is correct. The economy *can* produce more consumer goods and more capital goods at the same time.)

For the novice and old hand alike, it is essential to recognize and remember the assumptions behind various theories. If we don't, we may use the wrong theory, and make serious mistakes—just as the pilot who uses the wrong map may fly a plane into the nearest mountain top.

The distinction between "positive" and "normative" economics

The uses of theory are many, but they may be divided into two main families. **Positive** or **descriptive** economics aims at understanding how the economy works; it is directed toward explaining the way the world is and how various forces can cause it to change. **Normative** economics, on the other hand, deals with the way the world, or some small segment of it, ought to be.

A debate over a positive statement can be settled by an appeal to the facts. For example, the following is a positive statement: "There are millions of barrels of oil in the rocks of Colorado." This statement can be supported or refuted by a geological study. Another positive statement is this: "If 1 ton of dynamite is exploded 100 feet below the surface, 1,000 barrels of oil will be released from the rocks." Again, the facts can settle this point. By experimentation we can find whether this is true.

A *normative* statement is more complex; for example, "We ought to extract oil in large quantities from the Colorado rocks." Facts are relevant here: If there is no oil in the rocks of Colorado (a positive conclusion), then the normative statement that we ought to extract oil must be rejected for the very simple reason that it can't be done. But facts alone will seldom settle a dispute over a normative statement, since it is based on something more—on a view regarding appropriate goals or ethical values. A normative statement involves a value judgment, a judgment about what *ought* to be. It is possible for well-informed individuals of exemplary character to disagree over normative statements, even when they agree completely regarding the

facts. For example, they may agree that, in fact, a large quantity of oil is locked in the rocks of Colorado. But they may disagree whether it should be extracted. These differences may develop, perhaps, over the relative importance of a plentiful supply of heating oil as compared with the environmental damage which might accompany the extraction of oil.

In economics, some positive statements may be easily settled by looking at the facts. Among them is: "Steel production last year was 100 million tons," or, "Spending by state and local governments is 10 percent higher this year than last." But, where positive statements involve propositions about causation, they may be quite controversial, because the facts are not easily untangled. Many such controversial statements might be cited. For example: "If the quantity of money in the economy is increased by 10 percent next year, then inflation will accelerate"; or, "Continuing increases in government spending over the next 10 years will keep the unemployment rate lower than it would be if government spending were constant"; or, "Rent controls have little effect on the number of apartments offered for rent."

In evaluating such statements, economists (and other social scientists) have one major disadvantage compared with natural scientists. In many instances, experiments are difficult or impossible. For obvious reasons, no government will allow economists to try to find the effects of rent control by designing an experiment in which one large city is subjected to rent control while a similar city is not. Nevertheless, economists do have factual evidence to study. By looking at situations where rent controls have been imposed, they may be able to estimate the effects of those controls.

The differences between natural scientists and economists should not be exaggerated. In some instances, economic experiments are possible. For example, experiments have been undertaken to find if people work less when they are provided with a minimum income by the government. (The results will be reported in a later chapter.) Furthermore, while physicists, chemists, and geneticists can carry out experiments, not all natural scientists are in that happy position. To cite one example, astronomers observe; they do not experiment. And, until experiments with cloud seeding, meteorologists were likewise limited to observation.

Key Points

1 *Scarcity* is a fundamental economic problem. Because wants are virtually unlimited and resources are scarce, we are faced with the need to make choices.

2 The choices open to society are illustrated by the production possibilities curve.

3 Resources are not all uniform; for example, the land of Mississippi has characteristics different from the land of Minnesota. As a consequence, production normally involves increasing opportunity cost. As more cotton is produced, more and more wheat must be given up for each additional unit of cotton. As a result, the production possibilities curve tends to bow outward. (It is concave to the origin.)

4 The production possibilities curve is a frontier, representing the choices open to society if there is full utilization of the available resources of land, labor, and capital. If there is large-scale unemployment, then production occurs at a point within this frontier.

5 The economy can grow and the production possibilities curve can move outward if:

(a) Technology improves
(b) The capital stock grows
(c) And/or the labor force grows

6 By giving up consumer goods at present, we can produce more capital goods, and thus have a growing economy. The production of capital goods (investment) therefore represents a choice of more future production instead of present consumption.

7 For the poorest of the less developed countries, a choice between present consumption and growth is particularly painful. If they suppress consumption in order to grow more rapidly, people may starve. But growth is essential to raise a low standard of living.

8 Like other theoretical concepts, the production possibilities curve involves simplification. Because the world is so complex, theory cannot reflect the "whole truth." But, like a road map, a theory can be valuable if it is used correctly. In order to determine the appropriate uses of a theory, it is important to identify the assumptions on which the theory was developed.

Key Concepts

scarcity
goods
services
resources
factors of production
land

labor
capital
investment
entrepreneur
production possibilities
   curve

increasing opportunity
   cost
growth
takeoff
positive economics
normative economics

Problems

2-1   In Chapter 1, economics was defined as the study of how people make their living, of the problems they encounter, and of the ways in which these problems can be reduced. Frequently, economics is defined differently as the study of ''the allocation of scarce resources to satisfy competing human wants.'' Does either definition cover the study of unemployment? Which definition is broader?

2-2   ''Wants aren't insatiable. David Rockefeller's wants have been satisfied. There is no prospect that he will spend all his money before he dies. His consumption is not limited by his income.'' Do you agree? Does your answer raise problems for the main theme of this chapter, that wants cannot all be satisfied with the goods and services produced from our limited resources? Why or why not?

2-3   ''The more capital goods we produce, the more the U.S. economy will grow, and the more we and our children will be able to consume in the future. Therefore, the government should encourage capital formation.'' Do you agree or disagree? Why?

2-4   Does the United States have a moral obligation to aid India with its economic development? Nigeria? Brazil? China?

CHAPTER 3
Specialization, Exchange, and Money

> The . . . great achievement of money is that it enables man as producer to concentrate his attention on his own job. . . . The specialization and division of labour . . . would be impossible if every man had to spend a large part of his time and energies in bartering.
>
> **D. H. Robertson, *Money***

During the past century, economic progress has been marked by a huge increase in the quantity of capital, and by a flood of new inventions. First, the mechanical reaper and then the combine were invented to make the harvesting of grain quick and easy. Tractors have been introduced into farming; trucks speed the movement of goods; computers help in the design of products. A long and impressive list could be quickly compiled. The modern worker has not only more tools, but also much better tools than the worker of the nineteenth century.

The new tools have led to a significant increase in the degree of **specialization**. The nineteenth-century carpenter produced a wide range of furniture and related wood products, from jewelry boxes to caskets. (Indeed, occupations were sometimes combined, with the same individual acting as both carpenter and undertaker.) On the early frontier, the settler was largely self-sufficient. Families grew their own food, built their own homes, and often made most of their own clothes. Not so today. Most farms are specialized, producing only one or a few products, such as wheat, corn, or beef. The worker in a modern factory tends a machine designed to produce a single piece of furniture, or perhaps just a single leg of a piece of furniture. The results have not been an unmixed blessing. Modern workers are more prone to boredom, and they lack the sense of accomplishment enjoyed by the skilled workers of old as they saw their creations taking shape. But the results have undoubtedly contributed to efficiency: By specializing, the modern worker has become very productive.

Thus, the basic reason for specialization is obvious: It is efficient. To use some straightforward examples: It is efficient for the United States to import coffee and to export wheat or business machines to pay for this coffee. Coffee could be produced only with difficulty, and at a very high cost, in the United States. Similarly, it is efficient to produce steel in Pittsburgh and corn in Kansas. Kansans presumably could produce their own steel, but the cost would be prohibitively high. Specialization likewise takes place within a town or city: Barbers specialize in cutting hair, doctors in treating illnesses, and factory workers in producing goods.

EXCHANGE: THE BARTER ECONOMY

Specialization implies exchange. The farmer who specializes in raising beef must exchange beef (beyond the family's direct requirements) for furniture, clothing, and other needs. There are two kinds of exchange: barter, and exchange for money.

Under a barter system, no money is involved: One good or service is exchanged directly for another. The farmer specializing in the production of beef may find a hungry barber, and thus get a haircut; or find a hungry tailor, and thus exchange meat for a suit of clothes; or find a hungry doctor, and thus obtain medical treatment. A simple barter transaction is illustrated in Figure 3-1. In a barter economy, there are dozens of such bilateral (two-way) transactions: between the farmer and the tailor; between the farmer and the doctor; between the doctor and the tailor; and so on.

Clearly, barter is inefficient. Farmers can spend half their time producing beef, and the other half searching for someone willing to make the right trade. Barter requires a **coincidence of wants:** Those involved in barter must each have a product that the other wants. The farmer not only must find someone who wants beef, but that someone must also be able to provide something in exchange that the farmer wants. And, with barter, there is a problem of **indivisibility** or lumpiness. A suit of clothes—or an automobile, or a house—should be bought all at once, and not in pieces. To illustrate, suppose

that a beef farmer who wants a suit of clothes has been lucky enough to find a tailor who wants meat and is willing to make a trade. The suit of clothes may be worth 100 pounds of beef, and the farmer may be quite willing to give up this amount. The problem is that the tailor may not be *that* hungry, perhaps wishing only 50 pounds. In a barter economy, what is the farmer to do? Get only the jacket from this tailor, and set out in search of another hungry tailor in order to obtain a pair of pants? And, if the farmer does so, what are the chances that the pants will match?

EXCHANGE WITH MONEY

With money, exchange can be much easier. It is no longer necessary for wants to coincide. In order to get a suit of clothing, the farmer need not find a hungry tailor, but only someone willing to pay money for the beef. The farmer can then take the money and buy the suit of clothes. Because money represents **general purchasing power** (that is, it can be used to buy *any* of the goods and services offered for sale), money makes possible complex transactions among many parties. Figure 3-2 gives a simple illustration with three parties. But transactions in a monetary economy may be very complex, involving dozens or hundreds of participants.

Money also solves the problem of indivisibility. The farmer can sell the whole carcass of beef for money, and use the proceeds to buy a complete set of clothes. It doesn't matter how much beef the tailor wants.

In the simple barter economy, there is no clear distinction between seller and buyer, or between producer and consumer. When bartering beef for clothing, the farmer is at the same time both a seller (of beef) and a buyer (of clothing). In a monetary economy, in contrast, a distinction arises between seller and buyer. In the beef market, the farmer is the seller; the hungry tailor is the buyer. The farmer is the producer; the tailor is the consumer.

The sharp distinction which arises between

Figure 3-1
Barter

With barter, no money is used. The farmer exchanges beef directly for clothing. Transactions involve only two parties—in this case, the farmer and the tailor.

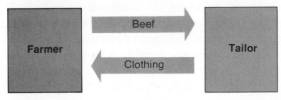

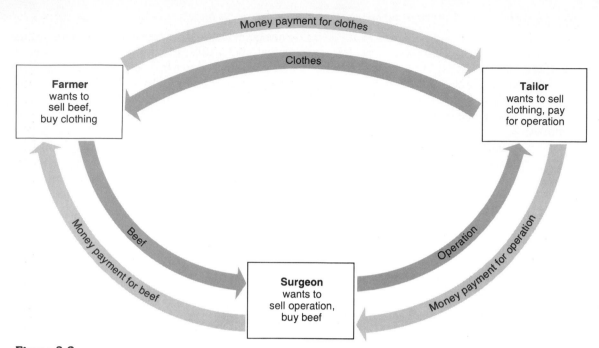

Figure 3-2
Multilateral transactions in a money economy

In a money economy, multilateral transactions among many participants are possible. The farmer gets clothing from the tailor, even though the tailor doesn't want to buy the farmer's beef.

the producer and consumer in a money economy is illustrated in Figure 3-3. Producers—or **businesses**—are put in the right-hand box; consumers—or **households**—in the left. Transactions between the two groups are illustrated in the loops. In the top loops, the transactions in consumer goods and services are shown. Beef, clothing, and a host of other products are sold in exchange for money.

In the lower loops, transactions in economic resources are shown. In a complex exchange economy, not only are consumer goods bought and sold for money; so are economic resources. In order to be able to buy food and other goods, households must have money income. They acquire money by providing the labor and other resources which are the inputs of the business sector. For example, workers provide their labor in exchange for wages and salaries, and owners of land provide their property in exchange for rents.

Although Figure 3-3 may seem complex, it involves substantial simplifications. There are large government transactions in our economy that have not been included in Figure 3-3. Remember the purpose of simplification discussed in Chapter 2—to show important relationships in sharp outline. Figure 3-3 shows the circular flow of payments; that is, how businesses use the receipts from sales to pay their wages, salaries, and other costs of production, while households use their income receipts from wages, salaries, etc., to buy consumer goods.

THE MONETARY SYSTEM

Because barter is so inefficient, people turn naturally to the use of money. In most societies, the government becomes deeply involved in the monetary system, issuing paper money and coins. But even if the government does nothing, a monetary system will evolve.

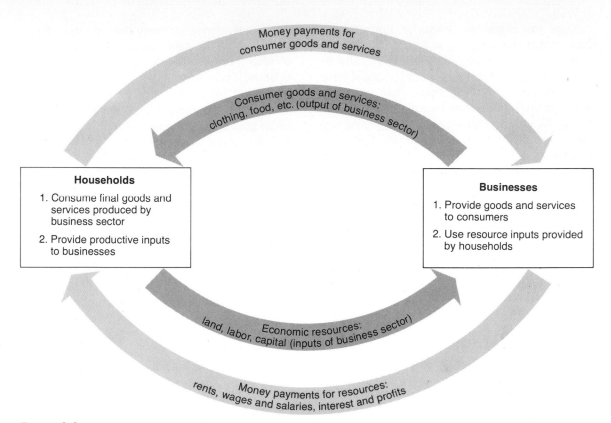

Figure 3-3
The flow of goods, services, resources, and money payments
in a simple economy
Monetary payments are shown in the outer loop. These pay for the flow of goods and
services and resources shown in the inner loop.

The very powerful tendencies for money to appear, and some of the important characteristics of a good monetary system, may be illustrated by a specific example of an economy that began without money: the prisoner-of-war camp of World War II.[1] Economic relations in such a camp were primitive; the range of goods was very limited. But some things were available: rations supplied by the German captors, and the Red Cross parcels which arrived periodically. These parcels contained a variety of items such as canned beef, jam, margarine, and cigarettes. Nonsmokers who received cigarettes were obvi-

ously eager to trade them for other items. The basis was established for exchange.

At first, trading was rough and ready, with no clear picture of the relative values of the various items. (In one instance, a prisoner started around the camp with only a can of cheese and five cigarettes, and returned with a complete Red Cross parcel. He did so by buying goods where they were cheap, and selling them where they were dear.) But as time went by, the prices of various goods tended to become stable, and all prices came to be quoted in terms of cigarettes. For example, a can of cheese was worth seven cigarettes. Not only did cigarettes become the measuring rod for quoting prices, but they were used as the common ***medium of exchange.*** Goods were bought and sold in ex-

---

[1]This illustration is based on R. A. Radford, "The Economic Organization of a P. O. W. Camp," *Economica,* November 1945, pp. 189–201.

change for cigarettes, even by nonsmokers. Nonsmokers were willing to accept cigarettes in payment, even though they had no desire to smoke; they knew that they would be able to use the cigarettes to buy chocolate, jam, or other items. In short, cigarettes became the money of the POW camp. This was a natural evolution; there was no government to decree that cigarettes were money, and no authority to enforce that choice. At other times and in other societies, other items have evolved as money: items as diverse as beads, playing cards, porpoise teeth, rice, salt, wampum, and even woodpecker scalps.

Monetary problems in the POW camp

Cigarette money made the primitive economy of the prisoner-of-war camp more efficient. But problems occurred, including problems quite similar to those of more advanced money systems. As part of the natural trend toward simplification, distinctions among different brands of cigarettes became blurred. Although all cigarettes were not equally desirable to smokers, all were equal as money. In paying for beef or other items, a cigarette was a cigarette. What was the consequence? Smokers held back the desirable brands for their personal use and spent the others. The less desirable cigarettes therefore were the ones used as money; the "good" cigarettes were smoked. This illustrates **Gresham's law.** This law, first enunciated by Elizabethan financier Sir Thomas Gresham (1519–1579), is popularly and loosely abbreviated: "Bad money drives out good." In this case, "bad" cigarettes drove "good" cigarettes out of circulation as money. (The good cigarettes were smoked instead.)

Gresham's law: **If there are two types of money whose values in exchange are equal while their values in another use (like consumption) are different, the more valuable item will be retained for its other use while the less valuable item will continue to circulate as money. Thus, the "bad" (less valuable) money drives the "good" (more valuable) money out of circulation.**

The tendency for every cigarette to be treated as equal to every other cigarette caused another monetary problem. As a cigarette was a cigarette, prisoners often pulled out a few strands of tobacco before passing a cigarette along. This corresponds precisely to a problem when gold coins circulate: There is a temptation to "clip" coins by chipping off bits of gold. And the cigarette currency became "debased": Some enterprising prisoners rolled cigarettes from pipe tobacco or broke down cigarettes and rerolled them, reducing the amount of tobacco in each. Similarly, governments have from time to time given in to the temptation to debase gold coins by melting them down and reissuing them with a smaller gold content. (Private entrepreneurs have had a strong incentive to do the same. But they have been discouraged throughout history by severe punishments against counterfeiting.)

But it was not clipping or debasement which led to the greatest monetary problems in the POW camp. As long as there was a balanced inflow of both cigarettes and other goods, the exchange system of the camp worked reasonably well. But, from time to time, the weekly Red Cross issue of 25 or 50 cigarettes per prisoner was interrupted. As the existing stock of cigarettes was consumed by smokers, cigarettes became more and more scarce. Desperate smokers had to offer more and more to get cigarettes; their value skyrocketed. To put the same point another way: Other goods now exchanged for fewer and fewer cigarettes. A can of beef which previously sold for 20 cigarettes dropped in value to 15, 10, or even fewer cigarettes. In technical terms, there was a **deflation**—a decline in the prices of other goods, measured in terms of money.

As cigarettes became increasingly scarce and prices continued to fall, prisoners tended to revert to barter in exchanging other products. Then, from time to time, thousands of cigarettes would arrive at the camp during a brief period. Cigarettes fell in value. In other words, the prices of other goods soared. Once again the unpredictability of the value of cigarette money caused a partial return to barter exchange. Thus, *the*

BOX 3-1

Why Cigarettes?

In the POW camp, cigarettes emerged as the commonly accepted money. Why cigarettes? Why not canned carrots or beef?

There were three reasons. First, although not everyone wanted cigarettes for his personal use, the market value of cigarettes was high. Thus, cigarettes were chosen over canned carrots because canned carrots were practically worthless. If carrots had been the "money," exchange would have been cumbersome, with prisoners lugging around many cans in order to make exchanges. *A good money is one whose value is sufficiently high that the individual may conveniently carry a considerable purchasing power.* Thus, in the broader society, the money that evolved was precious metals—silver, and particularly gold. Lead did not (generally) become money because its value was relatively low, and the use of lead would have been cumbersome. Of course, today our money is even more convenient than the precious metals: a $20, $50, or $100 bill may be carried easily and inconspicuously.

Thus, cigarettes were preferred to canned carrots. But why did cigarettes become money, rather than canned beef? Canned meat, like cigarettes, had a high value. Here, we come to the second and third reasons why cigarettes became money. A package of cigarettes is *easily divisible* into subunits—the 20 individual cigarettes—each of which is relatively *durable*. A can of beef, on the other hand, cannot easily be subdivided. If it is opened and cut up, the individual chunks will be messy and will quickly spoil. Moreover, a 2-ounce piece of beef is not easily distinguished from a 3-ounce chunk. The cigarette package, in contrast, can easily be divided into 20 individual cigarettes which are relatively long-lasting and easily identified.

Similarly, in the broader society, monies have developed which are easily divisible and durable. Precious metals, for example, are easily divisible into units of any size. And the small units of gold or silver are durable; indeed, much more durable than the cigarettes of the POW camp. But, in another respect, gold and silver are less desirable than cigarettes: As in the case of beef, an ounce of gold is not easily distinguished from an ounce and a half. Thus, governments became Involved In the monetary system, dividing quantities of gold into easily identified coins of specific weight and value.

The importance of subdivision also helps to explain the coexistence of gold and silver as money (for example, in the United States in the nineteenth century). Gold is easily divisible—up to a point. Gold coins of $50, $20, or $10 could easily be minted and were relatively convenient. But suppose the government wanted to mint a gold coin worth 25 cents. It would be so tiny that it would be easily lost. While the high value of gold made it an obvious choice for coins of high value, it was very inconvenient for the smaller denominations. Here, silver was the obvious choice: It was less valuable per ounce than gold.

In summary, the evolution of the "cigarette standard" illustrated a number of the characteristics which the item chosen for money should possess: It should be *sufficiently valuable* that a reasonably large purchasing power can be carried conveniently by an individual; it should be *easily divisible;* and it should be *durable.*

(Nevertheless, even outside the prisoner-of-war camp, the item which acts as money has not invariably met these qualifications. For example, items used as the means of payment are not always durable. In the nineteenth century, wage earners in the Staffordshire coal mines were paid partly in beer. In his book *Life and Labour in the Nineteenth Century,*† C. R. Fay observed: "This currency was very popular and highly liquid, but it was issued to excess and difficult to store.") ∎

†Cambridge: Cambridge University Press, 1945, p. 197.

monetary system worked smoothly only so long as a reasonable balance was kept between the quantity of money (cigarettes) and the quantity of other goods.

This story of the "cigarette standard" illustrates why a smoothly operating monetary system should be made up of money whose value is **uniform.** (Nonuniform money will lead to the operation of Gresham's law, with "bad" money driving "good" money out of circulation.) In the United States, the Federal Reserve System has the responsibility to assure that money is uniform; it is the institution which issues paper currency. It matters not whether the $1 bill I have in my pocket is crisp and new, or whether it is tattered and soiled. The Federal Reserve will replace it with a new bill of equal value when it becomes excessively worn. This means that it represents $1 in value to anyone. This uniformity in the value of each dollar bill obviously adds to the ease of exchange (and it means that Gresham's law does not operate in our modern economy). In accepting dollar bills, we need worry only about whether they are genuine; we need not quibble over their exact physical condition.

A second, and critical, responsibility of the monetary authorities is to ensure that there is the **proper quantity of money** in the system; neither too much nor too little. This will be an important topic in the campanion volume.

COMPARATIVE ADVANTAGE: A REASON TO SPECIALIZE

Money, the development of markets, and (perhaps equally important) the development of a sophisticated transportation and communications system, all make possible a high degree of specialization of production. They make specialization possible and relatively smooth; but they do not provide a reason *why* specialization is advantageous in the first place. At the beginning of the chapter, this question was raised, and the fundamental answer was given: Specialization can add to efficiency. It is now time to explain in more detail just *how*. A key concept in the

explanation is the **principle of comparative advantage.** To understand this principle, it is useful to look first at the simpler concept of **absolute advantage.**

A good tends to be produced in the place which is best suited for its production: steel near the coal mines of Pennsylvania, corn in the fertile fields of Iowa, bananas in the tropical lands of Central America, coffee in the cool highlands of Colombia, and so on. In technical terms, there is some tendency for a good to be produced in the area that has an *absolute advantage* in its production.

A country (or region, or individual) has an *absolute advantage* in the production of a good if it can produce that good with fewer resources (less land, labor, and capital) than other countries (or regions, or individuals).

This same principle applies to specialization among individuals within a city or town. Consider the case of the lawyer and the professional gardener. The lawyer is better at drawing up legal documents, and the gardener generally is better at gardening, so it is in the interest of each to specialize in the occupation in which he or she has an absolute advantage.

But the truth is often more complicated than this. Suppose a certain lawyer is better at gardening than the gardener; she's faster and more effective—in short, she has a "greener thumb." She has an absolute advantage in both the law and gardening. If absolute advantage were the key, she would practice law and do her own gardening as well. Does this necessarily happen? The answer: No. Unless this lawyer positively enjoys gardening as a recreation, she will leave the gardening to the professional. Why? Even though the lawyer, being an excellent gardener, can do as much gardening in 1 hour (let us say) as the gardener could in 2, she will be better off to stick to law and hire the gardener to work on the flowers and shrubbery. Why? In 1 hour's work, the lawyer can draw up a will, for which she charges $50. The gardener's time, in contrast, is worth only $5 per hour. By spending the hour on law rather than gardening, the lawyer comes out ahead. She earns $50, and can hire the gardener for $10 to put in 2 hours to get the gardening done. The lawyer gains $40 by sticking to law for that 1 hour. (This is explained in more detail in Box 3-2.)

The gardener also gains through specialization. Although he has to work 10 hours in order to earn the $50 needed to hire the lawyer to draw up his will, it would take him much more time to draw up the will himself. He would have to spend many hours—as many as 100, per-

---

BOX 3-2

Illustration of Comparative Advantage

A Assume the following:

  1 In 1 hour, the lawyer can plant 20 flowers.

  2 In 1 hour, the gardener can plant 10 flowers. (Therefore, the lawyer has the *absolute advantage* in gardening.)

  3 The lawyer's time, in the practice of law, is worth $50 per hour.

  4 The gardener's time, in gardening, is worth $5 per hour.

B *Question:*

How should the lawyer have 20 flowers planted?

  Option 1: Do it herself, spending 1 hour.

    Cost: She gives up the $50 she could have earned by practicing law for that hour.

  Option 2: Stick to law, and hire the gardener to plant the 20 flowers.

    Cost: Two hours of gardener's time at $5 = $10.

C *Decision:* Choose option 2.

    Spend the available hour practicing law, earning $50.

    Hire the gardener to do the planting for $10.

    Net advantage over option 1: $40.

D *Conclusion:* The lawyer has the *comparative advantage* in law. ■

haps—poring over law books just to learn the basic traps to avoid in drawing up a will. (And, even after spending the 100 hours, he could not be sure that he might not have missed something very simple that the lawyer learned in her many years of study.) Thus, by spending 10 hours on gardening and using the income to buy the lawyer's time, the gardener gains: He gets a better will than he could have gotten by struggling with legal books for a full 100 hours.

Thus, absolute advantage is not necessary for specialization. The lawyer has an absolute advantage in both gardening and law; the gardener has an absolute disadvantage in both. But the lawyer has a *comparative advantage* in law; the gardener has a *comparative advantage* in gardening. When the gardener and the lawyer stick to their comparative advantage, *both gain from specialization.*

British economist **David Ricardo** enunciated the principle of comparative advantage in the early nineteenth century to illustrate how countries gain from international trade. But comparative advantage provides a general explanation of the advantages of specialization; it is just as relevant to domestic as to international trade. Nevertheless, it is customary to follow Ricardo and consider this principle as part of the study of international economics. We follow the custom, and put off our more detailed analysis of comparative advantage to the chapter on international trade. For the moment, we note that the concept of comparative advantage is related to opportunity cost.

If two individuals (or regions, or nations) have different opportunity costs of producing a good or service, then the individual (or region, or nation) with the lower opportunity cost has the *comparative advantage* in that good or service.

The opportunity cost of the lawyer taking an hour to draw up a will is the alternative forgone. In Box 3-2, this is shown to be the planting of 20 flowers that she could do as an alternative. In contrast, the opportunity cost of the gardener producing a will is much higher. Drawing up a will would take 100 hours, in which he alternatively could plant 1,000 flowers. Therefore, the lawyer's opportunity cost of drawing up a will is lower than the gardener's (20 flowers vs. 1,000). Thus, the lawyer has the comparative advantage in law.[2] She will specialize in this, leaving the flowers to the gardener.

Comparative advantage, then, is the first great propellant driving the wheels of commerce (while money acts as the grease, making the machine run with less friction). But there is also a second fundamental reason for specialization.

ECONOMIES OF SCALE: ANOTHER REASON TO SPECIALIZE

Consider two small cities which are identical in all respects. Suppose that the citizens of these cities want both bicycles and lawnmowers, but that neither city has any advantage in the production of either good. Will each city then produce its own, without any trade existing between the two? Probably not. It is likely that one city will specialize in bicycles, and the other in lawnmowers. Why?

The answer is: *economies of scale.* To understand what this term means, first assume that there is no specialization. Each city directs half its productive resources into the manufacture of bicycles, and half into the manufacture of lawnmowers, thus producing 1,000 bicycles and 1,000 lawnmowers. But if one city specializes and directs all its productive resources toward the manufacture of bicycles, it can acquire specialized machinery and produce 2,500 bicycles. Similarly, if the other city directs all its productive resources toward the production of lawnmowers, it can produce 2,500. Note that each city, by doubling all inputs into the production of a single item, can more than double its output of that item from 1,000 to 2,500 units. Thus, economies of scale exist.

[2]It follows directly that the gardener has the comparative advantage in gardening: He gives up only one-thousandth of a will to plant a flower, compared to the one-twentieth forgone by the lawyer.

Economies of scale exist when a doubling of all inputs more than doubles output.

Even though neither city had any fundamental advantage in the production of either product, they can gain by specialization. Before specialization, their combined output was 2,000 bicycles and 2,000 lawnmowers. After specialization, they together make 2,500 bicycles and 2,500 lawnmowers.

While Ricardo's theory of comparative advantage dates back to the early nineteenth century, the explanation of economies of scale goes back even further, to Adam Smith's *Wealth of Nations* (1776). In Smith's first chapter, "Of the Division of Labour," there is a famous description of pin-making:

A workman not educated to this business . . . could scarce, perhaps, . . . make one pin in a day, and certainly not twenty. But in the way in which this business is now carried on, not only the whole work is a peculiar trade, but it is divided into a number of branches. . . . One man draws out the wire, another straightens it, a third cuts it, a fourth points it, a fifth grinds it at the top for receiving the head. . . . Ten persons, therefore, could make among them upwards of forty-eight thousand pins in a day. Each person, therefore, . . . might be considered as making four thousand and eight hundred pins in a day.[3]

What is the reason for the gain which comes from the division of pin-making into a number of separate steps? Certainly it is not that some individuals are particularly suited to drawing the wire, while others have a particular gift for straightening it. On the contrary, if two individuals are employed, it matters little which activity each is assigned. Adam Smith's "production

[3]Adam Smith, *An Inquiry into the Nature and Causes of the Wealth of Nations* (Modern Library edition, New York: Random House, 1937), pp. 4–5.

line" is efficient because of economies of scale which depend on:

1 The introduction of specialized machinery.
2 Specialization of the labor force on that machinery.

Modern corporations also derive economies of scale from a third major source:

3 Specialized research and development, which make possible the development of new equipment and technology.

In the modern world, economies of scale are very important as an explanation of specialization. They are a major reason why the manufacturers of automobiles, aircraft, and computers are few in number and large in size. It is partly because of economies of scale that the automobile industry is concentrated in the Detroit area, with Michigan shipping cars to other areas in exchange for a host of other products.

But economies of scale explain much more than the trade among the regions, states, and cities *within* a country. They also are an important explanation of trade *between* countries. For example, economies of scale in the production of large passenger aircraft go on (and costs continue to fall) long after the United States market is met. Thus, there is a major advantage to Boeing—and to the United States—in producing aircraft for the world market. And there are gains to the aircraft buyers, too. For example, Belgians can buy a Boeing 747 for a small fraction of the cost of making a comparable plane themselves.

In this chapter, the advantages of specialization and exchange have been studied. Exchange takes place in markets; how markets operate will be the subject of the next chapter.

Key Points

1 Specialization contributes to efficiency.

2 Specialization requires exchange. The most primitive form of exchange is barter. This has the disadvantage that it depends on a coincidence of wants.

3 Much more complex exchange, involving many participants, is feasible in an economy with money. Because exchange is so much easier and more efficient with money, money will evolve even in the absence of government action—as happened in the prisoner-of-war camp.

4 If the economy is to operate smoothly, money should be:

   (a) Uniform

   (b) Issued in moderate quantities (neither too much nor too little, compared with the quantity of goods and services to be bought)

   (c) Physically convenient (not bulky or easily lost)

   (d) Easily divisible into small denominations

   (e) Durable

5 There are two major reasons why there are gains from specialization and exchange:

   (a) Comparative advantage

   (b) Economies of scale

6 An example of comparative advantage is the lawyer who is better than the gardener at both law and gardening. Even so, she does not do her gardening herself, because she gains by specializing in law (her comparative advantage) and hiring the gardener to do the gardening (his comparative advantage).

7 Economies of scale exist if a doubling of all resource inputs leads to an output which is more than doubled.

Key Concepts

specialization	**indivisibility**	**debasement of the currency**
exchange	**general purchasing power**	**absolute advantage**
barter	**medium of exchange**	**comparative advantage**
coincidence of wants	**Gresham's law**	**economies of scale**

Problems

3-1 What are the major industries in your home town? Why did those industries locate there?

3-2 Suppose the government taxed all monetary transactions. Would such taxes cause a return to barter or to self-sufficiency? Does the government in fact tax monetary transactions? What are the consequences?

3-3 Suppose that one individual at your college is outstanding, being the best teacher and a superb administrator. If you were the college president, would you ask this individual to teach, or to become the administrative vice-president? Why?

3-4 Draw a production possibilities curve for the lawyer mentioned in Box 3-2, putting the number of wills drawn up in a week on one axis and flowers planted on the other. (Assume that the lawyer is willing to work 40 hours per week.)

*****3-5** Draw the production possibilities curve of one of the two identical cities described in the section on economies of scale.

*Problems marked with asterisks are more difficult than the others. They are designed to provide a challenge to students who want to do more advanced work.

CHAPTER 4
Demand and Supply: The Market Mechanism

Do you know,
Considering the market, there are more
Poems produced than any other thing?
No wonder poets sometimes have to *seem*
So much more business-like than business men.
Their wares are so much harder to get rid of.
Robert Frost, *New Hampshire*

Although some countries are much richer than others, the resources of every country are limited. Choices must be made. Furthermore, except on Robinson Crusoe's mythical island, every economy involves some degree of specialization. In every economy, therefore, some mechanism is needed to answer the fundamental questions raised by specialization and by the need to make choices:

1 *What* goods and services will be produced? (How do we choose among the various options represented by the production possibilities curve?)

2 *How* will these goods and services be produced? For example, will bicycles be produced by relatively few workers using a great deal of machinery, or by many workers using relatively little capital equipment?

3 *For whom* will the goods and services be produced? Once goods are produced, who will consume them?

The market and the government
Basically, there are two mechanisms by which these questions can be answered. First, answers may be provided by Adam Smith's "invisible hand." If people are left alone to make their own transactions, then the butcher, the baker, and

the brewer will produce the beef, bread, and beer for our dinner. In other words, answers may be provided by the ***private market.*** (In a market, an item is bought and sold. For example, a market existed in our simple illustration in Chapter 3, when a surgeon purchased beef from a farmer. When transactions between buyers and sellers take place with little or no government interference, then a *private* or *free* market exists.)

Second, answers may be provided by the ***government.***[1] The government's role may be quite limited, involving simply a modification of the operations of a market. For example, if the government were to tax heavy "gas-guzzling" cars, people would have an incentive to switch to small cars. Car manufacturers in turn would respond by producing more of the small cars and

---

[1]The market and the government are not the only mechanisms for answering these questions. For example, when a relief organization collects voluntary contributions of clothing or money for distribution to the poor or to the victims of a natural disaster, it is influencing who gets the output of society (Question #3). Similarly, within the family, a mechanism other than the market or the government is used to determine how the budget for clothing, etc., is divided among the family members. Nevertheless, the market and the government are the mechanisms on which economists concentrate in answering the three basic questions.

fewer of the large ones. Without becoming directly involved in the manufacture of cars, the government would thus be able to influence *what* goods are produced.

Taxes are not the only way that government may influence what will be produced. For example, Congress may pass laws which require new cars to have safety belts and other specific types of protective equipment. And the government may become directly involved in determining the type of output. Most notably, during wartime the government becomes a direct user of much of the output of the economy in the form of tanks, ships, and aircraft. Finally, the government may own and operate businesses. For example, while much of the electric power in the United States is produced by privately owned utilities, the government-owned Tennessee Valley Authority (TVA) is a large producer of electricity.

Conceivably, an economy might be designed to depend exclusively either on private markets or on the government to make the three fundamental decisions of *what, how,* and *for whom.* But the real world is one of compromise: In every actual economy, there is some mixture of markets and government decision-making. However, reliance on the market varies substantially among countries. In the United States, most choices are made in the market. By international standards, the government plays a restricted role, although this role has expanded substantially during the twentieth century.

Toward the other end of the spectrum, the economies of the Soviet Union, the People's Republic of China, and the countries of Eastern Europe rely heavily on government decision-making. As Marxist nations, they particularly object to having the private market determine for whom goods will be produced. They do not permit individuals to own large amounts of capital. Therefore, individuals do not receive large interest and dividend payments with which to buy a considerable fraction of the output of the economy. (In contrast, most capital is privately owned in **capitalist** or **free enterprise** countries such as the United States.)

In a **Marxist economy** where most capital

is owned by the state, the government is involved in detailed decisions as to which products will be produced with this capital. For example, the Soviet Union has a central planning agency which issues directives to the various sectors of the economy to produce specific quantities of goods. It would, however, be a mistake to conclude that government planning in the countries of Eastern Europe is a rigid and all-pervasive method of answering the three basic questions. Markets for goods exist in all these countries, and some nations (particularly Yugoslavia) allow many decisions to be made through the market. Thus, these countries too have **mixed economies,** although the mix between market and government decision-making is very different from ours.

A **capitalist** or **free enterprise economy** is one in which individuals are permitted to own large amounts of capital, and decisions are made primarily in private markets, with relatively little government interference.

A **mixed economy** is one in which the market and the government share the decisions as to what shall be produced, how, and for whom.

A **Marxist economy** is one in which most of the capital is owned by the government. (Individuals may of course own small capital goods, such as hoes or hammers, but the major forms of capital—factories and heavy machinery—are owned by the state.) Political power is in the hands of a party pledging allegiance to the doctrines of Karl Marx.[2]

---

[2]The rule by a Marxist political party is an important part of this definition, since there are a number of non-Marxist military dictatorships in which much of the capital is owned by the government—or by the generals who run the government. The term *state capitalism* is sometimes used to describe such a system.

The term *socialist* is sometimes applied to Marxist systems—as, for example, in the title "Union of Soviet Socialist Republics." However, we will avoid this term for the moment. Like the terms "liberal" or "conservative," the term "socialist" is ambiguous; it can mean quite different things to different people.

Because the market is relatively important in the United States, it will be our initial concern. (Later chapters will deal with the economic role of the government in the United States and with the Marxist economic system.) This chapter will explain how the market answers the three basic questions: What will be produced? How? For Whom?

THE MARKET MECHANISM

In most markets, the buyer and the seller come face to face. When you buy a suit of clothes, you talk directly to the salesclerk; when you buy groceries, you physically enter the seller's place of business (the supermarket). But physical proximity is not required to make a market. For example, in a typical stock market transaction, someone in Georgia puts in a call to his broker to buy 100 shares of IBM common stock. About the same time, someone in Pennsylvania calls her broker to sell 100 shares. The transaction takes place on the floor of the New York Stock Exchange, where representatives of the two brokerage houses meet. The buyer and the seller of the stock do not leave their respective homes in Georgia and Pennsylvania.

Some markets are quite simple. For example, a barbershop is a "market," since haircuts are bought and sold there. The transaction is obvious and straightforward; the service of haircutting is produced on the spot. But in other cases, markets are much more complex. Even the simplest everyday activity may be the culmination of a complicated series of market transactions.

As you sat at breakfast this morning drinking your cup of coffee, you were calling on products from distant areas. The coffee itself was probably produced in Brazil. The brew was made with water that perhaps had been brought to your residence in pipes manufactured in Pennsylvania and purified with chemicals produced in Delaware. The sugar for the coffee may have been produced in Louisiana, and the artificial cream manufactured from soybeans grown in Missouri. Possibly, your coffee was poured into a cup made in New York State, and stirred with a spoon manufactured in Taiwan from Japanese stainless steel which used Canadian nickel in its production. All this for one individual cup of coffee.

In such a complex economy, something is needed to keep things straight, to bring order out of potential chaos, and to make sure that all the coffee doesn't end up in New York and all the sugar in New Jersey. Market prices bring order by performing two important, interrelated functions:

1 Prices provide **information.**
2 Prices provide **incentives.**

To illustrate, suppose we start from the example of chaos, with all the coffee in New York and all the sugar in New Jersey. Coffee lovers in New Jersey would be desperate, and would clamor for coffee even at very high prices. The high price would be a signal, providing *information* to coffee owners that there were eager buyers in New Jersey. And it would provide them with an *incentive* to send coffee to New Jersey. In any market, the price provides the focus for interactions between buyers and sellers.

PERFECT AND IMPERFECT COMPETITION

Some markets are dominated by a few large firms; others have thousands of sellers. The "big three" automobile manufacturers make over 70 percent of the cars sold in the United States, with the rest of the sales being divided up among American Motors and a number of foreign firms. Such an industry, which is dominated by a few sellers, is termed an **oligopoly.** (The word "oligopoly" means "a few sellers," just as "oligarchy" means the "rule by a few.") Some markets are even more concentrated. For example, there is just one supplier of telephone services in your area; the telephone company has a **monopoly.** On the other hand, there are thousands of wheat producers.

A *monopoly* exists when there is only *one* seller. An *oligopoly* exists when a *few sellers* dominate a market.

The number of participants in a market has a significant effect on the way in which the price is determined. In the wheat market, there are thousands of buyers and thousands of sellers. The individual farmers know that each of them is producing only a tiny fraction of the total supply of wheat. They know that no one farmer can affect the price of wheat by holding his wheat back from the market. For each one, the price is given; the individual farmer's decision is limited to the number of bushels of wheat to sell. Similarly, the millers realize that they are each buying only a small fraction of the wheat supplied. They realize that they cannot, as individuals, affect the price of wheat. Each miller's decision is limited to the number of bushels to be bought at the existing market price. In the wheat market, where ***perfect competition*** exists, prices are determined by *impersonal market forces*. For the individual seller and the individual buyer, *there is no pricing decision to be made*. Every buyer and every seller is a ***price taker.***

Perfect competition exists when there are many buyers and many sellers, with no single buyer or seller having any influence over the price. (Sometimes, this term is shortened simply to "competition.")

In contrast, individual producers in an oligopolistic or a monopolistic market know that they have some control over price. For example, an automobile firm sets the prices of its cars. That does not mean, of course, that the company can set any price it wants and still be ensured of making a profit. It can offer to sell automobiles at a high price, in which case it will sell only a few cars. Or it can charge a lower price, in which case it will sell more cars. Similarly, the telephone company knows that it is large enough to influence its rates (although its freedom of action is limited by government regulation). On the other side of the market, some buyers may also be large enough to influence price. General

Motors is a large enough purchaser of steel to be able to bargain with the steel companies over the price of steel. When individual buyers or sellers can influence price, ***imperfect competition*** exists.

Imperfect competition exists when any buyer or any seller is able to influence the price. Such a buyer or seller is said to have market power.

(Note that the term "competition" is used differently in economics and in business. Don't try to tell someone from Ford that the automobile market isn't very competitive; Ford is very much aware of the competition from General Motors, Chrysler, and the Japanese. Yet, according to the economist's definition, the automobile industry is far less competitive than the wheat industry.)

Because price is determined by impersonal forces in a perfectly competitive market, the competitive market is simplest, and will therefore be considered first. The perfectly competitive market is also given priority attention because competitive markets generally operate more efficiently than imperfect markets, as we shall eventually show in Chapters 10–12.

THE PERFECTLY COMPETITIVE MARKET: DEMAND AND SUPPLY

We might as reasonably dispute whether it is the upper or the under blade of a pair of scissors that cuts a piece of paper, as whether the value is governed by utility [demand] or cost of production [supply].
Alfred Marshall,
Principles of Economics

In a perfectly competitive market, price is determined by **demand** and **supply.**

Demand . . .

Consider, as an example, the market for apples, in which there are many buyers and many sellers, with none having any control over the price. For the buyer, a high price acts as a deterrent; the higher the price, the fewer apples

An *industry* refers to all the producers of a good or service. For example, we may speak of the automobile industry, or the airline industry. (Note that the term "industry" can refer to *any* good or service; it need not be manufactured. Thus, we may speak of the "wheat industry" or the "hotel industry.")

buyers purchase. Why is this so? As the price of apples rises, consumers switch to oranges or grapefruit, or they simply cut down on their total consumption of fruit. Similarly, the lower the price, the more apples are bought. A lower price brings new purchasers into the market, and each purchaser tends to buy more. The response of buyers to various possible prices is illustrated in the ***demand schedule*** in Table 4-1.

Any demand schedule may be graphed as a ***demand curve.*** For example, the demand schedule in Table 4-1 is graphed as a demand curve in Figure 4-1 as follows: The quantity of the good (in thousands of bushels per week) is shown on the horizontal axis, and the price per bushel is shown on the vertical axis. In the demand schedule in Table 4-1, the first row (*A*) indicates that if the price were $10, consumers would be willing to buy 50,000 bushels of apples. This information is plotted in Figure 4-1 as point *A*. Similarly, points *B*, *C*, and *D* in Figure 4-1 represent the corresponding *B*, *C*, and *D* rows in Table 4-1.

When economists use the term "demand," they mean a whole demand schedule or curve

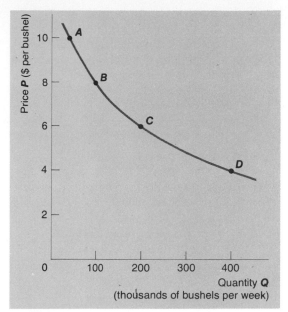

Figure 4-1
The demand curve

At each of the possible prices specified, there is a certain quantity of apples that people would be willing and able to buy. This information is provided in Table 4-1 and is reproduced in this diagram. On the vertical axis, the possible prices are shown. In each case, the quantity of apples that would be bought is measured along the horizontal axis. Since people are more willing to buy at a low price than at a high price, the demand curve slopes downward to the right.

(such as the one plotted in Figure 4-1). The demand schedule or demand curve applies to a *specific population* and to a *specific time period.* (Clearly, the number of apples demanded during a month will exceed the number demanded during a week. And the number demanded by the people of Virginia will be less than the number demanded in the whole Eastern United States.) In a general discussion of theoretical issues, the population and time framework are not always stated explicitly, but it nevertheless should be understood that a demand curve applies to a specific time and population.

A ***demand curve—*** or ***demand schedule—*** shows the quantities of a good or service which buyers would be willing and able to purchase at various market prices.

Table 4-1
The Demand Schedule for Apples

	(1) Price *P* ($ per bushel)	(2) Quantity *Q* demanded (thousands of bushels per week)
A	$10	50
B	$ 8	100
C	$ 6	200
D	$ 4	400

. . . and supply

While the demand curve illustrates how buyers behave, the supply curve illustrates how sellers behave; it shows how much they would be willing to sell at various prices. Needless to say, buyers and sellers look at high prices in a different light. Whereas a high price discourages buyers and causes them to switch to alternative products, a high price encourages suppliers to produce and sell more of the good. Thus, the higher the price, the higher the quantity supplied. This is shown in the **supply schedule** (Table 4-2) or, alternatively, in the **supply curve** (Figure 4-2). As in the case of the demand curve, the points on the supply curve (F, G, H, and J) are drawn from the information given in the corresponding rows of the table (that is, Table 4-2).

A *supply curve—or supply schedule—* **shows the quantities of a good or service which sellers would be willing and able to sell at various market prices.**

The equilibrium of demand and supply

The demand and supply curves may now be brought together in Figure 4-3. (See also Table 4-3.) To use the analogy of turn-of-the-century British economist Alfred Marshall, this figure shows how the two blades of the scissors jointly determine price.

The **market equilibrium** occurs at point E, where the demand and supply curves intersect. At this equilibrium, the price is $6 per bushel, and weekly sales are 200,000 bushels.

Table 4-2
The Supply Schedule for Apples

	(1) Price P ($ per bushel)	(2) Quantity Q supplied (thousands of bushels per week)
F	$10	260
G	8	240
H	6	200
J	4	150

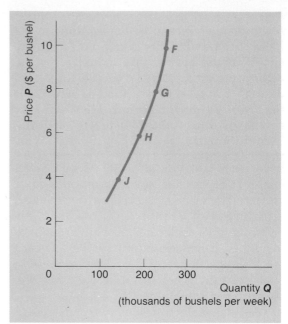

Figure 4-2
The supply curve for apples

For each of the possible prices specified, the supply schedule (Table 4-2) indicates how many units the sellers would be willing to sell. This information may alternatively be shown in this figure, which illustrates how the supply curve slopes upward to the right. At a high price, suppliers will be encouraged to step up production and offer more apples for sale.

An *equilibrium* **is a situation where there is no tendency to change.**

To see why E represents the equilibrium, consider what happens if the market price is initially at some other level. Suppose, for example, that the initial price is $10; that is, it is above the equilibrium price. What happens? Purchasers buy only 50,000 bushels (shown by point A in Figure 4-3), while sellers want to sell 260,000 bushels (point F). There is a large **excess supply,** or **surplus,** of 210,000 bushels. Some sellers are disappointed: They sell much less than they wish at the price of $10. Unsold apples begin to pile up. In order to get them moving, sellers now begin to accept a lower price. The price starts to come down—to $9, then $8. Still there is a surplus, or an excess of the quantity

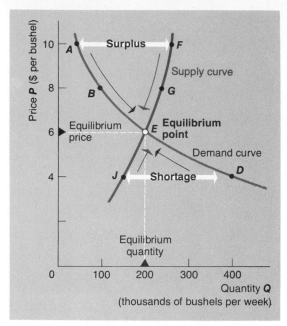

Figure 4-3
How demand and supply determine
equilibrium price and quantity
Equilibrium exists at point *E*, where the quantity
demanded equals the quantity supplied. At any higher price, the quantity supplied exceeds the quantity
demanded. Because of the pressure of unsold stocks,
competition among sellers causes the price to be bid
down to the equilibrium of $6.00. Similarly, at a
price less than the $6.00 equilibrium, forces are set
in motion which raise the price. Because the quantity
demanded exceeds the quantity supplied, eager buyers clamor for more apples, and bid the price up to
the equilibrium at $6.00.

supplied over the quantity demanded. (However, the surplus is now a more modest amount,
BG). The price continues to fall. It does not stop
falling until it reaches $6, the equilibrium. At this
price, buyers purchase 200,000 bushels, which
is just the amount the sellers want to sell. Both
buyers and sellers are now satisfied with the
quantity of their purchases or sales at the existing
market price of $6. Therefore, there is no further
pressure on the price to change.

An *excess supply,* or *surplus,* exists when
the quantity supplied exceeds the quantity
demanded.

Now consider what happens when the initial
price is below the equilibrium, at, say, $4. Eager
buyers now are willing to purchase 400,000
bushels (at point *D*), yet producers are willing to
sell only 150,000 bushels (at point *J*). There is
an *excess demand,* or *shortage,* of 250,000
bushels. As buyers clamor for the limited supplies, the price is bid upward. The price continues to rise until it reaches $6, the equilibrium
where there is no longer any shortage because
the quantity demanded is equal to the quantity
supplied. At point *E*, and only at point *E*, will the
price be stable.

An *excess demand,* or *shortage,* exists
when the quantity demanded exceeds the
quantity supplied.

Table 4-3
The Equilibrium of Demand and Supply

(1) Price *P* ($ per bushel)	(2) Quantity *Q* demanded (thousands of bushels per week)	(3) Quantity *Q* supplied (thousands of bushels per week)	(4) Surplus (+) or shortage (−) (4) = (3) − (2)	(5) Pressure on price
10	50	260	Surplus +210	Downward
8	100	240	Surplus +140	Downward
6	200	200	0	**Equilibrium**
4	400	150	Shortage −250	Upward

SHIFTS IN THE DEMAND CURVE WHEN "OTHER THINGS CHANGE"

The quantity of a product which buyers want to purchase depends on the price. As we have seen, the demand curve illustrates this relationship between price and quantity. But the quantity which people want to purchase also depends on other things. For example, if incomes rise, people will want to buy more apples (and more of a whole host of other products, too).

The purpose of a demand curve is to show **how the quantity demanded is affected by price, and by price alone.** When we ask how much people want to buy at various prices, it is important that our answer not be disturbed by other factors. In other words, when a demand curve is drawn, *incomes and everything else (except price) that can affect the quantity demanded must be held constant.* In the economist's jargon, we make the **ceteris paribus** assumption—that other things remain unchanged. (*Ceteris* is the same Latin word that appears in "*et cetera,*" which literally means "and other things." *Paribus* means "equal" or "unchanged.")

Of course, as time passes, other things do not remain constant. Through time, for example, incomes generally rise. When that happens, the quantity of apples demanded at any particular price increases. The whole demand curve shifts to the right, as illustrated in Figure 4-4. Since economists use the term "demand" to mean the whole demand curve or demand schedule, we may speak of this rightward shift in the curve more simply as an *increase in demand.*

Demand shifters

A shift in the demand curve (that is, a change in demand) may be caused by a change in any one of a whole host of "other things." Some of the most important are the following:

1 Income. When incomes rise, people are able to buy more. And people do in fact buy more of the typical or **normal good:** For such a good, the number of units demanded at each

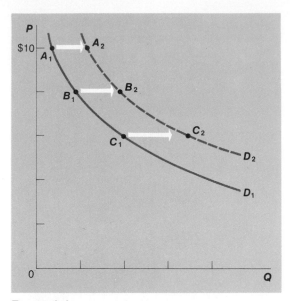

Figure 4-4
A change in the demand for apples

When incomes rise, there is an increase in the number of apples that people want to buy at any particular price. At a price of $10, for example, the quantity of apples demanded increases from point A_1 to A_2. At other prices, the increase in incomes also causes an increase in the number of apples demanded. Thus, the whole demand curve shifts to the right, from D_1 to D_2.

price increases as incomes rise. Thus, the demand curve shifts to the right with rising incomes, as illustrated in Figure 4-4.

There are, however, exceptions. As incomes rise, people may *switch away from margarine* and buy more butter, which they now can afford. When this happens—when the increase in income causes a leftward shift of the demand curve for margarine—the item is an **inferior good.**

If an increase in income	Shifts the demand curve for a good to the *right*	It is a *normal* good (or a superior good)
If an increase in income	Shifts the demand curve for a good to the *left*	It is an *inferior* good

2 Prices of related goods. A rise in the price of one good can cause a shift in the demand curve for another good. For example, if the price of pears were to double while the price of apples remained the same, buyers would be encouraged to switch to apples; they would buy a greater quantity of apples. Thus, a rise in the price of pears causes a rightward shift in the demand curve for apples. Goods such as pears and apples—which satisfy similar needs or desires—are **substitutes.** Other examples are tea and coffee, butter and margarine, bus and train tickets, or heating oil and insulating materials.

For **complements** or **complementary goods,** exactly the opposite relationship holds. In contrast to substitutes—which are used *instead of* each other—complements are used *together,* as a package. For example, gasoline and automobiles are complementary goods. If the price of gasoline spirals upward, people become less eager to own automobiles. The demand curve for cars therefore shifts to the left. So it is with other complements, such as tennis rackets and tennis balls, or cameras and film.

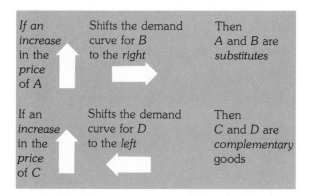

| If an increase in the price of A | Shifts the demand curve for B to the *right* | Then A and B are substitutes |
| If an increase in the price of C | Shifts the demand curve for D to the *left* | Then C and D are complementary goods |

Finally, many goods are basically *unrelated,* in the sense that a rise in the price of one has no significant effect on the demand curve of the others. Thus, bus tickets and butter are unrelated, as are coffee and cameras.

3 Tastes. As time passes, tastes change. Because they want to keep in shape, more people are jogging. This increases the demand for running shoes. Tastes, and therefore demand, are quite volatile for some products, particularly for fads such as skateboards.

This list covers some of the most important demand shifters, but it is far from complete. To see how it might be extended, consider the following questions:

1 If the weather changes, how will the change affect the demand for umbrellas? For skiing equipment?
2 If the President wears a hat during his inaugural drive up Pennsylvania Avenue, how might the demand for hats be affected?
3 If people expect cars to be priced $2,000 higher next year, what effect will this have on the demand for cars this year?

WHAT IS PRODUCED: THE RESPONSE TO A CHANGE IN TASTES

At the beginning of this chapter, three basic economic questions were listed. To see how the market mechanism can help to answer the first of these—*What* will be produced?—consider what happens when there is a change in tastes. Suppose, for example, that people develop a desire to drink more tea and less coffee. This change in tastes is illustrated by a rightward shift in the demand curve for tea and a leftward shift in the demand curve for coffee.

As the demand for tea increases, the price is bid up by eager buyers. With a higher price, growers in Sri Lanka (Ceylon) and elsewhere are encouraged to plant more tea. The equilibrium result, shown as point E_2 in Figure 4-5, involves a higher price and a greater consumption of tea. In the coffee market, the results are the opposite. At the new equilibrium (F_2), the price is lower and a smaller quantity is bought.

Thus, competitive market forces cause producers to "dance to the consumers' tune." In response to a change in consumer tastes, prices change. Tea producers are given an incentive to step up production, and coffee production is discouraged.

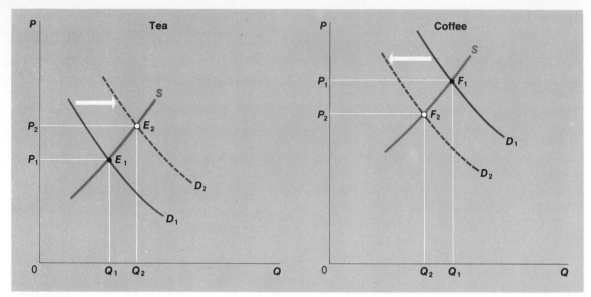

Figure 4-5
A change in tastes

A change in tastes causes the demand for tea to increase and the demand for coffee to decrease. As a result, more tea is bought, at a higher price. Less coffee is bought, and the price of coffee falls.

SHIFTS IN SUPPLY

But if the market makes producers "dance to the consumers' tune," the opposite is also true. As we shall now show, consumers "dance to the producers' tune," as well. Thus, the market involves a complex interaction, with sellers responding to the desires of buyers, and buyers at the same time responding to the willingness of producers to sell.

The supply curve is similar to the demand curve in one important respect. Its objective is to show *how the quantity supplied is affected by price, and by price alone.* Once again, the *ceteris paribus* assumption is made. When a supply curve is drawn, everything (except price) that can affect the quantity supplied is held constant.

Supply shifters

As in the case of demand, the "other things" that affect supply can change through time, causing

the supply curve to shift. Some of these "other things" are the following:

1 The cost of inputs. For example, if the price of fertilizer goes up, farmers will be less willing to produce wheat at the previously prevailing price. The supply curve will shift left.

2 Technology. If there is an improvement in technology, costs of production will fall. With lower costs, producers will be willing to supply more at any particular price. The supply curve will shift to the right.

3 Weather. This is particularly important for agricultural products. For example, a drought will cause a decrease in the supply of wheat (that is, a leftward shift in the supply curve), and a freeze in Florida can cause a decrease in the supply of oranges.

4 The prices of related goods. Just as items can be substitutes or complements in consumption, so they can be substitutes or complements in production.

We saw earlier that substitutes in consumption are goods which can be consumed as *alternatives* to one another, satisfying the same wants (for example, apples and pears). Similarly, **substitutes in production** are goods which can be produced as *alternatives* to one another, using the same factors of production. Thus, corn and soybeans are substitutes in production; they can be grown on similar land. If the price of corn increases, farmers are encouraged to switch their lands out of the production of soybeans and into the production of corn. The amount of soybeans they are willing to supply at any given price decreases; the supply curve for soybeans shifts to the left.

We also saw earlier that complements in consumption are used *together* (for example, gasoline and automobiles). Similarly **complements in production** or **joint products** are produced together, as a package. Beef and hides provide an example. When more cattle are slaughtered for beef, more hides are produced in the process. An increase in the price of beef causes an increase in beef production, which in turn causes a rightward shift of the supply curve of hides.

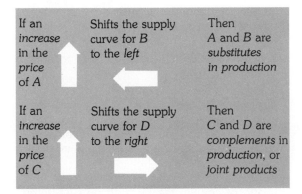

If an increase in the price of A	Shifts the supply curve for B to the *left*	Then A and B are substitutes in production
If an increase in the price of C	Shifts the supply curve for D to the *right*	Then C and D are complements in production, or joint products

The response to a shift in the supply curve

To illustrate how "consumers dance to the producers' tune," suppose that there is a frost in Brazil, which wipes out part of the coffee crop. As a result, the quantity of coffee available on the market is reduced. The supply curve shifts to the left, as illustrated in Figure 4-6. With less

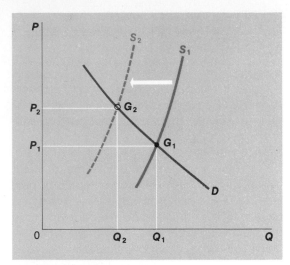

Figure 4-6
A shift in supply

A freeze causes a leftward shift in the supply curve for coffee. The result is a movement of the equilibrium along the demand curve from G_1 to G_2. At the new equilibrium, there is a higher price, and a smaller quantity is sold.

coffee available, the price is bid upward. At the new equilibrium (G_2), the price is higher and the quantity sold is smaller.

How do consumers respond to the change in supply? Because of the higher price of coffee, consumers are discouraged from buying. Some consumers may be relatively indifferent between coffee and hot chocolate, and may switch to chocolate because it is now less expensive than coffee. Others may simply reduce their consumption of coffee, buying it only for very special occasions. Because of the limited quantity, it is not possible for all those who might like to drink coffee to get it. Anyone who is willing and able to pay the high price will get coffee; those who are unwilling or unable to pay the price will not get it. Thus, *the high price acts as a way of allocating the limited supply among buyers.* The coffee goes only to buyers who are sufficiently eager to be willing to pay the high price, and sufficiently affluent to be able to afford it.

SHIFTS IN A CURVE AND MOVEMENTS ALONG A CURVE: THE NEED TO DISTINGUISH

Because the term "supply" applies to a supply schedule or a supply curve, a change in supply means a *shift* in the entire curve. Such a shift took place in Figure 4-6 as a result of a freeze in Brazil.

In that figure, observe that the demand curve has not moved. However, as the supply curve shifts and the price consequently changes, there is a movement *along* the demand curve from G_1 to G_2. At the second point, less is bought than at the original point. The quantity of coffee demanded is less at G_2 than at G_1.

The distinction between a shift in a curve and a movement along a curve should be emphasized. As the equilibrium moves from G_1 to G_2:

1 It is correct to say that "supply has decreased." Why? Because the entire supply curve has shifted to the left.

2 It is *not* correct to say that "demand has decreased." Why? Because the demand curve has not moved.

3 It is, however, correct to say that "the quantity demanded has decreased." Why? Because a smaller quantity is demanded at G_2 than at G_1.

A similar distinction should be made if the demand curve shifts. This is shown in Figure 4-7, based on the left panel of Figure 4-5. Here, it will be recalled, the demand for tea increased because of a change in tastes. The rightward movement of the demand curve caused the equilibrium to move *along* the *supply* curve, from E_1 to E_2. It is *not* correct to say that supply has increased, since the supply curve did not move. But the *quantity supplied* did change; it increased as the price rose.

The distinction between a *shift* in a curve and a movement *along* a curve is more than nit-picking. It is important in avoiding a classic error. History does not give us diagrams showing demand and supply curves, but it (some-

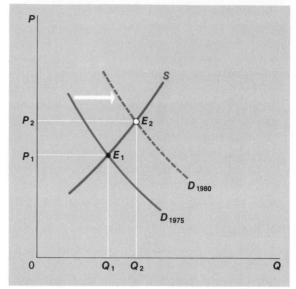

Figure 4-7
A shift in the demand for tea
This diagram, based on the left panel of Figure 4-5, shows that there is an increase in the quantity of tea supplied as the equilibrium moves from E_1 to E_2. However, supply does not change, since the supply curve does not move.

times) does give us quotations on prices and quantities. Suppose that, with a little research, we found that point E_1 in Figure 4-7 was observed in 1975 and point E_2 in 1980. If we are not careful, we might jump to the following incorrect conclusion:

The theory of the demand curve tells us that a rise in price should cause a fall in the quantity demanded. Between 1975 and 1980, the price rose, but so did the quantity. Therefore, the facts contradict the theory of demand.

But, of course, the facts do no such thing. The error in logic is this: Between 1975 and 1980, the demand curve *shifted*. As it shifted, equilibrium moved *along the supply curve*. Thus, the two points E_1 and E_2 trace out the supply curve, not the demand curve. Moreover, these two observations are exactly what we would expect as we move along a supply curve. When the price rises, so does the quantity. (Unfortunately, the results are seldom this clear.

The reason is that, as time passes, both the demand and supply curves may shift.)[3]

THE INTERCONNECTED QUESTIONS OF WHAT, HOW, AND FOR WHOM

In the previous pages, we have seen how two tunes are being played. Demand is the tune played by consumers, while supply is the tune played by the producers. And we have also noted how each group dances to the tune played by the other.

But if we now want to go beyond the question of *what* will be produced to the other questions (*How?* for *Whom?*), we must recognize that the world is even more complex. We don't merely have two tunes being played. We have a whole orchestra, with the tune played on any one instrument related to the tunes played on all the others.

The various pieces of the economy are illustrated in Figure 4-8, which adds detail to Figure 3-3 (in Chapter 3). The **product markets** for oranges, coffee, bread, etc., are shown in the upper box of the diagram; these are the markets on which we have concentrated thus far. But in the box at the bottom, we see that there are similar **markets for factors of production,** with their own demands and supplies. For example, to produce wheat, farmers hire workers and rent land. Thus, they create a demand for labor and land in the wheat industry. At the same time, individuals who work on wheat farms supply labor.

In answering the question, *What* will be produced? we began by looking at the top box, where the demand and supply for the various products are shown. If there is a large demand for tea and a small demand for coffee, we may expect much tea to be produced, and little coffee. But eventually we will also have to look at the lower box, which shows the demand and supply for the factors of production. Why is this relevant? Because the demand and supply curves in the upper box are influenced by what happens in the factor markets in the lower box.

As an example, consider what happens when oil is discovered in Alaska. To build the pipeline needed to get the oil out, workers have to be hired. As a consequence, the demand for construction labor in Alaska increases sharply. The wage rate in Alaskan construction shoots up, and workers flock in from the lower 48 states. The spiraling wage payments in Alaska (lower box) have repercussions on the demands for goods in Alaska (upper box). For example, the demands for food and housing in the upper box rise as a result of the increased earnings of construction workers in the lower box. (What happens to the price of a hotel room during the pipeline construction?)

How? and for whom?

To answer the question, *What* will be produced? we began by looking at the upper box of Figure 4-8. To answer the questions *How?* and *For Whom?* we begin by looking at the lower box.

The prices established in the lower box help to determine *how* goods will be produced. During the Black Death of 1348–1350 and subsequent plagues, an estimated quarter to a third of the Western European population died. As a consequence, labor supply was substantially reduced and wages rose sharply, by 30 to 40 percent.[4] Because of the scarcity of labor and its high price, wheat producers had an incentive to farm their lands with less labor. Wheat was produced in a different way, with a different combination of labor and land. The market mechanism was the way that the society in those

---

[3]Details: If the demand curve alone shifts to the right, then an increase in the price will be accompanied by an increase in the quantity sold (Figure 4-7). If, on the other hand, the supply curve alone shifts (to the left), then an increase in the price will be accompanied by a decrease in the quantity sold (Figure 4-6). If, finally, both the demand and the supply curves shift, we cannot tell whether an increase in price will be accompanied by an increase or a decrease in the quantity sold.

[4]H. Robbins, "A Comparison of the Effects of the Black Death on the Economic Organization of France and England," *Journal of Political Economy,* August 1928, p. 463.

days, as today, conserved its scarce supply of a factor (in this case, labor).

The answer to the question, *"For whom is the nation's output produced?"* depends on incomes. And incomes are determined by the interplay of supply and demand in the lower box in Figure 4-8. For example, the supply of doctors is small compared with the demand for doctors. The price of medical "labor" is therefore high; doctors generally have high incomes. On the other hand, unskilled labor is in large supply, and is therefore cheap. Consequently, the unskilled worker receives a low income. (For further detail on the demand and supply for labor, see Appendix 4-A.)

But, once again, we cannot look at only one box. There are influences from the upper box that must also be taken into account. For example, reconsider the Alaskan pipeline workers. We saw how the increase in demand for labor (in the lower box) drove their wage rate skyward. But that didn't mean that these workers lived like kings. Even though they had very high incomes, the Alaskan economy did not provide a large quantity of housing for them. Because of the tight supply conditions in the Alaskan housing market (upper box), housing prices soared. The construction workers' incomes went into paying these higher prices, rather than into a large increase in the quantity of housing. At least in terms of housing, these workers did not get a much larger share of the nation's output after all.

THE MARKET MECHANISM: A PRELIMINARY EVALUATION

There are thousands of markets in the United States, and millions of interconnections among the markets. Changes in market conditions are reflected in changes in prices. As we have seen, prices provide information to market participants; they provide them with incentives to respond to changing conditions; and they bring order out of a potentially chaotic situation—even though there is no individual or government bureaucracy in control.

Strengths of the market

In some ways, the market works very well. For example:

1 The market *gives producers an incentive to produce the goods that the public wants.* If people want more tea, the price of tea is bid up, and producers are encouraged to produce more. (However, where the government sets output targets, production may respond extremely slowly to changes in consumer tastes.)

2 The market *provides an incentive to acquire useful skills.* For example, the high fees that doctors charge give students an incentive to undertake the long, difficult, and expensive training necessary to become a physician.

3 The market *encourages people to use scarce goods carefully.* For example, when the coffee crop is partially destroyed by bad weather, the price is driven up, and people use coffee sparingly. Those who are relatively indifferent are encouraged to switch to tea. Even those who feel they must have coffee are motivated to conserve. With a high price of coffee, they are careful not to brew three cups when they intend to use only two.

4 Similarly, the price system *encourages producers to conserve scarce resources.* In the pasturelands of Texas, land is plentiful and cheap; it is used to raise cattle. In Japan, in contrast, land is relatively scarce and expensive. Because of its high price, it is used more intensively. Rice is grown rather than livestock.

5 The market involves a *high degree of economic freedom.* Nobody forces people to do business with specific individuals or firms. People are not directed into specific lines of work by a government official; they are free to choose their own occupations. Moreover, if people save, they are free to use their savings to set themselves up in their own independent business.

6 Decentralized markets provide *information on local conditions.* For example, if an unusual amount of hay-producing land in a specific county is plowed up to grow corn, then the price of hay in that county will tend to rise. The higher price of hay will signal farmers that they should

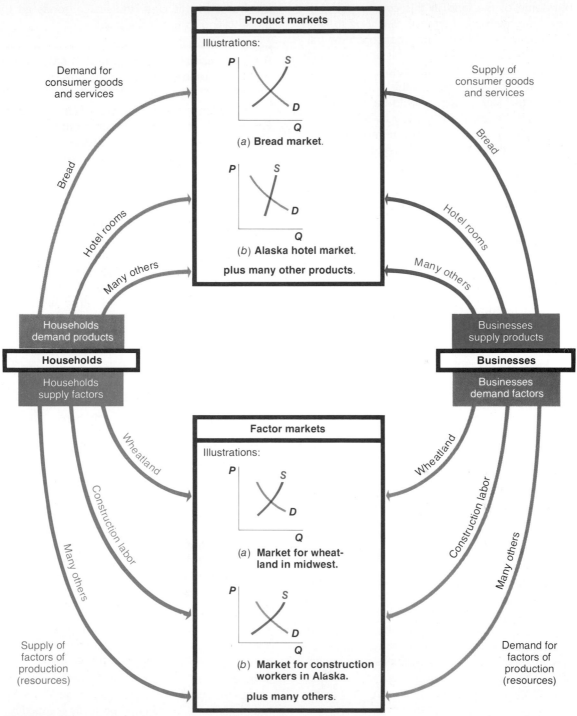

Figure 4-8

Markets answer the basic questions of what, how, and for whom

The product markets (top box) are most important in determining *what* is produced, and the factor markets (lower box) in determining *how* goods are produced, and *for whom*. However, there are many interrelationships among the demand and supply curves in the two boxes. For example, incomes change in response to changing demand and supply conditions in the lower box, and these changing incomes in turn influence the demand for products shown in the upper box.

put some of the land in this county back into hay. No government agency can hope to keep up-to-date and detailed information on the millions of localized markets like this one, each with its own conditions. (Note the amount of information that is relevant, even for this simple decision on whether hay or corn should be planted: the quality of the land, particularly its relative productivity in hay and corn; the number of cattle and horses that eat hay; the cost of fertilizer for hay and for corn; the cost of seed for each; and so on and on.)

In evaluating how well a market works, we should keep in mind the most important question of all: *compared to what*? Even a poor market may work better than the real-world alternatives. Thus, one of the strongest arguments for the market parallels Winston Churchill's case for democracy: It doesn't work very well, but it does work better than the alternatives that have been tried from time to time.

The alternative of price controls: Some problems Consider, for example, some of the problems which can arise if the government interferes with the market mechanism by fixing prices. Suppose, once again, that the coffee crop is partially destroyed by bad weather. If government controls prevent the price from rising, a shortage develops. Those who get to the store first are able to buy coffee at the low price. They may use the inexpensive coffee carelessly. But those who get to the store later find that coffee has been sold out; they have to do without completely.

Where government price controls result in shortages, people have an incentive to get to the store first, before their neighbors. In order to get scarce goods, they waste time standing in line. To use the quip applied to early post-World War II Britain, the society becomes a "queuetopia." The heavily regulated economies of Eastern Europe have had chronic shortages; queuing to buy scarce goods is common.

Moreover, as a result of price controls, goods may disappear from the regular distribution channels, and flow instead into illegal ***black markets.*** In this case, the scarce goods go to those willing to break the law.

A *black market* is one in which sales take place at a price above the legal maximum.

Price controls can create other problems. For example, the Polish Government in the late 1970s was anxious to prevent labor unrest, and therefore kept the price of bread fixed at a low price—so low that it was less than the price of wheat which went into making the bread. The result was that some farmers fed bread rather than grain to their livestock. Thus, the resources that went into making the bread from wheat were wasted. This does not happen in a market economy: Nobody is going to work to produce bread from wheat if the bread sells for a lower price. (Other problems which arise when the government fixes prices are discussed in Box 4-1.)

The market mechanism: Limitations and problems

While the market has impressive strengths, it is also the target of substantial criticisms:

1 While the market provides a high degree of freedom for participants in the economy, *it may give the weak and the helpless little more than the freedom to starve.* In a market, producers do not respond solely to the needs or the eagerness of consumers to have products. Rather, they respond to the desires of consumers which are backed up with cash. Thus, under a system of laissez faire, the pets of the rich may have better meals and better health care than the children of the poor.

2 An unregulated system of private enterprise *may be quite unstable,* with periods of inflationary boom giving way to sharp recessions.

3 In a system of laissez faire, *prices are not always the result of impersonal market forces.* As noted earlier, it is only in a perfectly competitive market that price is determined by the intersection of a demand and a supply curve. In many markets, one or more participants have the power to influence price. *The monopolist or oligopolist may restrict production* in order to keep the price high. (See Appendix 4-B.)

4 Activities by private consumers or producers may have *side effects.* Nobody owns the air or the rivers. Consequently, in the absence of government restraints, manufacturers use them freely as garbage dumps, harming those downwind or downstream. The market provides no incentive to limit such side effects.

5 In some areas, the market *simply won't work.* Where there is a military threat, the society cannot provide defense via the market. An individual has no incentive to buy a rifle for the army, since the benefits go to the society as a whole, not to the individual. Thus, defense is a prime example of a service which can be best provided by the government. The police and the judicial system are others. No matter how well the market works in general, people can't be permitted to "buy" a judge.

6 In recent years, a number of economists have expressed concern that the market economy of the United States has become *less flexible* than it used to be, and less able to adjust quickly to changing conditions. Tibor Scitovsky (of Stanford University and the University of California at Santa Cruz) has cited an important example, namely, "Our economy's failure, six long years after OPEC [the Organization of Petroleum Exporting Countries] had started flexing its muscles, to have taken even a first step towards substituting coal for oil, although idle capacity, unemployed miners, and coal deposits are all plentiful."[5]

7 In a system of laissez faire, businesses may do an admirable job of satisfying consumer demand as expressed in the marketplace. But why should these businesses be given high marks for *satisfying wants that they may have created in the first place* by advertising? In the words of retired Harvard Prof. John Kenneth Galbraith, "It in-

volves an exercise of imagination to suppose that the taste so expressed originates with the consumer."[6] In this case, the producer (not the consumer) is sovereign. According to Galbraith, the consumer is a puppet, manipulated by producers with the aid of Madison Avenue's bag of advertising tricks. Many of the wants which producers create and then satisfy are trivial: the demands for deodorants, automobile chrome, and junky breakfast foods.

(Without arguing the merits of each and every product, defenders of the market system have a substantial countercase, based in part on the question: Compared with what? If market demands are dismissed, who then is to decide which products are "meritorious" and which are not? Some government official? Should not people be permitted the freedom to make their own mistakes? And how can Galbraith assume that created wants are without merit? After all, we are not born with a taste for art or good music. Our taste for good music is created when we listen to the producer of good music, like the Boston Pops. Should the all-wise government official close down the Boston Pops, on the ground that it satisfies only the want which it has created? Furthermore, Galbraith exaggerates when he argues that business firms can control their sales through advertising. Even after an intense advertising campaign, a product may flop, as the Ford Motor Co. found when it introduced the Edsel automobile several decades ago.)

If these criticisms of the market are taken far enough, they can be made into a case for replacing the market with an alternative system in which the government directs economic activity. (However, defenders of the market argue that some of the criticisms—especially 2 and 6—do not make a case for more government interference. Rather, they argue that government activities have themselves added to the

[5]Tibor Scitovsky, "Can Capitalism Survive?—An Old Question in a New Setting," *American Economic Review,* May 1980, p. 3. Scitovsky attributes the inflexibilities not only to inherent problems in the market, but also, to an important degree, to government regulations.

[6]John Kenneth Galbraith, "Economics as a System of Belief," *American Economic Review,* May 1970, p. 474. See also Galbraith, *The New Industrial State* (Boston: Houghton Mifflin, 1967).

BOX 4-1

Rent Control

Next to bombing, rent control seems in many cases to be the most efficient technique so far known for destroying cities, as the housing situation in New York City demonstrates.

                                    Assar Lindbeck

New York City has had rent controls in one form or another since 1943, when they were introduced throughout the nation to protect industrial workers and the families of those serving overseas in the armed forces. (After the war, rent controls were abolished elsewhere in the nation.) Even if one wished to quibble with Lindbeck's devastating conclusion, the results cannot be considered encouraging.

The early effects of the imposition of rent controls are illustrated in the left panel of Figure 4-9. The maximum price which can legally be charged is set at P_1, below the free-market price of P_E. As a result, the quantity of housing demanded exceeds the quantity supplied; there is a shortage of AB units. As a consequence, it becomes difficult to find an apartment. When a renter moves out, there is a scramble to get the vacant apartment, and "knowing the right person" becomes a valuable asset. This basic conclusion—that it becomes hard to find an apartment when rents are controlled—is important.

But even bigger difficulties show up as time passes. Rent controls reduce the construction of new apartment buildings, because they reduce the rental income which owners can hope to receive. Furthermore, if rent ceilings are fixed at low levels, owners may let their buildings go without proper maintenance and repair. When the buildings eventually deteriorate to the point where they can't be rented, owners will abandon them (Lindbeck's bombing effect).

This longer-run effect is shown in the right panel, where the demand curve and the short-

Figure 4-9
Rent control

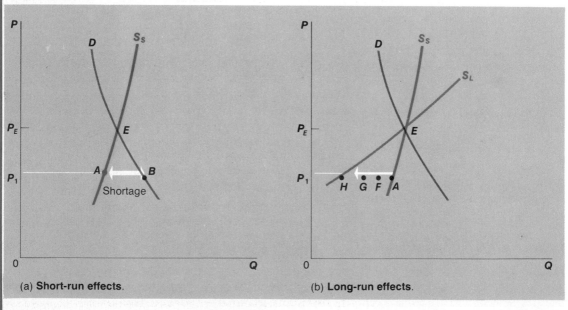

(a) **Short-run effects**.

(b) **Long-run effects**.

run supply (S_S) are copied from the left panel. During the first year of rent control, the quantity of apartments supplied is reduced to *A,* on the short-run supply curve (S_S). With the rent ceiling continuing at P_1, the effects become more serious as time passes. Because few new buildings are constructed and owners skimp on maintenance and abandon their older buildings, the quantity of apartments declines. After a few years, the number of apartments falls to *F,* and then to *G.* Finally it approaches point H on the long-run supply curve. (The long-run supply curve (S_L) shows the ultimate effect of permanent rent control.)

This illustrates the difficulties which can be created if rent controls are maintained over a long period. Over the short term, most tenants benefit from the control. Observe that tenants

pay a lower price, and they get about the same amount of housing at *A* as at the free-market equilibrium *E.* (Nothing much happens to the quantity of apartments supplied in the first year of rent control.) Over the long run, however, it is very doubtful that renters benefit after all. While they still pay a lower price, they have less housing at *H* than at *E.* It is very hard for newcomers to find a place to live. (Desperate apartment-hunters have been known to watch the obituary columns, calling perfect strangers in the event of a death in the family to find if an apartment is becoming vacant.) Furthermore, something happens that does not show up on the diagram: The housing that still can be rented at *H* may be shabby and run-down.

The other effect of rent control is that owners are clearly worse off, because their rental

income has fallen. Since both sides lose, a substantial case can be made against long-term rent control.

The problems here are, of course, reasonably obvious, and were recognized in New York City. Several steps were taken to alleviate the situation. First, in order to provide an incentive for new construction, rent control was applied only to existing apartments, and not to newly constructed apartments. Second, in order to give the owners enough income to maintain the buildings properly, provisions were made to raise rents through time. Apartment dwellers are a politically powerful group, however, so a number of rather interesting formulae were devised to protect the current tenants. Although the details of these formulae have varied from time to time, they contain one common element. The biggest upward adjustment in rent is permitted when an apartment becomes vacant.

This provision in turn led to another complication. The rent on a specific apartment came to depend less on its quality than on how recently it had changed occupants. This fact obviously made the rent control program harder and harder to defend as being "fair." Since the biggest rent increases occurred when tenants moved out, owners had an incentive to make life as miserable as possible for them. (Market incentives work. When the government puts a price on making tenants miserable, then owners will make tenants miserable.) Thus, it is not clear that the provision for increases in rents actually contributed to better maintenance.

The New York experience conveys a strong message. A sensible long-run program of rent control is very difficult to design. It is easier to see the problems than the solutions. There is an ominous long-term lesson for other parts of the country—such as Boston and a number of California cities—which have reintroduced rent controls during the 1970s. (Once introduced, rent controls are difficult to remove. Just as the major gains to tenants come in the first few years of rent control, so the major penalties to tenants come in the first few years of decontrol: Rents may shoot upward, and there is little short-term increase in the number of apartments for rent. Any politician considering decontrol may have to face a group of enraged tenant voters.) ∎

instability and inflexibility of the U.S. economy.) Marxist economists lay particular emphasis on the first and last points in their argument that the market should be replaced with central planning and government direction of the economy.

But the criticisms are also often made by those who seek to reform, rather than replace, the market system. The recent economic history of Western Europe, North America, and many other parts of the globe has to a significant extent been written by such reformers.[7] If the market does not provide a living for the weak and the helpless, then its outcome should be modified by private and public assistance programs. If wildcat banking causes economic instability, the government should take responsibility for a stable and sound currency in order to provide a healthy environment for the market system. Where monopolists have excessive market power, they should be broken up or their market power restrained by the government. Where there are side effects such as pollution, they can

---

[7]On the disturbing issue of whether liberal reform has piled burdens on the market system which it may not be capable of bearing, see Scitovsky's article cited in footnote 5. He raises the question (p. 5) of "how the capitalist state got itself into the business of undermining its own economic base."

be limited by taxation or control programs. In defense, justice, the police, and other areas where the market won't work or works very poorly, the government can assume responsibility for the provision of services.

Although the market is a vital mechanism, it has sufficient weaknesses to provide the government with a major economic role. This role of the government will be the subject of the next chapter.

Key Points

1 Every economy has limited resources and involves specialization and exchange. In every economy, a mechanism is needed to answer three fundamental questions:

    (a) What will be produced?

    (b) How will it be produced?

    (c) For whom will it be produced?

2 There are two important mechanisms for answering these questions:

    (a) The *market,* where individuals are free to make their own contracts and transactions.

    (b) The *government,* which can use taxation and spending policies, regulation, and government-owned enterprises to influence *what, how,* and *for whom.*

In the real world, all countries have "mixed" economies; that is, they rely partly on each of the two mechanisms. But the nature of the mix differs among countries. The United States places a relatively heavy reliance on the market. In the U.S.S.R. and other countries of Eastern Europe, broad areas of decision-making are reserved for the government.

3 *Prices* play a key role in markets, providing information and incentives to buyers and sellers.

4 Markets vary substantially, with some being dominated by one or a few producers, while others have many producers and consumers. A market is *perfectly competitive* if there are many buyers and many sellers, with no single market participant having any influence over the price.

5 In a perfectly competitive market, equilibrium price and quantity are established by the intersection of the demand and supply curves.

6 In drawing both the demand and supply curves, the *ceteris paribus* assumption is made—that "other things" do not change. Everything that can affect the quantity demanded or supplied (with the sole exception of price) is held constant when a demand or supply curve is constructed.

7 If any of these "other things" (consumer incomes or the prices of other goods) do change, the demand or supply curve will shift.

8 *What* the economy produces is determined primarily in the market for goods and services (the upper box of Figure 4-8). On the other hand, *how* and *for whom* are determined primarily in the factor markets (the lower box). However, there are numerous interactions among markets. The answer to each of the three questions depends on what happens in both the upper and lower boxes.

9 There is a substantial case to be made for the market system, because it encourages producers to make what people demand, and because it encourages the careful use of scarce goods and resources. But the market also has significant weaknesses, which provide the government with an important economic role.

Key Concepts

private market

central planning

capitalist economy

free enterprise

mixed economy

monopoly

oligopoly

perfect competition

imperfect competition

market power

demand

supply

equilibrium

surplus

shortage

ceteris paribus

demand shifter

inferior good

normal or superior good

substitutes

complementary goods

supply shifter

joint products

price control

black market

Problems

4-1 Figure 4-6 illustrates the effect of a Brazilian freeze on the coffee market. How might the resulting change in the price of coffee affect the tea market? Explain with the help of a diagram showing the demand and supply for tea.

4-2 In the subsection "*How?* and *For Whom?*" some of the effects of the discovery of oil in Alaska were considered briefly.

(*a*) Draw a demand and supply diagram illustrating what happened in the market for hotel rooms in Alaska. What happened to the price? To the quantity of hotel rooms?

(*b*) Do the same for the clothing market in Alaska. Do you conclude that the results were the same in the clothing and hotel markets? Explain.

4-3 The relatively high incomes of doctors give students an incentive to study medicine. Other than the expected income, what are the important things which affect career decisions?

4-4 It is often said that "the market has no ethics. It is impersonal." But individual participants in the market do have ethical values, and these values may be backed up with social pressures. Suppose that in a certain society, it is considered not quite proper to work in a distillery. With the help of demand and supply diagrams, explain how this view will affect:

(*a*) The demand and/or supply of labor in the alcohol industry.

(*b*) The demand and supply of capital in the alcohol industry.

4-5 Suppose that social sanctions are backed up by law, and that persons caught selling marijuana are given stiff jail sentences. How will this affect the demand and supply of marijuana? The price of marijuana? The quantity sold? The incomes of those selling marijuana?

4-6 In Box 4-1, rent control is discussed. Extend the analysis by describing (*a*) the effects of rent control on the city's tax revenues; (*b*) what will happen if rent control is imposed for 20 years, and then abruptly removed.

***4-7** "Rent control which applies only to structures in existence when the rent control law is passed will not affect new construction." Do you agree or not? Explain.

***4-8** Some writers of the New Left attack both the market system of the United States and the government bureaucracy which has been established in the Soviet Union. Is there any third option? Other than the market and the government, what mechanisms might be used to answer the questions of *what, how,* and *for whom?*

*Problems marked with asterisks are more difficult than the others. They are designed to provide a challenge to students who want more advanced work.

APPENDIX 4-A

THE DEMAND AND SUPPLY FOR
LABOR: THE MALTHUSIAN PROBLEM

If we wish to explain *specific* wage rates—for example, the high wage of construction workers in Alaska—we must look at that *specific* labor market. But we may also be interested in the average wage earned by all labor in an economy. In that case, we must look at the market for all workers.

When we do so, we follow the normal practice and assume that "other things are unchanged." Specifically, we assume that the average price of goods and services remains unchanged. Thus, a change in the wage represents a change in the *real* wage; that is, a change in the quantity of goods and services that the wage will buy. When we show an increase in the wage, the increase permits the worker to buy more goods and services. (It is not simply used up paying higher prices.)

The aggregate labor market is quite different from a specific market (like the market for construction workers). First, consider the supply. The supply curve for construction workers in Alaska slopes upward to the right: The higher the wage, the more workers are attracted from other industries and other states. In contrast, the supply of labor for the United States as a whole is approximately vertical (as shown in Figure 4-10). Even if the U.S. wage rate were to double, there would be little increase in the number of workers offering themselves for employment. The reason is that there are no "other industries" or "other states" from which workers can be attracted (although more workers might come in from other countries).

On the other hand, the demand curve for all U.S. labor does have the same general shape as the demand for labor in a specific industry. (It slopes downward to the right.) The higher the wage rate, the fewer jobs are offered. At a high wage rate, businesses have an incentive to use less labor (and more of other inputs, such as machinery) in the production of goods. Furthermore, with the prices of goods remaining stable (in line with the *ceteris paribus* assumption), an increase in the wage

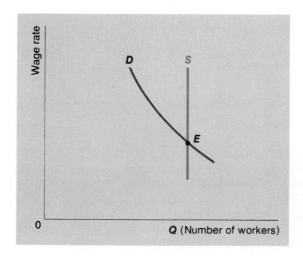

Figure 4-10
The aggregate labor market
For the labor market as a whole, the supply curve is approximately vertical. A doubling of wage rates will not cause a large increase in the number of people who are willing to work.

rate reduces the profitability of producing goods, and therefore causes a reduction in output and in the number of jobs offered. With the demand and supply curves shown, the equilibrium is at *E*.

Now, consider what happens through time. Population increases, and the supply curve for labor therefore shifts to the right. And forces are also at work causing the demand curve to shift. As time passes, the quantity of capital (machinery and equipment) increases, and this results in a rightward shift in the demand for labor. Why? As the quantity of machines and other capital increases, workers have more tools to work with. As a consequence, they can produce more goods; that is, their productivity rises. Therefore, employers are more anxious to hire workers, and are able to pay them a higher wage.

With both the demand and supply curves for labor moving to the right, the net effect on wages depends on the relative strength of the two shifts. Consider the two cases illustrated in Figure 4-11. On the left is Japan, where recent population growth has been small; the supply of labor has therefore moved only slightly to the right. At the same time, the Japanese have directed a large proportion of their productive capacity into the production of new factories and equipment. As a result of the increase in the quantity of capital, the demand curve for labor has moved rapidly to the right. The net effect has been a large increase in the Japanese wage rate.

In the second panel, a quite different situation is illustrated, namely, a problem which concerns a number of the poorer countries in which population growth has been very rapid. Improvements in medical services have cut mortality rates while birth

Figure 4-11
Shifts in the demand and supply of labor

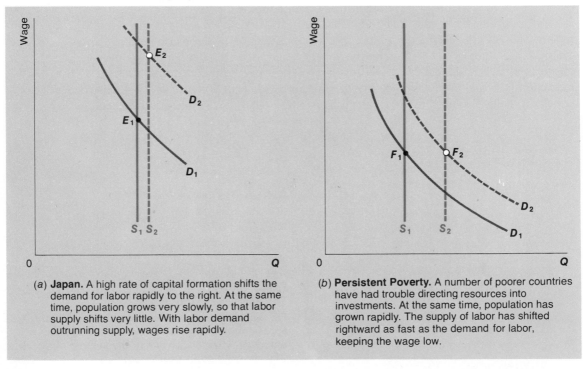

(a) **Japan.** A high rate of capital formation shifts the demand for labor rapidly to the right. At the same time, population grows very slowly, so that labor supply shifts very little. With labor demand outrunning supply, wages rise rapidly.

(b) **Persistent Poverty.** A number of poorer countries have had trouble directing resources into investments. At the same time, population has grown rapidly. The supply of labor has shifted rightward as fast as the demand for labor, keeping the wage low.

rates have remained high. As a result, the supply of labor has shifted rapidly to the right, to S_2. At the same time, a number of these countries have had trouble directing resources into the formation of capital. (Recall from Figure 2-6 that if they divert production away from satisfying their immediate consumption needs, the already low level of consumption may be depressed further.) As a consequence, there has been little increase in the capital stock, and the demand curve for labor has shifted out much less rapidly than in a country such as Japan. As a result, wage rates in a number of the poorest countries have risen very little, if at all.

Thus, we come to a very important conclusion: *The key to an increase in the real wage is an increase in productivity,* which comes mainly from *improvements in technology* and from an *increase in the capital stock at the disposal of the average worker.*

The Malthusian problem

There is a wide variation among the less-developed countries. In some, per capita output has risen rapidly in the past two decades; in others, it has remained relatively stagnant. The very poorest are haunted by the grim prospect described by the young English clergyman Thomas Malthus in his *Essay on the Principle of Population* (1798). Malthus emphasized the scarcity of natural resources—particularly land—which limits the production of food. Specifically, he argued that the output of food at best increases at an arithmetic rate (1, 2, 3, 4, 5, 6, and so on). However, the passion between the sexes means that population tends to increase at a geometric rate (1, 2, 4, 8, 16, 32, etc.):

It may safely be pronounced that population, when unchecked, goes on doubling itself every twenty-five years, or increases in a geometrical ratio. The rate according to which the productions of the earth may be supposed to increase, will not be so easy to determine. Of this, however, we may be perfectly certain, that the ratio of their increase in a limited territory must be of a totally different nature from the ratio of the increase in population. A thousand millions are just as easily doubled every twenty-five years by the power of population as a thousand. But the food to support the increase from the greater number will by no means be obtained with the same facility. . . .

It may be fairly pronounced, therefore, that considering the present average state of the earth, the means of subsistence, under circumstances the most favorable to human industry, could not possibly be made to increase faster than in an arithmetic ratio. . . . The ultimate check to population appears then to be a want of food, arising necessarily from the different ratios according to which population and food increase.[8]

Because of the tendency of population to outstrip food production, the income of the working class will be driven down to the subsistence level. During the nineteenth century, this proposition came to be known as the **iron law of wages.**

After the wage reaches the subsistence level, poor nutrition and starvation will keep population in check. There was a cruel implication to this theory: Public relief for the poor would do nothing in the long run to improve their condition. It would simply result in an upsurge in population; there would be more people to face starvation in the future.

[8]Thomas Malthus, *An Essay on the Principle of Population* (London, Reeves and Turner, 1888 edition), pp. 5–6.

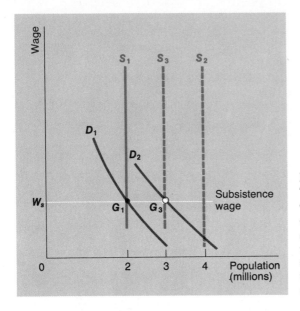

Figure 4-12
The Malthusian problem

The tendency for population to grow more rapidly than food production drives the wage down to the subsistence level at G_1. Thereafter, natural population growth would result in a wage rate *below* the subsistence. People starve, limiting the supply of workers to S_3, the number who can be paid the subsistence wage G_3.

The Malthusian problem is illustrated in Figure 4-12. Suppose that rapid growth has already driven the wage down to the subsistence level, as shown by the intersection of S_1 and D_1; the population is 2 million. Now, in the next 25-year period, population, if unchecked, would rise to 4 million (S_2). But food production can rise to no more than enough to support 3 million. Employers cannot pay 4 million a high enough wage to permit them all to survive; the demand for labor increases only to D_2. Starvation, war, or pestilence take their toll, keeping population down to the 3 million level that can be supported by the available food.

As a general forecast, Malthus' theory proved inaccurate: The standard of living in most countries has risen markedly in the past 200 years. Birth control has been a greater restraint on population growth than Malthus anticipated. And food production has increased beyond Malthus' expectation because of the technological revolution that has included agriculture as well as manufacturing. Nevertheless, Malthus' theory—that there can be a race between population growth and the ability to produce—is worth remembering in a world which is becoming more crowded. ■

APPENDIX 4-B

PRICE IS DETERMINED BY DEMAND AND SUPPLY CURVES ONLY IN A PERFECTLY COMPETITIVE MARKET

To see why it is only in a competitive market that the intersection of the demand and supply curves determines the price, consider the type of question which the supply schedule answers. If the price of apples were (say) $10 per bushel, how many apples would suppliers be willing to sell? This is a question which is relevant in a perfectly competitive market. Individual orchard owners indeed ask themselves how many apples they want to sell at the going market price. They know that they cannot affect that price, so each owner's decision is limited to the number of bushels to be sold.

But that is not the sort of decision a monopolist or oligopolist (like General Motors or Ford) has to make. It does not take the market price as given. Instead, it quotes a price for its product. For example, at the beginning of the model year, General Motors and Ford announce what the prices of their cars will be. Because these companies set their own prices—rather than respond to a given market price—there is no supply curve for the auto industry.

On the other side of the market, a similar complication can arise. The demand curve is a meaningful concept only if there are many buyers, with none having any influence over price. In such a case, the demand-schedule question is relevant. If the price is, say, $10 per bushel, how many bushels will buyers be willing to purchase?

But in a market with only one buyer (monopsony) or only a few buyers (oligopsony), the individual buyer *can* influence price. Therefore the question a monopsonist will ask is not, "How many units will I buy at the given market price?" but rather, "What price shall I offer?" Thus, for example, the only manufacturer in a small town will have monopsony power in the labor market, and will ask, "What wage rate shall I pay?" In such cases, where a single buyer sets market price rather than taking it as given, there is no demand curve.

The major market forms and the chapters in which they will be studied are outlined in Table 4-4. ■

Table 4-4
Types of Markets

Type	Characteristic	Is demand curve meaningful?	Is supply curve meaningful?	How is price determined?	Studied in Chapters
Perfect competition	Many buyers and sellers, with no single market participant affecting price	Yes	Yes	By intersection of demand and supply curves	4, 19–22
Monopoly	One seller, many buyers	Yes	No	By seller, facing market demand	23, 31
Monopsony	One buyer, many sellers	No	Yes	By buyer, facing market demand	31
More complex cases	Few buyers, few sellers	No	No	In complex manner	24, 31

Appendixes 4-A and 4-B

Key Points

10 The wage rate depends on the demand and supply of labor.

11 Increases in the productivity of labor will cause the demand for labor to increase. Increases in the quantity of capital are a principal cause of increases in the productivity of labor.

12 Population growth is the main cause of an increase in the supply of labor.

13 If the demand for labor shifts out faster than the supply of labor, wages will be pulled upward. If the supply shifts out faster than demand, the wage will be depressed. If the tendency for population to increase keeps the wage at a very low level and under downward pressure, the country faces the Malthusian problem.

14 Price is determined by the intersection of the demand and supply curves only in a perfectly competitive market.

Key Concepts

**supply of labor in a
  specific market**
**supply of labor in the
  nation as a whole**

productivity of labor
Malthusian problem
iron law of wages
monopsony

Problem

4-9 *(a)* Suppose you are the manager of a local drug store. What do you think the supply curve of clerks looks like?

  (b) What does the supply curve of labor facing General Motors in Michigan look like?

  (c) What does the supply curve for all labor in the United States look like?

  (d) Explain why the curves in parts *a, b,* and *c* have different shapes.

CHAPTER 5
The Economic Role of the Government

As new . . . problems arise beyond the power of men and women to meet as individuals, it becomes the duty of the Government itself to find new remedies.

Franklin D. Roosevelt

The defects and limitations of the market system, outlined at the end of Chapter 4, provide the government with an important role in the economy. In the words of Abraham Lincoln, a legitimate objective of government is "to do for the people what needs to be done, but which they cannot, by individual effort, do at all, or do so well, for themselves."

Government affects the economy in three principal ways: by *spending*, by *taxation*, and by *regulation*. For example, when the government *spends* for roads or for aircraft, then production is affected; more roads and aircraft are built. The primary function of *taxation* is to raise revenue for the government; taxes are an unpleasant necessity. But taxes may also be used for secondary purposes. For example, if the government wants to discourage the production of some goods, it can put a tax on them. (This will raise their price and lead consumers to buy less.) Third, the government can influence economic behavior through direct *regulation*. Regulations regarding seat belts and other safety equipment have affected the design of automobiles; safety requirements affect the way in which coal is mined; and government regulations limit the amount of pollution which manufacturers can discharge into the air and water.

(There is also a fourth way in which the government affects the economy: It runs some businesses. For example, the Tennessee Valley Authority produces electricity, and performs much the same function as a privately owned electric utility. In the United States, the government is less heavily engaged in running businesses than are many foreign governments. For example, in Western Europe, some steel and automobiles are produced by government-owned corporations. Because of its smaller importance in the United States, this fourth aspect of government activity is not studied in detail in this chapter.)

In contrast with the private market where people have an option of buying or not, government activities generally involve *compulsion*. Taxes *must* be paid; people are not allowed to opt out of the system when the time rolls around for paying income taxes. Similarly, government regulations involve compulsion; car manufacturers *must* install safety equipment. And compulsion sometimes exists even in a government spending program. Young people *must* go to school (although their parents do have the option of choosing a private school rather than one run by the government).

Later sections of this chapter will consider

how the government can use expenditures, taxation, and regulations to improve the outcome of the private market. As a preliminary, it is necessary to look at some facts—how the government role has expanded, and what the government is currently doing.

THE GROWTH OF GOVERNMENT EXPENDITURES

During the nineteenth and early twentieth centuries, government expenditures covered little more than the expenses of the army and navy, a few public works, and the salaries of judges, legislators, and a small body of government officials. Except for wartime periods when spending shot upward to pay for munitions, weapons, and personnel, government spending was small. As late as 1929, all levels of government (federal, state, and local) together spent less than $11 billion a year. Of this total, about three-quarters was spent at the state and local levels. Highway maintenance and education were typical government programs. Life was simple. (This does not mean, however, that a rigid policy of laissez faire was followed. Even during the nineteenth century, governments at both the state and local levels participated in some important sectors of the economy. For example, governments helped railroads and canal systems to expand.)

With the Depression of the 1930s, a major increase in government activity began. Distress and unemployment were widespread, and it was increasingly hard to believe that the workings of the private market would lead to the best of all possible worlds. During the decade 1929–1939, federal government spending increased from $3 billion to $9 billion. Part of the increase was specifically aimed at providing jobs through new agencies, such as the Civilian Conservation Corps (CCC). Then, when the United States entered the Second World War in 1941, huge government spending was required to pay for military equipment and for the salaries of military personnel.

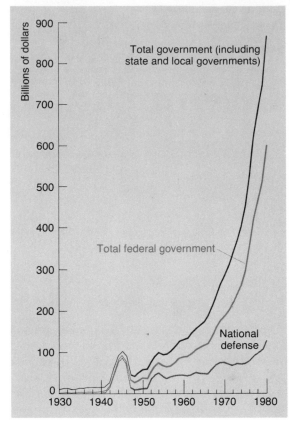

Figure 5-1
Government expenditures, 1929–1980
Federal government spending has risen particularly rapidly during military conflicts (from 1941 to 1944, 1950 to 1953, and 1965 to 1969). In the past decade, nondefense expenditures by federal, state, and local governments have accounted for the big increases in government spending.

When the war ended in 1945, the nation demobilized and government spending fell by more than 50 percent. But the decline was only temporary. Over the past three decades, spending at all levels of government has increased rapidly, to total no less than $869 billion by 1980 (Figure 5-1).

Government expenditures in perspective
Clearly, government spending has become very large. It is hard for the average citizen, accus-

tomed to dealing with a family budget measured in hundreds or thousands of dollars, to comprehend government budgets measured in billions. A billion dollars may be more meaningful if it is reduced to a personal level: A billion dollars represents about $4.50 for every man, woman, and child in the United States. Thus, with total budgets approaching $900 billion, our federal, state, and local governments spend almost $4,000 per person. The magnitude of a billion dollars may be illustrated in another way. When the government borrows $1 billion at an interest rate of 12 percent per annum, its interest payments amount to $325,000 per *day*.

Hugh Rutledge, writing in the *Indianapolis News,* has explained a billion this way:

"One billion seconds ago, the first atomic bomb had not been exploded.

"One billion minutes ago, Christ was still on earth.

"One billion hours ago, men were still living in caves.

"Yet, one billion dollars ago (in terms of government spending) was yesterday."

The rapid increase in spending has in part been a reflection of the additional responsibilities undertaken by government. During the 1930s, innovations included the social security system, whose principal function is the payment of pensions to retired people. More recently, the government has undertaken programs to provide medical assistance to the needy and to the elderly. Other programs to improve the lot of the needy have also grown rapidly. Furthermore, expenditures for weapons and other military purposes have remained high for the past three decades because of both the increasing complexity (and cost) of armaments and the cold war competition with the Soviet Union.

But the expenditures shown in Figure 5-1 can give a misleading impression of the size of the government. While the government is spending more and more, so are private individuals and businesses. For both the government

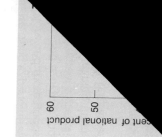

and the priv[...] reflect two n[...] and services[...] higher price[...] tures in bet[...] not in dollar[...] as a percen[...]

When v[...] in governm[...] dramatic. I[...] counts for a[...] ment's bud[...] cent of nati[...] percent by 1980, although there was a bulge during the escalation of the fighting in Vietnam. (In his initial budget proposals, President Reagan recommended that defense expenditures be increased to 6.2 percent of national product by 1984, reversing the downward trend.)

Government purchases versus transfers

A further complication in measuring the size of the government arises because of the two major categories of government expenditures: (1) government **purchases of goods and services**, and (2) government **transfer payments**.

Government purchases of goods include items such as typewriters, computers, and aircraft. The government purchases services when it hires schoolteachers, police officers, and employees for government departments. When the government purchases such goods and services, *it makes a direct claim on the productive capacity of the nation.* For example, when it spends $600 for a typewriter, then steel, plastic, rubber, and labor are used to manufacture the typewriter. Similarly, the purchase of services involves a claim on productive resources. The police officer hired by the government must spend time on the beat, and thus becomes unavailable for work in the private sector.

Government *transfer payments,* on the other hand, are payments *for which the recipient*

[1]The measure of national product—gross national product (GNP)—will be explained in Chapter 7 of our companion volume, *An Introduction to Macroeconomics.*

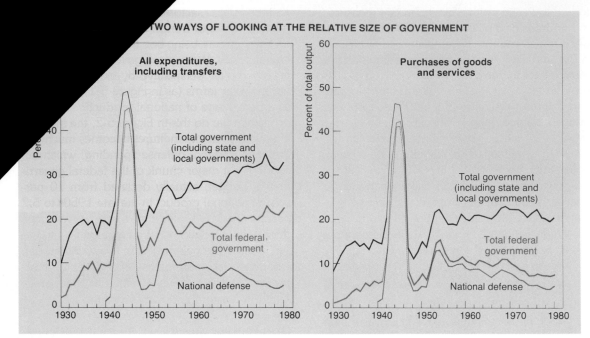

All expenditures, including transfers

Total government (including state and local governments)

Total federal government

National defense

Purchases of goods and services

Total government (including state and local governments)

Total federal government

National defense

Figure 5-2
Government expenditures (including transfers)
If we look at what the government takes for itself plus what it takes to redistribute in the form of transfers, then the government has laid claim to a larger and larger share of national product.

Figure 5-3
Government purchases of goods and services
However, government purchases of goods and services have not changed much over the past two decades, as a percent of national product.

does not provide any good or service in return. Welfare expenditures are transfer payments, and so are social security benefits received by the elderly.

In contrast with government purchases, transfer payments represent no direct claim by the government on the productive capacity of the nation. For example, when the government pays social security pensions to retired people, there is no reallocation of the nation's product away from the private sector toward the government sector. Unlike the typewriter company that manufactures a typewriter and ships it to the government to get the payment of $600, the social security recipient provides neither a good nor a service in return for the benefit. This does not mean, of course, that the social security system is unimportant. When the government collects social security taxes[2] from workers and

employers and pays benefits to retirees, the pattern of consumer spending is affected. The old have more to spend, and workers have less. As a consequence, producers find themselves faced with greater demands for the things that old people want, and with smaller demands for the things workers want. Although the social security system affects the amount of the nation's product that various individuals are able to purchase, it does not redirect the economy toward production for the government.

[2]Payments into the social security fund are sometimes called contributions, on the ground that individuals acquire a right to pensions and other benefits as a reward for their payments. But it is also correct to label the contributions as taxes, since they are involuntary payments which must be made to the government. (Furthermore, while there is some relation between the "contributions" and the benefits an individual will receive, it is not a close one.)

A *transfer payment* **is a payment by the government to an individual, for which the individual does not provide a good or service in return. Social security benefits, unemployment compensation, and welfare payments are examples of transfers.**

Figure 5-2 showed total government expenditures, *including transfers.* Another way of measuring the size of the government is to look only at government purchases of goods and services; that is, expenditures *excluding transfers,* as shown in Figure 5-3. These are the expenditures that make a direct claim on the productive resources of the economy. Observe that as a percentage of national product, government purchases of goods and services are approximately what they were two decades ago. Purchases by state and local governments have gone up, but these increases have been approximately matched by the declining percentage for the federal government.

We can thus get two quite different impressions of the government's size, compared with the size of the economy. If we look only at purchases of goods and services, then the percentage of national product going to the government has been quite stable (Figure 5-3) over the past two decades. If, on the other hand, we include transfers and look at total government expenditures (Figure 5-2), the government's percentage is increasing. The government is not directly claiming a larger and larger share of the nation's product for itself. But it is claiming a larger and larger share, to be *redistributed* in the form of social security, welfare, and other transfer payments.

The main trends of the past two decades, as shown in Figures 5-2 and 5-3, may be summarized. *As a percentage of national product:*

1 The combined total of purchases of goods and services by all levels of government has been stable. An expansion at the state and local levels has been approximately offset by a decline at the federal level.

2 Government transfers have risen rapidly. (This increase shows up in the contrast between Figure 5-2, which includes transfers, and Figure 5-3, which excludes them.)[3]
3 The expenditures allocated for defense have fallen.

THE BUDGET OF THE FEDERAL GOVERNMENT

Details on federal government expenditures, and on the taxes that finance these expenditures, are provided in Table 5-1. (This table includes both purchases of goods and services, and transfer payments.) While much of the federal budget continues to be directed toward military expenditures, a larger and larger percentage is going toward the meeting of human needs. Indeed, in 1974, income security (which includes social security benefits, unemployment insurance payments, and some of the federal welfare budget) passed national defense to become the largest single category of expenditure. Federal government expenditures for health have also risen rapidly, increasing from $13 billion in 1970 to $58 billion in 1980.

Federal receipts
On the receipts side, the **personal income tax** is the largest source of federal government revenue. This tax is levied on taxable personal income; that is, on the incomes of individuals

---

[3]More precisely, there are two sets of expenditures included in Figure 5-2 and excluded from Figure 5-3: (1) transfer payments to individuals, such as social security payments, and (2) interest on the debt.

Federal government expenditures for both these items grew rapidly between 1970 and 1980: transfer payments to individuals from $61 billion to $245 billion (for a total increase of 302 percent), and interest on the national debt from $14 billion to $53 billion (279 percent).

In contrast, federal government purchases of goods and services rose by only 107 percent during the decade, from $96 billion to $199 billion. (And, as we have seen, they declined as a percentage of national product. This was because the dollar value of national product grew even more rapidly, by a total of 165 percent.)

Table 5-1
The Budget of the Federal Government
(billions of dollars and percent)

| | 1980 actual | | 1982 proposals | | |
| | (1) | (2) | (3) | (4) | (5) |
	Billions of dollars	Percent of total	Carter proposals	Reagan proposals	Difference col. (4) compared to col. (3)
Budget outlays					
Income security	$193	33%	$255	$241	− 5.5%
Defense	136	23	184	188	+ 2.1
Interest on debt	65	11	90	83	− 7.8
Health	58	10	75	73	− 2.7
Education, training, employ-ment, and social services	31	5	35	26	−25.7
Veterans benefits and services	21	4	25	24	− 4.0
Transportation	21	4	22	20	− 9.1
Natural resources and envi-ronment	14	2	14	12	−14.3
All other	41	8	39	28	−28.2
Total budget outlays	$580	100%	$739	$695	− 6.0%
Budget receipts					
Personal income taxes	$244	47%	$332	$288	−13.3%
Social insurance contributions and taxes	161	31	215	215	0
Corporation income taxes	65	12	65	62	− 4.6
All other	50	10	100	85	−15.0
Total budget receipts	$520	100%	$712	$650	− 8.7%
Budget deficit					
(outlays minus receipts)	$ 60		$ 27	$ 45	

Sources: Council of Economic Advisers, *Annual Report, 1981,* p. 315; Office of Management and Budget, *Fiscal Year 1982 Budget Revisions* (March 1981), pp. 122, 127.

and families after the subtraction of exemptions and deductions.[4] For a married couple with no dependent children, the personal income tax in 1980 was levied at the rates shown in Table 5-2. (Under legislation passed in 1981, tax rates are to fall by one quarter by 1983.)[5]

Observe that, as income rises, the percentage of that income that has to be paid in tax also rises (Table 5-2, column 3); therefore, the income tax is **progressive**.

[4]In order to calculate your taxable income, you may subtract an exemption of $1,000 for you and for each of your dependents from your gross income. You may also subtract deductions for medical care, charitable contributions, interest payments, and taxes paid to state and local governments.

[5]The personal income tax is complicated; a number of details are left out of Table 5-2. For example, those with earned incomes of less than $10,000 may pay less than shown in the table, and the poorest may receive a payment from the government.

The **marginal tax rate** is shown in the last column; this is the tax rate on *additional* income. (It should not be confused with the *average* tax rate on *all* income in column 3.) In the tax bracket with income between $13,900 and $18,000, for example, the marginal tax rate is 21 percent. Within this bracket, if income rises by $100 (for example, from $14,000 to $14,100), $21 more must be paid in taxes. It is the higher and higher marginal tax rates (column 4) which pull up the average tax rate (column 3).

If a tax takes a larger percentage of income as income rises, the tax is *progressive*.

If a tax takes a smaller percentage of income as income rises, the tax is *regressive*.

If a tax takes a constant percentage of income, the tax is *proportional*.

While income taxes remain the largest single component of federal government revenues, social insurance taxes (to pay for social security and unemployment insurance) have been rising rapidly, and are becoming a larger share of federal tax revenues. Social security contributions, or taxes, are paid to finance old-age pensions, payments to the families of contributors who die or are disabled, and payments for Medicare (medical benefits for the elderly). In 1981, the tax stood at 12.25 percent of wages and salaries up to a maximum income of $29,700; half the tax is collected from the employer, and half from the employee. Social security taxes have been increased repeatedly in order to finance the rapid increase in social security payouts; the tax is scheduled to rise to 14.1 percent by 1985, and to 15.3 percent by 1990. (The maximum income subject to tax will also rise, with the amount of increase depending on the increase in wages.)

The social security tax is **regressive**. While it is collected at a flat percentage on incomes up to a limit of $29,700 (in 1981), any additional income is exempt from the tax. Thus, the tax constitutes a higher percentage of the income of an individual making $20,000 per year than of someone making $40,000.

Corporate income taxes constitute the third most important source of federal revenue. This

Table 5-2
Federal Income Taxes for a Married Couple with No Dependent Children, 1980

(1) Personal income	(2) Personal income tax	(3) Average tax rate (3) = (2) ÷ (1)	Marginal tax rate (tax on additional income)
$ 5,400†	0	0.0	14%
7,500	$ 294	3.9	16
9,600	630	6.6	18
13,900	1,404	10.1	21
18,000††	2,265	12.6	24
26,600	4,505	16.9	32
31,900	6,201	19.4	37
47,800	12,720	26.6	49
87,600	33,502	38.2	59†††
217,400	117,504	54.0	70†††

†There is a "zero tax bracket" of the first $3,400 per couple. In addition, there is an exemption of $1,000 per person; no tax is paid on the exemption. Thus, for a childless couple, taxes do not begin until income passes $5,400 (that is, $3,400 plus the exemptions of $2,000).
††Above $18,000, some of the brackets are omitted for brevity.
†††There is a maximum marginal tax rate of 50 percent on earned income (that is, income from wages, salaries, and professional fees). Rates above 50 percent applied to unearned income from interest, dividends, royalties, etc. (In 1982, the maximum rate on unearned income was reduced to 50 percent.)

tax is collected at a flat rate of 46 percent of all profits above $100,000. (Lower rates apply to the first $100,000.) Minor amounts of revenues are brought in by other taxes, such as excise taxes (on items such as alcoholic beverages and gasoline) and customs duties imposed on goods imported into the United States.

The government's revenues have fallen short of its expenditures in most years, including 1980. The government borrows the difference, mostly from corporations (including banks) and from individuals.

The early Reagan proposals

President Reagan's early budget proposals of March 1981 were aimed at reducing the size of government expenditures and cutting taxes. As can be seen in Figure 5-4, he proposed to reduce federal outlays below 20 percent of national product by 1984, and to reverse the upward trend of federal taxes as a percent of national product. (We emphasize that, for all years after 1980, Figure 5-4 shows *proposals*, not results. Many of the President's proposals must be approved by Congress.)

For details on the differences between Reagan's spending proposals and those of the outgoing Carter administration, refer back to Table 5-1, columns (3), (4), and (5). For defense, Reagan added to the already-substantial increases for 1982 recommended by Carter. For all other major sectors of the budget, reductions were made from Carter's recommendations. In percentage terms, the largest cuts were in educa-

Figure 5-4
Proposed budget changes of the early Reagan administration

In his first budget proposals, President Reagan recommended a cut in federal government spending as a percent of national product. He also proposed a reversal of the upward trend of federal taxes as a percent of national product.

(*Source:* Office of the White House Press Secretary, *President Reagan's 1982 Budget,* March 10, 1981, pp. 36–37.)

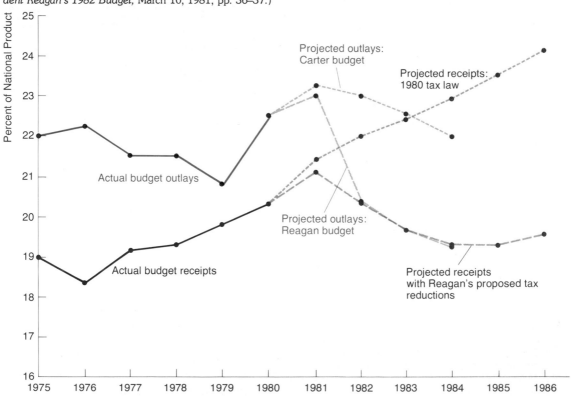

Table 5-3
State and Local Government Revenues and Expenditures
(fiscal year 1978–1979)

	Billions of dollars	Percentage of total
Revenues		
Revenue from federal government	$ 75	22%
Sales and gross receipts taxes	74	22
Property taxes	65	19
Individual income taxes	37	11
Corporation income taxes	12	3
All other	80	23
Total revenues	$343	100%
Expenditures		
Education	$119	36%
Public welfare	42	13
Highways	28	9
All other	139	42
Total expenditures	$328	100%

Source: Council of Economic Advisers, *Annual Report, 1981,* p. 321.

tion, training, employment, and social services (26 percent), and for natural resources and the environment (14 percent). In these two categories and in transportation, Reagan proposed to reduce expenditures in 1982 below actual expenditures in 1980 (column 1).

On the tax side, Reagan suggested personal income tax cuts which would reduce government revenues from this source by 13 percent, when compared to the 1982 proposals of the outgoing Carter administration.

STATE AND LOCAL GOVERNMENTS

Education is the biggest expenditure of state and local governments, accounting for 36 percent of the total in fiscal[6] 1978–1979 (Table 5-3). Highways and welfare account for other large chunks

of the budgets. (Some welfare programs, such as food stamps for the needy, are paid for entirely by the federal government. Other programs, among them Aid to Families with Dependent Children (AFDC), are partly financed by the federal government and partly by state and local governments.) Other important state and local expenditures are for police and fire protection, hospitals, and interest on the debt.

On the revenue side, states tax some of the same items as the federal government. Most states (and some local governments) have individual and corporation income taxes. Note, however, that income taxes provide a much smaller percentage of revenues for state and local governments than for the federal government. The two taxes that provide the largest revenues for states and localities are the sales tax (particularly important for state governments) and the property tax (the biggest source of tax revenues for local governments).

Revenue sharing
However, the biggest source of revenues for state and local governments as a group is not a

[6]The fiscal year is the year used in government or business accounts. Many governments and businesses begin their accounting years in March, July, or October, rather than on January 1.

tax at all, but rather grants from the federal government: Such grants amount to more than one-fifth of their total revenues.

Prior to 1972, virtually all federal government aid to states and localities took the form of **categorical grants**—that is, grants tied to specific programs such as special education for the handicapped. Not only did the money come with strings attached; it also required matching expenditures from state and local funds. In 1972, a new law was passed, providing for **general revenue sharing**—that is, grants from the federal government with (practically) no strings attached. The size of the grant for each state depended on (1) the state's population, (2) the tax effort of the state and its localities (that is, areas with the highest tax rates tended to get the largest grants), and (3) the state's per capita income. This third provision had the objective of directing funds to the neediest states. The second guideline was the most controversial, since it provided an incentive for state and local governments to spend the federal money, rather than use it to lighten tax burdens.

Revenue sharing involves grants from the federal government to state and/or local governments. Revenue sharing is *general* when it comes without restrictions on how it may be spent.

Categorical grants must be used for specific programs.

Block grants may be used in a broad area (such as education), and need not be spent on specific programs (such as reading programs for the handicapped).

General revenue sharing has not been very large, amounting to only $6 billion of the $75 billion which the states and localities received from the federal government in fiscal year 1978–1979. However, the basic idea of allowing the states and localities to decide how to spend funds was given a boost in early 1981. President Reagan proposed that restrictions on categorical grants be relaxed. Under this proposal, categorical grants would be combined into broader **block grants**. For example, instead of receiving grants for a number of *specific* education programs, states and localities would receive block grants to be used in the general area of education.

There were several reasons behind revenue sharing. The federal government wanted to encourage specific programs, and to help states and localities in financial difficulties to bear the burden of such programs. This was the basic reason for establishing categorical grants. The motivation for general revenue sharing was the view that there was a mismatch between the revenues and responsibilities of the federal government, on the one hand, and the states and localities on the other. Federal income tax revenues tend automatically to rise with a growing economy. But state and local tax revenues—based primarily on property and sales taxes—may grow less rapidly. Yet many of the responsibilities of government lie at the state and local level. Advocates of general revenue sharing hoped to use the tax powers of the federal government to lessen the financial burdens on state and local governments.

It is not so clear, however, that there is a basic mismatch between the tax powers and the responsibilities at the various levels of government. Observe, in Table 5-3, that the state and local governments, as a group, had a **surplus** of $15 billion in fiscal year 1978–1979. (Revenues of $343 billion were $15 billion greater than expenditures of $328 billion.) In the same year, the federal government had a **deficit** of $14 billion. Thus, critics of revenue sharing argue that the federal government has been sharing revenues which it didn't have.

If a government's revenues exceed its expenditures, it has a budget *surplus*.

If a government's expenditures exceed its revenues, it has a budget *deficit*.

If a government's revenues equal its expenditures, its budget is *balanced*. (The term "balanced budget" is often used loosely to mean that the budget is either in balance or in surplus; that is, revenues are at least as great as expenditures.)

The biggest mismatch seems to be, not between the federal government on the one hand, and states and localities on the other, but rather **among** states and localities. The tax revenues of some localities have risen rapidly, particularly where soaring real estate prices have led to large increases in real estate taxes. Other localities have had severe difficulties: New York and Cleveland are the two most notable examples. (During the 1970s, these cities got into financial crises where they were unable to make payments to holders of their bonds.) And some states are struggling to keep their budgets under control, while other states—particularly those receiving large revenues from oil wells or other natural resources—are in very strong financial positions. (Alaska's oil revenues are so large that that state intends to distribute some of the revenues to its residents.)

For the future, a major issue in revenue sharing will be the degree to which the federal government distributes grants to the particularly hard-pressed states and localities. (Canada and Australia have long had revenue-sharing programs aimed at helping the poorer provinces or states.)

GOVERNMENT REGULATION

The government budget, amounting to hundreds of billions of dollars, has a substantial effect on the types of goods produced and on who gets these goods. In addition, the government affects the economy through its regulatory agencies, such as the Environmental Protection Agency (EPA) that controls pollution. The cost of *administering* such agencies (which amounts to only 2 to 3 percent of the federal government's budget) is an inadequate measure of their importance. The cost to businesses of *complying* with these regulations is far higher. (For example, it costs a steel mill much more to install pollution control devices than it costs the EPA to administer the regulations.) And the gains to the public —in the form of cleaner air—are likewise much

greater than the small amounts which appear in the federal budget.

During the past century, a series of governmental agencies has been established to limit the most flagrant abuses of private business. In 1890, the Sherman Act declared business mergers that created monopolies to be illegal. Then the Federal Trade Commission (FTC) was established in 1914 in the belief that monopolies should be prevented before the fact, rather than punished after they are created.

But regulation goes far beyond the control of monopoly. For example, the Food and Drug Administration (FDA) determines the effectiveness and safety of drugs before they are permitted on the market. The financial shenanigans of the 1920s (which contributed to the collapse into the Depression) led in 1933 to the establishment of the Securities and Exchange Commission (SEC) to regulate financial markets. The SEC requires corporations to disclose information about their finances. (Joseph Kennedy—the father of the future president, John F. Kennedy— was appointed the first head of the SEC by Franklin Roosevelt.) Banks are extensively regulated by the Federal Reserve System, the Federal Deposit Insurance Corporation, the Comptroller of the Currency, and state regulatory agencies. The Federal Power Commission (FPC), Federal Communications Commission (FCC), and the Federal Aviation Administration (FAA) regulate power, broadcasting, and aviation.

In recent years, there has been an upswing in regulatory activity, with the addition of (among others) the Equal Employment Opportunity Commission (EEOC), the Environmental Protection Agency, the Commodity Futures Trading Commission (CFTC), and the Occupational Safety and Health Administration (OSHA).

In many areas, regulation is relatively uncontroversial. For example, few people complain about the government agency (the FAA) that certifies the airworthiness of aircraft. Similarly, there is widespread support for government regulation aimed at keeping unsafe drugs off the market. (The FDA blocked the use of thalidomide, a drug which caused birth defects in

Europe.) Each of the regulatory agencies was established to deal with a problem area where the free market had been tried and found wanting.

Problems with government regulation

However, doubts have set in after the flurry of regulatory activity of the 1960s and 1970s. For example, the FDA has been criticized for delaying the introduction of effective drugs that seem to be reasonably safe after extensive use in other countries. (No drug, of course, is *perfectly* safe—not even aspirin.) Hassles with regulatory agencies are considered a major distraction by business executives. In 1980, Eugene E. Jennings of Michigan State University surveyed 41 chief executive officers of corporations. Twenty-seven said they visited Washington at least once every other week. In a similar survey in 1971, only 5 of 39 said they went to Washington as much as once every other *month*.

The harshest criticism has been directed at the newer agencies, particularly the Occupational Safety and Health Administration. OSHA has been charged with harassing businesses and with a lack of perspective. While some industrial occupations remain hazardous, OSHA left itself open to ridicule by issuing detailed orders on the precise design of ladders and a solemn warning to farmers that they should beware of manure-covered cement floors (they're slippery).[7]

What is needed is a sense of balance. The private market mechanism has substantial defects. Corporations cannot on their own be counted on to pay sufficient attention to safety or to protect the environment from pollution. But government agencies also have defects; they are not run by superhumans capable of solving all our problems. At some point, we should be prepared to live with the defects of the market. In some cases, the cure may be more costly than the defects themselves.

Regulation in the public interest is made particularly difficult because of the political clout of producers. (This fact also complicates other types of economic policy, including government spending and taxation.) When regulations are being developed, the affected industry makes its views known forcefully. But the views of consumers and taxpayers are diffuse and often remain underrepresented. In an extensive study of regulatory agencies in 1977, the Senate Government Operations Committee concluded that the public is outnumbered and outspent by industry in regulatory proceedings. The committee chairman, Senator Abraham Ribicoff, observed that regulatory hearings "can be likened to the biblical battle of David and Goliath—except that David rarely wins." This conclusion should come as no surprise. For decades, an irreverent definition has circulated in Washington: A sick industry is one which cannot capture control of its regulatory agency.

The predominance of producer influence is not simply the result of a conspiracy of wealth. Rather, it is an intrinsic feature of a highly specialized economy. Each of us has a major, narrow, special interest as a producer; and each of us has a minor interest in a wide range of industries whose goods we consume. We are much more likely to react when our particular industry is affected by government policy; we are much less likely to express our diffused interest as consumers. Narrow producer interests are expressed not only by business, but also by labor. Unions concentrate their attention on events in their particular industry, even though the union members are also consumers, using a wide range of products. (We repeat: This prevalence of producer influence is primarily a result of modern technology and a high degree of specialization; it is not primarily a result of our particular system. It exists in a wide variety of political-economic systems, including those of Britain, France, Germany, Japan, and the Soviet Union.)

---

[7]An OSHA booklet offered the following infantile advice to farmers:

> Be careful around the farm. . . . Hazards are one of the main causes of accidents. A hazard is anything that is dangerous. Be careful when you are handling animals. . . . DON'T FALL.

THE ECONOMIC ROLE OF THE GOVERNMENT: WHAT SHOULD THE GOVERNMENT DO?

With government budgets reaching hundreds of billions of dollars, and with an extensive list of government regulations, the United States economy is clearly a substantial distance away from a pure market system of laissez faire. What principles and objectives guide the government when it intervenes?

In part, government intervention is based on deep social attitudes that are often difficult to explain. Thirty years ago, Americans could look askance at government-financed, "socialized" medicine in Britain. Yet at the same time they could consider British education "undemocratic" because many well-to-do Britons sent their children to privately financed elementary and secondary schools. The British, on the other hand, were proud of their educational system, and were puzzled by what they considered a quaint, emotional American objection to public financing of medical care. (During the past three decades, the gap between the two societies has narrowed, with increasing governmental involvement in medicine in the United States and some decline in the relative importance of privately financed education in Britain.)

The government intervenes in the economy for many reasons; it is hard to summarize them all. But we will look at five of the main ones.

1 The government provides what the private market can't

Consider defense expenditures. For obvious political reasons, defense cannot be left to the private market. The prospect of private armies marching around the country is too painful to contemplate. But there also is an impelling economic reason why defense is a responsibility of the government.

The difference between defense and an average good is the following. If I buy food at the store, I get to eat it; if I buy a movie ticket, I get to see the film; if I buy a car, I get to drive it. In contrast, if I want a larger, better equipped army,

my offer to purchase a rifle for the army will not add in any measurable way to my own security. My neighbor, and the average person in Alaska, Michigan, or Texas, will benefit as much from the extra rifle as I do. In other words, the benefit from defense expenditures *goes broadly to all citizens;* it does not go specifically to the individual who pays. If defense is to be provided, it must be financed by the government, which collects taxes to ensure that everyone contributes.

2 Externalities

An *externality* is a side effect (good or bad) of production or consumption. For example: When individuals are immunized against an infectious disease, they receive a substantial benefit; they are assured that they won't get the disease. But there is an *external benefit* as well, because others gain too; they are assured that the inoculated individuals will not catch the disease and pass it along to them. Similarly, there is an external benefit when people have their houses painted. (The neighborhood becomes more attractive.)

An *external cost* occurs when a factory pollutes the air. The cost is borne by those who breathe the polluted air.

An *externality* is a side effect of production or consumption. (Persons or businesses other than the producer or consumer are affected.)

An externality may be either *positive* (for example, vaccinations) or *negative* (for example, pollution).

Because of the effects on others, the government may wish to encourage activities which create external benefits and to discourage those with external costs. It can do so with the use of any of its three major tools: expenditures, regulations, or taxation. The government spends money for public health programs, for the immunization of the young. It has regulations on the types of automobiles which can be built, in order to reduce pollution. And taxes on gasoline or on polluting factories might likewise be used to discourage pollution.

The existence of an externality does not in itself make a compelling case for government action; the government should not be concerned with insignificant externalities or other trivial matters.[8] Thus, private incentives are generally enough to ensure that homes will be painted; the government does not usually intervene. However, there is growing concern over more serious externalities: While little was done about pollution two decades ago, major efforts are now directed toward cleaning up the air and water.

3 Merit goods

Government intervention may also be based on the paternalistic view that people are not in all cases the best judges of what is good for them. According to this view, the government should encourage **merit goods**—those that are deemed particularly desirable—and discourage the consumption of harmful products. People's inability to pick the "right" goods may be the result of short-sightedness, ignorance, addiction, or manipulation by producers. (Recall Chapter 4's brief discussion of Galbraith's views on created wants.)

In some cases, the government attempts merely to correct ignorance in areas where the public may have difficulty determining (or facing?) the facts. The requirement of a health warning on cigarette packages is an example. But, in other instances, the government goes further, to outright prohibition, as in the case of heroin and other hard drugs.

---

[8]The government does not always adhere to this rule of thumb. Many laws and regulations can be found that scarcely seem necessary. For example, spitting against the wind was made unlawful in Sault Ste. Marie, and punching a bull in the nose was prohibited in Washington, D.C. It is rather difficult to imagine how those particular laws' got on the books.

With a sufficiently grim imagination, we can perhaps guess how other unnecessary regulations were enacted, such as the Pittsburgh regulation against sleeping in a refrigerator, or the Arkansas law against the blindfolding of cows on public highways. These, and many other examples, may be found in Barbara Seuling's book, *You Can't Eat Peanuts in Church and Other Little-Known Laws* (Garden City, N.Y.: Doubleday, 1975).

The view that "the government knows best" is generally greeted with skepticism; the government intervenes relatively sparingly to tell adults what they should or should not consume. (Children are, however, another matter; they are not allowed to reject the "merit" good, education.) However, substantial government direction does occur in welfare programs, presumably on the ground that those who get themselves into financial difficulties are least likely to make wise consumption decisions. Thus, part of the assistance to the poor consists of food stamps and housing programs rather than outright grants of money. In this way, the government attempts to direct consumption toward housing and milk for the children, rather than (perhaps) toward liquor for an alcoholic parent.

4 Helping the poor

The market provides the goods and services desired by those with the money to buy, but it provides little for the poor. In order to help the impoverished and move toward a more humane society, programs have been established to provide assistance for old people, the handicapped, and the needy.

There is much resentment of the "welfare mess," and it does not all come from bigots who despise the poor. Because there were so many new programs introduced in a relatively brief period, particularly in the 1960s, it is perhaps inaccurate to speak of a welfare "system" at all; it's a patchwork. Recent presidents have struggled with this problem, and proposals for major change have included Nixon's family assistance program and Carter's welfare reform program (neither of which was enacted by Congress). One difficulty lies in how to reconcile conflicting objectives. How can help be given to the needy without weakening the incentive to work? How can assistance be guaranteed to abandoned mothers without giving irresponsible fathers an incentive to desert their families? How can the poverty-stricken be given a place to live without creating ghettos of the poor? There are no easy answers to such questions.

5 The government and economic stability

Finally, if we go back to the beginning of the upswing in government activity—to the Depression of the thirties—we find that the primary motivation was not to affect the kinds of products made in the economy, nor specifically to aid the poor. Rather, the problem was the quantity of production. With unemployment rates running over 15 percent of the labor force year after year, the problem was to produce more—more of almost anything would help put people back to work. Since the dark days of the 1930s, a major responsibility of the government has been to promote a high level of employment and stability in the economy.

TAXATION

The art of taxation consists of plucking the goose so as to obtain the largest amount of feathers with the least possible amount of hissing.
Jean Baptiste Colbert
Seventeenth-century French statesman

The major objective of taxation is to raise revenues—to obtain feathers, without too much hissing. But other objectives are also important in the design of a tax system.

1 Neutrality . . .

In many ways, the market system works admirably. Adam Smith's "invisible hand" provides the consuming public with a vast flow of goods and services. As a starting point, therefore, a tax system should be designed to be *neutral.* That is, it should disturb market forces as little as possible, unless there is a compelling reason to the contrary.

For the sake of illustration, consider a farfetched example. Suppose that blue cars were taxed at 10 percent, and green cars not at all. This tax would clearly not be neutral regarding blue and green cars. People would have an incentive to buy green cars; blue cars would practically disappear from the market. A tax

which introduces such a distortion would make no sense.

While this illustration is silly, real taxes do introduce distortions. For example, several centuries ago, houses in parts of Europe were taxed according to the number of windows. As a result, houses were built with fewer windows. To a lesser degree, the current property tax introduces a perverse incentive. If you have your house painted and your roof repaired, the government's evaluation of your house (the assessed value) may be raised and your taxes increased as a consequence. Therefore, property taxes encourage you to let your property deteriorate.

The problem is that every tax provides an incentive to do something to avoid it. So long as taxes must be collected, complete neutrality is impossible. The objective of the tax system must therefore be more modest: to aim toward neutrality. As a starting point in the design of a tax system, the disturbance to the market that comes from taxation should be minimized.

2 . . . and nonneutrality: Meeting social objectives by tax incentives

There is, however, an important modification which must be made to the neutrality principle. In some cases, it may be desirable to disturb the private market.

For example, the government might tax polluting activities, so that firms will do less polluting. The market is disturbed, but in a desirable way. Another example is the tax on cigarettes, which, in addition to its prime objective of raising revenue for the government, also discourages cigarette consumption. (Unfortunately, government policies are not always consistent. The government taxes cigarettes, forbids the advertising of cigarettes on TV, and requires health warnings on cigarette packages. But then the government turns around and subsidizes the production of tobacco.)

Taxation and regulation can be used to correct the failures of the private market. But the two approaches are quite different in one respect. Regulation aims at *overriding* the market mechanism, forbidding or limiting specific behavior on the part of business. Taxation aims at *using* the market mechanism, but making it work better. When there are externalities, such as pollution, the signals of the market are incomplete; businesses or individuals who pollute the air do not have to pay the cost. Taxation of externalities can improve the outcome of the market by making the signals facing businesses and individuals more complete: Taxation makes polluters pay a penalty, and gives them an incentive to reduce pollution.

3 Simplicity

To anyone who has wasted the first two lovely weekends of April sweating over an income tax form, simplicity of the tax system is devoutly desired. Of course, we live in a complex world, and the tax code must to some degree reflect this complexity. But, as a result of decades of tinkering, the U.S. income tax has become ridiculously complex. (See Box 5-1.) Indeed, it has become so complex that the Internal Revenue Service itself frequently gives incorrect answers to taxpayer inquiries.

4 Equity

Taxation represents coercion; taxes are collected by force if necessary. Therefore, it is important that taxes both be fair, and give the *appearance* of being fair. There are, however, two different principles for judging fairness.

The benefit principle This principle recognizes that the purpose of taxation is to pay for government services. Therefore, let those who gain the most from government services pay the most. If this principle is adopted, then a question arises: Why not simply set prices for government services which people can voluntarily pay if they want the services? In other words, why not charge a price for a government service, just as General Motors charges for cars? This approach may work—for example, for a toll road from which drivers can be excluded if they do not pay. But it will not work for public goods that benefit people even if they do not pay; for example, defense, disease control programs, and air traffic control. Everyone will enjoy them,

but no one will want to pay for them. It is the function of the government to determine whether such programs are worthwhile. Once the decision is made to go ahead, people must be required to support the program through taxes.

If the *benefit principle* of taxation is followed, it is up to the government to estimate how much various individuals and groups benefit, and to set taxes accordingly. (Individual citizens cannot be allowed to provide the estimates of how much they benefit personally; they have an incentive to understate their individual benefits in order to keep their taxes down.)

Ability to pay If the government sets taxes according to the benefit principle, it does not redistribute income. People are simply taxed in proportion to their individual benefits from government programs. If the government wishes to redistribute income, it can set taxes according to the *ability to pay*. The basic measures of the ability to pay are income and wealth.

If the government were to levy a progressive income tax and an inheritance tax, and at the same time provide assistance to those at the bottom of the economic ladder, it would substantially redistribute income from the rich to the poor. But the world is not so simple. The government levies many other taxes as well, and when they are all taken together, it is not so clear that the government is taking a substantially larger percentage of income from the rich than from the poor, as we shall see in the next section.

THE BURDEN OF TAXES: WHO ULTIMATELY PAYS?

It is difficult to determine who bears the burden of many of our taxes. For example, consider the relatively simple social security tax. Half this tax is deducted from the take-home pay of the worker. This half is regressive: An employee receiving $20,000 per year pays a larger percentage in social security taxes than does an employee receiving $50,000. But what about the other half of the tax which is levied on the

Meet Your Tax Code†

The Ways and Means Committee has before it this year [1976] a considerable list of proposed alterations in the nation's tax system. It is a fair bet, however, that the committee's tinkering will only further complicate that monument to obscurity, the Internal Revenue Code.

Abundant bafflement

When the federal income-tax law was written in 1913 as a section of the Underwood Tariff Act, it provided for a tax of 1 percent on income over $4,000, rising to 6 percent on income over $500,000. There were few loopholes. It was a pure tax designed to raise revenue. Even so, the measure was ominously verbose—8,000 words.

In the sixty-three years since, that section of a tariff act has grown into a monstrosity. Today's revenue code, with its multitudinous deductions, credits, special-treatment provisions, and exceptions to exceptions, runs to something like 1.5 million words. While the code also covers a variety of other taxes, the greater part of it deals with corporate and personal income taxes. Treasury Department regulations explaining the provisions of the code sprawl over close to 6,000 pages in six hefty volumes. In addition, it takes 110 volumes to contain the Internal Revenue Service rulings on what the regulations mean.

Regulations and rulings galore are necessary, for the Internal Revenue Code's verbosity is matched by its obscurity. Section 341(E), which deals with collapsible corporations, is famous for the challenge it poses to a reader. Connoisseurs regard its opening sentence of 600 words as a masterpiece of thorny writing. But many other passages can almost match it.

IRS instructions for filling out individual income-tax returns run to 150,000 words. The resulting taxpayer bafflement has made tax-return assistance a sizable industry. About half of the nation's 80 million tax filers use the services of tax preparers. At the seasonal peak in the early spring, some 250,000 Americans are gainfully employed in helping other Americans cope with their tax returns.

Throw the machine away

When legislators in Washington recognize a tax problem they tend to go at it obliquely rather than head-on. An illustrative example was the congressional reaction to the disclosure that 155 taxpayers with incomes in excess of $200,000 had paid no federal income tax at all in 1967. The Ways and Means Committee felt obliged to do something. But the committee did not proceed to tighten tax preferences that enable the rich to avoid taxes. Instead, the committee decided to impose what it called a minimum tax.

This proved to be exceedingly hard to comprehend—a major reason why the Tax Reform Act of 1969 was dubbed the Lawyers and Accountants Relief Act. The measure was also so ineffective that Congress felt constrained to rewrite it the following year. Each successive Congress has operated on this section again, and it is still weak.

Banker Walter Wriston, chairman of Citicorp, has come to the conclusion that "the tax machine has been so badly designed that no tinkering can help. It is time to throw the machine away." Both Wriston and [former] Secretary of the Treasury William Simon call for wiping away nearly all the deductions, preferences, credits, etc. and establishing a simple progressive tax, with hardly any ifs, ands, or buts in it. With nearly all avenues of tax avoidance closed off, rates could come way down.

Such an apocalyptic reform is probably not feasible in a complex economy. But certainly simplification of the Internal Revenue Code is long overdue. As Simon put it, "the present tax system is so riddled with exceptions and complexities that it almost defies human understanding." ■

†Abridged from *Fortune*, March 1976, p. 143.

BOX 5-2
What's Fair? The Tax Penalty on Marriage

Prior to the tax reform act of 1969, single people had a complaint. As the tax law was then designed, married couples got a tax break. For the married couple, each tax bracket was twice as wide as for a single person. Thus, for example, the single individual with an income of $15,000 was in the same tax bracket (that is, had the same marginal tax rate) as a married couple with an income of $30,000.

To meet the complaint of singles, the tax law was changed by the reform of 1969. No longer were brackets for married couples twice as wide as for single individuals. But this led to another complication. Consider two people (Jack and Joan), each with a $15,000 income, who married in 1980. After their marriage, they could no longer file as single individuals. And, as the tax brackets for marrieds were no longer twice as wide as for singles, their combined income of $30,000 pushed them up into a higher tax bracket. (Their marginal tax rate on additional income became 32 percent, compared with the 26 percent they would have paid as singles.)

Furthermore, this married couple faced other tax disadvantages. Rather than itemizing deductions for medical expenses, interest, etc., people are permitted to take a *standard deduc-*tion in calculating the amount of their incomes subject to tax. For singles, the standard deduction (also known as the *zero tax bracket*) is $2,300; for a couple, it is $3,400, or only $1,700 per person.

As a result of these provisions of the tax law, Jack and Joan found their taxes increased when they married. Compared with their unmarried friends (Dick and Jane), they paid $897 more in tax in 1980, as shown in Table 5-4. To avoid such a "marriage tax," which must be paid each year, some couples flew off in December to a Caribbean holiday. By getting divorced while there, they were able to save enough tax to pay for their holiday. (As a result of criticisms, Congress reduced the marriage tax. For a couple with a combined income of $30,000, the marriage tax had been even higher—$1,286—in 1976.)

(To see why such apparently preposterous results can creep into the tax law, study Problem 5-5, which illustrates how difficult, or even impossible, it may be to design a fair tax system.)†　■

†See also Alicia H. Munnell, "The Couple versus the Individual under the Federal Personal Income Tax," in Henry J. Aaron and Michael Boskin, eds., *The Economics of Taxation* (Washington: Brookings, 1980), esp. p. 249.

---

employer? Does the tax come out of the corporation's profits? Or is it passed on to the consumer in the form of higher prices? Or, possibly, this half may also fall on the worker: If there were no social security tax, the employer might be willing to pay a higher wage.

And, if the question of tax burden—of who ultimately pays—is complicated for the social security tax, it is even more complex for many other taxes. We simply do not have a very precise idea of who ultimately bears the burden of taxes.

The burden, or **incidence**, of all U.S. taxes —federal, state, and local—has been studied by several economists at the Brookings Institution (a Washington public policy research institution). They have made a number of estimates reflecting differences of opinion among economists as to who ultimately pays. On the "most progressive assumptions," the total tax burden rises from 22.4 percent of income for those with incomes between $5,000 and $10,000, to 51.9 percent for those with incomes between $500,000 and $1,000,000. On the "least pro-

Table 5-4
The Marriage Tax

	Dick	Jane	Jack	Joan
	(just friends)		(married)	
1 Gross income	$15,000	$15,000	$15,000	$15,000
1a Married couple's combined income			$30,000	
2 Standard deduction (zero tax bracket)	$ 2,300	$ 2,300	$ 3,400	
3 Personal exemptions	$ 1,000	$ 1,000	$ 2,000	
4 Tax paid on [(4) = (1)−(2)−(3)]	$11,700	$11,700	$24,600	
5 Tax	$ 2,352	$ 2,352	$ 5,601	
6 Combined tax for two people	$4,704		$ 5,601	
7 Marriage tax ($5,601−$4,704)			$ 897	
8 *Addendum:* Marginal tax rate on additional income	26%		32%	

gressive" assumptions,[9] the burden rises from 25.2 on incomes in the $5,000 to $10,000 range to 32.9 percent on incomes between $500,000 and $1,000,000.[10]

[9]According to the most progressive assumptions, property and corporation income taxes are paid by the well-to-do owners of property and corporations, and are not passed on to the public in the form of higher prices. According to the least progressive assumptions, corporation income taxes are passed on to the general public in the form of higher prices for the goods which corporations sell, and property taxes are passed on in the form of higher rents.

[10]Joseph Minarik, "Who Doesn't Bear the Tax Burden," in Henry J. Aaron and Michael Boskin, editors, *The Economics of Taxation* (Washington: Brookings, 1980), p. 74. The estimates cited, for 1970, are updates of earlier estimates by Joseph A. Pechman and Benjamin J. Okner for 1966.

Between 1966 and 1970, the tax system became more progressive. Accordingly, we may wonder if the system has been made still more progressive since 1970. Minarik and Pechman are currently studying this question.

Progressivity is much lower than one would expect on the basis of the income tax schedule (shown in Table 5-2) for two major reasons: (1) some other taxes are proportional or even regressive, such as the employees' half of the social security tax and a number of taxes at the state and local levels; and (2) tax "loopholes" allow higher-income groups to reduce their tax payments.

Tax loopholes

"Loopholes" are provisions of the law which permit the reduction of taxes. (Thus, those who use the loopholes are acting perfectly *legally* to *avoid* taxes, and should be sharply distinguished from those who act *illegally* to *evade* taxes, perhaps by padding their deductions or understating their incomes.) The term loophole clearly implies that the tax provision is unfair, and, as there can be strong disagreement over just what is fair (Box 5-2), there is likewise some disagreement over just what constitutes a loophole. However, here are some of the items which are often put on the list.

1 Investment tax credit

When a corporation or individual acquires business equipment, it is permitted to deduct 10 percent of the price of that equipment from its tax bill.

2 Tax-exempt securities

If you buy state or local government bonds, the interest income you receive from them is exempt from federal income tax. Similarly, interest income from federal government bonds is exempt from state and local taxes. Thus, individuals and corporations (including banks) can reduce their income taxes by buying government bonds.

3 Capital gains

When an asset is sold for more than it cost, the seller has made a capital gain. For example, if you buy General Motors stock for $2,000 and later sell it for $3,000, you have made a $1,000 capital gain. Capital gains are generally taxed at 40 percent of the rate for ordinary income from wages or salaries.

4 Deduction of interest

In calculating taxable income, individuals are permitted to deduct the interest which they pay on loans. This provision is of particular benefit to those who are making large interest payments on home mortgages.

A *tax credit* is a subtraction from the tax payable. (For example, if a $10,000 machine is bought, the 10 percent investment tax credit means that $1,000 can be subtracted from the taxes which must be paid to the government.)

In contrast to a tax credit, a *deduction* is a subtraction from taxable income. Suppose an individual pays $1,000 in interest on a home mortgage. This $1,000 can be deducted from taxable income. For someone in the 36 percent tax bracket, this results in a $360 reduction in taxes. (Note that the tax saving depends on the tax bracket. Thus, a $1,000 deduction reduces taxes more for someone in the 36 percent tax bracket than for a person in a lower bracket. Note also that the $1,000 deduction is worth only $360 to this individual, while a $1,000 tax credit is worth the full $1,000 in tax savings.)

These (and other) loopholes have led to much criticism. Jimmy Carter called the tax system a "disgrace to the human race" because of the many special exemptions and deductions. There are, however, three major complications that have so far prevented a comprehensive tax reform.

First is the disagreement over just what is fair. (This disagreement inspired Senator Russell Long to poetry. The typical attitude, he observed, is, "Don't tax you; don't tax me; tax the fellow behind that tree.")

The second complication is a political problem: Those who benefit from loopholes have an incentive to lobby to make sure they are not eliminated.

Finally, reform is complicated by the fact that fairness is only one of the major objectives in a tax system. Most of the loopholes were put in expressly to promote national goals which the proponents considered important. For example, the investment tax credit was introduced in the early 1960s at President Kennedy's request, to stimulate investment. In taxation, as in so many areas of economics, the policy maker is left with the problem of balancing conflicting national goals.

Key Points

1 The defects and limitations of the market provide the government with an important economic role. The government affects the economy through expenditures, taxation, and regulation.

2 In dollar terms, government spending has skyrocketed since 1929. However, as a percentage of national product, the growth of government spending has been much slower. Indeed, if only purchases of goods and services are counted, the government's share of national product has been quite stable over the past two decades.

3 Of the federal expenditures, transfer payments have risen much more rapidly than expenditures for goods and services.

4 Personal income taxes, social security taxes, and corporate income taxes are the main sources of revenue for the federal government. At the state level, sales taxes are the most important source of tax revenues. For localities, property taxes are the most important. States and localities also benefit from revenue sharing by the federal government.

5 Government regulatory agencies are active in many areas, regulating monopoly and protecting the public from misleading advertising, unsafe drugs, and pollution.

6 The primary reasons for government intervention in the economy are to:

(a) Provide public goods that cannot be supplied by the market because individuals have no incentive to buy them; individuals get the benefits regardless of who buys.

(b) Deal with externalities, such as pollution.

(c) Encourage the consumption of "merit" goods, and discourage or prohibit harmful products.

(d) Help the poor.

(e) Help stabilize the economy.

7 A number of objectives are important in the design of a tax system:

(a) In general, neutrality is a desirable objective.

(b) In some cases, however, the government should alter market signals by taxation. For example, a tax can be used to discourage pollution.

(c) Taxes should be reasonably simple and easily understood.

(d) Taxes should be fair. There are two ways of judging fairness: the benefit principle, and ability to pay.

8 The burden or "incidence" of taxes (that is, who ultimately pays the taxes) is hard to determine. But the rich don't bear as heavy a burden as the income tax rates suggest.

Key Concepts

regulation	regressive tax	externality
transfer payment	proportional tax	tax neutrality
income tax	revenue sharing	merit good
marginal tax rate	general revenue sharing	tax loophole
average tax rate	categorical grant	investment tax credit
progressive tax	block grant	capital gain

Problems

5-1 "That government governs best which governs least." Do you agree? Why or why not? Does the government perform more functions than it should? If so, what activities would you like it to reduce or stop altogether? Are there any additional functions which the government should undertake? If so, what ones? How should they be paid for?

5-2 "State and local governments are closer to the people than the federal government. Therefore, they should be given some of the functions of the federal government." Are there federal functions which might be turned over to the states and localities? Do you think they should be turned over? Why or why not? Do you agree with President Reagan, that it is desirable to reduce federal control by moving from categorical grants to block grants, to be used as the states and localities wish within a general area? Or is it desirable for the federal government to retain control by using categorical grants? Are there federal functions which the states are incapable of handling? Are there functions which the federal government can do much better than the states or localities?

5-3 The government engages in research. For example, the government has agricultural experimental stations, and during the Second World War, the government developed the atomic bomb through the massive Manhattan Project. Why do you think the government engages in these two types of research, while leaving most research to private business? Does the government have any major advantages in undertaking research? Any major disadvantages?

5-4 Consider two views of the tax system:

(a) "The government promotes social goals, such as education and the arts, through direct payments. It also promotes education and the arts by encouraging private giving. This is done by making gifts deductible from taxable income. Tax deductions may be an even more effective way of supporting education, the arts, and other desirable causes than direct government grants. Therefore, such deductions do not constitute 'loopholes.' Rather, they represent an efficient way of achieving important social goals."

(b) "The income tax is a mess. Homeowners get a tax break, but renters do not. The rich are able to escape taxes by making gifts to universities, the arts, and to charities. The only way to get equity into the system is to eliminate all deductions, and make all income subject to tax."

Which of these arguments is stronger? Why?

*5-5 Design what you consider to be a fair personal income tax schedule, giving the average and marginal tax rates at various incomes. Provide schedules for single individuals and for married couples. In your system, how much tax would each of the following pay:

(a) A single individual with a $10,000 income

(b) A married couple, each of whom makes $10,000

(c) A single individual with an income of $20,000

(d) A married couple, with one partner making $20,000 and the other having no income.

Would the taxpayers in each of these four categories agree that your tax is fair? (As a background for this question, reread Box 5-2. And good luck!)

---

*Problems with an asterisk (and particularly this one) are more difficult than the others. They are designed to provide a challenge to students who want to do more advanced work.

CHAPTER 6
Business Organization and Finance

Christmas is over
and Business is Business

Franklin Pierce Adams

The government is an important participant in the U.S. economy, regulating business and providing such public goods as roads, health services, and defense. But the primary productive role is played by private business. Businesses use the resources of society—labor, land, and capital—to produce the goods and services that consumers, the government, and other businesses demand.

In future chapters, we will study the behavior of businesses. How much do they produce? At what prices do they sell? What combination of land, labor, and capital do they use in the productive process? How do they respond to changing market conditions? Questions such as these are central subjects of any introductory study of economics. The purpose of this chapter is to provide background on the organization of businesses and the ways in which they obtain the money to finance expansion.

At the beginning of the 1980s, there were about 9 million businesses in the United States. Most were small, and were owned by an individual or family. Such small businesses predominate in certain sectors of the economy, such as restaurants, many services (plumbers, electricians), and some retailing operations. Some of them are here today, but will be gone tomorrow; small businesses are often high-risk ventures.

While most businesses are small, large corporations hire much of the labor force, use large

quantities of raw materials, and make most of the profits. Each May, *Fortune* magazine publishes a report on the 500 largest corporations; they regularly make over half the total profits of all U.S. corporations.

BUSINESS ORGANIZATIONS

There are three types of business organization: the **single proprietorship,** the **partnership,** and the **corporation.** The single proprietorship and the partnership are the most common forms of very small business, although even a one-person business may be a corporation. At the other end of the spectrum, large businesses are almost exclusively corporations. (There are exceptions. Large law firms, for example, are partnerships, and until recently, so were even the largest stock and bond brokerage houses on Wall Street.)

Single proprietorships and partnerships: Their advantages and problems

A single proprietorship is the easiest form of business to establish; there is little fuss or bother. If I decide to make pottery in my basement, I may do so. I can begin tomorrow, without going through legal and organizational hassles. (Not all businesses can be entered so informally. For

93

example, state and federal laws restrict banking and insurance to corporations having substantial assets. And local zoning laws and regulations may block or complicate the establishment of even the simplest business.) A single proprietorship has advantages for someone who wants to experiment with a new line of work—a fact that may explain why so many single proprietorships go out of business so quickly.

The single proprietorship is flexible and uncomplicated; the owner has no one else to consult. The proprietor buys the materials needed, hires any help that is necessary and can be afforded, and undertakes to pay the bills. The profits of the business belong to the owner, to be shared by no one (except the government, which collects its share in the form of personal income taxes paid by the owner).

But the single proprietorship has disadvantages. Most obviously, there are limits to how much one individual can manage. Consider a typical small enterprise, the gasoline station. In this sort of business, a single owner has problems. While help can be hired to operate the pumps, there are advantages in having someone around who is "in charge." Yet one individual would find it a crushing burden to try to be present during the long hours when a gas station is open. The obvious solution is to take on a partner, who will be jointly responsible.

Some partnerships are made up of just two people; others include dozens of partners. In a typical partnership, each partner agrees to provide some fraction of the work and some of the financing. (These shares need not all be equal. For example, a "silent partner" is one who provides financial support, but does not participate in the day-to-day running of the business.) In return, each partner receives an agreed share of the profits or suffers an agreed share of the loss. Again, the partnership is easily established; a simple oral agreement will do. However, this casual method is not recommended; it is a way to lose both business and friend. A formal partnership agreement, drawn up by a lawyer, can prevent much grief.

Both the single proprietorship and the partnership are simple and flexible, but they have the following major limitations:

1 If a proprietorship runs into difficulty, the owner can lose more than his or her initial investment. Personal assets, including home and car, may be lost in order to pay the debts of the business. In short, a proprietor has **unlimited liability** for all the debts of the business.

Similarly, partners have unlimited liability for the debts of the partnership; they can lose their personal assets as well as the money they originally put into the business. And, with a partnership, there is a particular form of risk: *Each partner is liable for the obligations undertaken by the other partner or partners,* and each partner runs the risk of being left "holding the bag" if the other partners are unable to meet their shares of the obligations of the partnership. Clearly, you should exercise great caution before taking on a dozen partners! (It is precisely because of this unlimited liability that partnerships are considered good form in the legal profession. A client has the assurance that *all* the partners will stand behind the acts of *each*.)

2 There is a problem of **continuity.** When a single proprietor dies, the business may too (although one of the children may take over the shop or farm and continue to run it). Continuity is an even more awkward problem in a partnership. Every time a partner dies, the original partnership automatically ends, and a new partnership must be formed. A new partnership agreement is likewise necessary whenever a new partner is admitted; and all partners must agree before any partner is allowed to sell his or her share of the partnership to a new party. These provisions are not surprising; after all, each of the partners will be liable for the acts of the new partner, and it is therefore only reasonable that each be given the right to veto the entrance of any new member.

3 There is the problem of **financing growth.** A partnership or proprietorship has a number of sources of financing: the personal wealth of the owner or owners; the profits made by the business which can be plowed back to purchase new equipment or buildings; the mortgaging of property; and borrowing from banks, suppliers, friends, and relatives. But it may be difficult to borrow the money needed for expansion. Lenders are reluctant to take the risks of lending large amounts to a struggling new enterprise.

Furthermore, it may also be difficult to bring in new owners to help with the financing. It is true that a carrot, in the form of a share of the profits, can be dangled in front of potential investors. But with the carrot comes a stick. In gaining a right to a share of the profits, a new partner also undertakes *unlimited liability* for the debts of the business. Consequently, outside investors will be reluctant to share in the partnership unless they have carefully investigated it and have developed an exceptionally high degree of confidence in the partners. This may make it very hard for a partnership to get the financing needed for expansion.

The corporation

The major advantage of the corporate form of organization is that it **limits the liability** of its owners: All they can lose is their initial investment. When new investors buy **shares** of the **common stock** of a business, they thereby acquire partial ownership of the business without facing the danger of unlimited liability. If the business goes bankrupt and is unable to pay its debts, the owners lose the purchase price of their shares, but not their homes or other personal property. By reducing the risks of investors, the corporate form of business makes it feasible to tap a wide pool of investment funds. Thus, the corporation is the form of business most suited to rapid growth with the use of outside funds.

Each *share of common stock* represents a fraction of the *ownership* (that is, a fraction of the *equity*) of a corporation.

Because corporations limit the liability of the owners, there is less legal protection for the creditors to whom the corporation owes money. If the corporation fails, its creditors (that is, those the corporation still owes money) cannot lay claim to the personal property of the owners. (Many corporations do, however, possess very large assets, cutting the risks of the creditors down to a low level.) Corporations must inform those with whom they do business of this limited liability; they do so by tacking to their corporate title the designation "Inc." or "Incorporated" (in the United States), or the more descriptive "Ltd." or "Limited" (in the British legal system). The French and Spanish use an even more colorful warning: Corporations' titles are followed by the letters S.A.—for *Société Anonyme,* or *Sociedad Anónima* (anonymous society).

Originally, in Britain some centuries ago, corporation charters were awarded only rarely, by special grants of the king and the Parliament. These corporations were granted substantial privileges; some were given special rights to conduct business in the British colonies—the East India Company, for example. During the nineteenth century, however, a major revolution occurred in business and legal thinking, and the modern corporation emerged. General incorporation laws were passed, granting to anyone the right to form a corporation. (See Box 6-1.) With a few important exceptions (such as banking, where governmental authorities retain control over the establishment of new banks), the formation of a corporation is a relatively straightforward and uncomplicated legal procedure.

In addition to limited liability, the corporation offers the advantage of continuity. In law, the corporation is a fictitious "legal person."[1] When one of the stockholders dies, the corporation survives; the shares of the deceased are inherited by his or her heirs, without the corporation's organization being disturbed. The heirs need not be concerned about accepting the shares, since they are not liable for the corporation's debts. Furthermore, the corporation survives if some of the stockholders want to get out

---

[1] In the late nineteenth century, this legal fiction was used by corporations to oppose government regulation. In a series of court cases, corporations argued that, as legal persons, they were shielded by the equal protection provisions of the Fourteenth Amendment to the Constitution.

What's a "Company Limited"?

In one of their lesser known nineteenth-century operettas *(Utopia, Limited)*, Gilbert and Sullivan undertook to explain the new concept of a "Company Limited." It was, they said, an association (if possible, of peers and baronets):

> *They start off with a public declaration*
> *To what extent they mean to pay their debts.*

And, of course,

> *When it's left to you to say*
> *What amount you mean to pay,*
> *Why, the lower you can put it at, the better.*

Thus, the best strategy for the founders of the company is to put up only a trivial amount of their own money—say, 18 pence:

> *If you succeed, your profits are stupendous—*
> *And if you fail, pop goes your eighteen pence.*

Of course, the company may fail:

> *Though a Rothschild you may be*
> *In your own capacity*
> *As a Company you've come to utter sorrow—*
> *But the Liquidators say,*
> *"Never mind—you needn't pay,"*
> *So you start another Company to-morrow!*

of the business. These stockholders can sell their shares to anyone willing to buy; there is no need to reorganize the company.

Corporation taxes

The profits of a proprietorship or a partnership are taxed as the personal income of the proprietor or partners. When a corporation is established, taxation becomes more involved. From the viewpoint of the shareholder-owner, the corporate form of business organization may involve either a tax advantage or a tax disadvantage.

Consider an illustration. A corporation with 1 million shares outstanding makes pretax profits of $10 million, or $10 per share. The corporation is taxed as a separate entity; its total corporation profits tax might amount to $3 million, or $3 per share. (The corporation income tax rate is 46 percent for all profits above $100,000 per year. But the effective tax rate is less than this percentage because of the investment tax credit and other detailed provisions of the tax law.) This leaves $7 million in after-tax profits, or $7 per share. Of this $7, the corporation might retain $5 for expansion of the business, and pay out the remaining $2 per share as dividends to the shareholders. In turn, the shareholders must include the dividends of $2 per share as part of their personal income, and pay personal income tax—at rates up to a maximum of 50 percent, depending on their tax bracket. From the viewpoint of the shareholder-owner, the disadvantage of this arrangement is that dividend income is taxed twice. First, it is taxed when it is earned as part of the total profits of the corporation. Second, it is taxed again when it is paid out in dividends and becomes the personal income of the shareholder.

But there also may be a tax advantage. Consider the $8 million not paid out in dividends. This income is taxed only once—and at a rate of only 30 percent.[2] (Remember: It is part of the $10 million in profits on which $3 million of tax is paid.) For wealthy shareholders in a high tax bracket, the 30 percent tax paid on the retained corporate profit is less than they would have to pay in personal income taxes if the business were a proprietorship or a partnership. Furthermore, for a small family-owned corporation, the tax advantage is even greater, since low tax rates apply to the first $100,000 of corporate profits. (The tax rate is 17 percent for the first $25,000 of profits; 20 percent for the second $25,000; 30 percent for the third; and 40 percent for the fourth.) Particularly for a new, growing business, there may thus be a tax incentive to incorporate. By keeping dividends low and plowing most of the profits back into the business, total taxes may be kept low.[3]

The double taxation of dividend income has drawn sharp criticism. Not only does a question of fairness arise, since profits going into dividends are taxed twice while profits retained for expansion are taxed only once. But a tax incentive is also provided for big corporations to grow even bigger: When profits are retained for expansion, double taxation is avoided. (Shareholders may be quite happy to have the corporation retain its earnings to finance growth, since they avoid the personal income tax which would be due if the corporation paid dividends. Although stockholders forgo dividend income in such circumstances, they own shares of a growing business; the value of their stock rises.)

The **integration** of the corporate tax with the personal income tax has been considered from time to time in the United States and other countries. With integration, corporate profits would be counted as personal income of the individual stockholders, whether the profits were paid out in dividends or not. (For example, in the earlier illustration, an owner of one share would pay personal income tax on the full $10 of profits—including profits retained by the corporation for expansion.) At the same time, the individual taxpayer would receive credit for the taxes paid by the corporation. (To continue the illustration, the $3 per share in taxes paid by the corporation could be subtracted by the shareholder from his or her personal income tax.) Thus, the tax law would "see through" the corporation. For tax purposes, the income of the corporation would be the income of the stockholders. And the taxes paid by the corporation would be counted as taxes paid by the individual stockholders. There would be neither a tax penalty nor a tax advantage from incorporation.

But integration raises a number of difficult technical questions. (In particular, the taxation of multinational corporations would become more complicated.) It is not clear that integration is administratively feasible.[4] Thus far, only minor steps have been taken to limit double taxation. (The first $100 of dividends received by individuals is exempt from personal income tax, and thus avoids double taxation.)

---

[2]At least, it is taxed only once now. If, at some time in the future, it is paid out as dividends, it will then be taxed again as personal income. In this case, the second round of tax is deferred, not avoided.

[3]The incentive to incorporate has been reduced by tax provisions which provide alternative ways of deferring taxes. For example, the Keogh plan permits the deferral of taxes on personal income put into a retirement fund. (After retirement, when the funds are used to provide the person with a pension, income taxes must be paid.)

[4]The problems are explained in detail in Charles E. McLure, Jr., *Must Corporate Income Be Taxed Twice?* (Washington: Brookings, 1979).

BOX 6-2
Who Controls the Corporation?

Because stockholders elect the board of directors, who in turn choose management, it would seem at first glance that the corporation is run in the interest of its stockholders.

However, things are not necessarily that simple. If its stock is spread among a large number of shareholders, a corporation may, in practice, be run by a group of insiders made up of the directors and senior management. The small stockholder's problem is akin to that of the consumer. In both cases, the stakes are not sufficiently great for the individual stockholder or consumer to make his or her views known forcefully. If you own only a few shares of a corporation's stock, it is probably not even worth your time and your travel expenses to show up at the annual meeting. What good would it do? If you have a suggestion, it is almost certain to be voted down anyway.

Furthermore, unless the corporation is doing very badly, you are likely to grant the management's request for your *proxy;* that is, you give them the authorization to vote on your behalf at the annual meeting. (This does not, however, mean that the management is immune from challenge: If the corporation's performance is weak, a dissident group of shareholders can get together. They may be successful in getting enough proxies to oust the old management. But this occurs only rarely. Throwing out management is a drastic step, which disrupts the everyday operation of the company. The standard advice given in the investment community is this: If you don't like the way the company is being run, don't fight management. Sell your stock. Vote with your feet.)

The separation of ownership and control was pointed out in *The Modern Corporation and Private Property* by A. A. Berle and Gardner C. Means, published in 1932. They found that the stockholding of 44 percent of the 200 largest U.S. corporations was so diffuse that no single family, corporation, or group of business associates owned as much as 10 percent of the stock. More recent work indicates that, by 1963, control was even more separated from ownership than it had been when Berle and Means wrote: What was true of 44 percent of the 200 largest corporations in the earlier period was by then true of 84.5 percent.

There is a great difference among companies. Until 1956, the Ford Motor Company was wholly owned by the Ford family. And even since the public offering of stock in 1956, the Ford family still controls the company. (A founding family or group may retain control by issuing different *classes* of common stock. One class, with restricted voting power, is offered to the public. The other class, with relatively great voting power, is retained by the founders. In Ford's case, class B stock amounts to only 11.5 percent of the total shares outstanding, but holders of this class have 40 percent of the voting power, giving them effective control of the corpo-

HOW A CORPORATION FINANCES EXPANSION

The corporation can obtain funds for expansion in the same way as a proprietorship or partnership; that is, by borrowing from banks or plowing profits back into the business. But a corporation also has other options. It can issue common stock, bonds, or other securities.

Common stock

When it sells additional shares of common stock, the corporation takes on new part-owners, since each share represents a fraction of the ownership of the corporation. As a part-owner, the purchaser of common stock not only receives a share of any dividends paid by the corporation, but also gets the right to vote for the corpora-

ration.) At the other extreme, American Telephone and Telegraph is owned by more than 3 million stockholders, none of whom owns as much as 1 percent of the total shares.

In cases where control is effectively in the hands of management rather than the owners, the question arises as to what difference this makes. There is an obvious community of interest between management and stockholders: Both groups want a corporation which is profitable. And management is obviously interested in the success of the corporation, since their jobs may be lost if the corporation goes under—or even if a poor performance leads to a successful proxy fight by a dissident group. (Even more

likely is a "revolt" by bankers, who may require the replacement of an incompetent management as a condition for renewing loans.)

But, while similar, the interests of management are not identical to those of stockholders. Management is interested in the preservation of their jobs. Therefore, they may be less likely to take risks than would stockholders. Furthermore, management—like a government bureaucracy—may be interested in growth for its own sake, even where growth does not contribute to higher profits. Why is that so? Because the importance of your position is in part measured by the number of people working for you. ■

tion's directors who, in turn, choose the corporate officers and set the corporation's policies. (On the question of who actually controls a corporation, see Box 6-2.)

Bonds

Rather than take on new owners by issuing additional common stock, the corporation may raise funds by selling bonds. A bond represents debt of the corporation; it is an I.O.U. that the corporation is obliged to repay, whether it is making profits or not. If the corporation doesn't pay, it can be sued by the bondholder.

A bond is a long-term form of debt which does not fall due for repayment until 10, 15, or more years from the time it was initially sold (issued) by the corporation (or government, or other issuer). Bonds usually come in large denominations—for example, $10,000. The original buyer normally pays the corporation a sum equal to the face value of the bond; in effect, the original buyer is lending $10,000 to the corporation. (The original buyer can resell the bond at more or less than the face value, depending on the market for bonds.) In return for the $10,000, the corporation is committed to make two sets of payments to the bondholder:

1 Interest payments that must be made periodically (normally semiannually) during the life of the bond. If the interest rate is, say, 14 percent per annum on a bond with a $10,000 face value, the interest payment will be $700 (that is, 7 percent) every 6 months.

2 A payment of the $10,000 **face value,** or **principal,** when the date of maturity arrives. That is, the corporation must repay the amount of the loan at maturity.

Since a bond commits the corporation to make the payments of interest and principal, it provides the purchaser an assured, steady income—provided the corporation avoids bankruptcy. Common stock, on the other hand, involves a substantial risk. During periods of difficulty, the corporation may reduce or eliminate the dividend, and the market price of the stock may plummet. But, while bonds provide more safety than stocks, they offer less excitement. Unlike the owner of common stock, the bondholder cannot look forward to rising dividends if the company hits the jackpot. The bondholder will get no more than the interest and principal specified in the bond contract. Generally, bonds are safe; but they are also dull.

Bonds are not the only type of debt which a corporation can issue. Securities issued with intermediate terms—of between 1 and 7 years to maturity—are generally known as **notes** rather than bonds. They are identical to bonds except for their shorter maturities. Securities with terms of less than 1 year are called **bills** or **commercial paper.** These are different from bonds or notes, since they provide no explicit,

periodic interest payment. Rather, the purchaser receives a return by buying bills at a **discount.** For example, a buyer paying $98,000 for a bill with a face value of $100,000 will get back $2,000 more than the purchase price when the bill reaches maturity.

Some investors desire an income-earning security "between bonds and stocks"; that is, one that will provide more safety than common stock, while still offering some of the excitement of stock (a larger potential return than bonds or commercial paper provide). These investors may choose *convertible bonds* or *preferred stock.*

Convertible bonds
Convertible bonds are like ordinary bonds, with one additional feature. Prior to a given date, they may be exchanged for common stock in some fixed ratio (for example, 1 bond for 10 shares of common stock). If the outlook for the corporation becomes very favorable, the holder of convertible bonds may exchange them for common stock, and thus own shares of the growing corporation. If, on the other hand, the company fails to prosper, convertible bonds may be held to maturity, when the bondholder will receive repayment of the principal.

Because the holder has the option of converting, the interest rate on convertible bonds is normally less than the rate on regular bonds, sometimes substantially less. Therefore, if you are thinking about buying convertible bonds, you have to weigh two conflicting considerations. The interest payments which you receive will be low. But you will have the option to convert into common stock, an option which may become very valuable in the event the business is successful.

Preferred stock
Preferred stock, like common stock, represents ownership, and not debt. The corporation is legally obligated to make interest payments to bondholders, but it is not legally required to pay dividends to preferred or common stockholders.

Preferred stockholders, however, have a claim on profits which precedes—or is "preferred" to—the claim of the common stockholder. The preferred stockholder has a right to receive specific dividends (for example, 10 cents per share) before the common stockholder can be paid any dividend at all. But, on the other hand, the preferred stockholder does not have the possibility of large gains open to the common stockholder. While the common stockholder may hope for rising dividends if the corporation prospers, the preferred shareholder will at most receive the specified dividend. (A rare form of stock, the *participating* preferred, provides an exception to this rule. It gives the holder the right to participate in the growth of the company's dividends.)

In any year, the corporation may decide not to pay dividends to either the preferred or the common stockholders. This creates a potential problem for the preferred stockholder. The voting control of the corporation is generally in the hands of the common stockholders. What is to prevent them from electing directors who will eliminate all dividends for a number of years, in order to accumulate funds and pay them all out in 1 year? If the preferred shareholders are confined to their specific dividend (say, $2 per share), then they will get paid only this 1 year; they will never recapture the dividends lost in the previous years. Instead, almost all the dividends will go to the common shareholders, who will thus be enriched at the expense of preferred shareholders. To prevent this abuse, preferred shareholders are often protected in several ways. (1) If dividends are not paid, they may get the *right to vote* for company directors. (2) Preferred shares may be *cumulative*. That is, if no dividends are paid for one or more years, they accumulate, and must *all* be paid before the common stockholder is paid *any* dividend. (3) Preferred shares may be *convertible* into common shares at the option of the preferred shareholder.

As a general rule, all types of securities— common stocks, preferred stocks, and bonds— may be resold by the original purchasers. Securities prices tend to reflect the judgment of buyers and sellers regarding the prospects of the corporation. Thus, for example, an announcement of a new product may make purchasers eager to buy the company's stock, and make present stockholders reluctant to sell. As a result, the price of the stock will be bid up. Purchasers also look at the position and performance of the company as indicated by a study of its financial accounts.

BUSINESS ACCOUNTING: THE BALANCE SHEET AND THE INCOME STATEMENT

Business accounts are valuable not only as a source of information for potential buyers of the company's stock or bonds. They also are an important tool for helping management keep track of how well the company is doing, and what it is worth. And businesses are required to keep accounts for taxation purposes.

There are two major types of business accounts:

1 The **balance sheet,** which gives a picture of the company's financial status at a *point* in time; for example, on December 31 of last year.
2 The **income statement** (also called the *profit and loss statement*), which summarizes the company's transactions over a *period* of time, such as a year.

The income statement records the *flow* of payments into and out of a company over a period of time. It is like a movie film that records the flow of water into and out of a bathtub. The balance sheet, on the other hand, is a still picture, showing the *stock* of water in the tub at a specific point in time.

The balance sheet
The balance sheet lists (1) the **assets** which a company owns, (2) the **liabilities** which it owes, and (3) the amount of **ownership** of the stockholders. Assets must be exactly equal to the total of liabilities plus ownership. To use a simple illustration: If you have a car worth $7,000 (an asset), for which you still owe $4,000 to the bank (your debt or liability), then $3,000 is the value of your ownership in the car.

The same fundamental equation also holds for a corporation:

Assets = liabilities (what is owed) + net worth (the value of ownership)

Assets are listed on the left side of the balance sheet; liabilities and net worth are on the right. Because of the fundamental equation, the two sides must add to the same total: **The balance sheet must balance.**

The *net worth* of a corporation—the value of the stockholders' ownership—is equal to the assets minus the liabilities of the corporation

---

As an example, consider the simplified version of the balance sheet of the Ford Motor Company shown in Table 6-1.

On the left-hand (asset) side, Ford has sizable assets in the form of cash (bank accounts), marketable short-term securities (such as government bills or commercial paper issued by other corporations), and accounts receivable (for

example, the value of cars which have already been delivered but not yet paid for). Ford naturally has large inventories of materials, such as tires, paint, glass, and parts, and of completed automobiles. Ford also has major assets in the form of land, plant (buildings), and equipment.

On the right side of the balance sheet, most of the liabilities of Ford are short term: amounts which Ford has not yet paid for its steel and other supplies (accounts payable); wages and salaries not yet paid for work already performed (accrued liabilities); and short-term debt (such as money owed to banks). In addition, at the end of 1979 Ford had an outstanding long-term debt of $1.3 billion. (If debt matures within 1 year, it is short term; in more than 1 year, long term.)

At the end of 1979, Ford's total assets were $23.5 billion, and its liabilities were $13.1 billion. The net worth—the ownership of all stockholders—was therefore $10.4 billion. Of this, $765 million had been paid in originally by stockholders purchasing shares of the company. But by far the largest part, amounting to over $9.6 billion, represented retained earnings; that

Table 6-1
Ford Motor Company Balance Sheet, December 31, 1979
(simplified, millions of dollars)

Assets			Liabilities and net worth		
1. Current assets		11,571	5. Current liabilities		9,263
(a) Cash	1,127		(a) Accounts payable and		
(b) Marketable securities	1,066		accrued liabilities	7,649	
(c) Receivables	2,724		(b) Short-term debt	977	
(d) Inventories	5,892		(c) Other	637	
(e) Other current assets	762		6. Long-term debt		1,275
2. Land, plant, and			7. Other liabilities		2,567
equipment		7,049	**8. Total liabilities**		———
3. Other assets		4,905	**(5 + 6 + 7)**		**13,105**
			9. Net worth (4 − 8)		**10,420**
			(a) Capital stock	765	
			(b) Retained earnings	9,655	
4. Total assets		———	**10. Total liabilities and**		———
(items 1 + 2 + 3)		**23,525**	**net worth (8 + 9)**		**23,525**

Source: Ford Motor Company, *Annual Report 1979.*

is, profits made over the years that had been plowed back into the business.[5]

At the end of 1979, there were 120.5 million shares of Ford common stock outstanding. (There were no preferred shares.) Each share represented an equity, or **book value,** of $86.65 (that is, $10,420 million in net worth ÷ 120.5 million shares).

The *book value* of a stock is its net worth per share. (It is calculated by dividing the net worth by the number of shares outstanding.)

If you are thinking of buying common stock of a company, its book value is one of the things that should interest you. If it has a high book value, you will be buying ownership of a lot of assets. But *don't get carried away by high book value.* If these assets happen to be machinery and equipment that can be used only to produce buggy whips or other items for which there is no demand, that high book value may not be worth very much; the assets may not earn much income in the future. (In fact, Ford suffered large losses in 1980, and the price of its stock fell below $20 per share.)

---

[5]"Retained earnings" may sound like a pool of funds which the corporation has readily available. However, this is generally not the case. Most retained earnings are not held in the form of cash; most are used to buy equipment or other items.

Suppose that, in the first year of its operation, a corporation earns $1,000, and retains it all. (It pays no dividend.) The $1,000 may be used to buy a new machine. Then, as a result, the following changes occur in the balance sheet:

Change in:

Assets		Net worth	
Machinery	+$1,000	Retained earnings	+$1,000

The retained earnings have not been held in the form of idle cash; they have been put to work to buy machinery. The machinery shows up on the asset side. When the retained earnings are included in net worth, the balance sheet balances.

Table 6-2
Ford Motor Company Income Statement for the Year 1979
(simplified, millions of dollars)

1. Sales		43,514
2. Less: Costs		42,015
(a) Costs, excluding items below	38,606	
(b) Depreciation	896	
(c) Selling and administrative costs	1,702	
(d) Employee retirement plans	811	
3. Income (profit) before taxes (1−2)		1,499
4. Less: Income taxes		330
5. Net income (net profit) (3−4)		1,169
(a) Dividends paid	468	
(b) Retained earnings	701	

Source: Ford Motor Company, *Annual Report 1979.*

The income statement

While the balance sheet shows the assets, liabilities, and net worth of a corporation at a *point* in time, the income statement shows what has happened *during a period of time*—for example, during a calendar year. A simplified version of Ford's income statement for 1979 is shown in Table 6-2.

In 1979, Ford sold $43.5 billion of cars, trucks, tractors, parts, etc. Costs of $42.0 billion are subtracted from sales to calculate income (profit) before taxes of $1.5 billion. Corporate income taxes were $0.3 billion, leaving an after-tax profit of $1.2 billion, or about $10 per share. Of this after-tax profit, $468 million was paid in dividends to stockholders ($3.90 per share), and $701 million was retained by the company. (Observe that the retained earnings in Table 6-1 are much larger than those shown in Table 6-2. The reason is this: The income statement in Table 6-2 shows only the retained earnings during the 1 year, 1979. In contrast, the balance sheet in Table 6-1 shows all retained earnings accumulated over the entire lifetime of the company.)

(We have used 1979 data in Tables 6-1 and 6-2 in order to show the typical situation in which a company is profitable. In 1980, Ford suffered an after-tax loss of $1.5 billion—the second highest in U.S. corporate history. That year was a terrible one for auto makers, whose sales fell sharply because of rising gasoline prices and surging imports of Japanese automobiles. Chrysler lost a record $1.7 billion, and even General Motors was in the red, suffering its first loss since 1921.)

Most of Ford's costs are reasonably straightforward. Ford pays wages to its work force, and buys steel, tires, parts, and materials from outside suppliers. These costs are included in the large cost subcomponent of $38.6 billion in line 2(a) of Table 6-2. But one cost item, **depreciation** [line 2(b)], needs to be explained. This represents the cost of plant and equipment used to produce automobiles and other items.

Depreciation

Consider the specific example of a machine acquired by Ford during 1979. This machine does not wear out during 1979; it will continue to be used in coming years. Therefore, in calculating the costs of production in 1979, it would be misleading to count the full purchase price of the machine. Instead, only a fraction is counted, with other fractions being allocated to future years while the machine is still in use.

The easiest way to allocate costs over a period of years is **straight-line depreciation,** which spreads the cost of the machine (minus its scrap value, if any) evenly over its estimated lifetime. For example, if a machine costs $10,000 and wears out in 5 years (with no scrap value), straight-line depreciation is $2,000 per year for 5 years. A more complicated method of spreading costs is **accelerated depreciation,** which allocates higher fractions of the cost to the early years, and lower fractions to the later years of the machine's life. (See Figure 6-1.)

Depreciation accounting is not an exact science. Not only does the useful lifetime of a machine depend on physical wear and tear, but it also depends on obsolescence, which cannot be accurately forecast. Even if a machine could

be permanently maintained in brand-new condition, it would eventually become obsolete; that is, its useful life would end as new and more efficient machines became available. (Obsolescence tends to be greatest for high-technology equipment. An early computer, built in 1946 at the University of Pennsylvania, contained 18,000 vacuum tubes, weighed 30 tons, and occupied a huge room, with other large areas needed for air conditioning. Now, a chip with equivalent computing capacity may be held on the tip of your finger.)

But an even greater complication arises because of the tax laws. Note that depreciation is a cost which is subtracted before taxable income is calculated (Table 6-2). Thus, firms have an incentive to increase their depreciation costs by estimating short lifetimes for their machines; they thus reduce their before-tax income and hence their tax bill. To prevent the government's loss of tax revenues, the law specifies the lifetime over which various types of equipment can be depreciated. (The law also regulates the degree to which depreciation may be "accelerated.") Thus, depreciation costs may be more dependent on the tax law than on how fast a machine in reality wears out or becomes obsolete. (A company may keep plant and equipment in use after they have been completely depreciated on its books.)

FINANCIAL MARKETS

As we have seen, corporations may finance expansion by retaining their profits or by looking outside for sources of funds. They may borrow from banks, insurance companies, or other financial corporations. Or they may issue additional stocks or bonds. Financial markets and financial corporations occupy a strategic role in the economy because they help to determine which businesses will receive the finances for expansion.

Financial corporations, such as banks, savings and loan associations, and insurance companies, are **financial intermediaries.** That is, they take small amounts of funds from a large number of people, pool these funds, and lend them in larger amounts to businesses, governments, or individuals. For example, a savings and loan association may receive 100 small deposits with an average size of $300. With the combined total of $30,000, it makes a mortgage loan to someone buying a house. In doing this, the savings and loan (S&L) provides a useful service. The home buyer is saved the trouble of trying to locate the 100 individuals who would be willing to put up small amounts. The people who provide the funds are saved the nuisance of lending directly to the homeowner and of collecting on the loan every month. In addition to handling the paperwork, the S&L investigates the credit-worthiness of the potential home buyer, thus limiting the risk that the loan will not be repaid. Similarly, banks and insurance companies take funds from deposits or insurance policies, pool them, and lend them to businesses, governments, or individuals who meet their standards of credit-worthiness.

Thus, a business that wants to borrow money may go to a bank or an insurance company. But what does a business do if it prefers not to borrow, and wants to raise money by selling its common stock instead? It may follow one of two courses. If it is a large corporation that already has many shareholders, it can give the current shareholders the rights or *warrants* to buy new stock at a specific price. Because this price is generally less than the current market price of the stock, the current stockholders have an incentive to exercise the rights—that is, to use the warrants to buy stock at the bargain price. Those who already have all the stock they want can sell the warrants to someone who wants to use them to buy the bargain stock. Thus, the corporation ends up by selling the new shares of its stock either to current shareholders or to those who have bought the warrants.

Figure 6-1
Depreciation ($10,000 machine, with 5-year life)
With straight-line depreciation, an equal amount of the machine's value is counted as a cost of production in each year of the machine's life. If accelerated depreciation is used, larger amounts of the machine's value are counted as a cost of production in the early years than in the later years.

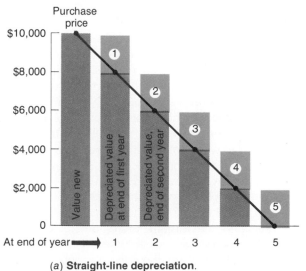

(a) **Straight-line depreciation**.　　　(b) **Accelerated depreciation**.

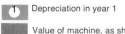 Depreciation in year 1

Value of machine, as shown on the company's books

Since a new company does not already have a large number of shareholders, it will use a different method of selling stock. It will approach an **investment bank,** a firm that markets securities. The investment bank looks for its profits in the markup between the price it pays to the company for the stock and the price at which it sells this stock to the public. The investment bank may simply undertake to sell as many shares as it can, up to the maximum the company is willing to issue. In this case, the company takes a risk: If buyers are unreceptive, few shares are sold and the company raises only a little money. However, if the investment bank is confident regarding the prospects of the company, it may **underwrite** the stock issue; that is, it guarantees the sale of the full issue of stock. If it is unable to find buyers for the whole issue, the investment bank will end up buying the shares itself. To limit its risk, the investment bank may bring in other investment banks to form a **syndicate** which jointly underwrites the new issue.

Investment banks may also underwrite corporation bonds. As part of their business, investment bankers keep close contact with pension funds and other large-scale purchasers of securities.

Financial markets: The objectives of buyers of securities

In some ways, the markets for stocks and bonds are similar to the markets for shirts, shoes, or automobiles. For example, just as the automobile dealer makes profits by the markup on cars, so the investment banker makes profits by the markup on stocks and bonds. But, in one very important way, the market for stocks and bonds is quite different from the market for shoes or cars. When you wish to buy a pair of shoes or a car, you can examine the available merchandise and make a reasonably good judgment as to its quality. You cannot make a perfect judgment, of course; you can't really be sure of the type of material used in the stitching in a shoe, and you can't really be sure that the brand new automobile will not turn out to be a lemon. Nevertheless, you can make a reasonably good judgment.

But when you buy a common stock, you are, in effect, buying a future prospect—something which is clearly intangible and about which it may be very difficult to reach an informed and balanced judgment. Similarly, when you buy a bond, you are buying a set of promises made by the bond issuer to pay interest and principal on schedule.

Because of the uncertainty of the future, purchasers do not simply choose the bond which has the highest interest rate; the credibility of the promise of the company to repay is also important. Indeed, purchasers of securities have three objectives to balance: return, risk, and liquidity.

Return is the annual yield, measured as a percentage of the cost of the security. For example, if a bond is purchased for $10,000 and it pays interest of $1,200 per year, then it yields 12 percent.

Risk is the chance that something will go wrong. For example, the company may go bankrupt and the bondholder may lose both interest and principal.

Finally, **liquidity** reflects the ability of the owner to sell an asset on short notice, with little cost and bother. A passbook account in an S&L is highly liquid: It may be withdrawn at any time for its full dollar value. (Thus, in addition to handling paperwork and evaluating borrowers' credit-worthiness, S&Ls and other financial intermediaries provide their depositors with liquidity.) At the other end of the spectrum, real estate or paintings are very illiquid. If you have to sell your home on short notice, you may have to accept a price which is much lower than you could get with a more lengthy selling effort.

While investors look for a combination of high return, low risk, and high liquidity, they do not all weigh the three objectives equally. Some (particularly those with steady incomes who are saving for the distant future) do not consider liquidity important, while others (perhaps those whose children are about to enter college) want to keep liquid investments on which they can draw in the near future. And different investors may have quite different attitudes toward risk.

The objectives of issuers of securities

A company raising funds also has three objectives to balance: to obtain funds in such a way as to achieve a high *return* for the corporation's stockholders; to avoid *risk;* and to assure the *availability* of money when it is needed.

A corporation balances risk and return when it chooses whether to issue stocks or bonds. In contrast with the view from the buyer's side, the view of the corporation selling securities is that *bonds* have a *higher risk* than common stock. If it sells bonds, interest payments must be made no matter how badly the corporation may be doing. Thus, large outstanding debt (large past sales of bonds) can put a corporation in a precarious position. If business slackens, it may be unable to meet large payments for interest and principal; the corporation may face bankruptcy. There is no such risk with common stock, since the company can cut dividends in the event of a downturn in business.

But, while it is safer for a corporation to issue stock, there is a disadvantage: Additional stock involves taking on new part-owners. If the company does well, the rising profits go partially to the new stockholders; the original stockholders must share their bonanza. In contrast, consider what happens if bonds are issued—that is, if the **leverage** of the corporation is increased. After the required payment of interest on the bonds, any large profits go only to the original stockholders. Thus, the more highly leveraged a corporation is, the greater is the uncertainty for its owners. Their potential gain is large, but so is their potential loss, including the possibility of bankruptcy.

Leverage is the ratio of debt to net worth. If this ratio is large, the corporation is highly leveraged.

As a group, stockholders and corporate managers tend to be optimistic. They consequently may try to maximize their expected gains by a high degree of leverage. Furthermore, limited liability provides an incentive for leverage. If things go well, stockholders can earn many times their original investment. But if things go poorly, they can lose their original investment only once.[6] Thus, a company may be highly leveraged in order to keep the potential gains in the hands of a few stockholders, while pushing off most of the risks onto a large number of bondholders (and others to whom the company owes money who will be left "holding the bag" if the company goes bankrupt). Thus, even though a company takes risk into account when it issues stocks or bonds, it has a temptation to discount the importance of risk, since someone else will suffer much of the possible loss.

If corporate managers were free to leverage to their hearts' content, the economy might be wildly unstable. (When businesses go bankrupt, their employees may be thrown out of work, and other businesses to whom they owe money may also go bankrupt.) Fortunately, however, there are limits to leverage. As leverage increases, the increasing risks to bondholders make them cautious. They become increasingly reluctant to buy that company's bonds unless the bonds yield a very high interest. If leverage becomes great enough, the company may find it impossible to sell bonds or to borrow from banks or others. Leverage is limited by the caution of lenders.

(However, the tax law gives corporations an incentive to increase their leverage by issuing bonds rather than stock. Interest paid on bonds and other loans can be subtracted as a cost in calculating taxable profits; consequently, interest payments reduce a company's tax. No such subtraction is permitted for dividends paid to stockholders: As we have seen, they are subject to double taxation. This incentive for leverage—which contributes to economic instability—provides another argument against the double taxation of corporate profits.)

---

[6]In their description of a "Company Limited" (in Box 6-1), Gilbert and Sullivan clearly recognized the advantage of leverage. The company with an equity of only 18 pence would be very highly leveraged. And profits on this 18 pence might well be "stupendous." If the company fails, "pop goes your 18 pence"—but that's all.

The final objective of corporations issuing securities is to assure the availability of money when it is needed. As a general rule, it is inadvisable to finance a new factory with short-term borrowing. It is unwise to have to keep repaying a short-term debt and borrowing money again each year to finance a factory over, say, a 20-year lifetime. In some of those years, funds may not be available to borrowers, or be available only at a very high interest rate. New factories should therefore be financed by long-term borrowing, or by the issue of additional stock, or by retained profits.

In order to ensure the availability of money for unpredictable requirements that can arise, a corporation may arrange a **line of credit** at a bank. A line of credit is a commitment by a bank to lend up to a specified limit at the request of the company. Similarly, builders may get commitments from savings and loan associations to provide mortgage money in the future. Such commitments allow builders to make firm plans for construction.

The bond market

Because security buyers balance risk and return, risky securities generally must have higher yields, or nobody will buy. This shows up in the bond market yields shown in Figure 6-2. Observe that the highest-grade corporate bonds, classified Aaa by Moody's Investors' Service, have lower yields than the more risky corporate bonds, classified Baa. (In judging the quality of bonds, investors' services consider such things as leverage and the stability of a corporation's earnings.) In turn, U.S. government bonds, which are free from risk of default, have lower yields than even the highest-grade corporate bonds.

Note also that the gaps between these three sets of bonds (U.S. government, corporate Aaa, and corporate Baa) are not constant. Most conspicuously, the gap between corporate Aaa and Baa yields shot up during the early 1930s. As the economy collapsed into the Depression, bankruptcies mounted; many shaky firms went under. The risks associated with the holding of low-grade corporate bonds rose, and conse-

quently their yields also rose compared to the yields on high-grade bonds. A similar, but less dramatic, increase in **risk premiums** took place during the recession of 1974, when the gap between the yields on corporate Aaa and corporate Baa bonds widened. (The gap between risk-free U.S. government bonds and corporate Aaa bonds also widened.)

A **risk premium** is the difference between the yields on two grades of bonds because of differences in their risk.

While the most important reason for differences in bond yields is difference in *risk,* several other influences are at work. There are very large quantities of U.S. government bonds outstanding, and the market for these bonds is very active, with relatively small selling costs. (The gap is small between the "bid" price, at which bond dealers are ready to buy, and the "offer" price, at which they are ready to sell.) Thus, U.S. government bonds provide a *liquidity* advantage; less loss results if the buyer has to turn around quickly and sell them. This is a second reason why their yield is low. A third reason is that U.S. government bonds (sometimes simply called U.S. governments) pay interest that is exempt from state income *taxes.*

The biggest tax advantage, however, lies with the state and local government bonds, whose interest is exempt from the large federal income tax. This important difference in tax treatment explains why yields on state and local government bonds are lower than on U.S. governments—even though U.S. government bonds are free from the risk of default while state and local government bonds are not. (In an extreme situation, the federal government has the constitutional right to print money to pay interest and principal on its bonds. State and local governments have no such right and may default on their debt, as the holders of Cleveland and New York City securities found to their sorrow during the 1970s.)

Finally, the most notable feature in the bond market is the general upward movement of all interest rates over the past two decades. This rise

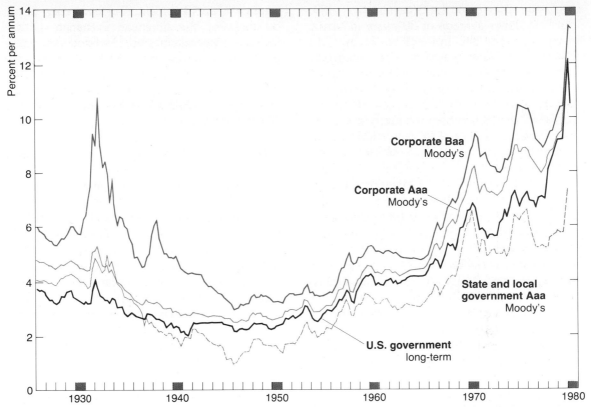

Figure 6-2
Long-term bond yields

The differences between yields on different securities reflect primarily differences in risk. (A notable exception is the low yield on state and local government securities, which reflects their tax-exempt status.) The rising trend of all interest rates in recent decades has been caused by a rise in the rate of inflation.

has been caused by the acceleration of inflation. When inflation is high, bondholders recognize that interest and principal will be repaid in the future when money is less valuable than at present. They therefore hesitate to purchase bonds unless interest rates are high enough to compensate them for the declining value of money.

The stock market

Stocks of major corporations already held by the public are usually bought and sold on the stock exchanges, the most famous being the New York Stock Exchange. Stockbrokers throughout the country maintain close contact with the exchanges, buying and selling stocks on behalf of their customers.

A *broker* acts as a representative of a buyer or seller, offering to buy or sell on behalf of clients.

Prices fluctuate on the stock exchanges in response to changes in demand and supply. Stock purchasers are interested in such things as the current and expected future profits of the corporation. Thus, stock prices may rise rapidly during periods of prosperity.

In the 1920s, the desire to "get rich quick" in the stock market became a national mania. With stocks rising, many investors learned that individuals, too, could use leverage to increase their potential gains; they borrowed large sums to buy stocks in the expectation that their prices would rise. Then came the Great Crash of 1929. The Dow-Jones average of 30 major industrial stocks fell from 381 in 1929 to 41 in 1932 (Figure 6-3). Many investors were wiped out. The stocks of the best corporations in America shared in the disaster. From a price of $396 in early September 1929, General Electric fell to $168 in late November, following the stock market panic, and to $34 by 1932. General Motors dropped from $72 to $36 to $8, and AT&T from $304 to $197 to $70.[7]

Another major upswing in the stock averages occurred in the 1950s and 1960s, with the Dow-Jones reaching 1,000 by 1966. During the 1960s, the U.S. economy had the longest continuous expansion on record. Common stocks promised a share in the nation's prosperity. And they were widely looked on as a hedge against inflation. After all, stocks represent ownership of corporations, and in a period of inflation, the dollar value of a corporation's plant and equipment should rise with the general increase in prices. This comforting viewpoint was plausible; but it was not borne out by unfolding events. From its 1966 high, the Dow-Jones retreated as inflationary pressures accelerated.

During the 1970s, stock market participants came to the view that inflation was very unhealthy for the economy, and signs of accelerating inflation were generally followed by declines in stock prices. As measured by the popular Dow-Jones average (shown in Figure 6-3), the stock market went nowhere during the decade: The average price of stocks was about the same in 1980 as it had been a decade earlier.

(However, while the stocks of major companies included in the Dow-Jones average turned in a mediocre performance, smaller stocks did better. In the 5 years ending in late 1980, the Dow-Jones average was up only 12 percent. Standard and Poor's broader index of 500 stocks was up 43 percent. And the average price of stocks on the American Exchange—which includes many energy stocks and stocks of smaller companies—was up more than 300 percent.)

CAPITAL MARKETS: TWO IMPORTANT PROBLEMS

The economic function of the markets for financial capital is similar to the function of markets for goods: They help to determine what will be produced in the economy. For example, if a company develops a new product for which there is a large demand, its profits will likely rise, and it will have little trouble in raising funds for expansion by borrowing or by issuing stock. In this way, the company will be able to quickly produce the item in demand.

There are, however, special problems in the capital markets. First, because of difficulty in getting information, money may be directed into the wrong industries or to the wrong firms. Second, private capital markets do not assure that there will be the right total quantity of investment in the economy.

The problem of information: Will funds go to the "right" industries?

Because securities involve future prospects—a promise of either future interest payments or a share of future profits—they are particularly difficult to evaluate. If promises are being bought, then the money may go to the slickest talker. History is full of artful swindlers, ranging from John Law (whose Mississippi Company first provided speculative riches and then financial disaster to its shareholders in eighteenth-century Paris), to Charles Ponzi, to 1970s-style con men like Bernard Cornfeld and Robert Trippet. (Ponzi used a masterfully simple scheme to swindle more than $10 million from Bostonians in 1919–1920: His operation declared large fictitious profits, and paid dividends on outstanding stock by selling new stock which investors snapped up because of the high "profits" and dividends. Cornfeld's Investors' Overseas Ser-

---

[7]For some of the drama of the collapse, see John Kenneth Galbraith, *The Great Crash, 1929* (Boston: Houghton Mifflin, 1961); or Frederick Lewis Allen, *The Lords of Creation* (New York: Harper, 1935), chap. 13.

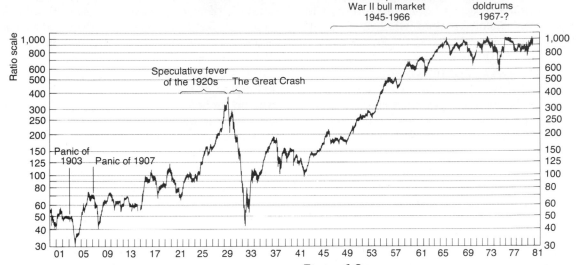

Figure 6-3
**The Dow-Jones industrial stock average,
1900–1981**

The biggest swing in stock prices, in percentage terms, took place during the expansive bull market of the 1920s and the sharp contraction (bear market) of 1929–1932. In the first two decades after World War II (1945–1966), average stock prices rose about sixfold. But between 1966 and 1980, there was no further gain; on average, stock prices were no higher in 1980 than in 1966. [Note: The figure is a ratio (or semilog) chart. As explained in Chapter 1, equal vertical distances represent equal percentage changes. For example, the distance from 100 to 200 is the same as the distance from 200 to 400.]

vice separated many Europeans from their savings. Trippet ran a Ponzi scheme, notable for the list of people swindled: It included Walter Wriston of Citicorp, one of the shrewdest bankers in America, from whom Trippet took $211,000.)

Financing that goes into hairbrained schemes represents not just a loss to individuals but a loss to society of the alternative projects which could have been financed instead.

Because it is so difficult for average investors to evaluate the prospects of a company (to know if they are dealing with a Ponzi), there is a strong case for regulations which require the disclosure of information by those issuing securities. In the United States, such regulations are enforced by the Securities and Exchange Commission (SEC). Before offering securities to the public, companies are required to issue a **prospectus,** which is a formal statement presenting information on the current position and the future prospects of the corporation. Publicly owned firms are required to make their accounts public and to announce publicly significant developments which may affect the price of their stock. (They are forbidden from "leaking inside information" to help their friends make a killing on the stock market.)

The SEC has prevented the type of financial buccaneering which marked the 1920s. (Cornfeld was induced to operate in Canada and Europe because of the strictness of SEC regulations.) Nevertheless, many investment projects are intrinsically risky. Thus, it is inevitable that large sums are sometimes channeled into honest projects that fail. For example, during the 1950s, the Ford Motor Company had a classic flop with its Edsel car. A number of large aircraft have also been financial failures, including an early jet airliner produced by General Dynamics. In spite of its impressive technology, the British-French supersonic Concorde is a major money-loser, in part because it is a fuel-guzzler designed in the days of cheap oil. In an uncertain world, each investment is an act of faith. The problem is to avoid investment decisions which are acts of *blind* faith.

Capital markets and the problem of instability

When an economy is operating at full employment, it is producing all, or nearly all, that it can with its limited labor force and capital stock. If additional investment is undertaken in one area, such as the production of a supersonic airliner, cutbacks must be made elsewhere. Participants in the financial markets evaluate risks, and thus tend to channel funds to the companies whose prospects they consider brightest. Consequently, the markets tend to direct funds toward the most productive pattern of new investments.

But consider the problem when the economy moves down into a recession or a depression. Then, there are large amounts of unemployed labor and unused plant and equipment. The decision to proceed with one investment (such as a bicycle plant) no longer requires that we forego an alternative investment (such as additional machinery for the auto industry). They can both be built by putting unemployed labor and unemployed equipment back to work. Indeed, if the downward slide of the economy is severe, there are available resources to produce a lot of additional capital goods of all sorts—and additional consumer goods, too. The important question ceases to be which of the competing investments is better; for example, would it be better to invest in the auto industry or the bicycle industry? Rather, the key question becomes: How do we get more investment in *both* the auto industry and the bicycle industry—and in other industries, too?

The private financial markets do a reasonably good job in determining relative risks and rewards, and thus do a reasonably good job of determining *which* investments will be undertaken. But they suffer major shortcomings in dealing with the problem of cyclical instability—the question of how much *total* investment should be undertaken. Consider what happened as the economy collapsed into the Depression of the 1930s. Stock market investors became panic-stricken as stock prices plummeted. At the very low prices of the Depression, the stock market was no longer an attractive place for corporations to raise funds. Any issue of stock in those days meant that current stockholders were practically giving away part of their ownership to new buyers. Similarly, with the widespread difficulties of business, risk premiums on bonds rose sharply. For much of the 1930s, there was no overall shortage of funds which banks and others had available for investment: The interest rate on risk-free federal government bonds was very low (between 2 and 3 percent). But funds were not cheap for many businesses because of extremely high risk premiums. As a result, investment was discouraged, and this deepened the Depression.

Low stock prices and high borrowing costs were not the only reasons that investment dried up during the Depression. Many business executives were so frightened that they would not have undertaken expansion even if funds had been available at very low interest rates. Their pessimism and lack of investment were not the result of a lack of information. During the 1930s, business was indeed faced with appalling prospects; an individual with perfect information would still not have invested. Regulations requiring the disclosure of information can help direct investment funds into the most promising projects, but additional information cannot be counted on to solve the problem of economic instability.

Because private financial markets do not necessarily result in a stable economy, the responsibility for stability has fallen to the federal government. How the government can fulfill this responsibility is a major topic in our companion volume, *An Introduction to Macroeconomics*.

Key Points

1 There are three forms of business organization: *(a)* single proprietorships; *(b)* partnerships; and *(c)* corporations.

2 Single proprietorships and partnerships are simple and flexible. On the other hand, the advantages of the corporate form of organization are *(a)* limited liability; *(b)* automatic continuity, even if one or more of the owners should die; and *(c)* better access to funds for financing growth.

3 A corporation can obtain financing by issuing (selling) common or preferred stock, and bonds (including convertible bonds).

4 There are two main types of business accounts. The *balance sheet* shows assets, liabilities, and net worth at a point in time. The *income statement* reports sales, costs, and profits during a period of time.

5 A financial intermediary takes funds from individual savers and pools these funds to lend to businesses, governments, or individuals.

6 The purchaser of securities balances three important objectives: *high return, low risk,* and *high liquidity.*

7 A company that issues new securities also tries to find the best balance among three objectives: (1) to keep the *return* of the corporation's stockholders as high as possible, (2) to avoid *risk,* and (3) to assure the *availability* of money when needed.

8 In general, bonds are less risky than common stocks for buyers of securities, and more risky for sellers of new securities. When corporations or individuals increase their debts, they thereby increase their leverage; that is, they increase their ratio of debt to net worth. While this raises their potential gain, it also increases their risk of bankruptcy, since they must make interest and principal payments no matter how bad business is.

9 Because stocks and bonds represent claims to future profits or interest payments, the evaluation of the issuer's prospects are extremely important for anyone buying a security. In order to protect the purchaser and to help direct funds into the projects where the returns are highest, the Securities and Exchange Commission (SEC) requires corporations to make relevant information available to the public.

10 Financial markets cannot be counted on to ensure the quantity of investment needed for full employment. The maintenance of a high level of employment is a responsibility of the federal government. (This role will be studied in future chapters.)

Key Concepts

single proprietorship	cumulative preferred stock	financial intermediary
partnership	balance sheet	savings and loan
limited liability	income statement	association (S&L)
corporation	assets	warrant
incorporated (inc.)	liabilities	investment bank
share of common stock	net worth	underwrite
equity (ownership)	short-term debt	syndicate
dividend	long-term debt	yield (or return)
double taxation of	retained earnings	risk
dividends	book value	liquidity
principal (or face value) of	profit	leverage
a bond	straight-line depreciation	line of credit
convertible bond	accelerated depreciation	risk premium
preferred stock	obsolescence	broker

Problems

6-1 For each of the following, state whether the sentence is true or false, and in each case explain why:

(a) If liabilities exceed assets, net worth is negative.

(b) If additional stock is issued at a price in excess of the book value, the book value of the corporation's stock will rise.

(c) In general, dividends plus retained earnings are greater than corporate income taxes.

(d) Dividends paid in any year must be less than after-tax profits.

6-2 Suppose you are an investment adviser, and a 50-year-old person comes to you for advice on how to invest $50,000 for retirement. What advice would you give? What advice would you give to a young couple who want to temporarily invest $10,000 that they expect to use for a down payment on a home 2 years from now?

6-3 If a corporation increases its leverage, what are the advantages and/or disadvantages for:

(a) The owner of a share of the corporation's stock

(b) The owner of a $10,000 bond of the corporation

6-4 "While private enterprise does make some mistakes and invest in losing projects, it is less likely to do so than the government. After all, business executives risk their own money, while government officials risk the public's money." Do you agree? Can you think of any investment projects that the government has undertaken which were particularly desirable? Might they have been undertaken by private businesses? Why or why not? Can you think of any government investment projects which were particularly ill-advised?

*6-5 In what ways do the interests of stockholders coincide with the interests of the managers of a corporation? Are there any ways in which their interests are in conflict? (See Box 6-2.)

*6-6 Consider a small corporation, with only two stockholders, which makes $100,000 in profits. On this, it pays $25,000 in taxes. The corporation pays no dividend; The $75,000 in after-tax profits is plowed back in the business to buy new equipment. Stockholder A, who owns 90 percent of the shares, has a high income, and is in a 60 percent marginal tax bracket. Stockholder B, who owns 10 percent of the business, is relatively poor, and pays personal income tax at a marginal rate of only 20 percent.

(a) Suppose now that the corporate tax and the personal income tax were "integrated." What would happen to the amount of income tax paid by each of the two individual stockholders? (Assume that the marginal tax brackets of the two individuals do not change as a result of integration.) Do you think integration would make the tax system more or less fair? Explain why.

(b) Individual A controls the company, and can decide whether dividends will be paid. Does the present tax law give this individual an incentive or a disincentive to pay out dividends? In what way are his interests in having the corporation pay dividends different from B's? How would the interests of A be changed by integration? Would his interests now be closer to B's? Explain.

*6-7 "High interest rates are needed to induce individuals or institutions to buy risky bonds. Similarly, high returns are required to induce corporations to invest in risky new ventures. Higher yields in response to risk are desirable, not only for the individual or corporation directly involved, but also for society. They discourage the waste of scarce resources on costly failures."

(a) Do you agree? Can you think of any exceptions, where the high risk premiums demanded by private investors discourage socially desirable expenditures? [Hint: We saw in Chapter 4 that the market mechanism does not necessarily work in a desirable way when there are side effects, or externalities. Are there ever side effects in investment decisions?]

(b) When New York City was in danger of default, the interest rate it had to pay to borrow money shot upward. Do you think that this increase was socially desirable? Argue the case for and against.

PART TWO

MICROECONOMICS: Is Our Output Produced Efficiently?

The *microeconomic* analysis that follows in Parts 2 and 3 will involve an examination of the individual firms that produce goods and services (like Ford Motor Company or the Florida orange grower) and the individual consumers who purchase cars and oranges. This study of the economy "in the small" is directed to the three questions: *What* is produced? *how* is it produced? and *for whom* is it produced? In Part 2 we will deal with the first two questions, just introducing the question of *for whom,* which will be taken up in detail in Part 3.

In Part 2 our focus will be on efficiency. One might well ask: "Because our companion volume (*An Introduction to Macroeconomics*) is devoted to the study of the broad aggregate in the economy, such as total unemployment and inflation, isn't it also devoted to the question of efficiency?" The answer is a clear yes. Historically, unemployment has been a major source of economic inefficiency. Idle labor and idle capital have meant the loss of output that could have been produced. We have also seen that severe inflation causes inefficiency. If the price system breaks down as a consequence of inflation and no longer gives the clear signals on which business planning must be based, decision-making deteriorates and the nation's output is less as a consequence.

Recognizing that these sources of inefficiency are important, we now turn our attention in Part 2 to the additional reasons why our economy is inefficient. To isolate these new sources of difficulty, we shall assume away the two great macroeconomic problems of inflation and unemployment. In other words, we now assume that there is no general rise in prices, nor large-scale unemployment. Even if these extremely favorable assumptions were realized, there would still be reasons why we might not be making the most of our productive ability. Specifically, we might be producing too much of one good and not enough of some other. That is one of the major problems to be studied in Part 2. ■

CHAPTER 7
Demand and Supply:
The Concept of Elasticity

When you have nothing else to wear
But cloth of gold and satins rare,
For cloth of gold you cease to care—
Up goes the price of shoddy.

Gilbert and Sullivan,
The Gondoliers

There isn't a farmer in the country who complains when he has a good crop. But some thoughtful ones may be concerned if everyone else has a good crop too. The reason is simple: A good crop nationwide will reduce the price; and that may hurt farmers more than the benefit they get from increased sales. Whether or not they will benefit or lose on balance depends on the *elasticity of demand.* This chapter is devoted to developing this concept, and to showing how important it is in answering such widely diverse questions as: Will a bumper crop result in higher or lower farm income? Does the consumer or the producer bear the burden of a sales tax? Why are agricultural prices unstable?

In this study of microeconomics, we begin by picking up the demand and supply curves which were developed earlier in Chapter 4.[1]

THE ELASTICITY OF DEMAND: WHAT HAPPENS TO TOTAL REVENUE?

Suppose the members of OPEC (the Organization of Petroleum Exporting Countries) are about to meet to negotiate over oil prices. Further suppose that one question they are ad-

*[1]As explained in the appendix to that earlier chapter, when both a demand and a supply curve are drawn in a diagram, we must be assuming perfect competition. However, if only one curve (demand *or* supply) is drawn, perfect competition need not exist. For example, the monopoly that provides local phone service faces a demand curve.

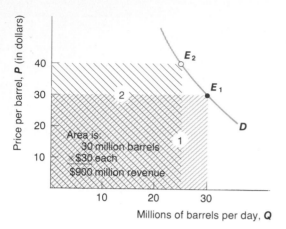

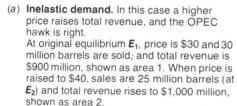

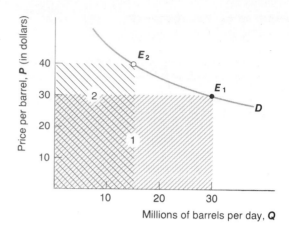

(a) **Inelastic demand.** In this case a higher price raises total revenue, and the OPEC hawk is right.
At original equilibrium E_1, price is $30 and 30 million barrels are sold; and total revenue is $900 million, shown as area 1. When price is raised to $40, sales are 25 million barrels (at E_2) and total revenue rises to $1,000 million, shown as area 2.

(b) **Elastic demand.** In this case a higher price reduces total revenue, and the dove is right. The initial equilibrium is again E_1, with $900 million of total revenue. But in this case the price increase has a quite different result. Since oil sales drop back so much, total revenue decreases to $600 million.

Figure 7-1
The elasticity of demand and total revenue: OPEC's oil pricing problem

dressing is: What will happen to OPEC's total revenue if the price is increased from $30 to $40 a barrel? An OPEC hawk argues that the price increase will have only a small effect on the quantity purchased; North America, Europe, and Japan will keep on buying oil regardless of its price. Therefore, if OPEC raises its price, its total revenue will also go up. On the other hand, an OPEC dove feels that another price increase will be the "straw that breaks the camel's back." Oil purchases will fall substantially as a result of conservation and the development of new oil supplies in other countries. Oil purchases will fall enough to more than offset the higher price, and OPEC revenue will therefore fall. Or so says the dove.

Who is right, the hawk or the dove? The two possibilities are illustrated in Figure 7-1. To understand the point in dispute, we must first show total revenue geometrically. For example,

if the initial equilibrium is at E_1 in panel a, what is total revenue? The answer is $900 million; that is, the *quantity* of 30 million barrels sold (the base Q) times the *price* of $30 a barrel (the height P). But base times height is the area of a rectangle—in this case rectangle 1 (shaded in gray). Similarly, we can sketch into the diagram the rectangles measuring the total revenue at other points on the demand curve.

Total revenue is the total quantity sold times the per unit price. Geometrically this is the rectangle enclosed to the southwest of a point on the demand curve.

Now let us return to our original question: When the price rises, will total revenue rise or fall? If demand is the curve shown in panel a, the OPEC hawk is right. A price increase will raise total revenue because the quantity sold holds up well; it does not shrink rapidly as the price increases. In this case, demand is **inelastic**. But if demand is the curve shown in panel b, the dove is right. A higher price will reduce total revenue because the quantity sold falls off rapidly. In this case demand is described as **elastic**.

If a change in price causes total revenue to move in the opposite direction (for example, if a rise in price causes a fall in total revenue), then demand is *elastic*.

If a change in price causes total revenue to move in the same direction, then demand is *inelastic*.

Although we can't be sure how the international oil market will respond to future price changes, we do know that in the past, to our great regret, panel a has told the story: Because the world demand for oil has been inelastic, the OPEC countries have been able to raise the price and thereby increase their revenue. Consequently, past increases in price have increased OPEC's revenue substantially.

ELASTICITY: THE RESPONSIVENESS OF QUANTITY DEMANDED TO PRICE

In comparing panels a and b, we see that elasticity is just a way of describing the responsiveness of demand to a change in price. For both curves, the price change is the same: an increase from $30 to $40. But the response of quantity demanded differs sharply. In the case of inelastic demand in panel a, the quantity responds only a little, while in the case of elastic demand in panel b, the response is very large. More specifically, in moving from E_1 to E_2 in panel b, total revenue falls because the quantity demanded decreases by 50 percent, which is more than the 33 percent increase in price. This suggests an alternative way to define elasticity: Demand is elastic if the quantity changes by a greater proportion than the price. Thus, we have the following definitions:

Elasticity of demand, ϵ_d

$$= \frac{\%\ \text{change in quantity demanded}}{\%\ \text{change in price}} \quad (7\text{-}1)$$

If ϵ_d is greater than 1, demand is *elastic*.
If ϵ_d is less than 1, demand is *inelastic*.[2]

---

*[2]Any numerical evaluation of elasticity between two points on a demand curve involves a minor technical problem. If we let ΔQ represent "change in Q," the percentage change in quantity in Equation (7-1) may be written $(\Delta Q/Q)\ (100\%)$. And if we similarly rewrite the percentage change in price as $(\Delta P/P)\ (100\%)$, our elasticity formula becomes:

$$\epsilon_d = \frac{(\Delta Q/Q)\ (100\%)}{(\Delta P/P)\ (100\%)} = \frac{\Delta Q/Q}{\Delta P/P}$$

This is a recasting of elasticity as a ratio of *relative* changes. Applying this formula in a straightforward manner to the movement from E_1 to E_2 in Figure 7-1a, we get a first approximation to the elasticity of demand:

$$\epsilon_d = \frac{5,000,000/30,000,000}{10/30} = .50$$

(Actually, since quantity is reduced, ΔQ is negative, and therefore ϵ_d is negative too. However, this negative sign is often omitted.)

The technical problem with this straightforward "first approximation" is the following. We used the initial E_1 values of $Q = 30,000,000$ and $P = 30$. But now suppose we had moved from point E_2 to E_1 on the demand curve. Initial values would now be those at E_2; in other words, $Q = 25,000,000$ and $P = 40$. You can confirm that this would result in the different calculation of $\epsilon_d = .80$. Obviously, we would like an elasticity description of the demand curve between E_1 and E_2 that is the same whether we start at E_1 or E_2. Rather than take either of the P, Q combinations used above, we take the average of the two; in other words, the average quantity $\bar{Q}$ and average price $\bar{P}$. Thus, elasticity of demand is calculated to be

$$\epsilon_d = \frac{\Delta Q/\bar{Q}}{\Delta P/\bar{P}} \quad (7\text{-}2)$$

$$= \frac{5,000,000/[(30,000,000 + 25,000,000)/2]}{10/[(30 + 40)/2]} = .64$$

As we expected, this falls between our two previous calculations of .50 and .80. Because this value is less than 1, demand is inelastic.

Since Equation (7-2) provides a way of calculating elasticity between two points separated by an arc of the demand curve, it is commonly referred to as the *arc elasticity* formula.

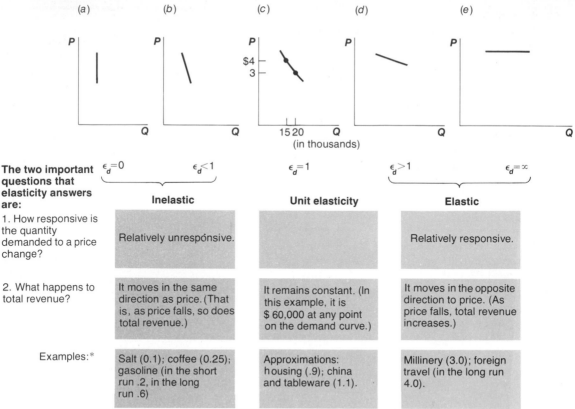

The two important questions that elasticity answers are:

	Inelastic	Unit elasticity	Elastic
1. How responsive is the quantity demanded to a price change?	Relatively unresponsive.		Relatively responsive.
2. What happens to total revenue?	It moves in the same direction as price. (That is, as price falls, so does total revenue.)	It remains constant. (In this example, it is $ 60,000 at any point on the demand curve.)	It moves in the opposite direction to price. (As price falls, total revenue increases.)
Examples:*	Salt (0.1); coffee (0.25); gasoline (in the short run .2, in the long run .6)	Approximations: housing (.9); china and tableware (1.1).	Millinery (3.0); foreign travel (in the long run 4.0).

Figure 7-2
Varying degrees of elasticity

*For numerical estimates of demand elasticity, including some of those given here, see H. S. Houthakker and Lester D. Taylor, *Consumer Demand in the United States* (Cambridge: Harvard University Press, 1966).

This elasticity equation is further illustrated by the five demand curves in Figure 7-2: The greater the response of quantity demanded to a change in price, the greater the elasticity. In panel *a* the elasticity of the completely vertical demand curve is zero because the quantity demanded is completely unaffected by price. [The elasticity ratio in Equation (7-1) is zero because its numerator is zero.] At the other extreme, the completely horizontal demand in panel *e* has infinitely large elasticity because even the smallest drop in price would result in an unlimited increase in sales.

In the intermediate case in panel *c*, quantity increases at the same rate as price falls; hence the numerator and denominator in Equation (7-1) are the same and elasticity is 1. This is referred to as **unit elasticity**.[3] Note how total revenue remains constant in this case.

In Figure 7-2, the flatter the curve, the more elastic it is. Can we conclude that this is always true? The answer is yes, *if the curves being compared pass through the same point* (such as E_1 in the two panels of Figure 7-1). This conclusion is significant enough to reemphasize:

If two demand curves pass through the same point, the flatter one is the more elastic.

*[3]An elasticity of 1 can be confirmed by using the precise calculation explained in footnote 2.

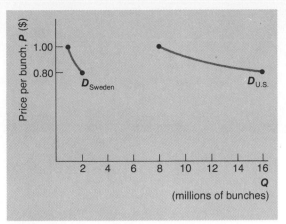

Figure 7-3
Why flatness alone does not indicate elasticity
The U.S. demand curve is flatter (that is, its slope is less), but the elasticity of the two curves is identical. The reason is that if the price falls by 20 percent, the quantity doubles in both cases. (In Sweden, it increases from 1 to 2, whereas in the United States, it increases from 8 to 16.)

This idea is important to remember. But it is also important to recognize that when two demand curves do *not* pass through the same point, elasticity *cannot* be judged merely by flatness. An illustration is provided in Figure 7-3: the demand for bananas in the small Swedish economy and in the large U.S. economy. Although U.S. demand is flatter, both curves have exactly the same elasticity. (In both cases, the quantity demanded increases by 100 percent when price falls by 20 percent.)[4]

---

[4]There are two other illustrations of why flatness and elasticity are not the same. The first is provided in Figure 7-2c. As we move left to right along this curve, its slope changes. But its elasticity does not. (It remains constant at 1.) The second is provided in Problem 7-5, where it is shown that as we move along a straight-line demand curve (with, of course, constant flatness), elasticity keeps changing.

ELASTICITY OF SUPPLY

Just as elasticity of demand indicates the responsiveness of buyers to a change in price, so elasticity of supply indicates the responsiveness of sellers. Supply is elastic if producers respond strongly to price changes, or inelastic if they respond weakly. The formula for supply elasticity is similar to the formula for demand elasticity in Equation (7-1):

Elasticity of supply, ϵ_s
$$= \frac{\% \text{ change in quantity supplied}}{\% \text{ change in price}} \quad (7\text{-}3)$$

Figure 7-4 shows five examples of supply elasticity. They range from the completely inelastic lack of response in panel *a* to the completely elastic response in panel *e*.[5] Once again, as in the case of demand, there is a simple rule connecting flatness and elasticity: *If two supply curves pass through the same point* (such as the lower left end of each supply curve in Figure 7-4), *the flatter one is the more elastic.* But otherwise, elasticity cannot be judged merely by flatness.

In contrast with demand (which traces out a curve if the elasticity is 1), supply is a straight line if the elasticity is 1. If extended, it would pass through the origin, as shown in panel *c* of Figure

---

*[5]To calculate the arc elasticity of supply between two points (*A* and *B*) in panel *d,* we use the same approach as in the calculation of the arc elasticity of demand (in footnote 2):

$$\epsilon_s = \frac{\Delta Q / \overline{Q}}{\Delta P / \overline{P}} = \frac{100/[(400 + 300)/2]}{1/[(9 + 8)/2]} = 2.43$$

Thus, this supply is confirmed to be elastic.

Despite the similarity in the calculations, there is one respect in which elasticity of supply and demand are quite different. Elasticity of demand indicates whether or not total revenue rises when we move to a new equilibrium on a demand curve. But there is no similar interpretation for supply: If we move to a lower-priced equilibrium on a supply curve (say from *B* to *A* in Figure 7-4d), price and quantity both decrease; hence total revenue falls regardless of the elasticity of supply.

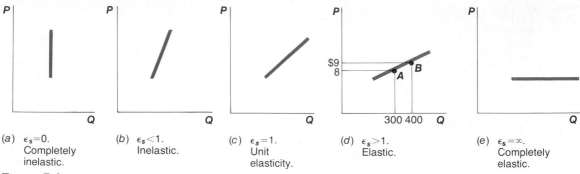

(a) $\epsilon_s = 0$.
Completely
inelastic.

(b) $\epsilon_s < 1$.
Inelastic.

(c) $\epsilon_s = 1$.
Unit
elasticity.

(d) $\epsilon_s > 1$.
Elastic.

(e) $\epsilon_s = \infty$.
Completely
elastic.

Figure 7-4
Different elasticities of supply

7-4. [On such a line, Q always changes in the same proportion as P. For example, if P doubles, Q also doubles. Hence, in this case the numerator and denominator in Equation (7-3) must be equal, and elasticity of supply is 1.] On the other hand, the straight-line supply curve shown in panel *b*, if extended, would pass through the Q axis; consequently, it is inelastic. (You should prove this in Problem 7-7.) Similarly, the supply curve in panel *d* is elastic because it would pass through the P axis. This, then, is the simple key to deciding whether a straight-line supply is elastic or inelastic: If extended, does it pass through the P or Q axis?

We now turn to the influences that determine elasticity of demand and supply. But first you may wish to consider in Box 7-1 how these elasticities may throw light on an important economic policy question: Who bears the burden of a commodity tax?

THE DETERMINANTS OF ELASTICITY

Why is the demand for some products highly elastic, while demand for others is inelastic?

Elasticity of demand

1 Luxuries versus necessities Whereas essentials such as electrical power or salt have an inelastic demand because purchasers can't avoid buying them, luxuries generally have a more

elastic demand. For example, luxuries such as foreign vacations have an elastic demand because purchasers can stop buying them if their prices rise. However, demand may be very inelastic for "superluxuries" bought by the very rich who may pay little attention to price. There is no better illustration than John Pierpont Morgan's comment that anyone who has to ask the cost of a yacht can't afford one.

2 Percentage of income Big items in a budget tend to have a more elastic demand than small items. To cite an extreme example, the demand for houses is more elastic than the demand for toothpicks. Purchasers may spend a week trying to negotiate a 1 percent lower price on a new house. But they won't even notice a 50 percent increase in the price of toothpicks. Thus, for small items like toothpicks, consumers are very insensitive to price.

3 Substitutability Items that have good substitutes generally tend to have a more elastic demand than those that do not. To illustrate, consider sugar and salt, items which are alike in many respects. Both are necessities, and both are small items in any budget. Yet sugar has a more elastic demand than salt because it has substitutes (such as honey), but salt does not. (Thus, salt has a low elasticity for all the reasons cited so far.)

4 Time The longer the time period, the more

elastic the demand becomes. For example, if the price of gasoline rises, the only immediate reduction in the quantity purchased will occur because existing cars are driven fewer miles. It takes some time for drivers to switch to smaller cars, and longer yet for the auto companies to design and build more fuel-efficient cars. But when they do, purchases of gasoline are further reduced: Demand is more price-responsive (elastic) in the long run than in the short.

Elasticity of supply

The elasticity of supply depends on the ability of producers to back away from the market if prices fall, and on their ability and willingness to expand sales if prices rise. Thus, elasticity of supply depends on:

1 The feasibility and cost of storage Goods that rot quickly must be put on the market (supplied) regardless of price; their elasticity of supply is very low. The same tends to be true of goods that are costly to store.

2 The characteristics of the production process Does an item have a close substitute in production? (That is, can the labor, land, and equipment used to produce it be readily switched into the production of another good?) If so, then supply will be elastic. For example, compare the elasticity of supply for wheat and for all grains taken together. In the face of a fall in the price of wheat, a producer may be able to respond by shifting fairly easily into a substitute grain like rye or corn; thus the supply of wheat is somewhat elastic. But if the price of all grain falls, a farmer may have much more difficulty in shifting out of grain production because there are no close substitute activities. Instead, the farmer will have to move into a less closely related activity, like raising beef. Thus the supply of grain, taken as a whole, is less elastic than the supply of wheat.

In contrast with substitutes (such as wheat and corn), other goods may be *joint products,* like beef and hides. (When you produce one, you get the other.) The decision to butcher a steer is influenced by the price of beef, but

hardly at all by the price of hides. Once the steer has been butchered, the (relatively unimportant) hide will be sold regardless of the price. In other words, the supply of hides is inelastic—because hides are a relatively unimportant joint product.

3 Time Time influences supply elasticity, just as it influences demand elasticity. In fact, this idea has already been encountered in our discussion of rent control in Chapter 4. It is only with the passage of time that the supply of apartments becomes more elastic, and rent control consequently has a more damaging effect. In Figure 7-6 on page 128, another example is shown—one used by the English economist Alfred Marshall in his discussion of the influence of time on supply almost a century ago.

Suppose demand for a perishable commodity like fresh fish suddenly rises from D_1 to D_2. The immediate effect on the first day in panel *a* is for price to rise to P_2. The reason is that after the boats return for the day, the quantity supplied is not influenced by price. Whatever has been caught (in our example, Q_1) is put on the market, regardless of price. (In Marshall's day, refrigeration was inadequate. Thus, there was no way suppliers could respond to a changed price by putting more or less on the market.) The immediate supply S is completely inelastic.

However, in the days that follow, the higher price induces fishing boat captains to increase their crews, and old retired boats are brought back into service. The quantity of fish caught and offered for sale increases. Thus, supply becomes more elastic in panel *b,* and price settles down somewhat to P_3. But this is not the long-run equilibrium. As more time passes, new boats can be built, and an even greater quantity of fish caught. Thus, in the long run, supply is even more elastic, as shown in panel *c*. The result is a further moderation of price, to P_4.

ELASTICITY AND THE SPECIAL PROBLEMS OF AGRICULTURE

Since the Great Depression of the 1930s, the government has supported the prices of many

BOX 7-1
Why Elasticity Is Important

Does a commodity tax fall more heavily on buyers or sellers?

To answer this question, consider the supply and demand for a good shown in Figure 7-5a. The initial equilibrium before the tax is at E_1, with 10 million units sold at a price of $3. Suppose now that the government imposes a sales tax of $1 per unit, which it collects from sellers. Who bears the burden of this tax?

The effect of this tax is to shift the supply curve upward from S_1 to S_2 by the full $1 amount of the tax. To confirm this, consider any quantity supplied—say, 12 million units. Point A on the supply curve S_1 tells us that before the tax, sellers would have to receive $4 per unit to induce them to sell 12 million units. This means that *after* the tax, they must receive $5 (at point B) in order to enable them to pay the government the $1 tax and still have the same $4 left. Thus, point B is on the new, after-tax supply curve S_2. And no matter what point we consider on S_1, the corresponding point on S_2 is always $1 higher. Thus, the entire supply curve shifts upward by the amount of the tax.

As a result of the tax, the equilibrium moves from E_1 to E_2, and the price rises from $3.00 to $3.20. Thus, buyers bear 20 cents of the burden; they pay 20 cents more per unit. Sellers bear the remaining 80 cents of the burden. (Their selling price has risen by 20 cents—from $3.00 to $3.20. But $1 of this must go to the government, so sellers get only $2.20 after tax.) The two arrows on the far left show how the $1 tax is split up into the 20-cent burden on buyers and the 80-cent burden on sellers.

The reason that buyers bear a lighter share of the burden in this case is because they respond more to changes in price than do sellers. (Demand is more elastic than supply.) However, in panel *b* the reverse is true. Here, sellers are more responsive to changes in price. (Supply is more elastic than demand.) As a result, sellers bear the lighter burden of the tax.

These conclusions can best be summarized if we think of two groups in a market, one buying, the other selling. Suppose one group (it doesn't matter which) takes the view: "We aren't keen to stay in the market. If the price moves against us, we can back away. In responding to price changes, we're flexible, sensitive, *elastic*." Suppose the other group feels: "We have no choice; we must stay in the market. Even if price moves against us, we can't back away. We're inflexible, unresponsive, *inelastic*." It is no surprise that this second group will bear most of the burden of a tax and will, in other situations as well, be in the more vulnerable position. ■

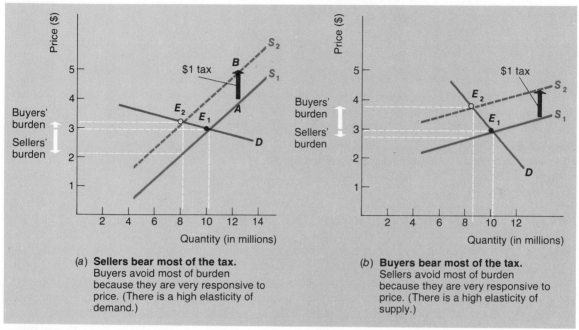

Figure 7-5
How the burden of a sales tax depends on the elasticity of demand and supply
In panel *a*, equilibrium of S_1 and *D* result in before-tax price of $3. As a result of the tax, supply shifts from S_1 to S_2 and the new equilibrium price is $3.20. Buyers pay 20 cents more—the burden of the tax that they bear. Sellers receive $2.20 (that is, the $3.20 market price less the $1 tax that they must pay the government). Thus they receive 80 cents less than the original $3—and this is the burden they bear. In panel *b*, supply is more elastic than demand, and consequently the after-tax price rises to $3.80. In this case, buyers bear 80 cents of the burden, and sellers only 20 cents.

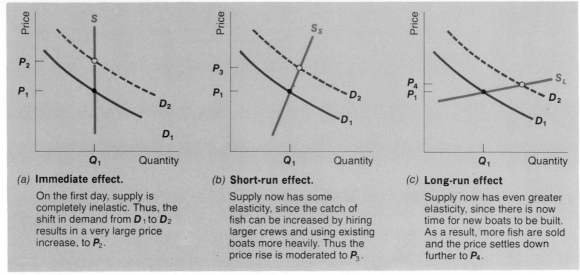

(a) Immediate effect.

On the first day, supply is completely inelastic. Thus, the shift in demand from D_1 to D_2 results in a very large price increase, to P_2.

(b) Short-run effect.

Supply now has some elasticity, since the catch of fish can be increased by hiring larger crews and using existing boats more heavily. Thus the price rise is moderated to P_3.

(c) Long-run effect

Supply now has even greater elasticity, since there is now time for new boats to be built. As a result, more fish are sold and the price settles down further to P_4.

Figure 7-6
How a price increase is moderated by supply response

farm crops. The government announces a support price, and stands ready to buy at that price. When market prices are weak, and farmers cannot get a higher price by selling on the private market, they can sell instead to the government at the support price. (For example, wheat sales were made to the government at the support price of $2.25 when the wheat market was weak in 1977.)[6]

Why does the government make this guarantee to farmers, but not to other producers? One reason is that agriculture has historically suffered from two special problems: Agricultural

prices have been unstable, fluctuating up and down from year to year; and they have shown a tendency to fall (compared with the prices of other goods). To understand each of these problems, we first ask: "What would happen to agricultural prices if there were no government intervention in these markets?" As we shall see, the concept of elasticity is very important in providing an answer.

Year-to-year price instability

In Figure 7-7, we show the problems that arise because agricultural demand and supply are inelastic in the short run (and because supply fluctuates from year to year depending on the weather). Demand for farm products is relatively inelastic because people must satisfy their appetite for food no matter what happens to price. Supply is also inelastic in the short run for several reasons: In some cases the product is perishable; in other cases the crop is already planted, and it is too late for farmers to respond much to a change in price.

In a normal year with demand D and supply

[6]The support program is, in fact, more complicated than this. The government stands ready to lend farmers an amount equal to the support price, provided they put up their wheat as collateral. If, after 11 months, farmers are unable to sell their wheat at a price above the support price, the loan comes due, and farmers forfeit their grain to the government rather than repay the loan.

In addition, the government in 1977 made direct payments to farmers to bring their total return up to $2.90 a bushel.

S_1, equilibrium is at E_1 with price P_1. But with a bumper crop and resulting supply S_2, equilibrium moves to E_2 and price falls all the way to P_2. In this example, a bumper crop cuts price by a third! Worse yet for farmers: The inelasticity of demand has meant that their income has been reduced (from the rectangle enclosed to the southwest of E_1 to the smaller rectangle to the southwest of E_2. This is the case that concerned the thoughtful farmer in the introduction to this chapter.) Similarly, you can confirm that a poor crop that results in equilibrium at E_3 will raise farm income. In short, because demand and supply are inelastic, relatively small variations in crop yield result in large price fluctuations. Moreover, the better the crop, the lower farm income may be as a result. (This point is illustrated further in Box 7-2.)

Figure 7-7
Short-run instability of farm price and income
In a normal year, inelastic demand D and supply S_1 result in equilibrium at E_1. But if there is a bumper crop and Q_2 is put on the market, equilibrium is at E_2, and price falls from P_1 to P_2. Because demand is inelastic, farm income is lower at E_2 than at the normal equilibrium E_1. But if there is a poor crop Q_3, equilibrium is at E_3 and farm income is higher than normal.

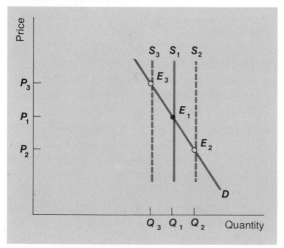

Long-run downward trend in price
The second farm problem is best understood by briefly considering our economic history. If we go back far enough, farming was our largest activity, with the majority of the population working on the soil. With old-fashioned techniques of agricultural production, an individual family could do little more than produce enough for itself.

But, with improvements in agricultural methods and technology, productivity increased. A typical farm family could produce more and more food: enough for two families, then three, then four, then more. Of course, as that happened, the number of people required on the farm to produce food fell to a smaller and smaller fraction of the population. This decline had effects that reached far beyond the farm. In fact, one of the essential requirements of our industrial development was the success of farmers in producing a food supply beyond their own needs. Without this capability the labor force necessary for a developing industry would never have been released from the task of grubbing a bare living out of the soil. It was no accident that the industrial revolution in Britain in the eighteenth century was preceded by a revolution in agricultural productivity. And that agricultural revolution has continued: The American farm family today supplies food for itself and for over 25 city families as well.

But this has been a mixed blessing for farmers, and once again elasticity is the key to understanding why. In panel a of Figure 7-8, E_1 represents the initial equilibrium in an earlier period, at the intersection of long-run supply S_1 and demand D_1, with demand being relatively inelastic because food is a necessity. Over many decades, D has been shifting to the right from D_1 to D_2 because of (1) the increase in the total food-consuming population and (2) the rising income of that population. But the effects of rising income have been fairly modest. Although consumers purchase more of almost everything as their incomes rise, their expenditures on food rise less rapidly than their expenditures on many

To Florida Citrus Growers, a Freeze Is a Blessing

In 1977, *The New York Times* carried the following story:†

The freezing weather in Florida's citrus belt will reduce this year's previously predicted bumper crop . . . but ironically it will ease the worries of growers who had feared they would lose money because of the surplus.

"Nature has bailed us out of a bumper crop," a spokesman for the Florida Citrus Commission said yesterday in a telephone interview. "The growers were going to lose money, but now the problem has been taken care of and an oversupply situation has been corrected."

In 1981 history repeated itself. The freezing weather came again, and destroyed an estimated 20 percent of the Florida orange crop. The wholesale price of concentrated orange juice immediately rose by 30 percent.

What do these events imply about the elasticity of demand for citrus fruit, and oranges in particular? ∎

†© 1977 by The New York Times Company. Reprinted by permission.

other goods. With rising income, people may double their expenditures on clothes and triple their expenditures on vacations, but they increase their food consumption by only a small amount. After all, how much more can anyone eat? Technically, we say that the **income elasticity** of demand for food is low; that is, food purchases respond weakly to an increase in income. (For more on income elasticity and other kinds of elasticity, see Box 7-3.)

On the other hand, over these same decades there has been an *even greater* shift in supply (from S_1 to S_2 in panel *a*) because of rapid improvements in farm technology, such as the development of new chemical fertilizers that have greatly increased yield per acre. With supply shifting more rapidly to the right than demand, price has fallen to a new equilibrium at E_2. But, as price falls, farmers—and even more important, their children—leave the farm to go into more highly paid activities in the city. And because they do, the proportion of the population on the farm falls. (Of course, this outflow of people from the farm also means that there is a less rapid increase in farm output than would otherwise occur. In other words, agricultural

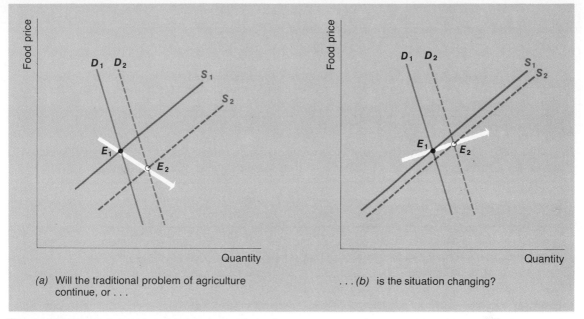

(a) Will the traditional problem of agriculture continue, or . . .

. . . (b) is the situation changing?

Figure 7-8
The long-run trend in agriculture
The classic problem of agriculture in panel *a* has been that supply has shifted to the right more rapidly than demand: hence, price has fallen. This situation may repeat itself in the future or it may, as some people predict, change to the situation shown in panel *b*. There, shifts in supply do not keep pace with shifts in demand, and price rises.

supply S_2 shifts less rapidly to the right. In turn, this means a less severe price reduction.)

Thus, in a nutshell, panel *a* illustrates the history of American agriculture: Because productivity has outrun demand, the proportion of the population on the farm has fallen. By becoming more and more efficient, American farmers are doing a great service to the public in terms of providing large quantities of food at a low price. But their very success in doing so has meant that farmers are producing themselves— or their neighbors—out of jobs.

Are we moving into a new era in agriculture?
Prices in American agriculture would be even more depressed were it not for our large exports

of food products. These exports became particularly important in the early 1970s as a result of crop failures in the Soviet Union and other parts of the world. Indeed, the buoyant demand for agricultural goods on world markets pulled up the international prices of wheat, soy beans, and other items, drawing the U.S. price of food up as well. Was this the first indication that we are moving into a new era of food shortage rather than surplus? Specifically, will the future world problem switch from the traditional one of supply outrunning demand, shown in Figure 7-8*a*, to the new problem, shown in panel *b*, where supply shifts less than demand, and food prices rise?

The argument that future food supply will lag behind demand has been advanced by a number of observers. Some of the reasons put forward are not very convincing—for example, the claim that we are facing a food crisis because the world is running out of land. In fact, studies indicate quite the contrary: Only about half the world's arable land is now being used, and much of the unused acreage has good agricultural

BOX 7-3

Other Elasticity Measures

The demand for any good is affected not only by its price, but also by many other influences such as consumer income. In this box we show how the elasticity concept can be used to measure the strength of these other influences as well.

Income elasticity of demand

Just as price elasticity measures how the quantity demanded responds to price changes, income elasticity measures how the quantity demanded responds to income changes. Formally,

$$\text{Income elasticity of demand} = \frac{\% \text{ change in quantity demanded}}{\% \text{ change in income}} \qquad (7\text{-}4)$$

Notice how this definition is similar to that of price elasticity in Equation (7-1). (Incidentally, when economists use the simple term "elasticity," they generally mean price elasticity.)

The American automobile is an example of a good with a high income elasticity of demand. Various estimates place its value between 2½ and 3; in other words, a 1 percent increase in income results in an increase in auto purchases of 2½ to 3 percent. On the other hand, the income elasticity of gasoline is about 1 and of tobacco is considerably·less (about 0.6). Thus the demand for tobacco is described as "income inelastic"; when income rises, tobacco purchases rise by a smaller proportion.

Income elasticity has another important interpretation. Recall that income is a "demand shifter"; when income rises, the demand (for autos or tobacco) shifts to the right. Income elasticity of demand measures the magnitude of that shift. In the case of automobiles, the shift is important, while in the case of tobacco it is far less so. (For a small category of goods—inferior goods—an increase in income shifts the demand curve to the *left:* Purchases decline as income rises. In such cases, the income

elasticity of demand is negative. The example cited in Chapter 4 was margarine. When incomes rise, people buy less, because they can now afford butter instead.)

Cross elasticity of demand

The quantity of a good demanded depends not only on its own price, but also on the prices of other goods. For example, the demand for cars depends on the price of gasoline. The **cross elasticity of demand** measures the strength of such effects. Specifically:

$$\text{Cross elasticity of demand} = \frac{\%\text{ change in quantity demanded of X}}{\%\text{ change in the price of Y}} \qquad (7\text{-}5)$$

If the cross elasticity is positive, the goods are **substitutes.** For example, beef and pork are substitutes: A 1 percent increase in the price of pork causes the quantity of beef demanded to increase by about 0.3 percent. (That is, it causes the demand curve for beef to shift to the right by 0.3 percent.) And a 1 percent increase in the price of butter causes the quantity of margarine demanded to increase by about 0.8 percent. Thus, butter and margarine are even closer substitutes than beef and pork.

On the other hand, if cross elasticity is negative, the goods are **complements.** For example, as a result of an increase in the price of gasoline, people drive less; the demand for cars is reduced. (In other words, the price of gasoline is a demand shifter, moving the demand for cars to the left. And cross elasticity measures the magnitude of this shift.)

To sum up: The algebraic *sign* of cross elasticity determines whether goods are substitutes (+) or complements (−); that is, whether an increase in the price of one shifts the demand for the other to the right or left. And the numerical value of the cross elasticity indicates the strength of this effect. ■

BOX 7-4

A Final Perspective on Agriculture: Is Falling Price the Sign of a Sick Industry?

Not necessarily. To see why, suppose that the price of a good you are producing has fallen by 50 percent. But, because of your higher productivity, you are now producing three times as many units as before (at the same total cost). Your income will be rising, rather than falling.

For a real-world example, consider IBM. Computer technology has developed rapidly over the past three decades: As already noted, a computer that once filled a room has now been replaced by a tiny chip. As a result, IBM and other producers have been able to cut computing prices drastically. Yet, despite falling prices, IBM's profits have still increased—because of the large increase in productivity.

For the American farmer, prices have also fallen—at least compared to the prices of other goods. By the late 1970s (but prior to the upswing in the last year or so of that decade) the ratio of prices farmers received to the prices they paid had fallen below 70 percent of the 1910–1914 average—that is, below 70 percent of **parity.**

Parity is the ratio of prices received by farmers divided by the prices paid by farmers (expressed as a percentage of the 1910–1914 value).

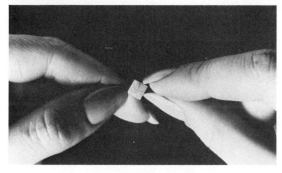

potential.[7] Moreover, recent advances in technology have allowed us to increase output by expanding our use of other inputs (like fertilizer) rather than land. For example, between 1957 and 1977 the acreage of U.S. land in peanuts remained the same, but our output of peanuts almost quadrupled. If this process continues, our future requirements for additional land may not be as great as is often supposed.

However, it is not so easy to dismiss some of the other reasons that food supply may lag behind demand. One is that productivity improvements in agriculture may not continue at their past rapid rates. It is very difficult to predict

[7]This is the conclusion reached by the Food and Agricultural Organization of the United States (FAO) in a 1969 study, *Provisional Indicative World Plan for Agricultural Development.* In another study, Leroy L. Blakeslee, Earl O. Heady, and Charles F. Framingham (*World Food Production, Demand and Trade,* Ames: Iowa State University Press, 1973) have estimated that only 3.4 billion of the world's 7.8 billion acres of potentially productive land are under cultivation.

Figure 7-9
The parity ratio, 1910–1980
The farm parity ratio which nose-dived during the Depression in the early 1930s, recovered to above its original 100 percent level during the '40s. However, since the early '50s, it has been on a downtrend.

(For how the parity ratio has changed over time, see Figure 7-9. Government price supports have prevented an even greater fall in this ratio.) But during this same period, the productivity of the farmer increased many times. For example, by the late '70s, one farmer was producing as many chicken broilers as eight produced in the mid 50s.‡ This allowed the price of chickens to

‡Even the productivity of the average cow had more than doubled.

fall *and* the income of the farmer to rise. In these circumstances, the low price of chicken was a poor indicator of what was happening to farm income—just as the low price of computing was a poor indicator of IBM's income. ■

productivity: On the one hand, new developments in genetic engineering may bring a rapid expansion in productivity and agricultural supply. On the other hand, the increase in food supply may be disappointing if we are unable to expand fertilizer production at past rapid rates because of limited supplies of oil (a key input in fertilizer production). Another concern is whether the serious crop failures in foreign countries during the 1970s were the result of unfavorable trends in the world's climate. But on this issue

even weather experts are divided; some believe our climate is warming up, others believe it is cooling off, while others believe that neither is happening and that, instead, the weather is just fluctuating more. Finally, to decide whether the future situation will be the one shown in panel *a* or panel *b* of Figure 7-8 requires projecting world food demand as well as supply. This projection requires answers to a number of difficult questions such as: Will the rapid population increases in the less-developed third-world countries continue, or will these countries begin to follow the lower birthrate patterns of the industrialized parts of the world?

It is extraordinarily difficult to predict such future developments; moreover, by the end of the '70s, no clear trend had yet emerged. By 1977, the American agricultural problem seemed to be shifting back from the scarcity problem earlier in the decade to one of surplus. As a result of three bumper years, the price of wheat fell about 50 percent between 1974 and 1977. In fact, the price was so low by 1977 that farmers were selling their wheat to the government for the guaranteed price, and the government stockpile of wheat was increasing rapidly.

However, surplus turned back to scarcity in 1980, when bad weather in major producing countries adversely affected crops. U.S. production of corn and soybeans fell by roughly 20 percent, Soviet grain production was 23 percent below target, and Australian wheat farmers suffered the worst drought of this century. Prices of wheat and soybeans rose sharply in the early summer of 1980. (The price of wheat then fell as the U.S. crop proved to be better than expected. But the price of soybeans stayed up.)

While buffer stocks had prevented an even more rapid increase in price, by 1981 they were beginning to be depleted. Another year or two of bad weather could cause severe shortages, with the much higher prices these would bring.

Thus, during the '70s there was no strong trend in agricultural prices. Rather, changing weather had caused substantial fluctuations. (The problems of agriculture are so important that we return to them in our discussion of perfectly competitive markets in Chapter 10.)

A final observation

Throughout this chapter, we have drawn demand and supply curves on the assumption that we know their shape and location. But often these are very difficult to estimate, for reasons described in the Appendix to this chapter.

Key Points

1 Demand elasticity indicates what happens to *total revenue* as price changes. For example, if demand is elastic, a reduced price will raise total revenue. But if demand is inelastic, a reduced price will lower total revenue.

2 Demand elasticity is also a measure of the *responsiveness* of quantity demanded to a change in price: the more responsive, the more elastic. Goods with high demand elasticity include large-budget items and items with close substitutes.

3 If two curves pass through the same point, the flatter one is the more elastic. But if they do not pass through the same point, there is no such simple relationship between flatness and elasticity.

4 Elasticity of supply measures the responsiveness of quantity supplied to a change in price; again, the more responsive, the more elastic. Goods with high supply elasticity include items that can be easily and cheaply stored and goods with close substitutes in production.

5 The elasticities of demand and supply are less in the short run than in the long run.

6 Year-to-year fluctuations in food prices are partly explained by inelasticity of demand. And, because of low demand elasticity, a bumper crop may lower farm income, while a poor crop may raise it.

7 The downward trend in farm prices relative to other prices has occurred in the past because of rapidly improving farm technology and our limited appetite for food. As a consequence, supply has tended to outrun demand. It is not clear whether this will continue, or whether the situation will be reversed, with food prices rising in the future.

Key Concepts

elastic demand
inelastic demand
unit elasticity of demand
total revenue as a $P \times Q$
   rectangle

relationship of demand
   elasticity to total
   revenue
elasticity of supply
joint products

price instability and its
   relation to elasticity
income elasticity of
   demand

Problems

7-1 At a time when the price of gasoline was $1 a gallon, a *New York Times* editorial stated that a 50-cent increase in its price would lower gasoline consumption by an estimated 10 percent. Does this imply anything about the elasticity of supply? Of demand? If so, what?

7-2 Suppose you are the manager of Fenway Park, home of the Boston Red Sox. You have been selling general admission tickets for $5 each, but because of the huge salaries that two of your star players have negotiated, you are losing money. The owners who have employed you may be millionaires, but they are concerned, and they press you to take action to increase total revenue. Specifically, they suggest that you raise the ticket price to $8. This suggestion bothers you—particularly when it leaks out to the newspapers. Not only do the sportswriters denounce the "greed" of the owners, they also argue that higher prices will backfire, causing fans to stay away in droves. As a consequence, gate receipts will be lowered, or so the sportswriters say.

How is this controversy related to the elasticity of demand? What assumptions are the owners making about elasticity? What assumptions are the sportswriters making?

7-3 Using the figure shown below, fill in the blanks.
Curve with greatest elasticity is _____
Next greatest elasticity is _____
Next greatest is _____
Lowest elasticity is _____
Unit elasticity is _____

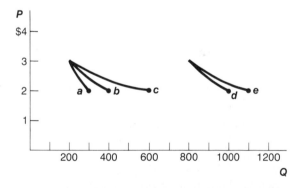

7-4 (a) Why didn't we define elasticity much more simply, as just the flatness of a curve; that is, elasticity = (the change in Q)/(the change in P)? (*Hint:* Plot exactly the same demand curve as in Figure 7-1a, but change the scale in which you measure price. Specifically, measure price in quarters, not dollars, so that E_1 and E_2 are now four times as high. What happens to elasticity? What happens to the flatness of D?)

(b) "Flatness is s poor measure because it depends on the arbitrary scale in which P (or Q) is measured." Is this statement true or false? Explain why.

*7-5 Using Equation (7-2) calculate the elasticity of the section AB in the demand curve shown below. Do the same for the section CE. Consider the following statement: "Since AB and CE have the same flatness, but different elasticity, this shows once again that flatness does not necessarily reflect elasticity." Is this true or false?

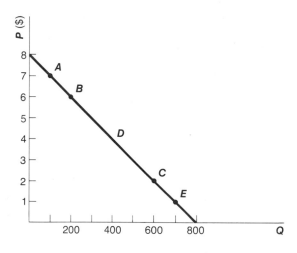

7-6 "Heating oil for homes has a greater elasticity in the long run than in the short." Do you agree? Explain.

7-7 In the next diagram, S represents any straight-line supply that, if extended, would pass through the Q axis. To show that S must be inelastic, draw a straight line to pass through the origin and any point R on the supply S. What is the elasticity of line OR? What, therefore, can be concluded about the elasticity of supply S?

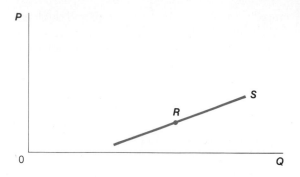

*7-8 Redraw Figure 7-5a on the assumption that buyers, rather than sellers, initially pay the tax. Does this affect the way the two groups bear the eventual burden?

*7-9 (Based on footnote 2 and Box 7-3.) In this diagram:

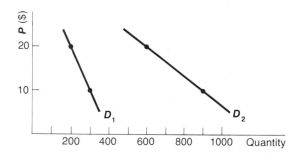

(a) What is the (price) elasticity of demand D_1 as price falls from $20 to $10? As price rises from $10 to $20?

(b) How does the elasticity of D_1 compare with that of D_2?

(c) Now suppose income has doubled and that demand has consequently shifted from D_1 to D_2. Calculate the income elasticity of demand.

*7-10 Would you expect the income elasticity of food to be higher or lower than that of restaurant meals? Explain.

APPENDIX

STATISTICAL DIFFICULTIES IN ESTIMATING DEMAND AND SUPPLY: THE IDENTIFICATION PROBLEM

First, consider demand: One method of estimating it is to observe how much of the good has been purchased in the past at various prices. (For example, the 1978 dot in Figure 7-10a tells us that quantity Q_1 was purchased in that year at price P_1.) If we are lucky we will observe a "scatter" of observations like the one shown in this diagram. A straight line fitted to these observations provides our estimated demand curve.

In panel b, we examine the underlying demand and supply curves that gave rise to these four "lucky" observations. Through the entire period of observation, the demand curve remained stable at D. But the supply curve shifted. For example, the 1975 observation was the result of the intersection of the demand curve and the 1975 supply curve S_{75}, while the 1976 observation was the result of the intersection of that same demand curve and supply, which had now shifted to S_{76}.

The reason that we were lucky in our scatter of observations in panel a was because they were generated in panel b in precisely this way—by a *stable* demand curve and a *shifting* supply curve. We have been able to "identify" demand because of shifts in supply. (As an exercise, set up an example where supply is identified by shifts in demand.)

But we will not usually be so lucky. Consider the more typical case shown in Figure 7-11 where the set of observations in panel a has been generated by the shifting supply and demand curves shown in panel b. Since both supply and demand

Figure 7-10
Special case when demand is easily estimated

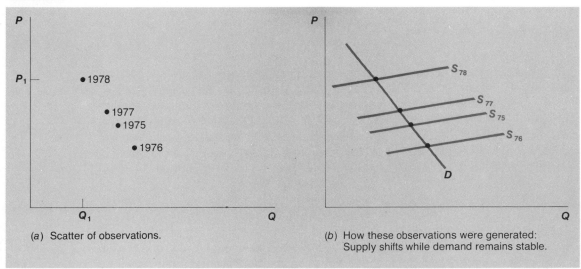

(a) Scatter of observations.

(b) How these observations were generated: Supply shifts while demand remains stable.

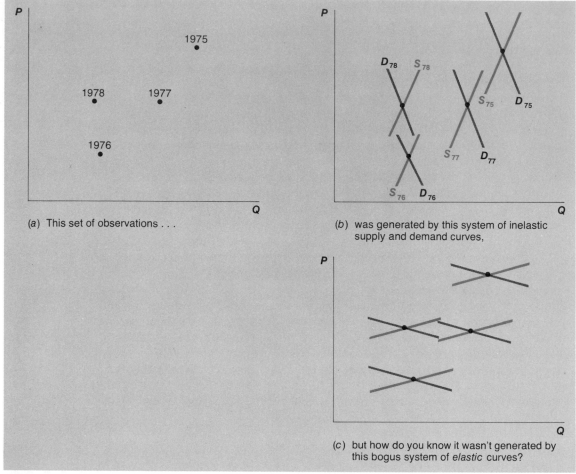

(a) This set of observations . . .

(b) was generated by this system of inelastic supply and demand curves,

(c) but how do you know it wasn't generated by this bogus system of *elastic* curves?

Figure 7-11
When demand estimation requires a special approach

shift in panel *b,* the result in panel *a* is a scatter of observations that gives us neither demand nor supply, but some apparently incomprehensible combination of both.

To emphasize the difficulty in this problem, in panel *c* we show a completely bogus supply and demand system that could have equally well generated the scatter in panel *a.* When all we have to work with is what we see in panel *a,* how in the world can we decide whether this scatter has been generated by the true, inelastic supply/demand system in panel *b* or the completely bogus, elastic system in panel *c*? Or by some other bogus system?

The answer is that the problem is indeed hopeless unless we can get more information. Specifically, we require information on how demand and supply shift.

If we have such information, supply and demand can be estimated using a complex statistical technique; but the highly simplified example in Figure 7-12 will illustrate the basic idea. Without further information, we can make no more sense out

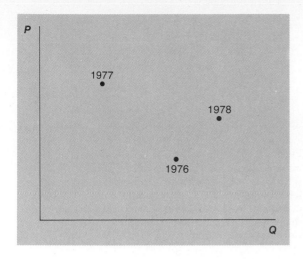

Figure 7-12
Can demand be identified?
This scatter seems hopeless. Without further information, it is.

of these three observations than we can out of the scatter in Figure 7-11a. (As an exercise show how this scatter could have been generated by several supply/demand systems, and that there is no way of knowing which is the true one.)

But now let us see how we *can* identify the true underlying supply/demand system if we have additional information on how each curve shifts. First, we know that demand shifts with income; specifically, suppose that an increase in income results in a parallel shift to the right of the demand curve. We then examine the figures on income and discover that it was the same in 1976 and 1977, but indeed did increase in 1978. This implies that the demand curve remained in the same position in 1976 and 1977, but shifted to the right in 1978.

Next consider supply. What might have caused it to shift? On investigation, we discover that there was a strike in 1977; this reduced the quantity supplied, shifting the supply curve to the left. Accordingly, we conclude that the supply curve was in the same position in 1976 and 1978 (when there were no strikes) but had temporarily shifted to the left in 1977.

This additional information allows us to eliminate all bogus supply/demand systems from further consideration. There is now only one supply/demand system that could have generated the observations in Figure 7-12, and that's the true one. As an exercise, you should try to discover it yourself before looking at the solution in Figure 7-13.

To sum up: We started out with an apparently incomprehensible scatter of observations that seemed to reveal neither demand nor supply. But, with some additional information on what causes demand and supply to shift, we were able to estimate both in Figure 7-13.

Of course, this simplified illustration can only provide a "feel" for the identification problem. In practice, estimating supply and demand (like estimating most other economic relationships) involves additional problems. For example: Each curve may shift in response to several influences (rather than just one). Thus, the demand for pork shifts not only with income but also with the price of beef. Such complications must also be taken into account.

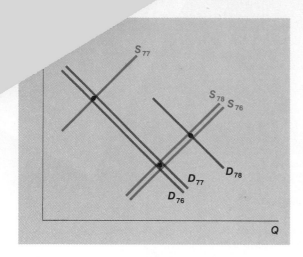

Figure 7-13
How demand (and supply) can be identified
With knowledge that there was a parallel shift to the
left in supply in 1977 and a parallel shift to the right
in demand in 1978, this supply and demand system is
the only one that can be fitted to the three observations in Figure 7-12.

Problem

7-11 Using Figure 7-13, show that shifts in supply identify demand, and that
shifts in demand identify supply. *Hint:* Show graphically the scatter that we would
have observed, and what we would (or would not) be able to identify, if:

(a) There had been no income increase in 1978, and therefore no shift in
demand.

(b) There had been neither an income increase in 1978 nor a strike in 1977, and
therefore no shift in either curve. ∎

CHAPTER 8
Demand and Utility

"Producers dance to the consumers' tune."
Reprise from Chapter 4

What is the tune that consumers play? Why do they demand certain products, but not others? What does a demand curve tell us about how consumers think and feel? Once we have answered these questions, we will be better able to understand how much consumers can be damaged by a fall in production. For example, how much are consumers hurt when a Florida freeze reduces the orange crop?

In Chapters 4 and 7 we have described and used the market demand curve. In this chapter we shall go behind it, to examine its fundamental characteristics. The first step is to see how the market demand curve is related to the *individual* demand curves of the many consumers who buy the product.

MARKET DEMAND AS THE SUM OF INDIVIDUAL DEMANDS

The total market demand for a good or service is found by summing the demands of all individual consumers, as illustrated in Figure 8-1. (In this example, two individuals represent the millions of consumers in the economy.) Bill Jefferson's demand in panel *a* shows how much he is willing and able to buy at various prices. Similarly, Barbara Washington's demand is shown in panel *b*, indicating her quite different view of the desirability of this product. At any given price,

say $1, we horizontally add the quantities demanded by each consumer in order to get the corresponding point on the market demand schedule in panel *c*. (Individual demand curves are labeled with a small *d*, and the market demand with a capital *D*.)

We now turn the spotlight on the individual consumer.

THE INDIVIDUAL CONSUMER'S DECISION: THE CHOICE BETWEEN GOODS

The consumer chooses between goods: for example, food and clothing. Should the consumer use a given income to buy more clothing and less food, or more food and less clothing? This choice between goods is a key decision for the consumer, and we will return to it in Box 8-1 and in the appendix.

However, it is also often useful to view the consumer as choosing, not between food and clothing, but between food and *all* other goods —in other words, choosing between food and money (since money can be used to buy all other goods). Of course, this decision between food and money is described by the individual's demand curve. (It tells us how much food will be bought at each price.) Let's consider what's behind this individual demand curve.

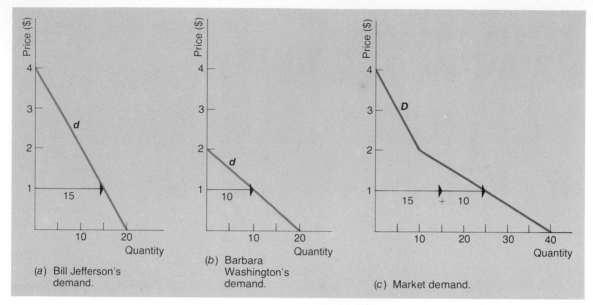

(a) Bill Jefferson's demand.

(b) Barbara Washington's demand.

(c) Market demand.

Figure 8-1

How individual demands combine to make up market demand

To find total quantity demanded at each price (for example, $1), horizontally add the quantities demanded by all individual consumers.

DEMAND AND MARGINAL UTILITY

A good is purchased because someone, somewhere, wants it. A demand for a product exists because it provides someone, somewhere, with satisfaction or utility. Indeed, **marginal utility** is the key concept underlying demand. By definition:

Marginal utility is the additional satisfaction an individual receives from consuming one additional unit of a good or service.

To illustrate, consider Lori Wahl, a student who is considering how many skiing lessons she should purchase this month. We ask her to evaluate how much utility or satisfaction she would receive from one lesson, from a second, and a third. Her reply might be: "The first lesson would clearly give me the most satisfaction; after all this study, I'm just dying to get away from it all for a day. The second would give me considerable pleasure, but not quite so much. And less again for the third lesson, since my appetite for skiing gets a bit jaded after a while. And so on."

The message she is giving us is the simple one sketched out in Figure 8-2: Her marginal utility decreases as she consumes more. Since eventually this must be true for any good or service, it is sometimes referred to as the *law of diminishing marginal utility*. But be careful with this "law." Although marginal utility must *ultimately* fall, it may rise at first. The first ski lesson may yield only pain, and skiing may not be enjoyable until the second, third, or fourth lesson. But eventually, as more and more lessons are purchased, marginal utility must fall: If she takes 10 lessons in one week, the tenth will provide less satisfaction than the ninth. (For simplicity, in our example marginal utility declines from the very first unit.)

So far, Figure 8-2 is imprecise (since we haven't yet put a unit of measurement on the marginal utility axis). Therefore, we press Wahl to be more specific about how highly she values each lesson. She is at a loss to do so until we point out that her evaluation of each lesson should be reflected in how much she would be willing to pay for it. Pursuing this line of reasoning, we ask her: "What would you be willing to pay for the first lesson?" When she replies, "Oh—$20," we continue: "And what would you be willing to pay for the second?" (More precisely, we might ask, How low would the price have to fall before she would be willing to buy two lessons?) In this case, her reply is $17. In this way, we get her to provide the information shown in Figure 8-3.

But since Wahl is very bright, she suddenly realizes: "Figure 8-3 not only shows my marginal utility. It's also my demand schedule d. It must be. At any price above $20, I won't buy any lessons. At $20 I'll buy just one: The first lesson is worth that much to me. Only if the price falls to $17 will I buy two lessons. And only if the price falls all the way to $13 will I buy three."

This relation between the marginal utility and demand schedules is an important one that we shall use frequently in the balance of this book. It can be expressed:

Figure 8-2
Diminishing marginal utility
Each purchase provides less additional satisfaction than the previous one.

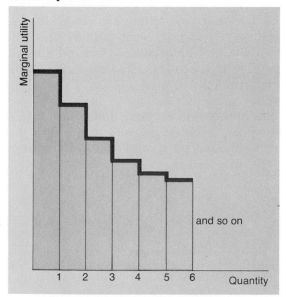

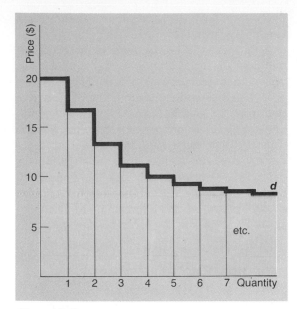

Figure 8-3
Diminishing marginal utility, as reflected in the consumer's willingness to pay less for each additional unit
The height of the marginal utility schedule in Figure 8-2 may be estimated by asking the consumer: "What is the maximum you would be willing to pay for each additional unit?" Thus, the demand schedule provides an estimate of marginal utility.

The height of a demand curve approximates the marginal utility of the good.

Notice that this statement, like so many others in economics, is only an approximation: Any good economist can tell you that this relationship is not an exact one.[1] Nonetheless, for

*[1]The problem is that we are measuring marginal utility in dollar terms, and this is an exact measure only if the marginal utility of money, our measuring rod, is itself constant. Otherwise, a measuring rod is being used that stretches or shrinks. Suppose, for example, that the price of cars falls and people spend less money on automobiles, leaving more for the purchase of other goods. As people increase their purchases of other goods, they get less marginal utility from each additional purchase. Therefore the marginal utility of money falls (because, after all, the utility of money depends on the utility of goods that money will buy). Thus, our measuring rod—namely, the marginal utility of money—is not constant.

many items it is a very close approximation (with exceptions being large-budget items, such as cars or houses). Using demand to represent marginal utility involves a logical problem not unlike the logical problems encountered in using gross national product as a measure of economic performance.[2] Just as we could not have gotten off square 1 in our macroeconomic analysis without using gross national product or some similar measure—while fully recognizing its deficiencies—so too it is useful in this elementary course to illustrate the idea of economic efficiency by calling on this demand/marginal utility approximation[3]—while also recognizing *its* deficiencies.

CONSUMER EQUILIBRIUM: HOW MUCH OF A GOOD TO BUY?

In Figure 8-4, Wahl's responses are reproduced from Figure 8-3. If the market price is $10 as shown, her demand curve tells us that she will buy 5 units; that is, her equilibrium will be at point *E*. But another way of describing this purchasing decision is to note that she will buy the first lesson since she values it at $20 (its approximate marginal utility) and it costs her only $10. Put another way, she would rather

[2]Indeed, it is easier to criticize using gross national product (GNP) as an approximation because of the problems with GNP cited in Chapter 7 of the companion volume and in particular because GNP can, in special circumstances, be a downright perverse measure. For example, when there is an increase in crime and more police are hired, GNP rises even though the society is worse off because of the higher crime rate.

[3]More advanced courses often use the more demanding technique of the indifference curve. This technique highlights a point noted earlier: The consumer chooses *between goods*. The elementary theory of indifference curves is presented in appendixes to this chapter and to Chapter 10.

Nevertheless, the approximation we are using here—measuring utility by the demand curve—is also often used in advanced work. For example, it is often used in the evaluation of government programs (in benefit-cost analysis). For a spirited defense of this approach—using demand curves as a research tool for measuring benefits rather than just a teaching tool—see Arnold C. Harberger, "Three Basic Postulates for Applied Welfare Economics: An Interpretive Essay," *Journal of Economic Literature,* September 1971, pp. 785–797.

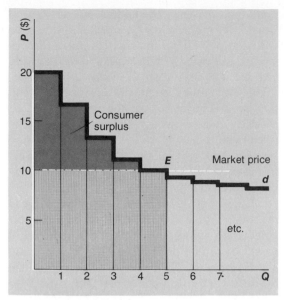

Figure 8-4
Consumer equilibrium and consumer surplus
The purchaser is willing to pay as much as $20 for the first unit. But she has to pay only the actual market price—$10. She thus receives a $10 consumer surplus on this first unit. Similarly, there is a consumer surplus on the second, third, and fourth units, also shown by the dark shading.

have the first lesson than use the $10 to buy some other good or service. Similarly, she will buy the second, third, and fourth lessons because she also values them above their $10 cost. But she will stop when she purchases the fifth because the $10 value she places on it is just equal to its $10 cost.[4] She has thus arrived at the important rule:

The consumer reaches equilibrium by increasing the purchase of a good until the value placed on the last unit falls to the level of its price.

For another view of consumer equilibrium, see Box 8-1.

[4]Since the cost of the fifth item is $10, just equal to its marginal utility, she will not really care whether she gets the fifth lesson or not. By convention, economists assume that this last, "don't care" unit is, in fact, purchased.

CONSUMER SURPLUS

Note that Lori Wahl is indifferent to the purchase of the fifth lesson, since the maximum amount she is willing to pay for it is exactly equal to its cost: $10. But this was not true of the fourth. For that lesson she would have been willing to pay $11. In other words, that fourth lesson provides more benefit ($11) than its cost ($10). She gets a surplus, or excess of benefit over cost, amounting to $1 on this fourth lesson. Similarly, she gets an even higher **consumer surplus** (of $3) on the third lesson. For all purchases, she gets the dark consumer surplus area shown in Figure 8-4.

Consumer surplus is the net benefit a consumer gets from being able to purchase a good. Geometrically, it is approximately[5] the dark area in Figure 8-4; that is, the area under the demand curve and above the price. Thus it is the difference between the maximum amount the consumer would be willing to pay and what actually is paid.

Now that we can visualize demand as a series of marginal utility bars, we hereafter approximate it with a smooth curve. With the preceding analysis of an individual's demand in hand, we can now turn to the market demand in Figure 8-5. (Remember, market demand is the sum of the demands of all individuals.)

Figure 8-5 shows how consumers benefit if the price of a good falls from $10 to $6, and they move from equilibrium E_1 to E_2. First, they enjoy a benefit of area 1 (equal to $1,600) because they can now buy the 400 units they originally purchased for $4 a unit less. Second, they also enjoy a consumer surplus of area 2 on the 200 additional units they are now purchasing.

Taking both sources of benefit into account,

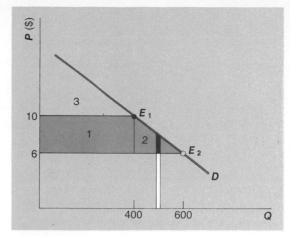

Figure 8-5

If market price falls from $10 to $6, consumer surplus increases by the shaded area 1 + 2

At the initial $10 price, consumers purchase 400 units at E_1. When price falls by $4, on these units alone they save $4 (400) = $1,600, shown as area 1. But they get a second gain as well. Because of the $4 price reduction, they move from E_1 to E_2, purchasing 200 more units. And on these units they get a consumer surplus of area 2. [To illustrate, we show one of these additional units, the five-hundredth. The $8 the buyer would be willing to pay for this unit is shown by the height of the demand curve; that is, by the white bar plus the black bar. But since this unit costs the buyer only $6 (the white bar), there is a consumer surplus of $2 (the black bar). All similar black bars in the 400 to 600 range make up triangle 2—the increase in consumer surplus because of these *new* purchases.] Thus, consumers have benefited (consumer surplus has increased) by both areas 1 and 2. To confirm this conclusion, note that consumer surplus at the original $10 price was area 3 (just as in Figure 8-4). But at a $6 price, consumer surplus is area 3 + 1 + 2, for a net increase equal to the shaded area 1 + 2.

we conclude that the consumers' situation has improved (consumer surplus has increased) by area 1 + 2. Thus

If the market price *falls*, there is an *increase* in consumer surplus equal to the horizontal area between the old and new price, and to the left of the demand curve.

---

*[5]Only "approximately" because we have measured marginal utility in dollars and, as already noted, this is not a perfect measure. Having noted this point twice, we will not belabor it. We will drop the word "approximately" in our references to consumer surplus.

BOX 8-1
Equilibrium for the Consumer: How to Choose Between Goods

So far in this chapter, we have been examining how much of a single good a consumer buys. But we now return to the question posed at the beginning of this chapter: How does a consumer choose between two goods? How much food and how much clothing should he buy? Or, more specifically, how many apples and how many cherries? The answer is: He should continue to purchase each good until the marginal utility received from the last dollar spent on cherries is equal to the marginal utility received from the last dollar spent on apples. To confirm this, suppose he has not done so. Specifically, suppose his marginal utility (per dollar of expenditure) is greater on cherries than on apples. In this case, he can make his given income go farther (provide more utility) by switching a dollar of expenditure from apples to cherries; the utility received from the additional cherries will exceed the utility lost on apples. And it will be in his interest to continue to switch purchases in this way until the marginal utilities are equalized. (Notice that they will equalize, because the marginal utility of cherries falls as he buys more, while the marginal utility of apples rises as he buys fewer.)

We can state his theorem in general:

A consumer will be in equilibrium if he extends his purchases in every direction to the point where the utility he receives from the last dollar of expenditure on one good is the same as that received from the last dollar spent on each of the others. In this way, he maximizes his utility from a given income. (8-1)

As a background for future chapters, the basic statement (8-1) is sufficient; it requires no further elaboration. But if you wish to pursue the idea further, it may be formally restated as follows: Consumer equilibrium requires that

$$\frac{\text{Marginal utility of cherries}}{\text{Price of cherries}} = \frac{\text{marginal utility of apples}}{\text{price of apples}}$$

or, putting this in symbols:

$$\frac{MU_{cherries}}{P_{cherries}} = \frac{MU_{apples}}{P_{apples}} \qquad (8\text{-}2)$$

For example, if a basket of cherries is twice as expensive as a basket of apples ($P_{cherries}$ is $8 while P_{apples} is $4) then in equilibrium the consumer needs to get twice as much marginal utility from a basket of cherries as a basket of apples. Suppose this is indeed the case: He gets 24 units of satisfaction from a basket of cherries, and only 12 from a basket of apples. Then we confirm that equilibrium exists because Equation (8-2) checks out:

$$\frac{24}{\$8} = \frac{12}{\$4}$$

Note from the left side of this equation that the consumer is spending $8 on cherries to get 24 units of utility; in other words, from each dollar spent on cherries, he gets $^{24}/_8$ = 3 units of marginal utility. And from the right hand side, he gets the same $^{12}/_4$ = 3 units of marginal utility from each dollar spent on apples. Thus Equation (8-2) is seen to be just a mathematical recasting of the basic principle (8-1): In equilibrium, the consumer gets the same amount of utility (in this example, 3 units) from a dollar's worth of cherries as from a dollar's worth of apples.

Alternatively, by rearranging (8-2) we can rewrite this consumer equilibrium condition as:

$$\frac{MU_{cherries}}{MU_{apples}} = \frac{P_{cherries}}{P_{apples}} \qquad (8\text{-}3)$$

In our example:

$$\frac{24}{12} = \frac{\$8}{\$4}$$

This is just a restatement of the same simple idea: In equilibrium the consumer must get twice as much utility from cherries on the left-hand side of this equation because cherries are twice as expensive on the right-hand side.

In the appendix we confirm in a more formal way that (8-3) does indeed describe consumer equilibrium. But again we emphasize: All that this equation is doing is to restate our basic principle of consumer equilibrium (8-1) in an alternative way. ■

Of course, the same proposition applies to a price increase:

If the market price *rises*, there is a *decrease* in consumer surplus equal to the horizontal area between the new and the old price, and to the left of the demand curve.

THE FLORIDA FREEZE: APPLYING THE ANALYSIS OF CHAPTERS 19 AND 20

As noted earlier in Box 7-2, cold waves in early 1977 and 1981 froze part of the Florida citrus crop. The effects of a freeze are illustrated in Figure 8-6. The harvest coming onto the market is reduced from the expected supply S_1 to S_2. This in turn means that prices are higher, with equilibrium at E_2 rather than E_1. Several groups of Americans are affected, as follows:[6]

Producers benefit Because demand for citrus fruits is inelastic, producers' revenue increases. As a group, they gain more from the higher price than they lose from the reduced harvest. (Of course, those producers who lose their entire crop are worse off. But their loss is less than the gain of other producers, who can sell their crop at a higher price.)

Consumers lose Because the price rises, consumer surplus is reduced by areas 1 + 2.

With producers benefiting and consumers losing, it is not immediately obvious how the nation as a whole is affected, on balance. However, a moment's reflection leads us to the following conclusion:

On balance, the nation loses When oranges freeze, we have fewer to eat; as a nation, we are worse off.

[6]To simplify this illustration, picking, shipping, and other costs of getting the oranges to market are ignored.

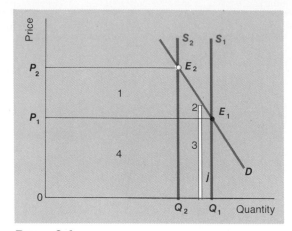

Figure 8-6
How Florida citrus freeze benefits producers but damages consumers and the nation as a whole
The bumper crop of S_1 would have resulted in equilibrium E_1, with price P_1. But because of a freeze, the supply coming onto the market is reduced to S_2. Consequently, equilibrium is at E_2, with price P_2. Producers' total revenue without the freeze (at E_1) would have been areas 3 + 4 (the rectangle to the southwest of E_1). But with the freeze shifting equilibrium to E_2, revenue is area 1 + 4 instead. Note that area 4 is common to both; thus producers gain area 1 from the freeze but lose area 3. Consumers have their surplus reduced by area 1 + 2 as a result of the increased price. For the nation overall, we must consider the effect on both groups:

Consumers	lose 1	lose 2
Producers	gain 1	lose 3
Sum indicates nation will	lose 2	lose 3

This overall loss to the nation of area 2 + 3 is easily confirmed. Consider *j*, one of the cases of fruit that freezes. The marginal utility it would have provided is the height of the white bar. If we sum all the similar bars throughout the range of lost output between Q_2 and Q_1, the result (area 2 + 3) is the total loss of utility because those oranges froze. *Warning:* Area 1 is a loss to consumers and a gain to producers. In cancelling it out in the tabled calculations above, we assume that area 1 is valued similarly by the consumers losing it and the producers receiving it—or at least similarly enough not to upset our conclusion. Although this is a reasonable enough assumption, it involves a value judgment. (This complication will be considered in more detail in Chapter 11.)

The various effects of a crop loss may now be summarized. Because demand is inelastic, producers as a group gain. (If demand were elastic, they would lose, of course.) But consumers and the nation overall lose regardless of demand elasticity.[7]

Now let us return to our conclusion that producers benefit from a freeze, and examine this more carefully. If you are an individual producer, it will not be in your interest to let your crop freeze. Nothing you can do as an individual affects price; and whatever the price may be, the more you have to sell, the better. But it benefits producers as a group if there is a freeze, because the resulting scarcity *does* affect price. This raises the question: If producers cannot get Mother Nature to restrict their supply, is it not in their interest to work together to do it themselves? The answer is yes. But in practice they may have difficulty in organizing to restrict supply. In turn, this may lead them to look instead to the government to introduce and enforce some form of collective supply restriction—for example, a government restriction on the amount of product that can be sold, or the number of acres that a farmer may plant. Such a restriction raises price and may also raise farm income, but what it does to consumers and the nation as a whole is quite another matter.

---

[7]If a good is produced for export (for example, Brazilian coffee), the nation as a whole may gain from a freeze. Thus, when frosts in Brazil reduced coffee supplies, prices soared in 1977. Brazil as a nation gained. The reason is that domestic producers benefited from the higher price. True, consumers lost, but they were mostly in foreign countries, not Brazil. In such cases, it may be in the national interest to restrict supply, as Brazil did during the 1930s by dumping coffee into the ocean.

Such supply restrictions should, however, be approached cautiously, even if a narrow national viewpoint is taken. In the long run, the demand elasticity may be much higher than in the short run. In other words, if coffee prices are kept high for a long period, people may switch to tea and decide that they prefer it. Furthermore, competing producers (in Africa or elsewhere) may be encouraged to increase production in response to higher prices.

EXTENSIONS OF DEMAND THEORY: TIME AND SEARCH COSTS

> Time is Money.
> **Ben Franklin**

In deciding to buy another unit of a product, the consumer compares the marginal utility the product provides with its cost. But cost is a broad term, covering more than just the purchase price. For example, car buyers consider not only the price of a car, but also the expected cost of gasoline, service, and repairs. And in evaluating repair cost, wise buyers take into account not only the expected repair bills, but also the time they may lose in going back and forth to the garage for repairs.

In deciding between two cars, this "time cost" may or may not be important. But in some purchases it can be critical.[8] For example, an airline ticket costs more than a cross-country bus ticket. But most people still fly; the reason is that flying takes less time. Moreover, as we would expect, airline passengers tend to have higher incomes than bus passengers. (Because they have higher incomes, their time is more valuable, so they are more likely to fly.)

Thus, time cost helps to explain consumption patterns—not only within the United States, but also among countries. In North America, we buy costly power appliances: they save us valuable time. In less wealthy countries, hand appliances are used instead. The extra time they require is of less consequence because the value of time is low in countries where income is low.

Heavy time costs may be incurred not only in the consumption of goods or services (such as travel), but also in the search for them. Thus we say that some products have greater **search costs** than others—and this may have an important influence over purchases. For example,

---

[8]A landmark—but very technical—early treatment of this issue was Gary Becker's "A Theory of the Allocation of Time," *Economic Journal,* September 1965, pp. 493–577.

people tend to buy gasoline at a convenient station; they do not generally search to save 1 or 2 cents per gallon.

Are we running out of time?

As our income increases, the opportunity cost of time rises; in other words, time cost increases. And as it does, it knocks some products right out of our consumption pattern. If you were to build an old fashioned washing machine, you would not be able to sell it now at *any* price. It would just take too much time for the buyer to operate; in other words, its high time cost dominates its price. As we become wealthier, we can expect that this will be true of a wider range of goods. Our problem will increasingly become a shortage of time, rather than of goods. More and more people will reach the situation of Jack Paar (Johnny Carson's predecessor as highly paid host on the *Tonight Show*): Paar complained that although he had been able to buy a houseful of electronic gadgets, he didn't even have time to turn them on, let alone play with them.

Conclusion: Does a recognition of time destroy consumer theory?

The answer is no, so long as we define the cost of a product to include both its price *and* its time cost. Bearing this in mind, we can restate our earlier decision-making rule in column 2 of p. 146 as:

The consumer reaches equilibrium by increasing the purchase of a good until its marginal utility falls to the level of its cost (with cost defined to include both its price *and* the time required to search for and use it).

If you have read Box 8-1, you can similarly see that the equations there could also be rewritten, again replacing price with cost to the consumer as we have broadly defined it. (To keep the argument simple in the balance of this book, we refer only to price; but we recognize that it includes time costs as well.)

Key Points

1 Marginal utility is the additional satisfaction derived from consuming one more unit of a good or service.

2 The height of the demand curve provides an approximate measure of marginal utility.

3 Consumers benefit when price falls. Specifically, the change in consumer surplus is the horizontal area to the left of the demand curve enclosed between the old and the new price.

4 When a crop is destroyed (by rot, frost, or whatever) producers may lose or benefit, depending on whether demand is elastic or not. The only firm conclusion is that consumers lose. So does the nation as a whole (unless it's an export item, such as Brazilian coffee).

5 To reach equilibrium, a consumer increases the purchase of a product until its marginal utility falls to the level of its cost—with cost defined to include not only price, but also time and search costs.

Key Concepts

Problems

8-1 Suppose each of three individuals has unit elasticity of demand for a particular good. Without drawing any diagrams, can you guess what the elasticity of the total market demand for this good will be?

Now draw diagrams showing how the market demand should be constructed. Is it flatter than an individual demand? Is it therefore more elastic? Explain.

8-2 Using your own example, explain why marginal utility eventually must fall.

***8-3** If the price of apples rises and of cherries remains constant, show from Equation (8-3) in Box 8-1 why the consumer is no longer in equilibrium. What action will he take to get into a new equilibrium?

8-4 Suppose that a substantial part of a lettuce crop spoils en route to market because of the producers' negligence. Will these producers suffer a loss as a consequence? Explain. How will consumers and the nation as a whole be affected? Would your conclusion be changed if the producers were insured?

8-5 What do you estimate the time cost of your education to be?

8-6 Consider two individuals—one who is retired, and one who is not. Both are wealthy and therefore equally able to purchase the world's most reliable (and most expensive) car. What influence(s) might make one of these buyers more likely than the other to buy this car?

APPENDIX

THE THEORY OF CONSUMER CHOICE: INDIFFERENCE CURVES

In this appendix, we develop an important principle introduced in Chapter 2 and emphasized in Box 8-1: Economic behavior involves a *choice between alternatives.* Consider an individual consuming unit—a single individual or household. Suppose, for simplicity, that the household is consuming only two goods, food and clothing. To analyse the decision it faces, we begin in Figure 8-7 and Table 8-1 with the concept of an ***indifference curve.***

To illustrate this concept, suppose that the household begins at a point chosen at random in Figure 8-7; say, point A, where it is consuming 3 units of clothing and 2 units of food. Then, to draw the indifference curve through A, we ask the following question: What other combinations of clothing and food would leave the household equally well off?

The household may inform us that it would just as soon be at point B, with 2 units of clothing and 3 units of food. In other words, if the household starting at A were asked to give up 1 unit of clothing in return for 1 more unit of food, it would respond that it doesn't care whether such a change takes place or not: The household is indifferent between points A and B. These two points are thus on an indifference curve.

On an ***indifference curve,*** **each point represents the same level of satisfaction or utility.**

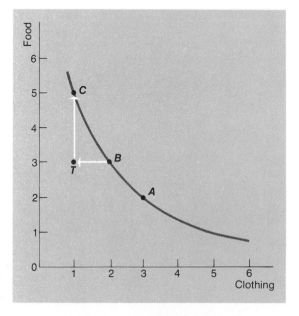

Figure 8-7
An indifference curve
An indifference curve joins all points where the household has the same level of satisfaction or utility.

Table 8-1
Combinations among which the Household Is Indifferent

Combi-nation	Clothing	Food	Amount of additional food required to induce house-hold to give up 1 unit of clothing (the marginal rate of substitution of food for clothing)
A	3	2	
B	2	3	1
C	1	5	2

Now let us continue the experiment, asking the household under what conditions it would be willing to give up one more unit of clothing. In moving upward and to the left from point *B*, the household recognizes that it is getting short of clothing, and has a lot of food. Therefore, it is willing to give up another unit of precious clothing only in return for a large amount (2 units) of food. Thus point *C*, representing 1 unit of clothing and 5 of food, is on the same indifference curve as *A* and *B*. Because the household is increasingly reluctant to give up clothing as its quantity declines, the indifference curve has the bowed shape shown.[9]

The marginal rate of substitution (MRS): The slope of the indifference curve

In moving from *B* to *C*, notice that the slope of the indifference curve is 2 (the rise *TC* = 2, divided by the run *BT* = 1).[10] This geometric concept has an important economic meaning. It is the amount of food (*TC* = 2) that is required to compensate for the loss of 1 unit of clothing (*BT* = 1). That is, it is the **marginal rate of substitution of food for clothing.**

The marginal rate of substitution (MRS) of food for clothing is the amount of food required to compensate for the loss of 1 unit of clothing. Geometrically, it is the slope of the indifference curve. (8-4)

The MRS (with its value of 2 in this case) is also the ratio of the marginal utilities of these two goods. That is,

$$\text{MRS} = \frac{\text{MU}_{clothing}}{\text{MU}_{food}} = 2$$

[9]Although indifference curves usually have a bowed shape, this need not always be the case. For example, a two-car family might be indifferent among the choices of *(A)* two Chevs, no Ford; *(B)* one Chev, one Ford; or *(C)* no Chevs, two Fords. Then, with Chevs on one axis and Fords on the other, the indifference curve joining points *A, B,* and *C* would be a straight line. The reason is that the family considers the two cars to be perfect substitutes for each other.
[10]Actually the slope of the indifference curve is −2, since the move from *B* to *C* represents a run of −1. But for simplicity, we ignore the negative signs that apply to all slopes in this appendix.

We can see why from our example: Since the household is willing to give up only 1 unit of clothing to get 2 units of food, it values clothing twice as highly as food. That is, its marginal utility of clothing is double its marginal utility of food. Formally, we can bring together the ideas in this section:

$$\frac{MU_{clothing}}{MU_{food}} = MRS = \text{the slope of the indifference curve} \qquad (8\text{-}5)$$

The indifference map

The indifference curve in Figure 8-7 is reproduced as u_1 in Figure 8-8. But recall that our starting point, A, was a point chosen at random. We might equally well have started at point F or G; there is an indifference curve that passes through each of these points as well. In other words, there is a whole family of indifference curves, which form the **indifference map** shown in Figure 8-8.

While all points on a single indifference curve represent the same level of satisfaction, points on another indifference curve represent a different level of satisfaction. The farther the indifference curve is away from the origin (to the northeast) the greater the level of satisfaction. Thus on u_3 the household gets a higher level of utility or satisfaction—that is, a higher level of real income—than on u_2. To verify this, note that no matter where on u_2 the household may be (say F), it can find a point on u_3 (such as G) that is preferred because it leaves the household with more of both goods. (And because other points on u_3—such as H—are equivalent to G, they must also be preferred to F.)

Incidentally, this illustrates the technique used by economists (and others) to show three variables in a diagram with only two dimensions. The three variables are the quantity of food, the quantity of clothing, and the household's utility. We can visualize

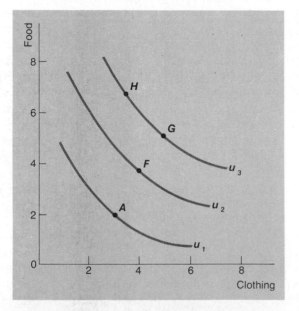

Figure 8-8
An indifference map
There is a whole set of indifference curves for the household, each curve representing a different level of utility. Thus u_2 represents a higher level of utility than u_1, and u_3 a still higher level.

this system of indifference curves as mapping out a utility hill, with each curve representing a contour line showing points with equal utility, just as a geographer's contour line shows points of equal height above sea level. And just as the geographer's contour lines cannot cross, so the indifference curves of a household cannot cross.

As the household moves from the origin to the northeast, it moves up the utility hill to higher and higher levels of satisfaction.[11]

The budget limitation

As we have seen, the indifference map reflects the household's *desires;* the household prefers G to F in Figure 8-8, and is indifferent between H and G. But the household's behavior depends not only on what the household *wants,* but also on what it is *able* to buy.

What the household is able to buy depends on three things: its money income, the price of food, and the price of clothing. If the household's income is $100, while the price of food is $10 per unit and clothing is $20, then the various options open to the household are illustrated by the **budget line** KL in Figure 8-9.

The *budget line* (or *income line* or *price line*) **shows the various combinations of goods that can be purchased by a household with a given money income and facing a given set of prices.**

If the whole $100 is spent on food at $10 per unit, the household can buy 10 units, as shown by point K. At the other extreme, if the household spends its whole $100 on clothing at $20 per unit, it can buy 5 units, as shown by point L. Similarly, it can be shown that any other point on the straight line KL will exactly exhaust the budget of $100. (As an exercise, show that this is true for point M.)

The slope of the budget line KL is

$$\frac{\text{the rise } OK}{\text{the run } LO} = \frac{10}{5} = 2$$

But this is the same as the price ratio of the two goods, that is,

$$\frac{P_{clothing}}{P_{food}} = \frac{\$20}{\$10} = 2$$

---

[11]One advantage of the indifference curve approach is that we don't have to worry about the units of measurement as we move up the utility hill. We know that curve u_3 represents more utility than curve u_2, but we don't need to know *how much* more. Specifically, with indifference curves, we are only making statements such as: "F is preferred to A, G is preferred to F, and G and H are equally desirable."

Thus, the indifference map involves simply an *ordering* of various consumption packages. This is called **ordinal measurement** in contrast to the more familiar **cardinal measurement** which actually specifies the size of any difference. (For example, a statement such as "F is 25 percent better than A" involves a cardinal measure. Such a measure is not necessary with the simple ordering represented by indifference curves.)

Avoiding the problems involved with cardinal measurement of utility was one of the main reasons why Nobel prizewinner J. R. Hicks developed the indifference curve approach in his *Value and Capital* (London: Oxford University Press, 1939).

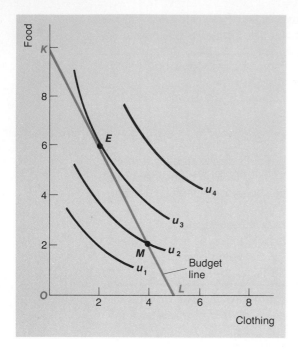

Figure 8-9
The equilibrium of a household with a budget limit
KL represents the household's budget limit. Each point on this line represents a combination of food and clothing that can be purchased, and that just barely exhausts the household's budget. Equilibrium involves moving along this budget line to the point (*E*) of tangency with the highest achievable indifference curve.

Thus:

The slope of the budget line is equal to the price ratio of the two goods. **(8-6)**

The household's equilibrium

Faced with the budget limit *KL,* the household purchases the combination of food and clothing shown at *E.* That is, it moves along the budget line to the point where that line touches the highest possible indifference curve, in this case u_3. Any other affordable purchase (like *M*) is less attractive because it leaves the household on a lower indifference curve (u_2 rather than u_3).

Consumers maximize their satisfaction or utility by moving along their budget line to the highest attainable indifference curve. This is achieved at a point of tangency such as *E* in Figure 8-9.

This conclusion allows us to bring several strands of the analysis together. The consumer is in equilibrium at a point of tangency, that is, a point where:

the slope of the indifference curve = the slope of the budget line.

Or, noting (8-5) and (8-6):

$$\frac{MU_{clothing}}{MU_{food}} = \frac{P_{clothing}}{P_{food}} \qquad (8\text{-}7)$$

Notice that this provides a confirmation of the argument in Box 8-1. Specifically, this equation confirms our earlier Equation (8-3).

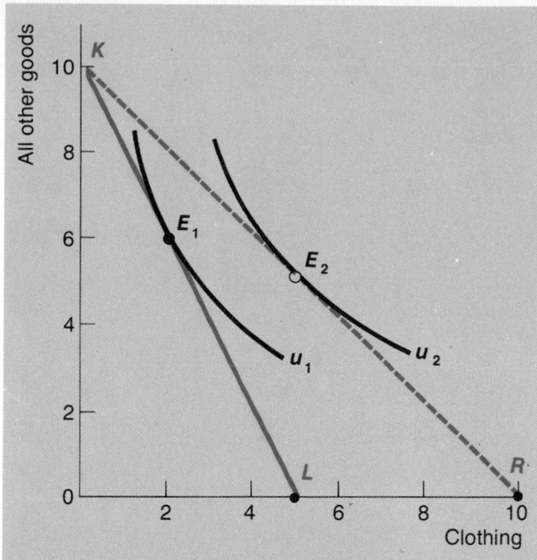

(a) Using indifference curves.

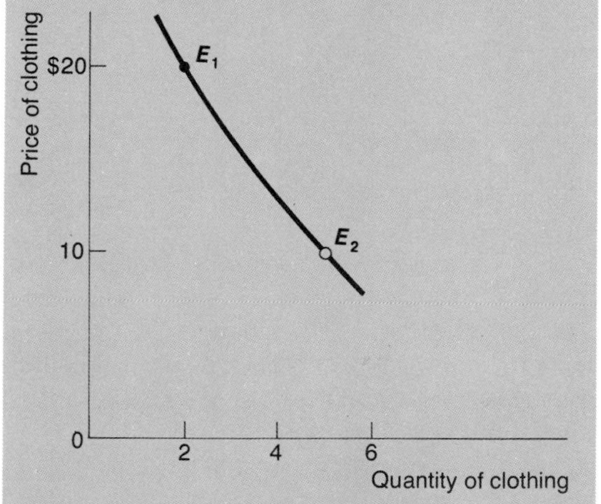

Figure 8-10
The effect of a fall in the price of clothing
As the price of clothing falls, from $20 to $10, the budget line rotates counterclockwise from *KL* to *KR*. As a result, the quantity of clothing purchased increases from 2 to 5 units. In panel *b* we graph exactly this same information about price and quantity; again we move from point E_1 to E_2. But in panel *b* these points define the consumer's demand curve.

(b) The corresponding demand curve for clothing.

In conclusion, we reemphasize that the budget line and the indifference map are independent of one another. The indifference map shows what the household wants; in defining the indifference map, no attention is paid to what the household can actually afford. What it can afford is shown by the budget line. When the indifference map and the budget line are brought together, the choice of the household is determined.

Deriving a demand curve from an indifference map
The indifference curve/budget line analysis is used in Figure 8-10 to show how the household responds to a fall in the price of clothing. When clothing was originally priced at $20 per unit, we have seen that the budget line was *KL* and the equilibrium

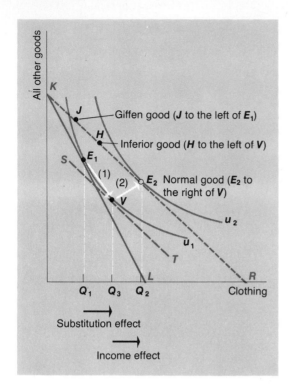

Figure 8-11
The substitution and income effects of a price reduction. (A detailed description of the move from E_1 to E_2 in Figure 8-10a)
With the fall in the price of clothing, there is a shift from equilibrium E_1 to E_2, which can be decomposed into two parts: Shift 1 from E_1 to V shows the substitution effect by holding real income constant. (V is on the same indifference curve as E_1.) Shift 2 from V to E_2 shows the income effect by holding relative prices constant. (The slopes at V and E_2 are the same.)

was E_1 (both reproduced from Figure 8-9). Now suppose that the price of clothing falls to $10, but the price of food remains unchanged. Because the price ratio has changed, the slope of the budget line changes. Specifically, the budget line rotates from KL to KR. (If all $100 is spent on clothing, the household can now buy 10 units at point R. But because the price of food does not change, the new budget line still ends at point K, as before.[12])

Faced with the new budget line KR, the household again searches for its highest possible indifference curve, finding it to be u_2 at the point of tangency E_2. The two points of equilibrium, E_1 and E_2, define the two points on the demand curve of the household, shown in Figure 8-10b. Thus the individual's demand curve can be derived from his indifference map.

The results of a price change: substitution and income effects
When the price of clothing falls, *ceteris paribus,* the household buys more clothing—for two reasons. First, clothing becomes cheaper compared to other goods. Consequently, the consumer *switches* from other goods to clothing. This is called the

---

[12]Because our simple example has only two goods (food and clothing), food may be interpreted as representing all goods other than clothing. In showing the relationship between the indifference curve diagram and the demand curve for clothing, it is customary to write "all other goods" on the vertical axis, as we have done in Figure 8-10a.

substitution effect. Second, when the price of clothing falls, the purchasing power of the consumer's money income rises. This allows the consumer to buy more of everything—including clothing. This increase in clothing is called the ***income effect***.

This distinction is illustrated in Figure 8-11, where we show how the movement in Figure 8-10a from E_1 to E_2—and the accompanying increase in clothing purchases from Q_1 to Q_2—can be broken down into the substitution and income effects. To look at the effects of substitution alone, we hold real income constant. That is, we keep the individual on the original indifference curve, u_1. But, at the same time, we allow the slope of the price line to change to reflect the lower price of clothing. Thus, we find a new price line, *ST*, parallel to *KR* (thus reflecting the new prices), but tangent to original indifference curve u_1 at point *V*. The *substitution effect* is the quantity change Q_1Q_3 associated with the move from E_1 to *V* (shown by arrow 1).

But, of course, the consumer does not actually move from E_1 to *V*; he moves from E_1 to E_2. The rest of the movement—from *V* to E_2 (arrow 2)—involves the *income effect*. Observe that a shift in the price line from *ST* to *KR* represents a change in real income alone; that is, it involves no change in relative prices. (The slope of *ST* and *KR* are the same.)

The *substitution effect* is the change in the quantity purchased which would occur as a result of a change only in relative prices, with real income held constant. (In Figure 8-11, it is the distance from Q_1 to Q_3.)
The *income effect* is the change in the quantity purchased which would occur as a result of a change only in real income. (In Figure 8-11, it is the distance from Q_3 to Q_2.)

Because of the shape of the indifference curve, the substitution effect following a fall in price *must* be positive. (Q_3 must be to the right of Q_1.) For the vast majority of goods—the normal goods—the income effect is also positive, as in the example already described in Figure 8-11. For the few goods which are *inferior,* the income effect is negative. In this case, an indifference curve is tangent to *KR* not at E_2, but instead at a point such as *H,* to the *left* of *V*. In other words, arrow 2 no longer points to the northeast, but instead points to the northwest. Accordingly, an increase in income *reduces* the quantity purchased.

[Economists have been fascinated with the logical possibility that a negative income effect might be sufficiently strong to more than offset the positive substitution effect; in other words, that an indifference curve might be tangent to *KR* at a point such as *J, to the left of* E_1. Such a case would certainly be extremely rare. One may have been observed by Victorian economist Giffen who studied the purchase of potatoes in a very poor economy. (In such a special case, a fall in the price of the staple food—potatoes—would greatly increase people's real income, thus allowing them to buy more meat and other expensive foods and actually *decrease* their purchase of potatoes. Notice that such a peculiar good—a so-called *Giffen good*— would have a strange demand curve; it would slope upward and *to the right.*] ■

CHAPTER 9
Costs and Perfectly Competitive Supply

In the last chapter, the consumer was king, deciding which goods would be produced, and which would not. But, in fact, it's a joint regency: The producer is also king. Goods aren't produced unless the consumer wants them *and* the producer can deliver them. In this chapter, we turn our attention to the producers.

In the last chapter, we stressed the *choices* open to consumers, specifically, the choice of *which* goods to consume. The producer likewise faces fundamental *choices:*

1 *Which* goods will the firm produce? And *how many* units of each?

2 *What combination of inputs* will the firm use in the production of these goods? For example, will an automobile manufacturer use a highly automated assembly line, with a great deal of equipment and only a few workers? Or less capital equipment, and more workers? Will the wheat farmer use a lot of fertilizer on each acre, or produce the wheat using more land and less fertilizer?

While these are the fundamental choices, producers in practice are constrained by their decisions of the past. For example, General Motors is committed to car production by its huge investment in plant and equipment. It does not have the option next month of producing

aircraft, or computers, or bicycles instead. Furthermore, GM is already committed not only on the kind of plant and equipment, but also on the *amount* of this capital it will have during the next month. (It is now too late to order new machines or build new factories.) For next month, GM has only one major production decision to make: *How many vehicles* will it produce with its present capital stock, and *how many workers* and how much material will it need to produce this number?

Thus, we distinguish between **short-run** decisions of producers, and their **long-run** decisions.

THE SHORT RUN AND THE LONG

In the short run, the firm is committed by past investment decisions; it cannot add to the amount of plant and equipment at its disposal. And it cannot switch to the production of another good.

In the long run, the firm can pick from the full menu of choices. It can reduce its capital committed to the production of a specific good —for example, by not replacing its automotive machinery as it wears out. Or the firm can acquire new equipment. Thus, in the long run, it can choose whether to produce in a capital-intensive manner—with many machines and few workers—or in a labor-intensive manner (many workers and few machines).

The *short run* is the period when the firm's quantity of plant and equipment is fixed.

The *long run* is the period when the firm is able to change the quantity of plant and equipment.

We emphasize that the distinction between the short run and the long is a logical one—the short run is whatever period plant and equipment are fixed. The short run cannot be identified as a specific number of weeks, months, or years. In some industries it may be many years; it takes that long to design and construct a large electric power plant, for example. In other industries, it may be only a matter of days: For example, a college entrepreneur can quickly buy a typewriter, and thus acquire the capital equipment needed to set up business typing term papers. Furthermore, the short run may be briefer for an expanding firm than for a contracting firm: An expanding firm may be able to acquire new equipment quickly. But a contracting firm may be able to reduce its capital stock only slowly: There may be no market in which it can sell its used machinery, and its capital stock may take years to wear out.

In order to simplify this chapter, we initially assume that there are only two factors of production: labor and capital. We ignore land and intermediate inputs (steel, parts, etc.) bought from other producers.

We also assume that, in making choices, business executives try to maximize their firm's profits. Of course, executives may also have other motives—for example, ensuring the security of their jobs, or increasing their own importance by expanding their operations and the number of people who work for them. But, to keep things simple, we focus on the important objective of profit maximization. Specifically, we assume that if a firm can increase its profits by making more of a good, it will do so. Or, if it can increase profits by producing less, that's what it will do.

THE SHORT-RUN PRODUCTION FUNCTION

First, we look at the short run, in which labor is the only input whose quantity can be changed. The decision facing the firm in the short run is this: How many workers should be employed, and how many units of output produced? As we shall see, the answer requires three steps. The first step is to estimate the firm's **short-run production function,** which shows the relationship between the quantity of labor used, and the number of units which can be produced. An illustration is given in the first two lines of Table 9-1.

The production function itself—lines 1 and 2—is straightforward. The first line shows the number of workers employed. The second shows the total product; that is, the total number of units produced. As the firm increases the amount of its labor input, it is able to produce more units of output.

Note also the third line, showing the **marginal product.** As we have seen earlier, "marginal" means additional. In this case, the marginal product is the additional output which is produced by adding one more worker. It is calculated from line 2. For example, when the fourth worker is added, total product increases from 18 units to 21. Thus, the marginal product of the fourth worker is 3 units of output. (This, and the other data given in Table 9-1, are illustrated in Figure 9-1.) As we shall see, an entrepreneur who wants to maximize profits will concentrate on what is happening *at the margin* (that is, on what happens when one more worker is hired, or one more unit of output produced).

The *marginal product of labor* is the number of additional units of output which result from the use of one more unit of labor.

The law of (eventually) diminishing returns

Observe in line 3 that, although the marginal product of the second worker is higher than that

Table 9-1
The Short-run Production Function
(The quantity of capital is fixed. Product is measured in units per week.)

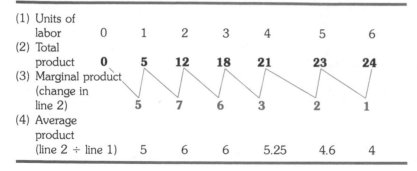

(1) Units of labor	0	1	2	3	4	5	6
(2) Total product	**0**	**5**	**12**	**18**	**21**	**23**	**24**
(3) Marginal product (change in line 2)		5	7	6	3	2	1
(4) Average product (line 2 ÷ line 1)		5	6	6	5.25	4.6	4

of the first, the addition of the third, fourth, fifth, and sixth workers results in a smaller and smaller marginal product. This is in keeping with the *law of (eventually) diminishing returns.* To explain this law, consider the example of a firm producing television sets with a given stock of

Figure 9-1
Total, marginal, and average product curves
The curves in this diagram correspond to the data in Table 9-1. The marginal product must eventually decline, in keeping with the law of eventually diminishing returns.

This figure also shows average product; that is, total product divided by the number of units of labor.

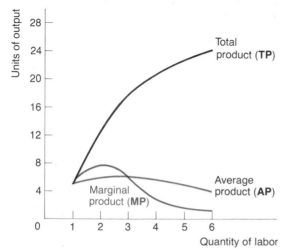

machinery. As it initially hires more labor, each additional worker increases the firm's output by a substantial amount. But ultimately, as its labor force grows and its equipment is operated closer and closer to capacity, an additional worker will add only a small amount to the firm's output. All the new employee can do is work on odd jobs or stand around waiting for one of the machines to be free. In other words, *marginal product must eventually decrease.*

The *law of (eventually) diminishing returns:* If more of one factor (labor) is employed while all other factors (like capital) are held constant, eventually the marginal product of that factor (labor) must fall.

This principle is easily confirmed in agriculture. As more and more workers are added to a constant amount of land—say, an acre—the marginal product of labor *must* eventually fall. If it did not, then the entire world could be fed from this single acre—or, for that matter, from your back garden.

COSTS IN THE SHORT RUN

To decide how much to produce, the firm's second step is to calculate its cost. In our simple example, the firm has two types of costs: capital costs and labor costs. In the short run, the firm cannot change its quantity of capital. Costs associated with the capital—for example, depreciation and interest on funds which were borrowed to buy equipment—are incurred regardless of how much is produced. (Indeed, they are incurred even if nothing is produced.) Accordingly, they are called *fixed costs,* or overhead costs.

But when the firm starts to produce, it incurs other costs as well. As its output increases, the firm requires more labor—as its short-run production function indicates. In other words, the firm's labor cost varies as the quantity of its output varies. For this reason, labor is called a *variable cost.* (The typical firm also has other variable costs—such as material inputs. But, as noted earlier, to keep the analysis simple we assume that no such material inputs are used.)

The firm calculates its variable cost, using information taken from its production function. To illustrate, let's return for a moment to the firm whose production function was shown in Table 9-1. If the wage rate is $300 per week, then the variable cost of producing 5 units is $300 (one worker is hired). And the variable cost of pro-

ducing 12 units is $600 (that is, two workers are needed, at $300 each).

For an entirely different firm, costs are illustrated in Figure 9-2a.[1] Fixed cost (shown by the lower white arrow) is always the same $35, regardless of what output may be. As we see, variable cost (illustrated by the upper white arrow) rises as output increases. *Total cost* is the sum of both fixed and variable costs; that is, the combined height of the two wide arrows. The numbers from which this diagram was drawn are set out in the first five columns of Table 9-2. (For the moment, the last three columns of this table can be ignored.)

Fixed costs **are incurred regardless of whether or not any output is produced.** *Variable costs* **are any costs above and beyond this; they increase as output increases.** *Total costs* **are the sum of fixed costs and variable costs.**

---

[1]We switch to a different firm because Table 9-1 does not give the detail needed to calculate variable cost for each of the units of output. (It allows us only to calculate variable cost for 5 units, or for 12 units, but not for the units in between.)

Table 9-2
Short-Run Costs of a Hypothetical Firm

Quantity q	Fixed Cost FC	Variable Cost VC	Total Cost $TC = FC + VC$	Marginal Cost MC = change in total cost	Average Cost** $AC = TC \div q$	Average Variable Cost** $AVC = VC \div q$	Average Fixed Cost** $AFC = FC \div q$
(1)	(2)	(3)	(4) = (3) + (2)	(5)	(6) = (4) ÷ (1)	(7) = (3) ÷ (1)	(8) = (2) ÷ (1)
0	35	—	35				
1	35	24	59	59 − 35 = 24	59 ÷ 1 = 59	24 ÷ 1 = 24	35 ÷ 1 = 35
2	35	40	75	75 − 59 = 16	75 ÷ 2 = 38	40 ÷ 2 = 20	35 ÷ 2 = 18
3	35	60	95	95 − 75 = 20	95 ÷ 3 = 32	60 ÷ 3 = 20	35 ÷ 3 = 12
4	35	85	120	120 − 95 = 25	120 ÷ 4 = 30	85 ÷ 4 = 21	35 ÷ 4 = 9
5	35	115	150	150 − 120 = 30	150 ÷ 5 = 30	115 ÷ 5 = 23	35 ÷ 5 = 7
6	35	155	190	190 − 150 = 40	190 ÷ 6 = 32	155 ÷ 6 = 26	35 ÷ 6 = 6
7	35	210	245	245 − 190 = 55	245 ÷ 7 = 35	210 ÷ 7 = 30	35 ÷ 7 = 5
8	35	295	330	330 − 245 = 85	330 ÷ 8 = 41	295 ÷ 8 = 37	35 ÷ 8 = 4

*The first five columns are graphed in Figure 9-2, and the last three in Figure 9-5.
**Rounded to the nearest dollar.

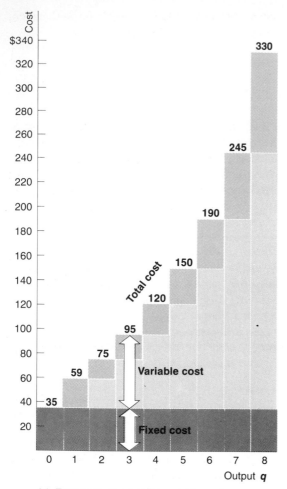

(a) Total cost=fixed cost+variable cost.

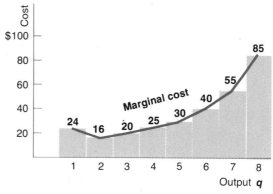

(b) Marginal cost: the increase in total cost.

Figure 9-2
Short-run costs of a hypothetical firm (drawn from Table 9-2)

In panel *a*, total cost is the sum of fixed cost and variable cost. Marginal cost indicates how much total cost is increasing, and is shown by the set of red bars in panel *a* or in panel *b*.

marginal cost (while business executives often call it *incremental cost*). Note how similar this concept is to marginal utility (the increase in utility because an additional unit is consumed) or to marginal product (the increase in output because an additional unit of input is used).

Marginal cost (MC) is the increase in total cost because an additional unit is produced.

Each of the red marginal cost bars in panel *a* of Figure 9-2*a* is now assembled on its own in

Observe that the red bars or "stairsteps" in Figure 9-2*a* show how total costs increase with each additional unit of output. Thus in producing its first unit of output, the firm's costs rise by $24, represented by the first red bar. In producing the second unit, its costs rise by $16, represented by the next red bar. Economists call each such bar

panel *b*. (This schedule can be viewed as "what would be left" if the supporting gray bars in panel *a* were removed and the red bars were allowed to settle down to the baseline.)

PROFIT MAXIMIZATION: MARGINAL COST AND MARGINAL REVENUE

In order to determine how much to produce to maximize profits, the firm now takes its third step. This step requires the firm to calculate its *marginal revenue* schedule.

Marginal revenue **(MR) is the increase in total revenue because an additional unit is sold.**

Suppose, specifically, that the managers wonder whether they should increase output by one more unit. They should, *if* their gain from doing so is greater than the cost. Their gain is the marginal revenue (MR)—the increase in total revenue from selling one additional unit. Their cost is the marginal cost (MC). So long as the marginal cost of the additional unit is less than its marginal revenue, the firm benefits (that is, increases its profit) by producing that unit. Therefore, a firm will continue to produce more and more units, until its marginal cost rises to the point where it is equal to its marginal revenue. Thus:

To maximize profits, the firm chooses the output where:
$$MC = MR \qquad (9\text{-}1)$$

This, then is the third and final step in the decision on how much to produce: Calculate marginal revenue, and choose the output where MR = MC.

Equation (9-1) represents the *general rule for maximizing profits,* regardless of the kind of market in which a firm operates (regardless of whether the firm is a monopolist or a perfect competitor). To provide a specific illustration of how Equation (9-1) determines the best output for a firm, we look first at a firm selling in a perfectly competitive market. (Firms in other kinds of markets will be studied later.)

THE SHORT-RUN SUPPLY OF THE PERFECTLY COMPETITIVE FIRM

Recall that the firm in a perfectly competitive market faces a given price. No matter how much or how little it sells, it cannot affect the price. Suppose, for example, that the firm faces a market price of $40. Its total revenue will be $40 from selling 1 unit; $80 from selling 2; and so on, as shown in column 4 of Table 9-3. (The first three columns are taken from Table 9-2.) With this total revenue, we see that its *marginal revenue* is $40, the same as the price; each time the firm sells one more unit, it gets $40 more in revenue, as shown in column 5.

For a firm in a perfectly competitive industry, marginal revenue (MR) is equal to price (*P*).

Profits are calculated in the sixth column, as total revenue minus total cost. Observe that the firm maximizes its profits by producing 6 units. This is the output where marginal cost equals marginal revenue; both are $40. We thus have an illustration of the general principle set out in Equation (9-1). Specifically:

A firm in perfect competition produces where
$$MC = MR = P \qquad (9\text{-}2)$$

Note that a decision to produce a greater output, say 7 units, would be a mistake. Since the seventh unit has a marginal cost of $55 but a price (marginal revenue) of only $40, producing it would cause a $15 reduction in profits.

On the other hand, if the firm is at an output below 6—say, at 4—expansion will be in its interest. (The marginal cost of the fifth unit is $30, and it can be sold for $40. Therefore, the fifth unit adds $10 to profits.)

But at 6 units, there is no tendency to expand or contract production, because margin-

Table 9-3
Profit Maximization by a Perfectly Competitive Firm Facing a $40 Price

(1) Quantity q	(2) Total Cost TC	(3) Marginal Cost MC	(4) Total Revenue TR	(5) Marginal Revenue MR	(6) Profit or Loss (6) = (4) − (2)
0	35		0		− 35
1	59	24	40	40	− 19
2	75	16	80	40	5
3	95	20	120	40	25
4	120	25	160	40	40
5	150	30	200	40	50
6	190	40	240	40	50* ⇐
7	245	55	280	40	35
8	330	85	320	40	− 10

*Profit is also at a maximum at 5 units of output. In cases like this, economists typically assume that the firm produces the larger output.

al cost MC is equal to price (that is, marginal revenue). Consequently, this is the equilibrium output for the profit maximizing firm.

This conclusion is illustrated in Figure 9-3: The firm facing a price of $40 supplies 6 units—that is, the amount shown by its marginal cost curve. (For an alternative view of this profit-maximizing decision see Box 9-1.)

The perfectly competitive firm's short-run supply: Its marginal cost curve

If price rises from $40 to $55, the horizontal price line in Figure 9-3 shifts up to this new, higher level. The firm responds to this higher price by increasing its output to 7 units, where MC is again equal to price. Or, if price falls to $30, it supplies 5 units; and so on. Notice that what we are doing is defining this firm's supply response; that is, how much it supplies at various prices. As price rises, it simply follows its marginal cost curve up; or if price falls, it follows its MC curve down.

Thus, just as marginal utility was the key to the demand curve in the previous chapter, we now see that *marginal cost defines the firm's supply curve*—provided the firm is producing anything at all. But it may not be: If price falls low enough, the firm will close down. The critical question therefore is: How far can price fall before the firm closes down and stops producing altogether?

Figure 9-3
A competitive firm produces where MC = price. (Marginal costs are for the firm shown in Figure 9-2)

Marginal cost MC is equal to price P at an output of 6 units. Since this output maximizes profit, it is the amount that this firm will supply.

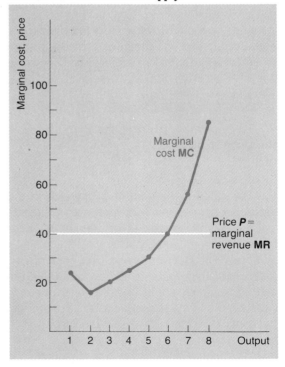

BOX 9-1

Another View of Profit Maximization: Total Revenue and Total Cost

Graphing a firm's marginal revenue and marginal cost curves in Figure 9-3 is not the only way we can visualize its profit maximization. We can alternatively graph its *total* revenue and *total* cost curves in Figure 9-4, and show its profit maximizing output on this diagram. Specifically, we first plot the firm's total cost curve, taken directly from Figure 9-2a. (There it was plotted as a series of bars, but here we draw it as a curve.) The firm's total revenue is also plotted as the straight line from the origin. This simply repeats an earlier message: Given the $40 price the firm faces, the first unit it sells yields $40 of total revenue, the first two units yield $80, and so on. Note that the slope of this line is equal to the price and to the marginal revenue.

Initially, if the firm produces only 1 unit of output, it operates at a loss of $19 shown by arrow *d:* Its $59 total cost exceeds its $40 total revenue. But as it increases its output, it moves upward to the right out of the red loss area into the black profit range where total revenue has risen above total cost. Finally, at 8 units or more of output, total cost rises above total revenue, and the firm again operates at a loss.

Where in the range between 2 and 7 units of output does the firm maximize profits? The answer is at 6 units, the output where its profit (the vertical distance *c* between the total revenue and total cost curves) is greatest.†

This is also the output where the slopes of the total revenue and total cost curves (specifically, the slopes of line segments *a* and *b*) are the same. We have already seen that the slope of the total revenue line is marginal revenue. Likewise, the slope of the total cost curve is marginal cost.‡ Thus, equating these two slopes is, in fact, equating marginal cost and marginal revenue—just as we did in Figure 9-3. ∎

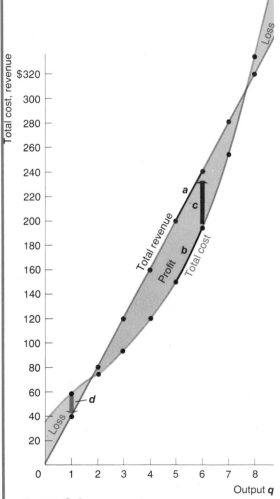

Figure 9-4
Another view of profit maximization by a perfectly competitive firm

†In the footnote to Table 9-3, we noted that profits were also at a maximum at 5 units, and that, in such cases, economists assume that the larger output is sold. We also assume here that the firm can't produce a fraction of a unit; for example, it can't produce 5½ units.

‡This is easily confirmed by referring back to Figure 9-2. The greater the marginal cost stairstep in that diagram, the greater the slope of the total cost curve in Figure 9-4. [Readers familiar with calculus will now see why it is a valuable tool in economics. Marginal cost is simply the first derivative (slope) of the total cost curve.]

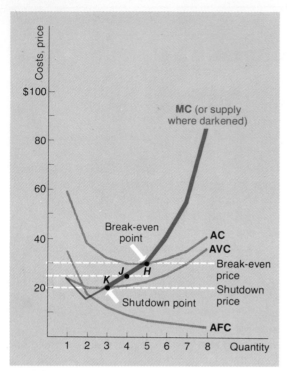

Figure 9-5
Drawing the firm's cost curves, and showing how they define its short-run supply

Marginal cost is reproduced from Figure 9-2. Average cost AC, average variable cost AVC, and average fixed cost AFC are taken from the last three columns in Table 9-2. The firm's short-run supply curve is shown as the heavy curve. It is that portion of its MC curve that lies above its AVC curve.

To throw light on this question, two new concepts are useful: (1) *average cost* (AC), or *average total cost* (ATC), defined as total cost divided by output; and (2) *average variable cost* (AVC), defined as variable cost divided by output. These two new concepts are calculated in the right-hand columns of Table 9-2, together with *average fixed cost* (AFC), defined as fixed cost divided by output. Then each concept is graphed, along with the MC curve, in Figure 9-5. Note that the MC curve cuts the AC curve where AC is at a minimum. (This must be so for reasons explained in Box 9-2. In that box we also explain the significance of AFC.)

Now consider what happens in Figure 9-5 if the price falls to $30. To identify its best output, the firm finds where MC equals the $30 price; this is at point *H*, where 5 units are produced. Observe that, at this point, average cost is at a minimum and is equal to price. Thus, the best the firm can do is to break even: The price barely covers AC, and profits are zero.

Next, suppose price falls even below $30, to say $25. If the firm produces at all, its output will be 4 units, at point *J*, where MC equals the $25 price. But this output involves operating at a loss, since *J* lies below the AC curve. (Specifically, the $25 price the firm receives does not cover the $30 average cost of producing each unit.) It sounds as though this firm will close down. But it does not; *even though it is operating at a loss at J, it still continues to produce in the short run.* The reason is that its $25 selling price more than covers its average *variable* costs. (That is, point *J* lies above AVC.) Therefore, it can completely cover its variable costs and still have some revenue left over to partly cover its fixed costs. And it is better to cover part of these fixed costs than to shut down and cover none of them at all.[2] Thus, so long as a firm is at least covering its variable costs, it continues to produce. That remains true so long as price is above the $20 level at *K*; but if price falls below this, the firm will not even be able to cover its variable costs, and it will close down.

Thus, *in the short run* (in the period when the firm is working with a fixed capital stock and cannot avoid these fixed cost commitments), the firm reacts to any given price by supplying a quantity that can be read off its marginal cost curve, *provided it is at a point above AVC.* In brief:

The firm's *short-run supply curve* is that part of its marginal cost curve that lies above its average variable cost curve.

[2]The reason is that bygones are bygones. The firm is saddled with those fixed costs; they are water under the bridge. (Hence, they are sometimes referred to as "past" or "sunk" costs.)

Table 9-4
The Evaluation of Costs and Profit

(a) By accountants			(b) By economists		
Total revenue		$102,000	Total revenue		$102,000
Costs (out-of-pocket)			Explicit (out-of-pocket) costs		
Labor	$10,000		Labor	$10,000	
Materials	59,000		Materials	59,000	
Rent	5,000		Rent	5,000	
Total	$74,000	$74,000			
			Implicit costs (income foregone)		
			Owner's salary	$24,000	
			Interest	1,000	
			Normal profit	2,000	
			Total costs	$101,000	$101,000
Accounting profit		$28,000	Economic (above-normal) profit		$ 1,000

This discussion may be summarized by describing the plight you may find yourself in someday if you are operating at a point like *J*. For example, suppose that you have inherited a house in another city, which you wish to rent out. You have to pay $200 a week of fixed costs (taxes, etc.) whether or not it's rented, and $40 a week of variable costs (utilities, etc.) if you do rent it. If you can get only $100 rent, should you rent the house or leave it vacant? The answer is: Rent it. True, you suffer a loss. But the $100 rent you receive more than covers the $40 of variable costs which you incur as a result of your decision to rent. Thus, you have $60 left over to cover some of the fixed costs, such as taxes. And that's better than leaving the house vacant and being stuck with *all* the fixed costs. Thus, your loss is less if you rent it than if you leave it vacant. Of course, in the long run you will not want to keep such a house, since you are suffering a loss. But in the short run—that is, until you can sell it—you are stuck. All you can do is your best, which is to minimize your loss by renting it.

But, of course, in the long run, when you have enough time to sell the house, your reac-tion as a supplier will be quite different. You will go out of this business, and stop renting altogether.

THE ECONOMIST'S CONCEPT OF COST: OPPORTUNITY COST

Before turning to the long run, let us briefly pause to see why the economist's definition of cost is broader than the more familiar definition that accountants use. To illustrate, suppose a friend who operates a store has asked you to analyze her business. Her breakdown of costs in column *a* of Table 9-4 seems to confirm her view that she has a good thing going. With revenue of $102,000 and costs of $74,000, she is earning an accounting profit of $28,000.

But you dig more deeply. You discover that she could earn a $24,000 salary by accepting a job from an insurance company. This is an *implicit cost* (or *imputed cost*) because it is not paid out of pocket. But we must include it, as we have done in column *b,* or we would not have an adequate picture of the true costs involved in operating this business (that is, the cost of all the

BOX 9-2
Two Important Influences on Average Cost

In this box we examine how a firm's average cost curve is influenced by its marginal cost curve and its average fixed cost curve.

1 The influence of marginal cost: Why a firm's costs are like a baseball player's average

Late in the 1980 season, Kansas City's George Brett had the best chance to hit the magic .400 (40 hits in each 100 times at bat) since the Boston Red Sox' Ted Williams did it with .406 in 1941. The numbers on the right show Brett's batting performance during 1 week in September. In the first three games against Chicago and Detroit he batted a disappointing .250 (one hit in each four times at bat). Since this marginal performance (shown in red) was below his average in the .380s, it pulled his average down. But in the next three games, his fortunes improved: He batted .500 or better. Since this marginal performance was above his average, it pulled his average up.†

So too with marginal and average costs. Until they reach their point of intersection *H* in

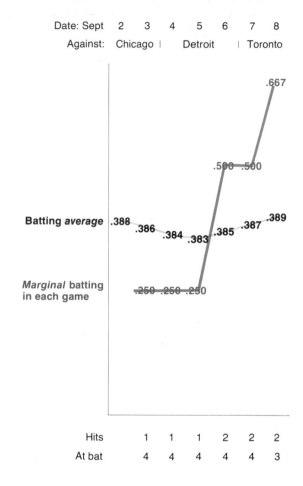

†Did Brett hit .400? Although the last three games shown here started him off on a hitting streak that carried him over .400 for a week in late September, he couldn't maintain the pace, and finished the season with .390.

---

resources used, including her own talent and energy). And we would not be able to judge whether she is doing as well in this business as she could in another activity (namely, working for the insurance company).

This implicit salary for her own effort illustrates the concept of **opportunity cost;** that is, the value of the best alternative forgone.

The *opportunity cost* of an input is the return that it could earn in its best alternative use.

Opportunity cost also indicates *how much an input must be paid to keep it in its present use.* For example, if your friend doesn't earn her opportunity cost (her potential salary in insur-

average fixed cost (AFC), calculated in the last column of Table 9-2. First, note that as output increases and we move to the right in Figure 9-5, AFC gets smaller and smaller. It must; after all, a fixed overhead cost (in this case $35) is being divided by an increasingly large output. As business executives know, increased volume means that overhead can be spread over a larger number of units of output. Thus, the overhead cost that has to be charged to each unit shrinks.

This is important because average cost AC (in column 6 of Table 9-2) is the sum of two components: average variable cost AVC plus average fixed cost AFC (in columns 7 and 8).‡ When AVC ceases to fall (in our example, at 2 units of output) AC continues to fall for a while because it is pulled down by its other component —the always-falling AFC. Moreover, the larger are fixed costs, the more influential AFC will be; that is, the longer it will continue to pull AC down. (To confirm, do the simple calculations in Problem 9-7.) Thus, high overhead industries—such as the telephone companies that require very heavy investment—tend to have falling average costs (economies of scale) over a wide range of output.

Figure 9-5, marginal cost is below average cost; hence, it is pulling AC down. But to the right of *H,* MC is above AC, and hence is pulling AC up. Since AC is falling until it reaches *H* but rising beyond, it must be at a minimum at *H,* where it meets MC.

2 The influence of average fixed cost (AFC)

Now consider how average cost is influenced by

‡This is easy to confirm: Just divide all terms in the equation TC = VC + FC by the quantity of output.

ance), she has an incentive to shift out of her present activity into the higher-return insurance business. This illustrates a point made early in this chapter: Producers make a *choice* as to what goods or services to produce (in this case, your friend chooses between retailing and insurance services).

You also discover that your friend has other opportunity costs which must also be included in column *b.* For example, she has a substantial amount of her own money tied up in this business. What would be her best alternative use of this money? She indicates that she would lend out part of it, thus earning $1,000 in interest. She would use the rest to buy part-ownership of a company in which she could earn a $2,000 profit. This last item—an opportunity cost of capital—is called **normal profit.**

We emphasize that whenever we draw a cost curve in this book, we include not only explicit out-of-pocket costs, but also implicit costs such as normal profit. Therefore, in our example, costs are the full $101,000 shown in column *b* of Table 9-4. This broad definition means that costs tell us how much all the resources employed by the firm could be earning elsewhere. Since her $102,000 of revenues exceed this $101,000 cost, she has earned above-normal profit of $1,000. (In economics, the word "profit" means *above-normal* profit unless otherwise stated.) It is this $1,000 "bottom-line" profit figure that allows you to judge that your friend does indeed have a good thing going: Her business not only provides her with an appropriate $24,000 income for her own effort and an appropriate return for the capital she has invested; it also provides her with $1,000 in addition. If present firms in an industry are making such (above-normal) profits, there is an incentive for other entrepreneurs to move their capital into this business, to get in on a good thing.

Economic profit is above-normal profit; that is, profit after taking account of all opportunity costs (including a normal profit return to invested capital).

Now suppose that salaries in other jobs increase. Specifically, suppose the insurance company increases its offer to your friend from $24,000 to $27,000. This increases the $24,000 owner's salary item by $3,000; and when column *b* is accordingly recalculated, the $1,000 of (above-normal) profit becomes a $2,000 loss. Your friend is no longer able to earn as much in this enterprise as in her best alternative activity. And (assuming she views this alternative line of work as equally interesting), she has an incentive to move.

Thus, *economic profit* (or loss) *provides a signal, indicating whether resources are being attracted to* (or repelled from) *an activity.*

THE LONG RUN

The production function and supply we have studied so far have applied only to the short run. That is, they have described a firm with a fixed capital stock of plant and equipment. But in the long run, the firm can change the quantity of capital. And this presents business executives with one of their most important decisions of all. Should the firm expand by acquiring new machines and building new factories? Or should it contract, by deciding not to replace its old capital as it wears out and becomes obsolete?

The long-run production function

Because the firm can change the quantity of capital in the long run, the options open to it are much broader than in the short run. The broader options are shown in the **long-run production function.** An example is given in Table 9-5.

Because the quantity of capital as well as labor is variable in the long run, this production function has two dimensions. From left to right, we show increases in the quantity of labor. In the upward direction, we show increases in the quantity of capital. Each number in the produc-

---

The *long-run production function* (or, more simply, the production function) shows various combinations of inputs and the maximum output which can be produced with each combination. For a simple firm with only two inputs (labor and capital), the production function can be shown by a two-dimensional table (like Table 9-5).

The *short-run production function* shows the relationship between the amount of variable factors used and the amount of output that can be produced, in a situation where the quantity of capital is constant. For the simple two-input firm, the short-run production function is one row in the long-run production function.

---

tion function indicates the maximum quantity of output that a hypothetical firm can produce with various specific combinations of inputs. For example, if the firm uses 3 units of capital (K) and 5 units of labor (L), it can produce 39 units of output. (For the moment, ignore the fact that some numbers in Table 9-5 are shown in red. The reason is explained in Appendix 9-A.)

Table 9-5 is, in fact, the long-run production function of the firm whose short-run production function was shown earlier in Table 9-1: Note that the earlier table now appears as the bottom row. In fact, this long-run production function is made up of *a whole set* of rows, with each representing a different short-run production function. Once the firm chooses how much

capital it will use, it is confined in the short run to operating along the corresponding row of this table. For example, if it chose 6 units of capital, then it is confined in the short run to the top line of the production function. But in the long run, it can move anywhere in Table 9-5.

COSTS IN THE LONG RUN

As we have just seen, the long-run production function is made up of a series of rows, each of which represents a short-run production function. For each short-run production function, there is a corresponding short-run average cost (SAC) curve. (S emphasizes that it applies to the short run.) Figure 9-6 illustrates four such curves.

Over the long run, the firm chooses the size of plant and equipment (and therefore the SAC curve) which minimizes its cost. Hence, for example, if it wants to produce output q_1, it chooses the plant and equipment required to operate on short-run curve SAC_C, and employs the number of workers needed to produce at point R on this curve. By picking point R, it chooses the lowest-cost combination of capital and labor. (For more detail on how firms choose the lowest-cost combination of inputs, see Appendix 9-A.) Alternatively, to produce q_2, it chooses the quantity of plant and equipment required for SAC_D and chooses the quantity of labor needed to produce at point S. Again, it chooses the least-cost combination of capital and labor. If we join all points like R and S, the result is the heavy long-run average cost curve (LAC). This is called an **envelope curve** because it encloses all the short-run SAC curves from below. (It's very easy for us to draw this curve now, but see Box 9-3 for the problems encountered by the economist who introduced the idea.)

Because there are many short-run SAC curves, rather than just the four illustrated, LAC forms a smooth curve. It shows the *lowest*

Table 9-5
A Hypothetical Firm's Production Function
This simplified production function shows the number of units of output a firm can produce from various combinations of inputs. For example, if it combines 2 units of labor with one unit of capital, element 2 in the bottom row indicates that it can produce 12 units of output.

Units of Capital (K)	1	2	3	4	5	6
6	24	35	42	47	51	54
5	23	32	39	44	48	51
4	20	28	35	40	44	47
3	17	24	30	35	39	42
2	14	19	24	28	32	35
→1	5	12	18	21	23	24

Units of Labor (L)

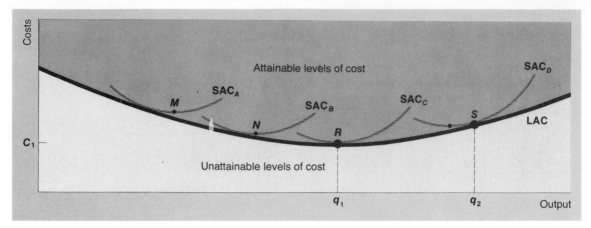

Figure 9-6
The long-run envelope cost curve
The SAC curves are the short-run average cost curves that apply if capital stock is fixed at various levels, *A, B,* etc. LAC is the long-run average cost curve that encloses all of them from below. It is the appropriate curve for a firm in its long run planning when it is free to select any quantity of capital. For example, to produce q_1, it would select capital stock *C*, thus operating on SAC_C at point *R* and keeping its average cost down to the lowest possible level (the height of *R*). Similarly, to produce q_2, it would select capital stock *D*, thus operating on SAC_D at point *S* and keeping its cost down to the lowest possible level at *S*.

average cost at which each output (such as q_1 or q_2) can be produced in the long run; that is, the period in which producers have the freedom to adjust their quantity of capital. Points in the light area below LAC cannot be achieved with present technology and with present factor prices. Points above LAC could be chosen. But a technically efficient firm rejects any such point in favor of a lower-cost point on the LAC. Note how LAC provides a summary of the relevant bits of information from each of the SAC curves. (Point *S* comes from one SAC curve, point *R* from another, and so on.)

Economies of scale

This concept is illustrated in the production function in Table 9-5. Suppose the firm doubles its labor force from 2 to 4 workers, and also doubles its capital from 2 to 4 units. As a result its output more than doubles, from 19 to 40; therefore it enjoys ***economies of scale.*** We emphasize that this is a long run phenomenon; it describes a firm that is able to increase its use of *all* factors of production.

Economies of scale **exist when an *x* percent increase in all inputs causes an increase of more than *x* percent in output.**

But in the short run, this firm may face diminishing returns. To illustrate, suppose it has 1 unit of capital, and is therefore confined to the

bottom row in the production function. As it doubles its labor force from 2 to 4, it does indeed encounter diminishing returns: The third worker has a marginal product of 6 units (18–12) while the fourth has a marginal product of 3 units (21–18).

Thus, a firm can face both economies of scale *and* diminishing returns. Although economies of scale are associated with falling costs, and diminishing returns with rising costs, they are not in contradiction. The reason is that the law of diminishing returns is a short-run concept that applies if one factor (capital) is held constant, while economies of scale is a long-run concept describing a situation where all factors are variable.

We can also illustrate the distinction between these two concepts in Figure 9-7, using

If You Have Had Trouble Drawing Curves in Economics, You Are Not Alone

The discerning reader will notice in Figure 9-6 that LAC touches the lowest short-run curve (SAC_C) at its minimum point. But it doesn't touch any other SAC curve at its minimum. For example, it touches SAC_A slightly to the left of its minimum point M.

This is such a subtle problem that it was missed by Jacob Viner, the economist who first developed the idea of the "envelope" curve. He asked his draftsman to draw an envelope curve to pass through the minimum point on each SAC curve. His draftsman knew that this couldn't be done, and said so. Viner insisted. So the draftsman presented him with a long-run curve which went through the minimum points on each SAC. But it clearly wasn't an envelope curve. (To confirm this, sketch a curve through the minimum points such as M and N, and you will see

that it is not the envelope curve LAC at all.) Viner permitted the erroneous diagram to appear in his article, complaining that his obstinate draftsman "saw some mathematical objection . . . which I could not succeed in understanding."[†]

There was a sequel. In the 1930s, Viner was unimpressed by Keynes' new theory of unemployment and income. On his arrival in North America, Keynes was asked to name the world's greatest living economist. He reportedly replied that modesty prevented him from naming the greatest, but the second greatest was surely Viner's draftsman. ∎

[†]Jacob Viner, "Cost Curves and Supply Curves," 1931; reprinted in George J. Stigler and Kenneth E. Boulding, *Readings in Price Theory* (Homewood, Ill.: Richard D. Irwin, 1952), p. 214.

the firm's cost curves. In the short run, with capital held constant, marginal costs must eventually rise, as shown by arrow f; the firm faces diminishing returns. But in the long run when all inputs can be increased, the firm moves along its LAC. For the firm shown here, the LAC curve slopes downward, and economies of scale exist.[3]

---

*[3]Although economies of scale are not formally defined in terms of a falling average cost curve, the two are closely related. To illustrate, suppose the firm in Table 9-5 purchases labor and capital at a fixed price, and the cost of buying two units of each happens to be $1,900. Since it produces 19 units, its average cost is $100. Now suppose it purchases twice as much labor and capital; its cost also doubles to $3,800. Since its output has more than doubled—to 40 units—its average cost is less than $100 a unit. As output increases, average cost falls.

In general, if the prices of inputs remain constant, economies of scale will result in a falling average cost curve. (If, however, the prices of inputs change, this simple relationship no longer holds.)

Figure 9-7

How a firm can face both economies of scale and diminishing returns

This firm faces diminishing returns, as shown by arrow f. (Its short-run marginal cost curve SMC_A rises because its capital stock is fixed at level A.) For this firm, there are also economies of scale, as shown by arrow e; its average cost LAC falls in the long run as it is able to increase its use of *all* factors.

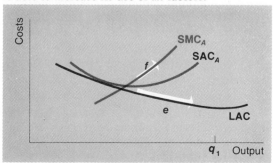

Thus we see once again that a firm can face both diminishing returns and economies of scale.

Returning to Figure 9-6, note that this firm continues to realize economies of scale until output reaches q_1, where the LAC reaches its minimum. This output where economies of scale are finally exhausted is larger in some industries than in others. For example, in autos, it is very large. Some estimates suggest this point is not reached until a firm is producing about 1 million automobiles per year.

Why do economies of scale exist? There are a number of reasons: Greater output means that workers can become adept at specialized tasks (like the workers in Adam Smith's pin factory). It also means that specialized machinery can be used in an assembly line operation. Greater output also means that large initial capital costs —such as the cost incurred by a telephone company in installing its lines, or the costs of a computer company in the research and development of a new product—can be spread over a greater volume of output; thus, the cost that must be attributed to each unit of output is reduced.

There are other reasons for economies of scale as well. With a greater output, a firm may be better able to use its talent. If a production line supervisor who can direct 20 workers is in charge of only 10, output and the number of workers employed can be doubled without requiring any more supervisors. In other words, as output doubles, this one important cost does not increase, so average cost tends to fall. Similarly, economies of scale may exist at the management level: The firm's executives may be able to handle more work and responsibility; as the firm grows and output increases, new managers are not required. Therefore, there is less management cost for each unit of output, and average costs tend to fall. Even if the firm has reached the point where doubling output does require twice as many managers, there may still be economies of scale if management is now able to specialize more. A person previously responsible for two areas of corporate planning may now need only be responsible for one. Management need no longer be "spread so thin," and consequently

may be able to do a better job.

With all these reasons for economies of scale, why are there ever **diseconomies of scale** (where LAC turns up, as it does at output q_1 in Figure 9-6)? The supervisor example provides a clue. Suppose output and employment, which have already doubled, now increase by another five times. In addition to the original supervisor, five new ones must now be hired. So far, it seems that average cost need not change, since there has been the same proportionate increase in both output and costs. But another person may now be required just to coordinate activities among the six supervisors. Thus as a company grows, new tiers of management may have to be created; and eventually a point is reached where management becomes unwieldy, and decision-making becomes too formal and slow;[4] there are just too many people between the vice president who makes the final production decisions and the workers on the line who carry them out. Consequently, average costs tend to increase.

The point where decision-making becomes unwieldy generally occurs much earlier in agriculture than in industry. Consequently, point R, where LAC begins to rise, is encountered at a relatively small output. One reason is that, on a relatively small farm, the owner-operator has the opportunity and incentive to make crucial decisions with great speed. If a ripe crop is threatened by a sudden turn in the weather, the farmer can drop everything and immediately harvest it. On the other hand, if this farm were part of a huge company, the crop could be lost

---

[4]General Motors' response to this problem of bureaucratic fossilization is an interesting one. It has been divided into several divisions: the Chevrolet division, Oldsmobile division, Cadillac division, and so on. Considerable independence is given to each division, and they are encouraged to compete with each other. The objective is to keep management sharp and responsive. In this way GM tries to avoid the disadvantages of bigness, while still enjoying its advantages. And for GM these advantages are substantial: It can capture economies of scale in R&D and production, because a new concept can be used by several divisions.

by the time decision-making worked its way through several echelons of management. (Nevertheless, farms reach their lowest cost at a much larger output now than they did several decades ago, in large part because of the development of new types of farm machinery.)

In our earlier discussion of the short run, we moved from short-run cost to short-run supply. Having looked at long-run cost, we now follow the same pattern and move on to long-run supply.

SUPPLY IN THE LONG RUN: THE PERFECTLY COMPETITIVE INDUSTRY

The discussion of long-run costs in the previous section was general, applying to firms in all types of markets (for example, monopoly or perfect competition). But when we come to drawing a supply curve, we focus on the perfectly competitive market.

The definition of perfect competition

We now require a more precise description of this form of market. So far we have only emphasized one of its characteristics.

1 *Each individual buyer and seller is a price taker.* That is, no firm can influence the price by deciding to increase or decrease its production; and no buyer can influence the price by deciding to increase or decrease purchases. Because each buyer and seller takes the market price as given, each concentrates on the *quantity* to buy or sell; there is no pricing decision for the individual market participant to make.

This first characteristic follows from two underlying assumptions:

a There are many buyers and sellers, with each buying or selling only a trivial fraction of the total market transactions.

b The product is standardized. For example, it doesn't matter to buyers whether they receive wheat produced in Minnesota or in Montana. (In contrast, hi-fi sets are not standardized. Therefore, this is not a perfectly competitive industry.)

In the study of the long run, another characteristic of a perfectly-competitive market should also be emphasized:

2 *An absence of barriers to entry;* that is, firms are *free to enter the industry.* An example of a barrier to entry has existed in the trucking industry: Truckers were required to have licenses, and the government granted new licenses only reluctantly. (Other examples of barriers to entry will be explained in later chapters.)

In a *perfectly competitive industry,* there are many buyers and sellers of a standardized product, with none having any influence over its price. And new firms are not prevented from entering the industry by barriers (such as government licensing).

Supply in the long run

Because long run supply is complicated by new firms coming into the industry (or old firms leaving) we must proceed in simple steps. Therefore, we first consider case A where: (1) all inputs are standardized (for example, all land is identical, all workers have the same skills, etc.); and (2) the industry is not very large in the economy, and, as a result, the expansion or contraction of this industry causes no change in input prices. As we shall see, the long-run supply curve of such an industry is perfectly elastic (horizontal).

Case A. Perfectly elastic long-run supply In Figure 9-8, we illustrate such an industry. In panel *b*, we assume that demand has been stable at D_1 for many years, and that the initial equilibrium E_1 is accordingly a long-run equilibrium, with 5,000 units being sold at price P_1.

Since we are assuming that all producers have access to identical factors (for example, all farm land is identical), all firms have the same cost curves. Figure 9-8a shows the costs of one of these firms—in particular, its short-run marginal cost or supply curve s_S. Suppose that, at initial price P_1, an individual firm produces 5 units, at point H (which corresponds to point R in Figure 9-6). Thus, there are 1,000 such firms

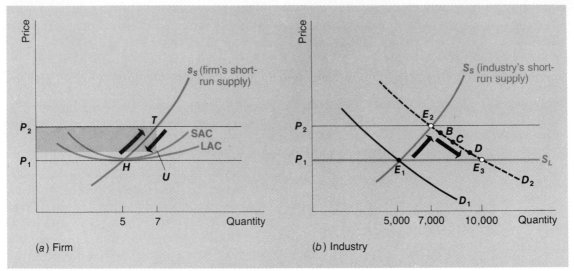

Figure 9-8
Long-run adjustment to an increase in demand

In this diagram, both the firm and the industry are initially at equilibrium at price P_1. The firm is at H, producing 5 units (left panel). The industry (right panel) is in equilibrium at E_1, with 5,000 units sold. (There are therefore 1,000 firms.) Now suppose that demand increases from D_1 to D_2. In the short run, the price rises to P_2, and firms in the left panel make gray-area profits because their selling price at T is greater than their average cost at U. New firms enter, supplying additional output. The price falls. In the long run, the price drops all the way back to P_1 at new equilibrium E_3. The individual firm in the left panel moves back to H; it no longer makes profits.

in the industry producing the initial total quantity of 5,000 units shown at E_1 in panel b. Because there are 1,000 such firms, the entire short-run supply for the industry S_S can be derived. At each price, the quantity supplied is found by multiplying the supply s_S of the individual firm by 1,000; in other words, the industry's short-run supply curve S_S in panel b is the horizontal sum of the 1,000 short-run supply curves of the individual firms.[5] Now consider what happens if demand increases to D_2.

[5] The argument is the same as we used in defining market demand by summing individual demands in Figure 8-1.

In the short run, the higher demand results in a new equilibrium in the right panel at E_2, with a higher price P_2. In the left panel, each firm moves up its short-run supply curve s_S to T, and makes a short-run profit equal to the shaded gray area: It makes a profit of TU on each of the seven units it produces. (This means an *above-normal* profit. Remember, normal profit is included in average cost.)

But this profit will attract new entrants. As new firms come in, more will be supplied in the right panel, and the price will begin to fall, first to B and then to C.

The new *long-run equilibrium* will not be reached until E_3; this means that the long-run supply curve S_L (which joins long-run equilibrium points like E_1 and E_3) is horizontal. Why is that? Because, according to our assumptions, new firms have access to the same quality factors of production, at stable prices. Therefore, new firms can enter with the same cost curves as existing firms. New firms continue to come into the industry as long as there are profits. Profits are not eliminated until the price falls back to P_1. At the new long run equilibrium E_3, 10,000 units are sold; there are 2,000 firms, each producing 5 units. (As the price drops back to P_1, each firm in panel a moves back down its supply curve s_S to point H, where it no longer makes a profit.)

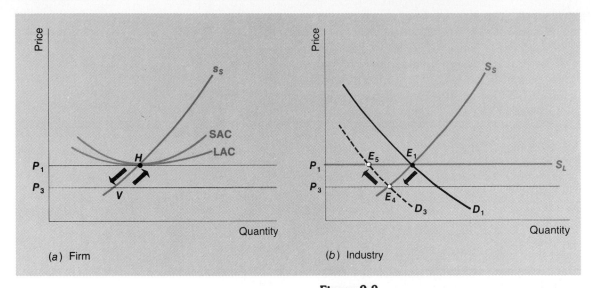

(a) Firm

(b) Industry

Figure 9-9
Long-run adjustment to a decrease in demand
In this diagram, the initial position is the same as in Figure 9-8. Now, however, demand decreases from D_1 to D_3. In the short run, the price falls to P_3, and firms (left panel) suffer losses. (The price is too low to cover average cost.) Some firms leave the industry, reducing the quantity of output in the right panel. The price recovers. In the long run, the price rises all the way back to P_1 at new equilibrium E_5. The individual firm which remains in the industry moves back up to H; it no longer suffers losses.

A similar argument applies if demand declines from D_1 to D_3, as shown in Figure 9-9. The industry in panel b moves to a new short-run equilibrium E_4, with price at the lower level P_3; individual firms in panel a move down their short-run supply curves from H to V. But the firms suffer losses there because the price is now less than average cost. Therefore, firms leave the industry. The quantity supplied decreases, and the industry moves gradually from short-run equilibrium E_4 to long-run equilibrium E_5. As price goes to P_1, the firms in panel a move up from V to H where they no longer incur a loss.

Note that the long-run supply curve S_L is much more elastic than the short-run supply curve S_S. Indeed, in this example, the long-run supply curve is perfectly elastic.

Case B. A rising long-run supply curve
Even in the long run, we would expect the supply curves of many industries to slope upward to the right. As an example, consider wheat, with the initial equilibrium E_1 in Figure 9-10. The long-run supply is not perfectly elastic, because all land is not the same quality (that is, land is not *homogeneous*). As more and more wheat is produced, farmers move to land which is less and less well suited for wheat, and they can produce on this land only at a cost

above P_1. In other words, new firms will be drawn into the industry only if the price remains above P_1. Thus, in the long run price will *not* fall back all the way to P_1; in our example, it falls back only to P_3.

To illustrate in more detail: In the short run, as demand increases from D_1 to D_2, equilibrium moves up the short-run supply S_S to E_2. At high price P_2, profits of existing firms encourage new firms to enter the industry. As in case A, the new entrants help to bring the price down—but only from P_2 to P_3. At P_3, the last firm to enter the industry is producing on relatively poor land, and is just able to cover its costs. With all the good land gone and only poor land remaining, there is no further incentive for firms to enter. Thus, the long-run supply curve S_L (joining long-run equilibrium points like E_1 and E_3) slopes upward. It is more elastic than the short-run supply curve S_S, but not perfectly elastic. (As the industry moves from E_1 to E_3, the adjustment of individual firms is explained in Appendix 9-B.)

Note that the height of the supply curve represents the *price required to draw additional resources into the industry*. For example, a price of P_3 is needed to draw enough resources into wheat to produce quantity Q_3. (In the previous case—of a horizontal long-run supply—no price increase was needed, because an unlimited supply of identical resources was available at constant costs.)

PRODUCER SURPLUS

Just as we examined how a price change will affect *consumer surplus* in the last chapter, we now consider how a price change affects producer surplus.

Figure 9-10
Long-run adjustment, with a rising supply curve

In this diagram, factors are not uniform in quality; some land is more suitable for growing wheat than other land. When demand increases from D_1 to D_2, the price rises to P_2 in the short run. The profits of existing producers encourages new entrants into the industry. And as new firms enter, the greater production of wheat causes the price to decline from P_2. However, it does not go all the way back down to P_1 because the new entrants are using land less well suited to wheat, and their costs are accordingly higher than P_1.

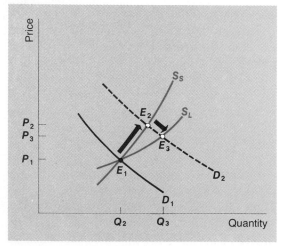

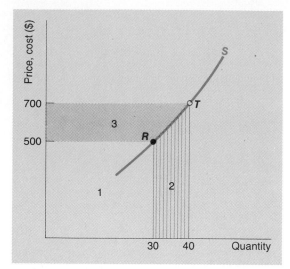

Figure 9-11
As price rises, producer surplus increases by the gray area

At initial price $500 and equilibrium R, 30 units are supplied for a total revenue of 30 × \$500 = \$15,000, shown as area 1. At a price of \$700, equilibrium moves from R to T and 40 units are sold, for a total revenue of \$28,000, or areas 1 + 2 + 3. Total revenue thus increases by area 2 + 3. But of this increase, area 2 represents opportunity costs of drawing new resources into the industry. Therefore, producer surplus has increased by area 3.

Consider what happens when the price rises from $500 to $700 in Figure 9-11. The equilibrium moves from R to T. And the total revenue of producers increases from area 1 to areas 1 + 2 + 3. In other words, factors of production receive additional revenues equal to areas 2 + 3. But of this increase, area 2 under the supply curve is a cost—specifically, an opportunity cost. (That is, it represents what is necessary to attract the additional factors of production into the industry.) That leaves factors of production with a net benefit—or increase in producer surplus—of area 3. Thus if the market price rises (falls), the increase (decrease) in producer surplus is estimated as the horizontal area between the old price and the new, and to the left of the supply curve.[6]

[6]In Appendix 9-C, we explain why this area is only an approximation of the increase in producer surplus, and not a precise measure.

This conclusion applies either in the long run or the short—depending on which supply curve we draw in Figure 9-11.[7] However, "who gets" the surplus can be quite different in the short run and the long. In the short run, we would expect the firms already in the industry to capture most—or perhaps all—of the producer surplus in the form of (above normal) profits. (It is such profits which attract new firms into the industry.)

In the long run, the producer surplus goes to factors like wheat land. As the price of wheat

rises and farmers are induced to produce on less and less suitable land, the rents on the more productive original wheat lands are bid up. Owners of these lands therefore get a windfall. In general, producer surplus goes to any factor or factors which are particularly suited to the good being produced. The prices of such factors are bid up as existing firms expand and new firms enter the industry.

Producer surplus **is any payment to factors of production in excess of their opportunity cost. (Whereas short-run producer surplus is likely to take the form of above-normal profit, long-run producer surplus goes to any factor of production—like, for example, high quality wheat land—that's particularly suited to the good being produced.)**

---

[7] It applies in the long run because, as we have just seen, the long-run supply curve represents opportunity costs (that is, what's required to draw additional resources into the industry). But the short-run supply curve likewise represents opportunity cost: The firm will be unwilling to supply one more unit of output unless the price covers the cost of attracting the variable inputs (labor, etc.) needed to produce that unit of output.

Key Points

1 The producer has a number of fundamental choices:

(a) Which good should be produced?

(b) How many units should be produced?

(c) What is the best combination of inputs to use?

2 In the short run, the firm cannot change the quantity of plant and equipment; it is committed by past decisions. Thus, the short-run decision is this: How many units should be produced, and how many workers are needed to produce this output? In the long run, the firm can change its capital stock, because all factors are variable.

3 The production function shows the maximum number of units of output which a firm can produce with various combinations of inputs.

4 To choose the profit-maximizing output, the firm takes three steps:

(a) It calculates its short-run production function.

(b) From its short-run production function, it calculates its costs—in particular its marginal costs MC.

(c) It calculates marginal revenue MR, and finds the output where MR = MC.

5 For a firm in perfect competition, the price is given; it is not affected by how much the firm decides to produce. For such a firm, P = MR.

6 Therefore, a firm in perfect competition maximizes profit where MC = MR = P (as shown in Figure 9-3).

7 A firm's short-run supply is determined by its short-run marginal cost curve, provided that the price is at least high enough to cover its short-run variable costs.

8 In measuring costs, economists use an "opportunity cost" definition. Thus, they include the explicit costs that accountants calculate, plus implicit costs, such as the normal profit on capital invested in the enterprise.

9 After all such opportunity costs have been covered, any remaining profit (that is, above-normal profit) provides an indication of how much more is being earned in this activity than in the next best alternative. If present firms are making such profits, resources tend to move into this industry. On the other hand, if present firms are not covering their opportunity costs (that is, if they are suffering an economic loss), resources tend to move out.

10 Long-run supply is more elastic than short-run supply.

11 If the long-run supply curve is rising, then an increase in demand results in a move to a higher-price equilibrium on the supply curve, and producer surplus increases. This change in producer surplus is represented by the area to the left of the supply curve between the old and the new price, in the same way as the change in consumer surplus in Chapter 8 was represented by the area to the left of the *demand* curve between the old and the new price.

Key Concepts

short run
long run
short-run production
   function
marginal product of labor
law of (eventually)
   diminishing returns
variable cost
marginal cost
fixed cost
total cost
average cost
average variable cost

average fixed cost
dependence of supply on
   marginal cost
marginal revenue
relationship of marginal
   cost to average cost
break-even point
shutdown point
economists' versus
   accountants' definition
   of cost
explicit versus implicit
   costs

opportunity cost
normal versus
   above-normal
   (economic) profit
long-run production
   function
envelope cost curve
economies of scale
short-run versus long-run
   supply
producer surplus
effect of a price change on
   producer surplus

Problems

9-1 "In the long run, all costs are variable." Do you agree? Explain, using machinery as an example of a cost that is fixed in the short run.

9-2 Recalculate Table 9-3 and find the profit-maximizing output for the firm if the price is:
   (a) $50
   (b) $30
   (c) $20

9-3 (a) Consider a firm operating at point R on the SAC and LAC curves in Figure 9-6. Does its short-run supply extend below R? If so, how far? If not, why not?

   (b) Suppose price falls below C_1. Explain how the firm (with the benefit of hindsight) would view its original decision to enter this industry. What would its output be in the short run, and in the long run? Is this another illustration of why supply is more elastic in the long run than in the short run?

9-4 "A firm that is facing diminishing returns (rising costs) cannot be facing economies of scale (falling costs)." Do you agree? Explain.

9-5 Explain why economists define costs to include normal profit. If additional profit exists, what does this tell us?

9-6 If a farmer in Kansas provides a statement of his costs to his income tax accountant, are there any opportunity costs he may miss? Explain.

9-7 Suppose the fixed cost of the firm in Table 9-2 is $10,000 instead of $35, while variable cost remains the same. What happens to MC? To AC? Does this support or refute our claim that "as fixed overhead costs increase in importance, AC tends to fall over a wider range of output"?

9-8 In Figure 9-8, the gray area measures the short-run profits which firms make as a result of an increase in demand. In Figure 9-9, demand decreases, and firms suffer short-run losses. However, the loss area was not shown in Figure 9-9. Sketch in this short-run loss area.

APPENDIX 9-A

THE FIRM'S PRODUCTION FUNCTION AND ITS CHOICE OF INPUTS

In this appendix we study in more detail a question posed at the beginning of the chapter: How does a firm decide which combination of inputs to use? For example, does it use a great deal of labor and little capital, or a great deal of capital and only a small amount of labor? Put this way, the decision applies to the long run (since it is only in the long run that the firm's capital can be changed); and the question is what point in its long-run production function (Table 9-5) is best. (But exactly the same type of decision is made in the short run when there are several variable inputs; for example, if the farmer is deciding on whether to use a lot of fertilizer and only a little labor, or vice versa.)

To decide what combination of inputs to use, the first step is to graph the production function.

Graphing the production function: Equal-output curves

First, note that several input combinations in Table 9-5 yield 24 units of output. These appear in red, and are reproduced to form the "output = 24" curve in Figure 9-12. Similarly, the "output = 35" curve is also extracted from Table 9-5. These equal-output (or in technical terms, iso-product) curves are very similar to the indifference (or equal-utility) curves in Figure 8-8. Just as the indifference map in that earlier diagram showed a whole family of indifference curves, each representing a higher level of utility as the household moved northeast from the origin, so the production function is a whole set of equal-output curves that also form a hill. As the firm moves to the northeast (using more inputs) it reaches higher and higher output levels. In one respect, however, the equal-output curves contain more information than indifference curves: Each equal-output curve represents a specific number of units of output (while all we know about indifference curves is whether they represent "higher" or "lower" levels of satisfaction).

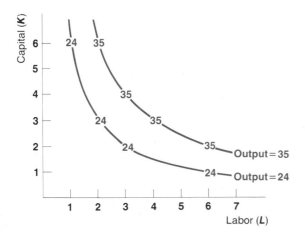

Figure 9-12
The production function in Table 9-5 graphed as a set of equal-output lines

To graph the production function, we extract the red numbers from Table 9-5. For example, each of the input combinations that yield 35 units of output in Table 9-5 is graphed in this diagram. When joined, they become the "output = 35" curve.

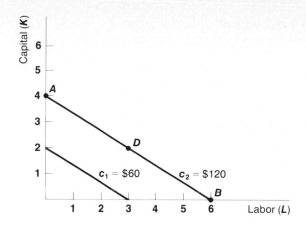

Figure 9-13
Equal-cost lines

If the price of labor is $20 per unit and the price of capital is $30, then c_2 is the equal-cost line that shows all combinations of these two inputs that can be purchased for $120. For example, combination D of 3 units of labor and 2 of capital costs 3($20) + 2($30) = $120; similarly, combination B costs 6($20) + 0($30) = $120. Parallel line c_1 is also an equal cost line, but it shows all input combinations that would cost $60. There is a whole family of similar parallel lines, each representing a different cost. If the price of labor relative to capital changes, then there is a whole new family of parallel lines with a different slope.

Graphing the price of inputs: Equal-cost lines

Maximizing profits requires not only the production function information we have just graphed, but also information on the price of inputs. How is this graphed? If the price of labor is $20 per unit, and the price of capital is $30, then straight line c_2 in Figure 9-13 is an *equal-cost line.* This shows all the combinations of labor and capital that can be purchased for a total cost of $120. (For example, this is the cost the firm will incur if it buys 4 units of $30 capital and no labor at point A. For more detail, see the caption to Figure 9-13.) Similarly, c_1 represents the input combinations that would cost the firm $60. Moreover, you can visualize a whole family of parallel lines showing successively higher costs for the firm as it moves to the northeast.

In Figure 9-14 we bring the previous two diagrams together. Curves q_1 and q_2 are from the firm's production function in Figure 9-12, while the solid straight lines are equal-cost lines from Figure 9-13. If the firm wishes to produce 24 units of output it will do so at least cost by using the input combination shown by E_2 (2 units of capital and 3 of labor). That is:

The firm selects the point on its equal-output curve that is tangent to an equal-cost line.

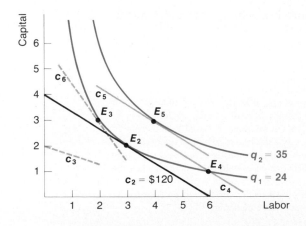

Figure 9-14
The firm's equilibrium is determined by its equal-output curves and its equal-cost lines

The least-cost way of producing 24 units of output is to select input combination E_2 where the equal-output and equal-cost lines are tangent. The firm then calculates its profit at E_2 by comparing its $120 cost with its revenue (24 units of output times whatever its selling price may be). Similarly, to produce 35 units of output, the firm selects tangency point E_5 and evaluates its profit there. Of these and similar tangency points, it selects the one with the greatest profit.

Any other way of producing this same output is rejected because it would be more costly. For example, the firm does not use input combination E_4 because this lies on higher cost line c_4.

Just as E_2 is the equilibrium for a firm wishing to produce $q_1 = 24$ units of output, E_5 is its equilibrium if it wishes to produce $q_2 = 35$ units of output. The final step for the firm is then to examine all equilibrium points such as E_2 and E_5 and select the one that will maximize its profits. This, then, is the way one can visualize the answer to our original question: "What point in Table 9-5 does the firm select to maximize its profit in the long run?"

The effect of a change in the price of inputs

If the relative price of labor and capital changes, there is a new family of equal-cost lines with a different slope. For example, if the price of capital rises from $30 to $60 while the price of labor is unchanged, you can confirm that flatter line c_3 is now the new $120 equal-cost line; and you can visualize the whole family of new equal-cost lines parallel to it. Thus,

The slope of the family of equal-cost lines depends on the relative price of the firm's inputs.

Thus, an equal-cost line for the firm is similar to a budget line for the consumer; its slope depends on the relative price of the items being purchased. Now let's suppose that capital has become *less* (rather than more) expensive relative to labor, and the equal-cost lines have therefore become steeper. Specifically, let's suppose the new set of equal-cost lines is C_6 and the family of lines parallel to it. To produce 24 units of output, the firm no longer uses input combination E_2. Instead it shifts to E_3, the point of tangency with one of its new equal-cost lines. This type of shift to the northwest will also occur along q_2 and all the other equal-output lines. Thus, no matter what its initial profit maximizing point, the firm moves northwest, substituting an input that has become relatively less expensive (capital) for the one that has become relatively more expensive (labor).[8]

Problem

9-9   With capital at $30 and labor at $20, how much less is the cost incurred by the firm that operates at E_2 rather than E_4 in Figure 9-14?

With capital at $20 and labor at $30, how much less is its cost if it operates at E_3 rather than E_2?   ∎

---

[8]Here is a real subtlety. Even though the change in relative price will put pressure on the firm to substitute capital for labor (the substitution effect) this does not guarantee that the firm will actually use less labor. To see why, suppose that the price of labor has remained unchanged, but the price of capital has fallen—and by enough to substantially reduce the firm's costs. This will encourage the firm to expand its output, in the process using more of *both* inputs. This is the cost reduction effect. If this effect is strong enough it may increase the firm's use of labor by more than the substitution effect decreases it; in such circumstances, the firm will employ more labor.

Note the similarity of the substitution and cost reduction effects in this production analysis to the substitution and income effects in the demand analysis in the Appendix to Chapter 8.

APPENDIX 9-B

LONG-RUN SUPPLY IN A PERFECTLY-COMPETITIVE INDUSTRY WITH NON-UNIFORM FACTORS OF PRODUCTION

The first three panels of Figure 9-15 display the long-run marginal cost curves of three wheat-producing firms. (For every long-run average cost curve—such as that shown in Figure 9-6—we may draw a corresponding marginal cost curve.) These three firms represent the large number which are either producing wheat, or are willing to start producing if the price rises high enough.

At price P_1, the only firm willing to produce wheat is firm A. It is the firm with the most suitable land for wheat, and is the only one which can produce with an average cost as low as P_1. Thus total industry supply in the last panel is just arrow f, the quantity supplied by firm A.

Price P_1 is not high enough to induce firms B and C to enter the industry. But suppose that the price rises. At P_2, industry supply is substantially augmented as firm B starts to produce and supplies the quantity indicated by arrow g. As price rises above P_2, market supply becomes the sum of the supply responses of firms A and B. (That is, it represents the horizontal sum of the long-run marginal costs for the firms which can cover their average costs.) Finally, at price P_3, firm C is just barely attracted into production, and market supply is shown by the three arrows representing the supplies of all three firms. Thus, the industry supply curve is the heavy line in the last panel, representing the horizontal sum of the supplies of the individual firms. It has an upward slope, because of differences in the quality of wheat land. ■

Figure 9-15
A rising long-run industry supply
At P_1, market supply is arrow f from firm A, the only firm producing at that low price. At P_2, A's supply is augmented by arrow g from firm B, since B is barely induced into production. (B cannot produce at average cost P_1 because it doesn't have as good land as firm A.) At price P_3, firm C also starts to produce (arrow k). Thus, at any price, industry supply S in the last panel is the horizontal sum of the supplies of all individual firms.

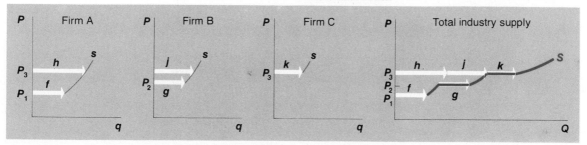

APPENDIX 9-C

INDUSTRY SUPPLY AND PRODUCER SURPLUS: SOME COMPLICATIONS

As we saw in this chapter, the long-run industry supply curve may slope upward because of different qualities of inputs (such as different qualities of wheat land). In this case, a rise in the price of the product results in an increase in producer surplus, which may be measured by the area to the left of the supply curve, and between the old and the new price. However, other forces may also affect the long-run slope of the supply curve, and these other forces make the area to the left of the supply curve a very imperfect measure of producer surplus. In this appendix, we consider several examples:

1 First, the long-run supply curve may slope upward even if all factors of production are of uniform quality (that is, they are homogeneous). Consider the supply of trucking services. As more and more trucks are operated, the roads may become congested. Trucks move more slowly, and the costs of the trucking companies rise on that account.

In this case, an increase in the demand for trucking may cause an increase in the long-run equilibrium price, *without any increase in producer surplus.* The higher price may not benefit *any* factor of production in the trucking industry; it may simply be dissipated in the higher costs resulting from road congestion.

2 Second, the long-run supply curve may slope downward even if all inputs are of uniform quality. Consider the case of a metal-fabricating industry made up of a number of competitive firms located in a small city near Chicago. As the industry grows, the costs facing each firm fall. This may occur, for example, because the supplier who is shipping unprocessed steel to this industry is now delivering to many more firms and is consequently able to reduce the charges to each. In other words, the supplier enjoys economies of scale, and passes part of the gains along to the firms using steel.

3 Finally, for an expanding industry there may be a combination of forces at work. For example, the long-run supply curve of the metal-fabricating industry may be horizontal because two sets of forces are balanced: The fall in the price of the unprocessed steel it is buying may be offset by the rise in the rents it has to pay on land which is increasingly in demand. In this case, an increase in output will be associated with an increase in producer surplus (the owners of land gain). But the horizontal supply curve would erroneously suggest that there is no producer surplus as a result of more production.

Thus, we illustrate the point made earlier in this chapter: The supply curve may be used only as a first approximation in calculating producer surplus. The area to the left of the supply curve may exaggerate producer surplus (case 1). Or producer surplus may occur, even when there is no corresponding area to the left of the supply curve (case 3). ∎

CHAPTER 10
Perfect Competition and Economic Efficiency

Under perfect competition, the business dodoes, dinosaurs and great ground sloths are in for a bad time—as they should be.

R. H. Bork and W. S. Bowman, Jr.

In the last chapter, we examined how perfectly competitive producers respond to the market price which they face. We now move from **describing the behavior** of firms in a perfectly competitive market to **evaluating the performance** of a perfectly competitive market from the point of view of society as a whole. We shall see that, under certain conditions, a perfectly competitive market provides a socially efficient result: Neither too much nor too little output is produced. In future chapters, we shall see why other market structures typically are *not* efficient. (For example, we shall see in the next chapter that monopoly is not efficient: Too little output is produced.)

PERFECT COMPETITION AND EFFICIENCY

We begin by concentrating on **allocative efficiency:** Is the right quantity of each good being produced? As we shall see, perfect competition provides allocative efficiency—*provided* two important assumptions are satisfied.

Two key assumptions
Thus far, we have made no distinction between the benefit a good provides to those who buy it

(its *private benefit* or private utility), and the benefit it provides to society as a whole (its *social benefit*). Often the two are the same. For example, the benefit to society of beefsteak is the benefit enjoyed by those who buy it and eat it; those who don't eat it don't enjoy it. But private and social benefit don't always coincide in this way. For example, the benefit to society of services provided by professional gardeners may include not only the satisfaction enjoyed by those who buy these services, but also the satisfaction of other individuals in the neighborhood.

But for now, we assume away this complication. We assume that the purchaser gets all the benefit from the good; the benefit received by the purchaser represents the total benefit to society. Thus:

Assumption 1. Social benefit is the same as private benefit. More precisely, the marginal benefit of a good to society as a whole (which we shall call MU_S) is the same as its marginal benefit (marginal utility) to those who buy it (MU). Therefore, the demand curve provides a measure both of private benefit and benefit to society.

$$MU_S = MU \qquad (10\text{-}1)$$

We make a similar assumption about cost:

Assumption 2. Social cost is the same as the private cost of producers. More precisely, the marginal cost of a good to society as a whole (MC_S) is the same as its marginal cost to producers (MC). Either can be read off the supply curve.

$$MC = MC_S \qquad (10\text{-}2)$$

Again this is often true: For example, the cost to society of producing wheat is generally just the cost incurred by wheat farmers. But again there are exceptions: The cost to society of paper may not only be the private cost incurred by the firm producing it, but also the cost to people downstream who suffer if the paper mill dumps polluting wastes into a river.

Such exceptions to these two assumptions are clearly important, and will be studied in Chapters 14 and 15. But for the moment we limit ourselves to the large number of cases where these assumptions are reasonably valid.

The idea of efficiency

In the previous two chapters, we have seen how the individual consumer picks the best quantity to buy, and how the individual producer picks the best quantity to sell. In either case, the activity is expanded until *its marginal cost equals its marginal benefit*. This principle is so fundamental in economics that it is not only the acid test of whether individuals (like consumers and producers) are operating at the level which is best for them. It is also the test of whether or not the economy as a whole is operating efficiently. In fact, the idea of efficiency in economics is based on precisely this concept:

Efficiency requires that an activity be run at a level where its marginal cost equals its marginal benefit.

If this condition is not met, a better solution can be found by either expanding or contracting this activity until its marginal cost *does* equal its marginal benefit. In other words, if this condition is not met, there is an efficiency loss.

Why the perfectly competitive market is efficient

Figure 10-1 illustrates how the decisions of many consumers and many producers in a perfectly competitive market lead to allocative efficiency. Note in the middle panel that supply and demand are equal at an equilibrium output of 100 units and a $10 price. At this equilibrium, the quantities purchased by individual consumers are shown in the panels on the left, while the quantities sold by individual producers are shown in the panels on the right. (Just as in Figure 8-1, we use only a few consumers to represent the very large number who participate in this market, and we do the same for producers.)

Consider the situation of an individual consumer in perfect competition. His marginal cost is the amount paid for one additional unit—that is, the price. As we saw in Chapter 8, he will consume up to the point where his marginal utility equals price; in other words, where his marginal benefit equals his marginal cost.

Moreover, in Chapter 9 we saw that the individual firm also equates its marginal cost and marginal benefit—with marginal benefit (marginal revenue) for a perfectly competitive firm being the price.

Thus, in a competitive market:

Consumers purchase until	$MU = P$	**(10-3)**
Firms produce until	$P = MC$	**(10-4)**
Therefore,	$MU = MC$	**(10-5)**

These three equations are illustrated in the three panels of Figure 10-2. Note especially that benefits are equal to costs at the margin in panel *c*, suggesting an efficient outcome. In fact, all that is necessary to ensure this is to add the two assumptions made in the previous section—that private and social evaluations are the same on both the benefit and the cost side. Then it follows from statement (10-5) above that, in a perfectly competitive market,

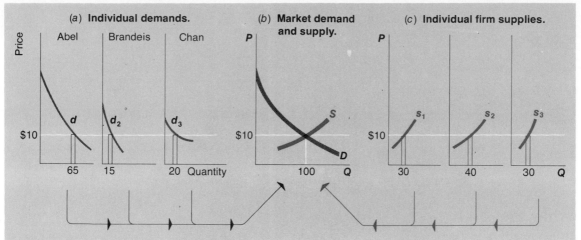

Figure 10-1
Individual consumers and producers in a perfectly competitive market
In panel *b*, market demand *D* reflects the individual demands in panel *a*, while market supply *S* reflects the supplies of individual firms in panel *c*. The perfectly competitive solution, where *S* and *D* intersect, is at a price of $10 and an output of 100 units. The bars in panel *a* show how each consumer continues to purchase until marginal utility MU equals the $10 price; and the bars in panel *c* show how each firm produces to the point where its marginal cost MC is equal to this $10 price. Since each consumer's MU is therefore equal to each producer's MC, any change in production or consumption would result in an efficiency loss.

$$\text{MU}_S = \text{MC}_S \qquad (10\text{-}6)$$

That is,

Marginal social benefit = marginal social cost

We do indeed have an efficient outcome from the point of view of society as a whole.

If private benefits are equal to social benefits, and private costs are equal to social costs, then the perfectly competitive equilibrium is efficient from an overall social point of view.

This proposition is so important that it is emphasized in Box 10-1.

Nonefficient quantities of output

To confirm that the perfectly competitive market is efficient, subject to the conditions we have specified, let us return to the competitive equilibrium of Figure 10-1. Suppose you are an all-powerful bureaucrat or czar and think you can improve on this competitive equilibrium. Specifically, suppose that you arbitrarily order that, instead of the equilibrium quantity of 100 units, 40 more units are to be produced and consumed. Try as you like, you cannot avoid a social loss on those additional units. On the one hand, they must cost more than $10; regardless of the firm (or firms) you select to produce them, that firm will have to move *up* its supply curve to a higher marginal cost. At the same time, those additional units will be consumed by individuals who value them at less than $10; regardless of whom you may select to consume them, those individuals will move further *down* their demand curves to the right, to a lower marginal utility. With the cost of each additional unit greater than $10, and the benefit it provides less than $10, there is a net social loss; that is, an efficiency loss. You thought you could do better; in fact, you did worse.

We can arrive at exactly the same conclusion using only the market supply and demand curves in the center panel of Figure 10-1, as

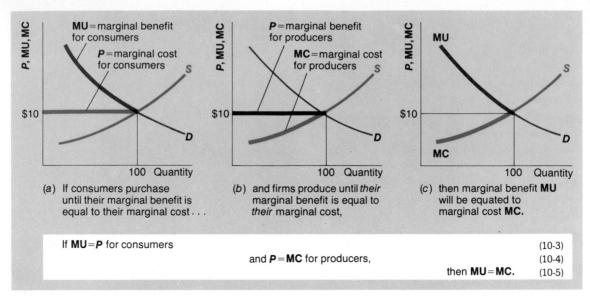

Figure 10-2
The competitive market: The equalization of marginal utility and marginal cost. (An elaboration of Figure 10-1b)

BOX 10-1
Conditions That Provide an Efficient Solution

Since MU and MC represent marginal private benefits and costs, and MU_S and MC_S represent marginal social benefits and costs, then:

If social and private benefits are the same,	$MU_S = MU$	(10-1)
and if consumers in a perfectly competitive market pick the quantity where marginal utility equals price,	$MU = P$	(10-3)
and if producers in a perfectly competitive market pick the output where marginal cost equals price,	$P = MC$	(10-4)
and if private and social costs are the same,	$MC = MC_S$	(10-2)
then Adam Smith's "invisible hand" works; the pursuit of private benefit results in benefit to society as a whole.	$MU_S \quad = \quad MC_S$	(10-6)

That is, there is a socially efficient solution. ■

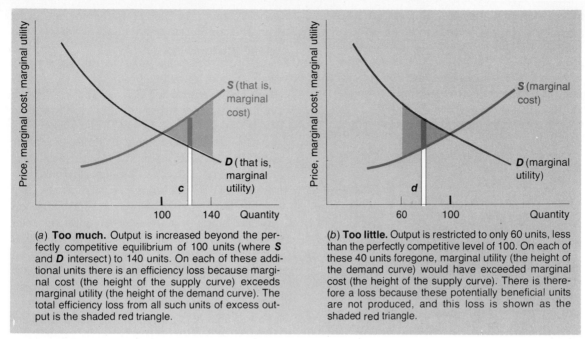

(a) **Too much.** Output is increased beyond the perfectly competitive equilibrium of 100 units (where **S** and **D** intersect) to 140 units. On each of these additional units there is an efficiency loss because marginal cost (the height of the supply curve) exceeds marginal utility (the height of the demand curve). The total efficiency loss from all such units of excess output is the shaded red triangle.

(b) **Too little.** Output is restricted to only 60 units, less than the perfectly competitive level of 100. On each of these 40 units foregone, marginal utility (the height of the demand curve) would have exceeded marginal cost (the height of the supply curve). There is therefore a loss because these potentially beneficial units are not produced, and this loss is shown as the shaded red triangle.

Figure 10-3
Inefficient quantities of output

reproduced in Figure 10-3. Again suppose output is expanded beyond the efficient, competitive quantity of 100 to the 140 units shown in panel *a*. To show the efficiency loss that results, consider a single unit, *c*, of this additional output. Its benefit to the consumer is shown by the white bar (the height of the demand curve); but its cost is even larger, as shown by both the white bar and the red bar (the height of the supply curve). Thus the net loss on this unit is the red bar. The sum of all similar losses on all the other excess units of output in the range between 100 and 140 is shown by the red triangle. This area is shaded red to represent losses, in contrast to gains which appear in black or gray.

On the other hand, suppose that for some reason output is less than the efficient quantity of 100 units—say, the 60 units shown in panel *b* of this diagram. To show the efficiency loss that results, consider one of the units that is no longer

produced, say *d*. Since its cost would have been the white bar (under the supply curve) and its benefit the white bar *plus* the red bar (the height of the demand curve), the net benefit to society of producing it would have been the red bar. Or to put the same point another way, society incurs the loss of this red bar because this potentially beneficial unit is not produced. And the sum of all such losses through the range of restricted output from 100 down to 60 is the red triangle. An illustration of a market in which too little is produced is provided by the rent control program described earlier in Box 4-1. When the government sets a low price, suppliers provide less than the equilibrium quantity, and the decline in quantity involves an efficiency loss similar to the one shown in Figure 10-3b.

This idea of an efficiency loss (sometimes called a deadweight loss) is so important to the study of microeconomics that you should be sure you have mastered Figure 10-3 before proceeding. In particular, we emphasize:

An *efficiency loss* occurs whenever there is a move away from the output where the marginal benefit (to society) is equal to the marginal cost (to society).

(A further discussion of efficiency is provided in Box 10-2 and in the appendix to this chapter.)

FREE ENTRY AND ECONOMIC EFFICIENCY

This conclusion—that a perfectly competitive market is efficient—depends on the absence of barriers to entry of new firms. To see why inefficiency may result if there are barriers to entry, consider the following example: Suppose that the third firm in Figure 10-1 has been blocked out of this market for some reason. (Suppose it's a firm that needs a government license, and it has been turned down.) Because its supply s_3 would not exist, total market supply in the center panel would be less, that is, lie to the left of S. The equilibrium output where this new supply intersects D would be less than the efficient quantity of 100. Potentially beneficial units of output would not be produced, because this third firm would have been unable to enter this market and produce them.

OTHER CONCEPTS OF EFFICIENCY

Thus far we have only shown how a perfectly competitive market can provide **allocative efficiency.** How does this market measure up in **technical efficiency**? Remember from Chapter 1 that technical inefficiency occurs when sloppy management results in high costs, that is, when firms produce at some point above their average cost curve rather than on it. (Recall from Figure 9-5 that the average cost curve represents the lowest costs with existing technology and existing factor prices.) The issue of technical efficiency is obviously important, even though economists often concentrate on the concept of allocative efficiency.

Perfect competition—with no barriers to entry—works toward technical efficiency as well as allocative efficiency. The fact that new firms can enter the industry puts pressure on existing firms to produce on their technically efficient AC curves or get out of business: If competitive firms don't adapt new technology and pick their lowest-cost combination of inputs, they may go the way of the dinosaurs. (Note in Figure 9-9 how perfect competition also puts pressure on firms to produce at the lowest point on their average cost curves. In that figure, the firms that survive in the long run all produce at the lowest point, H. This is also true of the firms in Figure 9-8.) In contrast to the firm in perfect competition, a monopoly firm may be protected from the pressures of competition. If it has a stranglehold on a market (because of a patent, for example), it can survive even if management is sloppy. (However, monopoly still does have an incentive to achieve technical efficiency; greater technical efficiency means greater profits. Therefore, in later chapters we will show monopoly firms producing on their technically efficient average cost curves.)

While a competitive market gets high marks for promoting allocative efficiency and technical efficiency, its superiority is less clear in a third kind of efficiency: **dynamic efficiency.** This term is hard to define, but it is applied to a market that encourages rapid innovation in the form of new products and new cost-cutting techniques. As we shall see in Chapter 13, there is considerable debate over whether or not some other forms of market are superior to perfect competition in this respect. (One argument is that large firms are the only ones able to finance the research necessary for many innovations.)

In conclusion, the competitive market scores high in two of the three aspects of efficiency. It is the first of these concepts—allocative efficiency—which will be the focus in the next few chapters. When you are considering whether some market is efficient or not, your first question should be: Are marginal benefits equal to marginal costs? Look at what's happening *at the margin.* (But Box 10-3 on page 201 shows why what's happening at the margin is not the last word.)

THE MARKET PRICE AS A SCREENING DEVICE

Every economy must have some device to determine who will consume a scarce good and who will not. In our economy, market price plays that role by acting as a barrier that must be overcome by buyers. In panel *a* of Figure 10-4, we see a competitive market in which 1,000 units are sold at a $15 price. In panel *b,* we see that this price has blocked out all potential consumers except those prepared to pay at least $15. In panel *c,* we see that this same $15 price also acts as a barrier to potential sellers, blocking out all but the lowest-cost producers. Unenthusiastic buyers and high-cost sellers are turned back, excluded from the market because of one simple criterion—they are unwilling or unable to meet the market price.

PREVIEW: PROBLEMS WITH THE COMPETITIVE MARKET

Thus far, we have provided a very rosy picture of how well perfectly competitive markets work. The examples of inefficient outcomes occurred when the government intervened to overrule the workings of a competitive market. When the government czar dictated output, too much was produced. And when the government set a rent ceiling, too little housing was produced. Indeed, up to this point, the analysis has had a very strong laissez faire message: The government should leave the market alone, its wonders to perform.

But this gives a distorted view of the American economy. In particular, for the free market to result in an efficient outcome, all four basic conditions listed in Table 10-1 must be met.

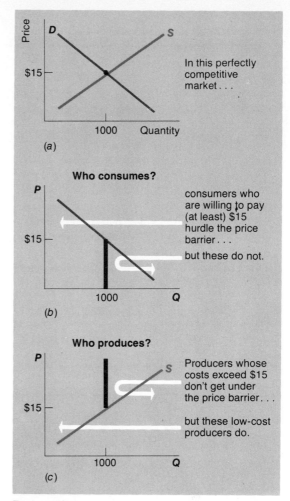

Figure 10-4
Price as a barrier that screens buyers and sellers in a competitive market

But, in practice, these conditions may be violated. (Table 10-1 shows how they may be violated, and the chapters that deal with each case.) When they are violated, the economy will operate inefficiently if it's left alone. Government intervention may make the economy work more efficiently, not less. Furthermore, *even when all four conditions are met,* the outcome will not necessarily be quite as good as this chapter has so far suggested, as we shall now see.

Table 10-1
How Four Basic Conditions Can Be Violated

	Condition	Will be violated if:	Considered in Chapter(s):
(10-1)	$MU_S = MU$	There are benefits to others than purchasers (neighbors enjoy a well-kept garden, for example)	15
(10-2)	$MC = MC_S$	There is pollution or other costs not borne by producers	14
(10-3)	$MU = P$	A single buyer has some influence over price (as may occur if there are only a few buyers)	19
(10-4)	$P = MC$	A single seller has some influence over price (as may occur if there are only a few sellers)	11, 12

BOX 10-2

Pareto and the Elimination of Deadweight Loss

With a bit of extra effort, we can increase our understanding of the important idea of efficiency.

A change that will make one individual better off without hurting anyone else is called a *Pareto-improvement*, named after the Italian economist Vilfredo Pareto who first developed this idea. If we have made all such Pareto-improvements, we arrive at a Pareto-optimum. This is exactly what economists mean by an efficient solution. It means that all deadweight losses have been eliminated, that is, all possible Pareto-improvements have been made.

The idea of a Pareto-improvement can be illustrated in Figure 10-1. Suppose that initially Brandeis has 1 less unit of output than we have shown there (namely, 14 units), while Chan has 1 more (21). A Pareto-improvement is now possible because we can make Chan better off without hurting anyone else (that is, without hurting Brandeis, the only other person who will

be involved). Here is how: Let Chan sell that 1 unit to Brandeis for $10. Chan benefits from this transaction. (Because he values his twentieth unit of $10, he values his twenty-first unit—the one he is giving up—at less than $10. So he benefits when he receives $10 for it.) At the same time, Brandeis has not been hurt because he values the unit he receives (his fifteenth) at exactly the same $10 that he pays for it.

This Pareto-improvement is possible because, initially, all producers and consumers did not value their last unit equally. But with this transaction, we have reached the perfectly competitive solution in Figure 10-1, where all consumers and producers *do* value their last unit equally (at $10). That is, the MU for all consumers is equal to the MC for all producers. So any further Pareto-improvement is impossible. Therefore this perfectly competitive solution is Pareto-optimal (that is, efficient). ∎

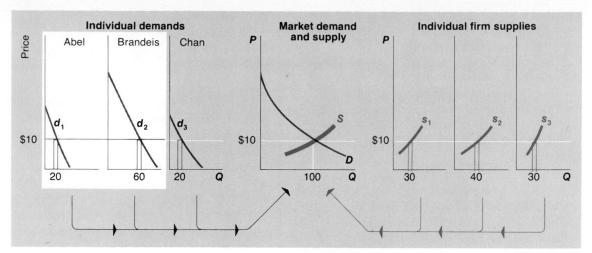

Figure 10-5
Another efficient, perfectly competitive solution
This figure is similar to Figure 10-1, except that Brandeis now has a greater income and demand than Abel and consequently consumes the greater quantity (60 units). This diagram also shows a perfectly competitive solution just as the one in Figure 10-1 does. Both are efficient, but which is better? The individuals concerned will have conflicting views. Abel prefers Figure 10-1 and Brandeis prefers Figure 10-5. But an economist examining this from the point of view of society as a whole cannot judge, because it is impossible to compare Brandeis' utility gain in moving from Figure 10-1 to Figure 10-5 with Abel's utility loss.

A RESERVATION ABOUT THE PERFECTLY COMPETITIVE SOLUTION: IT DEPENDS ON THE DISTRIBUTION OF INCOME

Returning to Figure 10-1, suppose that Abel has a higher income than Brandeis, and this is why he has the greater demand for this good. (Remember, demand depends both on desire for the product *and* ability to pay.) In Figure 10-5 we reproduce Figure 10-1, making only one single change: We suppose that the incomes of Abel and Brandeis are reversed. Brandeis now has the higher income and hence the higher demand, while Abel has the lower income and the lower demand, as shown in the white section. (Since nothing else need change,[1] the rest of Figure 10-5 has a shaded background.) In this diagram, just as in Figure 10-1, a perfectly competitive market yields an efficient solution. But it is a quite different solution. There is no way that economists can judge which of the two

solutions is better. All we can say is that both are efficient.

Abel and Brandeis, of course, will each have a clear opinion on which is better: Abel prefers Figure 10-1, where he gets most of this good (65 units), while Brandeis will prefer Figure 10-5, where *he* gets the lion's share. But from the overall point of view of society as a whole, there is no way to judge. True, if we could meter the heads of these two individuals and thus be able to say that, in moving from Figure 10-1 to Figure 10-5, Brandeis's utility gain exceeds Abel's utility loss, we might judge the pattern in Figure 10-5 superior. But this we cannot do, since *there*

---

[1]Market price need not be exactly the same $10 as in Figure 10-1; but this is an unimportant detail that does not affect the argument.

is no known way of comparing the utility of one person with the utility of someone .else.

To sum up: For each possible distribution of income, there is a different perfectly competitive solution. Each of these solutions is efficient; but we cannot demonstrate that one is better than the rest. The question of how income should be distributed is one that economists cannot answer (although we will throw more light on it in Chapter 23).

*ANOTHER RESERVATION: WHEN A COMPETITIVE MARKET PROVIDES MISLEADING SIGNALS

We have now dealt with the basic features of perfectly competitive markets. But there are a number of additional complications. For example, prices act as signals to which both consumers and producers react; but what happens if producers get the wrong message?

To illustrate this problem, recall from Figure 7-7 how a small shift in the supply of an agricultural product (perhaps because of crop failure or disease in a herd) will result in a substantial change in price. This instability may be compounded by the fact that there is typically a time lag (delay) between the decision to produce an agricultural good and its eventual delivery to the market. For example, wheat must be planted in the fall or spring for harvest in the summer; and the decision to breed cattle is often made several years before the beef is eventually sold.

In this situation, an initial disturbance may set off a cycle of price fluctuations, with price high one year, low the next, high the next, and so on. The idea is a simple one (and can be understood without necessarily consulting its detailed exposition in Box 10-4). Suppose that

*Note to instructors: In a short course, starred sections may be omitted without loss of continuity.

BOX 10-3

The Paradox of Value:

In *The Wealth of Nations,* Adam Smith presented a puzzle. One of the most valuable commodities is water; we simply cannot do without it. If necessary, we would be prepared to sell everything we own to acquire it. In contrast, we could easily do without diamonds or champagne. Yet water sells for a low price, while champagne sells for a high price. Is the world upside down?

This paradox is resolved in Figure 10-6. In the case of water, demand and supply result in a low price, P_W. True, demand for water is very great; but it is so plentiful (it can be supplied at such a low price) that we consume large quantities: We often use it to water the lawn or wash the car. At equilibrium E we consume gallons of water on which we place a low value, that is, a low marginal utility. (Remember that marginal utility is given by the height of the demand curve, and at equilibrium E this is only Q_1E.)

On the other hand, in the case of champagne, demand and supply result in a high price. True, the demand for champagne is not great. But it sells at a high price because its supply is limited by its high cost of production. Consequently, only the most enthusiastic buyers consume it, and on the last unit they consume, they enjoy a marginal utility of P_C. We conclude that the higher price of champagne is telling us that, *at the margin*—where we look at only the last unit consumed—*champagne has higher value* (higher marginal utility) *than water.*

But this is obviously only part of the story. The *total* value of water to society is our valuation, not just of the last glass we drink, but of *every* glass we drink, and the ones that keep us from dying of thirst are very valuable indeed. In fact, our valuation of one of those first glasses of water, say at Q_2, is extremely high; it is given by the height of the demand curve at Q_2 and we don't have enough room at the top of the dia-

What Happens at the Margin Is Not the Whole Story

gram to show this. But the same is not true of champagne; the utility from the very first glass of champagne *can* be shown in Figure 10-6. The total value to society is the utility we receive from *all the units we consume.* Thus we conclude that, *overall,* water is more valuable to us than champagne, even though its price is lower (its value *at the margin* is less). The paradox is resolved.

This water/champagne paradox should be kept in mind as we evaluate the efficiency of markets by concentrating on what's happening at the margin. We should remember that the units *before* we get to the margin may also be very important. ◼

Figure 10-6
How can the price of water be so low and the price of champagne so high?
In panel *a, D* and *S* result in equilibrium at *E,* with low price P_W and low marginal utility of water $Q_1E = P_W$. On the other hand, in panel *b,* the high cost of supplying champagne means that its price is at the much higher level P_C and its marginal utility is also at this higher level. If we view *only the last unit consumed,* champagne is more valuable than water. But when we consider *all units consumed,* our conclusion is reversed. For example, the glass of water at Q_2 that is drunk by someone almost dying of thirst has an enormous value. (The demand curve above Q_2 is so high it can't even be shown in this diagram.) All units of water, including those at the margin and those inside the margin, provide us with far more utility than all the units of champagne. In this sense, water is far more valuable.

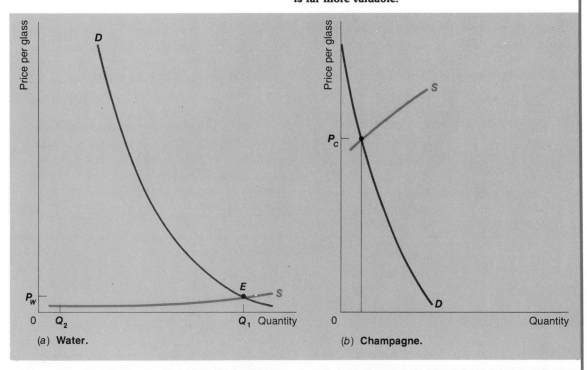

(a) **Water.**

(b) **Champagne.**

BOX 10-4

The Cobweb Cycle

Suppose that equilibrium has traditionally been at E, where long-run supply S and demand D intersect. If there is no shock to this system, price will continue at P, with production at Q. But now suppose that in the initial period some disturbance (perhaps a disease) reduces the total number of hogs marketed to Q_1. Also suppose that no more hogs can be produced for a year, so that the immediate supply is inelastic at quantity Q_1. In other words, immediate supply can be visualized as the tall arrow running vertically up from Q_1 and intersecting demand at the equilibrium point E_1. As a result, price is at the high level P_1.

In this initial year, farmers must decide on how many hogs to produce for the next year. Facing the very favorable price P_1, they respond by moving to point G on their supply curve, thus producing quantity Q_2. But when this large quantity comes on the market in the second year, the completely inelastic immediate supply (shown by the arrow pointing down toward Q_2) now results in a new equilibrium E_2, with low price P_2.

Of course, in this second year, farmers must decide what to produce for the third year. Facing low price P_2, they respond by selecting point H on their supply curve. But when this small quantity Q_3 is eventually produced and comes on the market in the third year, it results in an equilibrium at E_3, with price at the relatively high level P_3. Price, production, and consumption continue to bounce back and forth until the system again settles down to a long-run equilibrium at E.

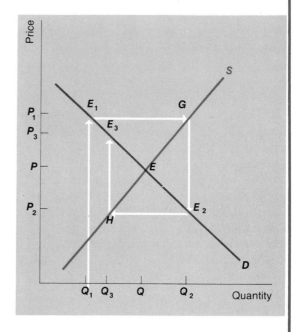

But things could be even worse. We leave you to confirm (Problem 10-6) that if supply S is elastic enough (and/or demand D is inelastic enough), the cycle will not converge to E, but instead will "explode," with price fluctuations becoming larger and larger.

The cobweb example provides a good illustration of a *dynamic problem;* that is, a problem in which *time must explicitly be taken into account.* Specifically, supply has a dynamic (time) element, since next year's supply depends on this year's price. ■

---

because of some initial disturbance, the price of hogs is unusually high. As a consequence, farmers expand hog production. When these hogs come to market at a later date, the result will be an oversupply, and the price will fall. In turn, the depressed price will induce farmers to switch out

of hogs, and this shift will lead in the next period to a shortage, raising the price up again to an abnormally high level. Thus the cycle continues as long as producers misread the market price signals and erroneously use today's price in making their production decisions. Even though this market is perfectly competitive, it follows a cyclical (cobweb) pattern and therefore does not work well. (The reason it is called a cobweb cycle will be readily apparent from a glance at the diagram in Box 10-4. The losses that result from this cobweb pattern are detailed in the next section.)

*SPECULATION AND PRICE INSTABILITY

There are several ways in which a cobweb cycle may be broken. First, after perhaps two or three dramatic price changes, farmers may recognize what is happening and accordingly stop making the erroneous assumption that today's price provides a good prediction of tomorrow's price. (Indeed, theoreticians who argue that there may be severe, continuing "cobweb" fluctuations have been criticized on the ground that they assume that farmers never learn.) The second possibility is that someone else recognizes this cobweb pattern and takes action that is not only personally profitable, but that also modifies the cycle and thus benefits society as a whole.

Speculation as a stabilizing influence
To illustrate how speculation works, suppose that price in a hog cycle has risen in the first year and fallen in the second. Now a bright individual suddenly realizes, "I've seen this happen before. This is that hog cycle again. Because price is low this year, a lot of farmers will be getting out of pork, and the price will be going up next year. I'm going to buy some of this year's cheap pork, refrigerate it, and sell it next year."

This will be a profitable venture (if the costs of storage, etc., are not too high), since the individual has discovered a way of putting into practice the advice any stockbroker will give: Buy cheap and sell dear. But this action not only benefits the purchaser; it also moderates the cycle. Why? The purchase of pork when it is cheap creates an additional demand that prevents its price from falling quite so far. And when pork is sold later at a high price, the additional supply prevents the price from rising quite so far. Thus the cycle is moderated by **speculation**.

Speculation is the purchase of an item in the hope of making a profit from a rise in its price (or the sale of an item in the expectation that its price will fall).

Basically, the case for speculation is as simple as that. But to nail it down more precisely, consider how the stabilization of price is beneficial from the point of view of society as a whole. Specifically, imagine the instance where not one, but many, speculators store pork in year 2 when price is low for sale in year 3 when it is high.

Panel a of Figure 10-7 shows the demand curve for pork, reproduced from Box 10-4. Year 2 is illustrated: In the absence of speculation, equilibrium is at E_2, with large output Q_2 and therefore low price P_2. Panel b shows year 3, with the same demand curve, but with smaller production Q_3. In the absence of speculation, equilibrium is at E_3, and the price is a high P_3. Now consider the behavior of speculators. In year 2 (panel a) they buy $Q'_2 Q_2$ units when the price is low, store them and sell them in year 3 when the price is high. In year 2 their purchases reduce the available supply from Q_2 to Q'_2. Therefore price rises from P_2 to P'_2. And their sale in year 3 increases the supply in that year, lowering the price from P_3 to P'_3. The cyclical swing in price has been almost eliminated: P'_3 is almost as low as P'_2. The only difference in the two is a margin of profit to compensate speculators for their storage and interest costs—and for the risk they have to run in a situation in which a wrong guess can cost them dearly. (The necessity of earning a profit also explains why they stop speculating when they do; any more speculation would further reduce the price difference in the two years and thus no longer leave them with an adequate profit.)

But this sort of speculation is not only profitable for speculators; it is also beneficial for society as a whole. True, reduced consumption in year 2 has reduced utility then, as shown by the red area in panel a; but there has been an even greater gray increase in utility in panel b, because of the increase in consumption in year 3. The reason for this difference is that units are being withdrawn from a "relatively sated" public

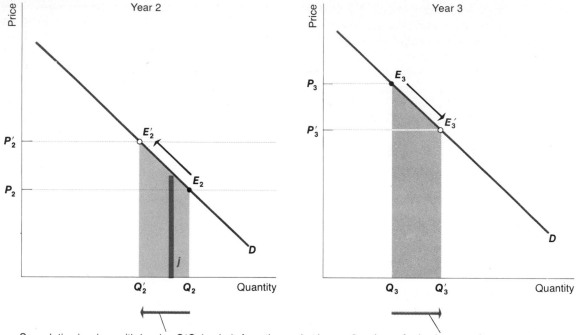

Speculation involves withdrawing $Q'_2 Q_2$ bushels from the market in year 2 and transferring it to year 3

in a year of glut (year 2) and provided to a "relatively eager" public in a year of scarcity (year 3). The difference between these two areas is a net benefit to society from this speculation. In short, speculation reduces the fluctuation in price—*and also the fluctuation in the quantity of this good.* [Without speculation, different quantities (Q_2 and Q_3) are consumed in each year; with speculation, roughly the same quantities are consumed (Q'_2 and Q'_3)]. It is by ironing out this fluctuation in quantities (by moving some of this good from a year of glut to a year of scarcity) that speculation provides its major benefit to society.

Of course, if this is a benefit that results from eliminating a cycle, it is also a loss from having a cycle rather than stable prices in the first place. This then provides a second major reservation about perfectly competitive markets: A failure of the timing and signaling mechanism may lead to price instability, as in the cobweb example. And if this is not ironed out by speculators, the free

Figure 10-7
How speculation may increase efficiency by stabilizing price
Without speculation, equilibrium in year 2 is at E_2 and in year 3 at E_3. (This particular example of fluctuating price is drawn from the cobweb cycle in Box 10-3, but it could equally well have been the result of other influences, such as varying weather conditions.) Speculation involves reducing the available supply on the market in year 2 from Q_2 to Q'_2 (as shown by the arrow) and transferring it to year 3, thus increasing the supply then by this same amount, from Q_3 to Q'_3. This raises price in year 2 and lowers it in year 3 until the two are almost equal. A typical unit j of reduced consumption in year 2 will reduce utility then by the solid bar in panel a; and the total loss from all such units of reduced consumption is the total red area. But the gain from increased consumption in year 3 is the gray area. The difference in these two areas is the beneficial effect of this speculation.

movement in price allowed by a perfectly competitive market may become a disadvantage—even though it is a great advantage in other circumstances. (For example, a freely moving price provides the incentive for shifting resources from one industry to another in response to changing consumer preferences.)

Speculation as a destabilizing influence

So far, speculators emerge from this discussion very much the heroes of the piece, but only because we have assumed that they predict the future correctly. But, of course, they may guess wrong; and if they do, their actions will result in a loss both to themselves and to society. For example, if they purchase and store this year on the expectation that there will be a greater shortage and higher price next year, and they are wrong (if, in fact, there is a glut and lower prices instead) they incur an obvious loss themselves. Moreover, from the viewpoint of society as a whole there is also a loss, because they will be moving supplies from this year's period of shortage (when they are badly needed) to next year's period of glut (when they are not). Thus, their individual success and their potential benefit to society depend on their ability to predict the future correctly.

There is another problem with speculation: The speculators we have described so far operate in a perfectly competitive way; each individual is unable to exercise any influence over price. The story is quite different for a speculator who attempts to **corner a market.**

Cornering a market is buying up enough of the commodity to become the single (or at least dominant) seller, and thus acquire the power to resell at a higher price.

In this case it is difficult to argue that society benefits. In fact, the price gyrations that result from such attempts may be costly, whether or not they succeed. For example, the heavy silver buying by Bunker Hunt and his brothers in 1979–1980 pushed the silver price up to record levels. By January 1980, silver was selling for more than $50 an ounce (up from about $10 in August 1979), and it was estimated that the

Hunt group held about one-sixth of the Western world's stock of silver. It seemed that the Hunts were trying to corner the silver market, but even that wasn't certain. (One investigator later suggested that they were just playing around—in a game of monopoly with real money.) But if they were trying to corner the market they did not succeed: In January, the market turned down, and a wave of selling drove the price back down to about $10 an ounce. Estimates of their loss during this price landslide ran as high as $1 billion. No one would pretend that such price gyrations were beneficial to the economy as a whole; indeed they severely dislocated industries such as photography that used silver.

*GOVERNMENT AGRICULTURAL PRICE SUPPORTS

One of the arguments for agricultural price supports is that the government thereby acts like the stabilizing speculators in Figure 10-7, preventing the severe fluctuations in price that would otherwise occur. (We've already seen that agricultural prices are unstable because these goods are sold in perfectly competitive markets where supply and demand are relatively inelastic, and supply may shift because of changes in the weather. Thus, without government intervention, the price of wheat could rise by 50 percent in one year and fall by 50 percent in another. This does not happen elsewhere in the economy: The prices of cars and clothing simply do not gyrate in this way.) Moderating such fluctuations in price is not only desirable for farmers, but for the economy as a whole.[2]

It is, however, difficult to evaluate farm programs because they can have two quite different objectives, as described on page 208.

[2]For a detailed examination of how far the government should go in stabilizing farm prices in a much more complicated context, see R. Edwards and C. P. Hallwood, "The Determination of Optimum Buffer Stock Intervention Rules," *The Quarterly Journal of Economics,* February 1980.

BOX 10-5
Forms of Farm Subsidy

In the absence of any government action, equilibrium in the wheat market in Figure 10-8a is at E_1, with farm income equal to the rectangle to the southwest of E_1 (that is, price P_1 times quantity Q_1). When the government announces it will support the price of wheat at a higher level P_2, farmers respond to this price incentive by moving up their supply curve from E_1 to E_2. At the same time, consumers are discouraged by this higher price and move back up their demand curve from E_1 to E_3. Thus at this higher price there is now an oversupply equal to E_3E_2 which must be purchased by the government at a cost to the taxpayer equal to the shaded area. Farm income has been increased from the original rectangle to the southwest of E_1 to the larger rectangle to the southwest of E_2 (that is, farmers now receive price P_2 on the Q_2 bushels they sell).

An alternative policy of equal benefit to the farmer is shown in panel b. In this case, the government again guarantees the same target price P_2 to farmers, who again respond in the same way by moving up their supply curve from E_1 to E_2. But in this case the government makes no attempt to maintain the market price at P_2 by buying up the surplus. Instead, it lets the market price "find its own level." And because Q_2 is coming onto the market, price falls to P_4. (The demand curve tells us that large quantity Q_2 will be purchased only at low price P_4.)

Farmers are being guaranteed P_2 per bushel by the government, but they are only getting P_4 from the market. The government must therefore put up the difference; in other words, it must pay a subsidy P_2P_4 to farmers for each bushel they sell. Multiplying this by Q_2, the number of bushels sold, yields the shaded area—the total subsidy paid by the government to farmers.

Farmers generally prefer the price support scheme in panel a; they view it as receiving a fair price for their wheat, whereas they sometimes regard b as a subsidy from the public purse. But in fact the two policies benefit farmers equally. (Under either scheme their income increases from the area to the southwest of E_1 to the area to the southwest of E_2.) Moreover, in its twin roles as wheat consumer and taxpayer, the public pays exactly the same amount for wheat under each program (that same area to the southwest of E_2).

There is, however, one good reason why the public will prefer panel b; it gets to consume more wheat (Q_2 rather than the Q_3 in panel a). This public preference for policy b clearly holds so long as the government has already accumulated enough to cover years of crop failure (as we assume in this box), and any additional agricultural produce it may accumulate will eventually either spoil or be sold at give-away prices. (To illustrate a give-away: Faced with the prospect that an accumulated butter surplus would otherwise spoil, the European Common Market sold it to the Russians for roughly *one-quarter* the support price its own citizens were paying. As you can imagine, European butter consumers were not amused.)

Because of the difficult theoretical issues involved, it is no surprise that actual policy has become obscure and complicated. Indeed, in the face of weak market prices in 1977, policies *a* and *b* were both used. As in panel *a*, the government had undertaken to support the market price of wheat at $2.25 a bushel, while at the same time adding some of policy *b* by paying farmers whatever further subsidy was necessary to raise their price to a target level of $2.90. This combined scheme was impossible to understand without a full grasp of each of its components, as set out in the two panels of Figure 10-8. (By 1979, the support price had been raised to $3.29 a bushel.) ∎

Figure 10-8
Alternative farm assistance programs
Under either program the government guarantees that farmers will receive P_2 per bushel. They consequently move up their supply curve from equilibrium E_1 to E_2. *In panel a,* the government fixes the market price at P_2. Consumers shift from E_1 to E_3. The difference in the amount produced (at E_2) and consumed (at E_3) must be purchased by the government. The cost it incurs is shown by the shaded area. *In panel b,* the government makes no attempt to support the market price. As a consequence price falls to P_4. But farmers have been guaranteed price P_2; therefore the government must pay them the difference ($P_2 P_4$) on each bushel. Since they are producing Q_2 bushels, the total payment is the shaded rectangle.

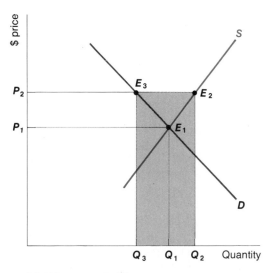

(a) Price support at P_2

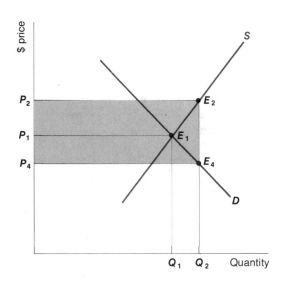

(b) Payment to farmers of $P_2 P_4$ for each bushel sold

Objective 1. To stabilize price and consumption

And let them gather all the food of those good years that come, and lay up corn under the hand of Pharaoh, and let them keep food in the cities.

And that food shall be for store to the land against the seven years of famine, which shall be in the land of Egypt; that the land perish not through the famine.

Genesis 41:35-36

To see how a government price support program can have the same favorable effect as the successful, perfectly competitive speculation in Figure 10-7, suppose that the government guarantees price at P'_2 in panel a. In a bumper-crop year it buys up Q'_2Q_2 thus keeping price up to the P'_2 support level. Then in a poor crop year of shortage, it can sell this accumulated stock, thus keeping price down to roughly this same level. In short, it moderates price fluctuations just as stabilizing speculators might, by moving goods from a period of plenty (panel a) to a period of crop failure (panel b). In the process the nation realizes the same efficiency gain.

This idea of an "ever-normal granary" has had a renewed appeal recently because of international developments. Our food prices can be sent shooting upward not only by a U.S. crop failure, but also by a crop failure abroad. Thus, the rapidly rising food prices of 1973 were a result of crop failures in the Soviet Union and elsewhere, and the increases in the government-guaranteed price which followed were designed partly to rebuild U.S. stocks to cover such contingencies. The objective was to accumulate buffer stocks not only to stabilize price, but also to provide a cushion against hunger in foreign countries that might encounter crop failures in the future.

Although this provides a case for government price guarantees, difficult questions remain. For example: Since the government price support has much the same effect in stabilizing price and quantity as successful private speculation, why can't private speculators do the job? If they can see a future shortage developing, why wouldn't they buy cheap now in order to sell dear in the future period of scarcity—in the

process moderating the fluctuation in price and quantity consumed?

To some degree, the question of who can do the better job of stabilizing price—private speculators or the government—reduces to the question of whether the government can predict future price as well as speculators can. If it can, then a government price support is the better way to stabilize price. (A government guarantee to farmers at planting time of the price they will eventually receive is the best way to induce the right production response—and private speculators cannot provide such a guarantee.) But many doubt that the government *can* predict as well as private speculators. After all, those in government are good at winning elections, whereas private speculators are good at predicting future price. (Those who aren't, lose money and go out of business.)

And even if the government *could* predict, it may not set price at that level, because it is pursuing another objective.

Objective 2: To raise average price

To isolate one issue at a time, assume that the problem of price instability does not exist; food is being produced at an efficient output, and the government has already stored away an ever-normal granary to cover the risk of bad crops here or abroad. In these circumstances, suppose the government introduces a price guarantee designed to raise, rather than stabilize, farm price (and hence farm income). Farmers respond to a high guaranteed price by producing more. There are two major effects. First, farm output has been increased beyond its initial perfectly competitive (and efficient) quantity, so that there is an efficiency loss. At the same time, there is also a transfer of income to farmers from taxpayers who must pay whatever subsidy is necessary to support the higher farm price. (Box 10-5 describes the two quite different forms a farm subsidy program may take. But in either case, the farmer benefits and the public pays.)

How, then, does one defend the idea of a price guarantee designed to raise farm income? One argument is that it will help cure farm poverty. But a price guarantee that subsidizes a bushel of wheat, rather than a poor farmer, is a very ineffective way of curing poverty, since it subsidizes the wealthy high-volume farmer much more than the poor low-volume farmer. The problem is not just that wealthy farmers get more income from the government than poor farmers; they often get a larger *proportion* of their income from government payments.[3] This raises the question: Shouldn't subsidies be designed to go to farmers who are poor, rather than farmers who produce a great deal of wheat?

We conclude that in analyzing government

[3]In *Food and Agriculture Policy* (Washington: American Enterprise Institute, 1977, p. 52) Luther G. Tweeten estimated that farmers with total sales of over $100,000 had an average income of $39,578, of which $8,867 (or 22.4 percent) was received in direct payments from the government. Farmers with sales between $2,500 and $5,000 had an average income of $6,832 (since many of the smallest farmers also had nonfarm sources of income), with only $588 (that is, 8.6 percent) coming from direct government payments.

In order to prevent too much government assistance from going to wealthy farmers, 1973 legislation limited the payments to any single farmer to $20,000 per year. (But in 1981, the government proposed removing this limitation.)

farm policies, the reason for a price guarantee is crucial. If the price guarantee is designed only to stabilize price by accumulating an ever-normal granary, then an argument can be made in its favor. But if, in addition, it is designed to raise the average level of farm prices, it becomes more difficult to justify. Moreover, this issue is complicated by the fact that the real objective of price supports is often to raise price, but they are promoted on the ground that they would stabilize price. How, then, can one tell which objective is being pursued? While there's no simple foolproof indicator, one important clue is this: If the accumulated surplus does not grow beyond the amount which may be needed to cover future crop failures, the policy may well be stabilizing and efficient. But if the surplus grows beyond this amount (or, equivalently, has to be kept down to this level by contrived disposal programs or by limits on production), price supports have been raising farm income. And if higher farm income is judged a desirable objective, we should search for more appropriate policies—policies that would more successfully cure farm poverty, without further enriching the already affluent large farmer.

Key Points

1 The efficient quantity of output from the point of view of society as a whole is where marginal social cost is equal to marginal social benefit.

2 If social costs are the same as private costs and social benefits the same as private benefits, a perfectly competitive market results in an efficient output. Thus, perfect competition eliminates deadweight loss; it allocates resources efficiently to satisfy human wants.

3 However, the wants that will be satisfied depend on how income is distributed. For each distribution of income, there is a different perfectly competitive result. And economics cannot clearly tell us which one is best.

*4 A problem with a perfectly competitive market is that its price signals may be misread, and

price may fluctuate as a result. An example is the hog cycle that occurs if producers erroneously assume that price this year is a good indication of what price will be next year.

*5 Private speculation or government price guarantees may be beneficial in a perfectly competitive market if on balance they reduce price fluctuations. Competitive speculators, if successful, tend to stabilize price. But those with larger resources who attempt to "corner a market" often have a destabilizing influence.

*6 If price supports are designed to raise (rather than just stabilize) price, they become more difficult to justify. They introduce inefficiency into the system, and they are a high-cost, relatively ineffective way of curing farm poverty.

Key Concepts

economic efficiency

private versus social benefit

private versus social cost

why perfect competition is efficient

efficiency loss

how price rations scarce goods

efficiency and the distribution of income

when market signals mislead

*cobweb cycle

*dynamic problems

*speculation

*when speculation is efficient, when not

*cornering a market

*agricultural price supports

*how price supports transfer income

Problems

10-1 "A perfectly competitive price that all buyers and sellers take as given is the key link in orchestrating production and consumption in an efficient way." Do you agree? If so, illustrate. If not, explain why.

10-2 According to Adam Smith, the pursuit of private gain leads to public benefit. Under what circumstances is this not true?

10-3 Apply the analysis of this chapter to show the triangular efficiency loss from the rent control policy described in Box 4-1.

*__10-4__ "Food has a higher value than gold because without food we would starve. Yet gold has a far higher price. That doesn't make any economic sense." Critically evaluate, showing how this involves Smith's paradox of value discussed in Box 10-3.

*__10-5__ What do you think of the argument that water is such an essential to human life that it should be provided free? If we were to do this, what would be the consequences? Would these consequences be greater or less dramatic in desert areas? Why is it that, in the case of air, we *can* follow this policy ("it's essential, so provide it free")?

*__10-6__ Redraw the cobweb diagram in Box 10-4, starting with these two changes: make S more elastic, and locate E_1 much closer to E. Does the resulting cycle settle down to E? How do you compare your result with Box 10-4?

*__10-7__ What are some of the pros and cons of government-guaranteed prices for farmers?

*__10-8__ If speculators guess wrong and buy a good in year 1 to sell in year 2 when it turns out to be even more plentiful and cheap, would their activities result in an efficiency gain or loss? Illustrate with a diagram. Would speculators realize a profit or loss?

*__10-9__ On March 5, 1980, *The Washington Post* reported:

Herbert Hunt, who did most of the talking during the day of testimony, insisted repeatedly that the brothers were not speculating in silver, but were investing in the metal because they believed it would become more valuable.

If you're working on the congressional staff and are asked to evaluate the statement, what would you say?

*__10-10__ If you are working for the U.S. government, and your only concern is to minimize the money the government has to pay out to farmers, which program in Figure 10-8 would you prefer, and why:

(a) if the demand curve passing through E_1 is very elastic?

(b) if demand is very inelastic?

(Recall that the payment made to farmers in each case is shown by the shaded area.)

*Problems marked with an asterisk are drawn from optional, starred sections of this chapter.

APPENDIX

ILLUSTRATING THE EFFICIENCY OF PERFECT COMPETITION WITH INDIFFERENCE CURVES

This chapter has shown that perfect competition results in efficiency in a simple economy in which social and private benefits are the same, and social and private costs are equal. To illustrate this point, we used demand and supply curves in Figure 10-3. We now show the same conclusion in an alternative way, using the indifference curves explained in the Appendix to Chapter 8 and the production possibilities curve introduced in Chapter 2.

Suppose initially in Figure 10-9 that producers are at point A on their production possibilities curve, making 500 units of clothing and 1,300 units of food. Suppose also that the prices of food and clothing are both $10 per unit. Then producers' income totals $18,000 [that is, ($10 × 500) + ($10 × 1,300)]. Producers are now on the $18,000 income line L_1, whose slope reflects the relative prices of the two goods, just like the slope of the budget line in Figure 8-9 or the equal cost line in Figure 9-13. Just as there was a whole family of equal-cost curves in Figure 9-13, we can visualize a whole set of parallel income lines such as L_1 and L_2 in Figure 10-9, each indicating successively higher income levels as producers move to the northeast. The objective of producers is to reach the highest one possible. Obviously, producers operating at point A on the $18,000 income line can do better by moving along the PPC to point E, which is on the $20,000 income line. (At E, they produce 1,000 units of each good for a total income of $20,000.) This is the best they can do.

Producers maximize their income by moving along the production possibilities curve to the highest attainable income line. This is achieved at the point of tangency shown in Figure 10-9.

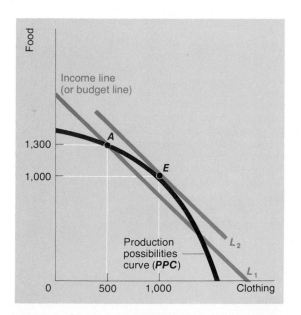

Figure 10-9
How producers maximize their incomes
The line representing producers' income goes through the point at which production is taking place. Its slope depends on the relative prices of the two goods. Producers attain the highest income line by producing where the slope of the production possibilities curve is the same as the slope of the income line; that is, at the point of tangency, E.

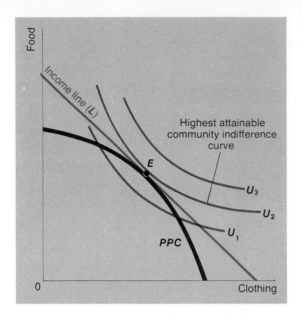

Figure 10-10
The competitive equilibrium
The competitive equilibrium occurs at *E*. Producers pick the point where the PPC is tangent to the highest attainable income line. Consumers pick the point where the income line is tangent to the highest attainable indifference curve. At this point, *E*, the production possibilities curve and the indifference curve are tangent. The maximum level of utility U_2 is achieved, given the productive capacity of the economy (shown by the PPC).

Now let's put this theory of producer behavior in Figure 10-9 together with our earlier theory of consumer behavior in Figure 10-9. In a perfectly competitive economy, in which every producer and every consumer takes prices as given, equilibrium is at *E* in Figure 10-10. On the one hand, producers maximize their income by moving along the production possibilities curve to the point (*E*) of tangency with the highest attainable income line *L*. At the same time, consumers maximize their utility by also moving to point *E*—because this is the point of tangency between their highest attainable indifference curve (U_2) and the income line *L*. Thus the community as a whole achieves an efficient solution, because at *E* it is producing the combination of food and clothing that lifts it to its highest attainable level of utility (U_2). Given the community's ability to produce (its PPC), there is no way it can reach a higher level of satisfaction than U_2 (like, for example, U_3); it's just not possible.

This, then, is our alternative illustration of the proposition established earlier in this chapter: A competitive economy leads to an efficient solution.[4]

[4]There must be a catch somewhere. According to this analysis, there is a single (unique) efficient solution (at *E*) and we already know from Figures 10-1 and 10-5 that there is not. (For each income distribution there is a different efficient solution.) This puzzle is resolved by noting that in Figure 10-10 we have drawn a set of indifference curves for the *community as a whole,* rather than for an individual household. And there are severe problems involved in defining such a community indifference system: There is no simple way of "adding up" the preferences of all the individuals in the nation. To illustrate, consider the simple, extreme case of a two-person economy: If I have all the income, then my preferences are the ones that count; if you have all the income, then it is your preferences that count. In other words, a community's preferences depend on who has the income. This means that there is no unique community indifference system. Nor, as a consequence, is there any unique efficient equilibrium; the equilibrium depends on how the nation's income is distributed. This is exactly the conclusion reached in Figure 10-5.

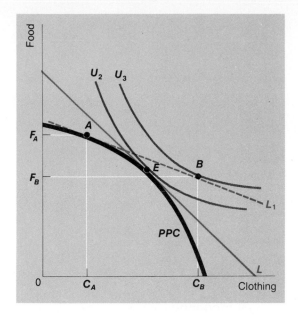

Figure 10-11
How markets adjust from an initial point of disequilibrium
If the relative price of clothing is originally below its equilibrium (that is, prices are those reflected in L_1 rather than L), producers will want to produce at A, and consumers will want to consume at B. As a result, there will be a shortage of clothing ($C_B - C_A$) and a surplus of food ($F_A - F_B$). Consequently, the relative price of clothing will rise until prices reach their equilibrium values, reflected in the slope of the income line L.

We emphasize again that this efficient solution results from producers on the one hand and consumers on the other responding independently to the competitive market prices reflected in the slope of the income line L.[5] This in turn raises the final, key question: Why does the competitive market generate the relative prices shown by L? To answer this question, suppose that initially the relative prices are those shown by line L_1 in Figure 10-11. (The lower slope of L_1 reflects a lower relative price of clothing.) Facing these relative prices, producers maximize their income by producing at A, the point of tangency between the PPC and income line L_1. But consumers try to consume at B, the point of tangency between income line L_1 and indifference curve U_3. However, they are in fact unable to reach point B, since the economy is incapable of producing this combination of food and clothing. (B is outside the PPC.) As a consequence, markets are out of equilibrium. The quantity of clothing demanded by consumers (C_B) exceeds the quantity supplied by producers (C_A); the price of clothing consequently rises. At the same time, the quantity of food demanded (F_B) is less than the quantity supplied (F_A); the price of food falls. As the relative prices of food and clothing change, the income line moves from L_1 toward L. In response, producers move from A toward E, while consumers move from B toward E. This movement continues until the income line becomes L, and producers and consumers have moved all the way to E. It is only then that demand and supply are brought into equilibrium. Thus, the equilibrium prices are indeed those reflected in line L. ∎

[5]To illustrate what can go wrong if producers do not act as perfect competitors, suppose that the producers of clothing form a monopoly and restrict the supply of clothing. In other words, the economy moves to the left of E in Figure 10-10, and it is no longer possible to reach indifference curve U_2. Consequently, the nation's utility is less than at the maximum (U_2).

CHAPTER 11
Monopoly

> The chief agency on which defenders of the market economy have relied to keep self-interest within useful bounds and prevent it from becoming oppressive is the system of free competition. Without it free exchange between unequals could still be a tyranny and its freedom a sham.
>
> **John Maurice Clark**

At one end of the market spectrum is perfect competition, with many sellers. At the other end of the spectrum is monopoly, with only one seller. (The Greek word *monos* means "single," and *polein* means "to sell.")

WHAT CAUSES MONOPOLY?

There are four major reasons why there may be only one firm selling a good:

1 Monopoly may be based on control over an input or technique. A firm may control something essential that no other firm can acquire. One example is the ownership of a necessary resource; an oft-cited illustration was Alcoa's control over bauxite supplies that allowed it to monopolize the sale of aluminum before World War II. Another example is the ownership of a patent, which allows the inventor exclusive control over a new product or process for a period of 17 years. (Patents are designed to encourage expenditure on research by allowing the inventor to reap a substantial reward.) When an existing firm owns an essential patent or exclusive control over a resource, new firms might like to enter the industry but they cannot; the industry remains monopolized.

2 Legal monopoly. It is sometimes illegal for more than one company to sell a product. Examples include the U.S. Postal Service: It is illegal for a company to set up in competition with the post office in the delivery of letters (but not in the delivery of packages). Similarly, a private bus company is sometimes given the exclusive right to service a community.

3 Collusive monopoly. If permitted by law, several producers may get together to form a single firm, or a single unified marketing operation in order to charge a higher price. (Their monopoly position will be maintained only if they are able to keep out new competing firms that may be attracted by the high price.)

4 Natural monopoly. A natural monopoly exists when economies of scale are so important that one firm can produce the total output of the industry more cheaply than could two or more firms. An example is the local telephone service. It is obviously cheaper to string one set of telephone wires down a street than two.

The prevalence of monopoly depends partly on how narrowly a market is defined. In the early 1970s, Boeing had a temporary monopoly in the jumbo jet market; the 747 still had no competition from other jumbo jets. But Boeing did not have a monopoly in the broader market for airliners, since it still had to compete with McDonnell-Douglas in the sale of smaller aircraft. (Even in jumbo jets, Boeing's monopoly was short-lived, as other manufacturers developed somewhat similar planes.) The telephone company has a monopoly of local telephone service, but not of the broader market for communications where it must compete with the mails and telegraph companies. Indeed, in the broadest sense, every producer competes with every other producer for the consumer's dollar. If you buy a new hi-fi, you may cut down on long-distance telephone calls to help pay for it. Thus, in a very broad sense, the telephone company is in competition even with the producer of hi-fi equipment.

But, if markets are defined in a reasonably limited way, significant areas of monopoly exist —in local telephone service, water, local gas service, and local electrical service, to name a few. Nonetheless, the importance of monopoly should not be overstated. **Oligopoly**—where the industry is dominated by a few sellers—is much more important in the U. S. economy. Some of the largest industries in our economy are oligopolies, including automobiles, large computers, aircraft, heavy construction equipment, large electrical generators, and steel. In spite of the importance of oligopoly, it is appropriate to consider monopoly first. Monopoly is the simpler form, and it provides a necessary background for the study of oligopoly.

NATURAL MONOPOLY: THE IMPORTANCE OF COST CONDITIONS

When discussing the problems that arise from the monopolization of an industry and the appropriate government policy response, it is essential to answer the question, "Is this industry a natural monopoly?" In other words, "Is the least expensive way to produce this good with one firm?" As we shall see, many of the questionable decisions by the government and the courts in dealing with monopoly have been the result of a failure to address this question.

The cost conditions which lead to natural monopoly are shown in Figure 11-1 (panel b), and are contrasted with the conditions which do not (panel a). The two products shown are assumed to have identical demand curves in order to highlight the difference in their costs— the central issue in explaining natural monopoly.

In the industry shown in panel a, a typical firm's long-run average cost curve (AC) reaches a minimum at only 10 units of output, a very small proportion of the total market. As a consequence, total market demand cannot be satisfied by one firm operating at its minimum cost. Instead, the least costly way of servicing this market is to have many firms producing just 10 units each. It is no surprise that perfect competition results.

In panel b, AC has the same minimum of $100, but the big difference is the much larger volume of output necessary for a firm to achieve this low cost. Unlike panel a where AC reaches a minimum and turns up at a very small volume, in panel b AC continues downward. The least expensive way of servicing the market is with one firm, and the stage is set for monopoly. By definition:

Natural monopoly occurs when the average cost of a single firm falls over such an extended range of output that one firm can produce the total quantity sold at a lower average cost than could two or more firms.

Why might costs continue to fall through much or all of the range needed to satisfy total market demand? The answer may be: high fixed cost (overhead). Local telephone, electric, water, and gas services are all natural monopolies, because the fixed cost in running telephone or electric wires, or in laying water and gas pipes, is very high relative to variable cost. (To illustrate what happens when fixed costs dominate, set fixed cost in Table 9-2 at $1,000, rather than just $35, and recalculate average cost. Notice how AC continues to fall as this $1,000 of fixed overhead is spread over a larger and larger number of units of output.)

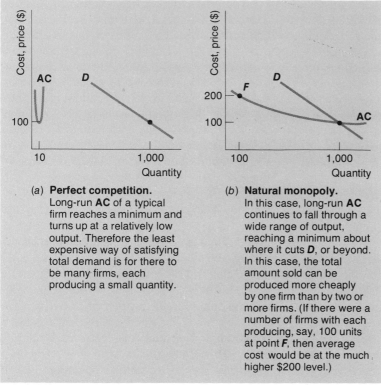

Figure 11-1
**How cost conditions can lead to
natural monopoly**

(a) **Perfect competition.**
Long-run **AC** of a typical firm reaches a minimum and turns up at a relatively low output. Therefore the least expensive way of satisfying total demand is for there to be many firms, each producing a small quantity.

(b) **Natural monopoly.**
In this case, long-run **AC** continues to fall through a wide range of output, reaching a minimum about where it cuts **D**, or beyond. In this case, the total amount sold can be produced more cheaply by one firm than by two or more firms. (If there were a number of firms with each producing, say, 100 units at point **F**, then average cost would be at the much higher $200 level.)

To verify that panel *b* tends to result in monopoly, suppose that initially a few firms are each producing 100 units at point *F*. This low volume results in a high average cost ($200) for each firm. An aggressive firm will discover that by increasing its output, it can lower its cost, and hence offer its product at a lower price than its competitors. Thus it can squeeze them out of business. In such a case of natural monopoly, competition tends to drive all firms but one out of the market.

The obvious attraction to the consumer of such price competition during the period in which the industry is being "shaken down" and the number of firms reduced is likely to disappear once the successful firm has eliminated all its competitors and has emerged as a monopoly. Because it is able to achieve economies of scale, its costs will be so low it need worry little about the entry of new competitors. (If such firms do appear, it can greet them with whatever price cutting is necessary to drive them into bankruptcy.) With little fear of present or future competition, the monopolist can then raise the price. Consumers of this product are at the mercy of the monopolist, except insofar as they are prepared to cut back their purchases in the face of a higher price. The question is: How high will the monopolist set the price? But before answering this question, we need to make one more distinction between perfect competition and monopoly.

THE DIFFERENCE IN THE DEMAND FACING A PERFECT COMPETITOR AND A MONOPOLIST

A perfectly competitive firm must take the market price as given. For example, an individual farmer never thinks of asking 1 cent a bushel more for his wheat, because he knows he won't get it; and he never offers to sell for 1 cent less, since he can sell all his wheat for the going market price. The farmer has no **market power.** As an individual producer among many, he is unable, by reducing the quantity he supplies, to have any noticeable influence on price.

The *market power* of a firm is its ability to influence its price (and thereby its profit).

To confirm that a farmer has no market power, suppose that the price in Figure 11-2 is $2, as determined by market supply and demand in panel b. The response of the individual farmer in panel a to this price is to supply 2,000 units. Now suppose he tries to influence the price. Specifically, suppose he reduces his supply by 1,000 units in the hope of making wheat scarce and raising its price. His move will reduce market supply in panel b, shifting S to the left, but by such a small amount (1,000 units) that this action won't even be noticed in the market. (If you try to draw the new supply curve, you will find you are just drawing a line over the old supply S.) Consequently market price, as determined in panel b, remains the same. The farmer has tried to raise the price, but this attempt to exercise market power has failed miserably. As an individual seller, he has no influence whatsoever over price, and this is reflected in the completely elastic demand curve he faces in panel a.

But the situation facing a monopoly is quite different, as shown in panels c and d. In panel d, total market demand is exactly the same as in the competitive case above. The only difference is that this market demand is now being satisfied

by a single monopoly firm; in other words, *the demand facing the individual firm in panel c is exactly the same as the total market demand in panel d.*

As a result, the monopoly can indeed affect price. To confirm this, suppose that it is initially selling at a $2 price. Because it is the only seller, this firm alone is supplying all the 2 million units sold (shown at point A in either panel c or panel d). Now suppose the monopoly tries to influence price by cutting its sales in half, from 2 million to 1 million units. The result is that price rises to $3. (The demand curve tells us that this is the price that buyers will pay if there are only 1 million bushels available.) Thus the firm moves from A to B on the demand curve. By restricting its output, it *is* able to make this good scarce and thus raise its price. (Alternatively, the firm could have made exactly this same move from A to B by quoting a $3 price, in which case buyers would purchase 1 million units.)

In short, the monopoly firm has market demand within its grasp. It can move along the market demand curve from a point like A to B, selecting the one that suits it best. On the other hand, the perfect competitor has no control over market price; instead, the individual firm faces its own completely elastic demand curve, and all it can do is select the quantity to sell. While the monopolist can raise the price, the perfect competitor must take price as given. The monopolist is a **price maker;** the perfect competitor is a **price taker.**

WHAT PRICE DOES THE MONOPOLIST SELECT?

Any firm, whether a monopolist or competitor, maximizes profit by selecting the output where marginal cost MC equals marginal revenue MR. As already recognized (in Figure 9-3), *marginal revenue for the perfectly competitive firm is the given market price at which it sells.* For example, marginal revenue for the perfectly competitive firm in Figure 11-2a is $2; no matter how many

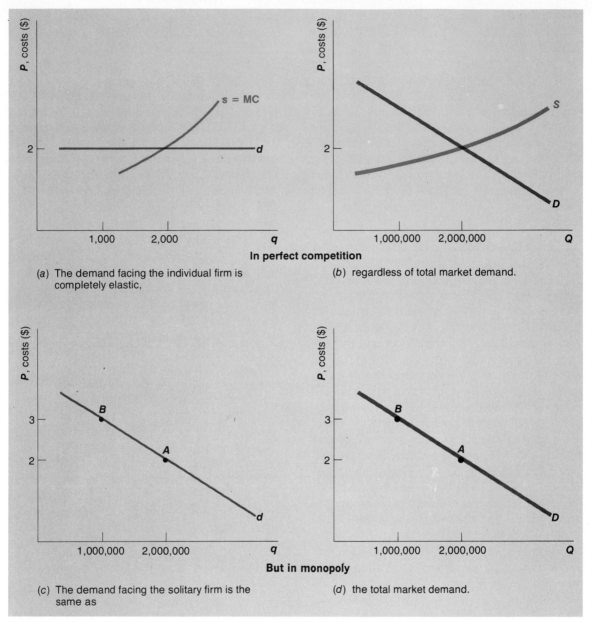

In perfect competition

(a) The demand facing the individual firm is completely elastic,

(b) regardless of total market demand.

But in monopoly

(c) The demand facing the solitary firm is the same as

(d) the total market demand.

Figure 11-2
The difference in the demand facing the monopolist and the perfect competitor
Note that the demand facing an individual firm in the left hand panels is shown with a light line and marked with a small *d*, whereas market demand in the right hand panel is shown with a heavy line and marked with a capital *D*.

units it sells, its revenue will increase by $2 if it sells one more. In other words, its marginal revenue schedule is identical to its completely elastic demand curve. *But for the monopolist, marginal revenue is not equal to the selling price.* This is such an important point that it deserves a detailed explanation.

What is the marginal revenue of a monopolist?

Suppose the monopoly firm in Figure 11-3 moves from *B* to *C* along its demand curve. At *B* it was selling 1 unit at a $50 price, but now at *C* it is selling 2 units at a price of $45 each. (Its average revenue AR is $45.) What is its marginal revenue, that is, the additional revenue it receives because it is selling 2 units rather than 1? To calculate the answer, note that the monopoly's total revenue from selling 1 unit was $50, but when it sells 2, its total revenue is $90. Thus, its revenue has risen by $40; this is its marginal revenue from the sale of the second unit. Note that this marginal revenue ($40) is less than the price ($45). This point is worth emphasizing:

For a monopolist, marginal revenue is *less than price.*

Table 11-1 shows the marginal revenue for the monopolist at each output. Total revenue is given in column 3, while column 4 shows how this total revenue changes for each successive unit sold. The resulting marginal revenue schedule is graphed in Figure 11-3.

The demand and marginal revenue curves now become the stepping stones needed to answer the question: How high does a profit-maximizing monopolist set price?

Monopoly output and price

To maximize profit, the monopoly follows the same policy as the perfectly competitive firm: It equates marginal cost MC with marginal revenue MR (but not with price, because for the monopolist MR and price are not the same). If it

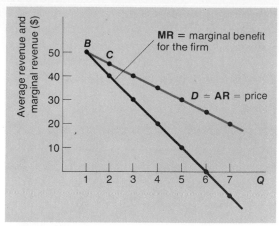

Figure 11-3
Why a monopolist's demand (AR) and marginal revenue (MR) differ (numbers are drawn from Table 11-1)
At point *B*, the monopoly sells 1 unit for $50. At point *C*, it sells 2 units for $45 each, for a total revenue of $90. The sale of the second unit increases its total revenue by $90 − $50 = $40. Its marginal revenue is thus $40. Another way to calculate this is to note that the monopoly receives a $45 price on the sale of the second unit; but from this it must deduct the $5 "loss" it must take on the first unit because it is getting only $45 for this, rather than the original $50.

(Note that the *D* and MR curves meet at the smallest quantity that can be sold—in our example, at point *B* where *Q* = 1 unit. This diagram therefore applies to a case such as radios or cars where it is impossible to sell less than 1 unit. However, in other cases—such as wheat—the units may be readily divided: It is possible to sell ½ of a ton, or 1/100 of a ton, or even less. Indeed, the smallest amount that can be sold is such a small fraction of a ton that, for all intents and purposes, the MR and AR curves will meet at the vertical axis where *Q* is zero. This case of perfect divisibility, with the two curves meeting at the vertical axis, is commonly used in economics.)

is not equating MC and MR, it can increase its profit by changing its output until the two are equal. An illustration of profit maximization is provided in Figure 11-4*a*, which shows the monopolist selecting output *Q*, where MC and MR intersect. Again we emphasize:

A monopolist—like a perfect competitor—maximizes profit by selecting the output where

marginal cost = marginal revenue

(But for the monopolist—unlike the perfect competitor—MR is *not* the same as price.)

With its output thus determined, what price does the firm then charge? In other words, what is the maximum price the monopoly can charge and still sell quantity Q? The answer is given by its demand curve, which indicates (at point E) that the firm can charge a price as high as P and still sell those Q units. This choice by the monopoly of output Q and price P is often referred to as its selection of the profit-maximizing point (E) on its demand curve.

Of course, a monopoly, like any other firm, must address another important question: Should it be in business at all? For the firm shown in this diagram, the answer is yes. In selling Q units, it makes a per unit profit of EV (the difference between its selling price E on the demand curve and its average cost V on the AC curve). Thus, a profit for a monopolist will exist so long as E lies above V, that is, so long as the demand curve cuts through (overlaps) the average cost curve, and does not lie entirely below it.

If EV is the monopoly's per unit profit, what is its total profit? The answer is the shaded area in panel b—that is, the per unit profit EV times PE, the number of units sold. Thus, these two

panels show two equivalent ways for the monopoly firm to maximize profit: In panel a, it equates MC and MR. Alternatively, in panel b, it selects the point E on its demand curve that maximizes the gray profit area. We shall use these two approaches interchangeably. The approach in panel b has been introduced because it clearly shows the profits which the firm is attempting to maximize. Moreover, it demonstrates both conditions that a firm must satisfy: It ensures (1) that the marginal condition MC = MR will be met, and (2) that the firm will not be operating at a loss (in which case it would go out of business in the long run).

Although a monopoly that equates MC and MR produces the best output *for the firm* (since it maximizes profit), a question remains: Is this the efficient output *for society as a whole?*

IS MONOPOLY EFFICIENT?

In general, the answer to this is no. A monopoly produces too little output, and the nation's resources are misallocated as a consequence.

But before we show the reason for such *allocative* inefficiency, we recall that there are also two other kinds of inefficiency: technical inefficiency and dynamic inefficiency. A monopoly may be *technically* inefficient: The firm may not be operating on its lowest possible cost curve. Because it has no competition, a monopoly may relax its cost controls, and resources

Table 11-1
How Marginal Revenue for a Monopolist Is Derived from Demand (Average Revenue) Information

(1) Quantity (Q)	(2) Price (P = AR)	(3) Total revenue (P × Q)	(4) Marginal revenue (MR)
1	$50	$ 50	
2	45	90	(90 − 50) = $40
3	40	120	(120 − 90) = 30
4	35	140	(140 − 120) = 20
5	30	150	(150 − 140) = 10
6	25	150	(150 − 150) = 0
7	20	140	(140 − 150) = −10

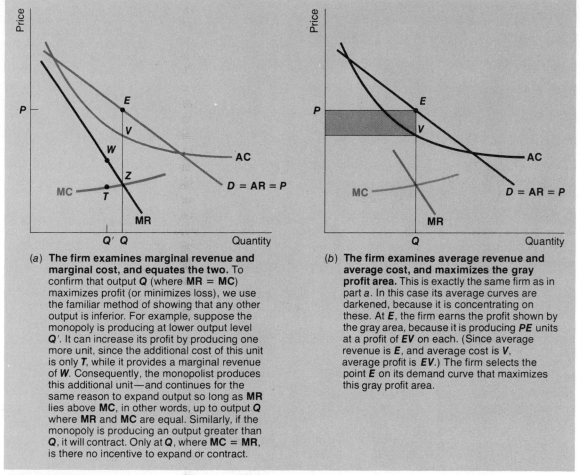

(a) **The firm examines marginal revenue and marginal cost, and equates the two.** To confirm that output **Q** (where **MR = MC**) maximizes profit (or minimizes loss), we use the familiar method of showing that any other output is inferior. For example, suppose the monopoly is producing at lower output level **Q'**. It can increase its profit by producing one more unit, since the additional cost of this unit is only **T**, while it provides a marginal revenue of **W**. Consequently, the monopolist produces this additional unit—and continues for the same reason to expand output so long as **MR** lies above **MC**, in other words, up to output **Q** where **MR** and **MC** are equal. Similarly, if the monopoly is producing an output greater than **Q**, it will contract. Only at **Q**, where **MC = MR**, is there no incentive to expand or contract.

(b) **The firm examines average revenue and average cost, and maximizes the gray profit area.** This is exactly the same firm as in part a. In this case its average curves are darkened, because it is concentrating on these. At **E**, the firm earns the profit shown by the gray area, because it is producing **PE** units at a profit of **EV** on each. (Since average revenue is **E**, and average cost is **V**, average profit is **EV**.) The firm selects the point **E** on its demand curve that maximizes this gray profit area.

Figure 11-4
Two equivalent views of the profit-maximizing equilibrium of a monopoly
(A third way is illustrated in Problem 11-4. This uses the *total* revenue and *total* cost curves in the same way that they were used to show the profit maximization of a perfect competitor in Figure 9-4.)

may be wasted as a consequence. In drawing our diagrams, we assume away this kind of inefficiency. But in doing so we should not forget: *Technical inefficiency in monopoly industries may be an important cost to society.*

The relationship between monopoly and *dynamic* efficiency is less clear. Large, monopolistic firms may have the greatest capacity to undertake research and development. And any firm has an incentive to develop a distinctive new product that will put it in a monopoly

position. (For example, Boeing had an incentive to develop the 747, because it provided the firm with a temporary monopoly of jumbo jets. Thus, monopoly is the payoff for innovation, and innovation is a source of growth.) In Chapter 13, we shall consider the dynamic effects of monopoly in more detail.

Now let us return to the central efficiency issue in this chapter: allocative efficiency (or just "efficiency," for short). Figure 11-5a illustrates an industry that is originally perfectly competi-

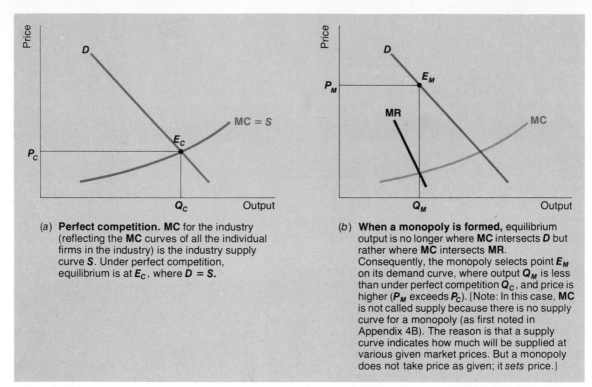

(a) **Perfect competition. MC** for the industry (reflecting the **MC** curves of all the individual firms in the industry) is the industry supply curve **S**. Under perfect competition, equilibrium is at E_C, where $D = S$.

(b) **When a monopoly is formed,** equilibrium output is no longer where **MC** intersects **D** but rather where **MC** intersects **MR**. Consequently, the monopoly selects point E_M on its demand curve, where output Q_M is less than under perfect competition Q_C, and price is higher (P_M exceeds P_C). [Note: In this case, **MC** is not called supply because there is no supply curve for a monopoly (as first noted in Appendix 4B). The reason is that a supply curve indicates how much will be supplied at various given market prices. But a monopoly does not take price as given; it *sets* price.]

Figure 11-5
The results of monopoly: restricted output and higher price

tive. (The least expensive way of producing this good is with many small firms; it is *not* a natural monopoly.) Now suppose in panel b that these firms get together (collude) to form a monopoly strictly in order to sell their product at a higher price. Specifically, in pursuit of this objective, let's suppose they form a single marketing agency. (An example is the marketing of dairy products described in Appendix 11-A.) Further suppose that the marketing arrangement leaves costs and demand unchanged; in other words, the MC and demand curves in the two panels of Figure 11-5 are the same.[1]

So long as the industry is perfectly competi-

tive (panel a) the marginal cost curve for the industry (MC) is the supply curve, and equilibrium is at E_C where supply equals demand. Output Q_C is produced and sold at price P_C. But when this industry is monopolized as in panel b, marginal revenue MR is now less than price, and the marketing agency maximizes the profits of the producers as a group by picking output where MC = MR. Thus, the new equilibrium is at E_M with smaller output Q_M and higher price P_M. Thus:

The monopolist sells a smaller quantity and charges a higher price than a perfectly competitive industry with the same costs and demand.

Because of monopoly, consumers suffer in terms of both price and quantity: At point E_M in panel b, consumers pay a higher price and enjoy less of this good than they did under perfect competition at point E_C. On the other hand,

[1]Demand may change if the marketing association advertises its product, but we ignore this complication.

producers benefit: Their ability to raise price provides them with an opportunity for profit that was not available when they were perfect competitors. Thus, monopoly damages the consumer interest, but benefits the producer interest. What is the net effect of monopoly on society as a whole?

The answer is that the monopolization of a perfectly competitive industry results in an efficiency loss which can be shown as follows: Since Q_C in panel *a* is the perfectly competitive output, it is efficient. Therefore, the smaller monopoly output Q_M must involve an efficiency loss; that is, a deadweight loss to society as a whole. This is confirmed in panel *a* of Figure 11-6, where the competitive equilibrium E_C and the monopoly equilibrium E_M of Figure 11-5 are reproduced in one diagram. The monopoly output Q_M is seen to be a standard case of "too little output," as first described in Figure 10-3*b*; thus the red efficiency loss here is exactly the same as in that earlier diagram. (The demonstration of that loss is briefly summarized in the caption to Figure 11-6*a*.)

Further insight into why this inefficiency occurs is provided in panel *b* of Figure 11-6. The marginal benefit to society (that is, marginal utility) of the good is reflected in its market demand. (This is true, regardless of whether the industry servicing that demand is competitive or monopolized.) The marginal cost of the good to society is also shown; it is the marginal cost of its production. Efficiency requires that a good be produced to output Q_C where these two are equal. This is what happens under perfect competition (right-hand arrow).

But if a monopoly is formed, it will sell less, since it equates MC with its marginal revenue MR, rather than with the marginal benefit to society D. Thus, when a monopolist makes a decision on the basis of self-interest, society suffers. Adam Smith's "invisible hand" fails in its task.

A final interpretation is that this efficiency loss under monopoly occurs because one of the conditions for efficiency (in Box 10-1) has been violated. Which one? The answer is: The mo-

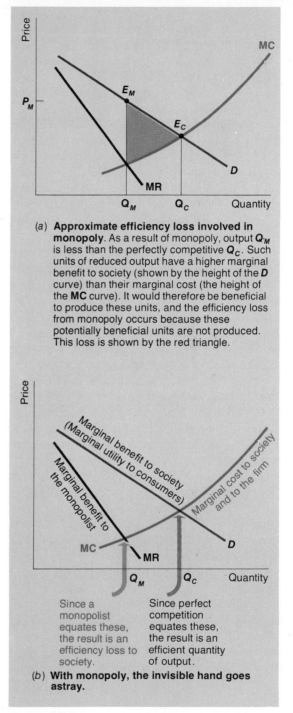

(a) **Approximate efficiency loss involved in monopoly.** As a result of monopoly, output Q_M is less than the perfectly competitive Q_C. Such units of reduced output have a higher marginal benefit to society (shown by the height of the **D** curve) than their marginal cost (the height of the **MC** curve). It would therefore be beneficial to produce these units, and the efficiency loss from monopoly occurs because these potentially beneficial units are not produced. This loss is shown by the red triangle.

Since a monopolist equates these, the result is an efficiency loss to society.

Since perfect competition equates these, the result is an efficient quantity of output.

(b) **With monopoly, the invisible hand goes astray.**

Figure 11-6
Monopoly vs. perfect competition

nopolist does not equate P and MC.[2] In the rest of this chapter and in the next, this is the issue we will continue to pursue: What happens if all the other conditions for an efficient solution hold, but the condition $P=MC$ is violated?

A reservation

The previous discussion seemed to lead to the clear judgment that society is harmed if a perfectly competitive industry is monopolized. This conclusion is generally correct. But it's not absolutely airtight, for two reasons. One is described in Box 11-1. The other involves the distinction between the **efficiency effect** and the **transfer effect** of a monopoly.

The efficiency effect is the reduction in efficiency associated with the production of a quantity that is too small. This effect has already been measured by the red efficiency loss shown in Figure 11-6a. The transfer effect occurs because the higher price charged by the monopolist results in a transfer from consumers who pay the higher price to the monopolist who pockets it. In criticizing monopoly because of its adverse effect on efficiency, we have thus far ignored the effect of the transfer. That is, we have implicitly assumed that the satisfaction the monopolist gains from, say, an additional $1 million is roughly equal to the reduction in consumers' satisfaction when they lose this sum. But it is possible that this assumption is wrong. The monopolist may get far more utility from this transfer than consumers lose. (Suppose, for example, that the product is something like a Rolls Royce, and the consumers who buy it are so wealthy they hardly notice the extra $1 million they pay for it. On the other hand, suppose that the owners of the monopolistic firm are widows and orphans who get enormous satisfaction from the additional $1 million. In this case, most people would conclude that the act of transferring income provides a net benefit. Moreover, it is conceivable

that such a benefit might offset the red efficiency loss in Figure 11-6a. Then our unfavorable judgment on monopoly would be upset.)

While this argument is logically possible, it is also somewhat strained; we have picked a special case.[3] Therefore, most economists would be prepared to argue that the monopolization of an industry typically results in a net loss to society.[4]

In passing, it should be pointed out that this problem of whether the $1 million is of equal benefit to buyers and sellers arises in evaluating almost any economic policy, whether it be controlling monopoly price, limiting pollution, or opening trade with foreign countries. Any such policy results in a change in some market price, and hence a transfer of income between buyers and sellers. Thus, any normative conclusion (on whether the policy is desirable or not) requires a working assumption of how people compare in their valuation of income.[5] Anyone unprepared to make such an assumption is restricted to positive economics—to an analysis of economic events, policies, and institutions, without any judgment on whether or not they have been beneficial to the community as a whole.

---

[3]Indeed, a negative transfer effect seems more likely: Isn't a dollar worth more to the typical consumer than to the typical monopolist?

[4]There is an additional cost of monopoly that we have not considered: To the degree that firms hire lawyers to help them establish or strengthen a monopoly position, then it's reasonable to argue that, from society's viewpoint, these legal resources are being wasted. (For a discussion of costs of this kind, see, for example, Richard Posner, "The Social Costs of Monopoly and Regulation," *Journal of Political Economy,* August 1975, pp. 807–828.)

[5]The same issue arises in macroeconomics. During any period in which the nation's per capita income increases, most Americans benefit, but a few are hurt. Any judgment that such an income increase has been of benefit to the nation overall involves a (reasonable) normative assumption about how people compare in their valuation of income. For more detail, see Arnold Harberger, "The Three Basic Postulates for Applied Welfare Economics: An Interpretive Essay," *Journal of Economic Literature,* September 1971, pp. 785–797.

---

[2]In our specific example, the monopolist in Figure 11-6a selects output Q_M where price P_M is about three times as high as MC.

The Theory of the Second Best

The conclusion that the monopolization of an industry results in a misallocation of resources is generally correct, but not always.

To understand why, consider industry X in an economy whose other industries are all perfectly competitive. If X is monopolized, not enough of X's output is produced, and too much of all the other goods. This is the standard conclusion.

But now suppose that all the other industries are themselves monopolized, but X is perfectly competitive. In this case, there will be too little output of the other goods, and too much X. What happens if industry X is now monopolized? This will reduce its output, and bring it back closer into line with the other industries; thus, the allocation of the nation's resources may actually be *improved*.

This is known as the *problem of the second best.* The first best economy is one in which all industries behave in a competitive way. If one industry is then monopolized, the economy becomes less efficient. But in a second best world —one in which some industries are *already* monopolized—it is unclear whether monopoly in yet another industry will make the economy more or less efficient. There is no simple answer to this question; the theory of the second best is quite complex.

The *theory of the second best* is the theory of how to get the best results in remaining markets when one or more markets have monopoly or other imperfections about which nothing can be done.

A second best argument is sometimes made in support of government policies to monopolize an agricultural industry. (See the milk example in Appendix 11-A.) Since the rest of the economy is pervaded by monopoly, so the argument goes, monopolizing agriculture may improve the nation's resource allocation. By and large, economists remain unimpressed with this argument and continue to recommend that we aim at the "first best" solution by reducing monopoly influence wherever it may be found. Hence, the theory of the second best is introduced here, not as a reason for encouraging monopoly in any specific sector, but rather as a warning that the economic world is seldom as simple as we might hope. ∎

GOVERNMENT POLICIES TO CONTROL MONOPOLY

In formulating policies to protect the public from monopoly, the government should begin with the question: "Is the industry in question a natural monopoly or not?" Suppose it is not, but results from collusion or from mergers which result in no cost reduction. This is the sort of situation described in Figures 11-5 and 11-6, where a clear case can be made for preventing monopolization—or, if it has occurred, for breaking it up. To achieve this objective, "antitrust" laws have been passed; they will be considered in Chapter 13.

In the balance of this chapter we concentrate on the other case, where the firm *is* a natural monopoly, with costs that fall as output expands. Breaking it up would be counterproductive. We don't need more than one set of telephone and electrical wires running down a street; nor do we need more than one set of water and gas pipes. If we had two or more firms in any of these activities, they would be duplicating the investment—the fixed costs—of the existing monopoly, and this would involve a waste of resources. In this case the appropriate policy is to allow the firm to continue as a monopoly, *but control its use of monopoly power.* The government can do so in either of two ways.

1 It may take over the function. For example, water and sewage disposal are generally provided by government corporations.

2 The government may let the monopoly continue as a privately-owned firm, but set up a regulatory agency to control its price. This is the way telephone service is typically provided in the United States.

In either case, the government is in control of the monopoly price. At what level should it set that price? To shed light on this question, consider the monopolist shown in Figure 11-7. We have already seen that a monopoly that is free to quote its own price will select point E_1 on its demand curve (at an output Q_1 where MC = MR). But this is not the socially desirable, efficient point E_2 (where MC = D = marginal utility). An appropriate government policy is to force the monopoly down its demand curve from E_1 to E_2. In theory, this can be done very simply by setting the maximum price that the firm can charge at P_2, the price at which its MC curve intersects the demand curve. This is called ***marginal cost pricing.***

Marginal cost pricing is setting price at the level where MC intersects the demand curve.

Since the regulated monopoly is now prohibited from raising price, it is forced to act like a perfectly competitive firm, taking price P_2 as given. Like the perfectly competitive firm, it will produce to point E_2, where its MC curve rises to the level of its given price P_2. Since E_2 is also the efficient point (where MC = D = MU), this policy has eliminated the original efficiency loss due to monopoly.[6]

Figure 11-7
Regulating monopoly price: The easy case
Without price regulation, the monopoly firm maximizes its profit by selecting point E_1 on its demand curve. (At this point, output is Q_1, where MR = MC.) If the government sets maximum price at P_2, the firm is forced down its demand curve to point E_2, with its output increasing to Q_2. This is the efficient output where the marginal benefit to society (D) is equal to marginal cost (MC). The efficiency gain from this policy comes from the elimination of the original "triangle" of monopoly inefficiency E_1E_2W. (This is the same sort of efficiency loss as the red triangle in panel a of Figure 11-6.) This policy also reduces monopoly profit: Since initially the monopolist maximized profit by selecting point E_1, any other point on the demand curve—including E_2—involves less profit.)

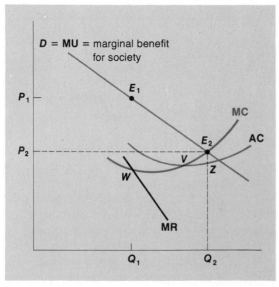

[6]This presents a puzzle: A government price ceiling increases efficiency in this example, but a government ceiling on rents reduces efficiency (as noted in our discussion of Figure 10-3b). How is this possible? The answer: The ceiling on rents moves an industry away from an efficient, perfectly competitive equilibrium. But in Figure 11-7, a price ceiling moves an inefficient monopoly at E_1 toward an efficient equilibrium at E_2.

Clearly, government intervention can be a powerful tool, since it can move an industry away from its free-market equilibrium. While this can be damaging if the industry is initially competitive, it can be beneficial if the industry is initially monopolized. For this reason, economists oppose price regulations in some circumstances, but favor it in others.

In summary, consider how well marginal cost pricing solves the monopoly abuse of producing too little at too high a price. The monopoly is forced to reduce its price, and it also increases its output. In addition, its monopoly profit has been reduced, though not necessarily eliminated. (Per unit profit of E_2Z still remains.)

Unfortunately, dealing with monopoly in practice is often not so easy. Although marginal cost pricing still allows a profit in the example shown in Figure 11-7, in other circumstances it may lead to a loss. In such a case, marginal cost pricing is not a satisfactory policy, since it involves setting a price ceiling that would eventually drive the firm out of business. Such an industry requires some other form of price regulation. This more difficult situation is dealt with in Box 11-2.

THE SPECIAL CASE OF DISCRIMINATING MONOPOLY: LETTING A MONOPOLIST ACT LIKE A MONOPOLIST—IN SPADES

The argument so far is that a monopolist should not be allowed to set a high price. But there is an interesting exception to this general rule.[7] Figure 11-8 shows the demand for the services of a doctor in a small town, along with her average costs (which, as always, include her opportunity cost—the income she could earn elsewhere). If she must quote a single price to all patients, she will decide not to go into this community. The reason is that her demand D does not overlap AC, so there is no single price she can select that will cover her costs. In short, even though she would be a monopolist and have the power to quote price, she would have no single price worth quoting. The best she could do would be to select a point like E on her demand curve, thus setting her fee at P and selling quantity Q.

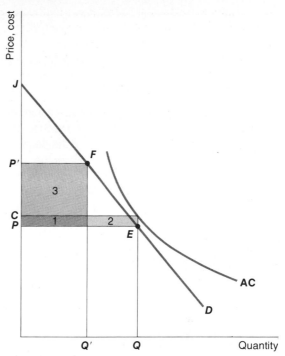

Figure 11-8
When discriminating monopoly may be justified
If the doctor (the potential monopolist) can charge only one price, she will not move into this town, because the demand D is not substantial enough to overlap AC. Any point such as E that she might select on D would thus leave her operating at a loss, shown by area 1 + 2, and she would stay away. On the other hand, she will move into town if she is allowed to discriminate, charging low fee P to the poor and high fee P' to the rich. On her Q' of services sold to the rich, she increases her income by area 1 + 3 which is more than enough to offset her original loss 1 + 2. Thus she can earn a profit—her benefit from discriminatory pricing. But her patients also benefit because they get a doctor and this provides them with at least some consumer surplus.

But she would still not cover her costs, because her price P would be less than her average cost C. (Specifically, her total loss, compared with what she could earn elsewhere, would be areas 1 + 2; that is, Q units sold at a loss of CP on each.)

Under such circumstances, this community goes without a doctor, thus losing potential

[7]This exception was explained by Joan Robinson in *The Economics of Imperfect Competition* (London: Macmillan, 1933), p. 203.

BOX 11-2
Unfortunately, Dealing with Monopoly Is Often Not So Simple

In Figure 11-7, average cost reached a minimum and turned up at point V *before* it reached the demand curve, that is, to the left of the demand curve. In Figure 11-9 we now consider the case where the average cost curve AC keeps falling until *after* it has crossed the demand curve. In this instance, the regulation of monopoly price involves substantial problems.

Average cost pricing

Suppose that we try to apply the policy that worked so well in Figure 11-7, and again try to drive the monopoly firm down its demand curve from its original profit-maximizing equilibrium at E_1 to the efficient point E_2, where MC = D = MU. As before, we attempt to do so by regulating price at P_2. But this policy will no longer work because it will turn the monopoly into a money-loser and eventually drive it out of business. (At E_2, it is operating below its average cost curve AC: The price P_2 that the firm receives is not enough to cover its average cost. The loss the firm would incur is shown by the red area.) The lowest price the government can set without eventually forcing the firm out of business is P_3, which will result in a new equilibrium at E_3. Here price is barely high enough to cover average cost; the firm just breaks even. This policy is called **average cost pricing.** Once again, the regulatory agency takes away the monopoly's power to select a point on its demand curve; the agency makes the decision on the appropriate point and makes it stick by regulating price.

Average cost pricing is setting price at the level where AC intersects the demand curve.

[*In theory,* break-even price P_3 should be easy for the agency to find. If the firm is earning an (above-normal) profit—as it would, for example, at E_1—then price is too high; so lower it. If

the firm is operating at a loss (for example, at E_2) then price is too low; raise it. This simple rule of thumb will bring the regulators to P_3, the price that just covers costs, including a fair return on the capital the owners have invested. *In practice,* however, P_3 is very difficult to determine, largely because of problems in defining (1) a fair percentage return to capital, and (2) the amount of capital invested—problems studied in Appendix 11-B.]

Finally, the effect on efficiency of average cost pricing is shown in panel *b* of Figure 11-9. If it were possible to move the monopoly all the way down its demand curve from E_1 to E_2 the result would be the now familiar triangular efficiency gain shown as areas 4 + 5. But since average cost pricing allows us to move this firm only part way—from E_1 to E_3—the gain is limited to area 4.[†]

Therefore, we conclude that since this policy of average cost pricing increases monopoly output from Q_1 to Q_3, it results in a *gain in allocative efficiency.* (Remember that unless we state otherwise, the word "efficiency" means "allocative efficiency.") Unfortunately, however, this policy, and any of the others discussed in this Box, may lead to a *loss in technical efficiency* (that is, the firm may not operate on its lowest possible cost curve). After all, why should the firm in Figure 11-9 strive hard to lower its costs,

---

[†]Robert A. Meyer and Hayne B. Leland conclude that the regulators of natural monopolies often do not succeed in "getting the price right"; that is, they select a price other than P_3 in our simple analysis in Figure 11-9*a*. Moreover, the effectiveness of regulatory agencies seems to differ widely between states. (See "The Effectiveness of Price Regulation," *Review of Economics and Statistics,* November, 1980 p. 566.)

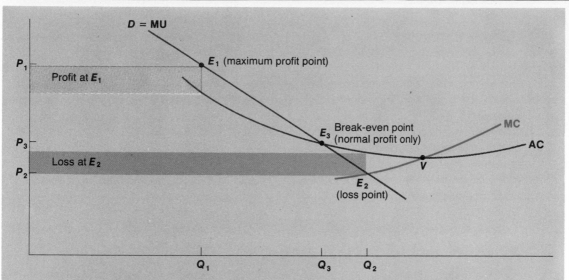

(a) **Average cost pricing.** An unrestricted monopoly would maximize profit by selecting point E_1 on its demand curve. (The profit it would earn is shown by the gray area.) Average cost pricing involves driving the monopoly down its demand curve to E_3, by setting a price ceiling at P_3. At this point the firm just breaks even, earning only the normal profit necessary to keep it in business. Marginal cost pricing (that is, setting price at P_2 in order to drive the monopoly further down its demand curve to E_2) is not feasible, because price P_2 is below average cost. Thus the firm would incur the loss shown by the red area, and eventually go out of business.

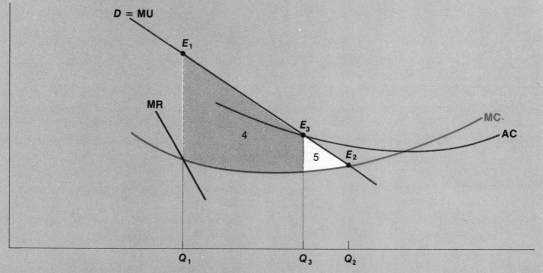

(b) **Efficiency gains that are achieved (4), and those that are not (5).** If it were feasible to drive the monopoly firm all the way down its demand curve from E_1 to E_2, then there would be an efficiency gain 4 + 5. But since the firm can be driven down only to E_3, the efficiency gain is limited to area 4.

Figure 11-9
Regulating monopoly price: The difficult case

when a reduction in costs will cause the regulatory agency to correspondingly lower price? Why shouldn't the firm's executives be allowed generous expense accounts, since such costs are simply passed on to consumers in the form of higher prices? No matter what the firm does, it isn't allowed to make a profit; so why should it tightly control its costs? (At best, it can earn a temporary profit only between the date it reduces its costs and the date the regulatory agency gets around to reducing its price.)

Government subsidy (with marginal cost pricing)

Another possible government policy to deal with the monopoly in Figure 11-9 is to force it all the way down its demand curve from E_1 to efficient point E_2 by marginal cost pricing, while at the same time paying the firm whatever lump-sum subsidy is necessary to cover its loss. In other words, a regulated price of P_2 drives the firm down its demand curve to point E_2 (thus capturing the entire possible efficiency gain 4 + 5), while a subsidy equal to the red area in panel a keeps the firm in business.

Although this policy may be attractive in theory, it raises such problems in practice that it is seldom used. (Subsidies to privately operated urban transit systems, however, have been justified along these lines.) For one thing, it is difficult for the public to understand why a government committed to controlling the market power of monopoly should end up subsidizing it. The point that the government is also regulating price (and thus eliminating monopoly profits) is difficult to explain to the public. Moreover, the policy of taking money out of the monopolist's pocket with one hand (the regulated price) while putting it back with the other (the subsidy) may strike the public as being inconsistent, even though it is not. In addition, the general problem in price regulation reappears here. So long as the government is committed to subsidizing the costs of

a monopolist, how can those costs be controlled? A firm may be very successful in holding costs down so long as it has to meet the test of the marketplace where failure means bankruptcy; but it may be far less successful in controlling its costs if it knows it will receive a subsidy for any loss it incurs.

Government ownership

The political problems involved in granting a subsidy are less severe if the government owns the monopoly, which it can then operate in the public interest at efficient point E_2. Again, taxpayers must subsidize the loss that results. Government-owned mass transit systems are often cited as examples. (Government subsidies cover more than half the costs of the typical large urban public transportation system.)

But there is no guarantee that such a publicly owned enterprise will be operated at the most efficient point E_2, since the objective of the government-appointed management may not be to increase efficiency so much as to redistribute income. (For example, the government may be trying indirectly to provide income—in the form of low-cost fares—to those who use the urban transport system.)

Finally, the same problem arises with government ownership as with the other policies discussed in this Box: So long as this firm's management receives whatever subsidy is necessary to cover its costs, it has inadequate incentive to keep costs down. There is a good reason why this may become a particularly serious problem in a public enterprise. Even in a private enterprise, the owners (stockholders) may have problems in controlling a management that is inefficient, wasteful, or pursuing its own interests at the expense of the owners' interests. But in a public enterprise this is even more difficult, because of the government bureaucracy that stands between the owners of the enterprise (the taxpayers) and its management. ∎

consumer surplus. Obviously, if there were some way for her to acquire part of this consumer surplus, it would be profitable for her to move in, and the community would benefit as well. She can do this if she is allowed to discriminate among her patients, selling her service at a higher price to some than to others. To illustrate, suppose she starts at initial position E, charging one price P to all her patients and incurring losses $1 + 2$. She can do better by discriminating; that is, by charging her first Q' patients (the wealthy ones) a higher fee, P'. This increases her income from these wealthy patients by areas $1 + 3$, more than offsetting her original losses $1 + 2$. Therefore, she is now able to more than cover her costs; with a higher income here than she could earn elsewhere, she decides to stay in this town.

In short, if she cannot discriminate, she will be forced to take an abnormally low income, and this community will lose a doctor. But if she is allowed to discriminate, she will earn a higher income, and stay in town. This is beneficial both for her and for her patients. In fact, it benefits even those patients who must pay the higher fee, because her presence provides them with a consumer surplus ($P'JF$) that they would otherwise have had to forego. Price discrimination is therefore justified in this case, because it benefits everyone concerned.

But even when price discrimination is desirable—as it is in this case—it may not be possible. To make different prices stick, the discriminating monopolist must be able to divide the market, thus preventing individuals who buy at the low price from turning around and selling to those who are charged the high price. In our example, the doctor can divide her market: A patient who buys a low-priced operation cannot turn around and sell it to a sick friend. On the other hand, a bus company may not be able to divide its adult market, charging some customers $10 and others $20. The reason is that those who are able to buy cheap $10 tickets can turn around and sell them to the others for some price (say $15) that benefits both groups. (But the bus company *can* divide its market between adults and children,

since an adult can't buy a cheap ticket from a child and use it on a bus.)

Finally, it should be reemphasized that it is possible to defend price discrimination by the monopolist in Figure 11-8 because she would be out of business otherwise (D does not overlap AC). But price discrimination is not justified in the normal case of monopoly where D does overlap AC and the monopolist is consequently able to earn a monopoly profit by quoting a single price. Indeed, an earlier section of this chapter explained why it may be inappropriate to allow such a monopolist to choose even a single price, let alone several. This is the type of monopoly that we shall concentrate on hereafter in this book—the classical monopoly which is able to produce profitably without discriminating, and sets price and output in a way that is damaging to the public interest.

DO FIRMS REALLY MAXIMIZE PROFITS?

The best of all monopoly profits is a quiet life.
J. R. Hicks

So far, it has been assumed that producers maximize their profit. But it should be recognized that they sometimes pursue quite different objectives. Sometimes, they may decide on a policy because it makes them look good to their stockholders. Sometimes, with the objective of expanding their market share, they may increase output beyond the profit maximizing point, provided they achieve some reasonable level of profit. (What often isn't clear is whether this is simply expansion for its own sake, or whether firms are giving up profit in the short run in order to increase it in the long run. For example, firms may want to grow in order to generate public confidence and thereby make it easier to sell their products in the future.) Alternatively, in order to avoid risk, producers may swing in the other direction, and "think small," only undertaking expenditures that will yield an assured high profit. Or they may follow a policy of "no change" solely because they enjoy the quiet life. For example, if they are earning large profits, why should they worry about changing their output and price just because their cost curves have shifted slightly? Or why should they worry about the minor loss incurred if they hire a few relatives?

Why not construct our economic theory using one of these other assumptions instead? The answer, in some cases, is that the assumptions are not specific enough. (For example, 10 business executives in identical circumstances, each pursuing the quiet life, might come up with 10 different decisions on output and price. And you can't construct a theory on that.) Even in those cases where a theory can be constructed, it will have the same flaw as profit maximization: It will not describe all economic decision-making. So we use profit maximization because this assumption is simple and precise enough to allow us to "get off square one" and construct a theory, and because it generally describes economic decision-making as well as any alternative assumption. But we recognize that in some cases it may not be as accurate a description of reality as we would like. And it is often only part of the story, since other objectives may also influence the decision-making process.[8] So we should be appropriately guarded in making claims for our conclusions.

Of course, if we have evidence that certain firms are pursuing some other objective (such as rapid growth), we may be able to adjust our profit-maximization conclusions in some reasonable way. For example, since high-growth firms tend to produce a larger output than profit-maximizing firms, we might ask: What does this greater output imply about price to the consumer? What are its effects on efficiency? How would producers respond to price regulation? And so on. The answers to some of these questions are straightforward, but others are not so clear. If we wanted to clarify them, we might even go one giant step further and construct a whole new theory from scratch, based on some other assumption than profit maximization. But that's a story for a more advanced course.

[8]For more detail on alternative theories of decision-making by the firm, see Robin Marris, *The Economic Theory of Managerial Capitalism,* (New York: Basic Books, 1968); and H. A. Simon, "Rational Decision-Making in Business Organizations," *American Economic Review,* September 1979, pp. 493–513.

Key Points

1 Monopoly means that there is a single seller. This situation may occur when a firm controls something essential to the production or sale of a good—like a patent, resource, or government license. Or it may occur if a number of firms combine in order to speak with one voice, so that they will be able to quote a single industry price.

2 Another important reason for monopoly is that a firm's costs may fall over such a wide range of output that total market demand can be most inexpensively satisfied by a single firm. This is a *natural monopoly.* Even when there are initially many firms in such an industry, they will tend to be eliminated by competition, with the single large firm that emerges able to undercut any present or future competitors.

3 A monopoly can do something a perfectly competitive firm cannot: Because it faces a demand curve that slopes downward to the right, it can quote the price at which it will sell.

4 Marginal revenue (MR) for a monopolist is not the same as price. The MR curve lies below the demand curve.

5 A monopolist maximizes profit by equating MC with MR, not with price. As a consequence, monopoly results in an inefficiently small output.

6 If the firm is not a natural monopoly—but instead is, say, the result of collusion—the government has available antitrust laws (described in Chapter 13) to break it up, or prevent it from forming in the first place.

7 If the firm *is* a natural monopoly, then breaking it up would raise costs. A preferred government policy is to set the maximum price the monopolist can charge. Facing this given price, the monopolist is forced into the price-taking role of the perfect competitor, and consequently increases output to a more efficient quantity.

8 A case can sometimes be made for allowing a monopoly to price-discriminate, that is, to charge a higher price to one group than to another. (A doctor in a small town, say, may charge a higher price to her wealthy patients.) Such discriminatory pricing may be justified if the good or service could not otherwise be produced.

Key Concepts

patent
legal monopoly
natural monopoly
collusive monopoly
oligopoly
market power

monopolist's demand
monopolist's marginal
 revenue
monopoly inefficiency
how monopoly raises price
 and reduces output

marginal cost pricing
discriminating monopoly
 (when justified, when
 not)
objectives other than
 maximizing profit

Problems

11-1 Which is closer to being a monopoly, American Motors or Rolls Royce? Answer the same question for the producer of bread in a small town or the producer of the wheat used in the bread. In each case, explain your answer.

11-2 Consider an indsutry in which the discovery and development of advanced machinery and technology mean that, as time passes, average costs for a firm tend to drift lower and lower. That is, through time the average cost for an individual firm moves from AC_1 to AC_2 in the following diagram. What do you think would happen in such an industry? Explain why. From the point of view of society as a whole, does the falling cost involve any advantages? Any disadvantages? In your view, how do these compare?

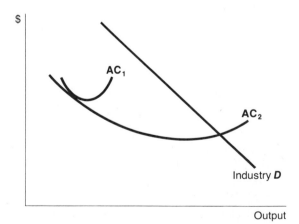

11-3 *(a)* If the firm with AC_2 in the diagram above is not regulated, would you expect that all the monopoly profits would go to the firm's owners? If not, who else do you think might eventually capture a share of these profits?

(b) Draw in the marginal cost curve that corresponds to AC_2. Show the best level at which to set regulated price. Explain why it is best.

*11-4 (This provides another way of viewing a monopolist's profit maximization, in addition to the two set out in Figure 11-4.) In the diagram below, note that the TC and TR curves for a monopolist are the same as for a perfect competitor in Box 9-1, except for one important difference: Because a monopoly faces a downward sloping demand curve, its TR is a curved rather than a straight line. (The TR curve is drawn from the data in Table 11-1, column 3.) Using the earlier approach in Box 9-1, describe how the profit maximizing output of this monopolist is determined. In particular, show geometrically why MC = MR.

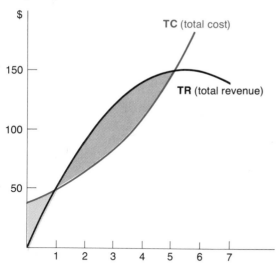

11-5 Given the cost conditions in the following diagram, name the price that would be set by a monopoly which is:

(a) Maximizing its profit

(b) Operating as a nonprofit organization

(c) Run by the government at an efficient output

If (a) and/or (b) are not efficient, explain why.

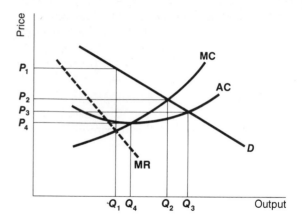

11-6 Does output Q in Figure 11-4b yield the monopolist the largest profit per unit of output? Explain why or why not.

*11-7 Evaluate the following policy recommendation: "The sole objective in dealing with monopoly is to eliminate excess profits. And this is easy to do. Just examine the firm's current operations, calculate its average cost (including normal profit), and set price at this level."

11-8 The following diagram shows the demand and the costs the government faces in providing a public utility service (say electricity) in a certain city.

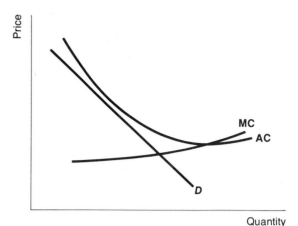

(a) If the government is interested only in maximizing the utility's profit (minimizing its loss), show the price it will set and how much it will produce and sell. Also show its profit or loss.

(b) Is this output the best from the viewpoint of allocative efficiency? If so, explain why. If not, show what the most efficient output is and explain why. What price does the firm set to achieve this output and what is its profit or loss at the efficient output?

(c) Suppose that this public utility is allowed to set discriminatory prices. It decides to charge the public a higher rate for its initial purchases while for any additional purchases it continues to charge the rate it set in question *(b)*. Could the public utility sell an efficient output and still make profits by following a policy of price discrimination?

(d) Do you see now why public utilities are sometimes allowed to set discriminatory rates?

(e) In the section "The Special Case of Discriminating Monopoly," it was observed that for successful discrimination a firm must be able to segregate its market and prevent resale among buyers. The doctor has no great problem in segregating her market. How about the public utility selling electricity?

11-9 Suppose the government owns the two monopolies shown in Figures 11-7 and 11-9. In the interests of efficiency, how should their prices be set? Would each firm operate at a profit or a loss? What government subsidies (if any) would be required? If two such monopolies are merged into a single government-owned firm, will it necessarily require a subsidy? Explain.

APPENDIX 11-A

GOVERNMENT MARKETING PROGRAMS: HELPING COMPETITORS TO ACT LIKE A MONOPOLIST

> Things are seldom what they seem,
> Skim milk masquerades as cream.
> **Gilbert and Sullivan,**
> **H.M.S. Pinafore**

A government agency set up to regulate a monopoly will force the firm to act like a perfect competitor, in the process driving it down its demand curve (Figure 11-7). But in some cases, the government acts in the opposite direction: A competitive industry may be provided with a marketing organization that allows the competitors to act like a monopolist and thus move *up* their market demand curve—something they cannot do by acting individually.

Point E_C in Figure 11-10a shows the equilibrium in a competitive industry before any attempt is made to monopolize it. The market price is $80, with 1,000 units being sold.

When a marketing association is formed, all producers speak with one voice and quote a higher price. Suppose the price the association decides on is $140, well above the competitive $80 level. The industry consequently moves up its demand curve from E_C to E_M. To make this higher price stick, the association must, like any monopolist, reduce sales from 1,000 units to 600. This cut implies that the individual firm illustrated on the right must decrease its output from 10 to a quota of 6. Therefore, the firm moves from F_1 to F_2. Despite the fact its output has been reduced, its increased price now allows it to earn a profit (shown as the shaded gray area).

The monopolization of this industry has had the expected results. Producers benefit from their newfound profit, while consumers lose because of increased price. On balance, there is an overall efficiency loss shown by the red area on the left.

However, there are strong pressures for such associations to come apart. While it is in the collective interest of all firms to restrict their output in order to raise price to $140, at this high price it is in the interest of the individual firm to *expand* output. In fact, at the $140 price set by the association, the firm on the right has an incentive to produce, not at F_2, but at B, the output where MC intersects this given price. The problem, then, for the industry association is how to compel each individual firm to operate in the collective interest at F_2, rather than attempt to pursue its own interest at B. This discipline is essential: If some firms start to produce more than their quota, more than 600 units will come onto the market, and price will fall. Moreover, getting existing firms to stick to their quotas is not the only problem: The entry of new firms, attracted by the above-normal (gray) profits, would also drive price down.

The problem of enforcing quotas and restricting entry often leads perfectly competitive producers of agricultural goods in the United States and elsewhere to seek a government marketing agency to do what a private producers' association may not

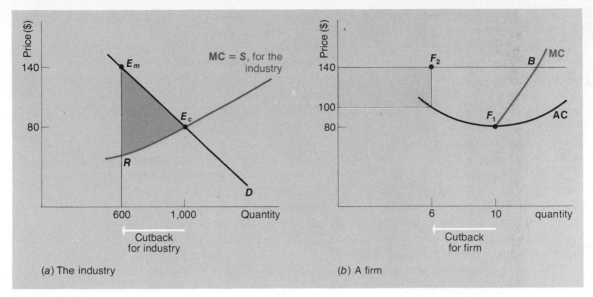

Figure 11-10
Effect of a producers' association or government marketing program on an industry and on an individual firm

Panel *a* illustrates a competitive industry. Market equilibrium is at E_C where $D = S$. Market price is $80, and there are 1,000 units supplied. When this industry is monopolized by a producers' association or government marketing agency, equilibrium moves from E_C to E_M. The association quotes a price of $140, with industry sales being reduced as a consequence from 1,000 units to 600.

In turn, the sales of the individual firm on the right must be reduced from 10 units to a quota of 6. This means that the firm moves from F_1 to F_2 where it makes the $240 profit shown by the gray area. (On each of its 6 units, it earns a $40 profit.) But the problem is that although this reduction in output has generated profits, each firm facing the given $140 price would like to increase its output. The firm shown would like to move from F_2 to B where MC = price. But such additional output would drive market price down; the industry would slide down its demand curve from E_M toward E_C. Moreover, with this price reduction, the profits of individual firms would also be reduced. (Of course, when there are thousands of firms in an industry—as in agriculture—a few can violate their quotas without disturbing price. But not many.) Thus disciplining firms to stick to their quotas is extremely important. This is one of the reasons why producers often prefer to have the government run the program.

be strong enough to accomplish. Since even a government agency may have difficulty in enforcing a quota on output, limitations are often placed, instead, on the acreage a farmer can plant (in the case of U.S. tobacco producers)[9] or on the number of hens that a poultry farm can maintain (in the case of Canadian egg producers). But such a quota system, even when enforced by government regulations, may spring leaks. For example, a number of Canadian egg producers were found with more hens than their quotas allowed. In fact, two of these individuals who "came up with egg on their face" were members of the board of directors of the marketing board that had set the

---

[9]For other U.S. agricultural products, acreage limitations are typically far less strict. Nonetheless, farmers may be required to set aside (idle) some acreage in order to qualify for government price support benefits (of the kind set out in Box 10-5).

quotas! There can be no clearer illustration of the problems of restricting output when producers' collective and individual interests are in conflict.

In the United States, there have been a number of examples of voluntary producers' associations. To cite one: By 1910, milk producers in certain regions of the country had privately banded together to gain bargaining power over their price. Their success was always limited by their inability to firmly control output coming onto the market, so that by the early 1930s they had become relatively ineffective. Under the pressure of very low milk prices in 1935, the government introduced its present system of "milk marketing orders," which guarantee the farmer a minimum price, depending on the use of the milk and the location. (These prices are not necessarily set at the monopoly level, but are the result of a political compromise. Except for California, the present price in any U.S. location depends on its distance from Eau Claire, Wisconsin, the heart of the U.S. dairy industry.) In addition to efficiency questions, there were unfortunate side effects when the government thus became involved in propping up price for a group of producers: The milk suppliers had an incentive to make campaign contributions to politicians with potential influence over their marketing program. Promises of large campaign contributions by milk producers to Nixon before the 1972 election were followed by a price increase for the industry, and this became the subject of a special Watergate-related investigation. ■

Problems

*11-10   Show the profit that the firm in Figure 11-10*b* would capture if it could get away with producing at point *B*. Is this an equilibrium if all firms try to do the same? Explain.

*11-11   How might an agricultural marketing association be defended by using the theory of the second best?

APPENDIX 11-B

AVERAGE COST PRICING: PUBLIC UTILITY REGULATION

When the theory of average cost pricing is put into practice in regulating a **public utility**, several problems arise.

A *public utility* is a natural monopoly in which many decisions (particularly pricing decisions) are regulated by a government agency. It typically provides an essential service to the public and often has high overhead costs because of the heavy investment it requires to deliver its product to the consumer. Examples include the companies that supply telephone service (via phone lines), natural gas (via pipelines) and electricity (via transmission lines).

How is average cost calculated?

Recall from Figure 11-9 that average cost pricing involves setting a price that will barely cover average costs (including normal profit); in other words, the objective is to keep the price low enough to prevent excessive monopoly profits, but high enough to provide a normal profit. But estimating a fair or normal profit for the owners involves estimating the amount of capital they have invested, and applying a fair percentage rate of return to that capital. (Profit = invested capital × percentage rate of return on that capital.)

(a) *What is a fair percentage rate of return on invested capital?* The answer to this should be: the opportunity cost of capital—the percentage rate of return it could earn elsewhere in the economy. Although regulatory agencies have given some consideration to earnings in other sectors of the economy, their rates of return have not matched rates elsewhere, perhaps because of tradition and a feeling that it is their responsibility to the public to keep their prices down. (This problem of a relatively low rate of return in public utilities has been made worse by a squeeze that results from inflation: It raises the costs of inputs for the utilities, but there is a regulatory time lag before they are allowed to raise their price.) In turn, the relatively low rate of return in public utilities has made it difficult for them to attract capital.[10]

(b) *What is the value of the capital invested (the "rate base")?* Should it be the *original* price which the firm paid for machinery and other capital, or their *present* replacement cost?[11] Because of inflation, it makes a lot of difference. The cost of

---

[10]It is often argued that this lower return is a reflection of the lower risk involved in public utility investment. True, there is no risk that the public utility will be driven bankrupt by competitors, since there are none. But public utility investment involves its own special kind of risk: the risk that the regulators will not adequately or quickly enough protect the investors' return from being eroded by inflation. (And as we shall see in Chapter 22, there is another very substantial risk involved in investing in a public utility using nuclear power: At any point, the government or the courts may force the firm to suspend or terminate its operations.)

[11]Adjusting for depreciation in either case.

replacing most equipment far exceeds its original cost years ago. Thus far, there is no clear consensus among the regulatory agencies on which method to use.

Other problems and reform proposals

Few would argue that regulation of a public utility should be abolished; it's the most reasonable way of getting the low costs offered by a natural monopoly while avoiding the worst monopoly abuses. But it is far from being problem free. It can be argued that regulation can be improved, both by making it more consistent, and by speeding up regulatory decisions (so capital-starved public utilities are caught less in an inflation squeeze). It is also important to ensure that regulation is being applied only to a natural monopoly and not to a (perhaps closely related) activity that is not a natural monopoly at all. For example, the provision of local telephone service is a natural monopoly and requires regulation. But certain other closely related activities—such as long-distance service and the production of telephones and telephone terminal equipment—may not be. ∎

CHAPTER 12
Markets between Monopoly and Perfect Competition

People of the same trade seldom meet together, even for merriment and diversion, but the conversation ends in a conspiracy against the public, or in some contrivance to raise prices.
Adam Smith,
Wealth of Nations

Monopoly represents the clearest form of market power; the monopolist is alone in the marketplace and has power to choose the price at which sales are made. But, if we look at such giants of American business as General Motors, IBM, and General Electric, we find that most of them are not monopolists. General Motors competes with Ford, Chrysler, Toyota, and Volkswagen; IBM has to contend with Control Data and Burroughs; and General Electric competes with Westinghouse (in the electrical generator market) and with Pratt and Whitney (in the jet engine market). ***Oligopoly***—where the market is dominated by a *few* sellers—is more significant in the U.S. economy than outright monopoly.

In this chapter we discuss oligopoly, concentrating on the difficult policy question it raises, and the various measures the government can use to control it. We also describe another kind of market that lies between monopoly and perfect competition: monopolistic competition. This will complete our discussion of the basic market forms.

OLIGOPOLY

The degree to which an industry is dominated by a few firms is measured by a ***concentration ratio***. Two such ratios are used; the first measures the proportion of an industry's output produced by its four largest firms; the second measures the output of its eight largest firms. Figure 12-1 shows that the auto and breakfast food industries are each dominated by the four largest firms. But some industries, like sporting goods, are not. (Moreover, while *production* of U.S. autos is highly concentrated, *sales* are much less concentrated because of substantial imports.)

Have these concentration ratios been getting larger or smaller over time? Back in 1951, MIT's Morris Adelman observed that "Any tendency either way, if it does exist, must be at the speed of a glacial drift."[1] Since then, concentra-

[1] Morris Adelman, "The Measurement of Industrial Concentration," *Review of Economics and Statistics,* November 1951, pp. 295–296.

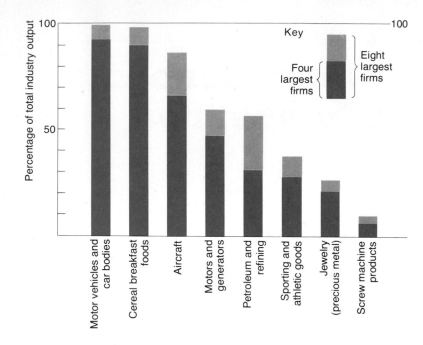

Figure 12-1
Importance of "big four" and "big eight" in selected industries, 1972. (Output is measured by value of shipments.)
Source: Bureau of the Census, *1972 Census of Manufacturers.*

tion seems to have been increasing, but by a barely discernible amount: It has been estimated that, over the long stretch of a quarter of a century prior to 1972, the (dark red) concentration ratio for 167 U.S. manufacturing industries increased, on average, from 40.9 to 42.7.[2] There seems to be no strong tendency for America's largest firms to eliminate their competitors and emerge as monopolists from the competitive

\

²See Willard F. Mueller and Richard T. Rogers, "The Role of Advertising in Changing Concentration of Manufacturing Industries," *The Review of Economics and Statistics,* February 1980, p. 90. These authors also provide estimates indicating that the slight increase in the overall average was the net result of a small decline in concentration in producer goods industries and a more marked increase in concentration in consumer goods industries—in part, because TV advertising made it easier for the few largest firms in a consumer goods industry to increasingly dominate their market. There have also been marked differences in concentration at a more detailed industry level. For example, prior to 1972, the dark red concentration ratio had fallen for motors and generators, had remained essentially constant for cereals, and had risen for motor vehicles.

struggle. Instead, oligopoly seems to be a stable form of market organization. It is not merely a temporary stop on an inevitable road to monopoly. What forces account for this stability? Why do a few firms grow so large, while none goes all the way to become a monopolist?

Part of the answer lies in the nature of costs. In many industries, there is an advantage of large-scale production: Average cost declines as output rises. A plant designed to produce 500,000 cars per year can operate at a much lower average cost than a plant designed to produce 100,000. But costs do not continue to fall forever. Once a plant is producing a million units, doubling its output won't significantly reduce its costs further.

When costs fall over a considerable range, they encourage the development of large firms. But when costs eventually begin to rise while each producer's output is still far short of satisfying total market demand, large firms are discouraged from growing even larger and developing into a monopoly. Thus, cost conditions may lead to **natural oligopoly.**

Natural oligopoly occurs when the average costs of individual firms fall over a large enough range so that a few firms can produce the total quantity sold at the lowest average cost.

This definition is illustrated in Figure 12-2b, where natural oligopoly is compared with perfect competition and natural monopoly.

But it is not just cost conditions that account for the persistence of oligopoly. Oligopoly represents a balance between forces that encourage concentration and those that work against it.

One of the strongest forces working toward larger and larger corporations is the incentive such firms have to acquire market power. The larger a firm becomes by internal growth or by buying out and absorbing its competitors, the greater its power to set price. (The fewer and smaller its competitors, the fewer sales they will be able to take away if the firm raises its price.) Thus, a firm in natural oligopoly, with no further incentive to expand because of cost reductions, may nonetheless seek to expand in order to push competitors out of the market and thus acquire more power to set price.

On the other side, the government provides a countervailing force that deters the expansion of firms, and discourages the monopolization of an industry. Specifically, the desire to protect consumers and competitors has led Congress to pass antitrust laws that prevent firms from establishing a monopolylike position.

The **product differentiation** which exists in many oligopolistic markets also discourages monopolization. A car is not just a car; there are many kinds—it's a differentiated product. For many years American Motors has enjoyed a near monopoly in the production of a very special kind of vehicle—a four-wheel-drive jeep.

Figure 12-2
Natural oligopoly compared with perfect competition and natural monopoly

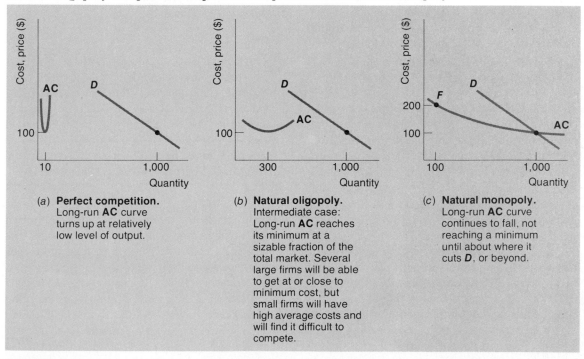

(a) **Perfect competition.** Long-run **AC** curve turns up at relatively low level of output.

(b) **Natural oligopoly.** Intermediate case: Long-run **AC** reaches its minimum at a sizable fraction of the total market. Several large firms will be able to get at or close to minimum cost, but small firms will have high average costs and will find it difficult to compete.

(c) **Natural monopoly.** Long-run **AC** curve continues to fall, not reaching a minimum until about where it cuts **D**, or beyond.

Paradoxically, the profits it obtained by its dominance in this small niche of the market saved it from bankruptcy, and thus prevented the broader auto industry from becoming even more concentrated. Likewise, product differentiation is important in many other oligopolistic industries. Control Data builds computers that are similar but not identical to giant IBMs. McDonnell Douglas builds planes that are similar but not identical to those of Boeing. (While product differentiation is significant in many oligopolistic markets, it is not important in them all. In the basic steel industry, for example, one company's product is much the same as another's.)

THE OLIGOPOLIST AS A PRICE SEARCHER

We have seen that oligopoly lies in the broad area between the polar cases of monopoly and perfect competition. At either of these two extremes, the firm is free of worry over how its competitors will react if it changes its price or output. The monopolist (by definition) has no competitors worth worrying about. On the other hand, the perfectly competitive firm has so many competitors that none will even be aware of any change it may make in its price or output. Since it provides such a miniscule part of the total market supply, its competitors won't even notice if it reduces the amount it is supplying. In contrast, in an oligopoly, each firm is very much aware of the other firms. Each recognizes that the others will notice any action it takes, and it must therefore worry about how they will react. If it reduces price, will its competitors follow? Will its action set off a price war? And where may this lead? In an oligopoly, the firms are mutually *interdependent;* each is very sensitive to the reactions of its competitors.

These three different types of market can be distinguished in a simple way. In perfect competition, firms are **price takers.** The individual firm has no influence over price, since it is determined by the impersonal forces of demand and supply. In monopoly, the firm is a **price maker.** By selecting a point on its demand curve, it chooses the price at which it will sell. In oligopoly, the firm is a **price searcher.** Although it has influence over price, this is limited by the possible reactions of its competitors.

Because an oligopolistic firm is in competition with several other large firms capable of vigorously responding to its actions, it must develop a marketing strategy. The world of oligopoly can resemble a chess game, with move and countermove. And, like a chess game, the outcome may be unpredictable. Once we enter the world of oligopoly, we leave behind the simple, definite solutions of both monopoly and perfect competition. Ever since Augustin Cournot's nineteenth-century study of duopoly (two sellers), it has been recognized that, when there are just a few sellers, the search for an equilibrium price can be complex. Oligopoly is one of the least satisfactory areas of economic theory.

For this reason, it is not possible here to do more than emphasize a few highlights. The first topic involves the situation where oligopolists recognize their common interest in raising prices and collude to act as though they were a monopoly. The second topic is the case where oligopolists abandon this common interest in pursuit of their own individual interests and the collusive arrangement comes apart.

Collusion

In the United States, collusion is against the law. The reason for such laws may be seen by looking at the economic effects of a **cartel,** the most formal type of collusion, where firms get together to gain the advantages of monopoly.

A *cartel* **is a formal agreement among firms about price and/or market sharing.**

As a simple example, consider a market where there are three similar firms. Although they maintain their own separate corporate identities, with their own plants and their own sales forces, suppose they get together to agree on a common price. In their collective interest, what is the best price to choose? The answer: the price which a monopolist would pick; that is, the price which will maximize their combined profits. Specifically, this price is determined in Figure 12-3 as follows. The marginal cost curves of the three

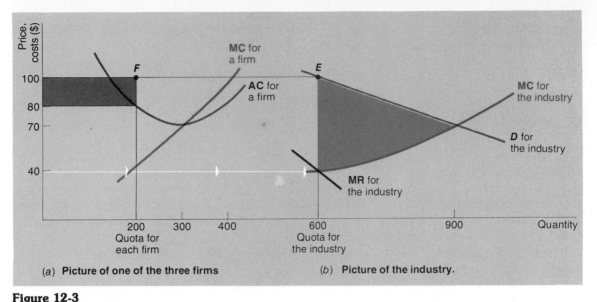

Figure 12-3
Collusion by three oligopolists
In panel b, MC for the industry is shown as the horizontal sum of the MC curves for the three individual firms on the left, and MR for the industry is calculated from industry demand D. The maximization of industry profit requires that output be set at 600 units (where industry MC = MR) and that price be set at $100. In other words, colluding oligopolists select point E on the market demand curve. How is the market of 600 units divided among the three firms? The simplest solution is to set a quota of 200 units for each, as shown in panel a. Thus each firm produces at point F, where it earns the gray $4,000 profit that results from the sale of 200 units at a $20 profit on each. (This $20 unit profit is the difference between the $100 selling price and the $80 average cost.) The problem is that the individual firm facing the given $100 price would prefer to sell more than its 200-unit quota. (It can sell an additional unit for $100, while its MC is only $45.) But if it does so, more than 600 units will be produced, and in panel b industry price will fall. If firms thus forget their *collective* interest in favor of pursuing their *individual* interest, the price-fixing arrangement comes apart. (For those who have studied Figure 11-10b, notice the similarity between the milk marketing program described there and the three colluding oligopolists in the present diagram. The only substantial difference is that in the earlier case there was such a large number of producers that they had little hope of managing and enforcing a private agreement, so they turned to the government. But in this present case, there are only three producers, so there is at least some hope of arriving at an agreement and making it stick.)

firms are added horizontally (as shown by the white arrows) to give the combined marginal cost curve for the industry. The highest profit is made at the point in panel b where this marginal cost curve cuts the industry's marginal revenue. (MR may be calculated from D for an industry, just as it was for a firm in Table 11-1.) This intersection of MC and MR determines the industry's profit-maximizing output of 600 units, while point E on the demand curve above indicates that the collusive price can be raised all the way up to $100.

This cartel benefits producers who have maximized their collective profit. (The profit each

realizes is shown by the gray area in panel a.) But from the viewpoint of society, this collusive arrangement presents the same problem as a monopoly. Too little is produced. For an efficient allocation of the resources of society, output should be raised from 600 units to 900, where marginal cost intersects the demand (marginal utility) curve. The efficiency loss from collusive pricing is shown by the red triangle (which is exactly like the triangular loss first explained in detail in Figure 10-3b). Thus in a cartel, just as in monopoly, Adam Smith's "invisible hand" fails, as Smith himself recognized. (See the quotation from Smith that introduced this chapter.)

The breakdown of collusion: The incentive to cheat

While a cartel may maximize profit by selecting price in the same way as a monopolist, it faces a problem that does not exist in monopoly. Because the cartel consists of more than one firm, some way must be found of dividing the market. This is necessary because the only way that the market price can be maintained at its profit-maximizing level of $100 in panel *b* is by restricting output to 600 units. (If the cartel members sell more, there will be downward pressure on price; that is, the industry will slide down its demand curve to the right.) There are a number of ways that participants can agree to limit sales. The market may be divided equally among all members (in this example, 200 units each), or it may be divided according to historical market shares, or by geographical area. For example, in the 1920s, two European firms agreed to carve up the market for explosives. Dynamit was allowed exclusive rights in certain continental European markets, in exchange for leaving British Empire markets to Nobel. (This was the firm of the same Nobel who established a peace prize.)[3]

From the viewpoint of the cartel members, the problem with such arrangements is that they tend to be unstable. Each firm in the cartel has an *incentive to cheat* by producing more than its allotted share.[4] To see why, note in panel *a* of Figure 12-3 that each firm is producing 200 units at a marginal cost of only $45. But the market price is $100; if a firm can steal a sale away from its competitors, it will increase its profit by $55. Thus, it has an incentive to step up sales efforts, or give secret price rebates in order to win customers. (Even if a firm grants a 30, 40 or 50 percent rebate on the selling price of $100, the return from the sale will still exceed the $45 marginal cost.) So the problem is seen to be this: The members of the cartel have a *collective* interest in keeping sales down in order to keep the price up. But each member firm has an *individual* interest, in conflict with the others, to sell more than its allotted share. If individual interests come to dominate, firms produce beyond their quotas, and the cartel's price collapses in a price war as firms fight over market shares. Because of the strength of the individual interest, cartels have tended to come apart after short and stormy histories.

Moreover, when there is a complete breakdown in a cartel, the struggle over markets may intensify. This is particularly true if the cost advantages of large-scale production have increased as a result of technological change. In this case, a natural oligopoly may be evolving into a natural monopoly. In the absence of government intervention, only one firm will ultimately survive. The question is, which one? Each firm wants to be the victor; each has an incentive to try to gain an advantage over its rivals by expanding rapidly to gain the lower costs from large-scale production. Excess supply is likely, with firms pushing frantically for sales. The result may be **cutthroat competition;** that is, selling at a price below cost in order to drive rivals out of business. In this struggle, the prize will probably go to the firm with the "deepest pockets" (the largest financial resources), which enable it to sustain the short-term losses while it is cutting the throats of its rivals.

[3] There are other ways of carving up a market. In the 1930s, Westinghouse agreed to pay General Electric a 2 percent royalty for the right to produce an improved light bulb, provided Westinghouse sold not more than one-third as many bulbs as GE. But if Westinghouse tried to increase its sales beyond this quantity, it had to pay a savage 30 percent royalty. You can imagine how effectively this agreement froze the relative shares of the market going to Westinghouse and GE.

Another form of collusion is a *bidding cartel.* For example, in isolated cases, some antique dealers in Britain have met together before the auction of a valuable item to set the price at which all of them but one would drop out of the bidding. This meant that their designated member who *was* left in the bidding was able to buy the antique for a bargain price at the expense of the seller. Why were the other dealers prepared to stop bidding at a low price? The answer: They knew that they would get their turn to make a bargain purchase.

[4] It is "cheating" as viewed by the other members of the cartel, but not as viewed by the public. More production will lower price and reduce the red efficiency-loss triangle.

A CASE STUDY OF COLLUSION: OIL

The most conspicuous and successful collusive arrangement of recent decades has been the Organization of Petroleum Exporting Countries (OPEC), made up of most of the major oil exporters, including many of the Middle Eastern nations, along with Indonesia, Nigeria, and Venezuela. These OPEC nations succeeded in raising the price of oil *by more than ten times,* from less than $3 a barrel in early 1973 to over $30 in 1980. (See Figure 12-4). The result has been far and away the greatest peacetime transfer of wealth between nations in history.

OPEC's success in 1973–1974 was particularly surprising because a number of experts thought it would fail. True, OPEC had one great strength: Oil buyers had to deal with its members, since there was no other major international source of oil. (Despite new discoveries, this remained essentially true throughout the '70s. See Figure 12-5, a 1978 map of international trade flows in oil, along with the world's known reserves. In particular, note the dominant position of Saudi Arabia.) With this control over the world's supply of internationally traded oil, the OPEC nations—and especially Saudi Arabia—have substantial control over their selling price.

At the same time, OPEC has always had an apparent weakness: In raising the price so rapidly, it seemed to have no system for setting production quotas. Without such quotas, how could OPEC prevent competition among its members from undercutting its price? The answer: There were a number of special features of the international oil market that made OPEC much stronger and more stable than the typical collusive arrangement.

Why OPEC was able to raise price successfully without setting production quotas

1 The international oil companies such as Exxon and Royal Dutch Shell were concerned with ensuring future supplies by maintaining good relations with OPEC members. They were therefore hesitant to encourage price cutting by switching away from a country with a high price to one with a somewhat lower price (although they have done this to some degree).

Furthermore, the major oil companies have no strong incentive to encourage price-cutting and a breakup of the cartel, since their profits have soared as a result of higher oil prices. (While OPEC has gotten most of the price increase, the oil companies have gotten a price increase on the oil that they produce and sell within the United States.)[5]

---

[5]On the other hand, it has been a difficult decade for the oil companies in two senses. First, the public has often blamed them for the price increases, even though it is the OPEC nations that have taken the lead in raising prices. Second, they are losing the control they used to have over international oil flows, as the OPEC members have increasingly cut them out in favor of selling directly to the governments of the oil-importing countries.

Figure 12-4
How the world price of oil has increased
There have been two periods of very rapid increases in the price of oil—1973–1974 and 1979–1980. But in between, oil price rose by less than the rate of inflation. (OPEC's real income per barrel of oil declined.)
Source: World Oil, August 15, 1980, p. 55.

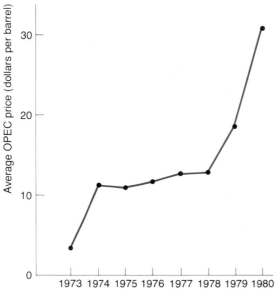

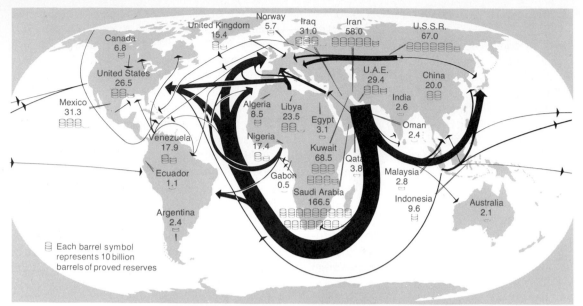

Figure 12-5

If you want to buy oil on the international market, OPEC is the place to go

OPEC dominates the supply of oil on the international market: The width of arrows represents the volume of international flows of oil in 1978. (Domestic flows are not shown. Two of the largest are from domestic producers to users within the United States and within the U.S.S.R.)

Source: Energy Information Agency, Department of Energy, *Annual Report to Congress, 1979,* vol. 2, pp. 37, 72.

2 The oil companies are further discouraged from switching between oil-supplying countries because oil has special chemical characteristics (sulfur content, etc.). Refineries designed for oil from one source are not always able to use oil from another.

3 The low short-run elasticity of demand for OPEC oil increased the incentive for OPEC nations to collude. They could raise price without a large short-run reduction in the quantity sold. And because sales held up well, there was less temptation for sellers to "rock the boat" by squabbling over market shares.

There are several reasons why the short-run demand for OPEC oil is inelastic. First, it is difficult to acquire substitutes for it: There isn't time to develop other forms of energy like solar or atomic power. Second, oil is essential. Evidence of this was provided in 1973 and 1979 when there were gasoline shortages. People in some states waited in line for hours before breakfast to acquire gasoline. And heating oil and other oil products that keep us from "freezing in the dark" are even more essential than gasoline. (Moreover, a supply of OPEC oil is even more critical for the Europeans and Japanese than for us. The Japanese have no signifi-

cant domestic sources of oil; they must import practically all that they use. At all times of the day and night, 365 days a year, the shipping lane between the Persian Gulf and Japan is punctuated every few miles with a gigantic tanker carrying the huge volume of oil necessary to fuel Japanese industry.)

The third reason why the short-run demand is inelastic is that oil represents only a small fraction of total costs. This is particularly true in manufacturing: Factories are willing, if necessary, to pay a much higher price for oil rather than shut down.

Finally, there was a fourth reason why the U.S. demand for OPEC oil was inelastic: The U.S. government kept the domestic price of oil from rising as fast as the world price. This meant that only part of any increase in OPEC price was passed on to American oil users. Therefore, Americans didn't reduce their consumption as much. In other words, the demand facing OPEC was less responsive to price (less elastic) because the U.S. government buffered Americans from the full impact of OPEC price increases. From OPEC's point of view, it seemed that Americans were willing to keep on buying oil with little regard for the price they had to pay. This made it easy for OPEC to raise price further. [This meant that the United States was caught in a vicious circle: The attempt to keep the U.S. domestic price down made it easier for OPEC to raise the world price; and the higher the world price (the higher the price of U.S. imports), the more difficult it became to hold the U.S. domestic price down.]

4 Not only was the elasticity of demand for oil low during the '70s. In addition, during the critical 1973 period when OPEC began its rapid price increases, the demand curve for oil was shifting out rapidly because of the boom conditions that existed then. Thus when OPEC began hiking the price, demand was both inelastic and growing.

5 At the same time, the OPEC *supply* of oil was being curtailed for noneconomic reasons. Because of the Arab embargo on sales to the United States and other countries supporting Israel in the 1973 Yom Kippur war, OPEC's oil exports fell by about 25 percent. This reduction in supply helped make the first rapid price increases of 1973 stick.

6 But as the '70s progressed, it became evident that there was another, even more important controlling influence over supply. Saudi Arabia, the largest producer for the world market, was adjusting its supply in order to control price. Specifically, whenever it appeared that a glut (oversupply) was developing on the world oil market, Saudi Arabia would cut back its own production. This maintained the world oil shortage that kept the price from falling. This was the main reason why OPEC was able over that decade to maintain a high price without resort to production quotas.

The key role of Saudi Arabia

Saudi Arabia is able to cut back its supply of oil because of its very special circumstances. Its population is small, and it has accumulated large assets from past oil sales. Therefore, it can afford to cut back its production at any time, keeping "its black gold in the ground." For example, by March 1975, in the face of weakening world oil price, the Saudis—with a capacity of 11.5 million barrels a day—had cut back their production to only 6.5 million. (However, the Saudis are now committed to ambitious and expensive development projects. And they want to keep a sizable cushion of foreign assets. Therefore, their freedom to cut back production may be less in the future than it was in the past.)

The Saudis have not only cut back production on occasion in order to keep the price up; they have also taken action on occasion to keep the price down. Why would they want to do this? The major reason is that they are concerned with maximizing their *long-term* gains, and a very high price of oil today would encourage importing countries to develop substitute forms of energy, thus weakening the demand for Saudi oil in the future. And the future of the oil market is a much greater concern for Saudi Arabia with its very large reserves than it is for some of the other OPEC countries with smaller reserves but larger populations and heavier financial requirements today.

How does Saudi Arabia keep the price from rising even faster than it does—that is, how does it keep other OPEC members from quoting even more rapidly escalating prices? The answer is by threatening to increase its supply or by actually doing so. Thus, for example, the Saudis successfully threatened a supply increase in 1977. And in late 1979 and 1980, they increased their output to reduce upward price pressures caused by the supply reductions following the Iranian revolution.[6] Nevertheless, the price more than doubled in 1979-80. (The problems associated with rapidly rising oil prices are considered in detail in Chapter 22.)

[6] According to some experts, part of this upward price pressure was caused by the Saudis' *own* earlier production cuts.

PRICING BY AMERICAN OLIGOPOLIES

We have seen that one of the ways oligopolists can try to avoid price wars is to form a cartel and agree formally on price. But within the United States this sort of collusion is illegal. How, then, do American oligopolists reduce the pressure of price competition? How do they avoid price wars and arrive at a reasonably profitable price? (Obviously, it is important for oligopolists to find answers to these questions. Equally matched giant competitors may face mutual exhaustion if they decide to slug it out by trying to capture markets with prices below average costs. In their exhaustion, they have a mutual interest in coming to a *modus vivendi*—to live and let live.)

One traditional explanation of why oligopolists can typically avoid price wars is that each firm may face a "kinked demand curve."

The kinked demand curve

The best way to understand this concept is to put yourself in the position of one of the three large oligopolists in an industry. If you cut your price, the other two competing firms are likely to take your act as a challenge. Since neither can afford to let you take away a share of its market, it is likely to meet your price cut with a price cut of its own. On the other hand, if you raise price, your competitors may consider this a golden opportunity. By keeping their own selling price stable, they will be able to capture a share of your sales. You therefore perceive that your competitors are behaving in a nonsymmetrical way: If you drop your price they will follow you, but if you raise your price they will not.

Figure 12-6 shows how this sort of behavior can lead to price stability. In this market, the three firms are assumed to be of equal size; each initially has one-third of total sales. Suppose your firm is the one illustrated. You know that if you change price and your competitors follow, you will retain your present one-third of the market. Thus you will move along the relatively vertical demand curve labeled d_f. (Note that at any price, say P_2, the quantity you sell on d_f is one-third of the total sales shown on the market demand curve D.) In other words, d_f is the

demand curve the oligopolistic firm faces *if* its competitors follow its price down *or* up.

However, d_f is relevant only if you quote a price *below* the existing price at E_1. If you quote a price *above* this—say P_3—your competitors will *not* follow. Instead, they will stand pat and you will lose part of your market to them, as shown by the red arrow.

Therefore, if you drop your price below E_1, you face demand d_f, while if you raise your price above E_1, you face demand d. In other words, the expected behavior of your competitors presents you with the kinked demand curve shown by the heavy lines in Figure 12-6.

The kinked demand curve shown by the heavy lines in Figure 12-6 is the demand the oligopolistic firm faces *if its competitors follow its price down but not up*.

Faced with this demand curve, how do you maximize profit? The likely answer: Select point E_1 where the kink occurs. Thus, you don't rock the boat. You continue to quote the price P_1 that you and your competitors have been quoting, and you service your safe traditional share of the market. Your profit is shown as the shaded gray area. (Experiment with other points on your kinked demand curve above and below E_1 and note that in each case your profit area is less. Moreover, also shift AC up or down a bit, and notice that E_1 remains your profit-maximizing point. Thus you tend to keep your price stable even though your costs change.)

The idea of a kinked demand curve was developed in the 1930s, and it has had continuing appeal as a way of explaining why oligopoly prices are stable, and, in particular, why they often remain firm during recessions when demand declines. (There are, nevertheless, important exceptions. In 1974, and again in 1980, some auto manufacturers offered rebates—in effect, price reductions—in order to increase their lagging sales.)

The theory of the kinked demand curve has been controversial. In the first place, it is incomplete. While it may *explain* price stability, it does not explain how price is established in the first

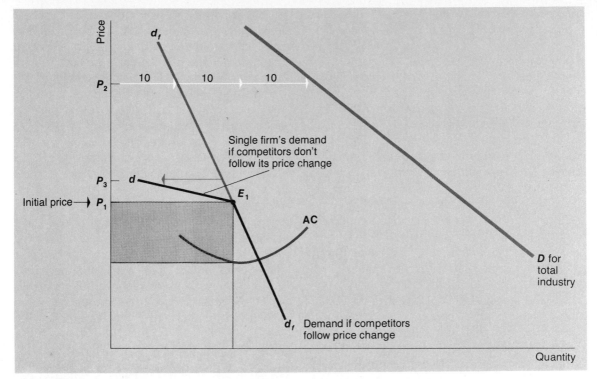

Figure 12-6
A kinked demand curve
Suppose that you have two equally large competitors, and your initial equilibrium is at E_1. If your competitors were to follow any price change you might make, the demand curve you would face would be d_f; regardless of the price you might quote, you would retain your basic one-third share of the market. (For example, if you were to quote price P_2 you would sell 10 units.) Unfortunately, however, you do not face d_f throughout its entire range, because your competitors will only follow you if you reduce price; so the only portion of d_f that is relevant is the heavily lined section below E_1. If you raise price the demand you face will be d. (Since your competitors do not follow you in this case, they will cut into your share of the market as shown by the red arrow.) To sum up: If your competitors follow your price change down but not up, you will face the heavy, kinked demand curve.

place. For example, in Figure 12-6, price remains at P_1 because it started out at P_1. But how did it get to be P_1 in the first place? It just sits there in this diagram unexplained, like the "smile without the cat" in *Alice in Wonderland*. The second difficulty with the kinked demand idea is that prices are not nearly so rigid as the theory suggests. As already noted, automobile prices have occasionally fallen. The same is true of steel prices: In late 1979, the steel companies provided discounts of 10 percent or more on some of their products. And, over the years, the prices of computers have been cut many times,

leaving them at only a small fraction of their earlier level. Furthermore, the 1970s were marked by many increases in oligopoly prices, another outcome which the kinked demand curve would not predict. Thus the kinked demand curve is more useful in providing insight into the pressures oligopolists face than in explaining how price is determined. Indeed, as a theory of price its relevance is limited because it explains something (price stability) that does not exist. Rather than try to explain why oligopoly prices are stable (when in fact they are not), it makes more sense to ask why oligopoly prices change in a reasonably orderly way. One answer is provided by the theory of *price leadership*.

Price leadership

Where collusion is illegal (as in the United States), the simplest way for firms to achieve an orderly change in price is for one firm to take the initiative with the others following.

To illustrate this price leadership concept in Figure 12-6, suppose that you are the price leader. Then the demand curve you face no longer has a kink. Instead, it is the line d_f throughout its entire length, because your competitors will follow your price change both down *or up*. In these circumstances, you will be able to lead the industry up to a new, higher price, provided you are confident that the other firms will in fact follow your lead.

If your leadership is thus assured, the result may approach that of a cartel. As leader, you will select the price that will maximize your own profits, and your choice may approximate the price that will maximize profits for the industry as a whole. However, as there is no formal agreement, the problem of "cheating" may be substantial. The leader may find others shaving prices (or providing rebates) in order to increase their market shares. For example, during this century, giant U.S. Steel has sometimes acted as price leader, and has not reacted to under-the-table price cuts by some smaller firms. (It was better to ignore them than to retaliate and risk leading the whole industry into a round of price cutting.) Consequently, these smaller firms were able to take advantage of U.S. Steel's price umbrella to cut into its markets: In 1910, U.S. Steel held almost half the market; but by the 1950s, its share had fallen to about one-third. Thus, while the giant in an industry may have an advantage from lower costs, the smaller firms may also have a major advantage: They may be able to compete aggressively without provoking competitive responses from the giant.

In practice, it may be quite difficult to identify any clear pattern of price leadership. There may be no consistent price leader; first one company may take the initiative in changing prices, then another. General Motors does not always announce its new model prices first; the initiative is sometimes exercised by Ford. And price leadership may be quite tentative. One firm may announce a price increase, to see if others follow. If they don't, the price increased will be withdrawn. (This sort of "trial and error" pricing may just be a way for the firm to test whether or not it can act as a price leader.)

Finally, even when oligopolists follow a pattern of price leadership, we cannot be certain that they are exerting monopoly power. If costs have generally risen by, say, 10 percent, an oligopolist may raise price by about 10 percent in the expectation that others will follow. Price leadership has apparently occurred; yet the firms may merely be defending themselves against rising costs, rather than exploiting monopoly power at the expense of the public. (For a way in which oligopolists may end up quoting the same price even though there is no price leadership, see Box 12-1.)

NONPRICE COMPETITION

Price is not the only way in which oligopolistic firms compete; they also compete, for example, by advertising and by attempting to provide a better product. These ways of competing are often preferred to price competition because they don't involve the risk of setting off a price war in which all participants lose.

Advertising

One form of nonprice competition is advertising. The firm that advertises has a simple objective: to make people want its product and buy more of it. That does not mean, however, that the more advertising the better. Since advertising must be paid for, it shifts up the cost curve. At some point, the firm will find that enough advertising is enough; any further expenditures would not pay for themselves in terms of increased sales.

In an oligopoly, the primary goal of advertising is often to capture the competitor's market. Thus, for example, the primary objective of Ford's advertising is to take sales away from General Motors and other auto companies. And,

Focal Point Pricing

Harvard's Thomas Schelling gives the following noneconomic example to illustrate how independent firms may end up quoting the same price even though there is no price leadership or overt collusion:

You are to meet someone in New York City. You have not been instructed where to meet; you have no prior understanding with the person on where to meet; and you cannot communicate with each other. You are simply told that you will have to guess where to meet and he is being told the same thing and that you will just have to try to make your guesses coincide. You are told the date but not the hour of this meeting; the two of you must guess the exact minute of the date for meeting. At what time will you appear at the chosen meeting place?†

Of the thousands of possible choices, Schelling discovered that a majority of people selected the information booth at Grand Central Station, and almost all chose high noon. Both are "focal points" because they provide the best guess of what the other party will do. So too with price: A retailer who wants to guess the price that competitors will charge in the range of say, $11.20 to $12.40, may well select the focal point $11.95. This price is based on the familiar tradi-

tion of "charging $12 but making it seem like $11." Thus, without any communication whatsoever between firms or any form of price leadership, this $11.95 focal point becomes the industry price. ■

†Thomas C. Schelling, *The Strategy of Conflict* (Cambridge: Harvard University Press, 1960), p. 56.

---

for its part, General Motors advertises to take sales away from Ford.

Advertising also increases the total market demand for the product. Thus, a monopolist such as AT&T advertises to increase the demand for long-distance calls. And some associations of perfect competitors advertise to increase total market demand, even though no single producer would find it profitable to advertise. (For example, the orange growers' association adver-

tises to encourage people to drink orange juice.) But the most heavily advertised products lie in the battleground between perfect competition and monopoly, where an advertiser like General Motors may benefit both by increasing the total demand for automobiles and, more particularly, by taking sales away from its competitors.

The social value of advertising is a controversial issue. On behalf of their industry, advertising agencies make the following points:

1 Advertising helps the consumer to make better decisions. It informs the public of new products and of improvements in old products. By informing consumers of what is available, it reduces search costs. For example, advertising may tell consumers where the bargains are, so they can save time and effort in shopping.

2 Advertising helps new producers to compete. By informing the public of a new product, it helps the producer to expand sales toward a high-volume, low-cost level. (A closely related point is that advertising stimulates research; if new products could not be advertised and sold in large quantities, the cost of their research and development could not be covered.)

3 Advertising supports our communications industry. Radio and TV are financed by advertising revenues. (If we didn't pay for our entertainment this way, we would have to pay for it in some other way.) Even the mundane classified ads play a significant role in the support of newspapers.

4 Advertising results in higher-quality products: The goodwill built up from past advertising of a brand name product may be an asset of great value for a firm—an asset it will be careful not to damage by turning out a shoddy product.

5 By encouraging the public to spend more, advertising stimulates production and creates jobs.

On the other side, critics respond:

1 Most advertising represents a waste. The heaviest advertising takes place in oligopolistic markets where firm A's major motive is to steal customers from firm B, and B advertises to cancel out the effects of A's advertising. After advertising, A and B share the market in roughly the same way as before. Little has changed, except that costs have gone up. As a consequence, consumers pay more for this product merely because it is advertised.

2 Where advertising is not a self-canceling waste, it is often pernicious, creating frivolous wants, distorting tastes, and increasing the materialism of a materialistic society.

3 Advertising often misinforms, and leads to lower-quality products. This occurs, for example, if firms are able to sell inferior products by falsely implying in their advertising that they are better. In this case, the cost of advertising includes both the waste in resources that go into making this claim *and* the cost to the public because it gets an inferior product.

4 Much advertising is offensive. We cannot listen to radio or TV without being bombarded with tasteless ads.

5 Advertising is a poor way to pursue the goal of full employment. If aggregate demand is too low, it should be increased by expansive fiscal and monetary policies.

Since it is difficult to compare these conflicting claims, our conclusion is that the statement that advertising involves "*all* loss" is too extreme, and so is the statement that advertising involves "*no* loss whatsoever." What do you think?

Other ways in which firms compete

In addition to advertising, there are other forms of nonprice competition. A firm can hire a larger sales staff in order to beat the bushes for customers. Or it can spend more on research, development, or design to improve the quality or attractiveness of its product. (This step may be welcomed by the consumer. But efforts to increase the appeal of a product may get out of hand. For example, in an earlier era when airlines were subject to price regulation and therefore had to find other ways to compete, Lewis Engman, the former chairman of the Federal Trade Commission, observed that the typical airline commercial was "like an ad for a combination bawdy house and dinner theater.") The typical oligopoly, such as an auto or appliance company, is locked in a struggle to match its competitors' price, *and* advertising, *and* sales force, *and* improvements in design and quality. Little wonder that the world of the oligopolist seems more competitive than that of the farmer, who may operate in a "perfectly competitive" market, but who never even thinks of a neighbor as a competitor. (But remember: According to the economist's definition, farming is the more competitive industry, since a single farmer has no influence whatsoever over price.)

BARRIERS TO ENTRY

Nonprice competition often creates barriers to entry. For example, if several large oligopolistic firms (like the auto companies) have been competing in the past by making huge expenditures on advertising, it may be almost impossible for a new firm to break into the industry unless it too has vast sums to spend.[7]

There are other barriers to entry into an industry as well. For example, existing producers may be associated with widely recognized brand names. (In some countries, the brand name "Kodak" is almost synonymous with "camera," and how do you compete with that?) Another advantage of existing producers is that they may get more favorable treatment from retailers. As an example, well-established Kellogg dominates sales of breakfast cereals because supermarket managers allocate it so much shelf space. At times, managers are so busy that they have even allowed the Kellogg sales representatives to come in and arrange their cereals display. In such cases, even General Foods may have trouble competing; so what hope is there for brand X? Thus a new entrant into the cereals market tends to be caught up in a vicious circle: It can't sell without shelf space, and it can't acquire shelf space until it can prove it can sell.

But the single most important barrier to entry is the fact that, in most oligopoly industries, costs fall over a wide range of output. In other words, economies of large-scale production make it very difficult for a small firm to compete. In order to get started, a new firm must have

"deep pockets"; it must have the financial resources to set up a productive facility large enough to move it quickly into the high-volume, low-cost range of production. (For this reason, new competition in oligopolistic markets often comes, not from struggling new firms, but rather from giants from other industries. For example, Xerox was faced with major new competition when IBM and Kodak entered the market for office copiers.)

If such barriers to entry are low or nonexistent, new firms freely enter. The result is no longer oligopoly (with a few sellers), but instead a quite different market form: monopolistic competition. This is the last type of market we will describe. As we do so, you can compare it with other markets in summary Table 12-1.

MONOPOLISTIC COMPETITION: LOW BARRIERS TO ENTRY

If the average cost curve stops falling and starts to rise when the firm is producing only a small fraction of the total industry sales, there is no cost advantage in being a giant, and many competitors enter the industry. This situation sounds like perfect competition, but it is not if firms are producing a *differentiated product*. In this case, the result is **monopolistic competition**. Because each firm is selling a somewhat different product, each has some control over price; if it raises its price slightly, it won't lose all its customers. Thus, it does not face the perfect competitor's perfectly horizontal demand curve. Instead, its demand curve slopes downward to the right. But because of the existence of many competitors, its control over price is not great. In other words, the demand curve facing the individual producer is quite elastic, as illustrated in Figure 12-7.

Monopolistic competition **exists when there are many sellers of differentiated products in an industry without barriers to entry. The demand curve facing the individual competitor is quite elastic, but not completely so.**

---

[7]Advertising tends to augment other advantages firms may enjoy from large size. (See A. Michael Spence, "Notes on Advertising, Economies of Scale, and Entry Barriers," *Quarterly Journal of Economics,* November 1980.) Thus it makes it easier for large firms to prevent small competitors from entering the industry.

Products can be differentiated even though they are physically the same. As an example, consider identical tubes of Crest toothpaste sold in stores in two different locations. Although the products are physically the same, they are not identical in all respects. The consumer will view one store's toothpaste as "better" (and will consequently pay a few cents more for it) because it is closer. Thus its location gives this store some control over price; it can charge a few cents more and not lose all its customers. But it doesn't have much control; if it charges a much higher price, buyers will bypass it to go to the less expensive (though less convenient) competitor.

It is relatively easy to get into retailing; a vast pool of funds is not necessary to buy a corner store or to run a gas station. Where existing firms are making above-normal profits, new entrants will come in, tending to eliminate these excess profits, as illustrated in Figure 12-7. Initially, the typical firm shown in panel a is operating at E_1

and earning the shaded gray profit. But, as new competitors enter and capture some of its sales, the demand curve it faces shifts to the left. (It gets a smaller and smaller share of the total market.) This process continues until its demand becomes tangent to the average cost curve, as shown in panel b. Faced with this new demand curve, the best the firm can now do is to select the point of tangency E_2, where it earns no excess profit. (Any other point on the demand curve would leave it operating at a loss.) Thus, free entry tends to eliminate above-normal profits for the run-of-the-mill firm in monopolistic competition.

Observe in panel b that monopolistic competition seems to involve inefficiency. At the firm's output of 80 units, MC ($70) is not equal to price ($90), so there is no reason to expect an efficient allocation of resources. Consumer demand could be satisfied at lower cost if there were fewer firms, each producing more (that is, if the typical firm in panel b were to increase its

Table 12-1
Types of Market Structure

Type of market	Number of producers and type of product	Entry	Influence over price	Examples
Monopoly	One producer; product with no close substitute	Difficult or impossible	Substantial (price maker unless price is regulated by government)	Telephone service
Oligopoly	(a) Few producers; little or no product differentiation	Difficult	Some (price searcher)	Steel Aluminum
	(b) Few producers; differentiated product	Difficult	Some (price searcher)	Autos Computers Cigarettes
Monopolistic competition	Many producers; differentiated product	Easy	A little	Most retail trade
Perfect competition	Many producers; undifferentiated product	Easy	None (price taker)	Wheat Some other agricultural products

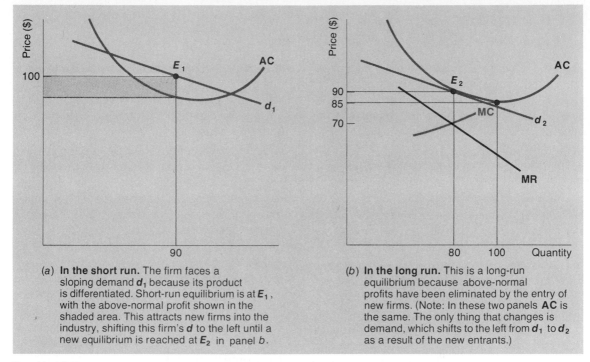

(a) **In the short run.** The firm faces a sloping demand d_1 because its product is differentiated. Short-run equilibrium is at E_1, with the above-normal profit shown in the shaded area. This attracts new firms into the industry, shifting this firm's d to the left until a new equilibrium is reached at E_2 in panel b.

(b) **In the long run.** This is a long-run equilibrium because above-normal profits have been eliminated by the entry of new firms. (Note: In these two panels **AC** is the same. The only thing that changes is demand, which shifts to the left from d_1 to d_2 as a result of the new entrants.)

Figure 12-7
Equilibrium for a typical firm in monopolistic competition

output from 80 units to 100, where its average cost is at the minimum $85 level). If the industry were reorganized in this way, wouldn't the result be a more efficient allocation of resources?

The answer is: Not necessarily. True, cost would be lower, and this would be an advantage for society. But there would also be a disadvantage: Since there would be fewer firms, consumers would have less choice. For example, a reduction in the number of retail stores would mean that those remaining could sell a larger volume, thus reducing their costs (and prices). But it would also mean that some customers would have to travel farther to shop. Perhaps the convenience of local stores is worth the slightly higher price we have to pay.

In short, when a product is differentiated, it becomes difficult to pin down the idea of effi-

ciency as simply as we did with an undifferentiated product (in Box 10-1). As a practical matter, no economist argues that the government should undertake broad regulation of firms operating in monopolistic competition. It is hard to make a federal case out of the inefficiencies (if any) that arise from monopolistic competition.

But this is not true of monopoly or oligopoly. (According to the informed guess of one authority,[8] the cost of inefficiency in such markets could exceed 6 percent of the value of the nation's GNP.) Here a federal case can be made, as we explain in the next chapter.

[8]F. M. Scherer, *Industrial Market Structure and Economic Performance* (Chicago: Rand McNally, 1970), p. 408.

Key Points

1 Many American markets are oligopolies, dominated by a few firms. In any such market, there is a substantial incentive for firms to collude so that they can act like a monopolist in raising price and restricting output. Such monopolization of an industry would lead to an inefficient allocation of the nation's resources.

2 A highly publicized example of collusion has been OPEC, which increased the world price of oil by more than ten times between 1973 and 1980. The result was the greatest peacetime transfer of wealth in history.

3 Our antitrust laws prohibit American firms from forming cartels, and from engaging in other forms of collusion that restrict competition. Nonetheless, there are forms of tacit collusion (such as price leadership) that are difficult to prosecute, and that may allow oligopolists to exercise monopolylike power.

4 Oligopolists often prefer to compete in ways other than cutting price. They may try to capture sales from rivals by large advertising expenditures, or by expenditures on research to develop better products.

5 When there are no barriers to entry (like patents or economies of large-scale production) and many small firms enter an industry, the result is monopolistic competition. This is similar to perfect competition except that firms are selling differentiated products. For this reason, each firm has some small control over price. (It faces a slightly sloping demand curve rather than the completely flat demand facing a perfect competitor.) Price *could* be reduced below the level that occurs in monopolistic competition, but only at the cost of providing consumers with less variety. Therefore, little case can be made for government controls.

Key Concepts

concentration ratio
natural oligopoly
product differentiation
collusion

cartel
incentive to cheat
kinked demand
price leadership

competition by advertising
competition in product
  quality
monopolistic competition

Problems

12-1 If there are only four large firms in your industry, explain why collusion would be in your economic interest as a producer. Explain how consumers of your product would be affected. Describe the problems involved in arranging a collusive agreement and in making it stick. Would the agreement be legal?

12-2 (For those who have studied Figure 11-10.) What is the difference between the monopolylike collusion involved in the cartel in Figure 12-3 and the monopolization of the milk industry in Figure 11-10? Why should the monopolization of an industry be outlawed in the first case, yet condoned—in fact, organized—by the government in the other?

12-3 What do you think would happen to the world price of oil if:

(a) Huge new deposits of oil were discovered off the U.S. coast?

(b) Huge new deposits of oil were located off the Saudi Arabian coast?

(c) There were major developments in nuclear technology, with fusion (hydrogen) power expected to become a major source of inexpensive energy by 1995?

(d) The U.S. government were to impose a 50 cents per gallon additional tax on gasoline?

(e) All countries were to raise gasoline taxes by 50 cents per gallon?

12-4 "Agricultrual prices are unstable, but other prices are stable." Evaluate this statement in the light of our discussion of kinked demand and our earlier analysis of agriculture in Chapter 7. To what degree do you believe this difference justifies agricultural price supports?

12-5 On balance, do you think that advertising is beneficial or damaging to society? Explain.

12-6 Manufacturers of cigarettes and producers of perfume both advertise. Do you think waste is involved in either case? In one more than the other? Discuss the possible benefits from advertising and the possible damage in each case.

12-7 If Chrysler goes bankrupt, the choice of U.S. consumers will be less. Does this provide a case for government assistance to Chrysler? (Aid has been provided in the form of loan guarantees. Thus the government risks picking up the tab if Chrysler does go bankrupt.)

12-8 Until a recent court decision, lawyers who cut their fees below the level allowed by their state bar association could be disbarred. How would you evaluate this regulation from an economic point of view?

CHAPTER 13
Government Regulation of Business

Th' trusts . . . are heejous monsthers built up be th'
enlightened intherprise iv th' men that have done so
much to advance progress in our beloved country.
. . . On wan hand I wud stamp thim undher fut; on
th' other hand not so fast.

**Finley Peter Dunne's characterization
of Theodore Roosevelt**

In the preceding two chapters, we have examined the problems that arise if firms are able to exercise market power, and we have seen that the government has a regulatory role to play in curbing that power. But in the last two decades government regulation has gone far beyond this traditional responsibility, and has now been extended to the promotion of safety and health in our workplaces, highways, and the environment. How successful have these various kinds of government regulation been? Did we, during the 1970s, attempt to regulate too much? Is there now some risk that in the 1980s we will try to regulate too little?

Government regulations on business fall into three major categories:

1 Antitrust laws to prevent firms from reducing competition by such acts as collusion or cutthroat pricing.

2 Regulatory controls over an industry's price and conditions of entry. Within this broad category, two quite different kinds of regulation should be distinguished:

(a) Regulation of a natural monopoly (that is, a public utility such as a power company or a phone company). Since this form of regulation has already been analyzed in Chapter 11 (especially Box 11-2 and Appendix 11-B) we will concentrate here on type *(b)*.

(b) Regulation of a naturally more competitive industry, such as trucking.

3 Quality-of-life regulation of health, safety, and working conditions. This type of regulation has grown most rapidly during the 1970s. Yale's Paul MacAvoy has observed that "The impact of price controls and health and safety regulation has grown in the 1970s so that for all intents and purposes the sector of the economy that could be termed 'fully regulated' has more than doubled in its share of GNP."[1]

We will look at each of the three types of regulation in turn, beginning with antitrust. (A fourth set, the regulation of energy, is deferred to Chapter 22.) Before studying the antitrust laws themselves, we consider the difficult economic questions which must be considered in developing an antitrust policy.

[1]*The Regulated Industries and the Economy* (New York: W.W. Norton & Co., 1979), p. 105.

I ANTITRUST POLICY: SOME PROBLEMS

In order to prevent the accumulation of market power, antitrust laws make the takeover of one firm by another illegal if it can be established that this would substantially reduce competition. On the same grounds, large existing firms can be broken up. But setting precise guidelines for taking this action is not an easy task. A number of problems complicate the life of the policy maker. For example, it is not certain that breaking up large firms will improve the performance of the economy. In business, big isn't *necessarily* bad.

Are there advantages of large size?

In a number of industries, the answer is yes, for several reasons:

1 Large firms can better afford R&D (Research and Development)   Because of their very large sales (and often because of the high profits they earn in oligopolistic markets), big firms may be able to finance large R&D projects that could not be undertaken by small firms. These expenditures benefit not only the firms that are thereby able to develop the profitable new products. Society as a whole also benefits as these new products become available. In his classic defense of large firms, Joseph Schumpeter wrote:

As soon as we go into details and inquire into the individual items in which progress was most conspicuous, the trail leads not to the doors of those firms that work under conditions of comparatively free competition but precisely to the doors of the large concerns—which, as in the case of agricultural machinery, also account for much of the progress in the competitive sector—and a shocking suspicion dawns upon us that big business may have had more to do with creating that standard of life than keeping it down.[2]

2 The attempt by firms to become large (specifically, their attempt to achieve a monopoly position) stimulates growth

Schumpeter argued that growth is the story of firms struggling to become large by the development of distinctive new products over which they have a temporary monopoly. To cite a recent example, Boeing acquired a temporary monopoly in jumbo jets through the development of the 747. Such innovations are an important source of growth.

According to Schumpeter, innovation may come not only from firms that are large, but also from firms that are small and seeking to become large. There is no question that small firms have generated much innovation. According to one study based on the first half of this century—much the same period that Schumpeter was describing—about two-thirds of the basic inventions were discovered by small firms or independent inventors.[3] For example, the oxygen furnace (one of the major twentieth-century innovations in basic steel) was invented, not by a giant U.S. firm, but by a small Austrian firm which was less than one-third the size of a single plant of U.S. Steel. Although large firms with their heavy R&D expenditures generate many innovations, so do smaller firms.

3 Large firms can capture economies of scale   In many industries, economies of scale can be fully realized only by very large firms. As already noted, in any antitrust decision on whether or not a monopoly should be broken up, a crucial question arises: Is this a natural monopoly based on economies of large-scale production? If the answer is yes, then breaking it up will raise average costs; a better policy is to regulate its price. On the other hand, if the firm is not a natural monopoly, it is appropriate to consider breaking it up.

The relevance of costs to antitrust policy has

---

[2]Joseph Schumpeter, *Capitalism, Socialism and Democracy* (New York: Harper, 1942), 3d ed., p. 82.

[3]John Jewkes, David Sawers, and Richard Stillerman, *The Sources of Invention* (New York: St. Martin's Press, 1958).

not always been recognized by the courts. Most notably, in the Alcoa case of 1945, Judge Learned Hand stated that the purpose of the antitrust laws is to "perpetuate and preserve, for its own sake and *in spite of possible cost,* an organization of industry in small units which can effectively compete with each other." (Italics are added.)

How can we resolve the conflict between Judge Hand's view that "small is good" and the view that, in the face of economies of scale, "big is better?" The proper answer may be a compromise: In defining antitrust policy it is an error to ignore economies of scale; but it is also a mistake to treat them as the only important factor. To see why, consider an industry where a few competing firms have been able to capture most, but not all, economies of scale. If economies of scale are the *only* consideration, then the policy should be "hands off": Allow one firm to drive the others out of business, monopolize the market, and capture even more economies of scale. But if this is permitted, the new monopoly that emerges will have to be regulated—with the whole set of difficulties this will create. Better to keep a number of firms in competition than to try to capture the last nickel of economies of scale by allowing the monopolization of the industry.

Thus one can agree with Judge Hand that a competitive organization of industry is beneficial, and this is the appropriate target. At the same time, costs in the form of economies of scale should also be considered—a point he rejected. If scale economies are important enough—as in the case of local telephone service—then an exception should be made: Monopoly should be allowed, but in regulated form. In short, when dealing with monopoly, policy makers should consider several issues, with costs being an important one.

A modern-day postscript should be added. In those industries which are now subject to intense foreign competition, large corporations are far less objectionable than they would be in an isolated economy. There are two reasons: (1) U.S. producers may be unable to compete with imports unless they are large enough to capture economies of scale. (With the flood of Japanese auto imports in 1980, nobody was talking about breaking up General Motors anymore.) (2) Because of competition from imports, the market power of U.S. giants is reduced; they are not as free to raise prices as they would otherwise be.

What is "unfair" competition?

In order to protect small competing firms, antitrust legislation is designed to limit a number of unfair practices, such as **cutthroat competition.** This occurs when a large firm attempts to drive its competitors out of business by pricing at less than cost. The large firm takes a loss in the short run, but it has the financial resources to do so; and, by outlasting its smaller competitors it can drive them into bankruptcy. (If the large firm has many products, the sale of its other items may provide more than enough profit to cover its losses on the products it is selling at cutthroat prices.) Once the cutthroat firm emerges as a monopolist, it can raise prices enough to more than recoup any earlier losses.

Cutthroat competition—sometimes called *predatory pricing*—is pricing below cost in order to drive competitors out of business.

In practice, it is difficult to draw a line between fair competition and unfair, cutthroat competition. One might think that a fair price is one that covers total costs (including a normal profit). But there may be problems in calculating total costs, particularly for a large firm producing many goods: It's not clear how some costs (such as overhead) should be allocated among its various products. Furthermore, even if a firm is pricing below costs, this doesn't necessarily mean that it is engaged in cutthroat pricing to eliminate competitors. In 1980, both GM and Ford suffered large losses—that is, they priced below average costs. But they weren't trying to "cut Chrysler's throat." Rather, they were frantically trying to hold their shares of the market in the face of stiff Japanese competition. Because of such real-world complexities, it is very difficult even to identify—let alone control—unfair competition.

What constitutes collusion?

In order to protect the consuming public, the antitrust laws prohibit collusive agreements by oligopolists to raise price. But collusion may be as difficult to identify as unfair competition. There may be exceptional cases, of course, where collusion has clearly taken place. For example, competitors may get together with the specific intention of fixing price and splitting up the market. In such cases, they can be sent to jail for their efforts. (See the electrical manufacturers' conspiracy described in Box 13-1.) But what action should be taken in more complex cases, where oligopolists with a common interest arrive at the same price without even so much as a wink or a nod because all firms follow a price leader? Certainly we cannot make it illegal to quote the current market price. If a firm's price "meets the competition," how can it be condemned? After all, doesn't a perfectly competitive producer (like the wheat farmer) sell at the going market price? Similar prices do not *prove* collusion.

ANTITRUST LEGISLATION IN THE UNITED STATES: A SUMMARY

Because of such complications, it is not surprising that the antitrust laws have been difficult and time-consuming to enforce. One notable example: On its last business day in early 1969, the outgoing Johnson administration filed suit against IBM for trying to monopolize the computer business. Twelve years later, the case was still in the courts—although there was finally some prospect that it would end some day. The government didn't even begin to present its case until 1975, and then took three years to complete it; one witness alone was on the stand for 78 days. At one point the Justice Department subpoenaed IBM for documentation that turned out to be, by the company's estimate, 5 billion pieces of paper that would take 100 lawyers 620 working days to produce. Little wonder that lawyers referred to the case as a "black hole" into which their careers might disappear without a trace.

Because of the complexities of antitrust laws, it is not possible to do more than note the most important ones:

The Sherman Antitrust Act (1890)

In response to the wave of mergers and the growing concentration of industry in the late nineteenth century, Congress passed the Sherman Act. It was direct and to the point. "Every contract, combination in the form of a trust[4] or otherwise, or conspiracy in restraint of trade" was declared illegal. It was likewise illegal to "monopolize, or attempt to monopolize, or combine or conspire . . . to monopolize" trade.

Teddy Roosevelt became the first "trust-busting" President. The surge of legal activity initiated during his presidency led to the breakup of Standard Oil and the American Tobacco Company in 1911.

The Clayton Act (1914)

The Clayton Act was intended to reinforce the Sherman Act by preventing the development of monopoly in the first place. To do so, it prohibited certain practices that are likely to lead to monopoly. Among other provisions, it:

1 Prohibited **interlocking directorates** designed to lessen competition. (An interlocking directorate exists when a director sits on the board of two or more competing firms.)
2 Prohibited **tying contracts** (sometimes called **full-line forcing).** Such a contract requires purchasers to buy other items in a seller's line in order to get the one they really want. Thus it helps a firm with a particularly appealing product to use it to monopolize the sale of other products.
3 Prohibited corporations from taking over an-

[4]The word "trust" has a long history. Before the Sherman Act, a favorite way to limit competition was to put common stock of different firms into a "trust," with an agreement for collective action and profit sharing. (The word "antitrust" is now used broadly to refer to any action against a powerful firm or group of firms.)

BOX 13-1

The Great Electrical Equipment Conspiracy, and Other Misdeeds

The classic case of price-fixing occurred more than two decades ago, when the manufacturers of heavy electrical equipment conspired to set prices, thereby raising the cost of almost every power-generating station built in the United States during that period. Senior officials from General Electric, Westinghouse, and 27 other firms ended up in court. Two million dollars in fines were eventually paid, and seven executives each spent 30 days in jail. (The personal cost was even more substantial. Almost as soon as the Justice Department began its investigation, the salary of one GE vice-president was cut from $127,000 to $40,000. While he was recovering from that shock, he was fined $4,000 and sent to prison for 30 days. When he got out, GE eased him out of the company altogether.)

Here is how *The Wall Street Journal* (Jan. 10, 1961) described the conspiracy in a passage that strangely echoes the words of Adam Smith, written over two centuries ago and quoted at the beginning of Chapter 12.

Many of the meetings took place at the conventions of the National Electrical Manufacturers Association and other trade groups. Rather typically, after a conventional and perfectly lawful meeting of some kind, certain members would adjourn for a rump session and a few drinks in someone's suite. It seemed natural enough that mutual business problems would be discussed—specifications, for example—and like as not prices would come up. In time it was easy enough to drift from general talk about prices into what should be done about them—and finally into separate meetings to fix them for everyone's mutual benefit.

One scheme they used was a form of bidding cartel. The firms agreed in advance on a complicated system in which each firm knew from the phase of the moon whether it should bid low or high on a contract. Each firm took its turn in being the winning low bidder. But, as in most

collusive schemes, the pressures to cheat were considerable, and for this reason General Electric finally dropped out. As one executive put it, "No one was living up to the agreements. . . . On every job someone would cut our throat; we lost confidence in the group."

In 1976 in another case, 47 executives from 22 companies pleaded no contest to federal charges of fixing the prices of cardboard boxes. Included were no less than the president of Container Corporation of America (annual sales at that time: about $1 billion). He was fined $35,000 and had to spend 15 days in jail—more precisely, 15 nights, since the judge allowed him out to work during the day.

Although it seems to have been getting more difficult for the Justice Department to get a conviction for price fixing, the penalty has become more severe when a conviction does occur: In 1975, the maximum jail sentence for an individual was increased from 1 year to 3, and the maximum fine for a corporation was raised from $50,000 to $1 million. By the late 1970s, American business executives were spending a record amount of time in jail for price fixing. (For more detail on this form of white collar crime and punishment, see "The Boss in the Slammer," *Forbes Magazine,* Feb. 5, 1979.) ■

other company by purchasing its common stock, if the takeover "substantially lessens competition." However, this provision was evaded by some firms that purchased the physical assets of the other company instead. (This loophole was not closed until the **Celler-Kefauver Antimerger Act** in 1950.)

The Federal Trade Commission Act of 1914

The Federal Trade Commission (FTC), a permanent board of five members, was set up in 1914 to deal with "unfair methods of competition." Like the Justice Department, the FTC can enforce the Clayton Act by taking alleged violators to court. (An example is a recent FTC suit against Exxon and other oil companies.) But in addition, the FTC was given some powers normally reserved to the courts; for example, it could issue cease-and-desist orders where it found unfair competition. However, the law did not define what "unfair" meant, and the courts made it clear that they, and not the FTC, would pass judgment on this question. Weakened by this court attitude, the FTC turned its attention in a different direction, to curbing misleading advertising and misrepresentation of products—responsibilities it was given by the **Wheeler-Lea Amendment** in 1938.

For many years the FTC was viewed by its critics as a relatively ineffective agency: "the little old lady on Pennsylvania Avenue." But this changed in the mid-1970s when one of its strongest critics became its chairman, and Congress increased the FTC's power to investigate and regulate whole industries rather than just single firms. By the late 1970s, the FTC had become so active that Congress reversed itself, and moved to curb its growing power.

These three acts, the Sherman Act, the Clayton Act, and the FTC Act, have formed the cornerstone of antitrust policy. (The electrical equipment conspiracy was prosecuted in 1960 as a violation of the Sherman Act.)

The other side: Legislation that tends to reduce competition, rather than increase it

Congress has passed several laws that have encouraged restraints on trade; they have put the interests of the producer above those of the consumer.

1 The Capper-Volstead Act (1922) provides immunity from antitrust laws to farmers who form cooperatives—provided these organizations do not engage in "undue price enhancement." (If they do, they can be disciplined by the secretary of agriculture—although the secretary has never used this power. However, the Justice Department several years ago filed suits against the three largest dairy cooperatives for collusive activities not exempted by this Act.)

2 The Robinson-Patman Act (1936) was designed to protect small firms in an industry from larger (often more efficient) competitors. In the words of co-sponsor Wright Patman, the act's objective was to "give the little business fellows a square deal" by curbing price cutting by large discount and chain stores. (It was therefore sometimes called the Chain Store Law.) Specifically, it was designed to prevent large stores from buying from suppliers at quantity discounts, unless such discounts were justified on the basis of actual cost economies. It also prohibited stores from selling to the public "at unreasonably low prices." Its major effect was to impede, though not prevent, the efficient development of retail trade.

3 The Miller-Tydings Act (1937) exempted **fair trade** contracts from antitrust laws, when such contracts are permitted by state law. (Under a fair trade contract, the manufacturer of a name-brand good could fix the price that retail stores charge the public.) During the 1960s and 1970s, manufacturers found it increasingly difficult to enforce such contracts, and, under heavy public attack, the fair trade exemption was ended.

Final observations

1   How should mergers be dealt with?   In deciding how much monopolization results from a merger, it is important first to recognize that there are three different types of merger. The kind that is most obviously anticompetitive is the **horizontal merger,** involving the union of firms which previously competed with each other. But a **vertical merger**—in which a purchasing firm merges with one of its suppliers—may also suppress competition by making it difficult for other suppliers to sell to the purchasing firm.

Both of these kinds of merger were illustrated in a 1962 case in which the Supreme Court disallowed a merger between the Brown Shoe Co. and T. R. Kinney. This was a vertical merger because shoe manufacturer Brown became a supplier to Kinney's retail stores. At the same time, it was a horizontal merger for two reasons: (1) both firms competed in manufacturing shoes; and (2) both firms competed in retailing shoes. Although the government lawyers were unable to argue convincingly that the merger would horizontally restrict competition in shoe *manufacturing,* they did successfully argue that the merger would horizontally restrict competition in shoe *retailing.* (In some retail markets, the new merged firm became the dominant supplier.) Moreover, the government lawyers also successfully argued that the merger would have unfavorable vertical effects: In the two years following the merger, manufacturer Brown increased its supply of shoes to Kinney's retail stores from zero to 8 percent of Kinney's sales. Thus the court concluded that Brown was using its relationship to Kinney to restrict other shoe manufacturers from selling to Kinney.

There is a third type of merger: a **conglomerate merger** where a firm joins another in a completely different activity. Whether such mergers adversely affect competition—and if so, by how much—is a controversial issue. A conglomerate merger may invigorate a weak company in an industry by providing it with new capital and more aggressive management. In such cases, competition can be enhanced. But a merger may help an already strong company to dominate an industry. This issue—considered in greater detail in Box 13-2—grew in importance during the successive waves of conglomerate mergers in the 1960s and late 1970s.

A **horizontal merger** is a union of firms in the same competing activity.

A **vertical merger** is a union of a firm and its supplier.

A **conglomerate merger** is a union of firms in unrelated activities.

---

2   "Workable competition"   During the late nineteenth century, antitrust legislation was launched on a wave of hostility toward giant corporations and their predatory, anticompetitive methods. But, since the days of the nineteenth-century "robber barons," there have been relatively few black and white situations. Antitrust history is largely the story of difficult gray areas.

At an early stage, in the 1920 U.S. Steel case, the Supreme Court put forth the "rule of reason." The Court held that mere size was no offense, and that giant U.S. Steel had not actually exercised monopoly power. But standards change. By 1945, the Court held that guilt does not require any overt act. In the Alcoa case of that year, the Court decided that even if a firm's actions might be otherwise reasonable, these actions are nevertheless illegal if they help the firm to maintain a monopoly position. For example, one reasonable business policy is to expand plant capacity in anticipation of increased demand. But the Court decided that such increases in capacity constituted a violation by Alcoa because they tended to block out potential new firms:

[Alcoa] insists that it never excluded competitors; but we can think of no more effective exclusion than progressively to embrace each new opportunity as it opens, and to face every newcomer with new capacity already geared into a great organization, having the advantage of experience, trade connections and the elite of personnel.

BOX 13-2
Conglomerate Mergers

International Telegraph and Telephone (IT&T) typifies the large conglomerate of the 1960s. It grew into a huge corporation by acquiring firms in unrelated activities: Sheraton (hotels), Grinnel (automatic fire sprinklers), C and C Cola, Avis (rent-a-car), Hartford Fire Insurance, and many others. Such conglomerate mergers have become increasingly important, especially since 1950 when the Celler-Kefauver Act tightened up antitrust control over horizontal and vertical mergers. As a result, conglomerates are now "where the action is."

What are the advantages and disadvantages of a conglomerate merger to: (1) the acquiring firm, (2) the "target" firm that is being taken over, and (3) society as a whole?

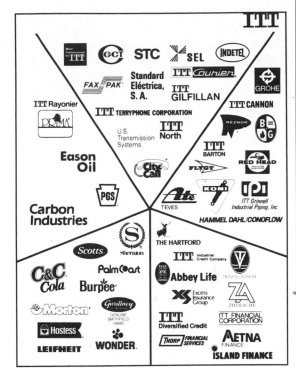

The interests of the acquiring firm: The urge to merge

Because of the tax laws, companies have an incentive to retain profits to finance internal growth, rather than pay them out as dividends to stockholders. (As we saw in Chapter 6, dividends are subject to tax twice—once when they are earned as corporate profit, and once when they are paid out as income to the dividend recipient. But retained earnings are taxed only once, as corporate profits.) If firms are generating large profits which cannot be used profitably in their current business, they have an incentive to "conquer new worlds" by entering new businesses. The easiest and cheapest way to do so may be to acquire an existing firm in another industry.†

Acquiring a new business may offer a challenging way for the firm to use its underutilized management talent. That is, expanding the firm may be a means of achieving economies of scale in management. Similarly, economies of scale may be available in R&D. For example, SAAB of Sweden produces both aircraft and automobiles, thereby reducing the design and engineering costs of each. Another reason for expanding into a new business is to diversify: If a firm is producing ski equipment with profits in the winter, its management may be interested in acquiring a tennis equipment company to provide profits in the summer. Finally, the firm's executives may just prefer to run a larger enterprise; they may enjoy size for its own sake.

A changing stock market price level provides firms with another reason to merge. Surprisingly, conglomerate mergers may be encouraged either by high stock prices or by low ones.

(Continued)

---

†Tax laws also can create an incentive for profitable firm A to take over a firm B which has suffered losses, because B's losses can then be used by A to reduce its taxable profit. Of course, A must take care that it is not acquiring a millstone—a company (B) that continues to run a string of losses in the future.

On the one hand, during the go-go days of the 1960s, high-flying companies with stocks selling at fancy price-earnings ratios could use their own overpriced stock as a way of paying for a new acquisition. (Because their own stock was so highly priced, they often could buy the other firms "cheaply"—that is, with relatively few shares of their own company.) On the other hand, the mergers of the late 1970s were quite different. The acquiring firm generally paid with cash, rather than its own stock. Why? At that time stock prices were low—often below book value. Thus, a firm could be acquired by purchasing its stock at a bargain price. (It was cheaper to buy the firm than to buy plant and equipment and enter an industry from scratch.)

The interests of the target firm

Existing owners (stockholders) of a firm may welcome a takeover bid by another firm, since they are typically offered more than the current market price of their stock. Thus in 1981, Dupont, Seagrams and Mobil became engaged in a bidding war to take over Conoco, the ninth largest U.S. oil company. Dupont won by offering almost $100 for Conoco shares that had sold for roughly half that price three months earlier, before the bidding began. Obviously, one game in the stock market is to try to identify and buy the stock of potential target companies before they actually receive takeover bids.

While the *owners* (stockholders) of a target firm may welcome a takeover bid, a quite different view may be taken by its *management*—the president, vice-presidents, etc., who run the company. (This conflict in views sometimes leads to a pitched battle in the stockholders' meeting.) Why would managers oppose a takeover? After all, they are frequently also large stockholders, and should welcome a takeover for this reason. But, *in their role as managers* they are more likely to resist, because the corporate reorganization that follows a merger may place their jobs in jeopardy. (In order to persuade managers to go along with the merger, they are

sometimes offered a "golden parachute" contract—that is, the right to a large financial settlement if they decide to "bail out" of the merged firm or if they are fired.) Managers may also be concerned that the direction of the company and the people employed in it may change as a result of a takeover. An example of successful resistance by the management of a target company occurred in 1979 when McGraw-Hill fought off a takeover attempt by American Express.

One of the ways the management of a target firm can resist a takeover is to accuse the acquiring firm of violating the antitrust laws by seeking to increase its control over some market. This charge can be backed up if the target firm can find some (perhaps relatively insignificant) market in which both firms already do business. (A farsighted management fearing a takeover may *put* itself in the same business by taking over a third firm.)‡

The interests of society

Benefits of conglomerate mergers   The basic argument for allowing conglomerate mergers is that they are the result of a search for business profit, and, *provided that competition is not restricted,* this profit is likely to imply an economic gain for society. (There are exceptions: for example, if the only gain from a merger is a reduction in taxes.)

To illustrate, consider a merger that does not restrict competition or reduce employment in the target company. If it increases efficiency in some way (say, by reducing per unit costs because of economies of scale), someone in society bene-

---

‡This has led the Justice Department to conclude that "the takeover phenomenon has produced negative side effects. Successful firms that fear they may become takeover targets have attempted to reduce their attractiveness by using accumulated cash to acquire other corporations in an effort to create antitrust conflicts with likely acquirers." *Report of the Attorney General: Conglomerate Mergers, Small Business and the Scope of Existing Anti-Merger Statutes* (U.S. Department of Justice, 1979).

fits: either the owners of the firm in the form of higher profits, or the labor force in the form of higher wages, or consumers of the product in the form of lower prices—perhaps all three.

Costs of conglomerate mergers If a merger does restrict competition, then, like any form of monopolization, it is likely to result in private profit for the firms but an efficiency loss to society. This is why the antitrust authorities, in evaluating a conglomerate merger, ask: "Would this merger increase the monopolization of any specific market?"

For several additional reasons, it has been argued that conglomerate mergers may be damaging overall. Size itself may be considered objectionable, especially if one considers the political implications of the concentration of power in the hands of conglomerates. (IT&T, in particular, did not provide reassurance on this point when it became involved in schemes to influence a presidential election in Chile.)

Conglomerate mergers may also have a long-term deterrent effect on entrepreneurship: The fear of an eventual takeover may discourage entrepreneurs from setting up and developing their own businesses. While this may be true in some cases, in others it is not. Some entrepreneurs set up a business in the *hope* it will be taken over; they view an attractive takeover offer as their eventual financial reward. They will particularly welcome a takeover if their business has reached a point where it is worth more to sell

than to continue to operate themselves. (This may occur if further expansion of R&D, production, and sales can be more easily and cheaply accomplished by a large acquiring company with greater facilities and with cheaper sources of cash.)

A final observation It is often assumed that a merger will increase market power only if merging firms are in the same market. But as noted earlier, a target firm *in a completely different market* may have its market power increased; one reason is that it now has access to the large financial resources of the conglomerate that acquired it. As a consequence, the target firm may be in a stronger position to drive out its competitors—for example, by predatory pricing below cost.

This concern is most valid if the target firm is one of the leading firms in its industry. But if it is not, then its expanded access to financial resources may significantly *increase* competition in its market. (There will then be, say, four major competitors in its industry, rather than the previous three.)

Thus, it is difficult to develop an overall policy for conglomerate mergers, just as it is for horizontal or vertical mergers. Because conglomerate mergers are less likely to restrict competition, the courts have tended to allow them—but not always. For example, a court judgment required IT&T to give up Avis Rent-a-Car. ∎

Between the permissive U.S. Steel decision in 1920 and the much tougher Alcoa decision in 1945, the pendulum had obviously swung a long way.

In the face of the need to balance the complex considerations of market power, tacit collusion, economies of scale, and the other issues which monopoly and oligopoly raise, it is too much to hope for a simple solution. Perfect competition is the perfect answer only in textbooks. In the real world, we must settle for "workable competition," where we gain many

of the advantages of large-scale business, but curb the more flagrant abuses. Harvard's Richard Caves has compared antitrust laws with traffic laws. Going 58 miles an hour in a 55-mile zone represents no calamity. But the police are there to catch the speeder who goes 65 or 70. The fact that we *might* get caught makes most of us drive a little more carefully. Similarly, the electrical machinery and cardboard-box cases described in Box 13-1 remind business executives that there is a jail cell awaiting the flagrant offender; they will be more careful as a result.

Moreover, fear of prosecution by the government is not the only discipline a business faces. A firm may also be sued by a competitor that has been damaged by anticompetitive practices. In such a civil antitrust suit, the court may award the injured party *three times* the amount of the damage. For example, after the electrical equipment executives were sentenced to jail for *criminal* price fixing, their companies were also taken to court in almost 2,000 *civil* suits. As a consequence, they had to pay about $500 million in damages. Obviously, this **treble damage clause** acts as a deterrent to antitrust violations.

II REGULATION OF PRICE AND ENTRY

. . . [In the] airlines it appears that the prime obstacle to efficiency has been regulation itself and the most creative thing a regulator can do is remove his or her body from the market entryway.
    Alfred Kahn, former chairman of the Civil Aeronautics Board

In Chapter 11, we examined in detail the strong case that can be made for government regulation of a natural monopoly such as the local telephone company. (Regulation forced the firm to act more like a perfect competitor facing a given market price.) Here we discuss a policy that is much more difficult to justify: government regulation of a naturally more competitive industry, such as the airline or trucking industry.[5] As will become evident, regulation in this case typically allows firms to act in a *less* competitive way. For example, regulation may reduce com-

petition by blocking the entry of potential new firms. Therefore it is no surprise that this form of regulation is often welcomed by the firms that are already in the industry. (A preview of some of the problems that arise is given in Box 13-3.)

A case history: The airlines

Until 1978, the CAB (Civil Aeronautics Board) regulated airline ticket prices and the routes serviced by each airline. By controlling routes, the CAB controlled entry: Between 1938 and 1978, the CAB turned down all the roughly 150 requests by new carriers to service trunk routes (long-distance routes between big cities). Thus, it limited the degree of competition facing airlines already servicing these routes. This was what led to the charge that the CAB was regulating the industry more in the interests of the regulated firms than of the general public.[6] In effect, the regulatory agency had taken on some of the responsibilities of a cartel manager by restricting entry, dividing up the market (the routes each airline serviced) and setting price. True, it did not set the high monopoly price that would be the target of a private cartel; but on the other hand, this special kind of "public cartel" offered two advantages not available to a private cartel. (1) Because it was administered by a government agency, there wasn't the problem of cheating that arises in a private cartel; the airlines were forbidden to undercut the prices set by the CAB. (2) It was immune from the antitrust laws that ban private cartels: Executives in the old regulated airline industry didn't have to worry about ending up in jail like executives in the nonregulated electrical equipment industry.

CAB price regulation came at a high cost to the traveling public. In California, where within-

---

[5]We are careful to describe the airlines only as an industry that is "naturally more competitive" than regulated monopolies such as the telephone or electricity companies. We recognize that without regulation it is far from *perfectly* competitive; most routes will support only a few airline companies. What keeps the industry competitive in any market (route) is not a large number of firms actually operating there, but instead the *easy entry* of potential new firms. Obviously, a plane now being used on a New York to Washington route can easily be switched to fly from New York to Chicago. In other words, any airline route is competitive in the sense that it is easily contested.

[6]One of the reasons that regulators may favor the interests of the industry is that they themselves have frequently held positions there. (The government's defense of appointing them to the regulatory agencies is that they are the leading experts because they have worked in the industry.) Even if regulators haven't previously come from the industry, they may want to get a job with it later—and often do. (Recent conflict of interest laws reduce, but do not eliminate, this problem.)

state airlines (notably Pacific-Northwest) were exempt from CAB regulation, the fare on the Los Angeles–San Francisco run in the mid-1970s was less than two-thirds the price on regulated routes of similar length elsewhere in the country. The CAB's role in keeping air fares high was further illustrated in 1974, when it rejected an application by a private British airline (Laker) to provide service between New York and London for little more than a third the economy rate then charged by other airlines. Finally, there were a number of studies that estimated a high cost of airline regulation, including one by the General Accounting Office (the investigative arm of Congress) which concluded that CAB regulation between 1969 and 1974 had cost air travelers $10 billion, or 29 percent of total airline revenue.

Thus, while the natural monopoly regulation of Chapter 11 has been designed to reduce industry price, regulation of this naturally more competitive airline industry kept price up. It is therefore no surprise when firms in this sort of an industry resist attempts to remove their regulation; often firms that don't have regulation will actively seek it.[7] For example, truckers of unprocessed agricultural produce at one time sought to be included in the regulated portion of the trucking industry.

At the same time, an industry may find regulation disappointing. Although the CAB controlled some forms of competition (price and routes which an airline could fly) it did not control others, such as the number of flights an airline could schedule on a route. Consequently, on routes serviced by several airlines, each competed vigorously to attract customers by offering more flights. This meant empty seats on many flights, and therefore high costs per passenger. Thus, non-price competition in activities not controlled by the CAB raised airline costs to the point where they dissipated much of the profit the cartelized industry might otherwise have earned. (Indeed, the airlines earned what the CAB considered a fair profit in only one year in every four.)

The cross-subsidization argument

There was another reason why the airlines were not more profitable: Although the CAB allowed them fares that earned a profit on their trunk routes between big cities, it also forced them to continue to provide service to smaller cities at a loss. Thus regulation resulted in "cross-subsidization" (one group of passengers being subsidized by another). Specifically, small-city travelers (who got service they would not have otherwise enjoyed) were being subsidized by travelers on trunk lines (who paid more for their tickets).

Indeed, one of the chief arguments of those who supported regulation was that it provided small-city passengers with convenient and safe service that would be dropped if regulation were to end. And by 1980, when regulations had been largely abolished, there seemed to be evidence to support this claim: The major airlines had given up their service to a number of smaller cities. However, this was more the result of soaring fuel prices than of deregulation. In 1981, the Council of Economic Advisers concluded that:

Higher energy prices have . . . made service to smaller communities by large aircraft an even less attractive financial proposition than it was earlier. However, the increased flexibility permitted by deregulation has helped to preserve air service to smaller communities by making it easier to substitute commuter carriers. Had this flexibility been unavailable, the short-run consequences would have been an enormous increase in Federal subsidies to the airlines, followed by the termination of service to many smaller communities.[8]

[8]*Annual Report, 1981,* p. 101.

---

[7]Firms with a new product may seek their own new agency, in preference to an existing agency that already regulates a similar good or service. The reason is that these firms may be severely restricted by the existing agency's regulations limiting new entry. For example, the airlines in the late 1930s sought their own new agency (the Civil Aeronautics Board), rather than leaving themselves to the mercy of the existing Interstate Commerce Commission (ICC) that regulated the railroads. (It's not clear how the airlines would have fared had they been forced to fight it out within the ICC against the powerful interests of their railroad competitors.)

BOX 13-3
The Parable of the Parking Lots

Producers have a natural interest to narrow the market and raise the price.

Adam Smith

Henry Manne, professor of law at the University of Miami, tells a simple parable to illustrate the problems of government regulation which protects existing firms by blocking the entry of new firms.†

Once upon a time in a city not far away, thousands of people would crowd into the local football stadium on a Saturday afternoon. The problem of parking was initially solved by a number of big commercial parking lots whose owners formed the Association of Professional Parking Lot Employers (APPLE). But, as time passed and crowds grew, every plumber, lawyer, and schoolteacher who owned a house in the neighborhood went into the parking business on Saturday afternoon, and cars appeared in every driveway and on most lawns. Members of APPLE viewed the entry of these "amateurs" into their business with no great enthusiasm, especially since some were charging a lower fee. Stories began to circulate about their fly-by-night methods, and the dents they had put in two cars (although, on investigation, it was discovered that denting was an equally serious problem in the commercial lots).

At a meeting of all members of APPLE, emotions and applause ran high as one speaker after another pointed out—in some cases, in a very statesmanlike way—that parking should be viewed, not as a business, but as a profession governed by professional standards. In particular, cutthroat price competition with amateurs should be regarded as unethical. The one con-

crete proposal, quickly adopted, was that APPLE members should contribute $1 per parking spot "to improve their public image, and put their case before the proper authorities."

No accounting was ever made of this money, but it must have been spent wisely, since within a few months the city council passed an ordinance to regulate industry price and to require that anyone parking cars must be licensed. But it turned out to be difficult for an independent house owner to get a license; it required passing a special driving test to be "professionally administered" by APPLE, a $25,000 investment in parking facilities, and $500,000 in liability insurance. Since every commercial lot found its costs consequently increasing by 20 percent, the city council approved a 20 percent increase in parking fees. (Within a year, APPLE had requested that the city council guarantee the liability insurance, so that people would have no fear of parking in commercial lots. One argument put forward by an APPLE spokesman was that this idea was similar in its intent to recent congressional legislation setting up an insurance scheme for stockbrokers.)

On the next football afternoon, a funny thing happened on the way to the stadium. Since police were out in large numbers to enforce the ordinance, driveways and lawns were empty and long lines of cars were backed up waiting to get into each commercial lot. The snarl was even worse after the game. Some people simply gave up waiting for their cars and had to return to retrieve them next day. (There was even a rumor that one car was never found.) In response, APPLE decided to go ahead with a "statistical-logistic study of the whole socioeconomic situation" by two computer science professors at the local university. Their report cited the archaic methods of the industry and pointed out that what each firm needed was fewer quill pens and more time on a computer.

† "The Parable of the Parking Lots," *Public Interest*, no. 23 (Spring 1971), pp. 10–15. Abbreviated with the author's permission.

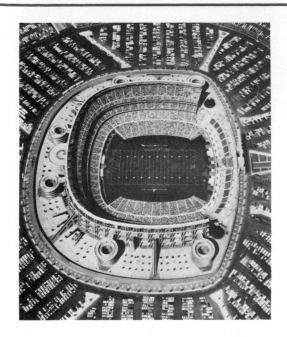

As the parking lots began to computerize their operations, it became quite clear that in the face of these rising costs, a further increase in parking fees was required. The increase was quickly approved by city councillors relieved that, in the modernization of the industry, they had finally found a solution. But, unfortunately, it was no solution after all. The problem, it turned out, was not so much deciding which car should be moved where, as actually moving it—and that continued to be done by attendants who had become surly and uncooperative because of the pressure they were facing.

Relief, however, did appear in two forms. First, many people got fed up with the hassle and started watching the game on TV. Second, small boys who lived in the houses closest to the stadium went into the car wash business on Saturday afternoon. They charged $5, but it was worth the price, since they guaranteed a top-quality job. (In fact, they guaranteed that they would spend at least 2 hours on it.) And they always had as many cars as they could handle, even on rainy days—in fact, especially on rainy days. ■

Deregulation

In 1978, Congress passed the Airline Deregulation Act. By the end of that year, passengers were benefiting from lower fares. In turn, lower prices resulted in more airline travel: In 1978, passenger travel increased by 40 percent as airline fares fell by 20 percent. Consequently, many of the empty seats were being filled and there was no substantial reduction in the number of flights. Thus, the worst fears of the aircraft manufacturers, airline pilots, and service personnel—that fewer planes would be flying, and their jobs would be in jeopardy—were not realized. At the same time, the airline industry was entering a state of competitive flux: Smaller airlines were not only "filling the gap" by moving into the small-city routes discontinued by the major airlines; they were also providing the majors with competition on the big-city trunk routes.

By 1980, some of the long-established airlines were under severe pressure from the small new companies. Some of the older lines—especially those that had expanded rapidly with deregulation—were in financial trouble. But to some degree this was the result of bad luck. The shakeout facing the airlines was much more severe because of a combination of external events: Following a crash in 1979, the Federal Aviation Administration grounded DC-10's for more than a month; between early 1979 and mid-1980, jet fuel prices more than doubled, forcing airline fares back up;[9] and this, along with the 1980 recession, reduced airline travel.

Consequently, during this period a key question was: "How much of the financial difficulty of the airlines was due to deregulation, and how much was due to these other pressures on the industry?" But many in the CAB and the airlines (including some who originally had opposed deregulation) were coming to the view

[9]During this period it was very difficult to estimate the effect of deregulation in lowering airline fares, because this influence was more than offset by the effect of higher fuel costs in *raising* fares. All that could be concluded was that, during this period, deregulation limited the rapid increase in airline prices that would have otherwise occurred.

that the airline companies—as well, of course, as passengers—had received some benefits from deregulation. For example, deregulation was allowing the airlines to move their equipment around quickly into more efficient routing patterns.

Deregulation of trucking

By 1980, the trucking industry was also being deregulated. Even before the deregulation law was signed on July 1, 1980, the Interstate Commerce Commission (ICC) had been making entry into the industry easier, and had been ending many costly regulations such as those that had restricted trucks from carrying certain items. (For example, one company was permitted to carry empty ginger ale bottles, but not empty cola or root beer bottles. Another could haul five-gallon cans, but not two-gallon cans.) Such regulations caused obvious inefficiency and were in direct conflict with the government's desire to conserve fuel.

As deregulation proceeded and competition increased, many trucking firms encountered severe financial difficulty, in some cases bankruptcy. (Some bankruptcies are to be expected when a regulatory system that has protected the inefficient is replaced by competition.) For trucking deregulation, the central issue was the same as for the airlines: "To what degree were the financial difficulties encountered by the industry a reflection of the expected shakeout from deregulation, and to what degree were they the result of the recession and skyrocketing fuel costs?"

III QUALITY-OF-LIFE REGULATION TO IMPROVE HEALTH, SAFETY, AND WORKING CONDITIONS

Whereas the price/entry regulation we have just discussed is imposed on a single industry (such as the airlines), quality-of-life regulation is usually imposed economywide, on all industries. (For a sample of these two kinds of regulation, see Table 13-1.) There is another significant difference in the two kinds of regulation: Whereas price/entry regulation often comes to promote the interests of the firms being regulated, quality-of-life regulation is generally opposed by regulated firms because it typically raises their costs and is considered a nuisance. Thus, quality-of-life agencies tend to reflect the views, not of the regulated firms, but instead of those who worked hard to have the regulations imposed. For example, OSHA (The Occupational Health and Safety Administration) tends to reflect the view of organized labor, and EPA (the Environmental Protection Agency) the views of environmental groups. (Pollution and the role of the EPA in controlling it are studied in the next chapter.)

Since quality-of-life agencies are pursuing important social objectives such as health and safety, we might assume that they operate in the public interest. They should, and often do; but not always.

Problems with quality-of-life regulation: Inadequate benefit-cost analysis

The improved health and safety standards that are designed to provide obvious benefits to society also involve substantial costs. For example, when firms are required to purchase safety equipment, their overhead costs rise. While the economywide evidence is that some of these higher costs are borne by the firms' owners or labor force in the form of lower income, much of this burden is passed on to customers in the form of higher prices. But in one way or another, the public pays for the health and safety benefits it receives.

Under what circumstances are we buying too little safety, and when are we buying too much? The answer is: We are buying too little whenever there are potential new safety regulations that would cost less than the benefits they would provide. And we are buying too much whenever the costs of some existing regulations exceed the benefits. Examples of too little safety may be found by going back to the 1950s, when there were few restrictions on the disposal of dangerous chemicals. An example of too much regulation (referred to as a "regulatory absurdity" by Charles Schultze, the Chairman of the Council of Economic Advisers under President Carter) was the 21 pages of fine print regulations imposed some years ago by OSHA on how to

Table 13-1
Alphabet Soup: A Sample of Washington's Regulatory Agencies†

"Market structure" agencies that control price and/or entry into an industry

1. *The Interstate Commerce Commission* (ICC, established in 1887) regulates rates and routes of railroads, waterway carriers, and most trucking companies. (Trucking regulation is now being reduced.)

2. *The Federal Maritime Commission* (FMC, 1936) regulates ocean commerce by overseeing price agreements between shipping companies.

3. *The Civil Aeronautics Board* (CAB) has regulated airline fares and routes since 1938. (By 1981, as a result of airline deregulation, its powers had been greatly reduced.)

"Quality-of-life" agencies that regulate health, safety, and working conditions

1. *The Food and Drug Administration* (FDA, 1931) regulates the labeling, safety and purity of food, and the safety and effectiveness of drugs.

2. *The National Labor Relations Board* (NLRB, 1935) regulates the labor practices of companies and unions. It adjudicates complaints of illegal or unfair labor practices by individuals, unions, or employers. In addition, it holds representation elections to deter-

mine which union, if any, will represent a group of workers.

3. *The Equal Employment Opportunity Commission* (EEOC, 1964) investigates complaints of racial, religious, or sexual discrimination.

4. *The National Highway Traffic Safety Administration* (NHTSA, 1970) regulates the safety of autos, trucks, buses, and other vehicles. For example, it orders the auto companies to recall and repair models with safety defects.

5. *The Environmental Protection Agency* (EPA, 1970) develops and enforces clean air and water standards, and controls noise and pesticide pollution. (It is described in detail in Chapter 26.)

6. *The Occupational Safety and Health Administration* (OSHA, 1971) regulates health and safety conditions in nongovernment workplaces.

7. *The Consumer Product Safety Commission* (CPSC, 1972) controls the design and labeling of goods to reduce injuries to consumers.

8. *The Mining Enforcement and Safety Administration* (MESA, 1973) enforces mine safety standards.

†For more detail on these and other regulatory agencies, see Paul W. MacAvoy, *The Regulated Industries and the Economy* (New York: Norton, 1979).

build a ladder, including such trivialities as how far the screws must be indented. While OSHA did eliminate nearly 1,000 outmoded or unnecessary regulations during the Carter administration, this example nonetheless still illustrates an important point: *A regulation cannot be justified simply because it is pursuing a desirable goal such as health or safety.* Instead, it should be subjected to a **benefit-cost** test.

Benefit-cost analysis is an estimate of the benefits and costs of a policy, and a comparison of the two. A benefit-cost test is the requirement that the benefits of a policy be at least as great as its costs.

All too often, the benefits of a new regulation are not estimated and costs are almost entirely ignored. Sometimes the fault does not lie with the agency that sets the regulations, but instead with the Congress that established the agency: For example, in the Clean Air Act and the Delaney Amendment to the Food, Drug and Cosmetic Act, Congress *prohibits* agencies from considering the costs of their regulations.

Costs of quality-of-life regulation

(1) The payment of salaries and other costs of operating the agencies By 1979 these costs were running in the range of $3–4

billion a year. Although this is a significant sum, it is relatively unimportant compared to the other costs of regulation.

(2) The costs firms incur in complying with the regulations   These include the costs to businesses that must install health and safety equipment (such as protective enclosures for machines); and the cost of the paperwork that firms must supply to the agencies. (At one point General Motors estimated that the documents it had to file to get its cars approved for one year would have made a stack 15 stories high.)

(3) Efficiency cost of regulation   There are many subtle effects of regulation on efficiency and productivity: The more time and effort that management spends in satisfying government regulations and in trying to influence its regulatory agency, the less time it has to develop, produce, and market its products.

But some of the effects are not so subtle. Regulations frequently lead to serious delay. For example, the testing and approval of a new drug by the Food and Drug Administration (FDA) now takes 5 to 7 years. The reason is that people in such an agency often develop a defensive "siege" mentality. They are faced with two conflicting objectives: (1) Get a drug out as quickly as possible so that it can begin to *save* lives; but (2) delay its release until it can be tested sufficiently to ensure that it is safe (so that it doesn't *take* lives). Faced with this choice, regulators often delay. They will be criticized less for delaying too long—and failing to save lives—than they will be for releasing a drug too soon, in which case its fatal effects may raise a political storm.

The FDA has recognized the cost of unnecessary delay—a particularly serious issue for anticancer drugs—and as a consequence, has set up a "fast track" for particularly promising drugs.

There are also costs of delay in other areas. As we shall see in Chapter 22, the long delays in acquiring approval from a regulatory agency have sometimes meant that energy-producing firms have had to abandon some investments altogether.

A final observation on costs

Regulation affects investment in another significant way: The more resources channeled into safety and antipollution equipment, the less that remain for equipment that produces more output. Thus, lost output in the future is the opportunity cost of investment in antipollution and safety equipment today. It has been estimated that by the mid-1980s there may be a sufficient buildup of this effect to reduce measured GNP by 3–5 percent.[10]

Even though such estimates are subject to considerable uncertainty, they suggest that the costs of quality-of-life regulation are now substantial. The question is: Have these regulations provided benefits sufficient to justify this high cost?

Benefits of quality-of-life regulation

Whereas costs of regulation can be expressed in terms of a decrease in GNP, the benefits of regulation cannot be expressed in terms of a higher GNP. (Regulatory benefits such as improved health or safety are not included in GNP calculations.) When benefits are measured one agency at a time, they have sometimes turned out to be disappointing. Statistical evaluations of OSHA have suggested that, at best, it has reduced accident rates by only a small amount.

On the other hand, EPA's regulations have generated considerable benefits, not only in resisting the trend towards a more polluted environment, but in some cases in even reversing it (as we shall see in the next chapter). Moreover, the introduction of safety requirements such as seat belts and stronger doors and bumpers by the National Highway Traffic Safety Administration (NHTSA) has apparently provided substantial benefits, since these regulations

---

[10]MacAvoy, *The Regulated Industries and the Economy*, p. 94.

were followed by a reduction in auto injuries and fatalities. This is even more impressive because, during this period, cars were becoming smaller and lighter—and for this reason less safe. (Thus, just preventing the safety record from getting worse represented substantial success.) However, it is difficult to sort out how much of this success can be attributed to these NHTSA regulations, and how much to other important influences such as the reduction in the speed limit and the decrease in the proportion of the population in the low-age category where accident rates are high.

Thus, while quality-of-life regulations have come at high cost, their benefits have been mixed: substantial in some cases, disappointing in others. This is perhaps no great surprise, since some agencies have not been required to assess the benefits and costs of the regulations they were imposing.[11]

An example where there may have been too much regulation is the case of saccharin, a very mild carcinogen that the FDA was required by law to ban. (The law required the banning of artificial carcinogens, regardless of the overall costs and benefits.) The benefit of this ban was less cancer. But its cost was the increase in heart disease of overweight people who were driven back to sugar. Thus, the ban on saccharin may have saved a few lives from cancer but lost as many—or perhaps more—from overweight.

By the late 1970s there was a growing view that regulators were trying to do too much;

accordingly, the agencies were under pressure to reduce existing regulations, and be more selective in introducing new ones.

Why benefit-cost analysis is not the last word

Benefit-cost analysis is not easy. For example, it is difficult enough to estimate that the cost of a certain regulation will be $4 million and its benefit will be the saving of 20 lives. But there is an even greater problem: Before these two figures can be compared, it is necessary to put a dollar value on the human lives that are saved. And how do you do *that*? (For some suggestions, see Box 13-4.) In many cases, the benefits and costs of regulations cannot be measured in a precise way.

As a consequence, opponents who want to abolish regulation sometimes use benefit-cost analysis as a debating point. They argue that we should not introduce (or continue) any regulation unless it can pass a rigid benefit-cost test—a near-impossible requirement in a world in which many benefits and costs simply cannot be measured precisely. This position is no more justified than the other extreme, held by those who argue that *any* regulation that improves human health or safety is desirable, and its costs should not even be considered.

The need for consistency

In the last analysis, a *judgment* must be made. And sometimes we are in a position to identify a desirable policy change, even when only fragmentary evidence is available. For example, an OSHA emission standard for coke ovens will be so difficult for industry to meet that its estimated cost will lie somewhere between $4.5 million and $158 million for *each* life it saves. Compare this with a regulation the government is *not* imposing—the elimination of railroad crossings which would save lives at an estimated cost of $100,000 each.[12]

---

[11]Toward the end of the Carter administration, and at the beginning of the Reagan administration, some moves were made toward requiring estimates of benefits and costs, as agencies were put under pressure to show that any new regulation would (1) provide significant economy-wide benefits; and (2) be **cost-effective,** that is, involve a lower cost than any other method of achieving the same result. (For example, it has been shown that a proposed OSHA regulation against on-the-job noise is not cost-effective, since ear protectors could provide similar hearing protection at less cost.) While these moves are in the right direction, they do not guarantee that a regulation will pass the crucial benefit-cost test: A regulation may be both cost-effective and provide very large benefits; yet its costs may still exceed its benefits.

[12]For these and other estimates, see Martin Bailey, *Reducing Risks to Life* (Washington, D.C.: American Enterprise Institute, 1980), p. 26.

BOX 13-4

The Eternal Puzzle: What Is a Human Life Worth?

The simple answer: An infinite amount. The miner trapped underground has a life which is priceless. Yet, we don't value our own lives this way. Were they to have infinite value, safety concerns would dominate all others. We would live as close as possible to our work and never drive a car, let alone take a trip to earn something as trivial as a few thousand dollars.

One method used to evaluate a life is earning potential—the expected amount the individual would have earned over the rest of his or her lifetime. By this measure, a life lost at age 20 is worth far more than a life lost at 40. This measure is far from ideal, since it measures the value of a *livelihood,* not a *life.*

An alternative approach is to start by asking, "What's the valuation of an individual who actually 'puts his life on the line?' " That is, how much more than the average wage must be offered to induce a worker to take a high-risk job like that of a lumberjack? Although this is probably the most promising way of evaluating a human life, it involves several difficulties. For example: (1) The higher wage indicates only how the workers who actually take these jobs value their lives. But isn't this far less than the valuation of the vast majority of the population who won't take such risky jobs because they value their lives more highly? (2) How much of the higher wage is compensa-

tion for the risk of death, and how much for the risk of injury? (The higher wage compensates for both, but we are only interested in evaluating the risk of death.) (3) These estimates are only meaningful if the people taking these jobs understand the risks they are taking. Is this so? Although there is quite surprising evidence that they do indeed fairly correctly rank the jobs from most risky to least, it isn't clear whether or not they consistently overestimate (or underestimate) the risks of all of them.

In a recent study, Martin Bailey of the University of Maryland looked at how workers act in risky situations. Their behavior suggests that they estimate the value of their own lives somewhere in the $200,000 to $700,000 range.[†] The imprecision of this estimate illustrates how difficult it is to place a value on a human life. ∎

[†]Martin J. Bailey, *Reducing Risks to Life: Measurement of the Benefits* (Washington: American Enterprise Institute, 1980).

Rachel Dardis (also of the University of Maryland) uses a different approach, examining how much consumers are willing to pay for fire detectors that reduce the risk to their lives. She concludes that the value of a human life is between $200,000 and $500,000—that is, in the bottom half of Bailey's range. Dardis, "The Value of Life: New Evidence from the Marketplace," *American Economic Review,* December 1980, pp. 1077–1082.

With just this information on the *cost* of saving a life, we can arrive at an important conclusion—even though we may have no information whatsoever on the *benefit* of saving a life. Specifically, we can conclude that government policy is inconsistent. It makes no sense to engage in *any* activity (saving lives or anything else) in an exceedingly expensive way (at least $4,500,000)—when one can achieve the same objective at far less cost ($100,000).

And if we have even the roughest sort of estimate of the benefit of saving a life—for example, if we know that this benefit falls anywhere between the $200,000 to $700,000 cited in Box 13-4—[13] we can go one large step further to a policy recommendation: Coke oven emission standards should be relaxed in favor of eliminating railroad crossings. By using society's limited life-saving resources to meet coke oven emission standards, we are missing the opportunity to save more lives in a less expensive way (by eliminating railroad crossings).

Thus, the payoff from selecting the least-cost life-saving method need not be expressed in terms of dollars saved. It can be measured in terms of lives saved—a more attractive approach for those who don't like to calculate *anything* in dollars when health or safety are at stake.

There are many other illustrations of regulatory inconsistency. For example: Why should saccharin have been banned outright by the FDA because it was a food additive, when there was no similar ban against *natural* foods that had cancer-inducing effects? And why stop at foods, and thus exclude tobacco, one of the stronger carcinogens?

But the problem of regulatory inconsistency goes far deeper than this. Agencies are often set up with objectives that are in direct conflict.

---

*[13]Actually, our argument still holds for an even wider range of values—specifically, so long as a human life is worth anything between the $100,000 railroad crossing estimate and the $4,500,000 coke oven estimate.

CONCLUDING OBSERVATIONS: REGULATORY CONFLICTS AND THE SHIFT IN ECONOMIC DECISION MAKING

Members of Congress are faced with a wide array of problems which involve large expenditures of their own time and public funds. It is no surprise, therefore, that when they encounter a problem that can *apparently* be solved by setting up a regulatory agency, they are inclined to do so. (Although this involves spending a minimum of taxpayers' money, the public still pays. But payment occurs in hidden ways, for example in a higher price for goods because producers incur a cost in complying with safety regulations. The public does not pay very much in the form of taxes that are easy to blame on politicians.)

As a result there is now a wide range of agencies with different objectives that are often praiseworthy, but that sometimes generate conflicts. For example, in pursuing its desirable goal of protecting the environment, the EPA encouraged the conversion of the nation's power plants from coal to less polluting fuels such as natural gas. But in pursuing *its* desirable goal of conserving scarce forms of energy, the Federal Energy Administration reversed the EPA's guidelines and urged the conversion from gas back to coal because coal is our most plentiful energy source.

[As an example of how firms can become entangled in conflicting regulations, consider the situation which faced AT&T and other telephone companies in California. Their Californian regulatory agency insisted that they pass on to their customers (via a price reduction) some tax savings they were getting from the Internal Revenue Service (IRS). But then the IRS ruled that they could not get this tax saving if they passed it on; they had to keep it in a reserve instead. Thus, the companies were caught in a Catch 22. They were receiving a benefit from IRS that they had to pass on to the Californian consumers; but as soon as they passed it on, the IRS wanted it back. AT&T's solution: Don't claim the tax sav-

BOX 13-5
Profit Maximization in a Regulated Economy

Even in an unregulated economy, the maximization of profits is a complex problem for a firm. Interrelated decisions must be made on which goods to produce, how much of each good to produce, and what inputs to use in the production process. Except in perfect competition—where the price is given by impersonal market forces—a pricing decision must also be made. So must decisions on how much to spend on advertising, improving product quality and design, and so on.

In a regulated economy, decision making is complicated further by the firm's relationships with the government and the courts. For example, a regulated firm may develop and price its products in a very special way: It may delay the announcement of a new product (or some other form of technological breakthrough) until the time when its regulatory agency is considering a critical ruling. The firm hopes to use this announcement to acquire public support, and thus indirectly influence the agency's decision. (American Telephone and Telegraph has been cited as an example.)† Alternatively, firms may try to gain support from their regulatory agency by strategically pricing their products, taking a loss on items sold to customers favored by the agency. A third method a firm may use to

influence its agency is to partially control the information it must submit: It may carefully select the facts it provides the agency. Or it may provide required information buried in a mountain of irrelevant material. Or it may submit required information with a warning that it is unreliable, and an assurance that better data are being assembled. Finally, its submission may be dressed up in a sufficiently technical form that the agency will have to set up a hearing to "get at the facts." (If regulatory agencies don't get at all the facts, their decisions may be overturned later by the courts.)

Finally, a regulated firm may put expert Washington legal firms on retainer or hire academic experts to do research studies, in order to make it difficult for them to testify against it in future hearings or court cases. And the firm's executives may seek to develop personal relationships with those in the regulatory agency, who will therefore think of how adverse decisions will affect their friends, rather than some impersonal company. (Such friendships may be easy to cultivate with regulatory officials who may eventually be interested in jobs with the regulated firm.)

Thus in a regulated economy, maximizing profit becomes much more complicated. Moreover, a new type of inefficiency arises, to the degree that the efforts and resources of firms are diverted away from producing goods and towards influencing their regulatory agencies. ■

†B. L. Owen and R. Braeutigam, *The Regulation Game: Strategic Use of the Administrative Process* (Cambridge, Mass.: Ballinger, 1978), pp. 5–6.

---

ing in the first place. But then the California regulators, annoyed that phone users in the state weren't getting a reduced price after all, forced the companies to lower their price to the level it would have been, had they got the tax saving and passed it on. AT&T then went to work lobbying in Washington to have the tax law changed.]

The rapid growth of regulation has resulted in a substantial shift in decision-making away from the economic marketplace. Business decisions that were once determined in the marketplace are now increasingly being influenced by the regulatory agencies and the courts. (For how this affects business decision-making, see Box 13-5.) The question arises: Could we not have done a less expensive and more effective job of pursuing the praiseworthy objectives of the regulatory agencies by continuing to rely on the market instead, but in a specially modified form? Answering this question is one of our major objectives in the next chapter.

Key Points

1 The government regulates business in three ways: *(a)* Antitrust laws are designed to keep markets competitive by limiting the accumulation of market power. *(b)* Regulatory agencies control price and conditions of entry into certain industries—including both natural monopolies (public utilities such as power or local phone companies) and more naturally competitive industries such as the airlines. *(c)* Other agencies regulate health, safety and working conditions economy-wide (across all industries).

2 Antitrust laws raise difficult questions. (For example, when is price cutting unfair? How do you know when firms are colluding?) Nonetheless, these laws have improved the competitive tone of American business, because violations can lead to jail sentences, to fines, or to civil suits from competitors for triple damages. The three main laws in the government's antitrust arsenal are the Sherman Antitrust Act, the Clayton Act, and the Federal Trade Commission Act.

3 Although government regulation may be the appropriate policy to deal with a natural monopoly, it is more dubious in industries such as the airlines. In such cases, the regulatory agency can be viewed as a legal way of "cartelizing" the industry by raising its price and dividing up its market.

4 A quality-of-life regulation cannot be justified simply because it is pursuing a desirable goal—even if this goal is saving lives. Instead, regulations should pass a benefit-cost test. But estimating benefits and costs is often difficult, and judgment must sometimes be substituted when good estimates are not available. (Insisting on the unrealistic requirement that any project pass a measured benefit-cost test is the position taken by some who oppose regulation on principle. But this position is as extreme as the opposing view, that any regulation that will improve health or safety should be undertaken regardless of cost.)

5 With the growth of regulation, economic decision-making is shifting from the marketplace to the government and courts.

Key Concepts

antitrust policy
advantages of size
how imports make an
   industry competitive
cutthroat competition
collusion

Sherman Antitrust Act
   (1890)
Clayton Act (1914)
Federal Trade Commission
   Act (1914)
laws that restrict
   competition

horizontal merger
vertical merger
conglomerate merger
workable competition
price/entry regulation
cross-subsidization
benefit-cost analysis

Problems

13-1 It sounds like a good idea to forbid any firm from predatory price cutting—that is, pricing to drive its competitors out of business. But consider the two examples below. In each case, do you think that the price-cutting action should be judged illegal (as it sometimes has been)?

(a) An efficient firm with lower cost than any of its competitors charges a lower price, and thus drives the less efficient firms out of business. This is an example of how our competitive system works: The more efficient take business away from the less efficient. Do you think this is a good system? If the less efficient are not driven out of business, what happens to the cost of producing goods?

(b) In a natural monopoly with economies of scale, the large, expanding firm finds its costs are falling; hence, it lowers its price and drives its small competitors out of business.

Do you see now why enforcing antitrust laws is difficult?

13-2 Which of the following agreements among firms in an industry do you judge desirable? Undesirable?

(a) An agreement to reduce output by 10 percent to end a glut on the market

(b) An agreement to quote the same price

(c) An agreement by the railroads to lay the same width of track

13-3 Does government encourage or discourage takeovers with

(a) its tax laws? (See Box 13-2.)

(b) its antitrust laws?

Explain your answer.

13-4 Suppose that, for the last 10 years, a government agency had regulated the prices of hotel rooms, thus preventing price competition among the big companies like Hilton and Sheraton. Suppose, also, that in return these companies had been required by the regulatory agency to maintain hotels in many smaller cities. Suppose the government is now considering an end to this regulation.

As an adviser to this industry, draw up a brief on how dangerous this action would be.

Now switch roles, and criticize the brief.

In your view, which is the stronger case? Do you think this example is similar to airline regulation? Why or why not?

*13-5** To understand cross subsidization better, consider a simplified example in which there are two individuals: A lives in a large city, B in a small one. Draw a diagram, showing what the demand curve of each individual for airline services might look like.

(a) Suppose that in the initial unregulated situation, A gets airline service at price P_1, while B gets no service. Show the consumer surplus (if any) for each individual.

(b) Suppose the following policy of cross-subsidization is introduced: B is forced to pay a price above initial price P_1 (and has consumer surplus reduced) in order to allow A for the first time to have airline service (and thereby enjoy a consumer surplus). Show how this policy may provide a collective benefit (an increase in the combined consumer surplus of both individuals taken together).

13-6 During the debate over trucking deregulation, *The Washington Post* (Mar. 2, 1980) quoted C. R. Looney, the traffic manager of PPG Industries, as follows:

I grant you some of these [truck] rates are a little higher than they should be, . . . but it is a trade-off we shippers should accept. There are so many different products [on which different rates might be set by truckers] that I just don't see how we could 'keep up' if rates were deregulated.

(a) Has this problem of confusing prices arisen in the airline industry since it has been deregulated? On balance, how would you weigh this problem against the gains of deregulation to the traveling public?

(b) Would you expect this problem of confusing prices to be greater or less in trucking than in airlines? How would this confusing array of trucking rates compare to the confusing array of prices consumers face on the many items they buy in a department store? Does this make a

case for regulating department store prices? Why or why not?

(c) Looney's bosses at PPG told Congress they favored deregulation. How do you explain the different views of Looney and top management?

13-7 Supporters of more strict government regulation of the economy have on occasion used the following argument: "A clean environment is a necessary precondition for any economic activity. Similarly, safety for the labor force is a necessary precondition for manufacturing. Thus these objectives must be achieved regardless of what their benefits and cost may be."

Do you agree? Explain why or why not.

13-8 Should a careless driver who runs into a railroad train be able to sue the auto maker for producing a car that involves an unreasonable safety risk? Should he be able to sue the auto company if he has bumped into another car at very slow speed and his engine has exploded as a consequence? If your answer differs in these two cases, how do you draw the line?

***13-9** What is the cost to society when a life is saved by OSHA's coke oven standard rather than by removing railroad crossings?

Express this cost in terms of the lives lost (that is, the additional lives that could have been saved if the resources put into complying with the coke oven standard had been put into removing railroad crossings instead).

CHAPTER 14
Problems of the Environment:
Pollution and Congestion

The fact that the nation's commitment to environmental cleanup will impose massive costs is in itself no reason to retrench on the commitment. But their very size does make costs a central factor in the design of control policy. The difference between inefficient and efficient control policies can mean scores, perhaps hundreds, of billions of dollars released for other useful purposes over the next several decades.

Allen V. Kneese and Charles L. Schultze

During the past two decades, we have become increasingly aware of the pollution of our environment. Water pollution poisons fish and can make them dangerous for human consumption. Air pollution causes the acid rain which is destroying life in some lakes in North America and Europe, and reduces the life expectancy of the residents of big cities by an estimated two years.[1] Ground pollution, caused by the dumping of poisonous chemicals in past decades (Box 14-1), has driven a whole community from its homes near Love Canal in upstate New York.

[1]Lester B. Lave and Eugene P. Seskin, *Air Pollution and Human Health* (Washington: Resources for the Future, 1977). The authors also estimate that controls over air pollution could increase the life expectancy of all Americans by almost one year. (To put this in perspective, between 1955 and 1980 U.S. life expectancy increased by about 3 years.)

POLLUTION: THE COSTLY JOB OF CONTROL

In order to reduce pollution, Congress has passed laws (such as the Water Pollution Control Act and the Clean Air Act) which:

1 Limit the pollutants a firm may discharge into the water, air, or earth. [The Environmental Protection Agency (EPA) has the responsibility for setting and enforcing these limitations.]

2 Limit the pollutants discharged by a *product,* such as the exhaust emissions discharged by automobiles.

3 Provide subsidies to municipalities for building waste disposal plants; and provide subsidies (in the form of tax reductions) to firms installing pollution control equipment.

The result has been substantial progress in cleaning up the environment. There are now

Chemicals and the Environment

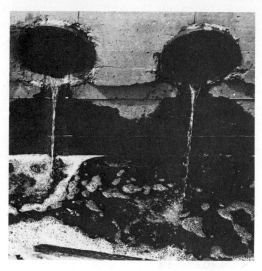

Chemical wastes have sometimes been dumped into a convenient stream, put into drums and then buried, or simply abandoned in a huge chemical "graveyard." Sometimes they have been spread far and wide over deserted country roads by speeding "outlaw trucks" that simply open their valves and let the chemicals slowly spill out. Often this dumping is done by a small firm hired by the large company that has produced the chemical waste. No questions asked; the less the large firm's executives know, the better. But ignorance will no longer be a defense: Congress is now acting to make all parties liable, and to ensure that chemical wastes will be tracked from the "cradle to the grave." ■

boutiques in Cleveland along the Cuyahoga, a river that used to be so loaded with pollutants that it twice caught fire. And even a critic of U.S. environmental policy concedes: "From the Appalachians to the Cascades, shy mountain streams that used to make their escape from paper-mill towns rafted with foam and stinking black with sulfite liquor now manage to sparkle a bit in the sunlight. Crab traps once more dangle from hardware-store ceilings of little towns up the Hudson."[2] The Great Lakes are cleaner and clearer, and fish are returning. Salmon have come back to the Penobscot River in Maine: People in Bangor claim to be catching 20-pounders during lunch hour.

But these tales tell only half the story. The EPA is to be judged not only by such instances where the environment has improved, but also by a number of instances where the environment has *not* improved—where EPA's sole "success" has been to keep the environment from

getting worse. It is important to recognize that success must be measured in these terms—in our ability to reduce pollution or to limit its growth. It is not reasonable to think in terms of eliminating it completely. A moment's reflection makes it clear why this would be an impossible objective. Even if we were to bring U.S. industry to a standstill by closing down every plant that did any polluting whatsoever, pollutants from millions of country barnyards and city streets would still wash into our streams. Since it is not possible to eliminate pollution, the practical questions are: How far should it be cut back? And what costs should we be willing to bear?

Before answering these questions, it is important to fully understand the various costs involved in pollution control. No matter how the clean-up is initially financed, the public eventually bears the burden in one way or another:

As taxpayers, we pay higher taxes because of the subsidies granted to firms installing pollution control equipment.

These subsidies cover only part of the cost of

[2]Tom Alexander, *Fortune*, November 1976, p. 129.

that equipment. But the remainder must also be borne by somebody—for example, by the firms that install the equipment, or consumers who have to pay more for the firms' products.

The most highly publicized cost occurs when jobs are lost because pollution-control standards force a plant to close down, or cause it to lose sales to imports. Even those who live closest to sources of industrial pollution (such as steel mills) often prefer pollution and jobs, if the alternative is a cleaner environment and unemployment. Comments from those who live close to a U.S. steel mill in Clairton, Pennsylvania are typical: "We're not against clean air, but we do need jobs and we do need U.S. Steel. . . . When the day comes that smoke stops coming out of those stacks, we'll all have to find another town."

Thus, in one way or another, the cost of controlling pollution touches us all. It is a large tab—no one really knows how large. Just to achieve the original clean-up standards set in the early '70s would have cost an estimated $40 to $60 billion a year. And since then several new problems have been discovered that are proving to be very costly to control—for example, the "ground pollution" from poisonous chemicals.

Because pollution is costly to control, we should try to use the least expensive methods available. Unfortunately, we have often not used these methods in the past; one of the major criticisms of EPA is that its pollution-control policies have been far too expensive. One of the objectives of this chapter is to show why. A second objective is to outline a better policy. (A worse policy, but one that is sometimes recommended, is described in Box 14-2.) But first, we consider why government intervention is necessary in the first place—why we can't count on Adam Smith's "invisible hand" to limit pollution.

POLLUTION: AN EXTERNAL COST

When pollution exists, private and social costs differ. For example, the costs of paper to society include not only the private or **internal cost** of production faced by the pulp and paper firm, but also the cost to those who live downstream and must put up with the wastes released into the river. While the pulp and paper firm has to pay

---

BOX 14-2

Why Not Control Pollution by Ending Economic Growth?

A no-growth policy would do no more than *stop the increase* in pollution; it would provide no reduction whatsoever in *existing* pollution. Thus, as a way of reducing pollution, a nongrowth policy would be inferior to our present policies: They have allowed us to reduce some kinds of pollution—by a quarter or a half, according to some estimates. (To have achieved such a reduction in pollution by reducing output would have required a massive reduction in GNP.)

Thus, as a way of reducing pollution, a limit on output would be extraordinarily expensive, yet ineffective. It is like killing a rat by burning half your house down. Even if you cure the problem, the side effects are appalling. Better by far to find a cure specifically designed to deal with the problem: If the problem is a rat, get a trap; if the problem is pollution, find a policy that directly reduces it. ■

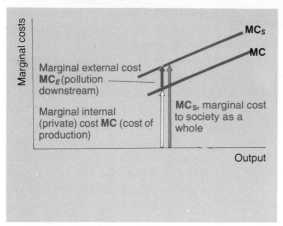

Figure 14-1

With pollution, private and social costs differ

The marginal cost to society of a good (the light red arrow MC$_S$) includes both the marginal *internal* cost to the producing firm (the white arrow MC) plus a marginal *external* cost not borne by the producing firm (the dark red arrow).

for internal production costs, any cost downstream is **external** to its operation, since this cost is borne by others.

Internal or private costs are the costs incurred by those who actually produce (or consume) a good.

External costs are those borne by others. Pollution is an example of an external cost (sometimes called a *spillover cost* or a *neighborhood cost*).

To analyze this problem, first consider the simplest possible example: Suppose that each unit of a good must be treated with a fluid that is then released into a river. In this case, each unit of output involves a constant external pollution cost, shown as the darkest red arrow in Figure 14-1. When it is added to the internal cost borne by producers (the white arrow MC), the result is the arrow MC$_S$, the marginal cost of this good to society. (MC$_S$ is a constant height above MC, reflecting our assumption of a constant per unit external cost.)

CONTROLLING POLLUTION: THE SIMPLEST CASE

When there is such an external cost, even a perfectly competitive market results in a misallocation of resources, as shown in Figure 14-2. In this figure, MC and MC$_S$ are reproduced from the previous diagram, and demand D represents, as before, this good's marginal benefit (either private or social). The perfectly competitive equilibrium is at E_1, with output Q_1 where demand D is equal to supply S_1 (with S_1 reflecting internal, private costs only, since these are the only costs faced by firms making the supply decisions). Since E_1 equalizes marginal benefit

Figure 14-2

Free-market efficiency loss when there is an external cost

Before the antipollution tax, industry supply is S_1, reflecting only the private (internal) costs of production facing sellers. This supply equals demand at E_1, with output at Q_1. But this output is inefficient because marginal social cost exceeds benefit for all units between Q_2 and Q_1. For example, the last unit Q_1 is not worth producing; its benefit (the white arrow under the demand curve) is less than its two costs to society (the white arrow plus the red arrow under the MC$_S$ curve). The efficiency loss is the sum of all such red arrows—that is, the red triangle. *After the tax r,* producers are forced to face both the internal *and* external costs, so that their supply curve shifts up from S_1 to S_2. D and S_2 now yield an equilibrium at E_2, with output Q_2. This is efficient because marginal social cost and benefit are equal. The efficiency gain from reducing output from Q_1 to Q_2 is the elimination of the red triangle.

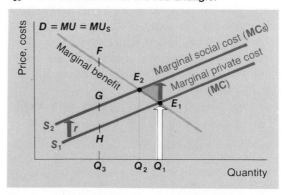

and marginal *private* cost S_1 only, it is not efficient. An efficient solution requires that marginal benefit be equal to marginal *social* cost S_2, and this occurs at E_2, at the smaller output Q_2. Thus we conclude that in a free, competitive market, *firms produce too much of a polluting good* (Q_1, rather than the efficient amount Q_2).[3] It is in society's interest to cut back production of this good and use the resources to produce something else.

To confirm that Q_1 is an inefficient output, note that the benefit from the last unit produced is the white arrow under the demand curve. But its cost is even greater, since it includes both its private cost (this same white arrow, as defined under the MC curve), and its external cost shown by the red arrow. Hence, this red arrow represents the net loss involved in producing this last unit Q_1. Since there is the same sort of loss involved in the production of each of the other "excess" units between Q_2 and Q_1, the total efficiency loss is measured by the red triangle.

In this instance, a relatively simple cure is possible: Impose a per unit tax on producers equal to the marginal external cost (the red arrow). Note that such a tax imposes a cost on producers equal to the cost of their pollution on others. Thus, the tax "internalizes" the externality; the producer is forced to face the external cost along with the internal cost. As a result of the tax, the supply curve shifts up from S_1 to S_2. (Remember: Supply reflects marginal cost, and this has risen by the amount of the tax that must be paid.) The new equilibrium is at E_2, where demand and new supply S_2 intersect. The new output of Q_2 is efficient because marginal *social* cost and benefit are equal. Finally, the efficiency gain from this tax policy is the red triangle, the original efficiency loss that has now been eliminated. In brief, as a result of this tax, society gets a benefit that the market would otherwise not deliver—cleaner water.

This is not the only suggestion for reducing

pollution. Another proposal is discussed in Box 14-3. A third suggestion is to set a limit on the output of polluting firms.

This limitation may or may not help to solve the problem; in fact, it may even be worse than doing nothing at all. For example, if output is limited to Q_3, as an exercise you can show that too little would be produced, and there would be a loss to society of triangle FE_2G. Since this loss exceeds the original loss, the cure in this case is worse than the original problem. You should also be able to show that an even stiffer restriction on output will result in an even greater efficiency loss. Thus, there is an advantage in using the market mechanism, rather than setting a limit on output. If the costs of pollution can be estimated and a tax of this amount imposed, the right amount of pressure can be applied to the market to push it back from the initial Q_1 to the efficient output Q_2.[4]

*CONTROLLING POLLUTION: A MORE COMPLEX CASE

In practice, policy makers face a number of complications omitted from our earlier example. In any particular air space (say, over Los Angeles) or any particular body of water (such as Lake Erie) the problem is not just one polluting industry (as in Figure 14-2), but many. Second,

---

[4]Rather than estimating pollution cost r, and then imposing a tax at this level, why not arrive at exactly the same solution by estimating and imposing output limit Q_2? The answer is that it is much more difficult to estimate Q_2 than r. The reason is that estimating Q_2 involves first estimating r, and then *in addition* estimating the location and elasticity of the supply and demand curves. (The more elastic these curves, the further to the left the output limit Q_2 should be set.) The task of locating these curves may be further complicated if they are shifting over time. Furthermore, *even if* the output limitation Q_2 is estimated correctly (a tall order) this policy will still be inferior to imposing a tax, because the clean-up costs will be greater—as we shall explain in point 2 in the next section.

*Note to instructors of short course: At any subsequent point you may leave this chapter without losing background essential for future chapters.

---

[3]In terms of our earlier analysis, a free market does not lead to an efficient solution because marginal private cost MC is not equal to marginal social cost MC_S. [Condition 10-2) in Box 10-1 is violated.]

pollution and output are not locked together in the fixed way assumed in earlier diagrams (where each additional unit of output generated a constant amount of pollution). In the more typical case, pollution may vary: A good may be produced with either a large amount of pollution (if wastes are dumped uncontrolled into the water or air) or a low pollution level (if wastes are somehow treated, or if less polluting fuels are used).

Consider a firm that installs purifying equipment to treat its wastes, or uses cleaner but more expensive fuels. This firm reduces pollution, but at a cost. This cost of reducing pollution for all firms in an area is shown in Figure 14-3 as the curve MCR. (R stands for reducing pollution.) It is drawn by first graphing point Q_1, the amount of pollution that will occur if it is not restricted in any way. As pollution is cut back, we move to the left up the MCR curve. At first, cleanup costs are low as the easy battles are won. (Pollution unit Q_2 can be eliminated at the low cost shown by the short red bar.) But the more pollution is reduced (that is, the more we move to the left in this diagram), the higher becomes the cost of further cleanup (the higher MCR becomes).

Until the last few decades, there were few restrictions on pollution. Therefore, any firm that could save costs by dumping its pollutants (rather than treating them) did so, and the result was pollution of about Q_1. Thus some of our lakes and rivers became public sewers.

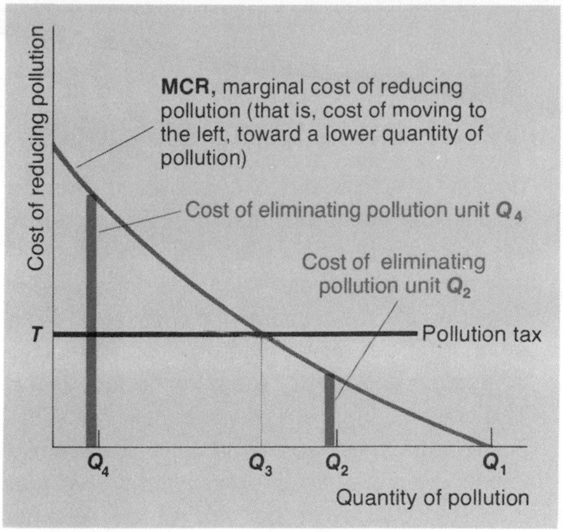

GOVERNMENT POLLUTION-CONTROL MEASURES

Now let's suppose the government wants to cut pollution in half—from Q_1 to Q_3 in Figure 14-3. Consider the policies which might be used.

1 A pollution tax

Assume that the government levies a pollution tax (sometimes called an effluent fee). Specifically, in Figure 14-3, suppose that tax T is charged for each unit of pollution emitted by a firm. Then firms eliminate pollution in the right-hand tail of the MCR curve. It costs them less to stop (for

Figure 14-3
The effect of a pollution tax

Q_1 is the amount of pollution that would occur in the absence of any control measure. As we move from this point back to the left along MCR, we see the cost of reducing pollution by one more unit (for example, by installing pollution-control equipment). Thus if pollution has been restricted all the way back to Q_4, any further reduction would require very expensive pollution-control measures, involving a cost shown by the tall red bar. If pollution tax T is imposed, firms voluntarily reduce pollution, moving from Q_1 to Q_3. So long as they are still to the right of Q_3, they will continue to reduce pollution because the cost of doing so (for example, the short red bar) is less than the cost of paying the tax. But they would not move to the left of Q_3. In this range, it costs them more to reduce pollution (the tall red bar) than to continue to pollute and pay the tax T.

example, the short red bar) than to continue to pollute and pay the pollution tax T. But pollution is reduced only to Q_3, where the tax line intersects MCR. To the left of this point, it costs firms less to pay the tax T (and keep polluting) than to reduce pollution at a cost, for example, of the tall red bar. So in this range, firms pay the tax and continue to pollute. (For detail on the difficult question of how high the tax should be set, see Box 14-4 on page 294.)

BOX 14-3

The Possible Role of Property Rights in Dealing With an External Cost

Couldn't the problem of "too much polluting production" by the upstream firms be cured by assigning those who live downstream the property right to clean water? Suppose, for example, that they can sue or charge the polluting firms an amount ($r per unit in Figure 14-2) that exactly compensates them for the damage they incur. The polluting firms are now in exactly the same position as they were when the government imposed a tax of $r; the only difference is that they are now paying this "tax" to the residents downstream instead of to the government. In either case they will voluntarily reduce their output from Q_1 to Q_2 where inefficiency has been eliminated. It seems as though proper assignment of property rights over the water is the key.

In an article on "The Problem of Social Cost" (*Journal of Law and Economics,* October 1960, pp. 1–43), Robert Coase went one step further. He argued that, strictly from the point of view of economic efficiency, it does not matter who holds the property rights. Specifically, it does not matter whether those downstream have the property rights and are compensated $r per unit by the polluting firms; or if the polluting firms have the property rights. In this case these firms would be free to dump waste into the river; but it will be more profitable for them to limit themselves, charging those downstream $r for every unit of pollutants they cut back.†

Thus, according to Coase, an externality like pollution arises because there is something

valuable (clean water) over which there are no property rights. So there is no market; clean water can't be bought and sold. Create property rights and you create a market that makes it at least possible for Adam Smith's invisible hand to work to reduce or eliminate inefficiency. Government intervention is not the only cure.

[It is enlightening to consider this analysis from another point of view: The problem with pollution is that something that used to be in unlimited supply (clean water) has now become scarce. Unless someone owns it and charges for its use, it will be used in wasteful ways. (The water will be used to carry off pollutants and the river will become a public sewer.) On the other hand, if someone does own the water and charges for it, its price will act as a monitoring device to direct it into its most productive uses. Moreover, *it doesn't matter who owns the water*—those living downstream, those firms located upstream, or the public as a whole. (Ownership by the public was the case described in Figure 14-2. On behalf of the public, the government extended its ownership over this water, and charged a fee of $r to firms that used it for waste elimination.) The point is that *someone* owns the water and charges for it. Only then will the water be used efficiently.]

But we emphasize: Coase's only claim is that it does not matter, *in terms of efficiency,* who owns the water. But in terms of equity, it obviously does matter: If property rights are held by downstream residents, they collect a fee from the upstream firm for any pollution added. But if the property rights are held by the upstream firms, *they* collect a fee from the downstream residents for any reduction in pollution.

Even though no claim can be made that the result is equitable, the conclusion that property rights and free bargaining may eliminate inefficiency is a very interesting one. It follows (with a

†Those living downstream will be willing to pay this $r per unit because this is how highly they value a cutback. (It's the cost to them of having the polluting output continue.) Also, since the polluting firms receive a $r per unit payment for reducing pollution, they will cut back to Q_2—for the same reason that they cut back that far in the face of the government's $r per unit tax. (It doesn't matter whether firms are paid $r per unit for cutting back, or are taxed $r per unit if they do *not* cut back. In either case they have the same incentive to cut back.)

number of reservations we shall come to directly) because the existence of inefficiency means that the two parties collectively lose. Therefore it is in their collective interest to get together and make a deal to eliminate this inefficiency. But this raises an even broader question: Why can't free bargaining also remove any *other* form of inefficiency, such as monopoly? Since monopoly makes the two parties collectively worse off, why don't they make a deal to avoid it? Specifically, why can't buyers compensate the monopoly firm to get it to lower its price and increase its output?

The answer is that there are problems ("transactions costs") in making such deals. How do a million buyers of a monopoly product organize themselves to make a payment to the monopolist? How do a thousand downstream residents on a river and the hundreds of polluting firms upstream organize themselves to make and receive payments? To illustrate, suppose the property rights to the water are owned by the polluting upstream firms. How do downstream residents get together to pay these firms to reduce their pollution? Specifically, how do the downstream residents keep some of their members from becoming "free riders," that is, people who are happy to have a payment made—and

their pollution thereby reduced—but who won't contribute themselves?‡

Another problem is: How do downstream residents know which firms are polluting the river and which are not? And if the downstream residents do reach an agreement with the polluting firms, how do they know that these firms have indeed reduced their pollution? Any attempt to solve these problems may involve substantial transactions costs.

For this reason, it is too much to expect that the existence of property rights and free bargaining will always lead to an efficient result. And even if it did, the question of equity would not be resolved: Who should pay the fee necessary to achieve efficiency, and who should receive it? Nonetheless, Coase's ideas are important because they help us to understand why externalities are a problem, and why government intervention is not necessarily the *only* solution. ■

‡These problems would be far less serious if the property rights are held, not by the upstream firms, but instead by the downstream residents; and if the payment (fine) to be paid to them by the upstream firms is set by the courts. Polluting firms would then respond to this fine just as they did to the tax in Figure 14-2. In fact, this policy is effectively the same as the pollution tax in that earlier diagram—except for one important respect: The residents downstream, rather than the government, receive the payment from the polluting firms. This sounds very equitable: The people downstream who are hurt by pollution are compensated for it. Unfortunately, this provides an example of how the objectives of equity and efficiency may conflict. This very equitable solution introduces a whole new source of inefficiency: Because of the compensation people receive if they locate downstream, more decide to do so. The pollution they consequently absorb represents a loss to society. In their location decision, people should take this pollution into account, and—other things equal—locate away from the river. But they won't take pollution into account if they are fully compensated for it by the polluting firms. Thus too many people locate downstream, and there is an efficiency loss to society. This loss is paid for, not by the new downstream residents who absorb the pollution (they are fully compensated), but instead by the polluting firms that pay the compensation, and by the public which pays higher prices for the products these polluting firms produce.

2 Requiring each firm to reduce its emissions

One might well ask: Why go to all the trouble of setting the pollution tax in Figure 14-3 when pollution could be cut by the same amount by a simple, direct control—by requiring every firm to cut its emissions by half? The answer is that although this approach would achieve the same reduction in pollution, it would involve heavier cleanup costs, as we shall now show.

Not all firms face the same costs in reducing pollution. With a tax, pollution is cut down in the least-cost way, by firms to the right of Q_3. (Note how the cost of eliminating pollution—the height of MCR—is less for these firms than for firms to the left of Q_3 that don't reduce their pollution.)[5] On the other hand, if all firms are required to cut their pollution in half, firms to the left of Q_3 must now also participate—at the high cost illustrated by the tall red bar.

Thus, the advantage of a pollution tax is that it "lets the market work." With firms reacting to the tax signal, pollution is reduced in the least expensive way and society devotes fewer real resources to the cleanup task.[6] The savings can be substantial. Allen Kneese and Charles Schultze have estimated that *a pollution tax would cost society 40 to 90 percent less than a policy of requiring all firms to reduce pollution by the same fraction.*[7]

---

[5]Allowing polluters to the left of Q_3 to escape the cleanup costs may sound unfair. But remember: They have to pay a tax.

[6]To simplify this illustration, we assume that any firm is either "completely to the left" of Q_3, or "completely to the right." In fact, of course, firms typically have some units of pollution on each side. "High-cost" firms have most of their units to the left of Q_3, and "low-cost" firms have most of their units to the right. But our conclusion still holds: The least cost way of cutting pollution in half is with a tax, with every firm eliminating only its pollution to the right of Q_3. Thus low-cost firms will be cutting their pollution by more than half, while the high-cost firms will be cutting it by less than half.

[7]Allen V. Kneese and Charles L. Schultze, *Pollution, Prices, and Public Policy* (Washington: The Brookings Institution, 1975), pp. 90, 99. Nevertheless, there are some cases where direct controls are appropriate. For example, it may be desirable to ban completely the emission of radioactive wastes that would damage the environment far into the future. (In this case, the appropriate tax would be prohibitively high, and equivalent to a ban.)

Which policy does the government use?

Surprisingly, the government relies principally on regulatory controls rather than letting the market work with a pollution tax. (A bill to set such a tax died in Congressional Committee in 1969.) Instead pollution limits are set for individual firms—a policy, as already noted, that involves large unnecessary cleanup costs.

Moreover there is a second problem. Air and water standards are set with little regard for the cost of reducing pollution (MCR). (In some cases the courts have interpreted the law as *prohibiting* the EPA from considering costs when setting standards.) Instead, the EPA tends to concentrate on what is technologically possible given existing pollution-control knowledge, and some of these measures are extremely expensive. Furthermore, the Clean Air Act, as amended, is designed to "protect and enhance" the quality of the nation's air—a worthy objective, except that the legislation has been interpreted to mean that the air should not be allowed to deteriorate significantly *anywhere*. As a consequence, even the states with the cleanest air have been encountering problems attracting new firms. This has blocked one avenue for reducing the overall pollution problem, namely, shifting firms from overloaded, highly polluted areas into regions with low pollution levels (where at least some of the pollutants could be "washed away" by natural processes).

Moreover, because pollution regulations have been so severe many firms have been in violation of air or water standards, and have been expending more of their efforts in fighting these regulations in the halls of Congress or the courts than in trying to find a pollution cure. In some cases, firms seem to be counting on the government to provide them with an eleventh-hour exemption from the law. For example, a threat to close down seven plants, employing 24,000 workers in Ohio's Mahoning Valley, induced the EPA to exempt them from water-emission restrictions. Such flip-flops have tended, at a minimum, to erode the credibility of the controls. And this has meant that standards have not been set in an even-handed way, but instead have been defined by a government under pressure to make last-minute changes.

Recently, there have been encouraging signs of a movement away from "command and direct" controls toward more efficient "let the market work" forms of control. One is to place a "bubble" over an area—an overall limit on the total pollution that is allowed (like Q_3 in Figure 14-3). Then a market is established in pollution rights: Any firm that reduces its pollution is provided with a right, or credit, which can then be sold to another firm that wants to expand but first must acquire such a credit to provide it with the right to pollute.

Such a system was introduced by the state of Maryland in 1980. This has the same effect as the pollution tax T described in Figure 14-3 (except that under this new scheme payments are made to firms reducing pollution, rather than to the government). And by 1981 the EPA was experimenting with taking the last step and setting up a system that *would* be the same as a tax; it was considering the sale of polluting rights.[8]

An alternative policy? Subsidizing pollution-control equipment

The federal government has provided grants to municipalities installing waste treatment plants, and has also provided subsidies in the form of tax reductions to firms installing pollution-control equipment. How effective are such subsidies?

In the first place, such subsidies are effective only if the equipment that is installed does a good job of reducing pollution. One of the problems has been that, after the government subsidizes the new installation, it pays little or no attention to how efficiently it is operated—in other words, how effectively it reduces pollution. (In some cases, the municipalities that have been subsidized to install expensive equipment have not even been able to cover its operating costs, and the equipment has fallen into disuse.)

The second problem with this form of subsidy is that it puts all the emphasis on end-of-pipe

treatment; that is, on the reduction of pollution as it is about to be discharged into the environment. But if a subsidy is justified for end-of-pipe treatment, it should be similarly justified for *any* reduction in pollution, regardless of how it may be achieved—for example, by the use of less powerful chemicals. Moreover, there is evidence that, in some cases, such alternatives may be far less costly. For instance, at a cost of only $1 million, the 3M Company introduced a less polluting process that saved the company over $10 million in waste disposal and other costs.

It may be concluded, therefore, that an end-of-pipe subsidy is too narrow an attack on the problem. And it will involve a cost to society if some firms do not use the lowest-cost method of controlling pollution, but instead switch to the end-of-pipe method solely because it is subsidized. The principle is a simple one. It is better to tell firms what to do than to give them detailed instructions on how to do it. (A regulation made as far back as the eighteenth century B.C. illustrates this principle perfectly. Hammurabi, King of Babylonia, set out a very simple building code. If a house fell down and killed an occupant, the builder of the house was put to death. All details for meeting this regulation were left to the builder.)

An even narrower approach to the problem is a government regulation that requires firms to install a *specific kind* of end-of-pipe purifying equipment. For example, consider the 1977 requirement that coal-burning electrical utilities install "scrubbers" to clean the smoke they were emitting. This tended to divert them from the more sensible solution of using cleaner Western coal. (So long as the government required scrubbers regardless, there was no incentive to use the more expensive, cleaner western fuel.) In turn, the continued heavy use of Eastern coal created a new problem: In the process of cleaning up the smoke from dirty coal, scrubbers generated liquid "sludge." Thus reducing air pollution created water pollution. Again we conclude: The preferred approach is to provide firms with a sufficient incentive to clean up, and let them, in the pursuit of profit, decide on the least-cost way of doing it.

[8]For more detail on this possible new direction of EPA policy, see the *Economic Report of the President, 1981* (Washington: U.S. Government Printing Office).

BOX 14-4

Pollution Control: Problems and Perspective

In Figure 14-3, tax T limits pollution to Q_3. An even higher emission fee would cut pollution back even more. The question we address in this box is: How far do we want to cut pollution back? In other words, how high should we set the pollution tax?

The problem of setting the right pollution tax

In Figure 14-4 we reproduce MCR from Figure 14-3, and also show MCP, the marginal cost of pollution to society. These two curves should not be confused. MCR is the cost of *reducing* pollution—for example, the cost of pollution-control equipment. On the other hand, MCP is the cost of *having* pollution; that is, the cost to us of foul air and contaminated water. As long as there is only a little pollution, the marginal cost of having it (MCP) is low. The first units of waste that are dumped into a stream generally break down and are absorbed by the environment. Similarly, the smoke from a campfire in a deserted area has no perceptible effect on the air. But as pollution builds up, additional emissions become increasingly noxious and costly; the MCP curve rises.

With these two curves, the best target is to cut back pollution to the point where MCP = MCR. Any other quantity is less desirable, as we can illustrate with the case where pollution is left completely uncontrolled and consequently reaches Q_1. For all units of pollution to the right of Q_3, MCP is greater than MCR, so it is a mistake to let this pollution occur. To evaluate the social cost of this mistake, consider one typical unit of this excess pollution, say unit Q_2. The cost of eliminating this unit of pollution (the height of the MCR curve, as shown by the white arrow) is less than the cost of letting it continue (the height of the MCP curve, as shown by the white *and* red arrows). Therefore, the net cost of allowing this unit of pollution to continue is the red arrow. If we sum the similar costs on all such units through the range Q_3 to Q_1, the result is the triangular red area—the loss to society of leaving pollution uncontrolled.

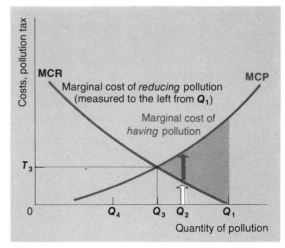

Figure 14-4
Efficiency loss from leaving pollution uncontrolled
MCR is reproduced from Figure 14-3. We also show MCP, the environmental cost of additional units of pollution. The best target level is to restrict pollution to Q_3, where MCR = MCP. To do so, a pollution tax is set at T_3.

On the other hand, a policy of cutting pollution back to the left of Q_3 also involves a loss. For example, if pollution is reduced to Q_4, one more unit involves little environmental cost (the height of the MCP curve above Q_4); but it is exceedingly costly to eliminate (the height of the MCR curve). Eliminating it is therefore a mistake. We conclude that the best target, Q_3, can be found only by taking both the cost of having pollution (MCP) and the cost of removing it (MCR) into account. (Once this target quantity Q_3 is determined, the necessary cutbacks can be achieved by setting pollution tax T_3.)

Unfortunately, this approach is not as easy as it may sound; one reason is the difficulty in estimating MCP. We do not know how dangerous many pollutants really are. Since we can only be very imprecise about MCP, our estimate of Q_3 (the right amount of pollution) is also very imprecise. Moreover, it needs to be continuously updated as new information on MCP becomes available.

Finally, the MCR curve shifts as our economy grows, as shown in Figure 14-5. This figure illustrates why pollution control is a much more pressing issue today than in the past, and why it will likely be even more important in the future.

Pollution in historical perspective

Why are we so concerned now with pollution, while a few decades ago we were almost totally unconcerned? Is the problem worse, or have we just awakened? And if it is getting worse, what can we expect 20 or 30 years from now?

In Figure 14-5, MCP is shown, along with MCR for three periods. MCR_{1960} cuts the baseline at Q_{1960}, the level of pollution that would have occurred had it been left completely unrestricted at that early date. Similarly, the other MCR curves indicate uncontrolled pollution levels Q_{1980} and Q_{2000} at those later dates. The red triangle marked 1980 shows the loss from a policy of leaving pollution uncontrolled today. (It is defined just like the red loss in Figure 14-4.)

Figure 14-5
Pollution in perspective
If we had not begun to deal with this problem, then unrestricted pollution would have increased (with growing GNP) from the past Q_{1960} to the present Q_{1980} to the future Q_{2000}. As a result, the loss to society of leaving pollution unchecked in each of these years is shown as the rapidly growing set of triangles marked 1960, 1980, and 2000. (Note that each of these triangles is defined between the relevant MCR and MCP curves in exactly the same way as in Figure 14-4.)

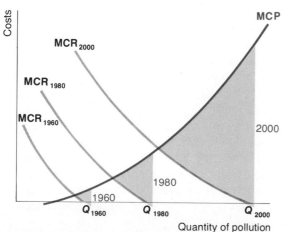

Now consider our situation in 1960. At that time, there were fewer factories clustered along any river and fewer cars spewing fumes into city air. So pollution was less severe. The result of leaving this pollution uncontrolled was the relatively small loss shown as the red triangle marked 1960. In those days, people did not think much about this problem.

Now let us look ahead to the future, to the year 2000. If industrial activity keeps growing, unrestricted pollution will grow to Q_{2000}, and the loss from failing to deal with it would be the very large red triangle 2000. There are several reasons why this loss builds up so rapidly. First, uncontrolled pollution tends to grow as output grows. Second, it may grow even faster, since more powerful chemicals and other materials are used as technology changes. Thus MCR shifts rapidly to the right. In addition, in the view of many experts, the MCP curve becomes steeper and steeper: The cost of pollution not only rises, but it does so at an increasingly rapid rate.

We emphasize that Figure 14-5 is not a prediciton of the future; it is merely a picture of what the future would have looked like *if* we had not taken action—or what it will look like if we give up our efforts to control pollution.[†] In this respect, pollution is similar to the public health problem in the nineteenth century. With the increase in urban population, lack of adequate sanitation produced a growing health problem that could equally well have been described by a diagram like Figure 14-5. The response to this challenge was the public health programs that prevented the "prophecy" in such a diagram from coming true. Similarly, pollution-control legislation can help to ensure that the prophecy in Figure 14-5 does not come true. ■

[†]Moreover, in this diagram as in any other economic model we have simplified. For example, we have assumed that pollution does not accumulate; in other words, that the cost of pollution depends only on how much occurs in the year in question. But pollution does accumulate. Heavy metal emissions from past years are with us today because they do not decompose with time. The same is true of certain pesticides that decompose very slowly. Our future problem could therefore be even more severe.

FUTURE PROBLEMS IN PROTECTING THE ENVIRONMENT

By the early '80s, the EPA was an embattled agency. It was under pressure from business because it was too harsh, and from environmentalists because it was too lenient. No sooner was it getting a handle on one problem, than it was hit with another. Consider just two of the new problems that had come to the fore in the previous decade: Is the world's outer atmosphere being damaged by air pollutants? And how can the 35,000 chemicals that are now being produced be controlled?

As we become increasingly aware of the problems that pollution can create, it becomes difficult to keep them in perspective and concentrate on the important ones. One reason is that the EPA is operating in an area of relative scientific ignorance. We simply don't yet know how dangerous many pollutants are. And this opens an area of severe conflict between the EPA and the nation's business. Who should bear the burden of proof? (1) Should the EPA have to prove that a waste product is harmful before restricting it? If so, we may today emit wastes which are in fact dangerous but have not yet been proved so. Or (2) should business have to prove that a waste product is *not* harmful before emitting it? If this rule were applied, waste disposal would become such an enormous problem that many firms could not survive, and many of those that did would be charging the public far higher prices.

One thing is certain: There will be continued conflict between business and the EPA; and this conflict is likely to increase as the problems the EPA has to deal with multiply. This is a further reason for the EPA to impose fewer of its own regulations and rely more on the marketplace—that is, replace its present system of detailed regulation with a tax incentive system that allows business to worry about the details. In other words, the government should be spending more of its effort in designing and building "better dams to control pollution" (such as a tax incentive system) and less on "putting a regulatory finger into every leak."

But in criticizing the government for not using the most effective pollution-abatement method, it is essential not to lose perspective: Abatement should be improved, yes; but abandoned, no. "Where would we be without an agency such as the EPA?" is an important question to keep in mind (as we have seen in Figure 14-5).

RECYCLING

One of the most promising ways to deal with pollution is to recycle wastes rather than dump them into the environment. Beer cans do not deface the landscape if they are reprocessed. Wastes that are recycled into the production process do not foul our rivers.

Figure 14-6 illustrates the potential benefits from recycling. The basic idea behind this diagram is the concept of *material balances:* On the left, production "sucks in" the materials it requires. Included are both new materials drawn up through pipe *a*, and recycled materials returned to the production process through pipe *c*. These materials pass through the production/consumption process and reappear in different form as "total materials out" on the right side of the diagram. Some of these residual "left-over" materials (such as chemical wastes) result from production, while some (like beer cans) are residuals from consumption.

This figure provides a framework for thinking about two important issues:

1 As our economic system expands, strains on the environment tend to increase both because more material is drawn up through pipe *a,* and because more pollutants are dumped back into the environment through pipe *b*.

2 We can help to cure the pollution problem by more recycling, that is, by directing more of the left over material on the right into pipe *c* rather than pipe *b*. Moreover, any success on this score will have a highly desirable side effect. The more our production/consumption requirements on the left can be satisfied by materials recycled through pipe *c*, the fewer natural resources will

Our economic system

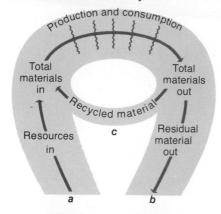

is based on our environment.

Figure 14-6
Recycling and the environment
The economic system in the upper half of this dia-gram uses the environment below by extracting re-sources from it through pipe *a* and returning residu-als back to it through pipe *b*. On the left, "total materials in" include both resources drawn from pipe *a* and recycled material from pipe *c*. On the right, "total materials out" that result from produc-tion and consumption are disposed of either by returning them into the environment through pipe *b* or recycling them through pipe *c*. For any given level of production and consumption, increased recycling (that is, diverting materials from pipe *b* to pipe *c*) provides two benefits: It reduces the residuals dumped into the environment through pipe *b, and* it reduces the natural resources that must be drawn out of the environment through pipe *a*.

have to be drawn from the environment through pipe *a*. In brief, recycling helps to solve two important problems at once: the problem of pollution and the problem of conserving natural resources. (We will return to a more detailed discussion of natural resources in Chapter 21.)

*CONGESTION AND THE AUTOMOBILE

Parking is such sweet sorrow.
Sid Caesar

Congestion can be analyzed in much the same way as pollution, since both are an external cost. An individual who decides to drive a car during congested periods takes into account costs like gasoline, and also the personal costs of aggrava-tion and delay. Since the driver must face these costs, they are internal costs. But the driver does not take into account the external costs—the increased aggravation and delay that *other* driv-ers encounter because one more car is on the road, making traffic jams a little more dense and parking spots a bit harder to find.

The problem is illustrated in Figure 14-7. During nonrush hours, drivers equate the mar-ginal costs (MC) and marginal benefits of driving (MB_1). Forty-five trips are taken, at equilibrium E_1. Traffic moves smoothly, and drivers face no congestion problems. But during rush hours, drivers put a much higher value on using the highway; in other words, the marginal benefit curve shifts up to MB_2. (Many drivers must get to work, and driving is the most convenient way.) Consequently, equilibrium shifts from E_1 to E_2 where 90 trips are being taken. Congestion is now a problem for two reasons. First, because each driver is now wasting time and gasoline on a congested highway, his own private cost of taking a trip has risen. (He is on the rising portion of the MC curve.) Second, since his car makes the congestion worse, other drivers also face an additional burden of aggravation and delay. This is the external cost of the trip he is taking, shown as the red arrow in Figure 14-7. Of course, when this cost is added to his private cost MC, the result is the marginal cost to society of having one more car on the road (MC_S).

The rush-hour problem is this: The decision by any driver to take a trip is based only on *private* cost MC rather than *social* cost MC_S. Thus equilibrium is at E_2 with too many cars on the road, and with an efficiency loss shown by the red triangle (as detailed in the diagram's

BOX 14-5

Public Transportation: What Price Should Be Charged?

Between the end of World War II in 1945 and the beginning of the rapid gasoline price increases in 1973, there was a major shift in America's traveling patterns: The use of public transit (railways, trolleys, subways, buses) fell, while the number of autos on the road increased many times. One important reason was the increase in wages that allowed more people to buy cars. (A higher wage level also meant a higher opportunity cost of time spent in waiting around for a bus, train, or any other form of public transit; this also induced people to buy more cars.) But the car is not a very good way of transporting large numbers of people, a point best illustrated by Thomas Liscos' observation that the 1 to 2 million people who commute to work daily in Manhattan could not get there by car even if the island were completely paved over. As our cities grow, public transit systems become the only way of handling the crush. (And public transit is also a way of keeping down oil consumption.)

An important question is: How should public transit be priced? Specifically, should fares be higher during rush hours than during off-peak periods?

Because of conflicting considerations, it is not possible to give a definitive answer. It might seem that, like a highway, public transit should carry a higher price during rush hours. After all, when an individual takes a bus or subway during rush hour, congestion is increased, and other passengers suffer as a consequence. This external cost can be internalized (that is, forced onto the individual who decides to travel) by raising rush-hour fares. Thus people will be induced to travel at less congested times.

But this is an incomplete answer. While people who have a choice should indeed be encouraged to travel in off hours rather than peak hours, some people have no choice: They

must travel to and from work during peak periods. They can't change the time they travel. All they can change is *how* they travel—by their own auto or public transport. In dealing with these people we should be using the opposite policy: Public transit fares should be *lowered* during rush hours to induce people to switch from autos to public transit, and thus reduce the congestion problem overall. (True, if a thousand people switch from their own cars to the subway, congestion will be increased there. But this will be more than offset by the reduction in congestion above ground because there will be a thousand fewer cars jamming the streets.) So we conclude that public transit pricing, like so many other economic policies, involves a conflict. One would like to raise rush-hour fares to induce people to travel at a different time; but at the same time, one would like to lower these fares to induce people to switch from automobiles to public transit. In the face of these conflicting pressures, which choice should be made? The answer depends on how these two pressures compare, and it is likely to differ from city to city. In "An Integrated Fare Policy for Transport in London," *Journal of Public Economics,* June 1978, pp. 341–356, Stephen Glaister and David Lewis suggest that rush-hour fares should be raised in that city. ∎

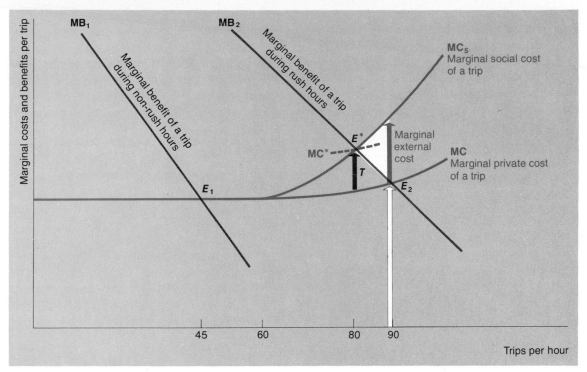

Figure 14-7
Traffic congestion and the case for tolls

During nonrush hours, equilibrium is at E_1 with fewer than 60 trips being taken. Traffic runs smoothly, and if one more trip is taken, that car on the road does not cause congestion delay; in other words, there are no external costs (MC and MC_S coincide). But during rush hours, drivers put a higher value on using the highway, so that the marginal benefit MB shifts upward and to the right to MB_2 with drivers thus taking more than the critical number of 60 trips. Because the highway is now congested, traffic is delayed, and private MC rises. (Each driver wastes his *own* time and gasoline in the traffic jam.) But in addition *other* drivers also suffer increased delay because of the trip he is taking. This external cost must be added to private MC to get marginal social cost MC_S. Private decisions by drivers equating MB_2 and private MC will result in equilibrium at E_2, with 90 trips being taken. But this is 10 more than the efficient number (80) where MB_2 equals social cost MC_S. The cost of congestion because of these 10 excess trips is the red triangle, for the following reasons: The last trip (the ninetieth) provides the benefit shown by the white arrow under MB_2. But the cost of this trip is the private cost (the white arrow under MC) *plus* the external cost to the other drivers (the red arrow). Thus, the net cost of this excess trip is the red arrow. When similar costs for the other 10 excess trips are summed, the result is the red triangular efficiency loss. If a toll equal to T is imposed on each trip during rush hours, then the private cost MC shifts up to MC^*. Private decisions equating MC^* with MB_2 now result in equilibrium at E^*, with the number of trips reduced from 90 to the efficient number of 80. The efficiency gain from this policy is the elimination of the previous red triangular loss.

caption). The way to avoid this loss is to reduce the number of trips from 90 to 80 by moving the equilibrium from E_2 to the efficient point E^* (where $MB_2 = MC_S$). This can be done by imposing a tax or toll T on each trip equal to the gap at E^* between MC and MC_S. Only then will each driver take into account not only his own

private costs, but also the external cost of his decision to other drivers. This general conclusion should, however, be qualified: Toll T adds to efficiency *only if* the benefit (the elimination of the red triangular loss in Figure 14-7) exceeds the cost of collection, including traffic delays at toll booths. (It has been suggested that toll booths be replaced with an electronic device or a TV camera that would read off the license plate of each passing car, along with the time of day. Then drivers would be sent a bill—like a phone bill—at the end of each month. Such electronic devices are already used by the railroads in monitoring their rolling stock.)

Note that, as in the case of pollution, the efficient solution does not involve eliminating congestion, but only reducing it. (In Figure 14-7, traffic is reduced to only 80 cars, not to 60.) Also note that the appropriate toll varies with the time of day: When MB_2 is high, reflecting the desire to travel in rush hours, the efficient toll is T. But when MB_1 is lower, reflecting the more limited desire to travel in nonrush hours, no toll is required. Thus, the appropriate toll is determined by the pressure of drivers to use the highway. Once set, the toll then relieves that pressure.

In describing such a toll, we have considered only the objective of efficiency. Of course, another objective of a toll may be to raise money to pay for the road. But in a congested area, the toll should not be set just for this money-raising reason. An example will illustrate why: Suppose that there are two bridges into a city, and that they are just barely able to handle the traffic without tie-ups. If a toll is set on each bridge to raise the money to cover its costs, there will be no toll on the old bridge that has already been paid for, but a high toll on the new bridge. As drivers consequently switch from the new to the old bridge, a traffic jam is created where none existed before.

Finally, there have been a number of other suggestions for reducing auto congestion. Each would reduce the problem, although generally in a somewhat less efficient way than a toll. These include proposals to: (1) Increase the tax on gasoline. This would reduce congestion by reducing the cars on the road anywhere, at any time. But this is a less effective policy since it does not deal directly with the problem of congestion on specific highways at specific times.[9] (2) Induce people to form car pools by levying a toll not on the car, but rather on the empty seats in it. (3) Provide a further incentive for car pools by reserving fast lanes on superhighways for cars with more than, say, two passengers.

[9]Although a gasoline tax is not the most effective policy to reduce congestion, it does help. And by reducing the number of miles people drive, such a tax has two other favorable effects: It reduces pollution from auto exhausts, and it reduces our demand for imported oil—thus making it more difficult for OPEC nations to raise prices so rapidly.

Key Points

1 Pollution is an example of an external cost, a cost that is borne not by the firm or individual producing or consuming the good, but instead by somebody else.

2 With the Clean Air Act and the Water Pollution Control Act, the government has imposed controls on the amount of pollutants firms can release into our air or water.

3 An alternative system of charging a pollution tax is generally superior, because it is a less costly way of reducing pollution. (The reductions in pollution are undertaken by the firms that can do so at the least cost.)

4 Such a pollution tax would also have been superior to another government policy that has been used: subsidizing firms (or municipalities) that install pollution-reducing equipment. Such a subsidy is too narrow an approach to the problem because it attacks pollution only at the "end of the pipe." Hence, opportunities to reduce pollution in less costly ways may be missed.

5 Recycling production or consumption wastes back into the production process helps solve two problems: First, less waste is dumped into the environment. Second, fewer natural resources need to be extracted from the environment to support our present production and consumption levels.

6 Highway congestion is another example of an external cost, because other drivers suffer delays and aggravation when an individual drives into a jammed-up road. Again, the most efficient policy is some form of tax, such as a toll, on this activity (provided the cost of collecting the toll does not outweigh the gains).

Key Concepts

internal (private) cost
external cost
social cost
inefficiency of free market
how a tax may increase
   efficiency
internalizing an
   externality

marginal cost of reducing
   pollution (MCR)
*marginal cost of having
   pollution (MCP)
pollution tax
pollution limits for
   individual firms
subsidization of
   pollution-control
   equipment

recycling
material balances
how the environment
   absorbs some pollutants
traffic congestion
how tolls affect efficiency

Problems

14-1 In 1977, after almost a week of oil spill, an oil blowout in the North Sea was finally capped by a high-priced, high-living American named Red Adair. Draw a diagram like Figure 14-1 to show the various costs involved in offshore drilling for oil. Determine whether the following costs are external or internal: (a) the expenditure by the oil companies on installing and operating drilling rigs; (b) the cost to the companies of hiring Red Adair; (c) the loss of marine life and the damage to beaches if oil spills occur that cannot be capped in time.

14-2 "When faced with a problem, economists have a natural inclination to suggest a solution that somehow utilizes the powerful magic of the price system; thus their solution for pollution control is a tax. On the other hand, lawyers have a natural inclination to set up regulations, and pass judgment on a case-by-case basis. And because lawyers make our laws, this is what has happened." Explain the economists' view, that this case-by-case approach of lawyers has increased the cost of pollution abatement. Is there a counterargument to be made for the lawyers' approach? Explain.

14-3 Critically evaluate the following statements:

(a) "Pollution taxes are immoral. Once a firm has paid its tax, it has a license to pollute. And no one should have this license."

(b) "Imposing a physical limit on the emission of a pollutant is like saying that you can do just so much of a bad thing and pay no penalty, but the moment you step over this line you will pay a large penalty."

(c) "There is no point in insisting on crystal-clear discharges into a river as muddy as the Mississippi."

(d) "Since it is impossible (and in any case, undesirable) to eliminate all polluting activities, the cost of pollution can be reduced if some polluting activities are moved into geographic regions where the environment can absorb most of the pollutants without noticeable effect."

(e) "Whereas a tax discourages a polluting activity, a subsidy to install pollution-control equipment does not. Therefore a subsidy should not be used."

(f) "There's no point in spending half our GNP cleaning up *potentially* cancerous chemicals when the public won't stop smoking (where evidence on cancerous effects is stronger).''

*14-4 Redraw Figure 14-4 appropriately to illustrate the two special cases where a pollution tax is not appropriate:

(a) Where pollution is no problem.

(b) Where pollution is so costly (as in footnote 7) that it should be banned outright.

14-5 Use Figure 14-6 to explain the various effects on the environment when cars were made smaller during the decade of the 1970s.

14-6 We have seen that the target rate of pollution is not zero. Do you think that the target rate of crime should be zero, or not? In other words, do you think we should expand crime prevention and hire police until the crime rate is driven to zero?

*14-7 (Based on Box 14-3.) The most equitable solution for air pollution is to have polluting firms pay a tax, not to the government, but instead to the nearby residents who suffer from pollution. Is this likely also to be the most efficient solution? Why or why not?

14-8 Show why completely eliminating congestion by cutting traffic back to 60 cars in Figure 14-7 would be worse than taking no action at all. Is it always true that the complete elimination of an externality is worse than no action whatsoever?

*14-9 Do you see any similarity between rush-hour tolls and peak-load (rush-hour) increases in the price of electricity? What do you think the efficiency effect of setting a high price for peak-load electricity would be?

*14-10 The government of an Italian city (which happened to be run by the Communist Party) subsidized the local public transportation system so that it could offer free rides, but only during morning and evening rush hours. Would such a subsidy work toward an efficient outcome? Why or why not? (Be careful! This is a complicated question.) Could there be objectives other than efficiency in this type of subsidy?

*14-11 In the final years of rigid airline regulation, about $100 million of the taxpayers' money was spent to ensure airline service to relatively small cities on lightly traveled routes. Supporters of regulation argued that this small-city service encouraged people to stay in small cities, and thus reduced congestion in big cities. Is this argument valid? Does it (a) reverse, (b) temper, (c) leave unchanged, or (d) strengthen your previous view about airline deregulation? Why?

CHAPTER 15
Public Goods

> There are certain goods that have the peculiarity that once they are available no one can be precluded from enjoying them whether he contributed to their provision or not. These are the public goods.
> **Robert Dorfman**

External or spillover effects can be either harmful or beneficial. Our earlier example of a bad external effect was the polluting of a river. The activities we now consider generate beneficial external effects. Examples already cited include the homeowner who plants a beautiful garden that neighbors also enjoy; or the individual who is vaccinated, thus protecting others as well from the spread of the disease.

EXTERNAL BENEFITS AND RESOURCE MISALLOCATION

If there are any spillover effects, whether they be spillover costs or spillover benefits, the free market will result in a misallocation of the nation's resources. For example, in Figure 14-2, we saw that if a good has a spillover cost a free competitive market results in too much output. In Figure 15-1, we now similarly show that if a good has a spillover benefit, then (as we would expect) a free competitive market results in too little output. (Before reading the detailed confirmation in the caption to Figure 15-1, you should try to prove this yourself. *Hint:* There are now external benefits to be added to the demand curve rather than the external costs that were added to the supply curve in Figure 14-2.) In this diagram we also show another expected result: A good with an external benefit should be

subsidized (just as a good with an external cost should be taxed). For example, when we subsidize vaccinations,[1] we are "internalizing an externality" in much the same way as when we taxed a polluter in Chapter 14. In that earlier example, the polluting firm that paid the tax was made to "feel internally" the external damage it was causing; so it did less. On the other hand, the purchaser of a vaccination who receives a subsidy is allowed to "enjoy internally" the external benefits it provides; thus vaccinations are encouraged. In either case, the *private firm or individual acts only after taking external effects into account.* This is as it should be.

Externalities may sometimes be internalized even without government action, but strictly as a result of private market forces. A private real estate firm will sometimes purchase a whole block of houses in a run-down neighborhood. Its renovation expenditure on each house raises the value of that house, and also provides a spillover benefit by raising the value of the other houses in the block as well. Once the firm has renovated all the houses in the block, it can capture both the internal and external benefits. For example,

---

[1]Because it is less complicated to administer, the government subsidy of vaccinations is typically in the form of a reduction in their cost (often to zero), rather than a grant paid to those who acquire them. But either form of subsidy has a similar effect in encouraging people to acquire more.

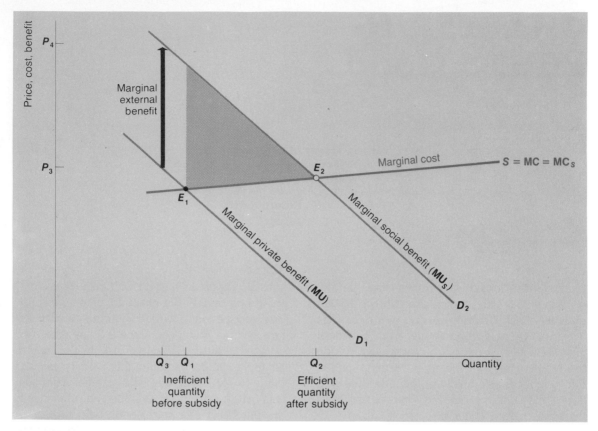

Figure 15-1

Efficiency loss when there is an external benefit

In this diagram we consider a product—such as vaccinations—that has external benefits but no external costs. The height of the market demand D_1 reflects how the actual purchasers value the vaccinations (that is, their own internal benefit because they don't get the disease). But there is also an external benefit (the arrow) enjoyed by nonpurchasers because the disease isn't passed on to them. When these two benefits are taken into account, the result is the marginal social benefit curve (MU_S).

A free, perfectly competitive market results in equilibrium at E_1, where marginal cost is equal to marginal *private* benefit (since this is the only benefit going to those who make the purchasing decisions). But the resulting quantity (Q_1) is not efficient. Instead, efficiency requires that marginal cost be equal to marginal *social* benefit, and this occurs at E_2, at a larger output Q_2. Thus we conclude that a free market does not produce enough of a good with external benefits. Specifically, the red triangle shows the efficiency loss if output is at the free-market quantity Q_1. All units of output between Q_1 and Q_2 have a

benefit—the height of D_2—that exceeds their cost shown by the height of S. Thus, producing them would result in a net benefit. *Not* producing them results in a net loss—as shown by the red triangle. [Alternatively, from our earlier analysis in Box 10-1, we confirm that inefficiency occurs because the condition that marginal private benefit (MU) equals marginal social benefit (MU_S) is violated.]

One possible way to eliminate this inefficiency is to provide purchasers with a per unit subsidy equal to the external benefit arrow, thus shifting the demand curve up from D_1 to D_2. (Demand shifts in this way because, for example, the individual initially prepared to pay only P_3 for unit Q_3 is now prepared to pay P_4—that is, the original P_3 plus the subsidy received from the government.) With this shift in demand, a competitive market does the rest. Its new equilibrium is at E_2, where supply and new demand D_2 intersect. Thus efficient output Q_2 is achieved. Finally, the efficiency gain from this subsidy is, of course, the red area—the original efficiency loss that has now been eliminated.

when it sells the first house, it can get a higher price because this house has been renovated; but it gets an even higher price still because the renovation of each of the other houses has provided an external benefit to this first house. Thus, while the firm may not find the purchase and renovation of just one house profitable, the purchase and renovation of the whole block may be—simply because the private firm is able to capture the spillover effects.

As another example, if a firm constructs a ski lift on a mountain, it will be able to sell tow tickets. These receipts will be an internal benefit to the firm. But the ski lift will also generate an external benefit in the form of greater pleasure for those eating at a nearby restaurant who enjoy watching people ski. The internal benefit to the ski-lift company from ticket sales may be insufficient to justify constructing the lift. But suppose the firm can buy the restaurant and, once the ski lift is built, start charging customers more. It thereby captures (internalizes) the external benefit it has created. It now becomes profitable to build the lift.

This suggests an alternative approach to spillovers: Allow economic units to join into large enough bodies so that decision-makers will take externalities into account. For example, heavy industry in a large city may result in a spillover cost of air pollution in the suburbs. If the city is expanded to include the suburbs, this cost will be internalized: All pollution—both downtown and suburban—will then have to be taken into account by the new, larger city government. Such an expansion of a city may also internalize externalities on the benefit side. For example, the city may decide to finance an orchestra or a theatrical company that cannot be justified unless the benefits provided to the suburbs can also be taken into account. (Note that this is only one argument for increasing city size. There are also arguments for decreasing the size of some cities. We are merely pointing out one economic influence that should be taken into account.)

Now consider a flood-control dam in a river valley. If a farmer were to build such a dam, he would enjoy an internal benefit since his own crops and buildings would be protected from floods. But such a benefit would be trivial compared with the enormous cost of constructing the dam. So no individual farmer builds it—even though its construction may be easily justified by the large external flood control benefits it would provide for the thousands of other farmers in the valley. If it is to be built at all, it will have to be built collectively—by a large group of farmers acting together, or by the government. Thus we come to the idea of a **public good**.

PUBLIC GOODS

One definition of a public good is "anything the government provides." But this is too broad a definition for our purposes,[2] since it includes all sorts of activities that could be undertaken privately but are provided by the government instead. (Public transport systems and the U.S. Postal Service are examples.) Since we are not interested in so broad a definition, we begin with the more narrow idea of goods—such as dams —that cannot be provided by the private market.

Since the idea of external benefits is important to our definition of a public good, we now compare in detail two of our previous examples. The first is hiring a gardener. Most of the benefits are internal, that is, they go to the family that hires the gardener to work on its own property. Therefore an unmodified free market works, at least to some degree: Individuals *do* have gardening done (although the amount is less than socially optimal).

Compare this with the example of a flood-control dam in a river valley. There are two important differences in this case. First, a free

[2]In fact, it is very difficult to define a public good. There are several definitions, each with some particular advantage over the others. For an alternative definition and further discussion, see Peter Steiner, "Public Expenditure Budgeting" in Alan S. Blinder, Robert M. Solow et al., *The Economics of Public Finance* (Washington: The Brookings Institution, 1974), pp. 241–360.

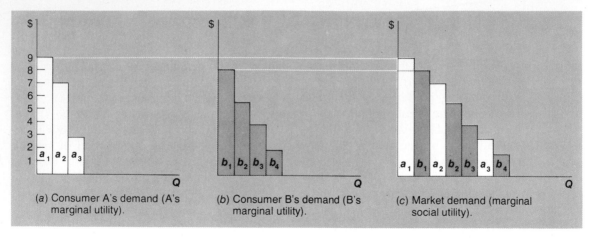

(a) Consumer A's demand (A's marginal utility).

(b) Consumer B's demand (B's marginal utility).

(c) Market demand (marginal social utility).

Figure 15-2
A private good

We horizontally sum individual demands in parts a and b to get market demand in part c. (At a price of $9, A buys 1 unit. If the price falls to $8, B also buys a unit. If the price falls to $7, A buys a second unit; and so on.) For such a private good with no external benefits, the market demand curve in part c represents marginal social utility.

market will not work at all. No dam will be built; there is no individual farmer who will do it. The reason is that the internal benefits of flood control he would receive are relatively small. Most of the benefits would be external—the flood control protection the dam would provide to *other* farmers in the river valley. Since no individual farmer will do it, any dam that is built will have to be constructed by the government. The second difference is more subtle: Once the government has built the dam, an individual farmer's benefit from it is the same as if he had built it himself.[3] This, then, is our more precise concept of a public good: It provides an individual with a benefit that does not depend on whether or not that person is the actual purchaser. Another illustration is a lighthouse. Once it is built, every ship is protected from the rocks, whether its owner has agreed to help pay for the lighthouse or not.

A *public good* provides benefits that are available to everyone; no one can be excluded from enjoying this good, regardless of who pays for it.

[3]Notice that this is not true of gardening, where the benefit to an individual *does* depend on who has the gardening done—himself, his neighbor, or someone far down the street.

The distinction between a public good and an ordinary private good is shown in the two diagrams above. In Figure 15-2 we illustrate a private good; the first two panels show each individual consumer's marginal utility. Each consumer would actually have to purchase and acquire the good in order to realize utility from it. As we saw in Figure 8-1, total market demand in panel c is obtained by a horizontal summation of the individual demands (marginal utilities) in panels a and b.

Figure 15-3 shows the alternative case of a public good, where all individuals can benefit from each unit produced. For example, consumer A gains utility a_1 from the first unit. But this same unit also provides consumer B with utility b_1. Since both individuals benefit from this first unit (both can, for example, see the warning beam from the same lighthouse) the utility provided by this first unit is a_1 *plus* b_1, as shown in the last panel. Thus, for such a public good, marginal social utility (MU_S) is found by vertical-

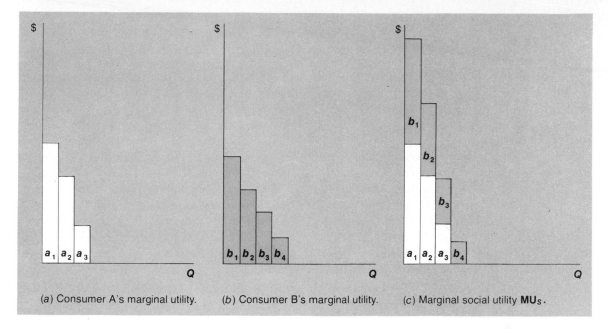

(a) Consumer A's marginal utility. (b) Consumer B's marginal utility. (c) Marginal social utility MU_S.

Figure 15-3
A public good

For a public good, we vertically add the individual marginal utilities in parts *a* and *b* to get the marginal social utility in part *c*. (The reason is that both consumers benefit from each unit.) With a public good, we thus stack utilities vertically—one on top of the other—whereas with a private good in Figure 15-2, we added utilities horizontally, putting one beside the other. (There may be some individuals who get zero—or even negative—utility from a public good. An example is the army. While most people place a positive value on the service it provides, some place a negative value on it. Any such negative valuations should be taken into account, thus reducing MU_S in panel *c*.)

ly adding the individual utilities (in contrast with the horizontal addition for a private good).[4]

But it is important to recognize that the

[4]In Figures 15-2 and 15-3, we have dealt with only the two extreme cases: a "pure" private good, which provides utility only to the purchaser, and a "pure" public good, which provides utility to all, regardless of who pays for it. There are, of course, many intermediate cases, where the purchaser gets most of the benefit, but others get some benefit. Illustrations of such intermediate cases were given in our discussion of external benefits in the first section of this chapter (for example, gardening and vaccinations).

resulting marginal social utility (MU_S) is not a demand curve in the ordinary sense. Nobody would buy the first unit if its price were $a_1 + b_1$. But if it can be produced at this cost or less, the first unit should be produced. And if the second unit can be produced for $a_2 + b_2$ or less, it should be produced too; and so on.

PROBLEMS IN EVALUATING THE BENEFITS OF A PUBLIC GOOD

Suppose that the final panel of Figure 15-3 shows the benefits of building a system of flood-control dams on a river; further suppose that the first dam would indeed cost less than $a_1 + b_1$, so that it should be built. Let us now examine in more detail our earlier claim that this public good can only be provided by the government. Why can't it be provided by private enterprise instead? After all, since the two farmers value it at $a_1 + b_1$, why doesn't some entrepreneur collect this amount from them and build the dam? (The entrepreneur would be collecting more than the cost of the dam and therefore could pocket a profit.)

To answer this question, note that our two farmers A and B represent thousands of farmers in the valley. (For other public goods as well, there are very large numbers of consumers.) Thus you can visualize MU_S as the vertical sum, not of two individual marginal utility curves, but instead, of thousands of them—with each individual curve being relatively insignificant. Now suppose that you are one of these individuals, and the private entrepreneur who is promoting this project asks you for your valuation of the dam. Specifically, he asks how much you would be willing to contribute to its construction. What would you reply? Clearly, you would have a strong incentive to understate your benefit, because you realize that it is very unlikely that your answer will influence the decision on whether the dam is built. You will either get a dam or not, depending on how the thousands of other farmers in the valley respond. All your reply will do is determine the amount that you will be contributing—and it's in your interest to minimize this. So you reply that you believe a flood-control system is exactly what this valley needs, and you believe your neighbors will value it very highly. But it will have little value to you; you personally are willing to pay very little for it.

Now, if the dam is built (as you secretly hope), it will cost you very little. Yet you cannot be excluded from enjoying its services: If the dam prevents a flood, your buildings and land will be protected. You get to be a **free rider**, enjoying the benefits without paying your share of the cost. The problem is that you will not be the only one with an incentive to ride free. Every other individual in the valley has exactly the same incentive, so that the entrepreneur gets a seriously biased response from everyone.

A *free rider* is someone who cannot be excluded from enjoying the benefits of a project, but who pays nothing (or pays a disproportionately small amount) to cover its costs.

Accordingly, the dam does not get built by the private entrepreneur. It is natural therefore to turn to the government, which can solve the free rider problem by forcing everyone to pay taxes to build the dam.

Although it can collect enough taxes to build the dam, the government still faces the problem of evaluating the benefits of the dam in order to decide whether or not it should be built in the first place. And in evaluating the benefits, the government, just like the private entrepreneur, encounters problems: It cannot simply ask people how highly they value the dam. If it were to ask you, and you believe that the government will build the dam without noticeably increasing your taxes, it will be in your interest to overstate your valuation (to increase the chance that the dam will be built). Thus, even though you previously told the private entrepreneur that the dam is worth almost nothing, you now turn around and tell the government it is worth $1 million to you (since you know you won't actually have to pay the $1 million). In short, estimates by individuals of what the dam is worth are unreliable, regardless of who is collecting them.[5]

Another approach, therefore, is to forget about canvassing people for their views and instead estimate benefits in some other way. For example, the government can estimate the increase in crops which would result from a flood-control dam. It can do so by examining past records to determine how frequently floods occur and the value of the crops lost in each

---

*[5]Devising some means of getting a better evaluation of public goods has become an important area of inquiry. One imaginative suggestion: Inform people that they will be taxed, but only if their individual valuation tips the scale in favor of building the dam. (Specifically, the tax paid by such an individual would be the cost of the dam, minus the sum of everyone else's evaluation.) Putting the question this way makes it less likely that people will provide a wildly inaccurate evaluation. In particular, it would prevent you from making your wild overestimate of a million dollars. Think about it: The more you exaggerate, the more likely it is that your answer will tip the scales in favor of the dam, and you will be taxed. *In addition,* the more you exaggerate, the higher your tax bill could be.

For more detail on this sort of tax—and in particular on the proposal of Edward H. Clarke, see T. Nicolas Tideman and Gordon Tullock, "A New and Superior Process for Making Social Choices," *Journal of Political Economy,* December 1976, pp. 1145–1159.

flood. This evaluation of benefits is then compared with the estimated cost of the dam.

There are, however, two potential problems with such a benefit-cost analysis. First, unless it is treated with care, it may be used to justify projects that the government has already decided to build for political reasons. For example, a dam may have been promised to a key group of voters in the last election campaign. And any government official with the task of justifying this dam may be able to do so by estimating its construction costs on the low side, and adding more and more benefits until the project is justified. These benefits might include the recreational services of the new lake and the human lives saved by flood control. While these may be important benefits, there is a wide range of values that can be placed on them, as we have already seen in our discussion of the evaluation of human life in Box 13-5.

There may be an additional complication in getting an accurate estimate if, as often happens, the engineers who expect to construct the dam are also the ones who are evaluating its benefits. There may be a real temptation for them to estimate the benefits on the high side in order to justify the dam, and thus create future income and employment for themselves.

OTHER PROBLEMS WITH GOVERNMENT EXPENDITURE DECISIONS

For several other reasons, public decision-making involves problems not encountered in the private sector.

1 The difficulty in reversing a public expenditure

In the private market economy, if we don't want big cars we don't buy them and they stop being produced. The reason is that an auto company would sooner admit its mistake than continue to produce large cars and lose money on them; hence the saying: "Don't throw good money after bad." In short, business executives will admit their mistakes to save their jobs. Not so in

the public sector, where admitting mistakes may *cost* politicians their jobs: If a government expenditure program is dropped, the opposition party may be able to use this "admission of error" to defeat the government in the next election. Furthermore, politicians do not personally suffer out of pocket when they continue questionable expenditures. This is another reason that they are less likely to admit a mistake and reverse an expenditure decision.

2 Voting politically for products is not specific enough

Our auto example suggests another important difference in public versus private decision-making. When you buy a small car, you register a clear and unambiguous vote for its production. But in the public sector, you vote for a dam (in theory) by voting for a political party committed to building it. In practice, it is not this simple; in fact, you may not get to vote on this issue at all. The reason is that in an election, you vote for a party with a whole set of policies. And you, like most other voters, may be voting for this party because of some other completely unrelated issue, like its foreign policy. It is therefore quite possible that the voters who have elected a government that has promised a dam don't really want the dam after all. In short, the political process of voting every few years is a relatively poor method for the public to express its preferences. The public is simply not voting often enough and specifically enough to provide a clear idea of who wants what. Compare this with the private market, where there is much more effective communication: Each day millions of decisions on millions of products are communicated to producers by consumers when they buy those products.

3 The incentive for politicians to support "special interest" groups

In making decisions, our elected representatives have a number of motives. For example, they may honestly be trying to promote the public interest, or at least what they believe to be the public interest. (Unfortunately, it's often not clear what the public interest may be; see Box

15-1.) Frequently their desire to serve the public is their reason for entering politics in the first place. But, once they enter politics, they can't accomplish anything without being elected. Thus, of necessity, all politicians—no matter how noble—must be concerned with getting elected or reelected. And one of the best ways to get reelected is to gain the backing of organized constituencies—or "special-interest" groups—who are able to deliver votes and/or financial support. In turn, the best way to get such backing is to support a program which is of intense interest to a group that benefits, but which is of far less concern to the public that has to pay. The special interest of most people is their job—the goods or services they are producing. (The source of our income is of intense interest to each of us.) Politicians seeking special interest support therefore pay particular attention to people as producers rather than as consumers (as we shall see, for example, in our discussion of tariff policy in Chapter 17).

4 Short-run, crisis-oriented decision-making

The desire to be reelected also leads politicians to favor policies with a cost that is hidden and a benefit that (1) is obvious and (2) will be realized before the next election. Why should politicians promote a policy that the public won't understand; or a policy that will provide benefits after the next election—and thus only help to reelect their successors? One of the reasons that politicians can take this limited short-run view is that a busy public cannot be adequately informed about the hundreds of issues on which politicians must decide. Thus politicians tend to put off tough, long-run decisions; and when they finally do take action, it is often in response to a crisis.

5 Problems in a government bureaucracy

Even if Congress has, with great foresight, made a decision that should benefit the nation overall, this policy must be administered by the appropriate government department (for example, the Department of the Interior, or the Department of Health and Human Resources). Each of these departments is a "bureau." That is, it receives its income from a granting agency (Congress) rather than the way a private firm does—from the sale of a product in the marketplace.[6]

a Difficulties in controlling a bureau's performance and cost   The government bureau typically is a monopolist in the provision of its service to the public. (Indeed, the reason the government may have taken over this activity may be that it is a natural monopoly.) But for precisely this reason it is difficult for Congress to judge its performance: There is no equivalent agency providing the same service with which it might be compared. Another difficulty is that a bureau's output can't be measured. Thus, for example, the Department of Agriculture can't be judged, like a private firm, on the number of bushels of wheat it produces, because it doesn't produce any. (This problem reaches right down through the ranks of the bureau. Difficulties in measuring output prevent senior members in a bureau from evaluating the productivity of their juniors.)

Because a bureau's performance is so difficult to evaluate, its costs are often hard to control. Its situation is quite different from that of a private firm under pressure to sell its product in the marketplace. Such a firm has great incentives to cut costs. These incentives come in the form of both a carrot (the desire to make profits) and a stick (the fear of bankruptcy if costs aren't kept in line). On the other hand, a bureau need not fear going broke. There is therefore far less pressure to keep costs down. An extreme example sometimes occurs at the end of a year, when a bureau's officials may feel under pressure to *inflate* costs by spending any remaining funds in their budget. (If they don't, their budget may be cut for the next year.) In short, because of inadequate cost cutting and performance standards, a bureau tends to become technically inefficient.

---

[6]Departments of large private firms may develop many of the characteristics of a bureaucracy, and, to the extent they do, the difference between the operation of a government department and a business is diminished.

Public Choice: What's "In the Public Interest?"

Majority rule is a basic principle of democracy. Surely we may take this simple and well accepted principle as a straightforward way of determining what is in the public interest, right? Not necessarily—for several reasons:

1 The problem of the oppressive majority

Under majority rule, if 51 percent of the public want a certain policy they can get it. It doesn't matter how small they value the benefit (as long as they get *some* benefit); nor does it matter how heavy the cost of this policy may be to the minority. Thus it is possible for majority rule to leave society as a whole worse off, with the benefits to the majority falling short of the costs imposed on the minority.

To illustrate, consider the following example.† 100 farmers in a community can only get access to a main highway by small connecting roads. It is in the interests of 51 of these farmers to vote to have only their own roads paved out of taxes collected from all 100 farmers. But this will inflict a loss on society if the 51 winners get only a small net benefit‡ while the 49 losers suffer a great deal from the tax they have to pay. Thus, majority rule may be defective.§ Like private decision-making, it can result in inefficiency—an overall loss to society.††

(Is there a better voting procedure than majority rule? The answer is that there are a lot of alternatives; but each involves some weakness or other.‡‡ For example, one could avoid the problem of the oppressive majority by requiring unanimous consent; then no policy could hurt anyone. But this rule is hopeless. By providing a veto to each individual, it paralyzes the government. Any policy that damaged even one voter would be vetoed. Rather than searching for a voting system which might conceivably be better than majority rule, a more common—and reasonable—approach is to protect minorities from an oppressive majority with a constitution, either written or unwritten.)

The example of the oppressive majority illustrates two additional points. (1) The government can redistribute income without transferring any cash. Suppose the farmers who get their roads paved receive more benefits than we have so far assumed. Specifically, suppose that they get net benefits from this policy roughly equal to the loss borne by the minority. In this case, the majority receives a large transfer from the minority—even though no cash transfer takes place between the two. (2) Members of a minority have a strong incentive to try to break down the existing majority coalition in order to form a new ruling coalition including themselves. For example, the 49 excluded farmers are likely to try to get two farmers to leave the present majority and join them. Then the newly formed coalition can turn the tables on the 49 who were in a majority but now find themselves out of

---

†This is a modified version of the example first suggested by Gordon Tullock in "Some Problems of Majority Voting" in K. J. Arrow and T. Scitovsky (eds.) *Readings in Welfare Economics* (Homewood, Ill.: Richard D. Irwin, 1969), pp. 169–178.

‡That is, their total benefit from the road, less the tax they pay.

§ However, majority rule may not be as inefficient in practice as theory might lead us to expect. The best evidence comes from Switzerland where many issues are decided by a referendum in which the public votes yes or no on a single issue. In a recent study of 100 such votes, Columbia's Eli Noam concluded that there were only a few instances in which the result was inefficient (that is, the minority lost more than the majority gained). See "The Efficiency of Direct Democracy," *Journal of Political Economy,* August 1980, pp. 803–810.

††Majority rule can be inefficient not only because such undesirable policies *are* introduced, but also because *desirable* policies are *not* introduced. (For example, a policy that would hurt the majority even slightly may be rejected, regardless of how much more it may benefit the minority.)

‡‡For a discussion of some alternatives, see Dennis C. Mueller, *Public Choice* (Cambridge: Cambridge University Press, 1979), especially pp. 49–58.

power. (Of course, the new coalition may then come under the same pressure from outsiders as the old; there may be a cycle of changing coalition patterns.)

2 The voting paradox: Why majority rule may lead to no clear winner

To illustrate this second problem, consider a population of only three individuals, faced with a choice among three options, A, B, and C. Suppose that Table 15-1 shows how each individual ranks each of these options. For example, the first column tells us that individual I prefers option A to option B, and B to C. In choosing among the options, what is the will of the majority?

If these individuals choose first between options A and B, a majority (individuals I and III) will vote for A. With A the choice so far, the only remaining question is how it compares to C. In voting between these two, the majority (individuals II and III) prefer C. So C is the final choice, reflecting the apparent will of the majority.

But now suppose that these individuals voted first between B and C. In this case, C is immediately rejected because individuals I and II prefer B. Thus the preference of the majority isn't

Table 15-1
The Voting Paradox:
Preferences of Three Individuals for
Alternative Policies A, B, and C

Choice	Individual I	II	III
First choice	A	B	C
Second choice	B	C	A
Last choice	C	A	B

clear at all; C may be the final choice or immediately rejected, depending on how the voting is set up.

Thus we conclude that in a world in which individual preferences differ, an important determinant of the final choice may be the political process itself (in this example, the political decision on which options will be voted on first). Thus the individual who sets a committee's agenda and/or controls the voting procedure may be able to control the result.§§

§§ This voting paradox, first described over a century ago, has been extended by Nobel Prizewinner Kenneth Arrow in *Social Choice and Individual Values* (New York: John Wiley, 1951).

In the absence of a profit motive, what incentives are there in a bureau? Government officials tend to substitute two other objectives: (1) the public interest (at least as they perceive it), and (2) their own interest, including establishing a public reputation, accumulating the power and perquisites of office, and—often most important—increasing the size of the bureau.[7]

[7]The objectives of officials in a bureau are discussed in detail by Anthony Downs, *Inside Bureaucracy* (Boston: Little Brown, 1967), pp. 81–111, and by W. A. Niskanen, Jr. (a member of President Reagan's Council of Economic Advisers) in *Bureaucracy and Representative Government* (Chicago: Aldine-Atherton, 1971), p. 38.

b The tendency for the government bureau and its budget to expand

There are several reasons why a government official might try to increase the size of a bureau. By increasing the number of employees, the official will seem to have more responsibility and thus may gain prestige. More employees may also mean more echelons of management—just as in a private firm—and therefore more jobs at the top; this in turn means improved prospects for promotion. Government officials may also seek more funds in order to serve the public or their constituency better; for example, the more funds going to the Department of Agriculture, the more benefits it can provide to the nation's farmers. And the

3 Logrolling

Logrolling occurs when two Congressmen agree: "You vote for my policy, and I'll vote for yours." How it works in a simple case with 3 voters is illustrated in Table 15-2.

The first row in this table indicates that policy A provides a benefit of 3 to individual I, and a cost of 2 to each of the other two voters. (It will obviously be I's pet project.)

In a simple majority vote, both policies are

Table 15-2
Logrolling
Benefits (+) or Costs (−) of Each Policy to Each Individual

	Individual		
	I	**II**	**III**
Policy A	+3	−2	−2
Policy B	−2	+3	−2
Net effect on each individual if *both* policies are passed because of logrolling:	+1	+1	−4

defeated. (Individuals II and III vote against policy A, and I and III vote against B.) But I and II have an incentive to get together first: II agrees to vote for I's pet policy A, if I will vote for II's pet policy B. Because of this agreement, both policies pass. As shown in the bottom row of this table, voters I and II both benefit; indeed that was the reason that they engaged in logrolling in the first place. But III loses—and by even more than the combined gain of I and II. Thus logrolling hurts the community overall, even though it benefits the "special interest" groups who engage in it (in our example, voters I and II).

(This is the classical example of logrolling; but there is another possibility. Change the two entries of +3 in this table to +5. Logrolling occurs again for exactly the same reason as before, and once again I and II benefit while III loses. The difference this time is that the combined gain of I and II exceeds III's loss; thus logrolling results in a net overall benefit for this community. Thus, logrolling isn't necessarily bad. In some cases, it may be the only way of achieving a socially desirable result.) ■

more its clients are thereby satisfied, the more they will put pressure on Congress if any attempts are made to cut the bureau's budget.

c Monopoly inefficiency: Public versus private Both a private monopoly and a monopolized public activity may result in technical inefficiency—that is, unnecessarily high costs. (They have less incentive than a competitive industry to keep costs down.) Both monopolies also involve allocative inefficiency (the wrong amount of output); but this inefficiency appears in two different forms. On the one hand, a private monopoly produces too little output and therefore employs too few resources. But a

public monopoly—a bureau—has natural tendencies to expand; thus it may employ *too many* resources.[8]

---

[8]In *The Affluent Society* (Boston: Houghton-Mifflin, 1958) John Kenneth Galbraith argues that the government is *not* too large a part of the economy. Indeed, he argues that in some respects the government is too small: Compared to a private business, it provides too few goods and services. One reason: Goods provided by private firms are advertised (with their consumption increased as a consequence), while goods provided by the government are not. Therefore, we overspend on autos, but underspend on parks. This raises the question: Do we spend too much on certain things the government provides but not enough on others?

BOX 15-2
A Review of Market Structure in the Last Five Chapters: How a Typical Firm's Costs Compare With Total Market Demand

Figure 15-4 shows how the kind of market that develops (whether it be monopoly, perfect competition, or whatever) is heavily influenced by the range over which the firm's average costs continue to fall. To highlight this point, we consider five different goods in the first five panels of this diagram. (We discuss the sixth panel later.) In almost all respects, these five goods are identical. In each case, total market demand is exactly the same, and average cost AC reaches a minimum at the same height, C. The only difference is, that, as we move left to right from panel to panel, AC reaches a minimum at an increasingly large output. Thus, in panel a, AC reaches a minimum at a very small output Q_1, while in panel e, AC reaches the same minimum height C at such a large output (so far to the right) that it cannot even be shown in the diagram.

In the case of perfect competition in panel a, market demand can be satisfied at minimum cost by a large number of producers. There is little role to be played by the government, since this market is generally efficient when left to its own devices. (We assume here that there are no complications, such as serious price fluctuations over time, or important externalities. If significant

externalities do exist, the government should generally tax to discourage external costs, or subsidize to encourage external benefits.)

Panel b is the case of natural oligopoly, where market demand can be satisfied at minimum cost by just a few firms. In such a market, a strong case can be made for the vigorous enforcement of antitrust laws to prevent either collusion or the merger of these firms into a monopoly.

In the case of natural monopoly in panel c, market demand can be satisfied at lower cost by one firm than by more than one. Here, the application of antitrust legislation to split up a single firm makes little sense, since the split would raise costs. A preferred approach is price regulation, which prevents the firm from charging a high monopoly price, while allowing it to gain the cost advantages of large scale production.

In panels d and e, costs have finally outrun demand. At no point do D and AC overlap, so there is no single price a firm can charge and still cover its costs. The appropriate government policy in either case is "hands off." If the gap between demand and costs is small enough, as in panel d, a discriminating monopolist (say, the

CONCLUDING OBSERVATIONS

Public goods and private goods

Box 15-2 compares a public good (in Figure 15-4, panel f) with private goods produced in various types of market. As we have discussed these various types of market structure, a recurring question has been "When does the private market work well, and when does it not?" We have seen that when the private market fails, a

case can be made for government intervention. But in the last three chapters it has become evident that government intervention is not a simple all-purpose solution either. In some circumstances government decision-making may also fail. Just because the private market is inefficient, it will not necessarily improve matters to have more government intervention. The government may improve things; or it may make them worse.

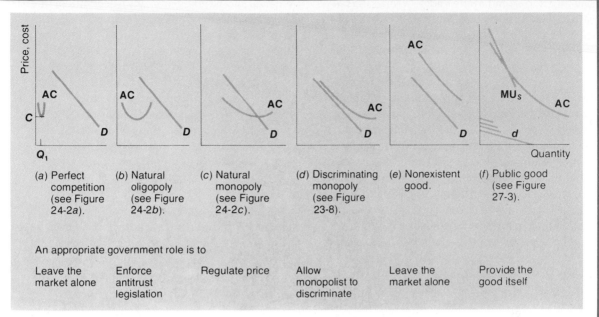

(a) Perfect competition (see Figure 24-2a).	(b) Natural oligopoly (see Figure 24-2b).	(c) Natural monopoly (see Figure 24-2c).	(d) Discriminating monopoly (see Figure 23-8).	(e) Nonexistent good.	(f) Public good (see Figure 27-3).

An appropriate government role is to

Leave the market alone	Enforce antitrust legislation	Regulate price	Allow monopolist to discriminate	Leave the market alone	Provide the good itself

Figure 15-4
The relationship of the costs of a single producer and total market demand

doctor in Chapter 11) may be able to cover her costs if she is able to charge different prices to different consumers. Since her services will not be available otherwise, the government should allow her to follow this policy.

But in panel *e*, cost outruns demand by such a large amount that even a discriminating monopolist cannot cover the cost of producing this good. In fact, the product will not even appear on the market; there is no economic justification for its production.

In panel *f*, we show a public good. In this case, we examine how its cost compares with its marginal social benefit curve, MU_s. (For specific details, see Problem 15-1*b*.) If the market is left to its own devices, no individual will purchase this good. If it is to be provided at all, the most obvious way is by the government. ■

Is the environment a public good?
One of the strongest cases for government intervention arises when the environment is being damaged.

There are several ways in which this can be prevented. If a firm is polluting the water or air, it should be taxed, as we saw in Chapter 14.

But suppose that the environment is deteriorating of its own accord; no firm or individual is at fault in any way. For example, suppose that a species of wildlife is dying off in the wilderness. In this case, the proper approach is to recognize that the preservation of this species is a public good (just like the construction of a dam in our example earlier in this chapter). Since no individual values the species highly enough to incur the cost of personally preserving it, the private market generally won't deliver. Although private conservation organizations may act, the ultimate decision on whether to save the species—and how much to spend in the effort—is likely to rest with the government. If the government does act, everyone can enjoy the resulting benefits.

How large would these benefits be? This question is not easy to answer. While most people would put some value on the preservation of a wildlife species, it is very difficult to say how much. As Harvard's Richard Caves has put it: "How highly should we value wombats, if they are so far from civilization that no one will ever see them, let alone eat them?" One answer is that we may place some value on them, even though we don't ever see them, just as we may place a value on an air-conditioning system even in a summer in which we never actually turn it on. This phenomenon is described as "option demand"—the desire to have an option, whether or not we exercise it. Thus we may want to keep open the option of seeing a species (or using it in medical research), even though we may never in fact exercise this option. Similarly, we may have an option demand for public parks which we may or may not actually visit. Option demand should be taken into account in the evaluation of environmental benefits.

Yet Caves' point is well taken: In discussing environmental protection, it is important to take a balanced view of the benefits and costs involved. For example, consider a caribou population that would be disturbed by the construction of an oil pipeline. A major cost would be involved in the extreme event that the pipeline were to cause the caribou to become extinct, since this action could not be reversed by future generations. But if there is no such risk of extinction, what is the difference between reducing the population of caribou by 5 percent and reducing the population of cattle by 5 percent by slaughtering them for meat? (Both policies provide obvious benefits: Killing cattle provides food, while laying pipelines is essential to provide heat and power.)

Again we conclude, as in Chapter 14, that keeping environmental damage down to an appropriately low level makes more sense than trying to avoid any damage whatever.

Key Points

1 If a good provides an external benefit, a perfectly competitive market will provide less than the efficient level of output. Government can induce the expansion of output to the efficient level by subsidizing buyers of this good by the amount of the external benefit. This "internalizes the externality" because buyers then personally enjoy not only the benefit the good provides to themselves, but also an amount equal to the benefit it provides to others.

2 No individual farmer would consider building a flood-control dam, because of its high cost and the fact that the benefits he himself would receive would be trivial compared with the benefits that would go to thousands of neighboring farmers. This, then, is the general idea of a public good: It is a good that will not be produced by the private market, but must be produced (if it is to exist at all) by the government.

3 An alternative definition is that a public good is one that can be enjoyed by everyone, regardless of who pays for it. For example, once a flood control dam has been built, no one can be excluded from enjoying its flood-control services.

4 Building such a dam is justified if its cost is less than the sum of its benefits to all the public.

5 In practice, there may be major problems in evaluating these benefits. Even if people have a clear idea in their own minds of what the benefits would be, they are unlikely to tell any government official (or, for that matter, any private entrepreneur). Therefore, the alternative approach of benefit-cost analysis is often used. For example, the benefit of flood control is estimated by looking at past records of how often floods have occurred and the damage they have done to crops. But it still remains extraordinarily difficult to estimate some of the benefits, like saving human lives.

6 When the government provides goods and services to the economy, a number of problems arise that are typically not encountered by private firms. First, it is more difficult for the government to reverse an error; politicians fear losing votes if they admit mistakes.

7 When the public buys privately-produced goods such as cars, producers have a clear-cut indication that this is what the public wants. But when the public votes for a party that has promised to, say, build a dam, it's not clear whether the public wants the dam or not. (It may have voted for the winning party for other reasons—such as its foreign policy.)

8 Politicians often make economic decisions not so much in the interests of the general public as in the interests of their specific constituency (or some group within that constituency). Moreover, they tend to favor policies with a payoff that is obvious and will be realized quickly—in particular, before the next election.

9 There is a natural tendency for a bureau and its budget to expand. One reason is that a bureau is typically not under the same cost-cutting pressure as a private firm which must sell its output on a competitive market.

10 There are two important ways to protect the environment. When it is being damaged by, say, a polluting firm, the proper approach is to tax that firm (as we saw in Chapter 14). But when the environment is deteriorating of its own accord (for example, if a wildlife species is becoming extinct), the preservation of the environment may be viewed as a public good. Thus, government protection of the environment is justified if the costs of this protection are less than the benefits it provides to all individuals in society.

Key Concepts

external benefits
how a subsidy affects
   efficiency
internalizing an external
   benefit
internalizing an external
   cost
a public good
marginal social utility for
   a private good and for a
   public good

private versus public
   decisions
difficulty in reversing
   public expenditures
why a political vote may
   not indicate what the
   public wants
special interest groups
lack of competitive
   pressures to cut costs in
   government

why government
   bureaucracies tend to
   expand
technical and allocative
   inefficiency in
   government departments
the environment as a
   public good

Problems

15-1 *(a)* On Figure 15-3c, draw a completely horizontal marginal cost curve at a height just above the top of bar a_2. Now show the number of units of this public good that the government should provide. (For example, how many dams should the government build in a flood-control network?)

(b) In Figure 15-4f, extend MU_S downward and to the right. Also extend curve AC to the right until it reaches a minimum, and then draw

in the corresponding MC curve. Show the amount of this good the government should provide.

15-2 If a freeway is to be built into a city, discuss the benefits and costs that you think should be estimated. Explain why making such estimates might be a difficult task.

15-3 Do you think national defense is a public good? Why? Do you think estimating its benefits is difficult? Why?

15-4 Suppose you are working for a government in the tropics, and a proposal is being considered to spray a wide area of territory for malarial mosquitoes. A critic states that such an expenditure is not justified, since if it were justified, a private entrepreneur would already have seized this opportunity. What position do you take?

15-5 (Review of the last two chapters.) Suppose the only three individuals who would benefit from a public good have the demand (marginal utility) schedules shown below. Assume also that each unit of this good involves a production cost of C and an external cost of K. Should this good be produced? If so, at what output?

15-6 Suppose that, instead of the per unit subsidy to the *buyer* shown as the arrow in Figure 15-1, the government provides exactly the same subsidy to the *seller*. Show the effect. Does this subsidy increase output to the efficient quantity? How does this policy compare with the policy of subsidizing the buyer?

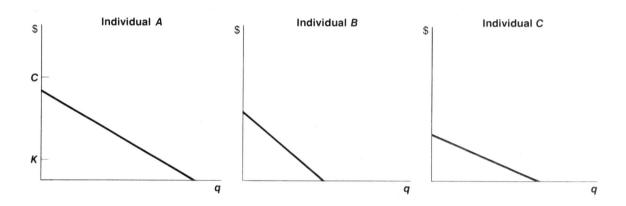

CHAPTER 16
The Gains from International Trade

Our interest will be to throw open the doors of commerce, and to knock off its shackles, giving freedom to all persons for the vent of whatever they may choose to bring into our ports, and asking the same in theirs.

Thomas Jefferson

Economic gains come from specialization. One of the reasons for the high material standard of living in the United States is our high degree of specialization. Steel is produced near the coalfields of Pennsylvania, wheat is produced in the Western states, and citrus fruits are grown in California and Florida. By such specialization, we are able to increase our total output of goods.

Just as specialization within the United States increases output and efficiency, so too does specialization among the United States and other countries. Specifically, international trade and specialization among the United States and other countries bring the same benefits as domestic specialization, first noted in Chapter 3: namely, the gains from comparative advantage and economies of scale. International trade also exposes domestic producers to increased competition and thus reduces their market power. Because of international trade, we are not only able to buy inexpensive foreign goods. We also can get goods more cheaply from domestic producers who must keep their prices down in order to meet foreign competition.

The major objective of this chapter will be to consider in detail each of these benefits from trade. But before doing so, we ask two questions.

WITH WHOM DO WE TRADE? WHAT DO WE TRADE?

The answers are provided in Table 16-1. From the first column, it is evident that the most important United States trading partner is Canada. (One reason is that distance and transport costs—natural deterrents to trade—are at a minimum in our trade with Canada.[1]) Japan is also a key trading partner, followed by the large countries in the European Economic Community and Latin America.

The right-hand side of the table indicates that we trade a wide variety of goods. Our exports include such diverse items as grain from Iowa and aircraft from Seattle. Our imports include base metals and other materials essential to American industry. And, for a nation on wheels, autos and oil account for an important

[1]Many Americans don't realize the importance of trade with Canada. The reason is that U.S. purchases from Canada include raw materials (base metals) and manufactured goods (telecommunications equipment) that are less familiar to the U.S. public than the consumer goods (watches, cars, and radios) that Americans buy from Europe and Japan. (Also, the cars that are bought from Canada are built by GM, Ford, and Chrysler, and are virtually indistinguishable from similar U.S.-built cars.)

319

Table 16-1
U.S. Merchandise Trade in 1980
(billions of dollars)

With whom do we trade?		What do we trade?	
Exports: U.S. sales to:		Exports	
Canada	$ 39.2	Grains	$ 20.8
Japan	20.8	Other agricultural products	21.2
European Economic Community (EEC)	53.6	Nonagricultural industrial supplies	64.2
Western Europe, except the EEC	14.1	Machinery	57.8
Eastern Europe	4.1	Civilian aircraft and parts	14.1
Latin America	38.8	Autos and parts	16.8
Australia, New Zealand, and South		Other consumer goods	16.4
Africa	7.1	All other	10.5
Other countries in Asia and		Total	$221.8
Africa	44.1		
Total	$221.8		
Imports: U.S. purchases from:		Imports	
Canada	$ 42.4	Coffee, cocoa, and sugar	$ 6.3
Japan	31.2	Other foods, feed, and beverages	11.8
European Economic Community	36.1	Petroleum and products	78.9
Western Europe, except the EEC	11.2	Other industrial supplies and	
Eastern Europe	1.4	materials	55.6
Latin America	37.4	Machinery	26.2
Australia, New Zealand, and South		Autos and parts	27.1
Africa	6.5	Other consumer goods	34.4
Other countries in Asia and		All other	8.8
Africa	82.9	Total	$249.1
Total	$249.1		

Source: Survey of Current Business (U.S. Department of Commerce), March 1981, pp. 52–55.

part of our trade: Our purchases of oil and its products made up almost a third of our total imports.

This, then, describes *what* and *with whom* we trade. Now let us return to the advantages we reap from trade. We consider three basic sources of gain: (1) increased competition, (2) economies of scale, and (3) comparative advantage.

MARKETS BECOME MORE COMPETITIVE, AND HENCE MORE EFFICIENT

Consider the monopoly firm in Figure 16-1. Initially, without international trade (panel *a*), this firm has the U.S. market all to itself. If it is

not subject to government regulation, it will be able to set a monopoly price. In panel *b,* we see what happens when trade is opened up. The potential demand facing the American producer is much larger, as shown by the total world demand curve. Therefore, the American firm is now able to go after foreign markets as well as the domestic market. But, it is no longer able to take the U.S. market for granted, since it faces stiff competition here from foreign producers. Thus, foreign trade can transform a natural monopoly in the domestic market (panel *a*) into a natural oligopoly in the world market (panel *b*). In the process, this firm's monopoly control of the U.S. market is broken, and its ability to exercise market power (charge a high price) is reduced. And as we have seen earlier, a lower more competitive price results in an improved allocation of resources, with a corresponding efficiency gain.

On the other hand, if the industry is originally a natural oligopoly, international trade can make it substantially more competitive. To illustrate, consider the U.S. firm in Figure 16-2 that, before trade, has about one-third of the domestic U.S. market. After trade is opened up in panel b, this firm will have a much smaller fraction of the market, because the market is now the whole world. Again, increased competition will tend to keep price down, with U.S. consumers benefiting. Furthermore, they gain in other ways as well, if the domestic producer is forced to compete in nonprice aspects, such as quality or design. Thus, the U.S. automobile industry has been pressured into producing smaller cars as a result of competition, first from European firms (in the late 1950s) and, more recently, from Japanese automakers.

ECONOMIES OF SCALE

In the face of economies of scale (falling average cost as output expands), there are two additional potential gains from trade.

New products become available

Specifically, international trade may make it profitable to produce goods which otherwise would not be produced at all. Figure 16-3a illustrates such a product. Demand is too low in the domestic economy to allow this good to be profitably produced. But when the foreign market becomes available, demand becomes large enough to cover average costs (the rightward shift in D makes it now overlap AC) and the item is introduced. An example is Boeing, which in 1980 exported about half its output. Without exports, Boeing would have had difficulty in covering the enormous design and tooling costs of its 747 jumbo jet; at the very least, its

Figure 16-1
How international trade breaks down monopoly power

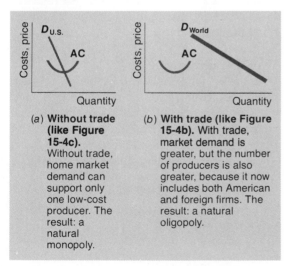

(a) **Without trade (like Figure 15-4c).** Without trade, home market demand can support only one low-cost producer. The result: a natural monopoly.

(b) **With trade (like Figure 15-4b).** With trade, market demand is greater, but the number of producers is also greater, because it now includes both American and foreign firms. The result: a natural oligopoly.

Figure 16-2
How international trade makes an oligopoly more competitive

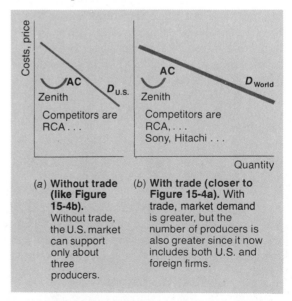

(a) **Without trade (like Figure 15-4b).** Without trade, the U.S. market can support only about three producers.

(b) **With trade (closer to Figure 15-4a).** With trade, market demand is greater, but the number of producers is also greater since it now includes both U.S. and foreign firms.

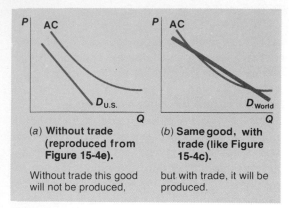

(a) Without trade (reproduced from Figure 15-4e).

Without trade this good will not be produced,

(b) Same good, with trade (like Figure 15-4c).

but with trade, it will be produced.

Figure 16-3
How international trade may create new products
The AC curves in these two figures are identical. But because of trade, the demand curve in part *b* is much farther to the right.

introduction would have been delayed. Perhaps it would not have been produced at all.

Existing goods can be produced more efficiently

Where there are economies of scale, trade results not only in the introduction of new products, but also in the more efficient production of old products. For example, European producers have been able to manufacture automobiles at larger volume and lower cost since the establishment of the European Economic Community. (Because tariff barriers have been eliminated within the EEC, a manufacturer in any member country can sell freely to buyers in all member countries.)

COMPARATIVE ADVANTAGE

Now suppose that there are no economies of scale; instead, suppose costs are constant. (The average cost curve is horizontal.) The theory of comparative advantage tells us that even in these circumstances, gains can be realized from international trade.

The basic idea of comparative advantage

has already been introduced in Chapter 3. Even though the lawyer cited there may be more skillful (that is, may have an absolute advantage) in both law and gardening, she does not do her own gardening. Instead, she concentrates on law, the activity in which she has a comparative advantage. By specializing in this way, she can acquire more gardening service than if she were to take the time to do it herself.

Internationally, the idea is exactly the same: Even though the United States may be better (that is, have an absolute advantage) in producing both aircraft and radios, it may be in our interest to concentrate on aircraft and other products in which we have a comparative advantage, and leave radios to other countries. By specializing in aircraft, we may be able to acquire more radios through trade than we could produce ourselves.

The idea of comparative advantage was developed in the early nineteenth century by David Ricardo, an English economist, financier, and Member of Parliament. In his simplified illustration of this idea, Ricardo assumed that markets were perfectly competitive, that there were no transport costs, that all production costs were constant, and that the only input was labor. He also assumed that there were only two countries (we shall call them America and Europe) producing two goods (we shall call them food and clothing).

Absolute advantage

As a preliminary, Table 16-2 shows the case where each country has an *absolute advantage* in the production of one good. In the first column, we see that a clothing worker in Europe can outproduce a worker in America (4 to 3), so by definition Europe has an absolute advantage in clothing. Similarly, in the second column we see that America has an absolute advantage in food, since an American worker can outproduce a European worker (2 to 1). The most efficient allocation of resources is to have America specialize in food and Europe in clothing as the calculations at the bottom of Table 16-2 confirm.

So far, it seems that each country specializes in the good in which it has an absolute advan-

Table 16-2
Illustration of Absolute Advantage:
Hypothetical Output per Worker in Europe and America

	Clothing	Food
America	3 units	2 units
Europe	4 units	1 unit

In the first column, Europe has an absolute advantage in clothing production because a worker can produce 4 units compared with only 3 in America. In the second column, America has an absolute advantage in food, because a worker here can produce 2 units, compared with only 1 in Europe. Both countries together can produce more total output when America specializes in food and Europe specializes in clothing.

To confirm, suppose specialization has not occurred; in other words, suppose that each country is initially producing both goods. Now suppose that they begin to specialize—America in food, Europe in clothing. Therefore, a worker in America is switched out of clothing and into food production. At the same time, a worker in Europe is switched in the opposite direction (out of food and into clothing). As a result of these two switches:

	Clothing output changes by	Food output changes by
In America	−3	+2
In Europe	+4	−1
Therefore, net world output changes by	+1	+1

tage. But this is not always so. We shall now show that the key to specialization is *comparative* advantage rather than absolute advantage.

Comparative advantage

Table 16-3 illustrates the more difficult case where one country, America (like the lawyer in Box 3-2), has an absolute advantage in the production of both goods. [An American worker outproduces a European worker in both clothing (6 to 4) and food (3 to 1).] Nonetheless, America —like the lawyer of Chapter 3—will not try to

Table 16-3
Illustration of Comparative Advantage:
Hypothetical Output per Worker in Europe and America

Product	Clothing	Food
America	6 units	3 units
Europe	4 units	1 unit

In the bottom row, one European worker can produce either 4 units of clothing or 1 unit of food. Thus, the opportunity cost of 1 unit of food in Europe is 4 units of clothing. In the row above, we see that an American worker can produce either 6 units of clothing or 3 of food. The opportunity cost of food in America is therefore $6/3 = 2$ units of clothing. (Notice how we calculate this opportunity cost by taking the ratio of the figures in the American row, just as we calculated the European cost $(4/1)$ from the figures in the European row.) Since the opportunity cost of food in America is less than in Europe, America has a comparative advantage in food and specializes in this good.

To confirm that this specialization will increase total world output, again suppose that each country is initially producing both goods. Now suppose they begin to specialize: America switches one worker out of clothing and into food, and Europe switches two workers out of food and into clothing. Then:

	Clothing output changes by	Food output changes by
In America	−6	+3
In Europe	+8	−2
Therefore, net world output changes by	+2	+1

satisfy its requirements by producing both goods itself. Instead, it will specialize in one and buy the other from Europe, as we shall now explain.

Our first step is to calculate the opportunity cost of food in each country. First, in Europe: The second row of Table 16-3 tells us that a European worker who is now producing 1 unit of food could, instead, be producing 4 units of clothing. In other words, in Europe *the opportunity cost of 1 unit of food is 4 units of clothing.* Since prices tend to reflect costs, we would expect these two goods to exchange in Europe for the same 1:4 ratio. That is, in the absence of international trade, 1 unit of food will exchange in Europe for 4 units of clothing.

On the other hand, what is the opportunity cost of food in America? The first row of Table 16-3 tells us that an American worker who is producing 3 units of food could instead be producing 6 units of clothing. In other words, in America the opportunity cost of a unit of food is $\frac{6}{3}$ = 2 units of clothing. Consequently, we would expect the two goods to exchange in America at this 1:2 ratio. That is, before trade, 1 unit of food will exchange in America for 2 units of clothing.

Since the opportunity cost of food in America is less (2 units of clothing versus 4 in Europe), we say that America has a **comparative advantage** in food. By definition:

A country's *comparative advantage* is the good that it can produce relatively cheaply; that is, at lower opportunity cost than its trading partner.

A similar set of calculations, again using the figures in Table 16-3, shows that in clothing, Europe has a lower opportunity cost and hence a comparative advantage.[2]

With this concept of comparative advantage in hand, we shall now see how both countries will benefit if they specialize in their product of comparative advantage and trade for the other —at any price ratio between the 1:2 price ratio which would prevail in an isolated America and the 1:4 in Europe. Suppose this price ratio— often called the "terms of trade"—is 1:3; that is, 1 unit of food exchanges internationally for 3 units of clothing. [The determination of this price ratio depends not only on the cost (supply)

conditions that we have been describing, but also on demand in these two countries. For example, the more strongly Europeans demand food (the U.S. export), the higher the price of food will be.][3]

Faced with an international price ratio of 1:3 (1 unit of food exchanging for 3 units of clothing) let's first show how America can benefit by specializing in its product of comparative advantage, food, and trading to satisfy its clothing needs. Specifically, for each American worker taken out of clothing production, America loses 6 units of clothing. However, that worker instead now produces 3 units of food, which can then be traded (at the 1:3 international price ratio) for 9 units of clothing—for a clear gain of 3 units of clothing. Similarly, Europe also gains by specializing in its product of comparative advantage— clothing—and trading it for food.[4]

To sum up this example, both countries gain from trade. America benefits by specializing in food (its comparative advantage) and trading for clothing. At the same time Europe benefits by specializing in clothing (its comparative advantage) and trading for food. [The reason that there are gains from trade is that the cost ratios in the two rows of Table 16-3 (namely $\frac{6}{3}$ and $\frac{4}{1}$) are different. If these ratios (that is, opportunity costs) were the same, there would be no comparative advantage and no gain from trade.]

The gain to the United States from trade may be illustrated in another way. Figure 16-4 shows the American production possibilities curve (PPC), derived from the U.S. figures in the first row of Table 16-3, assuming that there are 200 million workers in America. (For example, if they all work at producing clothing, each of the 200 million workers will produce 6 units for a total of 1,200 million units of clothing, as shown at point A.) In this simple Ricardian example, the

---

[2]In Europe the opportunity cost of clothing is $\frac{1}{4}$ of a unit of food ($\frac{1}{4}$ of a unit of food must be given up to acquire 1 unit of clothing). Similarly, in America the opportunity cost of clothing is $\frac{3}{6}$ = $\frac{1}{2}$ unit of food. With its lower opportunity cost of clothing, Europe has a comparative advantage in clothing. Notice in this simple two-country, two-good example that if America has a comparative advantage in one good (food), Europe *must* have a comparative advantage in the other (clothing).

[3]For more on the importance of demand, see footnote 5 on p. 326.

[4]In switching a worker from food to clothing production, Europe loses 1 unit of food. But that worker produces 4 units of clothing instead, and this output can be traded (at the 1:3 international price ratio) for $\frac{4}{3}$ = $1\frac{1}{3}$ units of food—for a gain of $\frac{1}{3}$ units of food.

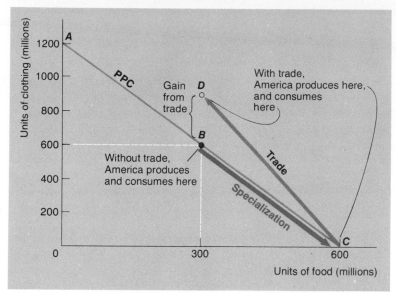

Figure 16-4
Gains from trade

America's production possibilities curve AC is derived from the first row in Table 16-3, on the assumption that there are 200 million workers in America. If
they all work at producing clothing (6 units each) the
200 million workers will produce 1200 million units
of clothing and no food at point A. On the other hand,
if they all produce food (3 units each) they will
produce a total of 600 million units of food and no
clothing at point C. Finally, suppose that half the
American workers produce food and half produce
clothing. Then the 100 million clothing workers will
produce 6 units each, for a total of 600 million units
of clothing, while the 100 million food workers will
produce 3 units each, for a total of 300 million units
of food. This combination of outputs is plotted as
point B. (The constant figures in the first row of Table
16-3 ensure that the production possibilities curve
AC is a straight line.)

Suppose that, without trade, America produces
and consumes at point B. When trade is opened,
America can (1) *specialize* in food, by shifting production from B to C, and (2) *trade* 300 units of food
for 900 units of clothing at the prevailing 1:3 international price ratio. Thus America can move from C to
D. Trade makes it possible for America to consume
at D, beyond the production possibilities curve AC.
(Of course, *production* cannot take place beyond the
PPC.) The American gain from trade is the increase
in clothing consumption from the original 600 units
at point B to the 900 units at point D. (In this
example, America's consumption of food remains
the same, but this need not necessarily be the case.
For example, in moving up the trade arrow, it may
stop at a point short of D. Then its gains from trade in
moving to this new point from original point B would
be both increased clothing *and* increased food.)

production possibilities curve is a straight line:
The opportunity cost of food in America remains
constant as we move down this curve: No matter
how much food we may be producing, we must
give up 2 units of clothing in order to produce 1
more unit of food.

Before trade, America will produce and
consume at a point on the production possibilities curve, such as B. With trade, America can
benefit by the following two steps.

1 Specialize. Shift production from B to C, as
shown by the red arrow. That is, produce 300
more units of food by giving up 600 million units
of clothing. Thus America concentrates on food,
the good in which it has a comparative advantage.

2 Trade. Trade these 300 million additional
units of food (at the 1:3 international price ratio)
for 900 million units of clothing. This second
step is shown by the gray arrow.

Wages and Trade

In our example, will wages be higher in America or Europe?

The answer is: In America, because labor is more productive here. (Remember, in Table 16-3 America has an absolute advantage in the production of both goods.) Because they can *produce* more goods, American workers can be *paid* "more goods," that is, a higher real wage. Moreover, Americans will have a higher real income whether or not the two countries trade. What trade and specialization make possible is an increase in real income in both countries. ■

As a result of this specialization and trade, America's consumption can rise from point B to point D. In other words, there are 300 more units of clothing available for consumption; this is America's *real income gain* (or efficiency gain) from trade.

In Figure 16-5a, we show that such a gain from trade exists even when opportunity costs are not constant; that is, in the more usual case when the production possibilities curve is not a straight line. This diagram also shows that, although trade induces a country to specialize, it will often not specialize completely: America moves from B to C, but not all the way to complete specialization at F. And one frequently observes this pattern: A country not only specializes in, and exports its product of comparative advantage—in this case, food. It also produces other goods as well—in this example, it produces *some* clothing at point C. (For details on why such a country will not specialize completely, see the caption to this diagram.)[5]

Comparative advantage thus leads to gains from trade. But why does comparative advantage exist? Why does America have a comparative advantage in wheat? One important reason is our large endowment of highly productive land, especially in the Midwest. Similarly, the reason that Saudi Arabia specializes in oil is its huge endowment of this resource. (As Figure 16-5 indicated, this is one of the most striking illustrations of how a nation's comparative advantage and trade are influenced by its resource endowment.) On the other hand, a country like India, with its huge pool of unskilled labor, tends to have a comparative advantage in activities that require a great deal of labor. Comparative advantage depends not only on such resource endowments, but also on skills and technology. For example, our highly developed technology gives us a comparative advantage in producing items such as computers and jumbo jets.

TRADE AND TECHNOLOGICAL CHANGE: THEIR SIMILARITIES

In Figure 16-5a we have seen that trade allows a country to consume at a point (such as D) that is

---

*[5]Figure 16-5a can also be used to show how demand too influences specialization and trade. (In this elementary treatment we have emphasized the other side of the coin: the importance of costs, as reflected in the production possibilities curve. But demand is important too.) Suppose there is an increase in both countries in the demand for food; as a consequence its price rises. Therefore, less food is needed to buy a given quantity of clothing. In other words, the trade arrow becomes steeper. Consequently it is no longer tangent to the production possibilities curve at point C, but instead at a point to the right, say G. G is therefore the best production point for this country. (The reason the point of tangency is best is given in the caption to Figure 16-5a.) Thus this country specializes even more, by moving from B not just to C, but to G. (And, of course, from point G, it trades up to the northwest along its new, steeper trade arrow.) To sum up: In response to increased demand, this country's production pattern changes; by producing even more food, it specializes to an even greater degree than before.

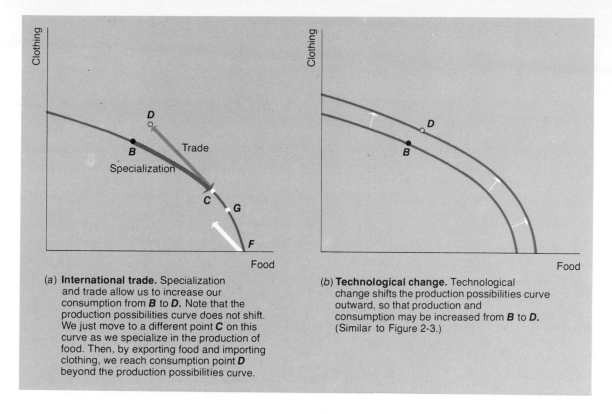

(a) **International trade.** Specialization and trade allow us to increase our consumption from **B** to **D**. Note that the production possibilities curve does not shift. We just move to a different point **C** on this curve as we specialize in the production of food. Then, by exporting food and importing clothing, we reach consumption point **D** beyond the production possibilities curve.

(b) **Technological change.** Technological change shifts the production possibilities curve outward, so that production and consumption may be increased from **B** to **D**. (Similar to Figure 2-3.)

Figure 16-5
Both trade and technological change allow us to increase consumption

(a) International trade. Specialization and trade allow us to increase our consumption from *B* to *D*. Note that the production possibilities curve does not shift. Instead we move to a different point *C* on this curve as we specialize in the production of food. Then, by trading food for clothing, we reach consumption point *D* beyond the production possibilities curve. (Why don't we specialize completely, by moving from *B* not just to *C*, but all the way to *F*? The answer is that we would then be trading along the white arrow, and this doesn't allow us to reach the high consumption point *D* that is achievable by specializing to *C* and trading along the gray arrow. For exactly the same reason that *F* is inferior to *C*, *any* other point on the production possibilities curve is also inferior to *C*. Therefore tangency point *C* is best.)

(b) Technological change. Technological change does shift the production possibilities curve outward, so that production and consumption may be increased from *B* to *D*. (Similar to Figure 2-3.)

beyond its production possibilities curve (PPC). True, *production* is always limited by the PPC, but consumption can be greater because of the gain from trade. In other words, international trade is the way for countries to break out of their production limitation and reach a point of consumption beyond it.

In panel *b* we see that technological change has the same effect of allowing us to move from point B to a higher point of consumption D. But it does so by shifting the production possibilities curve outward.

Trade and technological change are also alike in another significant respect. Though they generally provide a benefit to the nation as a whole, they do not necessarily benefit *every* group within the nation. Thus, there are often groups that object vehemently to trade or to technological change. For example, during the first period of rapid technological change in the textile industry about two centuries ago, workers feared that the new machinery being introduced would eliminate their jobs. (Some workers did indeed lose their jobs, even though machinery has ultimately made possible jobs with much higher productivity and pay.) This fear of job loss led some workers at that time to throw their wooden shoes (in French, *sabots*) into the machinery; hence, the word "sabotage" was coined. Similarly, international trade may displace textile workers, if production is shifted from textiles (where some markets have been lost to imports) to computers or jumbo jets (where we have a comparative advantage and export). Once again, those who are harmed may strongly object. In this case, they need not throw their shoes into the machinery; restrictions on imports are the way to seek protection. Thus, trade restrictions and sabotage are similar in one respect: Both prevent a general improvement in the standard of living in order to protect a specific group.

The temporary unemployment that follows either trade or technological change is a problem, but one that is frequently exaggerated. Workers displaced by technological change tend to be fairly quickly absorbed elsewhere, as are workers displaced by imports. This has been historically true in the United States. It has also been true in Europe, where the Common Market (the European Economic Community) has opened up trade among countries on a very large scale, but temporary unemployment has been less than expected.

While there are striking similarities between trade and technological change, there is an important difference. Technological change is permanent: Once the production possibilities curve shifts outward in Figure 16-5b, it doesn't shift back. In contrast, a trade gain is not necessarily permanent. If trade is sharply reduced (for example, because of the imposition of high tariffs) then most of the gains from trade are lost—that is, the country in panel *a* moves from *D* back toward point *B*.

THE VARIOUS EFFECTS OF INTERNATIONAL TRADE ON EFFICIENCY

While this analysis has illustrated the general case for trade, it is somewhat abstract since it lumps all American exports into a single food category and all imports into a single clothing category. Moreover, the only prices that exist are relative, barterlike prices. (For example, the price of 1 unit of food is 3 units of clothing.) Now, let us return to the more familiar world of supply and demand, where goods are sold for dollars. (For example, the price of a bushel of wheat may be $4.20.) Here, we shall no longer think in abstract terms of only two goods—a collective export (food) and a collective import (clothing). Instead, we examine one specific American export item (wheat) and one specific U.S. import item (woolens). In this more familiar frame of reference, we shall illustrate how trade increases efficiency.

Efficiency gain on a typical export: Wheat

Figure 16-6 shows the U.S. demand and supply curves for wheat. Without trade, equilibrium in the domestic market is at point *A*, where the nation's supply and demand intersect. Thus Q_A is produced at price P_A. At the same time, the price in the rest of the world is at the higher level *P*, reflecting the higher costs of producing wheat in foreign countries.

When trade is opened, U.S. producers discover that they can sell abroad at this higher price *P*, and they begin to do so. Moreover, since they can sell at *P* abroad, they will be unwilling to sell at any lower price in the home market. Thus the domestic price rises to the world level *P*.[6]

American producers, earning this more attractive price, expand their output. Specifically,

[6]More realistically, the American price rises to the foreign price, less transportation costs. But to keep this illustration simple, we assume that transport costs and other similar complications do not exist.

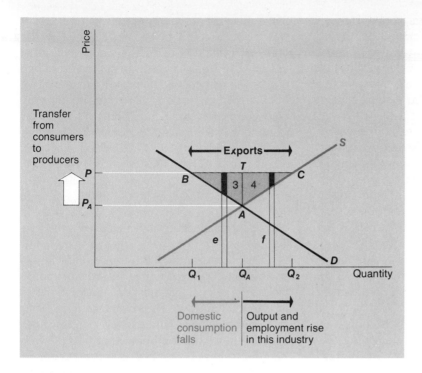

Figure 16-6
Detailed effects of the export of an individual good—wheat

With trade, price increases from P_A to P with Q_1Q_2 exported. Part of these exports come from reduced consumption (Q_1Q_A), with a typical unit shown as e. The consumer's valuation of this lost unit of consumption is shown as the hollow bar; the gain from exporting it instead is the export price P, that is, the hollow bar plus the solid bar. Thus the net gain on this unit is the solid bar, and the net gain on all such units of reduced consumption (in the range Q_1Q_A) is gray triangle 3. Exports also come from increased production (Q_AQ_2), with a typical unit shown as f. The cost of producing this unit is the hollow bar, while its benefit is the export price P, that is, the hollow bar plus the solid bar. Thus the net gain on this unit is the solid bar, and the net gain on all such units of increased production (in the range Q_AQ_2) is the gray triangle 4. Thus, the total efficiency gain from exporting is both these areas (3 + 4). But there is a transfer effect as well, shown by the white arrow on the left. Because price has risen, producers gain at consumers' expense.

they move up their supply curve from A to C, increasing their output from Q_A to Q_2. But, of course, consumers view this higher price quite differently. They move up their demand curve from A to B, thus reducing their consumption from Q_A to Q_1. In short, Q_2 is now produced and Q_1 is consumed, with the difference (Q_1Q_2) being exported. Thus, these U.S. exports come partly from increased production and partly from re-

duced domestic consumption. We now examine each of these effects in turn.

First consider one of the units of reduced consumption Q_1Q_A, say unit e. The consumer's valuation of this lost unit of consumption is shown as the hollow bar under the demand curve. (Recall that demand reflects marginal utility.) But the gain from exporting this unit is the export price P that is received for it, that is, the hollow bar plus the solid bar above. Hence, the net gain from exporting it, rather than consuming it, is the solid bar. The sum of all such solid bars throughout the relevant range Q_1Q_A is the gray triangle 3. This is the gain from switching goods from consumption to a more highly valued use, namely, export.

Next consider one of the units of increased production for export Q_AQ_2, say unit f. The cost of producing it is the hollow bar under the supply curve. (Recall that supply reflects marginal cost.) But the benefit from producing it is the export price P received for it, which is the hollow bar plus the solid bar. Therefore the net gain from producing it for export is the solid bar. The sum of all such solid bars through the relevant range Q_AQ_2 is represented by the gray triangle 4. This is the efficiency gain from expanding production for export.

The total gain from exporting is shown as the sum of both these effects; in other words, the total gray area in Figure 16-6. In simple terms, this gain indicates that wheat can be sold to foreigners for more than it costs to produce it, or more than is lost by switching it away from domestic consumption.

Of course, this gray area will represent an efficiency *loss* if producers are *not* allowed to export. It demonstrates that interference in a competitive world market may be damaging, in the same way that we have seen that interference in a competitive home market may be damaging.

Efficiency gain on a typical import: Woolens

A parallel analysis illustrates the gain from importing a specific item. Figure 16-7 shows the U.S. supply and demand curves for an import-competing product like woolens. Without trade, equilibrium in the domestic market is at point A, with price P_A and quantity Q_A produced and consumed. At the same time, the price in the rest of the world is at the lower level P, reflecting the lower costs of production there.

When trade is opened, U.S. consumers can buy imported woolens at this lower price P.

Since they will be unwilling to buy from American producers at a higher price (like P_A), the domestic price will fall to the world level P. At this lower price, U.S. consumers increase their purchases; they move down their demand curve from A to J, increasing their consumption from Q_A to Q_6. At the same time, domestic producers respond to lower price P by moving down their supply curve from A to H, thus reducing their output from Q_A to Q_5. In short, Q_5 is now produced in the United States, while Q_6 is consumed; the difference (Q_5Q_6) is the amount imported. Thus, U.S. imports result both in decreased production and increased consumption.

First, consider one of the units of decreased production Q_AQ_5, say unit j. The cost of importing it is the price P that must be paid for it, shown as the hollow bar. But because it is being imported, we save the cost of producing it ourselves, which is the hollow bar plus the solid bar (that is, its marginal cost as defined under the supply curve). Thus, the net gain from importing it, rather than producing it more expensively at home, is the solid bar. And the sum of all such solid bars over the relevant range Q_5Q_A is gray triangle 1. This is the gain from allowing imports to displace relatively inefficient, high-cost domestic production.

Now consider one of the units of increased consumption Q_AQ_6, say unit k. Its cost is the import price P shown by the hollow bar. But the consumer values it as the hollow bar plus the solid bar (its marginal utility defined under the demand curve). Therefore, the net benefit from this unit of increased consumption is the solid bar, and the sum of all such benefits is the gray triangle 2. This is the efficiency gain from allowing consumption to expand in response to a bargain international price.

The total efficiency gain on both accounts is the whole gray area in Figure 16-7. In simplest terms, this area shows that we can benefit by buying a low-cost import because it allows us to cut back our own inefficient, high-cost production; and it also allows us to increase our consumption of a bargain-priced good.

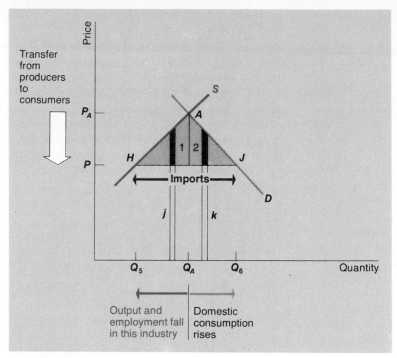

Figure 16-7
Detailed affects of the import of an individual good—woolens

With trade, price decreases from P_A to P, with HJ imported. This reduces home production by Q_AQ_5, with one such unit shown as j. The cost of importing it is the import price shown as the hollow bar. The cost saving because it is no longer produced at home is the hollow bar plus the solid bar. Thus the net benefit from importing it is the solid bar—and the benefit on all such units of reduced production (over the relevant range Q_AQ_5) is the gray triangle 1. Imports also result in increased consumption of Q_AQ_6, with a typical unit shown as k. The cost of acquiring it is the import price P, shown as the hollow bar; but it provides benefit (marginal utility) equal to the hollow bar plus the solid bar. Thus the net gain on this unit is the solid bar, and the net gain on all such units of increased consumption (in the range Q_AQ_6) is the gray triangle 2. Thus the total efficiency gain from importing this good is the entire gray area. But there is also a transfer effect, shown by the white arrow on the left. Because price has fallen, consumers gain at producers' expense.

HOW INTERNATIONAL TRADE ADVERSELY AFFECTS SOME GROUPS

While trade leads to an overall gain in efficiency, it is important to emphasize again that not all groups benefit. For example, in Figure 16-6, trade brings an increase in the price of wheat. As a result wheat farmers gain while consumers lose, with this transfer shown by the wide white arrow to the left of the diagram. (This is an important graphic device that will be used to show transfers throughout the rest of this book.)

On the other hand, the import in Figure 16-7 results in the opposite sort of transfer. Because it lowers price, consumers benefit while producers lose.

These benefits and losses to each group as a result of imports are shown more precisely in the alternative analysis set out in Figure 16-8.[7] Each

[7]Note to instructors: To a substantial degree, our analysis of transfer and efficiency effects in the balance of this book will be based on diagrams similar to Figure 16-7. But those who wish to supplement this with diagrams similar to Figure 16-8 will find several such diagrams in the Instructor's Manual.

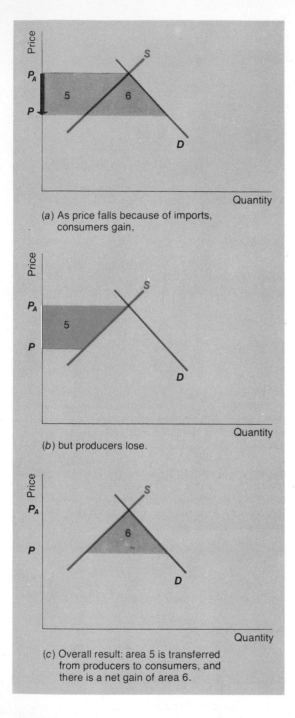

(a) As price falls because of imports, consumers gain,

(b) but producers lose.

(c) Overall result: area 5 is transferred from producers to consumers, and there is a net gain of area 6.

Figure 16-8
Detailed effects of an import of woolens. (An alternative to Figure 16-7)

panel in this diagram reproduces the U.S. supply and demand curves for woolens from Figure 16-7. The gain to the nation's consumers from a lower price is shown by the gray increase in consumer surplus in panel *a* (the area enclosed to the left of the demand curve). At the same time, producers are made worse off: They receive a lower price, and lose sales to imports. As a result, producer surplus is reduced by the red area in panel *b* (enclosed to the left of the supply curve).[8] Because this area 5 also appears as a gray gain in panel *a*, it is a transfer from the producers who lose it in panel *b* to the consumers who receive it in panel *a*. (This technique of identifying a transfer is important because it can be used on a wide variety of problems; for example, see Problem 16-8.) At the same time, area 6 in panel *a* is a gray gain *not* offset by a red loss. This net gain of area 6 is reproduced in panel *c*. This is, of course, exactly the same gray efficiency gain that first appeared in Figure 16-7.[9] (However, we repeat an earlier warning: In concluding that there will be an efficiency gain, we have assumed that the consumers' valuation of a $1 increase in income is roughly the same as the producers' valuation of a $1 reduction in income—or at least that they are sufficiently similar so that our conclusions are not upset.)

As a current example of how imports affect various groups in the United States, consider our imports of textiles from the Far East. The effect on American textile producers is clear. They are damaged because these imports depress the domestic price of textiles and reduce their sales.

[8]For a review of the basic idea of how consumer surplus changes as price changes, see Figure 8-5. For a similar review of how producer surplus changes (a concept we will also now be frequently using), see Figure 9-11.

[9]The method of Figure 16-8 can also be used to explain Figure 16-6 more fully. Specifically, as price rises in Figure 16-6:

    (*a*) Consumer surplus falls by $PBAP_A$.
    (*b*) Producer surplus rises by $PCAP_A$.
    (*c*) Thus, the net effects are a transfer of $PBAP_A$ from consumers to producers, and an efficiency gain of ABC.

At the same time, it is clear to American consumers that they benefit from a lower textile price. What is not always clear, however, is the net effect on the nation as a whole. But this analysis suggests that the overall effect is favorable, since the benefit to consumers more than offsets the loss to producers.

Finally, note that while output and employment fall in import-competing industries (Figure 16-7), they rise in export industries (Figure 16-6). When both these effects are taken into account, there is no reason to expect either a large increase or decrease in employment as a result of trade (although unemployment may rise during the adjustment period). We emphasize: The principal point of international trade—like technological change—is *not* to increase employment; it is to increase real income.

Key Points

1 In this chapter, a strong case has been made for international trade. (In the next chapter, we study the case for tariffs and other restraints on trade.)

2 There are three major sources of benefit from trade: *(a)* greater competition, *(b)* economies of scale, and *(c)* comparative advantage.

3 When trade is opened, countries specialize in certain products, increasing their output of these goods. If there are economies of scale, costs fall as a result of this increase in output.

4 Even if costs do not fall with rising output, trade will be beneficial if countries specialize in the goods in which they have a comparative advantage, that is, in those products in which they are relatively most efficient. We saw this not only in the Ricardian case where cost is constant, but also even in cases where cost (supply) rises as output increases (Figure 16-6).

5 Because trade lowers the prices of goods we import and raises the prices of goods we export, it hurts some while benefiting others. Consumers of imports benefit, while consumers of exported goods are harmed. (To some degree, but not completely, these are the same people, so that this transfer partly cancels out.) In addition, producers of exports benefit, while producers of import-competing goods are hurt.

6 International trade is similar in many respects to technological change. Both increase real income by allowing a nation to consume more: Trade allows a country to consume beyond its production possibilities curve, while technological change shifts the production possibilities curve out. Trade and technological change can cause the same sort of short-run unemployment until workers who have lost their jobs shift to new, more productive employment.

Key Concepts

specialization
increased competition
economies of scale
greater availability of
    products

absolute advantage
comparative advantage
opportunity cost
gain from trade
trade compared to
    technological change

exports: efficiency and
    transfer effects
imports: efficiency and
    transfer effects

Problems

16.1 "Foreign competition makes an industry more competitive." Should this result be viewed as an advantage or a disadvantage by *(a)* consumers of this good? *(b)* producers of the good? *(c)* the nation as a whole?

16-2 Suppose that the production of both X and Y involves economies of scale. Is it possible for both countries to benefit if Europe specializes in one and America specializes in the other? Explain your answer. Does this answer still hold if the cost curves for each good are identical in the two countries? (Hint: Review the discussion of economies of scale in Chapter 3.)

16-3 Return to Table 16-2, where costs are constant. *(a)* Change the "northwest" number 3 to 5. Does Europe now have an absolute advantage in either good? A comparative advantage in either? Draw a diagram like Figure 16-4 to show the potential American gain from trade (again assuming that there are 200 million workers in the United States and the international price ratio is 3:1). *(b)* Now change that same northwest number to 8. Which country now has a comparative advantage in food? In clothing? Are there potential gains from trade? Why or why not?

16-4 As a result of crop failures abroad in 1972–1973, world grain prices rose sharply, and, in response, U.S. grain exports increased. Consumers claimed that the resulting higher food prices in the United States were damaging to our economy, while producers claimed that they were beneficial. How would you evaluate these claims?

16-5 The following diagram shows the situation of Europe (the rest of the world) corresponding to the American situation in Figure 16-5a. Identify clearly:

(a) How Europe specializes when trade is opened.

(b) How Europe trades. Fill in details of how much of each good Europe exports or imports.

(c) Are there any lines or curves in this diagram that must be similar to those that appear in Figure 16-5a?

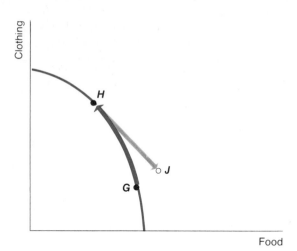

(d) Does Europe gain from trade? If so, how much?

16-6 "Economists say that international trade and technological change are similar—but they are wrong. Technological change increases our real income by making us more productive. Trade does not." Evaluate this statement.

16-7 (This problem looks ahead to Chapter 17.)

(a) Suppose that the United States and Europe become involved in a trade war, with each imposing such heavy restrictions on imports that trade between the two is eventually cut off altogether. Use Figure 16-5a and the diagram in Problem 16-5 to show the gains or losses each would suffer. Is a trade war a "zero-sum game" (what one country wins, the other loses)? Or is it like any other kind of war, with losses on both sides?

(b) Use two diagrams like Figures 16-6 and 16-7 to show in more detail how the United States would be affected by such a trade war.

***16-8** To see how the analysis of Figure 16-8 can be applied to an entirely different problem, consider the government price support policy for agriculture set out in Figure 16-8b.

(a) Use a series of colored diagrams like the panels in Figure 16-8 to show how the following

three groups benefit or lose: consumers; producers; U.S. taxpayers. (How much of the taxpayers' money does the Treasury pay out on the program?) By comparing these effects, indicate the transfers that take place, and in a final diagram, show the net, overall efficiency effect of this policy.

(b) Confirm this efficiency effect by noting how this policy affects output, and then applying the analysis of Figure 10-3.

CHAPTER 17
Tariffs and Other International Trade Issues

Protectionism is the institutionalization of economic failure.

**Former British Prime Minister
Edward Heath**

Despite the gains from trade explained in the previous chapter, no country follows a policy of completely free trade. Every nation restricts imports with trade barriers such as tariffs (taxes imposed on imported goods as they enter a country) or quotas (limits on the number of units that can be imported).

True, since the 1930s we have made great progress in reducing these trade restrictions. In the Kennedy Round of trade negotiations in the 1960s, the United States and other industrial countries cut their tariffs by about one-third. And, in the Tokyo Round agreement of 1979, these nations undertook to cut remaining tariffs by another third during the 1980s.

But negotiating trade barriers downward has been a long and arduous process. Despite these efforts, each country still retains substantial tariff and quota protection. There are two basic reasons: (1) Tariffs may be introduced for non-economic reasons. For example, a tariff may be imposed to protect an industry which might be essential to national defense in case of an emergency. (2) A country may restrict imports for special economic reasons, some of which are fallacious, but some of which may contain a kernel of truth.

NONECONOMIC EXPLANATIONS OF TARIFFS

The government may protect an industry for military or political reasons. Consider each objective in turn:

1 An industry may be essential for national defense

Two centuries ago, Adam Smith argued that national defense is an important goal. He maintained that, in pursuing this objective, we should be willing to protect our defense industries even if such protection involves an economic cost (that is, even if foreign countries have a comparative advantage in producing military supplies). This argument remains powerful more than 200 years later. Consider an extreme example: Even in the unlikely event that the Soviet Union agreed to sell us tanks more cheaply than we could produce them ourselves, we would not buy. Defense industries are considered essential.

(An important distinction can be made between consumer goods and weapons. Trade in consumer goods is mutually beneficial; both trading partners obtain more goods and therefore enjoy a higher standard of living. In the

336

military area, however, we cannot say, "the more weapons the better." Defense depends on a country's military strength *relative to* other countries. Indeed, if all countries have more weapons, we all may be worse off, not better off. Therefore, in the case of military equipment, no general case can be made that trade is beneficial.)

In protecting our defense industries, an important problem arises: Where do we draw the line? Do we protect just our military aircraft industry, or do we go one step beyond and protect our aluminum industry because it provides an input essential for military aircraft? Or do we take yet another step, and protect the textile industry, which produces military uniforms? Although the defense argument makes sense in some cases, it can be taken too far, since almost *every* industry makes *some* indirect contribution to national defense. (Furthermore, while we don't want to buy weapons from the Soviet Union, it does make sense to buy them from our allies—and sell other weapons to our allies as well: In this way, we can all gain economies of scale, which are generally very important in weapons production.)

2 People vote for their present jobs

Increased international trade means that some jobs are lost in industries whose sales fall because of competition from imports. But new jobs are created in export industries. The problem is that people are more concerned about the present jobs they may lose than the possibility of new jobs in an export industry. (After all, who knows for sure who will actually get these new export-based jobs?) So workers who don't want to take risks vote against increased trade; that is, they vote for the tariffs and other trade restrictions that protect their current jobs. Thus, too much attention may be paid to the employment that is lost from increased imports, and not enough to the employment that is gained from increased exports.

But even if we look only at imports, we remember from Figure 16-8 that the losses to producers from increased imports were more than offset by gains to consumers. By pointing this out, why can't a politician sell the idea of allowing imports in more freely?

The answer is that individuals tend to think and vote as producers, not consumers. To illustrate why, suppose that the import is shirts. There may be large benefits to consumers as a group from lower-priced shirts. But this gain is distributed widely among millions of purchasers, with each benefiting by such a small amount that nobody is likely to switch votes on this account. (Instead, consumers vote on issues which they view as more important.) On the producers' side, however, things are different. Here, fewer individuals are affected by increased shirt imports, but the effect on each individual—in both management and labor—is much more substantial. For people in this industry, the possible loss of a job will be important enough to determine how they vote; they become "one-issue" voters. In brief, producers vote for a tariff, while consumers scatter their votes around on a whole variety of issues, with only a few voting against the tariff. Therefore, the interest of consumers in free trade tends to be inadequately represented. (For a criticism of a policy that ignores the interests of consumers, see Box 17-1.)

A further reason that shirt producers may be able to exert strong political pressure is that they are not spread out all over the United States, as consumers are. Instead, they are concentrated in a few states or congressional districts. For members of Congress representing such districts, one very good way of getting political support may be to push for import restrictions on shirts. If they do, the shirt producers in these districts are likely to vote for them, while they will lose few votes of consumers. [Moreover, this is not just a political sleight-of-hand. From the narrow point of view of just the shirt-producing districts, duty-free imports of shirts may in fact be undesirable. The reason is that such districts bear much of the loss from duty-free imports (the red area in panel *b* of Figure 16-8). At the same time they receive little of the benefit (the gray area in panel *a*), because most consumers live elsewhere. So for these districts, losses from increased shirt imports exceed gains.] Thus, it is no great surprise if the members of Congress from shirt-

BOX 17-1

What Happens If the Consumer Is Forgotten: Bastiat's Negative Railway

The absurdity of ignoring the interests of the consumer has never been more eloquently stated than by the French economist Frederic Bastiat (1801–1850):†

It has been proposed that the railway from Paris to Madrid should have a break at Bordeaux, for if goods and passengers are forced to stop at that town, profits will accrue to bargemen, pedlars, commissionaires, hotel-keepers, etc. But if Bordeaux has a right to profit by a gap in the line of railway, and if such profit is considered in the public interest, then Angouleme, Poitiers, Tours, Orleans, nay, more, all the intermediate places, Ruffec, Chatellerault, etc., should also demand gaps, as being for the general interest. For the more these breaks in the line are multiplied, the greater will be the increase of consignments, commissions, transshipments, etc., along the whole extent of the railway. In this way, we shall succeed in having a line of railway composed of successive gaps, which we may call a Negative Railway. ■

†Abridged from Frederic Bastiat, *Economic Sophisms* (Edinburgh: Oliver and Boyd, Ltd., 1873), pp. 80–81.

producing districts go to Washington committed to restricting imports of shirts. And when they get there, they meet other members with similar problems: They too may be seeking protection for the goods produced in their own districts. The result is logrolling: The members from shirt-producing districts agree to vote to protect the products of other districts, in return for the promise of other members to vote for restrictions on shirt imports.

The result is continuous pressure in Congress for protection for industries that compete with imports. And when imports on a wide variety of goods are restricted, the shirt-producing district may well be damaged after all because of the higher prices of a wide range of imported goods. But the members from these districts may still be popular locally because they are remembered for their support for the protection of the shirt industry, rather than for their support for the protection of other goods.

Thus it is no surprise that some 200 years after the case for free trade was clearly stated by Adam Smith, protection still lives on. In fact, we might have even more severe trade restrictions except for two things: (1) Producers in export industries recognize their strong interest in international trade. Foreign countries are unlikely to buy our exports unless we buy imports from them. (2) The President is elected by all the people and carries a brief for the country as a whole. Most presidents in recent years have supported international initiatives to reduce tariffs.

ECONOMIC ARGUMENTS FOR PROTECTION

In an attempt to counter the strong case for international trade which dates back to Smith and Ricardo, advocates of protection have put forward a number of economic arguments. Some are fallacious, amounting to little more than weak rationalizations for protection, while others are stronger. The weakest arguments are considered first.

1 "Buy American because it keeps our money at home"

This argument is sometimes expanded to: "If I buy a transistor radio from Taiwan, I get the radio, and Taiwan gets the dollars. But when I buy a radio made in the United States, I get the radio and the dollars stay here." With a moment's reflection, we realize this argument can't be right because it applies to *all* of our imports. (It implies that we shouldn't be importing *anything,* and that is contradicted by the theory of comparative advantage.) Alternatively, we may show that it is wrong by noting that the Taiwanese do not work hard to produce radios for export merely for the joy of holding dollars. Like

you or me, they want to earn dollars to buy things. To a large extent, they use dollars to buy such things as machinery and food from us. In other words, when we import radios it is machinery and food that we give up, not dollars. Similarly, if we buy radios at home, we will *also* be giving up machinery and food. (Some of our own resources will have to be diverted from producing machinery and food to radios.) Which way of acquiring radios (from the Taiwanese or ourselves) will cost us less machinery and food? The answer was given in Chapter 16: Radios will cost us less—in terms of forgone machinery and food—if we buy them from the Taiwanese (provided, of course, that the Taiwanese have a comparative advantage in radios).[1]

This example has taught an important lesson. Whenever we encounter a theoretical argument for protecting a U.S. industry (such as radios) that superficially *seems* to be correct, ask yourself: Does it apply to *all* imports? If it does, then you can expect to find a logical fallacy in it somewhere.

2 "We can't compete with cheap foreign labor"

The reason wages are higher in America than in most foreign countries is that we are more productive. (Recall Box 16-1.) When we take into account both influences (our higher wages and our higher productivity) it does not necessarily follow that our costs are higher, and that we consequently cannot compete. True, we cannot compete with cheap labor in other countries in activities of their comparative advantage. But we can compete in activities of our comparative advantage, where our higher productivity more than offsets our higher wage. And this is where we should be concentrating. (On the argument that we will be unable to compete with foreign producers, see also Box 17-2.)

Foreign industries seeking protection from

---

[1]Chapter 18 in the companion volume discusses the situation where American expenditures in foreign countries are substantially greater or less than foreign expenditures in the United States. (In this case, our argument in this section is no longer so clear-cut; but it is still valid.)

The Petition of the Candlemakers

Sometimes the argument that we can't compete with cheap foreign labor appears in the slightly different form: "We can't compete with cheap foreign goods." This idea has never been more effectively criticized than by Frederic Bastiat over a hundred years ago. Here is his satirical description of an appeal by French candlemakers to the government to protect them from the free sunlight that was supposedly ruining their business:†

We are subjected to the intolerable competition of a foreign rival, who enjoys, it would seem, such superior facilities for the production of light, that he is enabled to inundate our national market at so exceedingly reduced a price, that, the moment he makes his appearance, he draws off all custom from us; and thus an important branch of French industry, with all its innumerable ramifications, is suddenly reduced to a state of complete stagnation. This rival is no other than the sun.

Our petition is, that it would please your honorable body to pass a law whereby shall be directed the shutting up of all windows, dormers, skylights, shutters, curtains, in a word, all openings, holes, chinks, and fissures through which the light of the sun is used to penetrate into our dwellings, to the prejudice of the profitable man-

ufactures which we flatter ourselves we have been enabled to bestow upon the country; which country cannot, therefore, without ingratitude, leave us now to struggle unprotected through so unequal a contest. . . .

Does it not argue the greatest inconsistency to check as you do the importation of coal, iron, cheese, and goods of foreign manufacture, merely because . . . their price *approaches zero,* while at the same time you freely admit, and without limitation, the light of the sun, whose price is during the whole day *at zero*?" ■

†Abridged from Frederic Bastiat, *Economic Sophisms,* pp. 56–60.

American goods sometimes turn this argument around as follows: "We can't compete with American labor, because it is more productive." Of course, the reply in this case is that, although U.S. labor productivity is higher, our wages are also higher. Thus, in many industries, our costs are not lower. True, other countries will not be able to compete in activities where our productivity is particularly great and where we consequently have a comparative advantage. But they can compete successfully in those other activities in which they enjoy a comparative advantage (that is, where their wage advantage exceeds our productivity advantage).

3 "Tariffs should be tailored to equalize costs at home and abroad"
This recommendation may sound plausible, but

it misses the whole point of international trade: *Gains from trade are based on cost differences between countries.* (It is to our advantage to import bananas or radios precisely because they can be produced more cheaply abroad than at home.) Eliminate cost differences and you eliminate the incentive to trade; and when you eliminate this, trade disappears. Thus, if we were to follow this recommendation, we would no longer be importing cheap bananas; instead we'd be producing them at home in greenhouses, with the costs of cheap imports from Central America being equalized by a high tariff. In other words, to the degree that we were successful in the (well-nigh impossible) task of tailoring tariffs to make costs precisely equal at home and abroad, we would lose the gains from trade we now enjoy. In a word: All that tailored tariffs would do is to strangle trade.

While these three arguments for tariffs are false, the following arguments do contain at least some element of truth.

4 "If we buy steel from Pittsburgh rather than from Japan, employment will rise in Pittsburgh rather than in Japan"

This statement may be true, particularly if there is large-scale unemployment in Pittsburgh. Why, then, does it not provide a very strong case for restricting trade, ranking in importance with the efficiency argument for free trade in the previous chapter? Why don't we use import restrictions to raise and maintain U.S. employment?

There are two problems with this suggestion. First, competition from imports may be one of the most effective ways of keeping an industry's price and wage level from rising rapidly. If the government becomes committed to providing an industry with whatever tariff it needs to protect it from losing sales and employment to foreign firms, what is to prevent the industry's price from rising rapidly, adding to inflation?

(This problem has recently been illustrated in the U.S. auto industry. By 1979, it was already losing sales to imports. Nevertheless, in the labor contract negotiated that year, it granted large wage increases—even though auto wages were already well above the average for U.S. manufacturing. The resulting increase in the price of cars was one of the reasons that the U.S. companies lost even more sales to imports. With large-scale unemployment among auto workers, the government was under great pressure to protect the industry. In 1981, the Japanese were persuaded to limit their auto exports to the United States. As a result, car prices rose even more. This raised the question: Why should other U.S. workers earning far lower wages be asked to subsidize autoworkers and auto companies by paying higher prices for cars?)

The second argument against restricting imports to raise employment is that our trading partners may retaliate by reducing their imports from us. To see why they might react in this way, suppose we restrict steel imports so that American purchases are switched from Japan to Pittsburgh. (This is often called a "beggar-my-neighbor" policy because we would be trying to solve our unemployment problem by shifting it to the Japanese.) In this case, the normal response of the Japanese may be to restrict their imports of *our* goods, and thus shift the unemployment problem back onto us.

In periods of worldwide recession, all countries are tempted to initiate a beggar-my-neighbor policy of increased protection; it is a tempting policy for them for exactly the same reason that it is a tempting policy for us. If all attempt to solve unemployment this way, the result will be a general disruption of trade. Unemployment may consequently rise, not fall. Thus, the increased U.S. protection from the Smoot-Hawley tariff of 1930 (combined with foreign retaliation) contributed to the worldwide depression. The Roosevelt administration undertook to reverse this destructive trend by pushing for the Reciprocal Trade Agreements Act, and by negotiating lower tariffs. (See Figure 17-1.)

If there is large-scale domestic unemployment, the cure should be sought in domestic monetary and fiscal policies (as discussed in Parts 2 and 3 of the companion volume), not in mutually destructive beggar-my-neighbor trade restrictions.

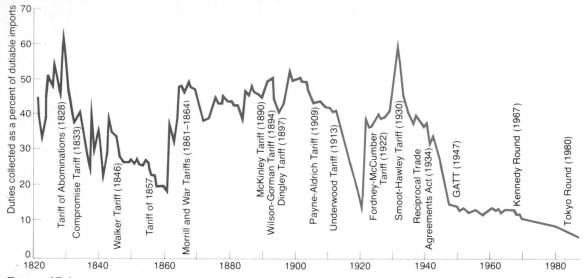

Figure 17-1
Average U.S. tariff rates

The United States has had high tariffs sometimes and low tariffs at other times. But since the 1930s, the trend has been down, so that now our tariffs average substantially less than 10 percent. Increasingly, the focus is on how non-tariff barriers restrict trade.
Source: Statistical Abstract of the United States.

5 "Restricting trade will diversify a nation's economy"

This is true; just as trade leads a country to specialize, restricting trade leads to the opposite: diversification. And isn't it a good thing for a country to diversify—to avoid putting all its eggs in one basket?

The answer is, perhaps. But for countries, like individuals, the risks from specialization are often more than offset by the gains. (The risk of a future oversupply of lawyers or doctors does not prevent individuals from taking up these specialized careers; their expected gains outweigh the risks they run.)

At the national level, an example of a high degree of specialization is Ghana's dependence on exports of cocoa, a product with a fluctuating price. It is true that Ghana's risks can be reduced by diversification. And diversification, in turn, may be encouraged by protecting new indus-

tries. But even for a country like Ghana, the argument must be balanced against the advantages of specialization—the gains from trade. Moreover, fluctuations in cocoa price work both ways: Whereas there is the risk that price may fall, there is also the possibility that price may rise. And in this case, the greater the degree of specialization, the greater the benefit. (Countries specializing in oil production have recently done exceptionally well.)

Finally, for an advanced industrial country like the United States, policies to diversify the economy are hard to justify: No matter how freely we may trade and specialize, our activities are still likely to remain remarkably diversified. The evidence is that we would not give up the production of a whole category of goods (like industrial products) to concentrate on another (like agricultural products). Indeed, it would be unlikely that we would give up even one industry (say sporting goods) in order to specialize in another (electrical machinery). Instead, the evidence suggests that trade leads to specialization in *certain kinds* of sporting goods, and *certain kinds* of electrical machinery. For large industrial countries, trade has not generally resulted in a narrow range of production activities.

6 "We need to protect our infant industries"

The basic idea here is this: A country may not be able to compete with other nations in an industry with economies of scale until this industry is well established and operating at high volume and low cost. This may be true even in an industry where the country will eventually have a comparative advantage and be able to produce very cheaply. This raises a question: Shouldn't such an industry be protected, so that it won't be wiped out by tough foreign competition during the delicate period of its infancy?

Although this line of reasoning is logically valid, it raises two practical questions: (1) How do you know that the only advantage of the foreign countries is that their industry is already established? For example, if a country is thinking of protecting an infant watch industry, how does it know that the only advantage of the Swiss and Japanese is that their industry is already established? Maybe they enjoy some basic advantage in watchmaking. If so, a watchmaking industry established elsewhere may never be able to compete. (2) When does an infant subsidy become an old-age pension? Industries that ask for protection as infants never seem to grow up, but instead become forever dependent on their tariffs. Such industries can become a real problem. Once established, they employ many people who vote; thus protection continues to go to them, rather than to the real infants who have not yet hired a large enough labor force to give them voting clout.[2]

7 "Restricting imports may reduce the price we have to pay for them"

This argument applies to goods in which the United States purchases a large amount of the world's supply. The idea is this: If the U.S. government imposes a tariff or some other trade restriction on such a good, say coffee, this reduces U.S. consumption of coffee. With U.S. imports falling, the world price of coffee falls. (There is less demand for coffee on the international market.) Thus, by restricting this import, the United States is able to acquire coffee at a more favorable price.[3] (Technically, this is sometimes referred to as *improving our terms of trade,* that is, reducing the number of units of exports we must give up in order to acquire a unit of imports.)

While the United States is a large enough purchaser to affect world price by such a restriction on its imports, this policy has limited applicability. Its strongest applicability is in the case of oil: A substantial cutback in U.S. import purchases from OPEC would tend to keep down the rate of increase in the world price of oil. However, in dealing with many of our other trading partners, such a policy of restricting our imports is unlikely to succeed. The reason is that they, like the United States, are large enough buyers in world markets that they too can play the same game. For example, if we restrict our imports from Europe to reduce their price, the natural reaction of the Europeans would be to restrict their purchases from us, thus driving down the price of *our* exports. With the price of both our imports *and* exports depressed, it is far from clear that on balance, we would benefit. The principal effect may be to reduce the volume of trade, with both ourselves and the Europeans being losers.

8 "Restricting imports reduces our vulnerability to a cut-off in foreign supplies"

Serious dislocations may occur if we become highly dependent on an import whose supply is suddenly reduced or cut off. For example, without imported oil, U.S. industry (not to mention

---

[2]A third practical question is this: If the industry will eventually be profitable, why shouldn't its owners cover any initial losses out of their future profits? (The answer may be that they are unable to raise the capital necessary to get them through the initial period of losses.)

[3]Although the United States as a nation pays a lower price to, say, Brazil, the price paid by individual U.S. buyers *rises*— because they must not only pay for the coffee, but also the tariff that goes to the U.S. government. (It is in response to this higher price they face, that individual U.S. buyers reduce their coffee purchases.)

U.S. auto owners) would face severe adjustment problems. One way of reducing this risk is to restrict oil imports so that we become less dependent on them. We return to a more detailed discussion of this policy later; but for now we note that it is difficult to make a similar case for restricting imports of other goods. The adverse effects of a supply disruption would be less severe, and supply disruptions would generally be less likely than for oil, where production is concentrated in the politically unstable Middle East. For example, in the extremely unlikely event that our textile imports from Asia were to be cut off, we could buy from Europe, or produce more textiles at home. Or we could rather easily cut back on our purchases, using our existing clothing longer. (In contrast, it is very difficult to reduce our consumption of oil quickly.)

Free trade versus protection: A summary

This discussion shows that we should never judge an issue by adding up the number of arguments for and against it. There are only a few arguments for free trade, but they are very impressive. A reduction in trade barriers:

- increases competition in our domestic market
- provides consumers with a wider selection of goods
- generates gains because of comparative advantage and economies of scale

Thus, it raises our standard of living.

On the other hand, there are many arguments for protection. But in summing them up, we first note that some are downright illogical. Moreover, even those that do have some element of truth (arguments 4 to 8 on the previous pages) don't provide a very strong case for U.S. protection—except perhaps in the special case of oil (to be studied in Chapter 22). The principal explanation for tariffs is not economic, but political: In the political process, producers' interests are generally given greater weight than consumers' interests.

THE DEVELOPMENT OF TRADE POLICY IN THE UNITED STATES AND ELSEWHERE

Figure 17-1 illustrates how U.S. tariff policy has changed in the past. Historically, liberalizing our trade has been a story of "two steps forward and one back." However, more or less steady progress has been made since the Smoot-Hawley Tariff raised U.S. protection to a peak during the Depression. In 1934, the Reciprocal Trade Agreements Act provided for **bilateral** (two-way) negotiations in which the United States and one other country would bargain down their tariffs against each other. Then, in 1947, the United States and 22 other nations signed the General Agreement on Tariffs and Trade (GATT). This was based on the idea of **multilateral** negotiations in which all participating countries would lower their tariffs. Since 1947, U.S. policy has, by and large, been to concentrate on this multilateral approach and to bargain down tariffs in GATT. (An important exception was the bilateral 1965 Auto Pact, in which the United States and Canada agreed to eliminate auto tariffs against each other.)

The European Economic Community (EEC)

In the late 1950s, the European Economic Community (EEC) was formed. Germany, France, Italy, Holland, Belgium, and Luxembourg (later joined by Britain and several other countries) agreed to form a common market by (1) introducing tariff-free trade among all participating nations; (2) imposing a common tariff against goods coming into the EEC from other countries; and (3) introducing other measures of economic coordination, such as a common policy of agricultural price supports.

One of the reasons for the formation of the EEC was that the member countries eventually wanted to move some distance toward political union. But they also had a strong economic motive: to gain the benefits of freer trade among themselves. Since its formation, the EEC countries have made substantial economic progress, although it is difficult to assess how much has been due to the formation of the EEC, and how much has been due to other influences. It is also difficult to assess how the EEC has affected outside countries like the United States. On the one hand, by inducing more rapid European growth, it has made Europe a better potential customer for U.S. exports. On the other hand, because the United States is not an EEC member, American firms now face the special problem of being outsiders in competing in the European market. (For example, before the EEC, American and German firms faced the same tariff barriers in selling in the French market. But since the EEC has been formed, U.S. firms still face a tariff when going into the French market. But competing German firms do not.)

The Kennedy and Tokyo Rounds of trade negotiations

By the early 1960s, there were several good reasons for the United States to promote the idea of reducing tariffs through a new "round" of multilateral negotiations. By reducing all tariffs (and in particular, the U.S. tariff and the new common European tariff) such a move would (1) reduce the U.S. problem of being an outsider in its trade with Europe; (2) promote closer political ties with Europe; and (3) provide the familiar gains from freer trade to all participants. The result of this initiative was the Kennedy Round of trade negotiations which, as we have already noted, resulted in the 1967 agreement to reduce existing tariffs on average by about 35 percent.

However, following this major success, the countries involved began to slide back into increasing protection. To counter this, and to achieve a further move toward freeing trade, there was a new set of negotiations during the 1970s—the Tokyo Round. This led to the 1979 treaty that is designed to cut tariffs, on average, by about one third in a series of steps during the 1980s. This treaty will also provide the industrialized countries with tariff-free trade in civilian aircraft. Moreover, it sets out new "codes" (regulations) to reduce—or at least limit—the growth of non-tariff barriers to trade.

Non-tariff barriers (NTBs)

The most familiar type of non-tariff barrier (NTB) is a quota that limits the quantity of a good that can be imported. (The Appendix shows why a quota may have many of the same effects as a tariff.) There are also many other, more subtle NTBs. For example, a country may impose complex and costly customs procedures or quality standards that deter imports. Or, it may have stiff health standards that must be met by imports. A health restriction may be justified: The gains to our health from such high standards may be worth the cost of reducing foreign imports. Nonetheless, a nagging question remains: Are such standards really being imposed to protect health? Or is their major purpose to protect domestic industries?

Another common NTB has been the preference granted by governments to domestic suppliers. Under the *Buy American* policy, for example, government purchasing agencies gave domestic suppliers a preference of at least 6 percent over foreign firms. (For products from labor surplus areas, the preference was 12 percent.) Foreign governments also gave preferences to their domestic producers when purchasing supplies. One of the major features of the Tokyo Round agreement was a reduction in this particular NTB.

As a result of this agreement, the United States at the beginning of 1981 waived the *Buy American Act* for most goods. At the same time, other countries signing the agreement—including such major trading partners as Canada, France, and Japan—likewise waived their preferences for domestic producers. (In particular, the large Buy Japanese preferences of the Japanese national telephone company were waived.)

THE MULTINATIONAL CORPORATION (MNC)

No discussion of trade would be complete without a description of two important developments—the growth of the multinational corporation and recent rapid changes in technology. (For more on technology, see Box 17-3.)

BOX 17-3
Changing Technology in the International Economy

Rapid technological change has complicated the traditional free-trade versus protection argument in the following way: In a stable, static world the most profitable course for a country is to concentrate on its comparative advantage. But in a world of rapid technological change, comparative advantage keeps changing. As a country switches from industry to industry in pursuit of its comparative advantage, the benefits of specialization may be eaten up by recurring turnaround costs (in the form of installing equipment and retraining labor in new industries).

After the Second World War, this argument was used to explain why some countries doubted their ability to benefit from growing trade with the technological leader, the United States. A simple analogy will illustrate: A rich and innovative man hires someone to fix his car, and pays well for the job. But as soon as the employee has bought the necessary tools and mastered the job, the rich man announces he has discovered a brilliant way to do it himself. Now he wants the employee to look after the electrical system in his house. As soon as the employee masters this, the rich man announces that he has invented a completely automatic, trouble-free electrical system so he can shift the employee into some other activity.

Throughout this process, the employee's wage may rise rapidly, since it is very profitable to be associated with a man of such wealth and genius. But the employee still faces problems. First, he is spending a lot of money in tooling up for new jobs, and is exhausting himself in learning how to handle them. Second, he may begin to wonder: "Given my employer's genius at replacing me, where will this all end? Will I eventually be shining his shoes for $50,000 a year?" So the employee begins to ask whether it would not be better to opt out of this game, even though quitting would mean a loss of income.

This sort of example was used to illustrate a problem faced by our trading partners. They agreed that free trade with us might maximize their income. But our rapid technological progress meant that their activities of comparative advantage were constantly changing, and made some of their economists wonder: "Is the real income gain from trade worth the turnaround costs? And who wants to be a fifth wheel anyway?"

This argument has recently become far less compelling because our trading partners (especially Germany and Japan) have reduced the technological gap and, in some activities, have taken the lead. Instead, the argument now appears in somewhat different form, as follows: With the development of the international economy, any technological change that occurs in one country can be copied, within a brief period, by producers in another country. An American innovation may give us a comparative advantage in a certain good, but it will last only until the production of this good is copied in some other country with lower labor costs. At this point, the United States moves on to producing and exporting another good in which it has made an even more recent technological breakthrough. Thus the comparative advantage of the United States is in technologically advanced activities, and these keep changing. Notice that this new interpretation focuses on the heavy turnaround costs incurred by the technologically advanced country. To return to our earlier analogy: The Europeans and Japanese have not, as they might have feared, ended up shining our shoes. Instead, they began by producing clothing and radios. But now they have moved up into producing cars and TVs, leaving clothing and radios for the new emerging industry in less developed places like Taiwan and Hong Kong. ■

Multinational corporations (MNCs) are firms with their head office in one country and subsidiaries in other countries. For example, Ford produces cars not only in the United States, but also in subsidiary companies in Britain, Germany, and other countries. Other countries have their multinationals too, like Royal Dutch Shell (owned principally by the Dutch and British).

Why does an American company become multinational? The traditional answer is that some firms go abroad to develop a source of a necessary raw material. But there are other important reasons as well. Once an American firm has developed a new product for the domestic market at great research and development (R&D) costs, it will want to sell the product worldwide. (By selling abroad, it will reduce the R&D costs per unit.) Moreover, an American company that has decided to sell its product in, say, Europe may also decide to produce it there, if this is cheaper than producing it in the United States and paying the shipping costs (including both the transatlantic transport cost and any European tariff).

Alternatively, U.S. firms may go abroad in search of lower wages: For example, they may go to Korea or Taiwan to produce goods requiring a great deal of labor. This has recently led American labor to complain that the multinationals are "exporting American jobs." In particular, labor has asked: "Why should the MNCs be allowed to transfer their technological know-how abroad, especially when much of it has been developed with the assistance of government funds provided by U.S. taxpayers?" This issue has become even more sensitive because of the recent tendency of U.S. MNCs to transfer more of their up-to-date technology to their foreign subsidiaries. Critics claim that this makes it easier for competing foreign-owned firms to copy this technology.

Multinational companies reply that you can't stop foreign competitors from copying your products. You can't prevent the spread of new technology. The most you can hope for, by keeping your technology "at home," is to prolong the normal "copying time"—but not by much.[4] You can't prevent these goods from eventually being copied and produced in low-wage countries. And if U.S. firms don't have subsidiaries there that do it, then the profits of Americans who own shares in these firms will be needlessly reduced. Furthermore, the technology which foreign countries gain from U.S. subsidiaries may be the best way to help these countries—better, say, than official assistance. Finally, foreign subsidiaries of U.S. firms create jobs in the United States. For example, auto engines, transmissions, and other parts are produced in the United States for export to General Motors' subsidiary that assembles cars in Canada. (About one-fourth of United States exports are such shipments by American firms to their foreign subsidiaries.)

Because of the resources which MNCs have at their disposal to set up new factories, they may make it easier for countries to get established quickly in their activities of comparative advantage. In other words, by making specialization easier, MNCs help increase world income.

However, the growth of multinational corporations has raised problems, mostly for the host countries in which the MNCs have established subsidiaries. For example, there is some concern that a large multinational may be able to acquire monopoly power in the host country's market. (On the other hand, the entry of a multinational may *reduce* the market power of an existing *domestic* monopolist.) Host countries are also concerned that they may become too dependent on foreign technology, and that their political independence may be eroded. For example, it is often felt that many of the most important decisions for a host country are not made there at all, but are instead made in foreign head offices. Furthermore, it is more difficult for

---

[4]Edwin Mansfield and Anthony Romeo (in "Technology Transfer to Overseas Subsidiaries by U.S.-based Firms," *Quarterly Journal of Economics,* December 1980, pp. 737–750) provide evidence that the transfer of technology to U.S. subsidiaries abroad may have substantially affected the length of this copying lag in some industries; but in most industries, it has not.

a host country's government to deal with a MNC than a domestic firm, because the MNC can more easily exercise the option of simply leaving the country to produce somewhere else. Finally, the image of multinationals has not been improved by the behavior of companies like Lock-heed. In an attempt to secure foreign defense contracts, Lockheed made payments to a number of politically influential people abroad. (No less than a former Japanese prime minister and a prominent member of the Dutch royal family were touched by this scandal.)

Key Points

1 Trade restrictions, such as tariffs or quotas, result in a loss of efficiency. (The gains from trade, discussed in Chapter 16, are eroded as trade is reduced.)

2 Trade restrictions on a good also transfer income from consumers to producers. One reason why countries have trade restrictions is that producers generally have more political power than consumers.

3 While many statements on the long list of economic arguments for protection are fallacious, some have a degree of merit. A less developed country, now exporting only a natural resource, may protect a domestic industry in order to diversify its economy, thus reducing its economic risks. An even stronger case can be made if that industry is a "promising infant," that is, an industry that will have a comparative advantage if only it can be firmly established. (The problem is, however, that such infant support frequently becomes an old-age pension.)

4 The United States, as a large buyer, might impose a tariff to reduce the world price of a good we buy (the "terms-of-trade" argument). But because other countries are likely to retaliate by imposing their tariffs on *our* goods, this is not a very strong argument for protection except, perhaps, in the special case of oil.

5 The same risk of foreign retaliation arises if we impose a tariff to try to cure a U.S. unemployment problem. Since this tariff would simply shift our unemployment problem onto our trading partners, their likely reaction would be to impose their own tariffs, thus shifting the unemployment problem back onto us—in particular onto our export industries.

6 Multinational corporations transmit new technology across national borders. Because of their ability to set up new plants quickly, they may make it easier for countries to find their activities of comparative advantage. For example, they often allocate labor-intensive activities to low-wage countries.

7 This in turn has led multinational corporations into conflict with U.S. unions that have accused them of exporting jobs. MNCs have also been criticized by host countries in which their subsidiaries are located. To illustrate: There is frequently political resentment that important economic decisions for host countries may not be made there at all, but instead in some head office located in a foreign country.

Key Concepts

tariff
quota
military argument for
   protection
political reason why
   protection continues

a tailored tariff
beggar-my-neighbor policy
diversification versus
   specialization
infant industry protection

protection to improve
   terms of trade
tariff retaliation
bilateral versus
   multilateral negotiations

General Agreement on
   Tariffs and Trade (GATT)
European Economic
   Community (EEC)

the Kennedy Round
the Tokyo Round
non-tariff barriers

Buy American
the multinational
   corporation (MNC)
subsidiary

Problems

17-1 In 1980, exports were equal to about 8.5 percent of U.S. GNP. They are more important for a number of other countries where they account for even higher proportions of GNP (over 20 percent in Great Britain, Sweden, and Canada).

Do you think the relatively low American percentage makes trade unimportant for the United States?

Which of these four countries trades most in *absolute* terms?

If the United States were, like Europe, split up into several countries, what would happen to the export/GNP ratio of each of these new countries?

*17-2 "The higher the tariff on an import, the more revenue the government collects." Is this statement true or not? Explain.

17-3 "Advertisers can try to persuade consumers to buy a good; but they cannot force them to buy. However, trade barriers involve the coercive power of the state: They can force consumers to buy the domestic product rather than the foreign product (unless the buyers are willing to do without altogether). Therefore, if we wish to protect the sovereignty of the consumer, trade barriers are a greater danger than advertising." Evaluate this statement.

17-4 Explain to what extent you agree or disagree with the following quotation: "Consumers not only fail to vote in their economic interest. Worse yet, they often don't even understand what their economic interest is. For example, consumers often react automatically to patriotic appeals like 'Buy American,' rather than ask critical questions like: 'Does the firm that is asking me to do this really have patriotic motives, or is it just trying to sell me an overpriced product?'"

*17-5 (a) Following Figure 16-8, show the effect of a "prohibitive" U.S. tariff that completely eliminates our import of a good.

(b) Using a similar diagram, explain the effects of a foreign tariff that prevents us from exporting a good.

(c) What are the effects if *we* prohibit our exports of this good? Why, then, might our government impose such a restriction? (In the face of rapidly rising world prices of soybeans in the early 1970s, we did indeed limit our exports of this good.)

*17-6 "Transport costs are like tariffs. Both deter trade. If either were reduced, countries would reap increased benefits from trade. Raising tariffs is much the same as going back to shipping goods in old, expensive clipper ships."

Do you agree? Why or why not? (Hint: Don't forget that the government collects revenues from tariffs.)

17-7 Do you think it would pay Australian cement manufacturers to spend a lot of money to promote a tariff on cement? Why?

APPENDIX

THE EFFECTS OF A TARIFF OR QUOTA
THAT REDUCES IMPORTS

Effects of a tariff

Typically, a U.S. tariff will not end our import of a good [as in Problem 17-5(a)], but will only reduce it. In Figure 17-2, we consider this case, looking at a situation where the world price remains unchanged in the face of a tariff. (That is, we assume that there are no terms-of-trade effects.)

Point A is the "no-trade" equilibrium while J is the free-trade equilibrium, with imports HJ. Now suppose that we impose a tariff t that reduces but does not eliminate this trade. In this case we would (correctly) expect an equilibrium somewhere between A and J, at a point like K. Thus, our tariff t raises price from the free-trade level P_W to P_t, shifts our equilibrium from J to K, and reduces our imports from the free-trade level HJ to RK.

The effects on all parties concerned are shown in panels b, c, and d. As the U.S. price rises from P_W to P_t, consumer surplus is reduced by the red area enclosed to the left of the demand curve in panel b, while producers benefit from an increase in producer surplus (the gray area 3 enclosed to the left of the supply curve in panel c). But now there is another effect, not encountered before, that is shown as area 4. This is the benefit to U.S. taxpayers because the U.S. Treasury is now collecting tariff revenue. (A tariff t, equal to RF, is collected on each of the RK units imported—for a total revenue of area 4.)

Since the two gray benefits in panel c also appear as red losses in panel b, they are transfers. Specifically, area 4 is the transfer from consumers (who pay more) to the Treasury (that collects the duty) while area 3 is a transfer from consumers to producers. But some of the red loss in panel b is not canceled out by gray gains in panel c. This balance is the net efficiency loss to society, shown as the two red triangles in panel d.[5] We conclude that a tariff results in these efficiency losses and a transfer from consumers to producers. Moreover, when a tariff only reduces (rather than eliminates) an import, there is another transfer as well—from consumers to taxpayers.

Effects of a quota

Trade may be restricted by a tariff or by a non-tariff barrier (NTB) like a quota. Such a restriction limits the number of units of a good that can be imported, and has many effects similar to a tariff. For example, in Figure 17-2a we saw that a tariff t raised price

---

[5]These two efficiency effects are marked 1 and 2 because they correspond to the two triangular efficiency effects first encountered in Figure 16-7. (We use red here to show the efficiency *losses* when trade is restricted. In earlier Figure 16-7, trade was being opened up, and the resulting *gains* were shown in gray. As an exercise, you should be able to confirm that triangle 1 in Figure 17-2d is the efficiency loss that results because inexpensive imports have been replaced by higher-cost domestic production, while triangle 2 is the efficiency loss that results because consumers have been prevented from purchasing this good at the lowest possible price.)

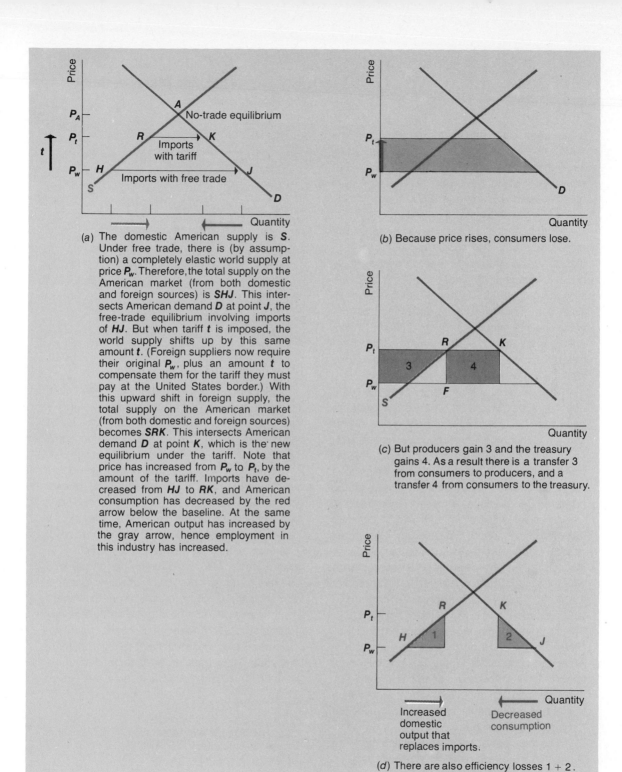

(a) The domestic American supply is **S**. Under free trade, there is (by assumption) a completely elastic world supply at price P_w. Therefore, the total supply on the American market (from both domestic and foreign sources) is **SHJ**. This intersects American demand **D** at point **J**, the free-trade equilibrium involving imports of **HJ**. But when tariff **t** is imposed, the world supply shifts up by this same amount **t**. (Foreign suppliers now require their original P_w, plus an amount **t** to compensate them for the tariff they must pay at the United States border.) With this upward shift in foreign supply, the total supply on the American market (from both domestic and foreign sources) becomes **SRK**. This intersects American demand **D** at point **K**, which is the new equilibrium under the tariff. Note that price has increased from P_w to P_t, by the amount of the tariff. Imports have decreased from **HJ** to **RK**, and American consumption has decreased by the red arrow below the baseline. At the same time, American output has increased by the gray arrow, hence employment in this industry has increased.

(b) Because price rises, consumers lose.

(c) But producers gain 3 and the treasury gains 4. As a result there is a transfer 3 from consumers to producers, and a transfer 4 from consumers to the treasury.

(d) There are also efficiency losses 1 + 2.

Figure 17-2 Effects of a tariff

BOX 17-4

Estimated Cost to the United States of Protecting Raw Sugar

It has been estimated that in 1970, under free trade, Americans could have purchased raw sugar in the world market at $110 a ton, and that equilibrium would have been at *J*. This would have involved U.S. imports of *HJ*, that is, 11.6 − 2.9 = 8.7 million tons.

But, because of an import quota of 5.2 million tons the total supply curve in the U.S. market was shifted to *S'* (the domestic supply curve *S* plus imports limited to 5.2 million tons). This intersected U.S. demand at equilibrium *K*. Thus, the quota not only reduced imports from *HJ* to the 5.2 million ton quota limit *RK*. It also raised price by $51 (that is, from the $110 free-trade level to $161). Thus the import quota was the equivalent of a $51 tariff.

Now let's see how various groups were affected. Area 3 was a $227-million transfer from consumers who were damaged by the higher sugar price to American producers who benefited from it. But because it was only a transfer from one American group to another, it was not a loss to the United States. The other three areas, however, did represent American losses. Area 1 was an efficiency loss of $79 million because low-cost imports were displaced by higher cost domestic production. Area 2 was an efficiency loss of $10 million because U.S. consumption was restricted: Sugar could not be purchased at the $110 world price by American consumers who valued it above $110 (but below $161). Finally, area 4 was also a loss to the United States—a $265-million transfer of income from American consumers to the foreign holders of import rights. (American consumers paid $51 more per ton for imported sugar, and foreign holders of quota rights received $51 more per ton for this same sugar.)

The total loss to the United States therefore was areas 1 + 2 + 4 = $79 million + $10 million

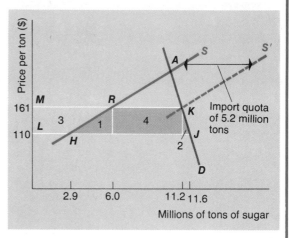

+ $265 million = $354 million.† Note in this case how the two efficiency losses were relatively small compared to the $265 million transfer of income from U.S. consumers to foreign quota holders.

Finally, suppose that the United States had not imposed this quota of *RK*, but had, instead, levied a $51 tariff. These two policies would have been equivalent in the sense that they would both have led to equilibrium at *K*, with imports of *RK*. Moreover, under either policy, effects 1, 2, and 3 would also have been the same. The difference would have been effect 4: Under a tariff, this $265 million transfer from the American consumer would have gone as tariff collections to the U.S. Treasury (and, hence, would not have been a loss to the United States). But under the quota, this transfer went to foreign quota holders, and hence *was* a loss to the United States.

†These estimates are from Ilse Mintz, *U.S. Import Quotas, Costs and Consequences* (Washington: American Enterprise Institute for Public Policy Research, February 1973).

In 1974 this quota was replaced by a tariff which you can visualize in the same diagram.‡ By 1978 it had become more restrictive than the 1970 quota, that is, it was raising the U.S. price from *L* to *above M*. Consequently, producers were receiving more protection, and the transfer (3) they were receiving from consumers was even greater. So too were efficiency losses 1 and 2. However, because the trade restriction was a tariff rather than a quota, area 4 was no longer a red loss to the United States. (Instead it was only a domestic transfer from U.S. consumers to the U.S. Treasury.)

The Federal Trade Commission has estimated the cost of this tariff to the United States as $365 million in 1978.§ ∎

‡President Ford reintroduced a quota in 1975, but it was so large that it was completely ineffective—a mere formality to prevent an increase in the tariff. In 1977 President Carter refused to reduce this quota to a level that would be effective. Thus in the late 1970s the quota could be ignored; the only effective restraint was the tariff.

§This figure, together with other more detailed estimates of the effects of this tariff, is given in M.E. Morkre and D. G. Tarr, *"Staff Report on Effects of Restrictions on U.S. Imports,"* Federal Trade Commission, June 1980, Chapter 6.

in the U.S. market from P_W to P_t, and thus reduced imports from *HJ* to *RK*. An equivalent, even more direct way of reducing imports by the same amount would be simply to ban any imports in excess of *RK*; in other words, impose a quota limit of *RK*. If we do this, the new equilibrium will again be at the same point *K*, just as it was with the tariff.

Therefore a quota of *RK* is sometimes referred to as the "quota equivalent of tariff *t*."[6] It leads to the same inefficiency in resource allocation as tariff *t*. Specifically, it raises price in the U.S. market, and so induces high-cost domestic production and decreased consumption. But there is one big difference. With a tariff, the higher price the consumer pays for imports goes to the U.S. Treasury in the form of the duty it collects (area 4 in Figure 17-2c). But *with a quota, no such revenues are collected.* Therefore this amount goes not to the Treasury, but instead to whomever is lucky enough to acquire the quota right to import [that is, to whomever is able to profit by (1) acquiring this good on the world market at cost P_W, then (2) shipping it into the United States, and then (3) selling it there at price P_t]. If these rights, or import licenses, are granted by the U.S. government to American importers, this windfall income 4 goes to the importers rather than to the Treasury. But if the quota rights somehow end up in the hands of the foreign firms that sell this good in the United States market, *this income goes to them rather than to the U.S. Treasury.* Consequently, this is a loss to the United States,[7] and this sort of quota becomes a much more

[6]Figure 17-2, with its demand and supply curves, assumes perfect competition. Tariffs and quotas are not so easily compared when competition is imperfect.

[7]One solution to ensure against this loss would be for the U.S. government to auction off these quota rights. Since the total revenue raised by the U.S. Treasury from this sale would be roughly area 4, such a quota would have effects similar to those of the tariff in Figure 17-2.

BOX 17-5
In Hong Kong, an Export Quota Is a Valuable Asset

In Hong Kong, there is a thriving market for the quota rights to export clothing to the United States. By the late 1970s, these rights were selling for about 10 percent of the value of the clothing. For example, the Hong Kong price for a quota to sell a sweater in the United States was about $1.50. Some Hong Kong exporters with large quotas found that it was more profitable to sell the quota rights than to produce the goods. So they closed down their factories and lived off the proceeds from the sale of their quotas. ■

costly protectionist device for America than a tariff. (For an example of how much more costly, see Box 17-4.)

This analysis throws light on an interesting recent policy issue. Rather than administer tariffs or quotas on our imports of textiles and color TVs and cars, the United States has pressed certain countries to agree to impose so-called "voluntary" quotas on their firms exporting to the United States. As a consequence, we have lost income 4 to these foreign firms exporting to us (as well, of course, as efficiency losses 1 and 2 that follow from any form of protection). Why then do we pressure foreign countries to impose these quotas? Why don't we impose our own import restrictions instead? The reason is that if we were to impose trade restrictions ourselves, then, according to GATT (the General Agreement on Tariffs and Trade), we would be subject to retaliation by the foreign country. (Because foreign producers get the windfall from export licenses—as illustrated in Box 17-5—"voluntary" export quotas are less damaging to foreign economies than American import quotas or tariffs. Thus, foreign countries may agree to quotas on their exports to the United States, rather than risk unilateral U.S. imposition of import restrictions.) ■

Problem

17-8 Using a multipanel diagram like Figure 17-2, explain the effects of the voluntary Japanese quota on TV exports to the United States that reduced their sales of TVs to this country by 40 percent.

PART
THREE

MICROECONOMICS: How Income Is Distributed

In Part 3, the central topic will be income distribution: *For whom* is the nation's output produced? We shall be asking questions such as: What determines the income that labor receives in the form of wages? What determines the interest and profit of capital owners and the rental income of landowners? Why does the heavyweight champion earn millions of dollars for every fight, while the nurse who looks after him in the hospital earns only a few thousand a year? And what policies can the government introduce if it wishes to change the nation's income distribution?

To answer such questions, we shall be turning our attention from the markets for goods and services to the markets for labor, capital, and other factors of production. Fortunately, many of the principles developed in analyzing the markets for goods in Part 2 can now be applied with appropriate modifications to factor markets. It will be no great surprise to find that factor markets are like product markets. Sometimes they operate efficiently; sometimes they do not. Therefore, while much of Part 3 will be new, much will be the application of the tools we developed in Part 2 to a challenging new set of problems.

In leaving Part 2, we reemphasize one of its important messages. Almost any government policy, from regulating a monopoly to imposing a tariff, will change a market price. And when a price changes, there are two effects: an **efficiency** effect,

and a **transfer** from one group to another. (For example, a price rise hurts buyers and benefits sellers; thus it causes a transfer from buyers to sellers.) When an economic policy is assessed, both its efficiency and transfer effects should be taken into account.

In the analysis of product markets in Part 2, the focus was on efficiency. But we have seen that a policy that increases efficiency cannot be judged on this ground alone; its transfer effect must also be recognized. When we shift our major focus to income distribution in Part 3, a similar conclusion is reached: Any policy designed to transfer income cannot be judged on this ground alone; its effect on efficiency must also be carefully examined. In the box that follows on the next four pages, we illustrate the two concepts of efficiency and income transfer by reviewing several diagrams from Part 2.

Whether or not you embark on this detailed, optional review, you should look at the diagrams in Figures 1 and 2 to get the general idea of their message. Figure 1 shows two policies with exactly the same transfer effects (white arrows) but completely different efficiency effects (shaded triangles). On the other hand, Figure 2 shows two policies with exactly the same efficiency effects (gray triangles), but completely different transfers (white arrows). Clearly, if we look at only the transfer effect *or* the efficiency effect—but not the other—we may get a very incomplete picture. ■

WHY BOTH EFFICIENCY AND TRANSFER EFFECTS MUST BE CONSIDERED

An important message from Part 2

To see how similar transfer effects can be accompanied by different efficiency effects, we reconsider the commodity tax in Figure 1. Then, to show how similar efficiency effects can be accompanied by different transfer effects, we will reconsider monopoly in Figure 2.

Reprise: The commodity tax on a good that pollutes and on one that does not

Panel *a* of Figure 1 shows the effect of a commodity tax on a good with no polluting side effects. Panel *b* shows this same tax applied to a good that does involve pollution. Otherwise, these two panels are identical. In both panels, the commodity tax will involve exactly the same set of transfers, shown by the broad white arrows. The reason that the transfers are identical is that in both cases, the tax shifts supply from S_1 to S_2, and equilibrium from E_1 to E_2. As a consequence, in each case consumers lose because the price they pay rises from P_1 to P_2, and producers lose because the price they receive (after paying the tax) falls from P_1 to P_3. But while consumers and producers lose, the U.S. Treasury gains in the form of increased tax receipts. Thus, in each panel, the broad white upward arrow shows the transfer from consumers to the U.S. Treasury, while the arrow pointing down shows the transfer from producers to the Treasury.

But, while transfers are the same in these two panels, the efficiency effects are quite different. Without pollution (panel *a*), the tax causes a red triangular loss of efficiency. But in the face of pollution (panel *b*), this same tax causes a gray triangular efficiency gain. (We assume the tax is equal to the marginal cost of pollution.) The reasons are detailed in the caption to Figure 1—but the basic idea is simple: In either case, the tax reduces output from Q_1 to Q_2. If there is no pollution (panel *a*), this output reduction

moves the economy *away from* the efficient output at Q_1, and this results in an efficiency loss. But when pollution exists (panel *b*) the efficient output is not Q_1, but rather Q_2; and the output reduction caused by the tax moves the economy *toward* this point, thus generating an efficiency gain.

Here is another way of seeing why this policy improves efficiency in panel *b,* but not in panel *a:* When pollution exists (panel *b*) the tax provides a benefit that does not exist in panel *a:* the benefit to the public of having a polluting activity curtailed.

These two panels contain an important message: In two sets of circumstances, a policy can have identical transfer effects, but completely different efficiency effects.

Reprise: The problem of monopoly

Figure 2 illustrates two ways in which monopoly output may be increased, thus increasing efficiency. In panel *a,* the traditional policy of price regulation is reproduced from Figure 11-7. The monopoly's initial equilibrium is at E_1. A policy of marginal cost pricing (that is, setting maximum price at P_2) will force the monopoly down its demand curve from E_1 to E_2, with the resulting transfer from the monopoly to consumers, as shown by the broad white arrow. In the process, monopoly output is increased from Q_1 to the efficient quantity Q_2, with the gray efficiency gain being the result.

Whereas in panel *a* the efficiency gain results from controlling the monopoly price, in panel *b* exactly the same efficiency gain is achieved by allowing the monopoly complete pricing freedom—including the freedom to charge different prices on different units. Suppose the monopoly is able to divide up its market and thus engage in price discrimination, just like the monopolist in Figure 11-8. However, where that earlier doctor-monopolist could divide the market into just two segments and thus quote only two prices, suppose that this present monopoly is in a strong enough position to quote a different price on each transaction. In other

Figure 1
Transfers the same, efficiency effects different:
The effects of a commodity tax . . .

(a) . . . if there is no pollution (based on Fig. 7-5)

(b) . . . if pollution does exist (based on Fig. 14-2)

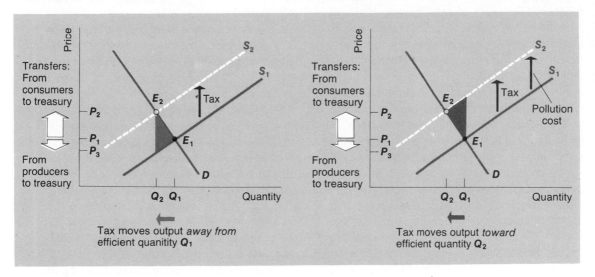

In both panels: Before the tax, equilibrium occurs at E_1, with price P_1 and output Q_1. The tax shifts supply up to S_2, thus shifting equilibrium to E_2. Consequently, output is reduced to Q_2 and price is increased to P_2.

panel (a)	panel (b)

Transfer effects

The burden of the tax is divided between consumers and producers. Consumers lose because the price they pay rises from P_1 to P_2. Producers lose because the price they receive (after tax) falls from P_1 to P_3. (Producers actually receive P_2, but out of this, they must pay the tax of P_2P_3.) Thus, there are two transfers: (1) the transfer from consumers to the treasury of P_1P_2 per unit (the white arrow pointing up); and (2) the transfer from producers to the treasury of P_1P_3 (the white arrow pointing down).

Transfer effects

Exactly the same as in panel a.

Efficiency effect

In this case, there are no externalities, so that D represents marginal benefit to consumers *and* to society, while S_1 represents marginal cost to producers *and* to society. Since D and S_1 are equal at output Q_1, this is efficient. Since the tax reduces output to Q_2, it results in an efficiency loss.

Efficiency effect

Because pollution costs exist, the marginal cost of this good to society is S_2 rather than S_1. Since S_2 intersects marginal benefit D at E_2, Q_2 is the efficient quantity of output. By reducing output from Q_1 to this efficient quantity Q_2, the tax generates an efficiency gain, shown by the gray triangle.

words, in dealing with the very first buyer, this monopoly refuses to sell even one unit unless it receives the maximum price that the buyer is prepared to pay, namely, the thin price arrow *a*. The monopoly then turns to the next buyer and similarly extracts *b*, the maximum price that the second purchaser is willing to pay. Thus the monopoly continues to work its way down its demand curve, exercising the ultimate degree of market power by squeezing every last nickel from every buyer along the way.† Because it can thus price each unit all the way up to its demand curve, it is able to convert its demand curve into a marginal revenue curve. For example, price *b* on the monopoly's demand curve is also a point on its marginal revenue curve, because its additional revenue from selling the second unit is *b*.

Such a monopoly will not stop at E_1, but instead will continue to *F*, where its marginal cost MC now equals its new marginal revenue D. (To confirm this, observe that the monopoly selling at point E_1 will receive a marginal revenue equal to Q_1E_1. Since its marginal cost is only Q_1W, it will continue to expand production.) Therefore, in panel *b* the monopoly increases its output from Q_1 to Q_2, the efficient level, just as in panel *a*. Hence, there is exactly the same gray efficiency gain.

By now, you may be very uneasy about the way the monopoly in panel *b* is able to benefit from discriminatory pricing. The large transfer from consumers to this monopoly is shown by the broad white arrow pointing up. (The height of this arrow is the average of the price increases the monopoly is now charging its original customers.) Note how this contrasts with the transfer

in panel *a*, which was in exactly the opposite direction because the monopoly was forced to lower its price.

[Note that there is one big difference between the discriminating monopolist discussed here and the discriminating monopolist in Figure 11-8. In that earlier diagram, the doctor-monopolist was not able to produce at all unless she could discriminate. (Her *D* was always below AC.) And it was better for consumers to be able to buy her services at a high price than not to be able to buy them at all. But there is no such justification for discrimination here, since the monopolist in Figure 2*b* is initially able to produce profitably at E_1 without discriminating.]

Panel *b* also illustrates why *monopoly profits may provide a poor indication of how monopoly distorts resource allocation* (that is, how it reduces efficiency). When the monopoly in panel *b* increases its profit by price discrimination, this does not increase the monopoly distortion in resource allocation. Quite the contrary: It eliminates this distortion altogether.

The message of Figure 2 may be recapped. The outcomes of the two panels involve exactly the same gray efficiency gain. But the transfers are completely different. Whereas the forced reduction in price in panel *a* transfers monopoly profit back to consumers, the unfettered exercise of monopoly power in panel *b* allows the monopolist to profit even more at the expense of consumers.

Conclusions

Any economic policy can have two effects: a transfer and an efficiency effect. If we consider only one of these effects, we will miss an important part of the total picture. For example, if we were to look only at the transfer effects in Figure 1, we would conclude: There is no difference between these two cases. And we would miss the completely different effects on efficiency. Or, if we were to look only at the efficiency effects of the two policies in Figure 2, we would conclude that they are the same. And we would miss their completely different transfer effects. ■

---

†Since one individual may appear in several locations on the demand curve, the monopoly must be able not only to quote a different take-it-or-leave-it price to each individual; but also, in dealing with one individual, it must be able to quote a different price for each purchase. Obviously, no firm does discriminate so completely. But the basic idea in this analysis still holds for firms that price-discriminate to a less complete degree. (For example, surgeons may have a widely varying set of rates.)

Figure 2
Efficiency effects the same, transfers different

(a) **Regulating monopoly price (based on Fig. 11-7)**

(b) **Allowing the monopolist to discriminate completely (based on Fig. 11-8)**

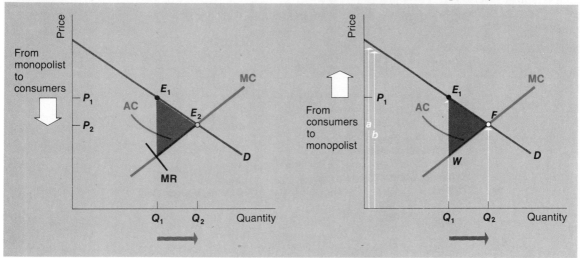

Original equilibrium is at E_1, with the monopoly selling output Q_1 at price P_1.

panel (a)

A price ceiling set at P_2 drives the monopoly down its demand curve from E_1 to E_2.

panel (b)

This discriminating monopoly prices "right up to its demand curve," charging the first buyer *a,* the second *b,* and so on. This allows it to convert its demand *D* into a marginal revenue curve. Hence, when it works its way down to E_1 it does not stop, since its marginal revenue (Q_1E_1) is still higher than its marginal cost (Q_1W). Instead it continues to produce to *F,* where these two are equal.

Transfer effect

Since the price consumers pay is lowered from P_1 to P_2, there is a transfer from the monopolist to consumers shown by the broad white arrow.

Transfer effect

Since the monopoly is able to squeeze a higher price (*a, b,* etc.) out of its original consumers, there is a transfer from consumers to the monopoly. (In fact, all the original consumer surplus is transferred to the monopoly.)

Efficiency effect

Output is increased from Q_1 to the efficient quantity Q_2, where marginal cost equals marginal benefit *D.* The resulting efficiency gain is shown in gray.

Efficiency effect

Exactly the same as in panel *a.*

CHAPTER 18
Wages in a Perfectly Competitive Economy

Last week a premature blast went off
And a mile in the air went big Jim Goff.
. . . .
When the next payday came around
Jim Goff a dollar short was found
When he asked "What for," came this reply
"You're docked for the time you was up in the sky."

Thomas F. Casey, "Drill Ye Tarriers, Drill"

The wage rate is the price of labor; and the market for labor is somewhat similar to the market for a good, such as wheat. Of course, these two markets are far from being completely the same. Labor is not just a commodity; labor involves *people*. Thus, there are major policy issues in labor markets which do not arise in the markets for other inputs or for final products. For example, if manufacturers wish to abuse their machines, that is pretty much their own business; the cost will come when the machines wear out quickly, and no major issue of public policy arises. Not so for labor. If a mine owner wishes to abuse workers by sending them to hazardous, dust-filled mines, the health of human beings is affected; the government has the right—and the responsibility—to intervene to set health standards. Or consider another example. Some business executives have peculiar quirks with respect to their products. In the early days of the automobile, Henry Ford's attitude was, "You can have any color of car you want—so long as it is black." No question of public policy arose; Ford paid for his views when he lost sales to competitors who were willing to give consumers their choice of colors. In contrast, personal quirks in the market for labor can be pernicious. If an employer just doesn't like some racial groups, the government may reasonably intervene to enforce nondiscriminatory hiring. Machines have no rights; but workers do.

Although the labor market is different in these respects from other markets, it may still be analyzed with some of the familiar tools we have already developed. What influences affect labor demand? What influences affect supply? In what circumstances does a free labor market result in an efficient wage rate and employment level, and in what circumstances does it not? [An economy cannot be efficient overall unless it has both efficient product markets (as described in Chapter 10) *and* efficient factor markets—including the labor markets described in this chapter.] Other issues dealt with in this chapter include the policy question: Can the government intervene in the labor market to transfer income to labor, just as it sometimes intervenes in a product market to transfer income from one group to another? And when it does, what effect does its intervention have on efficiency?

A PERFECTLY COMPETITIVE LABOR MARKET

In this chapter, we will study a perfectly competitive market for labor in a specific industry. Such a labor market has characteristics similar to a perfectly competitive product market:

1 Workers are mobile—they are not prevented from moving from one industry to another;

2 There are so many buyers of labor service (employers) and sellers (workers) that none has any market power to influence the wage rate; and

3 Labor is standardized. All workers are equally skillful, and equally productive in the industry being studied.

In Appendix 18-A we relax the first assumption, that workers are mobile. Specifically, we examine the economic effects of a rigid type of racial discrimination, where blacks are not mobile because they are not allowed into jobs traditionally held by whites. In the next chapter we turn our attention to assumption 2 and examine what happens when this condition is not met. What is the result when workers form a labor union in order to raise the wage rate? Or when employers with market power are able to influence the wage in the other direction? Finally, in Chapter 20 we relax the last and most unrealistic assumption—that all workers are equally productive.

But in our initial task of describing a perfectly competitive market—in which all three assumptions *do* hold—we now address the question: What determines the demand for labor? Although our main focus in this chapter is in the labor market in a specific *industry* (such as bicycles), we first set the stage by examining the labor demand by a single *firm* (the individual bicycle producer).

LABOR DEMAND AND PRODUCTIVITY

In the United States, real hourly wage rates are now approximately five times as high as they were in 1900. They have increased because of rising labor productivity.

The *real* wage is the nominal (or dollar) wage rate adjusted for inflation. The statement that the real wage is five times as high now as in 1900 means that an hour's wage will now buy five times as many goods and services as in 1900.

To more precisely describe the concept of labor productivity and examine its role in determining wages, consider the firm in Table 18-1 with a given stock of plant and machinery.

In the first two columns, we see how this firm can increase its physical output (column 2) by hiring more labor (column 1).[1] In column 3, the **marginal physical product** of labor is calculated, as we would expect, by noting how much total product in column 2 increases as each additional worker is hired. For example, hiring the second worker increases output from 5 to 12, or by seven units.

But the firm is even more interested in how its revenue increases as it hires more labor. These figures—showing the *value* of the marginal product of labor—are displayed in column 5. For example, hiring the second worker yields $140 of additional revenue, that is, the seven additional units that worker produces times the $20 price of each unit. (Notice that in this table we are assuming that the firm not only hires in a competitive *labor* market, but also sells its output in a competitive *product* market, where price is constant at $20.) In its decision-making, the firm is concerned with the value of labor's contribution in column 5. We refer to it as the **marginal productivity of labor** and graph it as the black curve in Figure 18-1.

The **marginal physical product** of labor is the additional number of units of output a firm can produce because it has hired one more worker.

The **marginal productivity** of labor is the dollar value of its marginal physical product.

---

[1] These figures come directly from the firm's short-run production function (Table 9-1) which is the same as the last row in its long-run production function (Table 9-5).

Table 18-1
Marginal Productivity of Labor†

(1) Number of workers	(2) Total physical product	(3) Marginal physical product (change in column 2 because one more worker is hired)	(4) Price per unit of product	(5) Value of marginal product, that is, marginal productivity of labor (MPL) (5) = (3) × (4)
0	0			
1	5	5	$20	$100
2	12	7	$20	$140
3	18	6	$20	$120
4	21	3	$20	$ 60
5	23	2	$20	$ 40

In this hypothetical example, marginal physical product falls, provided that more than two workers are hired (column 3). Thus, beyond the second worker there are diminishing returns to labor. This table is based on the short-run production function in Table 9-1.

†Shown for a hypothetical firm with a given capital stock and selling in a competitive market at a constant price.

How many units of labor will the firm hire? If the wage paid to each worker is the $60 shown by the red line in Figure 18-1, this firm will stop hiring when it has employed four workers. (The fifth won't be hired because that worker would provide only $40 of additional revenue but would cost $60 to hire.) In general:

In a perfectly competitive equilibrium, the profit-maximizing firm hires labor to the point where the marginal productivity of labor equals the wage rate. (Moreover, this idea applies in general: Using exactly the same reasoning, the firm hires *any* factor of production to the point where its marginal productivity equals the payment that must be made for it. Another example will be given in Figure 20-1.)

It now takes one more step to show that the firm's marginal productivity of labor curve represents its demand for labor. We have already seen that point T on its MPL curve is also a point on its demand curve (since, at a $60 wage, the firm hires four workers). Similarly, any other point on this MPL curve, say V, is also a point on

the firm's demand curve. (At a $40 wage, the firm hires five workers.) With the points on the MPL curve representing corresponding points on the labor demand curve, the two curves coincide.

Finally, you should now work through Problem 18-1 to see how the firm's income is divided between the wages it pays to labor and the amount it has left over to pay interest, profit, and rent to other factors of production. This will be a useful introduction to our discussion later in this chapter of how income is divided.

What causes a shift in labor demand?
Another way of asking this question is: What causes a shift in the marginal productivity of labor schedule in column 5 of Table 18-1? There are two reasons. First, the price of the firm's product (column 4) may change. If it rises from $20 to $30, then all the marginal productivity figures in column 5 will correspondingly rise, causing the demand for labor to shift upward to d_2 in Figure 18-2. Examples of such a shift in demand include the increased demand for carpenters resulting from an increase in the price of

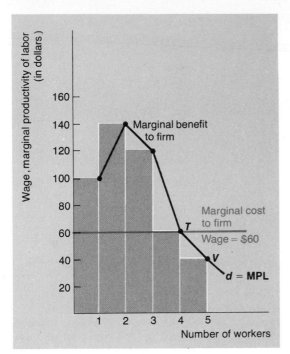

Figure 18-1

A firm's demand for labor is the marginal productivity of labor (drawn from column 5 of Table 18-1)

The points on the MPL curve represent points on the firm's demand curve. For example, point T on the MPL curve is also on the demand curve, because at a wage rate of $60, the firm hires four workers.

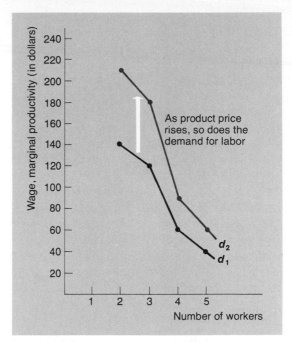

Figure 18-2
The firm's derived demand for labor

d_1 is the marginal productivity of labor when product price is $20. (It is calculated in column 5 of Table 18-1, and has already appeared as d in Figure 18-1.) d_2 is the marginal productivity of labor if product price rises to $30. (This is a recalculation of column 5 in Table 18-1, with $30 replacing $20 in column 4.)

houses, and the increased demand for farm labor following an increase in the price of wheat. Both these examples illustrate the *derived demand* for labor. In these industries, labor is demanded, not for its own sake directly, but for the goods and services it produces.

Derived demand **exists when a good or service is demanded because of its usefulness in producing some other good or service. Thus, there is a derived demand for labor to produce cars, and for land to grow wheat.**

The second reason that the demand for labor may shift up (that is, the MPL values in the last column of Table 18-1 may increase) is that labor may become physically more productive.

In other words, its marginal physical product in column 3 may increase. Such an increase can result from an expanded use of *capital* or an improvement in *technology*. For example, if additional machines are installed in a factory (more capital is used) the existing work force may be able to produce more.[2] If a new type of machine is designed or a better layout for the factory is discovered, technology is improved, and workers consequently may be able to pro-

[2]In Table 9-5, suppose the amount of capital employed is increased from one unit to two. We now read along the second last row rather than the last row. Regardless of how much labor is employed, more output is produced. (Each output figure in the second last row is larger than the corresponding figure in the last row.)

duce more.[3] Often changes in the quantity of capital come hand in hand with improvements in technology. For example, when a larger, technologically superior aircraft is introduced, the airlines that purchase it are thereby using improved technology. But they are also increasing their capital stock (so long as they replace each old plane with one of the new, larger ones). For both reasons, the productivity of pilots increases.

(Some improvements in technology result in a lower demand for labor in specific industries. For example, when new weaving machinery was introduced during the industrial revolution, many textile workers lost their jobs. But in the long run, even such "labor-saving" improvements bring increased demand for labor and higher wages in the economy as a whole, as we shall see later in Box 19-1.)

The labor market for an industry

Now let us turn from the labor demand by a firm to the labor demand by an industry. In a perfectly competitive economy, the industry's demand for labor will be the sum of the demands by the individual firms in somewhat the same way that the market demand for a good (in Figure 8-1) is the sum of the demands of individual consumers.[4] Such an industry demand curve for labor (D) is shown in Figure 18-3, along with the industry supply curve, S, which will be described later.

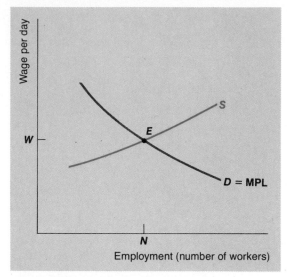

Figure 18-3
Determination of an industry's wage rate
In a perfectly competitive labor market, the wage rate W is determined by the intersection of the demand and supply curves for labor.

---

[3]Such a technological change means that all numbers in the production function (Table 9-5) increase.

*[4]In fact, the industry's demand for labor is not exactly the horizontal sum of the demands by the individual firms. To see why, note that if the wage rate falls, each firm hires more workers, as shown by the individual labor demand curves. But this increased hiring results in increased industry output, which depresses the price of that output. This in turn shifts the labor demand curve of each individual firm. (Remember, each of these curves is drawn on the assumption that output price remains constant.)

In short, the individual demand curves we are trying to sum do not remain fixed. In ignoring this problem, we recognize that the statements we make from now on will only be approximations. (As one might expect, there are many other examples of such complicated feedbacks in economics.)

MARGINAL PRODUCTIVITY AND THE DIVISION OF INCOME

One of our major interests in Part 3 is to see how the nation's income is divided, and the marginal productivity of labor curve (the demand for labor) can throw light on this issue. Specifically, in this section we shall show how the income share going to labor and the income share going to other factors of production in an industry can be read off the MPL curve shown in Figure 18-4.

Suppose equilibrium in this labor market is at E, with wage W (reproduced from Figure 18-3). What is the value of the industry's total output?[5] The first worker produces output with a value of a, the bar on the left in Figure 18-4; the second produces b, and so on to the last worker,

---

[5]More precisely, the industry's value added, that is, the value of the industry's output after deducting the costs of all its inputs purchased from other industries (like the cost of steel to the auto industry). Throughout this analysis we define value of output in this value-added sense.

who adds *j*. Thus, the total value of output is equal to the shaded areas 1 + 2. (We assume that nothing can be produced unless some labor is employed.)

What part of this total goes to labor? The answer is area 2, since wage *W* is paid to each of the *N* workers employed. Thus, if the labor market is competitive, we can summarize how the value of the industry's output is distributed in the following two statements:

Labor receives income equal to the wage rate times the number of workers employed. This labor income is the rectangle to the southwest of the equilibrium point on the labor demand curve (marginal productivity of labor curve).

Area 1 is what remains after labor is paid. It is what employers have left to distribute to other factors of production: interest and profit to capital, rent to land, and so on. Thus:

After labor is paid, all other factors of production together receive the triangular area enclosed to the northwest of the equilibrium point on the labor demand curve.

These two conclusions can now be used to analyze some of the effects of a controversial government policy: the minimum wage.

THE EFFECT OF A MINIMUM WAGE

The Fair Labor Standards Act of 1938 set a minimum wage of 25 cents an hour, covering 43 percent of the nonagricultural labor force. Since then the minimum wage has been increased over 10 times, and its coverage more than doubled. (However, not all workers in the industries covered by this legislation receive the minimum wage, because some firms do not comply with the law. One reason: For firms that are first offenders and that do not falsify data, the penalty for breaking the law is sometimes less than the cost of complying with the law by paying the minimum wage.)

The purpose of the minimum wage has been to raise labor income and thus reduce the poverty problem. What effect has this legislation had? To answer this question as simply as possible, we initially assume that the minimum wage applies to all industries, and we continue our assumption of a perfectly competitive economy.

We concentrate on a typical industry that has been paying a low wage, and is required to come up to the minimum by the law. In Figure 18-5*a*, the initial equilibrium E_1 corresponds to equilibrium *E* in Figure 18-3. Employment is N_1 and the wage rate W_1. If a minimum wage is set above this at, say W_2, firms facing more expensive labor move up their labor demand curve from E_1 to E_2, reducing their hiring from N_1 to N_2.

How the minimum wage affects various groups in the economy

Does the minimum wage achieve its objective of increasing labor income? The answer is: Not necessarily, because it has two conflicting effects. On the one hand, labor income increases because the wage rate rises. But on the other

Figure 18-4
An industry's marginal productivity of labor curve and the distribution of income
Total income earned by all factors of production is area 1 + 2. Of this, area 2 is paid to labor, and area 1 goes to other factors of production.

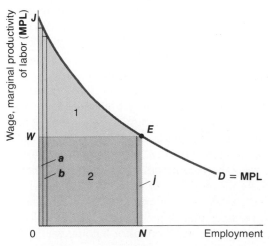

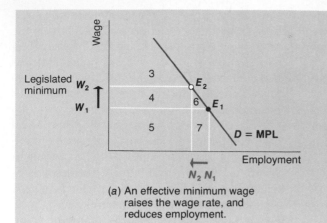

(a) An effective minimum wage raises the wage rate, and reduces employment.

(b) Labor gains and loses: Gain 4 goes to workers who still have jobs. But those who no longer have jobs lose 7.

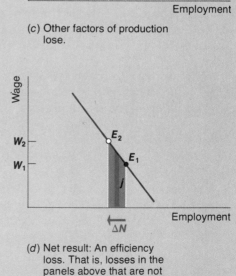

(c) Other factors of production lose.

(d) Net result: An efficiency loss. That is, losses in the panels above that are not offset by gray gains.

hand, labor income decreases because $N_1 N_2$ workers lose their jobs. According to the first of our two earlier summary statements on income distribution, labor's initial income at E_1 was areas 5 + 7, but at the new equilibrium E_2, labor income has become area 5 + 4. Thus, labor's income has increased by area 4 (workers who still have a job receive a higher wage). At the same time, labor income has decreased by area 7 (workers who have lost their jobs no longer receive any wage). Both these effects are shown in panel b of Figure 18-5.

What happens to the income of other factors of production? Initially, income to other factors was areas 3 + 4 + 6 (the triangular area to the northwest of equilibrium E_1 in panel a). But at the minimum wage equilibrium E_2, this income shrinks to area 3. Thus, other factors lose income 4 + 6, as shown in panel c.

From this analysis we see that a minimum wage will not necessarily transfer income from other factors of production to labor. True, it does reduce the income of other factors, as shown by the red area in panel c. But it does not necessarily raise the income going to labor, since the red loss and gray gain in panel b may cancel out. The elasticity of demand for labor is the key: If it is inelastic, then labor income overall will rise; but if it is elastic, then labor income will fall.

Figure 18-5
Effects of a minimum wage in competitive conditions

What is the evidence? Recent studies indicate that labor demand is inelastic as shown in Figure 18-5.[6] Therefore the labor force overall benefits from a minimum wage: The increase in income of the winners who retain their jobs (area 4) exceeds the reduction in income of those who lose their jobs (area 7). There is therefore some redistribution of income from other factors of production to labor.

How the minimum wage affects teenagers and minorities

In our overall assessment above, the workers who lose their jobs because of the minimum wage should not be forgotten. Who are they? The answer often is: minority groups who tend to be "last hired, first fired"; and teenagers who lack work experience and skills. (Teenage minorities get the worst of both worlds.) Because the teenage unemployment rate is more than double the rate for adults, a number of economists have suggested a "two-tiered system," with a lower minimum wage for teenagers than for adults.

But such special treatment for teenagers has been opposed by labor unions on the ground that employers might lay off adults with families to support, in order to hire teenagers at a lower wage. Moreover, if teenagers are given special treatment because of the disadvantage they face (inexperience), why shouldn't other groups with problems be given special treatment to encourage their employment as well? For example, why not also give special treatment—a lower minimum wage—to workers who are near retirement, who may have lost some of their mental or physical sharpness? With a two-tiered system that gives special treatment only to teenagers, people near retirement would have to face a double problem: They would have to convince potential employers that they are not only worth the standard minimum wage, but also that they should be hired instead of low-wage teenagers.

[6]In "How Elastic is the Demand for Labor?," *Review of Economics and Statistics,* November 1980, p. 518, Ken Clark and Richard Freeman estimate that the demand for labor is about 0.4 or 0.5. (Earlier studies had estimated it to be even lower.)

The minimum wage and economic efficiency

In panel *d* of Figure 18-5 we see how a minimum wage results in a red efficiency loss. (As before, this is any area that appears in the panels above as a loss to one group without being a gain to another.) To confirm the efficiency loss in panel *d,* observe that the thin red bar *j* shows the nation's output forgone because that worker is left unemployed by the minimum wage; and the total red area is the output forgone because of all the workers who have lost their jobs. This is the now familiar efficiency loss that results when a market—in this case, a labor market—is moved away from its perfectly competitive equilibrium.

In evaluating the U.S. minimum wage legislation, we should add several important qualifications. If workers dislike taking risks, they may prefer the situation before the minimum wage (when a low-paying job was easy to find) to the situation afterward, when the wage is higher but they run the risk of losing their jobs. Thus, by increasing the risk facing the labor force, a minimum wage may cost more than Figure 18-5 suggests.

The labor force may find a minimum wage disappointing in another respect: The gain to workers who keep their jobs may be less than gray area 4. This will occur if employers who have to pay the higher wage cover the cost by cutting back on some of the other benefits they provide to their labor force—in particular, on-the-job training. Again, this has important implications for teenagers. We have already seen that minimum-wage legislation may hurt teenagers because some lose their jobs. Now we see that even those who hang onto their jobs may be hurt, because they may lose on-the-job training opportunities.

On the other hand, there are several important reasons why a minimum wage may turn out better than Figure 18-5 suggests.

1 This figure is based on the assumption that all jobs are subject to this legislation—that workers who lose their jobs have "nowhere else to go" and become unemployed. But in the United

States there are jobs which are not covered by minimum wage legislation. To the degree that the unemployed find them, the efficiency loss is reduced; it is less than the red area in Figure 18-5d. (Also, the income loss of these workers is less than area 7 in panel b.)

2 The minimum wage may force employers to increase labor productivity. Because labor costs more, employers will be under pressure to use it more effectively.

3 Our unfavorable assessment of the minimum wage in Figure 18-5 depends critically on the perfectly competitive assumption that before the minimum wage is introduced, employers have no market power which enables them to keep wages low. But this is often not the case. *When employers do have market power, our conclusions in Figure 18-5 may be reversed: A minimum wage may lead to greater efficiency, greater employment, and a much larger transfer from other factors of production to labor.* (In the next chapter, we will explain why.)

THE SUPPLY OF LABOR FOR AN INDUSTRY

The labor supply for an industry, first shown in Figure 18-3, is now reproduced for more detailed examination in Figure 18-6. As the wage rate rises from W_1 to W_2, the labor supplied to this industry increases from N_1 to N_2 as workers are drawn in from other industries by this increasingly attractive wage rate. As a specific example, the labor supply curve tells us that when the wage rate rises to W_3, worker a is drawn into this industry.

In order to persuade the worker to move, the wage rate W_3 will have to be high enough to cover the individual's **transfer price.** Specifically, the wage will have to be high enough to compensate the worker for:

1 The wage paid in the industry from which the worker is moving

2 Costs of moving (both financial and psychological)

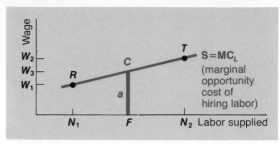

Figure 18-6
Supply of labor for an industry
The rising supply curve for labor shows how an increase in the wage paid by an industry increases the number of workers seeking jobs there. Moreover, the height of the supply curve at any point like *C* reflects the opportunity cost of hiring another worker (*a*) in this industry—that is, his or her productivity in the previous job. Thus, the supply curve for labor reflects the opportunity cost of hiring one more worker (just as the supply curve for a product reflects the cost of producing one more unit of output).

3 Differences in the attractiveness of the new industry, compared to the industry in which the worker was previously employed.

Item 2 need not be very great. It may be zero—if the worker is moving from one factory to a factory next door, and needs to make no change in residence or commuting arrangements. Item 3 may be either positive or negative: If the new job is less attractive, a higher wage will be needed to induce the worker to move. If, on the other hand, the new job is considered more attractive, the worker may be willing to come for a *lower* wage rate than in the old job. (More detail for items 2 and 3 will be given in Box 18-1.)

For the moment, we focus on the first item, which is usually the most important. The wage in the industry from which the worker is moving was also the worker's previous marginal productivity. (Remember, the previous employer would have equated marginal productivity and the wage rate.) So the height of the bar *FC* represents the value of the output worker *a* was producing in his or her alternative activity—the opportunity cost of having this worker in this industry. Thus, we conclude that:

The height of an industry's labor supply curve provides a measure of the opportunity cost to society when another worker is hired in that industry.

(In this chapter and the next, we concentrate on the supply of labor facing an individual industry; as its wage rises, labor is drawn in from other industries. But in some circumstances, it is appropriate to consider, "What is the supply of labor for the *economy as a whole?*" This question is studied in Appendix 18-B.)

THE "INVISIBLE HAND" IN A PERFECTLY COMPETITIVE LABOR MARKET

Does Adam Smith's "invisible hand" work in factor markets as it did in product markets? Specifically, if a labor market is perfectly competitive and is left alone, will it lead to an efficient result?

Panel *a* of Figure 18-7 illustrates the quantity of employment N_1 and wage W in a perfectly competitive labor market. This is efficient be-

cause it satisfies our criterion; the marginal benefit of any activity (in this case, hiring labor) must be equal to its marginal cost. This is confirmed in panels *b* and *c* by showing that any other solution is inefficient. (This analysis is described

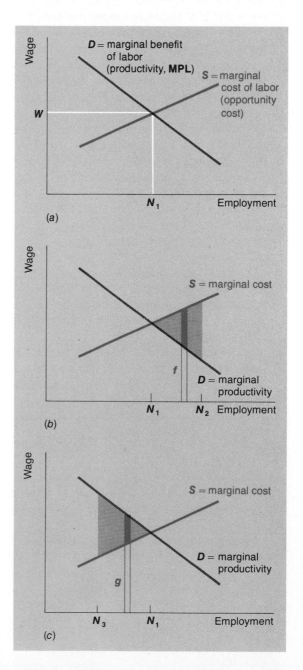

Figure 18-7
Why a perfectly competitive labor market is efficient

(*a*) At the perfectly competitive amount of employment N_1, there is an efficient number of workers in this industry—because *D* (the marginal benefit of hiring another worker) is just equal to *S* (the marginal cost of hiring another worker).

(*b*) N_2 is inefficient. There are too many workers in this industry—individuals like *f* whose productivity here (the empty bar) is less than elsewhere (empty bar plus solid bar).

(*c*) N_3 is also inefficient. There are too few workers in this industry. Employment should be increased by hiring workers like *g*, whose productivity here (the empty bar plus the solid bar) is greater than elsewhere (the empty bar).

BOX 18-1

Adam Smith's "Invisible Hand" in the Labor Market

Our earlier analysis of Smith's "invisible hand" in a product market (Figure 10-3) is extended to a factor market in Figure 18-8. If all individual employers and employees make decisions that are in their own self-interest, the result will be in the public interest (at least in the sense that the outcome is efficient). In panel a, producers hire labor up to the point where they maximize their profit. In panel b, workers pursue their own self-interest by offering their labor services to this industry so long as the wage they receive (W) is greater than their reward elsewhere (MC_L). The result in panel c is an efficient one for society, made possible because of the key role played by a perfectly competitive wage rate. It is the employers' reaction to the given market wage in panel a and the worker's reaction to this same wage in panel b that bring MPL (the marginal benefit to society) and MC_L (the marginal cost to society) together in panel c. So long as no single individual on either side of the market can influence W, it is the key in orchestrating the actions of employers and employees in an efficient way.

In Figure 18-8, we have assumed that the height of the supply curve for labor measures productivity in other industries from which labor is being drawn. (We have been focusing on item 1 in the section on the supply of labor for an industry.) But what about the other items which determine the height of the supply curve; namely, costs of moving and the pleasantness of the jobs (items 2 and 3)? Do they upset the conclusion that a competitive market is efficient? The answer is no.

Here's why. Costs of moving can be important—for example, if a worker has to travel from one city to another to take the new job. Resources are used in trucking the worker's furniture and other possessions from one city to another. It is not efficient for the worker to move unless the productivity (and the wage) in the new industry is sufficiently higher to compensate for the move. But it must be—otherwise the worker won't move. Accordingly, the operation of the market leads to the efficient result.

Likewise, complication 3 does not cause inefficiency. Suppose that the new job is more attractive, and therefore the worker moves even though the wage (and productivity) is less. The market value of output will fall; this seems to be an undesirable move. But that is not so. For economic welfare, we should count more than the goods and services produced. It is also very

concisely because it is so similar to our earlier demonstration in Figure 10-3 that a perfectly competitive market *for a good* yields an efficient result.)

On the one hand, suppose that for some reason employment is greater than N_1, say N_2 in panel b. Let f represent one of these units of "excess employment." The benefit from employing this worker in this industry is the worker's marginal productivity, as given by the empty bar under the labor demand curve. But the cost of employing this worker is the value of the output no longer produced in the worker's alternative activity: This is given by the empty bar plus the solid bar under the supply curve. The difference is the solid bar, which is the efficiency loss to society because the worker is in this industry rather than a higher-productivity job elsewhere. The total efficiency loss to society for all such excess workers in the range N_1N_2 is the red triangle.

On the other hand, at employment N_3 in

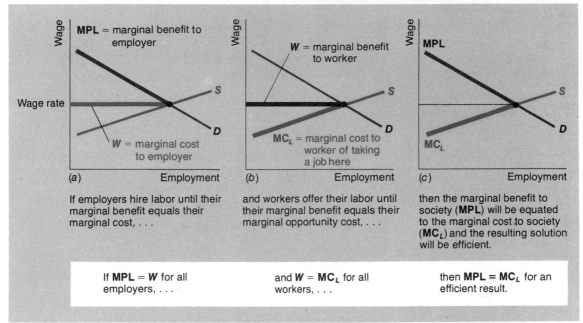

If **MPL** = **W** for all
employers, . . .

and **W** = **MC**$_L$ for all
workers, . . .

then **MPL** = **MC**$_L$ for an
efficient result.

Figure 18-8
How the pursuit of private benefit in a
perfectly competitive labor market results in
an efficient outcome for society as a whole
(Compare with Figure 10-3)

important for people to enjoy their jobs. If the
pleasantness of the new job at least compensates for the lower wage (that is, the lower
productivity), no loss of efficiency occurs. But the
pleasantness of the new job must compensate—
otherwise the worker won't move. Once again,
we confirm the efficiency of the competitive
market. ■

panel c, there are too few workers in this industry. To confirm, consider one worker g who
might be employed in this industry, but is not.
The cost of employing this worker here is the
value of this individual's output in the alternative
activity, shown by the empty bar under the
supply curve; but the benefit from employing
the worker is the marginal productivity in this
industry, shown by the empty bar plus the solid
bar under the demand curve. The difference is
the solid bar which represents the worker's

greater productivity in this industry than elsewhere; this is the output that is lost because he or
she is not employed here. Finally, the total
efficiency loss to society is the red triangle—the
sum of all such losses over the range $N_3 N_1$. In
brief, this efficiency loss occurs because workers
are not hired in this industry even though they
would be more productive here than elsewhere.

To sum up: There is an efficiency loss if
employment in this industry is greater or less
than the perfectly competitive quantity N_1 in

panel *a*. (For further detail on this point, see Box 18-1.) Thus, this analysis confirms the clear analogy between the labor market for an industry, where perfect competition generates efficient employment and wage rate, and a product market (discussed earlier in Chapter 10) where perfect competition generates efficient output and price.

Some complications

As always, we can make no claim that perfect competition necessarily results in the "best of all possible worlds." It satisfies only one of our important objectives: the *elimination of deadweight inefficiencies*. But it does not address the question: How equitable (fair) is the resulting distribution of income between labor and other factors of production? (We will consider this important and difficult question in Chapter 23.)

While perfectly competitive labor markets are efficient in theory, complications arise in practice if there are any external spillover costs or benefits. (Externalities can arise in a labor market just as in a product market; for example, see Problem 18-7.) But the most substantial complication of all is that, in practice, labor markets seldom are perfectly competitive because buyers or sellers of labor have the market power to influence price (the wage rate). When they do, there is no longer any reason to expect that a free market will lead to an efficient result, as we shall see in the next chapter.

Key Points

1 Demand for labor reflects the marginal productivity of labor. In a competitive labor market where no individual buyer or seller of labor has any influence over the wage rate, a firm will hire labor until the marginal productivity of labor equals the wage rate.

2 Demand for labor in an industry, say textiles, may shift because of an increase in the price of textiles. Thus, the demand for labor is "derived" from the demand for textiles. Or, labor demand may shift as a result of increased use of capital, or the discovery of a new technique.

3 If labor markets are competitive, minimum wage legislation that raises the wage rate will also reduce employment and will therefore result in an efficiency loss. The total income of labor may either increase or decrease.

4 The supply of labor for an industry reflects the (approximate) opportunity cost of labor, that is, the output workers could have produced in other industries.

5 Adam Smith's "invisible hand" works in a perfectly competitive labor market just as it does in a perfectly competitive product market: If all market participants (employers and employees) pursue their individual economic gain, the result is an efficient solution for society as a whole. To get this efficient result, we must assume perfect competition. That is, we must assume that neither buyers nor sellers of labor can influence the wage rate (the issue addressed in the next chapter).

Key Concepts

real wage
marginal physical product
  of labor
marginal productivity of
  labor (MPL)
why labor demand reflects
  MPL

derived demand
share of income paid to
  labor
share of income paid to
  other factors

minimum wage
opportunity cost of
  labor MC_L
why labor supply reflects
  opportunity cost
labor market efficiency

Problems

18-1 In Figure 18-1 we concluded that, at a $60 wage, this firm hires four workers.

   (a) What, then, is its total revenue? (Use the background data in Table 18-1.) How much remains after its wages have been paid; that is, how much does the firm have left over to pay interest, rent, and profit to its other factors of production?

   (b) From the bars in Figure 18-1, show

      (i) the firm's total revenue;

      (ii) the part of this revenue paid to labor;

      (iii) the part that is left for other factors of production.

18-2 The firm's MPL curve in Figure 18-1 is drawn on the assumption of a given $20 price for the firm's output. But now suppose that because of decreased consumer demand for this output, its price falls to $10. Show graphically what happens to the firm's MPL curve. Does the firm change its employment? If so, by how much? Is this a further illustration of how "producers dance to the consumers' tune"? Explain.

18-3 James O'Hara, the Chairman of the Congressional Minimum ·Wage Study Commission, criticized the proposal to have a lower minimum wage for teenagers than for adults:

> The payment of a subminimum wage to a particular age group is so at conflict with . . . the requirements of social justice that it ought to be rejected as a policy option

even if we thought it would substantially reduce youth unemployment.

Do you agree that it would be unjust to have a lower minimum wage for teenagers, even if it would increase teenage employment? Explain why or why not. (Alternatively, explain the case that can be made on each side.)

18-4 Because of a special commonwealth association, Puerto Rico has many close economic ties with the United States. What do you think of the idea of Puerto Ricans imposing the U.S. minimum wage on their island? In answering this question keep this in mind: Because of low labor productivity and a rapidly growing labor supply, Puerto Ricans have historically had a wage rate substantially lower than in the continental United States.

   Would such a common minimum wage result in a more severe unemployment problem in Puerto Rico or the continental United States? In your view, should the Puerto Ricans have a minimum wage below the U.S. level? What do you think of the idea of setting a minimum wage in Puerto Rico low enough so that it would not cause any unemployment there? If it were set at this level, would it achieve the objective of reducing poverty by raising wages?

18-5 Would a minimum wage be more likely to raise the total income of labor if the elasticity of demand for labor is low rather than high? Explain why or why not.

30-6 "The wage rate acts as a screening device that determines where scarce labor will be employed and where it will be not." Illustrate this idea, referring if you like back to Figure 10-4. (Use the example of labor that is hired to build apartment buildings but not hired to hoe field corn.)

30-7 Suppose that the people in a large city judge that external benefits result when musicians are hired for a symphony orchestra. (Musicians are thought to make an important indirect contribution to the cultural life of the community merely by living there—in addition, of course, to the direct contribution they make whenever they play in a concert.) If a symphony orchestra is being organized by a private entrepreneur who requests a subsidy from the city government, how would you advise the government to decide?

APPENDIX 18-A

DISCRIMINATION IN THE LABOR MARKET: AN INTRODUCTION

Demand and supply curves can be used to identify some of the economic consequences of racial discrimination (although discrimination also creates social, moral, and political problems which cannot be dealt with in such a simple framework). What happens if employers favor whites for the better positions, and offer only inferior jobs to blacks, even though they may have equal skill and training? Although the example we use is discrimination against blacks, the analysis also applies to discrimination against women or any other group.

To set the stage, the left panel of Figure 18-9a shows the situation in an economy in which there is no discrimination. Notice that we are now describing the labor market for the economy *as a whole,* rather than for a single industry. (Discrimination is an economy-wide problem.) Thus, the demand curve D includes the demands of *all* hiring firms in the economy. The supply curve S is vertical—a reasonable first approximation for the economy as a whole. [An industry's supply curve in Figure 18-3 slopes upward to reflect how workers can be drawn in from other industries. But for the economy as a whole, there are no "other industries" from which labor can be drawn. We therefore take the labor force as given, resulting in the vertical supply. (The labor supply for the economy as a whole is studied in more detail in Appendix 18-B.)]

In the labor market shown in Figure 18-9a, wage W is paid to N workers—N_W whites and N_B blacks. No distinction is made between them; that is, in hiring workers, employers are "color-blind."

What happens if discrimination is introduced into this market? Specifically, consider the extreme case where employers no longer hire blacks to do the same jobs as whites in the main labor market, but hire them instead only for low-productivity, dead-end jobs.

In this extreme case, there are now the two quite separate labor markets shown in part *a* of this diagram—the one on the left for whites, and the one on the right for blacks. This is an example of a **dual labor market.** In the main labor market, supply

shifts from S to S_W because this market is now for "whites only"; the wage rate consequently rises from W to W_W. In the black labor market shown on the right, demand for labor D is low, reflecting the fact that the only jobs available are low-productivity tasks. Supply in this market is S_B, representing blacks who have nowhere else to go. Consequently, the wage rate is W_B, substantially less than the wage W that blacks received before discrimination.

The effects of such discrimination on each group and on the overall efficiency of the economy may be summarized:

1 Black workers lose. Because their wage rate falls from W to W_B, their total wage income falls from area 3 to area 6. (They may also suffer higher unemployment, which does not show up in this diagram.)

2 White workers gain. Because their wage rate rises from W to W_W, their total wage income rises by area 1 (that is, it increases from area 4 to area 4 + 1).

3 Owners of other factors of production lose. Specifically, the income earned by capital and other non-labor factors of production in the main labor market decreases by areas 1 + 2. (This income before discrimination was areas 7 + 1 + 2, but afterwards it is only area 7.) Of this, area 1 is a transfer from other factors to white workers receiving a higher wage.[7] (The loss 2 incurred by other factors may be roughly offset by new income 5 that they receive from the ghetto market.)

4 There may be little effect on whites overall. Because non-labor factors of production (like capital) are owned mostly by whites, there may be little effect on all whites taken together. True, white wage earners gain area 1; but this is just a transfer from other white-owned factors.

5 There is an efficiency loss. When we turn from the transfer effects to the efficiency effects shown in part b of this diagram, we see that the total product of the economy falls. As black workers are forced out of the main labor market, production falls by the red area. This is only partially offset by their new (gray) production in the ghetto market into which they have been segregated. The difference is the reduced total output of the economy, that is, the efficiency loss that results from discrimination.

6 This efficiency loss is borne primarily by blacks. Because there is little net effect on whites overall, blacks suffer most and perhaps all the efficiency loss from discrimination. [To confirm this, notice that the reduction in black income (from area 3 to 6 in panel a) is essentially the same as the efficiency loss—the red area less the gray area in panel b.]

Measuring the effects of discrimination

Barbara Bergmann of the University of Maryland has provided detail on how discrimination against blacks raises the income of white labor (area 1 in Figure 18-9).

---

[7]This leads to the following puzzle: While discrimination may be in the economic interest of white *workers*, this analysis suggests that it is not in the interest of *employers* representing other factors of production (such as their own capital, stockholders' capital, etc.). Why, then, do employers continue to discriminate? One possible answer will be given in Box 19-3.

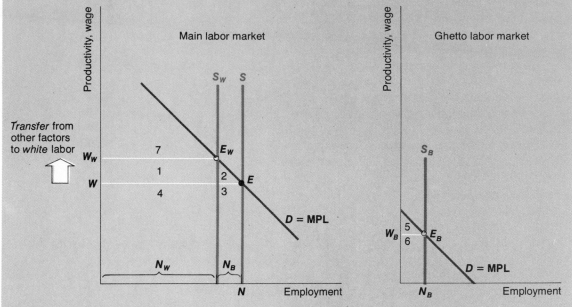

(a) **How discrimination affects wages and incomes.**

    In a color-blind market *without discrimination,* equilibrium is at **E** in the left panel. The wage received by all workers is **W,** with N_W whites and N_B blacks employed. *With discrimination,* blacks are forced into the ghetto market on the right, where equilibrium is E_B. Thus black wages fall from **W** to W_B and the wage income of black workers falls from area 3 to area 6. Meanwhile, the forced departure of blacks from the main labor market on the left reduces labor supply there from **N** to N_W, thus raising wages of whites from **W** to W_W, and raising the wage income of white workers by area 1 (that is, from area 4 to areas 4 + 1).

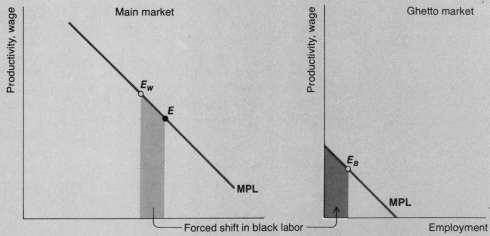

(b) **The efficiency effects of discrimination**

    As a result of the forced departure of black labor from this main labor market, there is lost output of the red area under the marginal productivity curve. This is more than . . .

the output (gray area) produced by black labor when it is hired in this low-productivity ghetto market. The efficiency loss is the difference in these two areas—the reduced output of black labor because it is shifted from high- to low-productivity jobs.

Figure 18-9
An introduction to the economics of labor-market discrimination

In an article in the *Journal of Political Economy* (March 1971, pp. 294–313), she estimated that the income of white males in the lowest education bracket (less than an elementary school education) was increased by somewhere between 7 and 10 percent. Moreover, the income of poorly educated white females was raised by an even greater amount—between about 10 to 15 percent. (Generally speaking, discrimination has a smaller percentage effect on the income of more highly educated workers, whether they be male or female.)

In examining how blacks were affected, Bergmann estimated that discrimination reduced black labor income by about 25 to 40 percent. (In our model, this means that area 6 was about 25 to 40 percent smaller than area 3.) Finally, in evaluating the overall efficiency loss (the difference between the red and gray areas in part *b*), she estimated that over the economy as a whole, labor market discrimination was unlikely to reduce total national income by more than 1½ percent.

There is evidence that during and since the 1967–1969 period on which Bergmann's estimates were based, there has been a substantial reduction in income differentials. In the first twelve years following 1964 (when Congress passed the Civil Rights Act making discrimination in employment illegal) approximately one-third of the income difference between black and white males was eliminated.[8]

However, some of this progress may be an illusion. In an article in the *American Economic Review,* (September 1979, p. 553), Edward Lazear provides evidence that some employers who are legally forced to raise black wages compensate by reducing on-the-job black training. Thus blacks get higher current wages, but in exchange sacrifice future wages. (Notice that some employers seem to be reducing on-the-job training as a way to "partially escape" not only from the minimum wage law—as we saw earlier—but also from the antidiscrimination laws.)

Discrimination against blacks in the housing market[9]

Blacks have a lower standard of living not only because labor market discrimination lowers their wage but also because discrimination in the housing market can increase the price they have to pay for a place to live, as illustrated in Figure 18-10.

Suppose the races are segregated, with blacks in the central core area and whites in the suburbs beyond. Any increase in the white population can be accommodated by an expansion of new housing into the surrounding countryside. But an expansion of black population encounters resistance at the white boundary—in particular, the reluctance of whites there to rent or sell to blacks. Moreover, population pressure in the black area may build up as blacks move into the city from depressed rural areas. This pressure raises the price blacks have to pay to the point where whites near the border are finally willing to rent or sell to blacks. Thus, blacks pay more than whites—with the difference in price being the amount that whites require to overcome their reluctance to deal with blacks. (How can a houseowner sell to blacks at a higher

[8]Richard B. Freeman, *Labor Economics,* 2d ed. (Englewood Cliffs, N.J.: Prentice-Hall, 1979), p. 100.

[9]This discussion of housing draws on Edwin Mills, *Urban Economics* (Glenview, Ill.: Scott Foresman, 1972), pp. 169, 170.

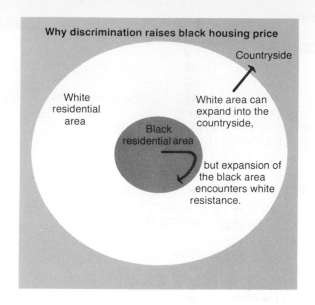

Why discrimination raises black housing price

Countryside

White
residential
area

Black
residential area

White area can
expand into the
countryside,

but expansion of
the black area
encounters white
resistance.

Figure 18-10
Housing discrimination
The white residential area can expand, but the black area is surrounded by white neighborhoods.

price than whites? The answer is that the owner quotes a price above the market value, and accepts a lower bid if it is made by a white, but not if it is made by a black.)

Exceptions to this pattern may occur. For example, prices in the white area next to the black core may even temporarily fall if panicky whites try to sell quickly. (In the past, such panic was sometimes induced by real estate agents who engaged in the now illegal practice of "block-busting." This is the practice of selling one or two houses in an all-white block to blacks, and then using high-pressure scare tactics on the remaining whites to stampede them into quick sales "while there is still time." The incentive for real estate agents to engage in this practice was the commission they made from the rapid turnover of homes.) ■

Appendix 18-B

THE ECONOMY-WIDE SUPPLY OF LABOR

In Figure 18-9a, the economy-wide labor supply was shown as a vertical line, S, to reflect a given labor force for the economy as a whole. But there are two reasons why the supply curve may not be completely vertical after all—why the total amount of labor supplied in the economy may respond to a change in the wage rate:

(a) The *labor participation rate* may change. That is, there may be a change in the proportion of the population in the labor market.

(b) There may be a change in the average *number of hours worked* by the existing labor force.

For an individual deciding how much time to spend on leisure and how much on work, a wage increase exerts two conflicting pressures:

1 The **substitution effect:** Since the reward for work (the wage rate) has increased relative to the reward from leisure, people have an incentive to substitute: more work, less leisure.

2 The **income effect** works in the opposite direction. A higher wage means higher income, and thus allows workers to acquire more of everything they want: not only more goods, but also more leisure. In acquiring more leisure, they work less.

Which of these two conflicting effects dominates? We cannot be sure. As Figure 18-11 is drawn, the two are exactly balanced at wage W_3, where the quantity of labor supplied is at a maximum. But if the initial wage is lower than this, the substitution

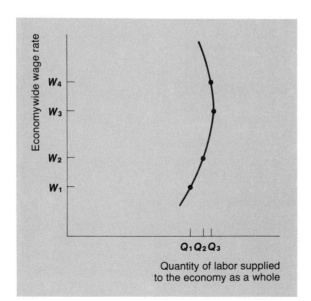

Figure 18-11
The supply of labor in the economy as a whole (not just in a single industry)
At low wage W_1, an increase in the wage to W_2 results in an increase in the quantity of labor supplied (from Q_1 to Q_2). However, at some higher wage rate (W_3) workers achieve a high enough income that any further increase in the wage rate will allow them to afford not only more goods, but also more leisure. In other words, an increase in the wage rate induces them to work less; the quantity of labor supplied is reduced.

effect dominates: As wages rise (from W_1 to W_2), people work more (Q_2 rather than Q_1). On the other hand, at a wage above W_3, the income effect dominates: A further increase in the wage (to W_4) causes a *reduction* in the amount of labor supplied. In this range above W_3, the labor supply curve is described as "backward bending." ■

Problem

18-8 The efficiency loss that occurred in Figure 18-9 can be viewed as the result of splitting the labor market into black and white segments with different productivity in each. Explain why a similar efficiency loss occurs, at least to some degree, in the U.S. labor market because of its geographical divisions. (Because workers find it difficult and costly to move, they often stay in low-wage and low-productivity areas, rather than move into higher-productivity areas.) Is it therefore true that barriers to labor mobility impose a cost on the economy? Do you see now why a policy of increasing labor mobility may increase the efficiency of the economy even when it doesn't reduce unemployment? (In fact, it may also reduce unemployment.)

CHAPTER 19
Wages in Imperfectly Competitive Labor Markets

> Trade unionism is not socialism. It is the capitalism
> of the proletariat.
>
> **George Bernard Shaw**

In this chapter we study how the labor market departs from perfect competition. On the supply side, workers in many industries have formed unions in order to influence wage rates and working conditions. On the demand side, employers frequently have some control over the wage rate. An extreme example is a firm that is the only employer of industrial labor in a small town.

When market power exists on both sides of the market, the result is *bilateral (two-way) monopoly*. This is the situation that we wish eventually to study in this chapter. But, in order to work up to this complicated subject, we address two preliminary questions: What happens if there is market power only on the supply side of the labor market? And what happens if there is market power only on the demand side?

First, we look at unions. Although one of their major objectives is to exercise market power to increase wages, they have other significant roles as well.

LABOR UNIONS: THE BENEFITS OF COLLECTIVE ACTION

It is sometimes said that the competitive market "has no memory, and no future." In such a market, people are hired or fired simply on the basis of what they can do *today*. But, in the real world, people work not only for the wage they receive today, but also in order to ensure a secure job for the future. In other words, people have a *stake* in their jobs. An important role of the union is to protect the stake of the workers, to give them a collective voice not only in the setting of wages but also, more generally, in the conditions of employment. With the backing of unions, workers are protected from arbitrary changes in the "rules of the game" by management. Workers express their *voice* by joining together in a union.[1]

Workers gain several advantages when they get together in a union, rather than "standing alone": (1) A single worker may have difficulty even getting management to listen, let alone negotiate to remove a grievance. (2) Management may retaliate against an individual who is complaining. (The courts' interpretation of U.S. labor law is that workers acting collectively are protected from management retaliation, but as individuals they are not.) (3) Even if an individual were to succeed in negotiating a change, it is unlikely that it would be worth the effort. Most of the benefits would go to other workers. In this sense, the resolution of a labor grievance is a public good; *all workers benefit, regardless of who negotiates it.* Negotiations are therefore undertaken collectively—by a union.

[1]This section draws heavily on Richard B. Freeman and James L. Medoff, "The Two Faces of Unionism," *The Public Interest,* Fall 1979, pp. 69–93.

Job security is important to many workers, particularly those who have reached 50 and would have difficulty finding another job. Thus, one major objective of a union is to negotiate clear rules on the conditions under which workers can be laid off or discharged. **Seniority rules** protect those who have been on the job longest and have the most to lose if they are discharged.

Seniority rules give preference to those who have been longest on the job. Individuals with seniority are typically the last to be discharged or laid off, and the first to be rehired.

Without seniority rules, older workers might be in a vulnerable situation. Over the years, they may have slowed down. In the absence of seniority rules they might be the *first* to be laid off. Thus, union-negotiated rules can be viewed as a way of reducing older workers' vulnerability; in turn this provides younger workers with assurances about the future so that they can commit themselves to an occupation more completely than they could in a timeless, impersonal, perfectly competitive market. Unions also negotiate for pleasanter and safer working conditions.

In the past, unions have focused their attention on wages and on conditions on the "shop floor." In the future, will union representatives take positions in the nation's boardrooms? Germany is experimenting with **codetermination:** Labor and management have an equal number of seats on the board of directors, with the owners making the decision in the event of a tie. This experiment has had mixed success. It has improved communication. But both sides have reservations: Management feels that labor representatives sometimes waste time by raising "shop-floor" issues (such as plant ventilation) and sometimes leak secrets (such as proposed plant layoffs). On the other hand, labor members of the board complain that the owners are in control because of the extra vote they get in the event of a tie. And rank-and-file workers fear that their board members may begin to think like managers and soften their demands for higher wages and better working conditions.

In the United States, Douglas Fraser, the president of the United Auto Workers (UAW), was elected to Chrysler's board of directors in May 1980, marking the first time a union leader has sat on the board of a major U.S. corporation. Although this does represent a precedent of sorts, it was more an act of desperation to save a near-bankrupt company: Chrysler gave the union president a seat on the board in exchange for the UAW's agreement to defer several hundred million dollars in wages and benefits.

While unions have the important function of negotiating on this broad range of issues, one of their central roles has always been to exercise bargaining power in order to raise wages—including fringe benefits such as pensions, health insurance, or paid vacations. (We use the term "wages" broadly, to include all such benefits paid for by the company.)

Collective bargaining

There are two kinds of unions in the United States.

1 *Industrial unions,* such as the United Auto Workers, draw on all workers in a specific industry or group of industries, regardless of the workers' skills.

2 *Craft unions,* such as the plumbers' or carpenters' unions, draw from *any* industry, provided the workers have a common skill.

Both types of unions engage in **collective bargaining.**

Collective bargaining is any negotiation in which workers are represented collectively, by a union, in bargaining over wages, fringe benefits, hiring policies, job security, or working conditions.

In addition to direct negotiations over pay rates, unions may attempt to raise wages indirectly in a number of ways. For example, unions may:

1 Lobby for a higher legal minimum wage. (Because of traditional wage differentials among jobs, an increase in the minimum wage may create upward pressures on wages above the minimum as well.)

2 Negotiate shorter workweeks and early retirement. (Such steps reduce the supply of labor, and thus put upward pressure on wages.)

3 Negotiate with employers to hire only union members, and then limit union membership by imposing such barriers to entry as high initiation fees or long periods of apprenticeship. (This approach, which also restricts the supply of labor, is most commonly used by craft unions.)

In each case, a union may have objectives in addition to higher incomes. For example, a shorter workweek may be desired for its own sake, and apprenticeship may be a way of screening bumbling amateurs out of dangerous occupations. [Not surprisingly, motives are sometimes mixed. The charge has been made that the American Medical Association (AMA) has acted like a craft union. For many years—prior to its change in policy about two decades ago—the AMA used its power to limit the number of medical schools, and even forced schools which had been approved to limit the number of students they admitted. While the stated reason for this tough policy was to improve the quality of medical service, it also restricted the supply of doctors and increased their incomes.]

Before examining the detailed economic effects of unions, we first briefly review the long struggle to establish unions in the United States.

LABOR UNIONS: THEIR HISTORICAL DEVELOPMENT

You must offer the American working man bread and butter in the here and now, instead of pie in the sky in the sweet bye and bye.
The philosophy of early labor leader Samuel Gompers (as described by Charles Killingworth)

The beginning of the American union movement dates back to an era in which a relatively powerless labor force lived in poverty, or near to it. In the last third of the nineteenth century, the Knights of Labor emerged, hoping to become the one great organization that might speak for all labor. Like the labor movement in England and a number of other European countries, the organization sought to make labor a unified force for radical political change.

But American workers have never been sympathetic to such an overt political objective. The Knights disappeared, to be replaced in the 1880s by the American Federation of Labor (AFL), led by Samuel Gompers and devoted to the bread-and-butter issues of improving wages and working conditions, rather than to pursuing a political class struggle. When asked what labor wanted, Gompers had a simple answer: "More."

The bread-and-butter approach remains an important characteristic of American labor. While unions sometimes support Democratic candidates, they often remain uncommitted, and on occasion support Republicans. Thus, American labor has not followed the common pattern in England and some other European countries of formal, close association with one political party.

Since its early beginnings, the history of American unions can be divided into the three periods sketched in Figure 19-1: (1) an initial low-membership period until the mid-1930s, (2) rapid growth for the next decade; and (3) the period since World War II.

The period before the Great Depression

Until the early 1930s, unions developed in a hostile climate. On the one hand, business executives strongly resisted any attempts to unionize their firms, and would frequently retaliate against pro-union workers by firing them and then blacklisting them with other potential employers. They would also sometimes use so-called *yellow-dog contracts:* A worker had to sign a commitment not to join a union in order to get a job.

An important question was how the courts would treat labor-management disputes. In particular, in light of the Sherman and Clayton antitrust acts, would they view unions as re-

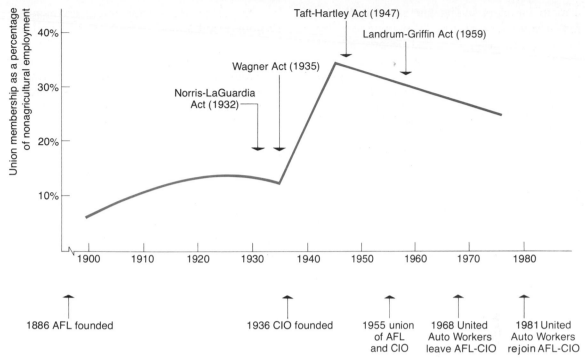

Figure 19-1

Major trends in U.S. union membership (relative to total employment)

American union membership remained low until the mid-thirties, then rose rapidly until the end of World War II. Since then, union membership has grown less rapidly than the labor force.

(*Source:* Department of Labor, *Handbook of Labor Statistics.*)

straints on trade? Judgments either for or against unions seemed possible: On the one hand, a union could be viewed as a restraint on trade, since it is a combination of workers seeking to raise wages, just as a collusive oligopoly is a combination of sellers seeking to raise price. On the other hand, the Clayton Act seemed to exclude unions by stating that "labor is not an article of commerce." By and large, the courts' judgments during this early period did not favor labor.

For several reasons, union growth was thwarted during the 1920s and early 1930s. The AFL lost ground because it remained firmly committed to the idea of craft unionism on which it was founded. Therefore, it did not adequately appeal to the increasing number of unskilled workers in mass-production industries, such as steel and autos. Moreover, there was growth in employer resistance to unionism. Employers introduced paternalistic schemes providing labor with relatively generous benefits in an attempt to demonstrate that workers would do better outside a union than in. And, as a result of growing court hostility toward unions, employers were allowed to use injunctions (court orders) to prevent unions from picketing, striking, or pursuing almost any other activity judged threatening to business. (Sometimes the courts issued injunctions without even hearing the union case.)

The period of rapid union growth before and during the Second World War

In the depths of the Depression in the 1930s, Congress passed several laws that improved the climate for unions. The first was the **Norris-LaGuardia Act** of 1932 that prevented employers from using what had become a prime weapon in the struggle against unions: the injunction. Court intervention in a labor dispute was to be limited to protecting property and preventing violence.

In 1935, the **Wagner Act** (National Labor Relations Act) moved the government from a position of neutrality to one that favored labor. This act had three key provisions:

1 It declared the legal right of workers to form unions.

2 It prohibited employers from a number of unfair labor practices, such as firing or blacklisting pro-union workers.

3 It established the National Labor Relations Board (NLRB) to control unfair labor practices by employers and to resolve disputes among unions. For example, the NLRB is empowered to hold elections in which workers decide which of two or more competing unions will represent them.

There is no question that the Wagner Act achieved its objective of removing the barriers to union growth: During the decade that followed, the proportion of the labor force that belonged to unions almost tripled. There was a second important reason for this growth. In 1936, several union leaders, led by John L. Lewis, split away from the AFL because of its concentration on craft unions. They formed the Congress of Industrial Organizations (CIO), a collection of *industrial* unions. Between 1936 and 1945, the CIO had great success in unionizing autos, steel, and other mass-production industries. (In 1955, the two unions resolved their differences and rejoined forces in the new AFL-CIO.)

The postwar period

Since World War II, unions have ceased to grow at the rapid rate of the preceding period. In fact, although their membership has grown moderately, it has not grown as rapidly as the labor force, so that the percentage of workers in unions has actually declined. There are several reasons for this.

First, heavy industry (where union membership tends to be most solidly concentrated) has had declining employment relative to other sectors of the economy. There also has been a shift in industrial jobs to the South, where unionism is weaker than in the North. In addition, attitudes toward unions have undergone change. Postwar unemployment rates have been much lower than during the 1930s, and this decline has weakened the commitment to unions. (During the Depression, workers felt desperately powerless and looked to unions for protection.) And unions may have overplayed their hand during the Second World War. During the early war years, unions had added muscle in the form of a rapidly increasing membership. By 1944 they were flexing that muscle in a series of strikes that many of the public viewed as damaging to the war effort. The feeling that unions were becoming too powerful contributed to the passage of the **Taft-Hartley Act** in the face of stiff union opposition.

The Taft-Hartley Act (1947) Just as the Wagner Act twelve years earlier had dealt with "unfair" employer practices, the Taft-Hartley Act now attempted to outlaw "unfair" union practices. For example, it prohibited **closed shops** in industries engaged in interstate commerce. (Since only union members could be hired in a closed shop, it provided a union with veto power over who could be hired.) The Taft-Hartley Act also prohibited jurisdictional strikes (conflicts between unions over whose members will do specific jobs). It also forbade the "checkoff" of union dues unless workers agree to it in writing. (With a checkoff, employers collect dues for the union by deducting them from workers' paychecks.) In addition, the Taft-Hartley Act included provisions to increase the financial responsibility of union leaders. For example, it required pension funds to be kept separate from other union funds, and required union leaders to provide both their own membership and the National Labor Relations Board with detailed information on how union funds were being spent. The act also contained a provision to delay strikes which "imperil the national health or safety." Specifically, the U.S. president was empowered to seek a court injunction in such circumstances to require strikers to return to work for an 80-day cooling-off period.

But the most controversial provision of the Taft-Hartley Act was contained in its famous section 14(b). This recognized state **right-to-work laws** which forbid compulsory unionism, and thus make the **closed shop** and the **union shop** illegal. About 20 states—mostly in the South—have passed such laws. Union leaders consider section 14(b) to be overtly anti-union, and they have worked hard for its repeal. Indeed, opposition to 14(b) is considered an acid test of whether a politician is pro-union or not.

A *closed shop* means that a firm can hire only workers who are already union members.

A *union shop* permits the hiring of nonunion members, but requires workers who are not yet members to join the union within a specified period (such as 30 days).

A *right-to-work law* outlaws the closed shop and the union shop in favor of the *open shop* (in which there is no requirement to join a union).

The Landrum-Griffin Act This act was passed in 1959 by a Congress that was concerned over union corruption and wished to increase the restraints on union leaders. Among other stipulations, union officials were prohibited from borrowing more than $2,000 of union funds; the embezzlement of union funds became a federal offense; and restrictions were placed on ex-convicts seeking union offices. This act also sought to make union decisions more democratic by strengthening the power of members to challenge their leaders through the ballot box: It required regularly scheduled elections of union officers by secret ballot, with every member being eligible to vote. Moreover, a member's right to participate in any union meeting was guaranteed, and any member was given the right to sue a union that tried to withhold any of these privileges. While it is difficult to judge how effective this legislation has been in limiting union corruption, one conclusion is clear: It has still not completely solved the problem. (In the last two decades, workers have found that it is not only their boss who may end up in the slammer; it may be their union leader as well. In an extreme example in the late 1960s, Joseph Yablonski challenged Tony Boyle for the leadership of the United Mine Workers. After losing the election, Yablonski threatened to expose irregularities within the union. On December 31, 1969, an intruder murdered him, his wife, and his daughter in their sleep. In 1974, Boyle was convicted of arranging this murder, and was sentenced to three life terms in jail. In two subsequent retrials, he was convicted again.)

LABOR UNIONS: THE EXERCISE OF MARKET POWER

Since unions bargain over wages and working conditions for their membership, they must be included in any realistic analysis of the labor market. In this section we consider the effects of a union that exercises its market power to (1) raise the wage rate, and (2) ensure employment for its members.

The economic effects when a union negotiates higher wages: A first approximation

We begin by assuming that employers have no market power on the other side of the market. In other words, employers take the wage rate as given.

Suppose that, with no union, equilibrium in a perfectly competitive labor market for an industry is at point E_1 in Figure 19-2. Now assume that this industry is unionized—that is, the workers who supply labor form a monopoly (a union) to raise their wage rate. (In the United States, unions seem to raise wages by roughly 10–18 percent; that is, union members earn, on average, about 10–18 percent more than nonunion

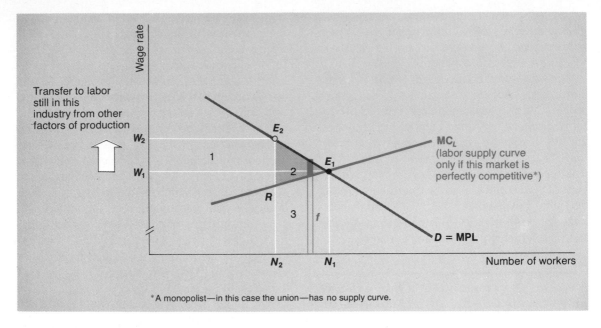

Figure 19-2

The effects of unionizing an industry in a previously competitive labor market

When a union is formed, equilibrium moves from the perfectly competitive point E_1 to E_2. (The union raises the wage rate to W_2, and employers respond by reducing employment to N_2.) As a result, there is a transfer from other factors of production to workers who are still employed. The direction of this transfer is shown by the white arrow; its amount is area 1.

Triangle 2 is the resulting efficiency loss. It is explained by following the analysis in Figure 18-7c. Consider worker f who has been laid off. His productivity in this industry was the empty bar plus the solid bar (the height of the demand curve). But his productivity elsewhere—his opportunity cost—is only the empty bar (the height of the MC_L curve). So when he loses his job in this industry and must take a job elsewhere, the lost productivity is the solid bar. Triangle 2 is the lost productivity from all such laid-off workers in the range $N_1 N_2$ who must shift to lower productivity jobs.

(Notice that the efficiency loss is only area 2. Why isn't it area 2 *plus* 3, like the loss with a minimum wage in Figure 18-5, panel *d*? We have already seen that the minimum wage loss in that earlier diagram would be reduced to the degree that unemployed workers find jobs elsewhere. And in the present case of the unionization of an industry, workers do get jobs elsewhere, where their earnings and productivity are shown by area 3. Therefore, area 3 is not a loss. Accordingly, the net loss is only red triangle 2.)

workers in comparable activities.[2]) In our example in Figure 19-2, suppose the union raises the wage rate from W_1 to W_2. (The enforcement of this higher wage requires "union discipline." Members must not be allowed to offer their labor services for less than W_2.) Faced with wage W_2, employers react by moving up their demand curve from E_1 to E_2. Because the union has raised wages, employment is reduced from N_1 to N_2.

Now consider the transfer and efficiency effects of this policy. The transfer is shown by the white arrow on the left of this diagram. Because

[2]See Richard B. Freeman and James L. Medoff, "The Two Faces of Unionism," p. 78, and C. J. Parsley, "Labor Union Effects on Wage Gains: A Survey of Recent Literature," *Journal of Economic Literature,* March 1980, p. 20.

Wesley Mellow ("Unionism and Wages: A Longitudinal Analysis," *Review of Economics and Statistics,* February, 1981, p. 51) estimates that the union effect is slightly less than this. However, Greg J. Duncan and Frank B. Stafford (in "Do Union Members Receive Compensating Wage Differentials?" *American Economic Review,* June 1980, p. 370) estimate that the union's effect is even greater, but estimate that most of this greater effect is compensation for less attractive working conditions—a faster pace, a more structured work setting, and so on.

of the higher wage, workers who still have jobs in this industry benefit, while other factors of production lose. At the same time, there is an efficiency loss shown by the red triangle (as detailed in the caption to Figure 19-2). This loss occurs because employment has been reduced from its perfectly competitive, efficient amount at N_1 to N_2, and displaced workers have had to move to industries where their productivity is lower.

But again, notice that in arriving at any such conclusion on efficiency in Part 3, we must make assumptions similar to those made in Part 2. For example, we assume that perfectly competitive conditions exist elsewhere in the economy. And we also keep in mind that, although we can make the statement that the move from E_1 to E_2 is inefficient, we cannot make the stronger statement that this move "is damaging overall to the economy" without making some assumption about how the winners and the losers compare in their evaluation of income. Remember: As always, efficiency is desirable; but it's not the whole story.

Finally, note that the similarity of labor and goods markets, first noted in the previous chapter, continues to hold. In particular, Figure 19-2 shows that the monopolization of a labor market is similar to the monopolization of a product market in Figure 11-6a, except, of course, that we are now talking about the wage and employment of labor rather than the price and quantity of a product.[3]

*[3]However, there is an important reason why we cannot analyze monopoly in a labor market in exactly the same way as we analyze monopoly in a product market. In a product market, a monopoly firm will take into account any loss of sales (reduction in output) that results from its high price. But in a labor market, it is not clear how fully a union will take into account any reduced employment that results from its high wage. This may be particularly true if the industry is growing and if the high wage does not displace any of the *current* union members, but instead reduces only the number of *new* workers coming into the industry. This difficulty prevents us from determining the level of W_2 by applying the standard analysis of monopoly in Chapter 11, where MC is equated to MR. (The union may not care much about the MC and MR of additional new workers.) Therefore, we cannot be specific about how much a union will try to raise the wage rate.

Featherbedding: The economic effects

Any idiot can decide whether to hire one or two boys to wash his car. But the head of Britain's largest car company can't decide whether 1,000 or 2,000 workers should be employed on an assembly line.
Overheard in an English pub.

As well as raising the wages of its members, a union may seek to protect their jobs. This may become a prime objective if employment is shrinking (for example, because demand for the product has been falling off, or laborsaving machines have been introduced). There are two principal ways that a union may try to prevent the loss of jobs. One is to negotiate a reduction in the number of hours in a standard workweek; if all workers work fewer hours, no worker need be laid off. (Moreover, if the union is able to negotiate a sufficient increase in the per hour wage rate, its members may not suffer any income reduction; they may work less for the same pay.)

The second way that a strong union may deal with falling employment is to use its bargaining strength (by striking, if necessary) to negotiate a *featherbedding* agreement. One example is the agreement that standby musicians be hired when nonunion musicians are performing. Another example occurs when newspapers, provided with advertising copy that is completely typeset, then have to turn around and hire union members to set this type again. This "bogus type" is never used.

Featherbedding is the employment of labor in superfluous jobs.[4]

Historically, the most famous example was provided by railroad firemen, who used to shovel coal to keep the fires burning in the old steam

[4]Featherbedding as defined by the Taft-Hartley Act (payment for work not actually performed) is illegal. Here we are concerned with a broader definition that includes cases where workers are on the job, but the work is contrived. (That is, the job would not exist were it not guaranteed by the union-management contract.)

locomotives. But with the development of the diesel engine—which has no fire—their jobs disappeared. Yet their employment remained guaranteed by a union contract. Another, more recent example has arisen in the airlines. Although large airliners have traditionally required three crew members in the cockpit, the FAA has judged that only two are now required on some of the new models with more advanced electronic equipment. But the Airline Pilots Association has threatened to suspend service unless there are three crew members in the cockpit. They state that the problem is one of safety: A larger crew is better able to watch out for other aircraft. The airlines reply is that this is just featherbedding.

In this case it may be difficult to sort out how much of the problem is safety and how much is featherbedding. But other cases are more clearcut. For example, the use of "bogus type" is featherbedding pure and simple. What is the effect of such superfluous work? The answer is that it generally keeps employment in that industry higher than in a perfectly competitive market.[5] Specifically, it keeps employment at N_2 in Figure 18-7b on p. 371, rather than allowing it to fall to the competitive amount N_1. And it leads to an efficiency loss which is at least as great (and often greater) than the red triangle shown in that earlier diagram. (That triangular efficiency loss was based on the assumption that employers use the extra workers they hire as productively as possible. However, many featherbedding contracts require employers not only to hire more workers, but also to assign them to low- or zero-productivity tasks, such as the setting of "bogus type." This makes the efficiency loss even greater.)

Is this judgment on featherbedding too severe? Because it protects workers who might otherwise have difficulty in getting another job, isn't it a way of introducing compassion into the economic system? The answer is yes, but it is a bad way to do it. Far better to ease labor's shift into other jobs than to have society carry an overhead of unproductive employment into the future. [A common way of negotiating the end to a featherbedding contract is for the company to guarantee that all those individuals now holding jobs will continue to be employed; but they will not be replaced. Although this may be a costly solution, it does guarantee that the problem will disappear as the present work force reaches retirement age. This is far superior to a featherbedding contract, where the inefficiency doesn't disappear when people retire because they keep getting replaced in useless jobs. (More on the relation between efficiency and compassion is provided in Box 19-1.)]

HOW UNIONS INCREASE EFFICIENCY: THE OTHER SIDE OF THE COIN

In our analysis so far, we have seen how a union may reduce efficiency by negotiating a monopoly increase in wages that results in less employment. But this is only part of the story; a union may also have *favorable* effects on efficiency.

1 By providing workers with a collective voice, a union makes it possible for them to improve their working conditions rather than quitting. Thus there may be less labor turnover, less disruption in the workplace and lower hiring and training costs.

2 Unions can improve the morale of the work force, and improve communication between workers and management; this may lead to better decision-making.

3 Even in its role of raising wages, a union may increase efficiency rather than reduce it. It is true that raising wages does reduce efficiency (by the red triangle in Figure 19-2) *but only if market power is held solely by the union*. We shall now show that if market power is initially held by *employers* on the other side of the market, then the formation of a union may be a desirable counterbalance that *increases* efficiency.

---

[5]This is not always the case, however. The "bogus type" requirement contributed to the death of newspapers in a declining industry. It therefore may have resulted in fewer newspaper jobs (even though it may have kept up the number of typesetting jobs).

BOX 19-1

The Conflicting Objectives of Compassion and Efficiency

Two centuries ago, at the beginning of the industrial revolution in Britain, laborsaving machinery was introduced into the textile industry. Displaced workers in those days had much bleaker prospects than today: It was harder to find another job. And without a job, a family faced severe malnutrition, or worse. Consequently, there were riots in which workers (the Luddites) broke into the factories, destroying the new laborsaving machines. While recognizing their plight, we must ask: Suppose they had succeeded? Suppose laborsaving machinery had been banned, and their primitive handcrafting jobs guaranteed? If they and their heirs had been successful in thwarting technological change, wouldn't our situation today be very much like theirs two centuries ago? And if so, what progress would we have made against the problem that concerned them most: poverty?

Although laborsaving machinery may create transitional unemployment, it creates far better jobs in the long run. When bulldozers are introduced, whole armies of workers with shovels lose their jobs. But in the long run, this is highly beneficial both for society and also, in most cases, *for the workers who initially lose their jobs.* This is not only true of the ditchdiggers who get higher-paying jobs driving the bulldozers. It is also true of the other ditchdiggers, who get jobs in new, growing industries (aircraft, electronics, etc.). These jobs exist because the introduction of bulldozers and other machines increases our ability to produce, and therefore raises our income and purchasing power; this in turn means that we can afford to buy goods that did not exist before.

In brief, society benefits because the labor force is engaged in more productive activities than ditchdigging. Because machines now perform menial jobs, we produce and consume

more. This example illustrates why we should not automatically choose compassion over efficiency, but instead, should search for policies that combine both. Historically, economic progress—our increased level of efficiency—is the reason that we now have the income to be able to afford more compassion than we could have 200 years ago. We are now wealthy enough to ensure people against the extremes of poverty that had to be faced in earlier, less productive eras. The point is a simple one: We should exercise compassion, but not in ways that thwart progress because they lock in inefficiency. ∎

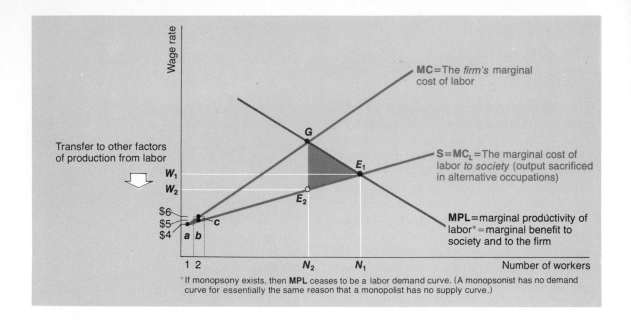

*If monopsony exists, then **MPL** ceases to be a labor demand curve. (A monopsonist has no demand curve for essentially the same reason that a monopolist has no supply curve.)

MONOPSONY: MARKET POWER ON THE EMPLOYERS' SIDE OF THE LABOR MARKET

Employers typically quote the wage rate they will pay. In doing so, they frequently do not act like perfect competitors who take a market wage as given. Instead, they exercise market power to keep the wage rate down.

To analyze this situation, we initially assume exactly the same perfectly competitive market that we began with in Figure 19-2, with equilibrium at E_1 reproduced in Figure 19-3. But this time, instead of introducing monopoly (a single seller, in the form of a union) we introduce **monopsony** (a single buyer—that is, a single employer of labor). What happens if this single employer quotes a lower wage rate (while workers on the other side of the market act as perfect competitors, taking this wage rate as given)? Specifically, suppose that the employer quotes a wage W_2 below the perfectly competitive wage W_1. In response to wage W_2, some workers leave this now unattractive industry for other jobs; in other words, they move down their supply curve from E_1 to a new equilibrium at E_2. (Details on

Figure 19-3
Effects when a perfectly competitive labor market is monopsonized

When a monopsony is formed, equilibrium moves from the perfectly competitive point E_1 to E_2. (Because the monopsonist quotes lower wage W_2, fewer workers offer their labor services—and employment falls from N_1 to N_2.) As first explained in Figure 18-7c, there is the efficiency loss shown by the red triangle, as some workers shift into lower-productivity jobs in other industries. Finally, the lower wage results in a transfer from labor to other factors of production, as indicated by the white arrow on the left.

how the employer will select the precise wage W_2 are given in Box 19-2.)

The transfer effect of the employer lowering the wage is shown as the white arrow to the left of this diagram. Workers are paid a lower wage, and other factors of production benefit as a consequence.[6] At the same time, there is the red triangular efficiency loss, because employment is less than its perfectly competitive amount at N_1.

[6]Note to instructors: Figure 19-3 (and others in this chapter) may be supplemented with a multipanel analysis (similar to Figure 18-5) that shows how each group in the economy is affected. Details are given in the *Instructor's Manual*.

BOX 19-2

How Far Does a Monopsonist Try to Reduce the Wage Rate?

To choose the wage rate that will maximize its profits, the monopsonist first calculates MC (its marginal cost in hiring more labor) from the supply of labor S. This calculation is illustrated in the lower left hand corner of Figure 19-3: From the S curve we see that the firm must pay $4 an hour to hire one worker (bar a), and $5 an hour to hire two (bar b). But the firm's marginal cost of hiring the second worker (MC) is not $5, but is instead $6—the $5 bar b that it must pay the second worker, *plus* the additional dollar (bar c) it must pay the first worker to raise his or her wage from $4 to $5. Thus, the marginal cost of labor to the monopsony firm (MC) lies above the supply curve of labor S.

To maximize profit, this firm hires labor to the point G where its marginal cost of hiring labor (MC) is equal to its marginal benefit from hiring labor (MPL, labor's marginal productivity). With its desired employment thus being N_2, what's the lowest wage it can quote? The answer is W_2, which is the point on the S curve above N_2. [At this wage rate, the supply curve S indicates that just exactly the desired number of workers (N_2) will offer their services to this firm.]

However, one important qualification must be made. The choice is this simple only when labor is unskilled, and needs no training. If the firm has to train new workers, then workers are obviously no longer identical: Experienced workers are more productive than new workers. In such circumstances, the firm might wisely decide not to try to get workers cheaply. By offering more than wage W_2, the firm can reduce turnover and training costs. One example of such behavior occurred in the early days of the Ford Motor Company, when Ford offered a wage above the going rate—and thus got the pick of the labor force.

[This box provides another view of why inefficiency (the red triangle) arises from an employment level of N_2: Note that the marginal cost of labor *for the firm* (MC) is *not* the same as the marginal cost of labor *for society* (S, the output labor could produce in another activity). And the private firm is equating the marginal benefit of labor (MPL) to its *own* marginal cost MC, rather than to *society's* marginal cost S. Notice how this analysis of monopsony inefficiency parallels the analysis of monopoly inefficiency in Figure 11-6; in each case inefficiency arises because *the marginal benefit to society is not being equated to the marginal cost to society.*] ■

This loss occurs because the workers between N_1 and N_2 who leave this industry go to less productive jobs elsewhere. (An example of an even stronger exercise of monopsony power is given in Box 19-3.)

How does monopsony in the labor market arise? There are several possible answers: There may be just one firm hiring labor in a small town. Or employers might band together to form a bargaining association to depress wages and thus increase their own income. Here we see another example of Adam Smith's "invisible hand" gone astray: The monopsonist's pursuit of private benefit does *not* lead to public benefit. Quite the contrary: It leads to the efficiency loss shown by the red triangle in this diagram.

In reality, there are few cases in which monopsony occurs in its pure form (only *one* buyer). There is more likely to be a small group of employers, that is, an oligopsony (a few buyers). In quoting a wage rate, each firm has some latitude; but to a greater or lesser degree it is influenced by the wages quoted by competing firms. On the one hand, competition among

Monopsony and Discrimination in the Labor Market

Monopsonists who use their market power to depress the wage rate of their entire labor force may go one step further and reduce even more the wage paid to a specific subset of their workers (for example, minorities). To illustrate, consider the monopsonistic firm that has used its market power to depress the wage rate in Figure 19-3 from the perfectly competitive level W_1 to W_2. It may then go one step further and offer minorities an even lower wage. Such discrimina-tion may be in the economic interest of the firm for the same profit-making reason that induced the doctor to charge different fees in Figure 11-8.

But this example of racial discrimination is *unlike* another described earlier in Figure 18-9, at least in one important respect: Here discrimi-nation *is* in the interest of the employer who practices it, whereas it was not in the firm's interest in the situation described in Figure 18-9.

these firms may leave each with very little latitude—that is, very little influence over the wage it can quote. In this case, the wage may be close to the competitive level W_1. But if the few oligopsonists collude (either overtly or by such covert means as "wage leadership"), they may together lower the wage rate well below W_1—at or near the level W_2 that a monopsonist would choose.

Although monopsony in its pure form (only one buyer) is rare, there has been one notable example: the monopsony power that the owners of baseball clubs used to have in buying the services of their players.

Monopsony and baseball salaries

I don't understand why grown men play this game anyhow. They ought to be lawyers or doctors or garbage men. Games should be left for kids.

Ted Turner, owner of the Atlanta Braves

One reason grown men play baseball is because of the high income it offers, especially since the monopsony power of club owners like Ted Turn-er was broken in 1976. Before this, the "reserve clause" had made each major league owner a monopsonist, since a player could not sign a contract with any other major league team. But,

beginning in 1976, a player in certain circum-stances could become a free agent and negotiate with other clubs. Figure 19-4 shows what hap-pened. A comparison of the before-and-after salaries of these players indicates the remarkable way that the monopsony power of the reserve clause had depressed players' salaries. And con-firming evidence has continued to pour in. In 1979, free agent Nolan Ryan signed a 3-year contract for $1 million a year. But as any baseball fan knows, even this became peanuts a year later. (See Box 19-4.)

[The reserve clause was obviously bad for the players. But was it bad for the game? Owners in small cities argue that, without the reserve clause, teams in large cities like New York will be able to use their larger gate receipts to "buy a world series" by bidding away all the superstars from smaller cities like Cincinnati. Games will become lopsided. Thus, competition among clubs for players will destroy competition be-tween teams on the playing field and ruin the game. To support their case the owners point to the World Series of 1977 and 1978 as omens of things to come. Both were won by the New York Yankees, rich in superstars signed from other clubs. One of these—Reggie Jackson—hit three home runs in the final 1977 Series game. And big-city Philadelphia, led by Pete Rose who had

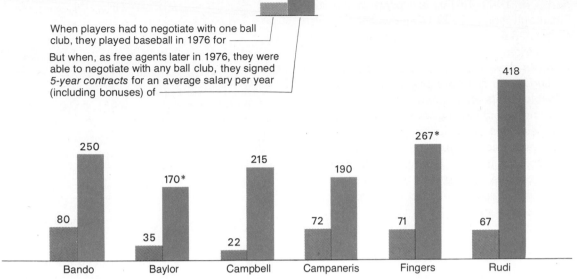

When players had to negotiate with one ball club, they played baseball in 1976 for ⎯

But when, as free agents later in 1976, they were able to negotiate with any ball club, they signed *5-year contracts* for an average salary per year (including bonuses) of ⎯

	Bando	Baylor	Campbell	Campaneris	Fingers	Rudi
Free agent	250	170*	215	190	267*	418
Reserve	80	35	22	72	71	67

*Annual average over a *six* year contract

Figure 19-4
How monopsony (the reserve clause) depressed baseball salaries. (Numbers in $000s, rounded.)

Multimillionaires in Baseball: The Dave Winfield Story

In 1980 the baseball world was astonished when the New York Yankees signed free agent Dave Winfield to a contract worth an estimated average of $1.5 million to $2 million *per year for ten years.* This salary was due to Winfield's escape, as a free agent, from the monopsony power of the reserve clause: His salary in San Diego the previous year was only $350,000. (To get some idea of Winfield's "before-and-after" situation, just increase the height of both bars for Baylor in Figure 19-4 by *ten times.*) Further evidence that Winfield's high salary was due to his free agent status was to be found in the much lower salaries of equally good (or arguably better) players still held in the grip of the reserve clause. For example, Ron Guidry, a Yankee teammate and one of the best pitchers in baseball, was receiving only an estimated $250,000 a year. And Baltimore's Eddie Murray—with a higher batting average than Winfield, and more yearly home runs and runs-batted-in—was earning just $150,000 a year. ■

been bid away from Cincinnati, won the World Series in 1980. (In an exception to the rule, Pittsburgh won in 1979.) The owners have also contended that the huge salaries that result from these bidding wars are unfair, since the superstar who can draw the crowds is paid far too much relative to the first-class player who is also very valuable to his team. Owners argued that they could not avoid bidding wars—stars attract fans. But they could not at the same time bid for stars, pay reasonable salaries to other players, and still make profits. In 1981, a baseball strike occurred when owners insisted that the status of free agents be changed in order to control the bidding wars for stars.]

The effects of unions reconsidered

We are now in a position to show why our criticism of unions, which held if markets were initially competitive, is no longer necessarily justified if there is monopsony power on the other side of the market.

Figure 19-5 shows how a union that raises wages can actually raise, rather than lower, economic efficiency. This will occur, for example, if a monopsonist has already lowered the wage rate from the competitive level W to W_1. At this lower wage, fewer workers have been offering their labor services to this industry. Therefore, the monopsonist has reduced employment in this industry from N to N_1 (moved the equilibrium from E to E_1), with a consequent efficiency loss of areas $1 + 2$. If a union is now formed and raises the wage rate from W_1 to W_2 (moving the equilibrium from E_1 to E_2), the efficiency loss is reduced from areas $1 + 2$ to just area 2. In other words, the formation of this union results in an efficiency gain of area 1. (Of course, formation of this union has also benefited union members by recapturing some of the income previously lost to the monopsonist.)

Thus, the following case can be made for unions: By forming a union in a labor market dominated by monopsonistic employers quoting a take-it-or-leave-it wage rate like W_1, workers send a representative to the bargaining table

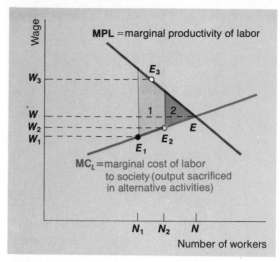

Figure 19-5
How inefficiency may be reduced if a union raises wages in a monopsonized labor market
Before the union, the monopsonist sets the wage rate at W_1; with equilibrium at E_1, there is an efficiency loss of $1 + 2$. When the union is formed it raises the wage to W_2. Equilibrium moves from E_1 to E_2, some employment is restored, and the efficiency loss is reduced to area 2. In other words, this increased wage improves efficiency by area 1. It also transfers income from the monopsonist to labor. But if the union pushes the wage up past the competitive wage W—for example to W_3—equilibrium will be moved away from E to E_3, and efficiency will be reduced once again.

who can counter by presenting the same sort of take-it-or-leave-it offer to management: "If you do not accept our wage claim, then we will strike your firm, withdrawing all workers from the job and closing down your operations." Thus the union allows workers to speak from a position of strength, and the wage will be negotiated between union and management. Typically, it will lie somewhere between the two initial "take-it-or-leave-it" offers of the two parties. Only in this way can labor exercise what Harvard's Kenneth Galbraith calls **countervailing power** to prevent the wage from being depressed to a level like W_1 in Figure 19-5. And if labor thus raises its wage from W_1 to W_2, it will be promoting its own interest *and* increasing overall economic efficiency.[7] Moreover, union practices like picketing are a means of increasing the union's countervailing position of strength by ensuring that the union is effectively speaking for all labor, and that the employer cannot hire substitute labor.

A complication

Such is the case for unions. But it does not justify all exercise of market power. If a union gets very strong and pushes the wage up beyond W toward W_3, equilibrium will shift away from E toward E_3 and efficiency will once again be reduced.

Thus, the typical policy problem in the labor market is not that one side has market power and the other does not, but rather, that the relative power of the two may be imbalanced. If the government is pursuing the objective of making labor markets more efficient, it should be very careful if it is reducing the bargaining power of one group and not the other. If the market power of the group that is already in the weaker position is being reduced, this government action will be making the problem of imbalance worse, rather than better.

This discussion also allows us to sharpen up our earlier conclusion about a minimum wage. If a minimum wage raises the wage rate in Figure 31-5 from an existing very low level like W_1 toward the competitive level W, employment and efficiency in this labor market will be increased, rather than decreased. On the other hand, if the minimum wage is set at a higher level and therefore raises the wage rate *away from W* and toward W_3, employment and efficiency will be reduced. Therefore, a useful guideline for a minimum wage is to set it near the competitive wage level in most industries. (This guideline is difficult to put into practice because competitive wage rates are difficult to estimate, and they differ among industries.)

BILATERAL MONOPOLY: RELATIVE BARGAINING POWER

When both sides have market power (as in Figure 19-5), they will push in opposite directions. While the employer tries to keep the wage rate down close to W_1, the union tries to push it up close to W_3. The outcome will depend on the bargaining power of the two sides; we cannot tell by looking at the MC_L and MPL curves precisely where the final solution will be.

Which side has the stronger bargaining position?

To see the importance of bargaining power, suppose that there is only one company in a mining town, and that it faces an ineffective union representing only a minority of the workers. In this case, the company will be in a good position to keep the wage low. On the other hand, if there is one union facing a number of employers, the union may have the stronger bargaining position. It is sometimes suggested that this is the situation in the auto industry (although Ford and GM can scarcely be considered weak bargaining adversaries).

If the United Auto Workers (UAW) judges that its negotiations with the industry are not proceeding in a satisfactory way, it typically threatens to pull its workers out on strike in one of the auto companies, say Ford. If it does so, Ford workers on strike will get income support from a union strike fund drawn from workers from all the auto companies. But the company being struck (Ford) does not get the same sort of support from the other companies in the indus-

---

[7]This is another example of the *theory of the second best*, first encountered in Box 11-1. If there is only a single firm in a small town, it will inevitably be able to exercise monopsony influence over the wage rate. The economist's "first best" efficient solution (perfect competition on both sides of the market) is simply not possible, no matter how desirable it might be. Instead, we must look for a second best solution. This may involve workers forming a union in order to influence price and thus counterbalance the power that the monopsonist already enjoys on the other side of the market.

try.[8] True, Ford may get moral support from the other firms, but they still go on selling cars and cutting into Ford's market. And therein lies Ford's problem. If it is shut down by a strike and unable to produce cars, it will find that its share of the market is being eroded and that its profits are falling. In fact, a strong union may have the power to drive a company bankrupt—and sometimes this does happen, although not by design.

(Workers rightly regard driving a firm out of business as "overkill," since this would destroy their jobs. Consequently, a union is unlikely to pick as its target one of the financially weak companies in an industry; American Motors is not a prime target of the UAW. If a firm is already close to bankruptcy, a strike threat may be very ineffective. It may be met only by the resigned observation: "If we agree to your wage demand, we go bankrupt. If we don't and you strike, we go bankrupt. There is nothing we can do." And the negotiations end there. Consequently, the union will select as its target a company that is reasonably sound financially—one that is both able to afford a sizable wage increase, and can be hurt a great deal by a strike without being driven bankrupt.)

STRIKES

The bargaining position of either side can also depend on its ability to outlast the other in a long strike. For example, the credibility of a strike threat by a union depends in part on the size of its strike fund. If this has been depleted by earlier strikes, the union is in a weak position. The company can play a strong hand, making a low offer (close to W_1) and sticking close to it, with the knowledge that the union cannot afford to strike. On the other hand, a company will be in a weak bargaining position if *it* cannot afford a strike. This may be the case for several reasons:

1 A construction company that has to pay heavy penalties for delay in completing a project may be forced to capitulate to a union strike threat.

2 A firm producing a perishable good or service may be in a weak bargaining position because sales and profits lost during a strike may be lost forever. ["Perishable" is used broadly, applying not only to physically perishable goods (such as fruit) but also to a good that goes out of date. For example, if a newspaper cannot deliver today's edition, the papers become worthless.]

Of course, firms producing goods that are not perishable are in a much stronger position—especially if these firms have accumulated large inventories, and can consequently keep selling right through a strike. It is no accident that before critical wage negotiations, companies try to build up inventories, just as unions try to build up strike funds.

The cost of a strike

Strikes are costly to both sides: to labor in the form of lost wages, to management in the form of lost sales and profits. To illustrate, suppose that, in the absence of a strike, the wage is W in Figure 19-6, with employment N. Then a strike that reduces employment to zero involves a temporary cost in terms of lost output valued at areas $1 + 2$. Labor loses income 1 (its wage W times employment N) while the income lost by other factors is the remaining area 2. (Note that this is only the short-run cost of a strike, since it applies only so long as labor and other factors of production do not seek employment elsewhere.)

Since both parties face a substantial loss in the event of a strike, it is often assumed that when a strike does occur, it is the result of an error in judgment by at least one of the conflicting parties. That need not be the case, as we will see in the next section.

---

[8]Sometimes industries make exceptions. An example was the 1958 pact by the airlines: If one were struck, the others agreed to share their revenue with it, in order to increase its strength in resisting union demands. The companies' objective was to prevent the union from picking them off one at a time.

Transit Strike in the Big Apple

When a strike of transit workers closed down the New York subway and bus systems in 1980, economic life in the city was snarled. Retail sales fell by about 30 percent, and absenteeism more than doubled. But even for those who managed to get to work, the cost was high: Pin-striped executives resorted to roller skates, and thousands walked across the Brooklyn bridge, cheered on by the mayor. Thousands of people took to bicycles; some lines at air pumps were 45 minutes long. The only bright spot: Serious crime was down 23 percent; the muggers too had trouble getting to work. ■

Labor-management negotiations to avoid strikes

Case *a* in Figure 19-7 illustrates the overwhelming majority of situations: Labor and management should be able to find a wage to agree on,

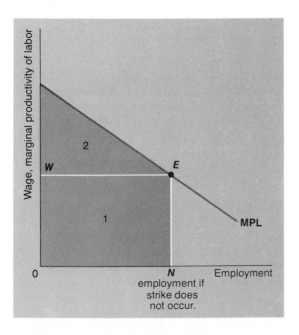

and thus avoid a strike. The range of wages acceptable to management (arrow M) and the range of wages acceptable to labor (arrow L) overlap through the shaded range W_1W_2. Any wage rate in this positive, shaded "contract zone" is acceptable to both parties. (Remember: The term "wage rate" includes fringe benefits.) The actual negotiations may begin with labor demanding W_4 and management offering W_3. To the public, it appears that they are far apart, and there is little hope of an agreement. But as the negotiations proceed, both sides compromise, trading off one claim against another. (Often

Figure 19-6
Short-run cost of a strike to labor and other factors of production

Without a strike, the value of total output in this industry is area 1 + 2, as first noted in Figure 18-4. Labor earns area 1, and other factors of production earn 2. But *if a strike does occur,* both these income areas are lost. (The cost may be less if some of the production lost during a strike can be made up after the strike is settled; or if, in anticipation of the strike, the firm is able to increase its output and inventories.)

neither party will officially concede anything; this may be viewed as a sign of weakness. Instead, each simply remains silent on a claim made by the other, and this "trade" is thereafter mutually recognized.) Thus management "moves up its arrow M" and labor moves down its arrow L, until they reach a point of agreement at, say, W_5. (Often they may not move much until just before a strike deadline, when both parties work furiously to reach a settlement.) In settling on W_5, management's negotiating team claims success; labor has been negotiated all the way down from its original demand of W_4. The union is also able to claim success; it has negotiated management all the way up from its original offer of W_3.

Following this pattern (or one similar to it) most labor negotiations result in an agreement; a strike is avoided. But of course the highly publicized cases are those where a strike *does* occur. How does this happen? One answer is shown in panel *b* where L and M do not overlap. There is *no* wage acceptable to both parties, regardless of the negotiating skill they may display. We return to that case in a moment, but first we explain why a strike may occur even in panel *a* (where there *is* a mutually acceptable range of wage rates). Two reasons have been cited:

1 One of the parties may have some extraneous objective. For example, a company may want a strike as a means of weakening or destroying workers' support for their union. Alternatively, the union may want a strike in the belief that it will improve labor solidarity and morale. Or, either side may want a strike as a way to increase its long-run credibility—as a means of establishing that when it threatens a strike in future negotiations, it is not bluffing.

2 One of the two parties may engage in poor bargaining strategy. For example, suppose that management's initial offer is far below W_3—in fact, so low that it is viewed by labor as an insult. The anger that results may sour the negotiations enough to cause an unnecessary strike. An alternative bargaining error by management is to make an initial offer that is too *generous*. Specifically, suppose management initially offers W_1,

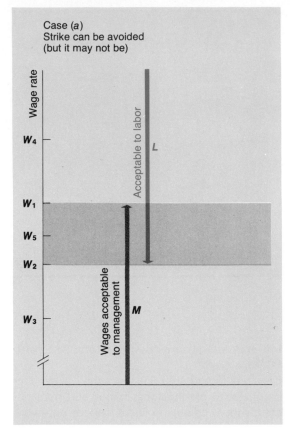

Figure 19-7
Some of the reasons why strikes occur

and states that this is its final, best possible offer (which it is; note that W_1 is right at the top of arrow M). The problem is that the union leaders may not believe it. They may view it as a standard opening offer and attempt to negotiate it up. When this attempt fails, a strike occurs because the union cannot accept W_1. (It will look foolish to its membership if it has gone through weeks or months of trying to negotiate the company up and has been unable to budge it an inch. It will seem that management has dictated the wage from the beginning, and all that the union has done is to make concessions. Why do the workers need such a union?) Thus, although management has been very generous in offering W_1, it has inadvertently caused a strike because it

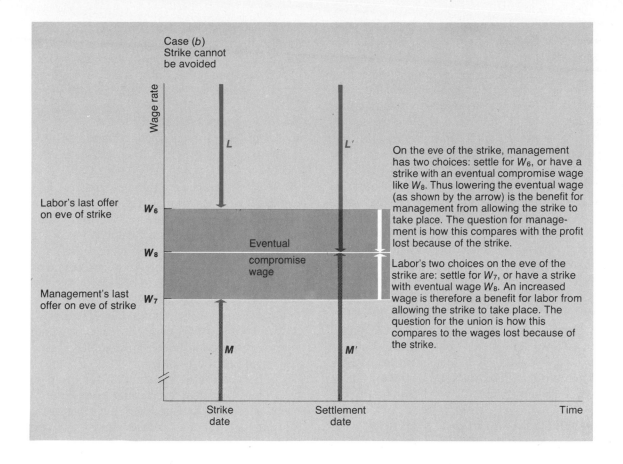

Case (b)
Strike cannot
be avoided

Wage rate

L

L'

Labor's last offer
on eve of strike

W_6

On the eve of the strike, management has two choices: settle for W_6, or have a strike with an eventual compromise wage like W_8. Thus lowering the eventual wage (as shown by the arrow) is the benefit for management from allowing the strike to take place. The question for management is how this compares with the profit lost because of the strike.

Eventual
compromise
wage

W_8

Labor's two choices on the eve of the strike are: settle for W_7, or have a strike with eventual wage W_8. An increased wage is therefore a benefit for labor from allowing the strike to take place. The question for the union is how this compares to the wages lost because of the strike.

Management's last
offer on eve of strike

W_7

M

M'

Strike
date

Settlement
date

Time

has not "played the negotiating game."[9] It has not followed the cardinal rule of "giving the other side a ladder to climb down."

Thus, even when there is a positive contract zone of acceptable wage rates (W_1W_3), an agreement may not be achieved because of inept negotiating. In the words of Lloyd Reynolds of Yale University:[10]

Negotiators may stake out firm positions from which it is later difficult to retreat, may misread the signals from the other side, [or] may be unable to surmount the tactical difficulties of graceful concession.

[9]This tactic of quoting a high initial offer and sticking to it is called "Boulwarism" after a former vice president of General Electric, who used this policy without success.

While economic forces set the background and help to define the limits within which the negotiated wage will fall (W_1W_2), collective bargaining has some of the characteristics of a poker game: The wage negotiated is very much the product of the bargaining skills of the participants. And without minimal skills, there may be no bargain at all.

As already noted, the final reason that a strike may occur is that a positive contract zone does not exist—as in *case b* in Figure 19-7. In this situation a strike cannot be avoided, because the positions (arrows) of the two parties do not overlap. On the *eve* of the strike, there is no

[10]*Labor Economics and Labor Relations,* 7th ed., (Englewood Cliffs, N.J.: Prentice-Hall Inc., 1978), p. 447.

wage that is acceptable to both. Each party would rather have a strike than agree to the other side's last offer.

But the longer the strike goes on (the farther we move to the right in this diagram), the more likely each side is to modify its previous strong position—that is, the more the two arrows L' and M' approach each other: Workers on the picket lines increasingly feel the financial pinch of lost wages. Similarly, management sees its losses mount. Both recognize that the other *does,* in fact, mean business. Thus L' and M' eventually meet and the strike is settled, at a compromise wage such as W_8. But precisely because W_8 *is* a compromise wage, it is more attractive for each side than its opponent's last offer before the strike (as the white arrows indicate). Thus, achieving a more attractive wage is an incentive for each side to accept a strike rather than to capitulate to the other on the eve of the strike. (Sometimes, one side "loses a strike," and is forced to settle at or very near the pre-strike offer of the other. In this case, it has made a mistake by not settling earlier.)

The frequency of strikes

Although strikes do occur, they are infrequent. The annual percentage of working time lost in strikes during the 1960s and 1970s was never greater than 0.5 percent, and averaged about 0.2 percent. Thus, the average worker spends less than 1 day a year on strike.[11]

[11]Wildcat strikes—sudden walkouts by small groups of workers—are uncommon in the United States. This is fortunate, since such strikes can be much more disruptive than a full-scale strike that follows a breakdown in union-management contract negotiations. Wildcat strikes may be the result of unions that are too weak to prevent their members from taking actions that harm the workers in the industry as a whole.

While they are rare in the United States, wildcat strikes have been a major problem in Britain, and have contributed to the decline of the British automobile industry. For example, when British Leyland was struggling to halt the rapid decline in its market share in early 1978, six vehicle inspectors walked off the job in a dispute over the condition and color of the overalls provided by the company. Forty other inspectors stopped work in sympathy; as a result 3,600 workers were laid off. Car production worth $3 million was lost, and the company's sales shrank even further.

However, strikes may be more costly than this figure suggests. They may result not only in lost output in the industries where the strikes occur; they may also inflict spillover costs on other industries.

Spillover costs of a strike

To illustrate, suppose that when the tire industry is on strike the value of the lost output and income *in that industry* is shown as area 3 in Figure 19-8a (exactly the same as areas 1 + 2 in Figure 19-6). The loss may not end here: As tire supplies are depleted, auto production may be delayed or dislocated. This disruption involves a cost to the auto industry and inconvenience to the car-buying public. Since these are costs that are not incurred by any firm or individual in the tire industry, they are spillover (or external) costs of the strike and are shown as area 4. In short, if a strike occurs in the industry, it will involve both internal cost 3 to the industry plus external cost 4 elsewhere in the economy.

In panel *b* we see that the situation could be far worse. If one or more auto companies is eventually forced to shut down, the value of the lost output in the auto industry and the inconvenience to the public (area 4) may far exceed the value of the lost output in the tire industry (area 3). In this case, the cost of a strike to society (areas 3 + 4) overwhelms the cost (3) to those in the industry in which the strike takes place.

Other illustrations abound. When mine workers go on an extended strike, the external cost of a coal shortage to electrical power stations and their customers may exceed the costs to owners and labor in the mines. In a 1976 strike in California canneries, the income lost in these factories represented only a small part of the total cost. Far more important was the loss to the state's farmers: $10 million worth of tomatoes and $15 million worth of peaches and apricots had to be left to rot because the canning factories were closed down. Moreover, because so much of the nation's supply of canned fruit and vegetables comes from California, the American consumer also had to bear a cost in the form of higher prices.

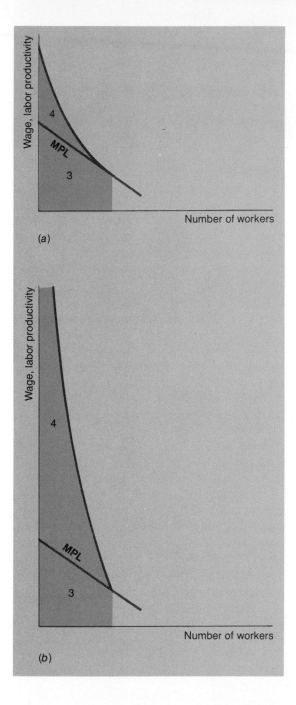

(a)

(b)

Figure 19-8
Spillover cost of a strike

(a) **When a strike occurs in tire production, area 3 shows the internal cost to the industry—the value of the lost output of tires. Area 4 shows the additional external cost to the public, and in particular to the auto industry where production is dislocated because tire supplies have dried up.** *(b)* **If the shortage of tires becomes so severe that auto companies have to lay off workers, the spillover cost of a strike (area 4) may be far more severe than the internal cost to the tire industry (area 3).**

over how area 3 is to be divided, we are losing area 4. Something is very wrong.''

Thus a number of ways have been sought to prevent strikes when negotiations between labor and management break down.

Last resort procedures to prevent strikes
As noted earlier, the Taft-Hartley Act empowered the President to seek a court injunction imposing an 80-day "cooling-off period" to delay a strike which threatens the national health or safety. (Although this provides time for labor and management to negotiate a settlement, a strike may still occur after the 80-day period.)

To assist deadlocked negotiations, the Federal Mediation Service has been established. *Mediation*—or *conciliation*—involves the appointment of an impartial third party to study the situation and suggest a compromise settlement. Although mediators cannot make binding recommendations on how the conflicts will be settled, they may be very helpful in resolving disputes for several reasons: A mediator may be able to (1) discover a solution that the two contending parties have overlooked; (2) find out who is bluffing and who is not, thus reducing the risk of a strike because one side has miscalculated the true position of the other; or (3) provide a means of saving face for parties that are otherwise locked into highly publicized positions from which there is no graceful retreat. For example, a union can go back to its members and say: "We were taking a tough negotiating position until that mediator arrived." Thus, the two parties may be able to achieve a settlement because

Thus, the general public has a stake in a strike decision in any specific industry. But the public is not represented in the negotiations that lead to a strike. Its attitude is often: "While labor and management in this industry are fighting they are able to shift the responsibility (blame) onto the mediator.

If mediation fails, a second, more forceful technique is **voluntary arbitration:** Labor and management submit their conflict to an impartial third party, and *commit themselves in advance* to accept the arbitrator's decision. (Provisions for voluntary arbitration are included in many collective bargaining agreements, as a way of settling disputes over the interpretation of the terms of the agreement.)

A third, and much more drastic, approach has been sometimes suggested: **compulsory arbitration,** whereby the government *forces* both parties to submit their dispute to an arbitrator, who then decides on a binding settlement. Although this seems like a simple solution, it has caused bitterness in countries which have relied on it.

DISPUTES INVOLVING PUBLIC SERVICE EMPLOYEES

The most damaging strikes are usually those with large external or spillover costs. These costs tend to be particularly great in the public sector. When subway workers go on strike, lost income of these workers and the transit authority (area 3 in Figure 19-8b) is trivial compared with area 4—the spillover cost of tying up the city's economic activity (as illustrated earlier in Box 19-5.) Serious spillover costs similarly result from a strike of garbage collectors or firefighters.

Public service employees sometimes argue that, unless they unionize, their monopsony employer (the government) can exercise too much market power in setting their wage rate: They must accept whatever "take-it-or-leave-it" contract the government offers. Accordingly, public service employees have recently been organizing at a rapid rate: Membership in public service unions increased from just over 1 million in 1960 to more than 6 million in 1978. By 1981, a single union—the American Federation of State, County and Municipal Employees

(AFSCME)—had grown to 1.3 million members, and had become the largest of the unions affiliated with the AFL-CIO.

This growth in their unions' strength is one of the reasons why the balance of market power may now be tipping towards public servants. But there are other reasons as well:

1 The threat of a strike by public service employees becomes a very potent weapon. Whereas a strike in the private sector puts pressure on employers to settle because of the income they will lose, a strike in the public sector—such as a sanitation or transit workers' strike—puts pressure on the employers (the government) because of the votes it may lose from an irate, suffering public.

2 A government may find it easier than a private employer to raise the funds necessary to pay a higher wage. For example, the government may increase taxes, or borrow. Another way to avoid a strike may be to provide a generous increase in pensions,[12] a relatively painless measure because it commits a future—rather than the present—government to pay employees when they retire. Thus, it has appeal to politicians whose major concern is to win the next election. New York City proved how painful the long-run consequences of such a policy may be: By 1975, "the chickens had finally come home to roost." Wage and pension commitments (combined with other major problems, such as large welfare expenditures) drove the city to the brink of bankruptcy, where it was saved only by state and federal government aid.

3 In private industry a strike may drive a firm out of business. Thus, strikers run the risk that their jobs may disappear, and this prospect acts as a restraint on labor demands. But there is far

[12]In a recent study ("Wages and Unionism in the Public Sector: the Case of Police," *Review of Economics and Statistics,* February 1981, p. 59), A. Bartel and D. Lewin conclude that unionization of the police seems to have been more effective in increasing fringe benefits than salaries.

less restraint of this kind in the public service. True, a strike may cost the government an election. But this is a serious problem only for the government officials who are voted out of their jobs. It is far less of a threat to public service workers whose jobs are likely to exist no matter who wins the next election. This puts a public service union in a strong bargaining position.

4 Public employees (and their dependents) may become a significant percentage of the voting population. This weakens the resistance of elected officials to their demands.

At every level of government—federal, state, and local—strikes of public service workers are generally illegal. Nonetheless, some civil servants do walk off the job or withdraw their services in more subtle ways, such as reporting in sick. State and local workers striking illegally have generally not been punished. But in the summer of 1981, President Reagan fired 12,000 air traffic controllers who struck in violation of the law.

Should public employees be allowed to strike? It is easy to answer no: If trash collectors go on strike, pollution may threaten public health. If firefighters or police go on strike, people may die in fires or be victimized by criminals. In the face of such strike threats, a government may feel almost forced to meet labor demands. Surely no group of individuals should hold this sort of power over the public.

Unfortunately, however, the problem is not quite so simple. If workers are not allowed to strike, they may reasonably demand some other mechanism for achieving a fair wage. One promising approach adopted by the federal government is to provide civil servants with salaries equal to those in comparable private sector jobs. But this provides neither a simple nor a complete solution. One difficulty is considered in Problem 19-6; another is the problem of defining what is meant by a "comparable" private sector job. And what downward adjustment, if any, should be made to government salaries because of attractive pensions and greater job security?

WAGE DIFFERENCES: WHY DO THEY EXIST?

In answering this question, we shall draw together and expand on some of the points made in the last two chapters.

1 First, there may be **_dynamic differentials_** in wage rates. For example, if there is an increase in the demand for construction workers in Alaska, their wages will rise above wages earned elsewhere; a dynamic differential is created. Eventually, this higher Alaskan wage will attract workers from other parts of the country, and the wage in Alaska will settle back toward the wage level elsewhere; the dynamic differential disappears. Thus, such differentials are only temporary; the speed with which they disappear depends on the mobility of the nation's labor force.

A _dynamic wage differential_ arises because of changing demand or supply conditions in the labor market. It tends to disappear over time as labor moves out of relatively low wage jobs and into those that pay a relatively high wage.

2 Some of the Alaskan wage differential may not disappear over time; to some degree wages may remain higher in Alaska to compensate for some disadvantage of working there (perhaps the colder climate). Similar **_compensating wage differentials_** may arise in jobs offering less security or less pleasant working conditions.

Compensating wage differentials may result if labor views some jobs as less attractive than others. (Employers have to pay a higher wage to fill the unattractive jobs.)

For example, jobs with high stress pay about 10 percent higher wages, and repetitive jobs may also pay higher wages. On the other hand, unpleasant jobs sometimes do not carry the higher wage one would expect. Instead, they may just have a higher turnover rate. This suggests that there may be a pool of available workers who take jobs without realizing they are unpleasant; and when they do realize it, they are more likely to quit.

3 Some wage differences reflect **monopsony or monopoly power.** Thus, workers in a small town with a single industrial employer (monopsonist) tend to receive a lower wage. On the other hand, workers who are exercising market power through a union tend to get higher wages. A particularly high wage may be received by workers who are not only able to exercise market power in their own labor market (through a strong union), but who are also employed by a firm with monopoly influence over its product market. For example, workers at General Motors have been able to earn a high wage not only because they have a strong union (the United Auto Workers) but also because they work for a company that has been able to earn oligopoly

profits in the car market. In other words, their strong union has been able to negotiate wage increases out of GM's oligopoly profits in the car market. (When the auto companies' oligopoly power was reduced in 1980–1981 by competition from imported cars, the result was not only losses for the car companies, but also pressure on the UAW to forgo wage increases won in earlier negotiations. The companies no longer were earning oligopoly profits that could be shared with labor.)

4 Other departures from perfect competition may result in wage differentials. For example, **barriers to entry** in the form of long apprenticeship requirements may keep wages up in some crafts. And **discrimination** against blacks or women can keep their incomes low.

5 Finally, wage differences exist because people have different **talents, education and training.** This is a major topic in the next chapter.

Key Points

1 Labor markets are often imperfect. Workers form unions to exercise monopoly power on the supply side of the market. On the other side of the market, employers may exercise monopsony power. Examples include a government that hires public service employees and a private firm that is the only major employer in a small town.

2 Unions provide labor with a collective voice. In collective bargaining, unions promote the interests of their workers by pressing for such improvements as *(a)* better working conditions, *(b)* seniority rules to protect long-time workers, and *(c)* higher wages.

3 If a union is formed in a perfectly competitive labor market, then to the degree that it raises the wage rate, it transfers income to labor from other factors of production. There is an overall efficiency loss because some workers are not hired in

this industry even though they would be more productive here than elsewhere.

On the other side of the market, if employers acquire monopsony power and lower the wage below its perfectly competitive level, there will be the same sort of efficiency loss. But, while the efficiency effects of monopoly and monopsony will be similar, their transfer effects will be in opposite directions. When a monopsonist lowers wages, the transfer is *from* labor *to* other factors of production.

4 If a labor market is already monopsonized by a single employer, efficiency will not necessarily be reduced if a union is formed to raise the wage rate. In fact, if the union's market power is used only to offset the market power of the employer, efficiency can be *increased.*

5 A union may increase efficiency in other ways, too. By providing workers with a collective voice, it may improve their working conditions. Costly turnover of the labor force is reduced as a consequence. A union may increase productivity by improving morale and communication between labor and management. On the other hand, a union may negotiate featherbedding rules which reduce efficiency.

6 Bilateral monopoly occurs when market power exists on both sides of the labor market: Unions with monopoly power bargain with employers with monopsony power. The wage that results will fall between the high wage an unopposed union would seek and the low wage an unopposed monopsonist would offer. But, within these limits, it is impossible to predict precisely where the wage rate will be set. However, it will be heavily influenced by the bargaining power of each side. (For example, a large union strike fund will increase the union's bargaining power, while a large inventory of finished goods will increase the bargaining power of management.) Bargaining is also affected by the negotiating expertise of representatives of labor and management. An incompetent negotiator who won't provide the other side with a face-saving compromise may prevent an agreement from being reached.

7 Membership in public service unions has grown rapidly in recent years. Such a union may have a strong bargaining position, particularly if it provides an essential service. To avoid a strike, a government employer may be willing to tax or borrow to meet a wage claim that would drive a private employer out of business.

Key Concepts

industrial union
craft union
collective bargaining
closed shop
union shop
right-to-work law
open shop
Taft-Hartley injunction
transfer and efficiency effects of a union

transfer and efficiency effects of monopsony
featherbedding
bilateral monopoly
why a union may decrease or increase inefficiency
relative bargaining power of union and management
losses to each side from a strike

why strikes occur
spillover costs of a strike
mediation
voluntary arbitration
compulsory arbitration
dynamic wage differentials
compensating wage differentials

Problems

19-1 "Monopsony in the labor market may have exactly the same effect on efficiency as a union." Is this possible? Explain. Would the transfer effects be the same in the two cases? (If you have studied Figure 2 in the introduction to Part 3, show how the two cases in the present example can involve identical efficiency effects, but entirely different transfer effects.)

19-2 In the case of monopsony, which efficiency condition in Box 18-1 has been violated? Explain.

19-3 In Figure 19-5, suppose that the initial wage rate in a unionized labor market is at W_3. If employers form a bargaining association and successfully negotiate a lower wage rate, show how efficiency is affected. Consider two cases: What happens if the association negotiates the wage down to W_2? Down to W_1?

19-4 Do you think that, as capital accumulates, the bargaining power of workers vis-á-vis management increases or decreases? Which workers can more effectively threaten to strike: Workers who would be leaving bulldozers idle? Workers who would be laying down their shovels?

19-5 Which union in each of the following pairs has the greater bargaining power? In each case, explain why.

(a) A union of workers on the New York subway or a union of workers who build the trains.

(b) A firefighters' union or an elementary teachers' union.

(c) An elementary teachers' union or a university professors' union.

(d) An airline pilots' union, or an intercity bus drivers' union.

19-6 "Tying wage increases in the public sector to wage increases in private industry will not necessarily equalize wages. All it will do is keep them the same if they start out equal. If public sector wages are initially less than the private sector wages, tying wages in this way only guarantees that inequities will be preserved." Do you agree? Do you think it is fair to pay both public and private employees the same wage if public employees have a greater guarantee of job security? If not, explain why and give an estimate of the differential you consider desirable.

*19-7 Explain how the theory of the second best applies to labor forming a union in a market that is already monopsonized.

CHAPTER 20
Other Incomes

> Buy land. They ain't making any more of the stuff.
> **Will Rogers**

About three-quarters of national income goes to labor in the form of wages and salaries. The remaining quarter goes to the owners of other productive factors—capital and land.

There are several forms of income from capital. First, interest income is received by those who provide **debt capital;** that is, those who lend money to businesses (or others) to finance the purchase of machinery or the construction of new buildings. (One way to lend a firm money is to buy its bonds. Another way is to lend money to a bank or other financial intermediary which in turn lends it out to the firm.) Second, profits are earned by those who own **equity capital;** that is, those who own small businesses outright, or who own shares of a corporation's stock. Although the individual who is buying stocks and bonds may view them quite differently, in this chapter we emphasize their similarity. Both represent a way in which people can contribute to the expansion of the nation's capital, and receive income in return.

Income is earned not only on physical capital, such as machinery and buildings, but also on **human capital.** An example is the human capital you are now accumulating in the form of an education. Your expenditure of time and money today will increase your productivity in the future and hence increase your income. Thus, an investment in human capital is like an investment in a machine or some other form of physical capital: It is an expenditure today that is expected to pay off in the future. (But, as we shall see, you shouldn't be too optimistic about this payoff.)

INTEREST: THE RETURN TO DEBT CAPITAL

To begin, let's suppose that firms finance investment only by borrowing. Borrowing takes place in the *market for loanable funds* where lenders (suppliers of funds) and borrowers (demanders of funds) come together. Like a competitive commodity market, a perfectly competitive market for loans can be studied with supply and demand curves.

How the demand and supply of loans determines the interest rate

Figure 20-1 shows the demand curve for loans by firms seeking the money to invest in plant and machinery.[1] (Hereafter, we refer simply to machinery.) Just as we have already seen that the demand for labor depends on the marginal productivity of labor, so too the demand for loans to buy machinery depends on how productive that machinery will be, that is, on the **marginal efficiency of investment** (MEI) shown in this diagram. Suppose bar *a* on the far left of Figure 20-1 represents the investment in machinery with the highest return (MEI) of 15 percent. (For example, consider a machine which costs $100,000 and wears out completely after only one year. If this machine generates enough sales to cover labor, materials, and

---

[1]People who need loans to buy houses or cars also participate in this market, but in this simple introduction we avoid such complications.

411

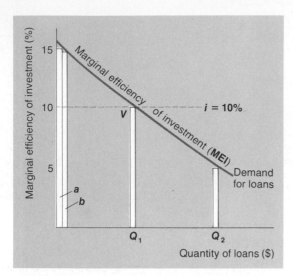

Figure 20-1

The marginal efficiency of investment and the demand for loans

Investment opportunities are ranked in order, starting with those yielding the highest return on the left. The resulting MEI schedule is also the demand for loans. For example, if the interest rate is 10 percent, then firms will demand Q_1 of loans. They keep borrowing to point V, where the marginal benefit of borrowing (the MEI schedule) is equal to the marginal cost of borrowing (the interest rate).

administrative costs, plus $115,000, then it provides a rate of return of 15 percent.)

The next most attractive investment is b, which can earn a 14½ percent return; and so on. The result is the marginal efficiency of investment curve (MEI). This curve also represents the demand for investment loans. For example, if the interest rate is 10 percent, then Q_1 of loans will be demanded: Firms will wish to invest in all the high-return opportunities to the left of V, but none to the right where the return has fallen below the 10 percent cost of borrowing money. (Detail on the MEI is given in Chapter 12 of the companion volume, in the section entitled "The Interest Rate and Investment Demand.")

Recall from Chapter 18 that firms in a perfectly competitive economy hire labor to the point where its price (the wage rate) is equal to

its marginal productivity. Similarly, in a perfectly competitive economy the firms in Figure 20-1 acquire capital to the point where the price (the interest rate) equals the marginal efficiency of investment.

In Figure 20-2, the demand for investment loans (MEI) is reproduced from Figure 20-1, together with the supply of funds by lenders. This supply indicates how much businesses and households are willing to provide at various interest rates.[2] For example, the 6 percent interest rate that would just barely induce individual f to save and lend reflects how highly she values this money in its alternative use—current consumption. Individuals who value current consumption more highly won't be induced to save and lend until the interest rate rises above 6 percent. Therefore, they appear further to the right in this supply schedule. They are often described as having a stronger **time preference;** that is, they have a stronger preference for consuming now rather than in the future.

In a perfectly competitive capital market, equilibrium is at E, where demand and supply intersect. In this example, the equilibrium rate of interest is 8 percent.

It is important to emphasize that this 8 percent interest rate reflects the height of the demand curve at E. In other words, *the marginal efficiency of investment is 8 percent.* We can take $1 worth of goods today and invest it to produce $1.08 of goods next year. *Since capital is productive, present goods can be converted into a larger amount of future goods.*

Through investment, present goods can be *exchanged for* a larger amount of future goods. Thus present goods are *worth more* than future goods, with the interest rate telling us how much more.

[2]In this analysis, we ignore a number of macroeconomic complications, including the effects of the banking system on the supply of loans. These complications were studied in Chapters 10 to 12 of the companion volume.

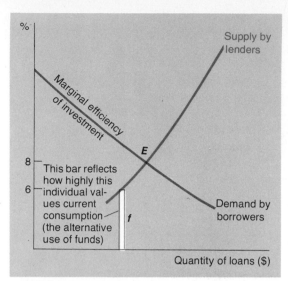

Figure 20-2
The market for loans

The demand for loans is reproduced from Figure 20-1. It reflects the marginal efficiency of investment. The supply of loans depends on how highly lenders value money in its alternative use—consumption. The equilibrium is at E with an 8 percent interest rate.

Roundabout production, with interest as the reward for waiting

Investment is often described as **roundabout** or **indirect production.** Rather than using resources today to produce consumer goods directly, society produces an even greater amount of consumer goods *indirectly* by a roundabout method: First, resources are used to produce capital goods, and then this capital is used (together with labor and land) to produce consumer goods.

The greater quantity of consumer goods that is eventually produced in this way is the incentive for undertaking roundabout production. But roundabout production is not possible unless some people are prepared to defer their consumption today. That is, people must be willing to save. This is necessary in order to release the resources that would otherwise go into producing consumer goods, and allow these

resources to produce capital goods instead. For their decision to defer consumption—to wait before enjoying their income—savers receive an interest return. Thus, the interest rate can be viewed as a *reward to savers for waiting,* just as the wage rate is a reward to labor for its time and effort.

How risk affects the interest rate

Although there is only one interest rate shown in Figure 20-2, in fact there are many rates of interest. A very large and financially sound corporation will be able to acquire loanable funds at a relatively low interest rate, since lenders view this loan as relatively risk-free. But a company in shaky financial condition will have to pay a higher interest rate to compensate lenders for the greater risk they have to take in this case. Thus, the interest rate shown in Figure 20-2 may be viewed as the ''base rate of interest'' that applies to a risk-free loan; as such, it is the best simple measure of the marginal efficiency of investment. Even though we continue to concentrate on this base rate, we should keep in mind that it reflects a whole array of interest rates on loans of varying risk.

As we have seen in earlier chapters, an important question in product or labor markets is: What happens if the government intervenes to impose some restriction? This is also an important question in the capital market (the market for loans).

Effects of an interest rate ceiling

Figure 20-3 shows what happens in a perfectly competitive capital market when the government imposes a ceiling on the interest rate that can be charged by banks. Original equilibrium (before the ceiling) is shown at E_1, with the interest rate at i_1. If the government now sets a ceiling below this rate, say at i_2, the market no longer clears: There is a shortage of funds, E_2F. Unsatisfied borrowers cannot find loans.

One of the arguments in favor of an interest rate ceiling is that it will reduce the burden of interest payments that must be paid by the relatively poor individuals and small firms that

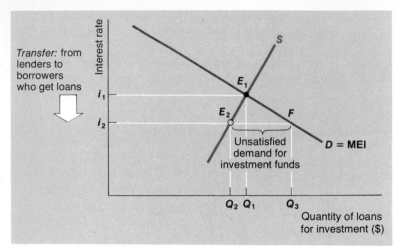

Figure 20-3 labels: Interest rate (y-axis), S, E_1, i_1, E_2, F, i_2, Unsatisfied demand for investment funds, $D = MEI$, Q_2 Q_1 Q_3, Quantity of loans for investment ($), Transfer: from lenders to borrowers who get loans

Figure 20-3
Effects of an interest rate ceiling

Before the interest rate ceiling, equilibrium in this competitive capital market is at E_1, with Q_1 of investment funds loaned out at interest rate i_1. When a ceiling of i_2 is imposed, borrowers are attracted by the lower rate and seek Q_3 of loans. (Borrowers try to move down their demand curve from E_1 to F.) But only Q_2 are available because lenders, discouraged by the reduced interest return, move down their supply curve from E_1 to E_2. Thus, equilibrium moves from E_1 to E_2, loans are reduced from Q_1 to Q_2, and there is Q_2Q_3 unsatisfied demand for loans. By lowering the interest rate that lenders receive and borrowers pay, the interest rate ceiling results in the (white arrow) transfer from lenders to those borrowers who get funds.

must borrow. And the lower interest rate does result in a transfer from lenders to borrowers—but only to those borrowers lucky enough to get loans. (This transfer is shown by the white arrow on the left.) However, there is no guarantee that this redistribution will "help the poor." Some of the largest borrowers who get the "bargain" loans may be the rich who borrow to finance their big homes and business ventures. And some of the borrowers who are left unsatisfied may be the poor, who suffer as a consequence.

Moreover, this interest rate ceiling has two unfavorable effects on efficiency. First, it reduces the quantity of loanable funds available for investment from Q_1 to Q_2. This shift in the market away from its initial, perfectly competitive equilibrium results in the efficiency loss shown by the familiar red triangle in Box 20-1. This problem—that there are now too few investment funds available—is not the only reason for an efficiency loss. Another reason is that the wrong investors may get these limited funds. Box 20-1 explains why in detail.

In a nutshell, the reason is that loans have to be rationed. [At interest ceiling i_2, demand for loans (Q_3) exceeds supply (Q_2).] Bankers may ration the limited supply of funds by a first come, first served procedure, or some more complex method. But whatever the method, there will be a second efficiency loss unless the funds are rationed out to exactly the right set of borrowers

—that is, those borrowers to the left of Q_2 in Figure 20-3, who have the investment projects with the highest productivity (MEI). Unfortunately, there is no guarantee that this will happen. Because the interest rate is so low, borrowers in the range Q_2Q_3, with lower productivity investments, will also be trying to obtain funds, and some may succeed. If this "rationing error" does occur, then the second efficiency loss results: In the market for investment funds, high productivity investments lose out to low productivity ones.

This second source of inefficiency (above and beyond the red triangle in Box 20-1) may be summarized as follows: In an unrestricted, perfectly competitive capital market, the interest rate is a price that allocates funds to the most

BOX 20-1

The Inefficiency of an Interest Rate Ceiling

The market for loanable funds in Figure 20-3 is reproduced here, along with the ceiling that reduces the interest rate from i_1 to i_2. This policy is likely to have several adverse effects on efficiency. First, because suppliers of funds (savers) are discouraged by the lower interest rate and provide fewer funds (arrow a at the bottom of the diagram) economically justified investment projects like g are "knocked out"—they cannot be undertaken. But this involves a loss because the cost of this project would have been only the empty bar under the supply curve (the cost to the lender of having to reduce consumption) while its benefit would have been the empty bar *plus* the solid bar under the demand curve (the productivity of this investment). Thus the net loss because this project is canceled is the solid bar. And the efficiency loss from all such cancellations (that is, those in the range shown by arrow a) is the red triangle. Thus, the principle previously established in the market for goods and for labor—that a shift away from a perfectly competitive equilibrium (such as E_1) will result in an efficiency loss—is now shown to hold in a perfectly competitive market for investment funds as well.

But the efficiency loss will be limited to this red triangle *only if* the investment projects knocked out by a lack of funds are those (like g) in the range a. If this is not the case, there will be a second efficiency loss. To illustrate, suppose, for example, that project j on the left is the one that is knocked out, not g. (The promoter of g may have been able to borrow by being more persuasive to a banker who is rationing loans.) An even greater efficiency loss is now involved

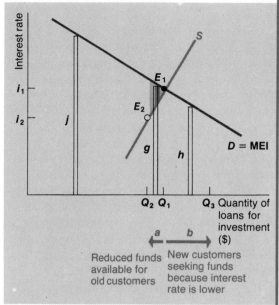

because an even more productive investment (j rather than g) is knocked out.

Moreover, this inefficiency may be even more serious. It's quite possible for j to lose out, not to g, but instead to an even lower-productivity project like h. In fact, h's productivity is so low that h would not even be considered at the original interest rate i_1; nobody would try to borrow to undertake it. The only reason someone is now applying for funds for h is the attraction of the artificially low interest rate. And if h gets funds rather than j, the efficiency loss from this rationing error—the reduction in the nation's output—will be even more severe. [Now this loss will be the difference in j's (tall bar) productivity and h's very low productivity.] ■

productive investment projects. But when an interest rate ceiling is imposed, some other allocating device must be used, and there is then a risk that the wrong set of projects will get the funds.

(Moreover, this is a general problem that applies to other cases of price fixing as well, such as our earlier example of rent control. Not only does rent control result in fewer apartments for rent. In addition, the wrong people may get the apartments. For example, a retired couple may continue to hang on to a choice New York apartment even though they now spend 9 months a year in Florida and would give up the apartment if they had to pay the higher free-market rent.)

Once again we conclude: If we wish to transfer income from the rich to the poor, changing a market price like the interest rate may be an unwise way to do it. In the first place, an interest ceiling may be an ineffective form of transfer because it may not move income from the rich to the poor at all. (The statement that "borrowers benefit, therefore the poor benefit" involves two possible errors: First, borrowers as a group may not benefit, since some no longer get funds. Second, many borrowers are not poor.) Moreover, an interest ceiling may have damaging effects on efficiency. Isn't it better for the government to do any transferring directly, by taxing the rich and subsidizing the poor? The answer is yes, *provided* the government can do so without incurring large efficiency losses of a different sort (an issue to be discussed in Chapter 24).

NORMAL PROFIT: A RETURN TO EQUITY CAPITAL

So far in this chapter we have assumed that all investment projects are financed by borrowing. Now let's broaden our analysis to include "equity finance," that is, funds a firm raises by selling its stock. (A third source of funds is retained earnings.) Those who buy stock obtain a share of the ownership and future profits of the firm.

In Chapter 9, we drew a distinction between two kinds of profit. First, **normal profit** reflects opportunity cost—the return necessary to induce and hold funds in one activity rather than another. Second, **above-normal profit** is any additional return beyond this. We defer discussion of above-normal profit to a later section, and concentrate here on normal profit.

For those who provide equity funds, what is their normal profit? That is, what is the opportunity cost of these funds? The answer is the return the funds could earn in their best alternative use. But the alternative to buying stock is to buy interest-bearing securities. Thus, normal profit is the base rate of interest plus an appropriate premium for risk—a risk which may be substantial because the entire amount that is put into the ownership of a firm may be wiped out. (Profit is sometimes described as a reward for risk-taking. But it is more than this, since it must also include a base rate of return needed to attract funds away from interest-bearing alternatives.)

We can now recast Figure 20-2 in the more general form shown in Figure 20-4, which represents the total market for investment funds. Now *D* includes the total demand by business for investment funds (whether these funds are raised by borrowing or by the sale of stock), while *S* is the corresponding supply. The result-

Figure 20-4
The market for investment funds
(a generalization of Figure 20-2)

Whereas Figure 20-2 showed only borrowing, the diagram here shows two ways that business may raise funds: by borrowing or by equity finance (the sale of stock). *D* is the demand for funds (in either debt or equity form) to finance new investment, while *S* is the corresponding supply of funds. In equilibrium, the base rate of return—in the absence of risk—would be *r*. But in a risky world, the return any specific business must actually pay for the funds it raises will be *r* plus an appropriate amount to compensate the lender for risk.

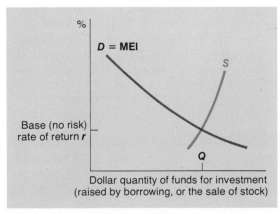

ing equilibrium Q is the quantity of both debt and equity funds provided by savers to those who invest.

THE ROLE OF FACTOR PRICES

We have examined the pricing of two factors of production—labor and capital. We now pause briefly to consider how factor prices influence both the individual firm's decisions on using these factors, and the allocation of these factors across the economy as a whole.

How factor prices influence decisions by individual firms

In its decision-making, a firm must address several issues. On the one hand, it must decide on how much labor and how much capital equipment it will use. But at the same time, it must also decide on which goods to produce and how much of each. To illustrate, suppose the wage rate rises; the firm decides to use less labor and more capital. (It substitutes a relatively less expensive factor of production, capital, for a more expensive one, labor.) Moreover, because of the higher wage, the firm may also reduce the output of its final products, especially those requiring a great deal of labor. (As a further example of how factor and product decisions are interrelated, suppose the price of one of its products rises. In response, the firm will increase its output of this good by hiring more factors of production and/or by shifting production away from one of its other outputs.) In short, the firm's decisions on what to produce and the amount of factors to employ are not separate decisions. Instead, they are all *elements of one overall decision.*

How factor prices influence the allocation of scarce resources throughout the economy

Just as the price of a good acts as the screening mechanism for deciding who will consume it and who will not (Figure 10-4), so a factor price acts as a monitoring device to determine how a scarce resource will be used. For example, the wage rate acts as a screen to determine the particular activities in which society's scarce labor will be employed. In a competitive, fully employed economy, a wage rate rising with productivity conveys a clear message to those producers who can no longer afford to hire. The message is: Society can no longer afford to have its scarce labor employed in your activity; there are now too many other, more productive pursuits. This may seem harsh, but it is the sign of economic progress. Think back, for a moment, to all the things that labor used to do, but no longer does. At our current high wage rates, it doesn't pay to hire workers to hoe field corn anymore, as in the "good old days." And household servants have almost vanished.

Similarly, we have seen how the interest rate is a market price that acts as a screen to determine in which particular activities investment will take place. And when that screening device is replaced by another (for example, the rationing that occurred under the interest rate ceiling in Figure 20-3), investment funds are unlikely to go into the most productive activities.

THE RETURN TO HUMAN CAPITAL

Income is earned not only by investment in machinery and other physical capital, but also by investment in *human capital*—the acquisition of skills, training, and education.[3] In many essential respects, an investment in human capital is similar to an investment in physical capital: Current consumption is reduced in the expectation of higher future income and consumption. For example, students give up the income they could make if they were not busy studying; they live frugally in the hope that the education will

---

[3]For a sample of the work by three of the early contributors in this field, see G. S. Becker, *Human Capital: A Theoretical and Empirical Analysis, with Special Reference to Education* (New York: National Bureau of Economic Research, 1964); Jacob Mincer, *Schooling Experience and Earnings* (New York: National Bureau of Economic Research, 1974); and T. W. Schultz, *The Economic Value of Education* (New York: Columbia University Press, 1963).

BOX 20-2
Who Should Invest in Apprenticeship Training?

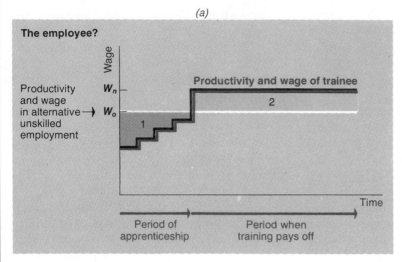

(a)

The employee?

Wage

Productivity and wage of trainee

W_n

Productivity and wage in alternative → W_o unskilled employment

1

2

Time

Period of apprenticeship

Period when training pays off

In panel *a,* the trainees' wage (the red line) is always kept the same as their productivity (the black line). Therefore, the investment in the initial apprenticeship period (area 1) is not made by the employers. Instead it is made by the trainees who take a lower wage during this period than the wage W_o that they could earn in alternative jobs. They also get all the later payoff from the investment (area 2), since the wage W_n then is higher than the W_o they would earn without the training.

In panel *b,* the trainees bear none of the cost of the investment, nor do they capture any of the payoff from it. Throughout, their wage remains the same W_o that they would have earned in other jobs. It is now the employers who pay the total cost (area 1), since, during the apprenticeship period they get less productivity from the trainees (black line) than the wage they pay them (red line). In theory, employers also get the later payoff from this investment (area 2) when the productivity of the trainees exceeds their wage.

pay off in higher income after graduation. Similarly, apprentices may be willing to work for abnormally low wages if they are receiving training that is likely to lead to a better job.

By recognizing the importance of human capital, we are recognizing that everyone in the labor force is not equally productive; we are relaxing our earlier assumption in Chapter 18 that labor is standardized. In fact, the quality of labor depends on the amount of education, skill, and experience that various individuals have

acquired. Some have a lot of human capital, others very little. Frequently their incomes reflect this.

Who pays for the investment in human capital? In the case of education, much of the investment is undertaken by the individuals who spend their time studying instead of earning an income. But governments also invest: Federal, state, and local governments all help to finance education. One justification for these expenditures is that it is only fair to provide educational

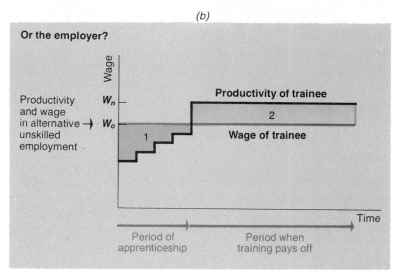

(b)

Or the employer?

Productivity and wage in alternative → unskilled employment

Wage

Productivity of trainee

W_n

W_o

2

1

Wage of trainee

Time

Period of apprenticeship

Period when training pays off

But the problem for employers is that they may not get this later payoff, since workers may leave once their training is completed. Specifically, workers may be attracted away by another employer offering higher wage W_n. (Such an offer is likely, since this is now what their services are worth.) This risk that employees will leave once their training is complete reduces the incentive for employers to undertake investment in human capital, even though it might yield high returns to society in terms of greater labor productivity.

[These two panels represent the two sharpest alternatives. But in practice, other more complicated arrangements are often introduced. For example, even employers who pay the whole training cost (as in panel *b*) almost always give the trainees some of the eventual payoff 2, in order to keep them from leaving.] ■

opportunity for all. Another is that education provides not only a benefit to those who acquire it, but also spillover benefits to others in society as well. For example, if a highly educated doctor discovers a new vaccine, it may not only increase the discoverer's own income, but will also benefit the public which now has protection from a disease. In the face of such spillover benefits, the unaided free market may not provide enough investment in human capital and research, so the government also contributes.

On-the-job apprenticeship or training in industry also represents an investment in human capital. There are several ways the initial cost of this investment may be covered. For example, individual workers may accept a low wage during the apprenticeship period when their productivity is still low. (As noted in an earlier chapter, the possibility of using this arrangement is limited by the minimum wage laws.) Alternatively, employers may pay apprentices a standard wage and thereby bear the initial costs of this investment. But this option raises a serious problem for employers (Box 20-2), since they are investing in an asset (skill or training) which they do not own. The workers are not slaves, and they can always quit and go to work elsewhere, taking the training with them. (Of course, the ease with which they can do so depends on how specific their expertise is to the company that trained them.) This is another reason why there may be underinvestment in human capital: Employers may not invest as heavily in training programs as they would if workers would guarantee to stay on the job and thus allow employers to "get their money back."

Human capital and discrimination

You do not take a person who for years has been hobbled by chains, and liberate him . . . and then say, "You are free to compete with all the others," and still justly believe that you have been completely fair.

Lyndon Johnson

The problem of low income for members of a minority group may reflect far more than present discrimination by employers. It may also be the result of the past inability of the minority to acquire human capital. Such a group may be caught in a vicious circle. To illustrate: Past discrimination has meant that some minorities have been paid lower wages. As a consequence, they have been unable to provide equal educational opportunity for their children, who in turn are paid lower wages—even by an employer who doesn't discriminate. In other words, they remain at a disadvantage "even if those making important economic decisions are without prejudice."[4]

One way of breaking this vicious circle is to ensure equal educational opportunity for minorities. Indeed, to make up for past discrimination, special efforts are now being made under affirmative action programs to get blacks, other minorities, and women into training programs and positions where they can accumulate human

[4]Henry Aaron, *Politics and the Professors* (Washington, D.C.: Brookings Institution, 1978) p. 43.

capital. How far affirmative action should be extended to "reverse discrimination"—whereby minorities and women are given preferential treatment—is a very controversial legal, moral, and social question, which has reached the Supreme Court.

[In the 1978 Bakke case, a California medical school was sued by a rejected white applicant who claimed to have better qualifications than some nonwhites who had been admitted. While upholding affirmative action in principle, the court seemed to back down in this specific case; it ordered Bakke admitted. However, in 1979, the court ruled against a white worker, Brian Weber, who wanted the court to order his admission into an industrial training program. (Weber claimed, like Bakke, to have been excluded because slots were reserved for blacks.) The court has obviously had difficulty with this issue—no surprise, since it has no simple, clean solution.]

Measuring the return on human capital: What is a university education worth?

Acquiring a university education involves a cost for a student in terms of fees and expenses, plus the income that could have been earned by working instead. What is its future payoff? In 1969, those with a university education were earning, on average, about $4,600 more per year than those with only a high school education. But by 1974–1975, this gap had narrowed to roughly $3,200, showing that the economic value of a college education had fallen. By the early 1980s, the gap seemed to be stabilizing.

Why did the financial rewards for a university education fall during the 1970s? The most important reason seemed to be the increased supply of university-trained people. Unprecedented numbers were being graduated, both because of the population bulge at the university age level and because an increasing proportion of that population was going to university. At the same time, the demand for university graduates was not increasing at the same pace—partly because of shrinking job opportunities in education, one of the areas of employment that requires a university degree. (Elementary schools,

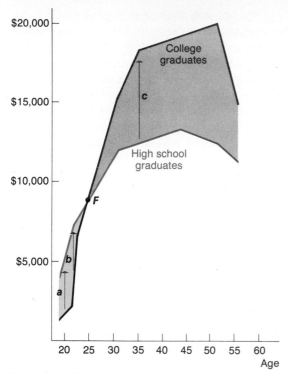

Figure 20-5
Age profile of people's incomes, with and without a college education
Earnings over the life cycle for high school graduates and college graduates. (Comparisons are for white males in 1973.)
Source: Richard B. Freeman, *Labor Economics* (Englewood Cliffs, N.J.: Prentice-Hall, 1979), p. 39.

high schools, and universities had already increased their staffs to handle the bulge in population.)

Suppose we wish to calculate a percentage rate of return on a human investment like a college education. This can be done in much the same way as we would calculate a percentage rate of return on a physical investment like machinery: We compare its initial costs with its eventual payoff, in terms of a higher income. Figure 20-5 shows the income pattern of those with a college degree and those without.

What is the cost of a college education? First is the income forgone during the actual period of study. This cost can be visualized as a set of arrows like *a*, one for each year spent in college. But that's not the only sacrifice college students make. Even after their education is complete, their average incomes at first are below the incomes of people without a degree, who have 4 years of experience and seniority instead. (This cost to college students is the set of after-college arrows like *b*.) However, this income disadvantage of college graduates disappears fairly quickly. By their late 20s (at point *F*), they have caught up. And by their late 30s, they have gone well ahead (arrow *c*), and they stay ahead.

Thus, the costs and benefits of a university education can be summed up as follows:

1 The *costs* include both (*a*) the income forgone during university and the later "catch-up period" (the red area in this diagram); plus (*b*) the cost of residence, tuition, etc. (not shown in this diagram).
2 The *benefits* are in the form of a higher income later (the gray area).

With this information in hand we can then answer the key question: "When college graduates eventually get the income benefits shown in gray, what percentage rate of return are they earning on their investment (their tuition, sacrifice of income, etc.)?"

Unfortunately, such calculations raise some complications which should be clearly understood. For example, can we really say that the higher income of university graduates (the gray area in Figure 20-5) is all due to their university education? The answer is no. One reason for their higher earnings is that they are, on average, more talented and hardworking. (They aren't dropouts.) Thus, even without a college education, they would still earn more on average. Accordingly, one task is to figure out how much of their higher income should be attributed to their college education and how much to their greater talent and perseverance. A second difficulty is that the *private* rate of return to the individual acquiring an education is not the same as the *social* rate of return to the nation as a whole. (For adjustments in the private rate necessary to estimate the social rate, see Box 20-3.)

Why Private and Social Returns to Education Differ

In order to estimate the social return to investment in higher education, we would ideally take the estimated private rate of return, and

1 Adjust it *upward,* to take account of any external benefits (like the spillover benefit from the education of the doctor who discovered a new vaccine).

2 Adjust it *downward* to take account of government subsidies to higher education. (These are a cost of the investment to society, but not to the private individuals being educated.)

Taubman and Wales† provide evidence of another reason why private and social rates of return differ. According to these authors, employers pay university graduates more, not only because education has made them more productive, but also because it has given them a "credential." In other words, education acts as a screening device that tells employers which individuals have the capacity and diligence to learn. Although this credential provides university graduates with a private return (a higher income), there may be little corresponding benefit for society as a whole. This tends to lower the social return for education compared with the private return. ■

†P. Taubman and T. Wales, "Education as an Investment and as a Screening Device," in F. T. Juster (ed.), *Education, Income and Human Behavior* (New York: McGraw-Hill, 1975) pp. 110–116. Our discussion of the returns to education also draws on Richard B. Freeman, "The Decline in the Economic Rewards to College Education," *Review of Economics and Statistics,* February, 1977.

Studies that attempt to take some of these complications into account indicate that the private rate of return to an individual from acquiring an undergraduate degree is about 8 to 10 percent per year, while the social rate of return is probably less—perhaps as low as 4 percent. (For those who incur the much heavier cost of continuing on to a Ph.D., the private rate of return on this extra effort is only about 2 percent.) Moreover, these studies confirm that the rate of return to a university education has been falling through the years, not only because of the decrease in its benefits (the higher income eventually earned) but also because of an increase in its costs (such as tuition). By the mid-1970s, the rate of return on this particular form of human capital seemed to have fallen well below the rate of return on investment in physical capital.

Of course, one should also take into account the additional benefits of a university education as "consumption," rather than "investment." For example, it provides many individuals with a greater appreciation of history and literature. One might also evaluate the psychological benefits well-educated people receive because they have more interesting and challenging jobs. (Even if the income were the same, it would be pleasanter to design a bridge than to pour the cement.) Then, too, jobs may come with what the British call "perks" (perquisites). For example, expenses-paid business trips are often fun. But on the other hand, those at the top often work very hard, under great pressure.

The complex nature of wages and salaries

In the preceding section we have seen why an individual's wage or salary may reflect far more than just a basic wage rate. For example, an individual's income may be higher because of education. Or, it may be higher because of some specific talent or ability: Bjorn Borg was born with a great natural ability to hit a tennis ball; others are born with a special talent for solving equations.

Figure 20-6 illustrates this idea. An initial point of reference is provided on the left by the base income of $15,000 earned by an unskilled

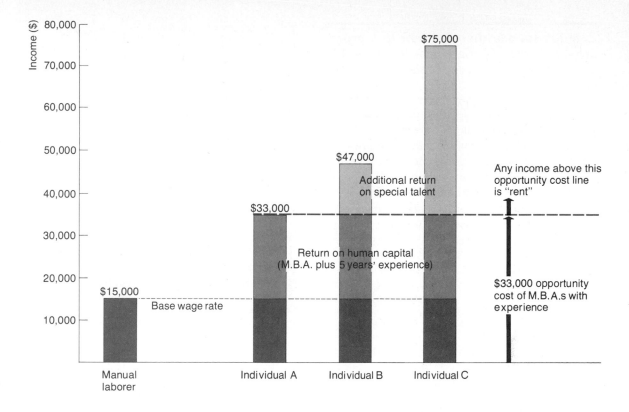

Figure 20-6
Dividing income into its components

The three individuals on the right have the same qualifications—an MBA plus 5 years experience—and the same $33,000 opportunity cost, shown by the red dashed line. Any surplus income above this is rent, shown in light gray. Thus, *A* earns no rent, *B* earns $14,000 rent, and *C*—with the greatest natural talent for the job—earns $42,000 rent.

laborer with no special talent or training. The remaining three individuals work for a large firm. Individual *A* is educated up to an M.B.A. and has 5 years' experience. He earns $33,000 income; this is also what he could earn in an alternative occupation. (This includes the $15,000 base wage plus an $18,000 return on his education and experience.) In other words, $33,000 is his income, and also his opportunity cost. Individual *B* has exactly the same education and experience as *A*, and the same $33,000 opportunity cost. But her income is another $14,000 higher because she has a special flair for solving the firm's problems. Finally, individual *C* has exactly the same education, experience, and opportunity cost as *A* and *B*. But he has an even more incisive mind in dealing with the problems encountered by this firm. His income consequently is a hefty $75,000.

Three components of income can be distinguished:

1 The $15,000 base income for unskilled work.

2 The $18,000 extra income that these individuals could earn in other jobs because of their education and experience.

The first two components represent opportunity cost. The last one does not:

3 Additional returns to those with special talents. This third item falls under the economists' broad definition of **rent.**

Economists use the term *rent* **in a broad sense, to identify the return to any factor of production in excess of its opportunity cost.**

Thus, rent is the gap between what a factor *is* earning and what it *could* earn elsewhere. Expressed this way, we see that there are two reasons why an individual's income might include a very large rent component. (1) The income he or she *is* earning may be very high. (2) What he or she *could* earn elsewhere is low. We continue to focus on the first reason here, while the second is considered in Box 20-4.

RENT

What do Luciano Pavarotti, Jack Nicklaus, and an acre of Iowa farmland have in common?

The answer to this question is: Like business executive *C* (Figure 20-6), they all earn an economic rent because of their superior quality. Pavarotti has an exceptional voice. Nicklaus plays outstanding golf. An acre of Iowa land yields large quantities of grain.

Rent on agricultural land, based on differences in quality

All economic analyses begin with the cultivation of the earth. . . . To the economist, . . . the green plain is a sort of burial place of hidden treasure, where all the forethought and industry of man are set at naught by the caprice of the power which hid the treasure. . . . Thus is Man mocked by earth his stepmother, and never knows as he tugs at her closed hand whether it contains diamonds or flints, good red wheat or a few clayey and blighted cabbages.

George Bernard Shaw

Figure 20-7 shows three plots of land with no alternative use but to grow a crop. In other words, their opportunity cost is zero. It therefore follows from the preceding definition that any income they earn is rent. In this special case, the economist's and the public's definition of rent coincide: It is the income earned by land.

Relatively poor land *C* has such low productivity that with a $3 price of wheat, it has just

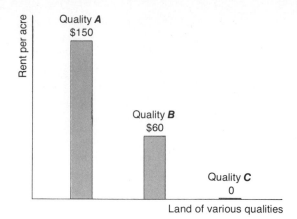

Figure 20-7
Rent based on differences in quality of land (based on wheat price of $3 per bushel)
Marginal land *C*, which is just barely fertile enough to cultivate, earns no rent. High-productivity land *A* earns the highest rent.

been brought into cultivation. The value of the wheat it produces is barely sufficient to cover the costs of fertilizer, machinery, the farmer's time, and other inputs. Therefore, it earns no rent. Land *B* is more fertile soil that grows enough wheat per acre to pay for other inputs and leave $60 per acre; that is, its rent is $60 per acre. Land *A* is even more productive and earns a rent of $150.

Of course, the rent on these plots of land depends on the price of wheat. Suppose that, because of crop failures elsewhere in the world, the price of wheat rises from the initial $3 a bushel (in Figure 20-7) to $4. The result is shown in Figure 20-8. Land *C*, which previously earned no rent, now does. And the rents earned by plots *A* and *B* increase. Land *D* is now the marginal land, just brought into cultivation and earning a zero rent.

*Another example of rent: The income from mineral deposits

A mineral deposit may also earn an economic rent. To confirm this statement, reinterpret Fig-

Note to instructors of short courses: The rest of this chapter is made up of optional sections. Any of the starred sections may be omitted without losing continuity.

ures 20-7 and 20-8 as follows. Mineral deposit A is a rich vein of ore, easy to reach. Mineral deposit B is also a rich vein of ore, but difficult to reach and extract. Deposit C is of poorer quality and so difficult to reach that it is initially (in Figure 20-7) barely being mined. In Figure 20-8 we see how an increase in the price of ore increases the rent earned on each of these deposits and induces the mining of low-yield deposit D for the first time.

*Rent on land because of its location

Land may yield economic rent not only because of its fertility, but also because of its location. To illustrate, land A in Figure 20-9 is in the prime business district of a city and can be used in a highly productive way. A business might wish to locate there for a variety of reasons: It might want to be close to suppliers and competitors so

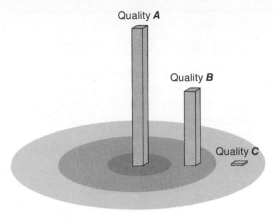

Figure 20-9
Rent based on differences in the location of land

Compare with Figure 20-7. Because of its greater convenience and lower transport costs, land A earns a higher rent than land B. Land C, in a relatively poor location, earns no rent.

Figure 20-8
How rents increase when the price of wheat increases

This figure is the same as Figure 20-7 except that the price of wheat has risen from $3 to $4 per bushel. Because of this increased price, all existing plots of land earn greater income—that is, greater rent. Moreover, less productive plot D is brought into cultivation for the first time.

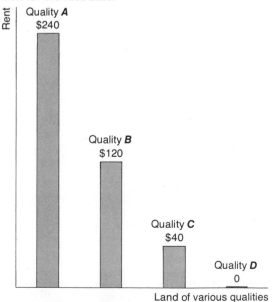

that it can easily keep up with new developments and innovations in the industry. Or, it might wish to have access to the large labor pool that exists in this area of high-density population. Or, it might wish to be close to the population center in order to reduce the cost of transporting its product to market.

For all these reasons, location A earns a rent. Land B is less attractive since it is not in this prime district, and it earns a smaller rent. Finally, land C earns no rent because it is even farther away and therefore involves even higher costs of inconvenience and transportation.

These blocks in Figure 20-9, just like the bars in Figure 20-7, give us a picture of how rents compare. And because the selling price of land depends on the rent it can earn (as we shall shortly see in more detail), these blocks also give us a picture of how land prices over an urban area will compare. (Although the heights of the blocks have been drawn to reflect rents and land values, they may also provide some rough indication of where the tallest buildings will be constructed. The reason is that constructing each additional square foot of office space eventually becomes more and more expensive as a building gets higher and higher. Consequently, if land is

BOX 20-4
Rent and Opportunity Cost

Rent is defined as the difference between what a factor *is* earning and what it *could* earn elsewhere (its opportunity cost). The three business executives in Figure 20-6 had the same ($33,000) opportunity cost, but different incomes; so they had different rents. Here, we consider individuals who have the same *income* but different *opportunity costs*. Differences in

rent occur in this case as well, as we shall now show.

In Figure 20-10(a) we show a labor market in which all individuals have the same productivity, and the same salary Y. But opportunity costs vary: Remember, the supply of labor S reflects opportunity cost—the potential earnings of individuals in other jobs. Thus, individuals a and b

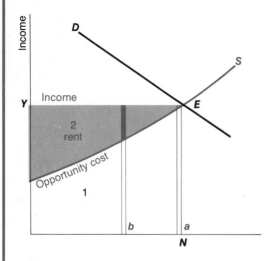

(a)

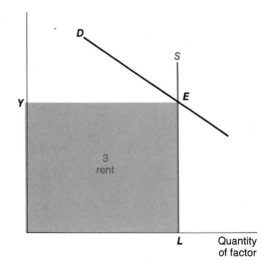

(b)

Figure 20-10
Rent of a factor of production that (a) has an alternative use (such as labor), and (b) one that does not (such as some types of land)

(a) All individuals in this panel earn the same income Y, but they have different opportunity costs (as given by the height of the supply curve S). The difference between the two (income and opportunity cost) is rent. For individual b, this is the dark bar, while for individual a, it is zero. For all individuals collectively, it is the red area. (b) None of the plots of land in this panel has any other use. Each has zero opportunity cost, and their supply is completely inelastic. Therefore, their entire income 3 is rent.

have different opportunity costs, as shown by the two empty bars. Therefore their rents will vary.

To show this in detail, first consider individual *a*. She has barely been attracted into this industry by income *Y*, since this is what she can earn elsewhere (her opportunity cost). Because there is no difference between her income and her opportunity cost, she earns no rent.

The situation for individual *b* is different. His opportunity cost (potential income elsewhere) is shown by the lower empty bar. The difference between this and his *actual* income *Y* is the red bar; this is his rent. Visualizing similar red bars representing the rents of other workers, we conclude that the rent earned by all *N* workers in this industry is the shaded triangle 2.

To sum up: The *N* workers in this labor force, all earning salary *Y*, have a total salary income of areas 1 + 2. Of this, area 1 is their opportunity cost, while area 2 is their rent.

The income of any other factor of production can similarly be divided into opportunity cost and rent components. In particular, we are interested in the land shown in panel *b* which has a completely inelastic supply because it can't be used for anything but agriculture. (Quantity *L* will be supplied no matter what its price may be.) Because it can't earn anything in any other use (its opportunity cost is zero) *all* its income 3 is rent.†

Finally, we can recap our discussion of rent with the simple example shown in Figure 20-11, which illustrates how an individual can earn rent because *(a)* he's very good at what he's doing (the issue addressed in the main text), or *(b)* he's

†As factor supply becomes less elastic, we can visualize it as rotating around *E* in a counterclockwise direction. (We move from panel *a* toward panel *b*.) Rent becomes a more and more important part of income.

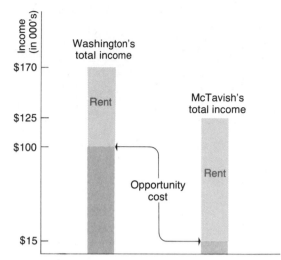

Figure 20-11
Why rent depends both on (1) how good a factor is in its present use, and (2) how bad it is in any other use
Washington has more basketball talent, and earns a higher salary. If the opportunity costs of the players were the same, Washington would earn the higher rent. But their opportunity costs are not the same. In fact, McTavish's is so much lower that rent makes up a larger part of his income than Washington's.

very bad at anything else (the issue addressed in this box). Washington is a better basketball player than teammate McTavish, and his higher income reflects this. If they had the same opportunity costs, Washington would have a higher rent. But they don't. Whereas Washington's opportunity cost is $100,000 (his potential salary playing football instead), McTavish has no other talent than basketball. His opportunity cost is the bare $15,000 that he could earn in manual labor. Because his opportunity cost is so low, almost all his income is rent; indeed, for this reason there's a higher rent component in his income than in Washington's. ■

cheap, you buy more land and build sideways. But if land is expensive enough, you conserve it by building up. Thus, buildings tend to be tallest in the prime, most expensive locations.)

*Above-normal profit as a rent

Since above-normal profit is defined as a return above opportunity cost, it is, by definition, a rent. The most obvious illustration occurs in the case of monopoly, with the shaded area in Figure 11-4 sometimes being referred to as a **monopoly rent.** It exists because entry by new firms into the industry is restricted. Therefore, it is a rent on whatever restricts entry. For example, it may be rent on a government license that is granted to one firm (or a few) and that blocks out other potential competitors. Or, it may be rent on a patented product that other firms cannot copy. Or, if there are economies of scale, the existing firm may earn a rent since no other firm can afford to enter.

*HOW RENTS ARE CAPITALIZED

If land plots A and B in Figure 20-7 are put up for sale, we would expect A to sell for a higher price; it will be more valuable because of the higher rent it can earn. This is generally true: Higher rents result in higher land values. But can't we be more precise about how the value of land is determined?

If you had the money and you were interested in buying land B in Figure 20-7, how much would you be willing to pay for it? Bear in mind that, as an alternative, you can always purchase bonds (or stocks) instead, and earn a rate of return of, say, 6 percent. Because the rent of land B is $60 per year, you should be willing to pay about $1,000 for it. This gives you the same 6 percent rate of return on your land (a $60 return on $1,000) as on the alternative of buying bonds. Moreover, the competition of other potential buyers who feel the same way will ensure that the price of land B will settle at about $1,000—so long as the rent on B is expected to remain at $60 per year.

But when the rent on land B doubles in Figure 20-8 to $120, the value of this land will also change; it will also roughly double to about $2,000, with the rate of return left unchanged at 6 percent (that is, a $120 return on $2,000). To describe this process, we say that an increase in rent is **capitalized** in the value of the asset (land).

In practice, there are many complications. In particular, the price of land will be affected not only by present rents, but by expected *future* rents too. If a single year's rent increases by 20 percent, the price of land may increase by more than 20 percent if people expect rents to continue rising.

[How an income flow—like rent or interest—is capitalized in the value of an asset—like land or a bond—is given in Box 11-1 in the companion volume. (The "capitalization of an income flow" is just another way of saying "the calculation of the present value of an income flow.")]

The fact that land prices reflect rents leads us to be skeptical of any government program to raise farm income by raising the price of commodities, such as wheat. Its major effect may be to cause higher rents (a shift from Figure 20-7 to 20-8) and consequently a higher value for farmland. Thus, its benefit tends to go to the owners of farmland when the price supports are introduced. By and large, it does not go to those who want to farm by renting land. And, if new farmers purchase the land, they will be passing their eventual income increase from farming over to those who sell the land at a high price. Paradoxically, the higher wheat price may make farming *less* attractive for newcomers: They now have a greater problem of raising the money necessary to purchase the higher-priced farm land. Thus, government price supports designed to "help out the small farmer" may, in fact, keep those of limited means out of farming altogether.

Moreover, serious problems arise even for those who do raise the necessary funds to get into farming by borrowing heavily on a big mortgage. They will be able to earn a living—and make those big mortgage payments—only if the government price-support program continues. So these farmers *of necessity* become strong supporters of the government program;

without it, food prices would fall, and they would no longer be able to make their mortgage payments. In short, when government support programs are introduced, they benefit one group—those who initially own the land. But if these initial owners sell it, they are "out-of-reach": For example, if they have retired to Florida on the proceeds of their land sale, they cannot be damaged if the farm support program is then reversed. Instead, the damage all falls on the *new* owners.

Other economic rents—besides those on land—may also be capitalized. The number of taxis in New York is limited: A driver must have a "medallion" to operate a cab. Because this requirement makes taxis scarce in New York, the fares collected by each taxi are greater. But this higher income (rent) becomes capitalized in the value of a medallion. By 1980 the price of a medallion had risen to $68,000, that is, to *10 times* the cost of a cab. (See Box 20-5.) Thus, someone who wants to own and operate a cab in New York faces the same problem as the Midwestern farmer. He may be able to do reasonably well once he gets into the business, but how in the world does he raise the money to get started in the first place?

Finally, taxi medallions raise this issue: Rather than let the medallion owners benefit from the policy of restricting the number of cabs, would it not have been better for New York to auction off the rights to operate cabs only for 1 or 2 years at a time? Then the city would have been able to collect the rents. Moreover, individual drivers could now enter the industry far more easily. They would have to buy only the right to operate a cab for 1 or 2 years, rather than the far more expensive right to operate it permanently (the cost they now incur when they buy the medallions).

*Taxing rent

Rent has always been a natural target for taxation. About a century ago, Henry George built a powerful single-tax movement on the idea that nothing should be taxed but land rents. (His book *Progress and Poverty* sold millions of copies, and he almost won an election as mayor of New York.) Why, asked George, shouldn't we tax land rents, since they represent a pure windfall? Owners obviously don't produce the land, nor do they work for their rental incomes. Instead, they just hold the land and become wealthy from "unearned increments" as the population increases and rents rise. George argued that the land rents belong to the public as a whole and should be taxed away from the owners and used for public purposes.

George's case was based not only on equity, but also on efficiency. A levy on land rents is one of the few taxes that need not distort resource allocation. Even if half the rent on land is taxed away, it will still remain in cultivation. What else can the owner do with it? And because the quantity of land in use is not affected, there is no reason to expect an efficiency loss. (Compare this with a tax on any other factor of production. For example, a tax on wages can affect the incentive to work, and might thus affect the amount of work done.)

However, George's proposal to tax land rent raises two serious difficulties—in addition to the obvious problem that, as a single tax, it would not raise enough money to cover today's large government expenditures. First, if present owners paid the current high price when they bought their land, rents are not a windfall to them at all, but just a reasonable return on their large initial expenditure. (Why tax those who bought land, and not those who bought stocks or bonds instead?) The only windfall is to the previous owners who sold the land for a high price. But they may now be living in Bermuda, beyond the reach of the taxing authority. Second, in practice it may be impossible to separate the rent on land from the return to buildings. (If you tax a landlord's income, you will be taxing *both*.) But to an economist, the return to buildings (or any other improvements on the land) is not a "rent" at all. Instead, it is a return to *capital*, and it cannot be taxed without causing distortion and inefficiency. For example, a tax on the returns from apartments will discourage the construction and maintenance of such buildings for the same reason that rent control did in the example in Chapter 4.

BOX 20-5

If You Want Investment Advice, Don't Ask Your Broker—Ask Your Cabbie

Seats on the New York Stock Exchange are like taxi medallions. They are limited, and as a consequence, they are valuable. However, as a result of a disappointing stock market and the abolition of minimum brokerage fees, the price of a seat on the Stock Exchange plunged from $515,000 in 1969 to $40,000 in 1977. During the same period, a taxi medallion doubled in value, and had become worth more than a seat on the Stock Exchange. By 1980, a medallion was worth $68,000, which isn't bad for something that was worth less than $10 in 1941.

In the "good old days," fathers sometimes launched their sons in business by buying them a seat on the Stock Exchange. Nowadays, buying them a cab might be a better investment. And perhaps we should think the unthinkable: If you want investment advice from someone with a proven track record, should you ask your stock broker—or your cab driver? ■

Key Points

1 Those who provide the nation's capital receive income in several forms. For example, those who own businesses receive a profit income. Those who lend money to businesses to purchase plant or equipment receive an interest income.

2 In a perfectly competitive capital market, the interest rate is determined by the demand and supply of loanable funds. Demand reflects how productive these funds will be when they are invested (the marginal efficiency of investment). Supply reflects how highly savers value money in its alternative use—consumption.

3 Because capital is productive, present goods can be exchanged for even more future goods. Therefore, present goods are worth more than future goods. The interest rate indicates how much more.

4 The interest rate also acts as a screening device that allocates funds to investment projects with the highest productivity. A government ceiling that lowers the interest rate below its perfectly competitive level results in two kinds of efficiency loss: *(a)* It reduces the total funds available for investment, and *(b)* it may result in these funds being allocated to the wrong set of projects. It also results in a transfer from lenders to those borrowers who are able to get loans.

5 Income is earned not only on machinery and other forms of physical capital, but also on human capital, that is, on skills, training, and education. The individuals who own the human capital are not the only ones who bear the initial cost of the investment. Governments also invest by subsidizing education, and businesses invest by subsidizing training programs. An inadequate past opportunity to accumulate human capital is one significant reason why the income of minority groups is depressed.

6 The return from an investment in a university education has been estimated as about 8 to 10 percent for the individual who acquires it, but perhaps as low as 4 percent for society as a whole.

7 Economists define rent as the return to any factor of production above its opportunity cost. Those with superior talents in any occupation, whether business or basketball, earn a rent.

8 Land also earns a rent—except for plots that are not cultivated or have just barely been brought into cultivation. The most fertile plots earn the largest rent. If the price of wheat (and other crops) increases, rents on all cultivated plots of land rise and new plots are brought into cultivation.

9 Rent is also earned on land because of its location. Mineral deposits similarly earn rent, with the richest, most accessible deposits earning the highest rents. Above-normal profits earned by a firm are also a form of rent. In the case of monopoly, these rents are typically due to something (such as a patent or a government license) that blocks entry by potential competitors.

*10 The higher the rent earned by an asset (like a plot of land), the higher its value; thus, rents are "capitalized." This in turn has important implications for any agricultural price support policy that raises rents and therefore the price of farms. Although such a policy obviously benefits those who own farms, it won't necessarily increase the income of those who want to buy farms and work them. Quite the contrary: It tends to discourage new entrants by increasing the initial cost of buying a farm.

Key Concepts

debt and equity capital

physical and human capital

marginal efficiency of investment (MEI)

why present goods are worth more than future goods

base (risk-free) rate of interest

transfer and efficiency effects of an interest rate ceiling

misallocation due to rationing of funds

normal and above-normal profit

substitution between factors of production

interest rate as an allocator of investment funds

human capital and discrimination

affirmative action programs

private and social returns to education

economists' broad definition of rent

rent on land due to differences in fertility

*rent on land due to location

*monopoly rent

*capitalization of rent

Problems

20-1 (Review of Chapters 18, 19, and 20.) Why are wages and salaries higher in the United States than in most other countries? Why are our other forms of income also higher? The highest per capita incomes are not in the United States or Western Europe, but in some of the smaller states along the Persian Gulf. Why?

20-2 When economists speak of labor, capital and land as factors of production, resources such as oil are included in the broad "land" category. Explain how the rapidly rising price of oil in the 1970s affected (a) decisions by individual firms on the combination of factors they would use, and (b) the mix of final goods that was produced. (Use plastics and fertilizer—which both require a large quantity of oil to produce—in your answer.)

20-3 "In a world in which labor is free to switch jobs, there will be inadequate investment in human capital in the form of job training." Do you agree? Explain why or why not. How might our minimum wage laws be changed to reduce this problem? Would such changes raise other problems?

20-4 Explain why the armed services have subsidized the university education of students who sign up to serve for several years after graduation. (Explain why your answer is similar to one of the cases in Box 20-2.)

20-5 Why might a firm pay a very high salary to attract an executive from a competing firm?

20-6 In Figure 20-6, does individual A receive more income than a manual laborer because of rent? Does B receive more than A because of rent? Explain your answer.

20-7 The public's idea of rent does not coincide with the economist's definition. How are the two concepts different? Give an example of (a) a return which an economist considers rent, but the public does not; (b) a return which the public considers rent, but the economist does not; and (c) a return which both consider rent.

20-8 Do you think that rent is an important or an insignificant part of the income of the following:

(a) Robert Redford

(b) An elevator operator

(c) A textile worker

20-9 Are these statements true or false? "An increase in the price of oil not only stimulates the search for oil. It also brings previously uneconomic sources of oil into production. But it does not affect rent on existing oil fields." Correct whatever statements are false, if any.

*20-10 Suppose that all the agricultural land within 100 miles of Kansas City is equally fertile. Suppose also that all corn must be sold in Kansas City, and that the cost of transporting it there depends only on distance. What pattern of land rent would you expect over this area?

*20-11 Suppose New York City imposed its taxi restriction by allowing only a restricted set of *individuals* (Smith, Gonzales, etc.) to drive cabs. Would rents be generated in this case? If so, who would earn these rents?

*20-12 The number of doctors is limited because anyone practicing medicine must have a license. Are rents generated in this case? To whom do they go? Is the objective of licensing to affect doctors' income, or is there some other reason?

*20-13 According to Henry George's single-tax idea, taxes on land rent would not affect efficiency even if they reached rates of 50, 90, or 95 percent. Do you agree? Why or why not? Does George's argument apply to other forms of rent? For example, would a 95 percent tax on above-normal profits affect efficiency? Why or why not?

*20-14 When Dave Winfield decided to play baseball he turned down offers to play pro football (where, let's suppose, he might be now working for $100,000 a year) and basketball (for $500,000 a year). Divide his current income (of, say, $2 million a year) into rent and opportunity cost.

CHAPTER 21
Natural Resources, Conservation, and Growth

The . . . economy of the future might be called the "spaceman economy," in which the earth has become a single space ship, without unlimited reservoirs of anything.

Kenneth Boulding

Land is one of our most valuable and durable natural resources. When the soil is used, it is not "used up"—provided, of course, it is given reasonable care and protection. The amount that will be available next year will be the same, whether we use it today or not. But the same thing is not true of most other natural resources. The amount of iron ore that will be available in the future depends on how much we use today. And the amount of timber that we can cut 10 years hence depends on how much we cut today.

This chapter focuses on these resources, like iron ore or timber, whose future supply does depend on the current rate of use, and where questions of conservation are therefore important. Are we using these resources too fast? Are we taking the attitude: Why should we worry about future generations—what have they ever done for us? Do our expanding industrial requirements, along with our finite and shrinking resource supplies, put us on a collision course that will soon bring us to our knees, as some observers have predicted? And what can economics tell us about how rapidly we should be using up our scarce natural resources?

THE EFFICIENT USE OF RESOURCES: AN INTRODUCTION

A simple market for a privately owned natural resource (timber) is illustrated in Figure 21-1. Here, S reflects the direct cost of harvesting timber—the wages of lumberjacks, the cost of hauling, etc. But another cost of cutting it this year is that it cannot be cut next year. Supply curve S' takes into account this cost as well. For example, the price required to induce the owner of unit a to sell today—the **reservation price** —includes the empty bar (the harvesting cost) *plus* the solid bar (the amount necessary to compensate for the future reduction in the available harvest).

The *reservation price* of a resource includes both the cost of harvesting or extracting the resource today, *and* the amount necessary to compensate for the reduction in the resource available in the future. (For details, see Box 21-1.)

The demand for timber D in Figure 21-1, like the demand for any other input, depends on

434

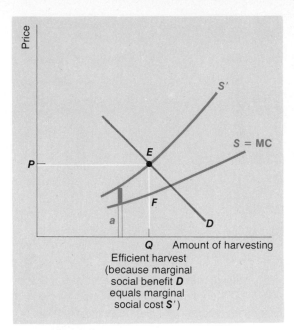

Figure 21-1

Market for a privately owned natural resource

The supply S' of this natural resource depends not only on the marginal cost of harvesting it (as illustrated by the empty bar) but also on the necessary compensation to the owner for the reduced crop available in future years (the red bar). Provided that the resource is privately owned, both these costs will be taken into account and the equilibrium will be at the efficient point E.

its marginal productivity—for example, the productivity of timber as it is used by the construction industry. Equilibrium in a competitive timber market will be at E, with price P and quantity Q of timber cut. This is efficient, because the marginal benefit of cutting timber (its marginal productivity, given by the height of D) is equal to the marginal cost [the height of S', which includes both the cost of harvesting (QF) and the cost of having a reduced stand of timber available in the future (FE).]

This competitive market provides an efficient solution because we have assumed that the forests are *privately owned*. There are owners with *property rights* who have an interest in taking the future into account. Thus, they have a clear incentive to see that the cutting takes place

in a sensible manner—that is, in a way that takes account of future costs FE, and also recognizes other conservation concerns like protecting the small trees that will make up the "next generation" harvest.

If forests were common property that anyone could cut down, the result would be quite different. You can guess, quite correctly, that uncontrolled cutting might be a conservation disaster: Anyone could use a chain saw in the free forest, and the only cost that would be taken into account would be the harvesting cost S. Individuals cutting down trees would have little regard for the loss to future harvests. ("If I don't cut it now, someone else will.") Too much would be cut down today, and valuable timber would be sold at too low a price.

PROBLEMS WITH A COMMON PROPERTY NATURAL RESOURCE: FISH

To see why conservation may become a serious problem when there are no property rights, consider fishing. While many forests are the property of individuals or corporations, the oceans are not. The result is shown in Figure 21-2. Since people who fish do not own the schools of fish, they have little reason to take into account the damage they are doing to future catches. (After all, each boat takes too small a catch to affect the future fish population.) Thus, they respond to supply curve S rather than S', and take no account of how fishing today affects the fish available for future catches. The result is an equilibrium at E^* rather than E. Too many fish are caught.

The efficiency loss that results because fish are a common property resource is shown as the familiar red triangle. This is easily confirmed by considering b, one of the "excess" fish caught. The marginal benefit of catching b is shown as the empty bar under the demand curve, while its marginal cost (including the effect on future catches) is shown as the empty bar plus the red bar under the S' curve. Thus, the net loss from

BOX 21-1

What Influences an Owner's Reservation Price?

Some of the major influences on reservation price are:

1 The **expected future price** of the natural resource. The greater the expected price of timber next year, the greater the owners' incentive to leave timber standing, "in the bank" so to speak. Therefore, the higher will be the reservation price they will require before they will allow the timber to be cut today.

2 The **expected future cost of harvesting** the resource. The higher the expected cost of cutting the timber next year, the less incentive the owner will have to leave the timber standing, and the lower will be the reservation price. Obviously, if this expected future cost is high enough, it could eat up the entire future price of the timber, thus eliminating its future value. In this case, the owner has no incentive at all for leaving timber uncut, and curve S'' coincides with curve S in Figure 21-1.

3 The **interest rate.** The higher the interest rate, the greater the valuation of present goods relative to future goods and the greater the incentive to acquire timber today, when it is highly valued. In other words, the higher the interest rate, the lower the incentive to leave timber standing, and the lower the reservation price.

4 The **rate of growth of the forest.** If the forest has become fully mature—that is, if it is no longer growing—the owner will acquire no more timber by letting it stand for another year, and will therefore have a lower reservation price.

For simplicity, we have assumed that the owner's decision is only whether to cut the timber this year or next year. But, of course, the issue is not so clear. Instead, the problem is to find the efficient pattern of harvesting over the next n years. And if the owner is engaged in replanting the forest (rather than simply letting it grow up itself, as we assume here), this is another important cost to be taken into account. ∎

catching this fish is the red bar, and the sum of the losses on all the other "excess" fish caught over the range QQ^* is the red triangle.

One way to eliminate this loss is to tax those who catch fish according to the damage they do to future catches—in other words, tax them (or charge them a fishing fee) high enough to raise

their supply curve from S to S'. This would result in the efficient catch Q. Notice how close this is to our analysis of external costs in Chapter 14. (For other policies to reduce a harvest to a more efficient quantity, see Box 21-2.)

In Chapter 16, we cited the advantages of free trade in goods, In that discussion we saw a

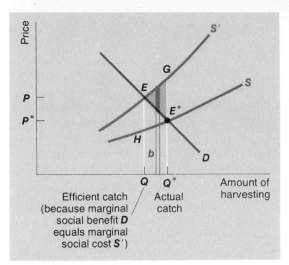

Figure 21-2
Market for a common property resource
This case is exactly the same as the one shown in Figure 21-1, but with one exception. Here the natural resource is not privately owned. (Anyone can catch fish in the ocean.) Since there are no owners to take the future into account, the supply response is S rather than S'. Equilibrium is thus at E^* rather than E, and the harvest is at Q^* rather than the efficient quantity Q. The result is the red efficiency loss.

number of impressive reasons why an "open border" may be in a nation's interest. But in the case of extracting a natural resource like fish, there is a problem with an open border. In fact, free and unrestricted access of all comers to a fishing area can destroy a nation's attempt to conserve by controlling the catch made by its own people. Thus, recent attempts by a number of countries to extend their property rights over fish by expanding their territorial limits should be judged, not only in terms of the obvious issue of whether domestic or foreign fishing boats will get this year's catch, but also in terms of the more subtle issue of whether this policy is aimed at conserving the resource. (The difficult task of conservation is complicated by the fact that fish swim. No matter how carefully a nation may protect them, they may be caught outside its territorial waters.)

The question of territorial rights has now become a difficult policy problem, involving

many countries (including the United States) in international disputes. In the 1970s it led Britain and Iceland close to military conflict in a "cod war," touched off when Iceland unilaterally extended its territorial waters to 200 miles. Iceland's reason was that the population of cod had fallen by one-third, and overfishing might lead to a disaster like the near disappearance of herring a few years before. (The seriousness of the threat to the cod population was a controversial issue. As the British news magazine *The Economist* pointed out, cod and herring are different kettles of different fish: The short-lived herring can be decimated by one bad spawning season, but cod have about 8 years to spawn.) British fishing boats, long accustomed to fishing off the coast of Iceland, continued to do so. Iceland sent out gunboats to cut the British fishing nets. When an Icelandic gunboat fired shots toward a British ship, it was rammed and forced back into harbor. In the best nineteenth-century tradition, the British then sent in the Royal Navy, in a scene reminiscent of an old Hollywood movie.

Disagreements over the extension of territorial waters from 12 to 200 miles also arose *within* the United States, between two groups of fishermen. Those on the East Coast favored an extension to 200 miles; they wanted protection from competing foreign boats off the East Coast. But an extension was opposed by West Coast fishermen who were less concerned with foreign competition off the U.S. coast than with being able to fish in foreign waters themselves—in particular, in the waters off Latin America. (They recognized that, if the United States extended its territorial waters, they would not be able to object to a similar extension by Latin American countries. In fact, the United States did extend its territorial waters to 200 miles in 1977.)

*The idea of maximum sustainable yield
While the preceding analysis has highlighted the important issue of common property versus private ownership of resources, in many respects

---

*Instructors of short courses may omit this section.

BOX 21-2

Policies to Control the Use of a Common Property Resource

The problem is: How can harvesting be restricted today in order to prevent a damaging shortage tomorrow? To illustrate, we turn from commercial ocean fishing to sport fishing—say, for bass or trout in an inland lake (where there may be exactly the same case for conservation).

1 The option we have already suggested is for the government to impose a price restraint by levying some sort of tax or fishing fee. One example is a requirement that anyone who fishes must have a license. (Even more appropriate, were it not for difficulties in its administration, would be a fixed charge per fish caught.)

2 The second option is for the government to impose various *non-price restraints*. Examples abound: It may limit each person's catch. Or, it may limit the fishing season, prohibiting any fishing whatsoever at certain times. (The off-season is typically defined to minimize the disturbance to spawning.) In other cases, more peculiar non-price restraints have been imposed. In certain areas of Alaska, salmon fishing is illegal unless it is done in a boat no more than 32 feet long, and the maximum number of nets each person can use is carefully specified.

3 A third option, which may be feasible for a small lake but not for an ocean, is to put fishing rights under private ownership. The idea is to get the new owner to preserve his asset by reducing the catch from Q^* to Q in Figure 21-2. (He might do so by charging a fee of EH on each fish caught.) This "creation of a property right" is sometimes cited as a way of allowing resources to be allocated efficiently by a free market that would not work well otherwise.

But in practice, this policy raises two difficulties. The first is a transfer problem: How do you deal with the new owner, who now can reap the ownership benefits from a resource which was previously publicly owned? (One possibility is for the government to auction off this ownership to private individuals. The government would thus reap the ownership benefits.) The second problem is this: In controlling the fishing in a lake, the new owner will have monopoly power (unless there are many other lakes with other competing owners nearby). How, then, can we be sure that this monopolist will cut back the catch from Q^* only to Q, the desirable quantity from a conservation point of view? Why won't the owner, like any other profit-maximizing monopolist, exercise market power by cutting back the catch even further? If this occurs, private ownership will not bring an efficient solution after all. ■

It is an oversimplification. In Figure 21-3 we examine some other resource issues. This diagram shows how the *growth* in a fish population (on the vertical axis) depends on the *size* of the population (on the horizontal axis). Point D indicates that the maximum size of the population is 10 million fish. When this point is reached, there are so many fish that their population will not increase further: For each new fish, an existing one will die. If there is no fishing, the fish population will grow toward this number, but not beyond. To confirm this, note that at any point to the left of D, such as K, the fish population will grow (by the height of K). As a result, the population will be greater in the next period, causing a movement to the right, which will continue as long as the yield curve lies above the axis. But, once D is reached, there is no further growth in the number of fish.

There is no reason why a hungry human race should be particularly interested in this "no fishing" solution. (There is little satisfaction in knowing that the sea is as full of fish as it can possibly get.) Instead, let us consider a point like C that does involve fishing. Here the fish population is $X_C = 2$ million, and is increasing by $Y_C = 1\frac{1}{3}$ million fish per year. At this point, we can take out the natural increase of $1\frac{1}{3}$ million fish year after year without reducing the 2 million population. Hence, this curve is known as the **sustainable yield** curve, or more simply, as the **yield curve.**

Sustainable yield is the amount of a renewable resource (like fish) that can be harvested while still leaving the population constant.

The highest point on this curve, M, represents the *maximum sustainable yield*. This is a point of particular interest, because it shows the maximum number of fish (in this case, 2 million) that can be caught on a continuing basis without depleting the parent stock. To harvest fish at this maximum rate requires a parent population of 5 million (measured along the horizontal axis). As a first approximation, preventing the resource from falling below this 5-million quantity is what economists mean by conservation.[1] (They do not generally mean keeping this fish population at its greatest possible size of 10 million.)

Of course, for some resources and in some periods, conservation may not be necessary. The situation long ago, before large-scale commercial fishing, is illustrated by a point like K, with the ocean almost as full of fish as it could get. As human population and our demands on

Figure 21-3
Sustainable yield curve

This curve shows the tendency of a fish population to increase. For example, point C indicates that a population of 2 million fish will grow by $1\frac{1}{3}$ million per year. This is the number we could catch and still leave the population intact. At first this curve rises. The larger the fish population, the greater its natural increase. However, this increase reaches a maximum at M, where a fish population of 5 million generates an annual increase of 2 million. This 2 million is the *maximum sustainable yield*, the largest number that can be caught per year and still leave the fish population constant. To the right of M, the yield curve falls as the ocean becomes increasingly crowded with fish. When the population of fish reaches 10 million (point D), the ocean can support no further increase.

[1]The best conservation target need not be precisely M. On the one hand, the best target may be to the right of M if this substantially reduces the costs of fishing. (By letting the fish population grow, we make the fish easier and cheaper to find.) On the other hand, the interest rate tends to pull the target to the left of M. The reason: In taking so many fish out of the sea today that we deplete the population from 5 million to, say, 4 million, we consume fish now at the cost of an even greater quantity of fish in the future. This sort of trade may be justified if we value fish more highly today than in the future. The interest rate tells us that this is in fact the case.

Because these two influences—the cost of catching fish and our higher valuation of present fish—are pulling us in two opposing directions, we may view M as a good approximate target.

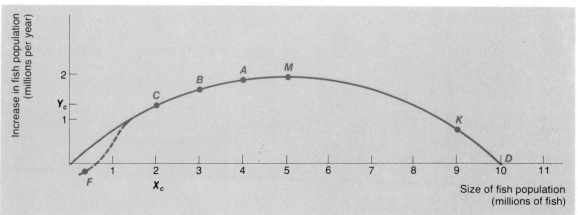

the seas increased, the fish population was reduced by heavy commercial fishing; there was a move to the left in this diagram. However, so long as the fish population still remained above 5 million (that is, to the right of the maximum sustainable yield at M), there was no conservation problem. As we harvested more, the fish population fell, but it became more able to regenerate itself. (That is, the natural increase—as shown by the height of the curve—became greater as we moved from K toward M.) It is only if we reach M, where the fish population is only 5 million, that we begin to encounter problems. If at this point we continue to harvest more than the natural increase, we will continue to reduce the fish population (shift left from M). But now, with each such shift, the fish population becomes less able to regenerate itself; that is, each shift to the left moves us to a lower point on the yield curve. If we do not limit our catches, we may risk extinguishing a whole species, just as we very nearly extinguished the buffalo. (And fishing out an ocean is not just a theoretical possibility. As already noted, this almost happened with herring in 1969 as a result of the development of larger, more efficient fishing boats. And the introduction of sonar for chasing down whales has endangered some types of whale.)[2]

To sum up: The maximum sustainable yield (M) and the population (5 million) on which it is based provide the approximate targets for efficient harvesting and conservation. Of course, if a species is so plentiful that it is at a point like K, there is no need to restrict catches; there is no economic conservation problem.

---

*[2]If the yield curve is like the dashed curve in Figure 21-3, heavy fishing may do irreversible damage to the species. Suppose that we have fished the population down to a quarter-million fish, and are consequently at point F. There are still some fish, but they cannot find other fish to spawn. There is no longer a natural increase. Instead, there is a natural decrease in population. (F lies below the horizontal axis.) Thus, once we have reached a point like F, the population will eventually die out on its own even if we stop fishing altogether. Clearly, the first rule of conservation should be to prevent such irreversible disasters.

THE CONSERVATION OF NONRENEWABLE RESOURCES

Even with a resource such as timber or fish that is **renewable** (it reproduces), a rapid harvest can eventually exhaust the resource. But exhaustion becomes an even more serious specter if the resource is *nonrenewable*. Examples include oil and copper ore. (Although new oil supplies may be created, this requires eons of years, so that, for all practical purposes, we consider oil nonrenewable.)

There is a finite quantity of each nonrenewable resource, and if we continue to use a constant amount each year, we will ultimately exhaust the available supply. Moreover, this day of reckoning will tend to come sooner because, with population growth, the amount we extract does not stay constant, but may grow instead.

Simple projections spell disaster
Anyone who projects the present rate of world population growth into the future finds that our requirement for nonrenewable resources is on a collision course with their available supply. Within the next hundred years or so, something must change. A number of models have been developed to show that, on our finite planet, today's trends in population growth and resource use cannot continue long into the future. For example, a computer-based study in 1972 concluded that:

If the present growth trends in world population, industrialization, pollution, food production, and resource depletion continue unchanged, the limits to growth on this planet will be reached sometime within the next one hundred years. The most probable result will be a rather sudden and uncontrollable decline in both population and industrial capacity.[3]

If present trends continue, by the middle of the twenty-first century disaster will be upon us—or, more precisely, upon our grandchildren.

[3]Donella H. Meadows and others, *The Limits to Growth* (New York: Universe Books, 1972), p. 29.

But does it make any sense to assume that present trends *will* continue for a century? After all, if we are prepared to project present trends, we can bring the world to an end much more dramatically than this, and we don't need a computer to show it. Any simple illustration will do. For example, if we project from a period in which the fruit fly population is growing, we can in a matter of a relatively few years bury the earth 2 miles deep in fruit flies. Any such projection provides an illustration, not of good economics or biology, but of the mathematical magic of mechanically compounding a rate of growth.[4] A far more challenging and rewarding intellectual exercise is to ask: Why will the population of fruit flies eventually stop growing? Why will major changes in our present economic and social system occur?

Adjustments as resources become scarcer

What changes can we expect in our present pattern of life as a growing population presses on a shrinking resource supply?

Change 1: Substitution in production As demand presses on available supply, the prices of resources rise and producers substitute other inputs. For example, the price increases that occur as the supply of oil is depleted make people turn to other sources of energy, such as solar energy, wind energy, or alcohol. (They may not be economical yet, but they are becoming so as the prices of oil and natural gas continue to increase. In fact, Brazil is already making use of significant amounts of alcohol as a supplement for gasoline.)

Change 2: Induced innovation The higher the price of oil, the greater the economic incentive to improve existing substitutes and to develop new ones. Thus, it is not just a case of switching to known substitutes. In addition, sub-

stitutes not yet known may be discovered. Think of how the development of plastics has reduced our requirement for metals.

Change 3: Substitution in consumption As the price of energy rises, consumers buy smaller cars, turn down their thermostats, and insulate their homes more thoroughly. As forests have been cut down and quality wood has become more expensive, consumers have turned to furniture made with veneers.

Change 4: Changes in population growth Population growth cannot be projected far into the future because the rate of population increase will be modified by the economic pressures that build up. As our planet becomes more crowded, bringing up children becomes more expensive—and this may influence the typical couple's decision on family size. Moreover, the population growth rate may fall for other reasons that have little to do with economics. In the highly industrialized countries, birthrates have recently been dropping because of changing social attitudes toward the family and children, and because of the development of birth control methods. True, much of the world's population is still in the less developed countries, where the rate of increase is still high in some countries. Reasons for this continued high rate include poverty (parents view children as a way of providing for their old age), a decline in death rates (because of better medical services), and religious or social objections to birth control. But these influences are likely to weaken. Living standards are rising (slowly), and death rates cannot continue to fall as rapidly in the future as in the past.

With the increasing scarcity of resources, there is a major problem. But it is not the problem of some future resource Doomsday. (There are far more plausible reasons than resource scarcity for the human race to face Doomsday before the year 2100—particularly if we are unable to control nuclear weapons.)

What, then, is the nature of the resource problem? Basically, it is one of *cost* and

---

[4]To confirm the magic of compound growth, consider this: We will give you a million dollars, if you will give us just 1 cent today, 2 cents tomorrow, 4 cents the next day, and so on for just 1 month.

BOX 21-3

Dynamic Efficiency in Pricing a Nonrenewable Resource†

How high should a nonrenewable resource be priced in order to ensure that our future requirements can be met? Although this is a difficult question, we can isolate some of the issues with the following simplified example. Suppose we have a limited quantity of a metal that will be completely replaced in 2 years by a cheaper plastic substitute of equal quality. The objective, then, is to completely use up the available supply of the metal in the next 2 years in the most efficient way. (Because cheaper plastic will then become available, there is no need to save any metal beyond this date.) How should it be priced this year and next year to achieve this objective?

The answer is to select resource prices P_1 and P_2 in the 2 years as shown in Figure 21-4, so that the following two conditions are met:

1 The quantities used in the 2 years should exactly add up to the total available supply Q. In other words, $Q_1 + Q_2 = Q$.

2 Price P_2 should be higher than P_1 by a gap AB equal to the interest rate. Thus, if the interest rate is 5 percent, P_2 should be 5 percent higher than P_1.

Why does this price pattern result in the efficient allocation of this resource over time? The answer is that efficiency requires that we value the marginal productivity of a ton of metal the same in both years. (Otherwise we would be able to increase output by switching a ton of metal from the year of low productivity to the year of high productivity.) But hasn't this efficien-

†This box is based on Harold Hotelling's classic article that stimulated the study of natural resource economics a half century ago: "Economics of Exhaustible Resources," *Journal of Political Economy,* April 1931, pp. 137–175. For a summary of the research that this article inspired, see S. Devarajan and A. C. Fisher, "Hotelling's 'Economics of Exhaustible Resources': Fifty Years Later," *Journal of Economic Literature,* March 1981, pp. 65–73.

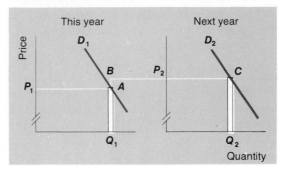

Figure 21-4
Efficient pricing pattern for a nonrenewable resource over 2 years
Efficient pricing requires that the gap AB between prices in the 2 years be equal to the interest rate. Efficiency also requires that the amount of the resource used up ($Q_1 + Q_2$) be equal to the total quantity available. (Note that there is no reason for D_1 and D_2 to be the same; in fact, they are quite different in Figure 21-5.)

cy criterion been violated, since the marginal productivity of a ton of metal this year (as defined under demand curve D_1) is bar Q_1A, while its marginal productivity next year is the higher bar Q_2C? The answer is no: *We value these two marginal productivities equally because they are earned in two different years.* Remember from Chapter 20 that we value goods this year more highly than goods next year, with the interest rate measuring the difference. When we accordingly raise the value of this year's Q_1A by the interest rate, we see that it is worth exactly the same as next year's Q_2C. (It was precisely to make these values equal that we separated P_1 and P_2 by the rate of interest.)

To sum up the message of Figure 21-4: The fixed supply of this resource is efficiently allocated if we use Q_1 this year and Q_2 next. This is what will occur in a competitive market if prices are P_1 and P_2 in the 2 years. We make no claim that this is the price pattern that will necessarily prevail; in fact, it may not. For example, if the supply of this resource is controlled by a small number of producers they may, like any other oligopolists, use their market power to set prices above P_1 and P_2. [True, higher prices will mean that some of this resource will not be used up by the end of year 2, when it will be displaced by

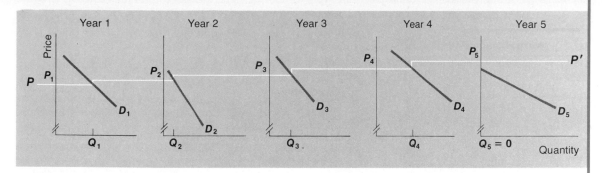

Figure 21-5
Efficient pricing pattern for a nonrenewable resource over a longer period

This figure extends Figure 21-4. Determining the efficient pattern of price and resource use over time may be viewed as fitting a price "staircase" PP' to the demand curves, with the restriction that $Q_1 + Q_2 + Q_3$ . . . be equal to the fixed remaining supply. As before, the height of each step in this staircase is the interest rate.

substitutes. But the oligopolists will still have maximized profits because of the increased price on the amount that they actually *do* sell. This is an obvious extension of our conclusion (in Chapter 12) that it may be profitable for colluding oligopolists to raise price, even though they sell less as a consequence.]

In Figure 21-4, it has been assumed that the resource will be completely replaced by a substitute in 2 years. Figure 21-5 extends this analysis to the case where the resource is replaced after a longer period.

The resource in Figure 21-5 is replaced by a substitute after year 4. This does not necessarily mean that a substitute eliminates all demand in succeeding years. In fact, there is still demand for the metal in year 5, namely, D_5. But the point is that it lies below P_5; the inexpensive substitute has "stunted" the demand for this metal. Of course, another reason that demand may be stunted may be that public taste turns against this resource; thus our use of it could end for this reason as well. An example is coal: Home furnaces were quickly converted away from coal about half a century ago, not only because oil and gas substitutes were developed, but also because no one wanted to shovel coal any more.

There are three crucial but highly unpredict-

able influences that will affect the efficient pricing pattern:

1 If existing deposits of the resource turn out to be less plentiful than expected, there will be less Q to distribute over time, and the whole price "staircase" PP' will shift upward. (As this happens, note how the quantity demanded each year is reduced into line with the reduced supply.) On the other hand, if new deposits are discovered, there will be more Q available, and the price staircase will shift down.

2 Price staircase PP' will shift if demand turns out to be different from what is expected. For example, if future demand is greater than expected, the price staircase will shift up.

3 The price staircase will shift down (or up) if substitutes are developed more (or less) rapidly than expected; and it is very difficult to predict just when the development of substitutes will, in fact, occur. For example, it is very difficult to estimate when—if ever—nuclear fusion (as opposed to present-day nuclear fission) will become a major source of energy. But this is important to know, because the best rate of oil use today depends on when this substitute becomes available. [Another complication in the case of oil is that it may be easier to develop substitutes for some of its uses (energy) than for others (plastics production).]

Thus, in practice, it is very difficult to pin down specifically the efficient pricing and allocation pattern for any resource. But this box has highlighted some of the important considerations that should be taken into account. ■

technology. Oil provides an example. Energy substitutes are available, but they are costly. Technology and increasing oil prices determine when existing substitutes become economical and how rapidly new substitutes are developed. A second example is one of our most essential resources, but one that we frequently take for granted: fresh, clean water. If we run out of it, we will be forced to tap a more expensive source of supply than our lakes and rivers: the ocean, where the supply is unlimited. But the use of seawater would involve the enormous cost of purifying and transporting it. Our problem is to keep these potential future costs in mind when we make decisions today, to ensure that we do not use our resources carelessly and wastefully. The more intelligently we conserve resources and the more we develop substitutes, the less the future cost of resource scarcity will be.

The central question, either in the case of resources or fruit flies, is therefore not, What would happen if current trends were to continue for 100 years? but rather, What is the likely process of adjustment? And even more to the point, What is the best path of adjustment? What can we do to make the process of adjustment work smoothly in terms of encouraging the discovery and development of substitutes? And finally, are we pricing resources high enough today to protect our interests tomorrow? (For a detailed analysis of this question, see Box 21-3.)

RESOURCES, THE ENVIRONMENT AND ECONOMIC GROWTH

In earlier chapters, several arguments for growth have been considered:

1 Unemployment is likely to be less severe in a rapidly growing economy.

2 Growth makes it easier to solve the poverty problem. Growth brings an across-the-board increase in income that lifts many families out of poverty; it can be a "rising tide that lifts all boats." Moreover, growth makes it easier to change the *relative* position of the boats—to increase the percentage of the nation's income that goes to the poor. It is far easier to provide for the poor if the total income pie is growing than if it is not (and any gains to the poor must be taken from someone else).

3 Growth increases not only our own future income, but also the income of our children.

However, as already noted, this third point should not be overstated. If history is any guide, technological improvements will make our children wealthier than we are, no matter what growth policy we follow. As MIT's Robert Solow points out: "Why should we poor folk make sacrifices for those who will in any case live in luxury in the future?"

Moreover, growth has recently been criticized on other grounds as well: It depletes our resources and increases the pollution in our environment. Do these arguments justify slowing growth (or, as some suggest, setting a target growth rate of zero)? In an earlier chapter, we argued that a nongrowth policy was a poor way to attack the pollution problem, both because ending growth would involve an enormous cost and because it would be relatively ineffective since it would not deal directly with the pollution problem. (It would only prevent pollution from growing, but it would not cut it back.) There are similar reasons for being skeptical of a no-growth policy to conserve our resources. It would involve great cost, and it would not directly attack the problem of resource scarcity. (Even if we were to end growth completely, we might still continue to deplete our resources too rapidly.) Better to deal specifically with the resource problem by encouraging the discovery and development of substitutes, and by ensuring that resources are expensive enough to induce us to cut back adequately on their use.

In short, a policy of slowing growth is not specific enough to cure any single problem (like resource depletion, pollution, or congestion). However, there is one overall argument for slowing growth: Although it would not solve any *one* of these problems, it would tend to make *all* of them less severe.

Finally, in assessing the growth-versus-antigrowth debate, a helpful question to ask is this: Would the arguments now used against growth have applied equally well a hundred years ago? If so, has our growth over the past century been a mistake? Some people argue that, if we could, we should turn back the clock; but many others would disagree. This is a judgment that you will have to make for yourself. But in comparing the past with the present, don't forget the simple things we take for granted today. Before deciding in favor of the idyllic pastoral life of a century ago, ask yourself this: What would you think of a world without aspirin —let alone penicillin?

Key Points

1 If a resource (such as timber) is privately owned, its supply will reflect not only the current cost of harvesting or extracting it, but also the amount necessary to compensate the owner for the adverse effect of present harvests on future resource supplies.

2 If a resource such as fish is not privately owned, boat captains will take no account of how this year's harvest will affect future harvests, and the result is an efficiency loss: Too much is harvested today.

3 In an attempt to limit the current catch of fish, the government may impose various restrictions, such as fishing licenses or off-season limits on fishing. In the case of ocean fishing, some governments have extended their territorial waters to limit the catch of foreign vessels. (It is difficult, however, to sort out how much of this territorial extension is a desire to conserve and how much is a desire to protect domestic vessels from foreign competition.)

4 Special problems arise when a resource is nonrenewable. (Timber and fish are renewable because they reproduce themselves. But resources like oil and copper do not.) If current rates of consumption continue, we must someday exhaust our nonrenewable resources. This simple observation has led to a number of "Doomsday studies" that predict the collapse of our economic system. However, a problem with many of these studies is that they take inadequate account of price adjustments: As such resources become scarcer, their prices rise; this encourages conservation and stimulates the search for substitutes. An important question is: Are today's prices of nonrenewable resources high enough to ensure that existing supplies will not be used up too quickly and that the development of new substitutes will be encouraged?

Key Concepts

renewable resource
nonrenewable resource
reservation price
privately owned resource

common property
resource
territorial limits
sustainable yield curve

maximum sustainable
yield
induced innovation

Problems

21-1 Suppose 50 boats are fishing in an ocean area. Would there be any reason for the government to allow the boat owners to sign an agreement restricting the amount each catches? Is it possible that restricting the catch, which began as a conservation measure, may become a means of exercising market power? Explain.

21-2 The problem of efficient timing in harvesting timber is illustrated in the diagram below. For example, point A indicates that if we wait 15 years before harvesting again, an acre will yield 10 units of timber. Which point represents a forest in which there is no longer any timber growth? Would you cut timber every 15, 30, or 66 years? Explain. (Assume that cutting and replanting costs are negligible.)

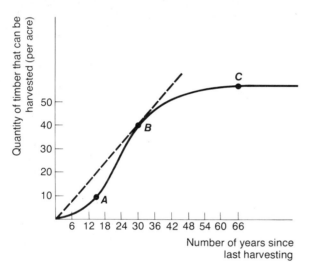

Number of years since last harvesting

21-3 Doomsday models typically project a constant rate of growth of population and resource usage, and hence forecast disaster. What economic forces tend to cause a change in the use of raw material resources? What forces affect the rate of population growth?

21-4 Equity among generations seems to suggest that we should not sacrifice much for our children, since they are likely to be wealthier than we are, regardless of what we do. But how, would you evaluate the following counterargument? Historically, each generation has sacrificed for the next. Is it fair for any generation to opt out of this process and thus become a "free rider," receiving benefits from the previous generation, but making no attempt to pass on benefits to the next?

*21-5 In Figure 21-5, explain how conservation measures may be taken too far. Specifically, explain why it would be a mistake to cut back consumption 1 unit below Q_1 in year 1 in order to conserve that unit for use in year 5. Also, show why it would be a mistake to ignore conservation concerns and use 1 unit more than Q_1 in year 1.

CHAPTER 22
Energy

Keeping fuel prices artificially [low] . . . subsidizes
excessive consumption, inhibits exploration and development of supply, and misrepresents the worth
of [energy-saving] technological changes.
Thomas C. Schelling

In 1973, the Arab-Israeli War led to a 6-month
Arab embargo of oil exports to the United States
and other nations considered friendly to Israel.
The Organization of Petroleum Exporting Countries (OPEC) used the occasion to increase the
price of a barrel of oil from less than $3 to more
than $11. In 1979–1980, the Iranian revolution
and war between Iraq and Iran disrupted the
world's oil supplies; OPEC jacked the price of oil
up to more than $30 a barrel. Somehow our
economic future has become linked to unpredictable political events in a few countries halfway around the world. How did we get into this
situation? And what can we do about it?

In previous chapters, we have seen that it is
impossible to study economic policy today without encountering the effects of the soaring international price of oil. For example, higher energy
prices pushed costs up in 1973–1974 and 1979–
1980, and led to the paradoxical situation where
inflation accelerated as the economy headed
into recession. And rising oil prices have led to
such huge trade imbalances among nations that
the stability of the international financial system
has been brought into question.

In this chapter we study the U.S. policies
that have been developed in response to this
higher price. What were the consequences of the
policy of keeping the price of oil within the
United States below the world level until early
1981? What are the pros and cons of the
decision to allow the U.S. price to rise to this
level? Should the U.S. price be *above* this? And

what alternative energy sources are available?

In answering these questions, we will be
drawing on a number of the economic tools we
have already developed in this book. Particularly
valuable will be an understanding of issues such
as opportunity cost (Chapter 2), oligopoly collusion (Chapter 12), environmental costs (Chapter
14), international trade (Chapters 16 and 17),
resource pricing (Chapter 21), and the analysis
of the efficiency and transfer effects of price
changes that has been a main theme throughout
the microeconomics part of this book.

THE INTERNATIONAL MISMATCH OF
OIL PRODUCTION AND OIL USE

The soaring price of oil has made us all acutely
aware of the "resource problem": We cannot
count on plentiful supplies of basic materials at
cheap prices. But, while world consumption of
oil has increased rapidly during the past three
decades (with the U.S. increase shown in Figure
22-1), the world is not about to "run out of oil,"
at least not in the near future. In the two decades
before the first oil price explosion in 1973–1974,
new reserves were found more rapidly than oil
was being used, with the result that the world's
proven reserves rose from about 24 times the
current annual consumption to about 30 times.
While U.S. reserves (which had peaked in 1970)
fell during the rest of the 1970s, new reserves

found elsewhere in the world were more than making up for this decline (Figure 22-2).

The most conspicuous feature of the world oil market is this: *Much of the consumption is in one set of countries* (in particular, North America, Europe, and Japan). But *much of the production is in another* (the OPEC countries) which have used their market power to push up the price. This imbalance of production and consumption—which leads to the huge international trade in oil shown earlier in Figure 12-5—is illustrated in Figure 22-3. The pie charts on the left indicate how oil comes from OPEC, and will continue to do so in the future. The pie chart on the right shows how oil is used heavily by the advanced industrialized countries. Thus, on the one hand, the Middle East countries produce over a third of the world's oil, while

consuming less than 2 percent. On the other hand, Japan consumes 8.2 percent of the total, yet produces practically none. The United States consumes almost a third of the world total, while it produces a much smaller fraction. Accordingly, the United States imports a large quantity of oil. (See also Figure 12-1.)

It has not always been so. The United States did not become a net importer of oil until the late 1940s. And as late as 1960, U.S. imports were little more than 10 percent of the oil consumed. One reason for the small quantity was that so much of U.S. needs could be satisfied by home production. (In fact, to protect the domestic oil industry, the government imposed import quotas to hold back a flood of cheap foreign oil. And it restricted the output of domestic producers to keep the price from collapsing in the face of excess capacity.)

However, the era of substantial self-sufficiency was coming to an end. While consumption continued to grow, U.S. oil production peaked in 1970. The result was a sharp rise in U.S. imports, particularly after the relaxation of import quotas in 1970. The rising U.S. imports added to the already strong demand for international oil caused by the international boom in

Figure 22-1
Estimated U.S. petroleum consumption and imports, 1949–1980

With few exceptions, U.S. oil consumption has increased from year to year over the last three decades.
(*Source:* Energy Information Administration, Department of Energy, *Annual Report to Congress, 1980,* vol. 2, p. 49.)

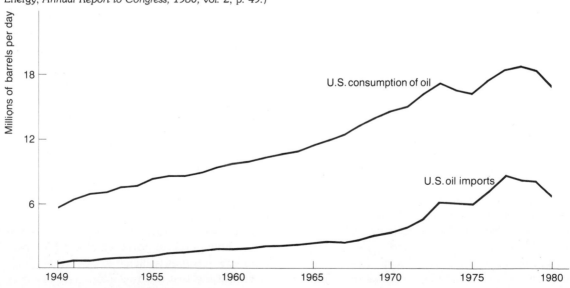

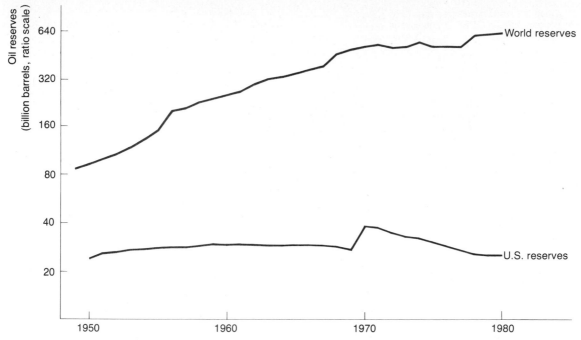

Figure 22-2
Proved U.S. and world oil reserves, 1949–1980

U.S. reserves remained stable from the early 1950s until 1969. In 1970, there was a large increase (Alaskan oil), followed by a slow decline. This decline in U.S. reserves was more than offset by new oil discoveries in other countries; proved world reserves increased during the late 1970s.

(*Sources:* Energy Information Administration, *Annual Report to Congress, 1980,* vol. 2, pp. 41–43; *World Oil,* various issues.)

economic activity. The stage was set for OPEC to flex its muscles.[1]

OPEC had been established on September 6, 1960—an event which was considered so unimportant at the time that it was not reported until September 25 by *The New York Times* in a brief four-paragraph story. During its first decade, OPEC was ineffective. But by 1973 its time had come. The rapid increase in oil prices is a well-known story.

OIL IN THE OVERALL U.S. ENERGY PICTURE

Oil is not, of course, the only source of energy in the United States. But it is the most important,

[1]A brief history of the oil problem may be found in Robert Stobaugh and Daniel Yergin, *Energy Future,* Report of the Energy Project at the Harvard Business School (New York: Random House, 1979), Chaps. 1–2. Further detail is provided in Craufurd D. Goodwin, ed., *Energy Policy in Perspective: Today's Problems, Yesterday's Solutions* (Washington: Brookings Institution, 1981).

accounting for roughly half our energy use. In the longer-term perspective—shown in Figure 22-4—the shift from one energy source to another has been striking. Until a century or so ago, wood satisfied most of our energy needs. Then coal became king, supplying more than half our energy requirements until the Second World War. Now it accounts for only about a fifth, and has fallen in importance behind not only oil, but also natural gas. Hydroelectric power and nuclear power are relatively small components in the overall picture.

By the late 1970s the United States had become dependent on oil to satisfy half its energy needs. Since roughly half its oil was

(*a*) Since the world's reserves are
concentrated in OPEC countries

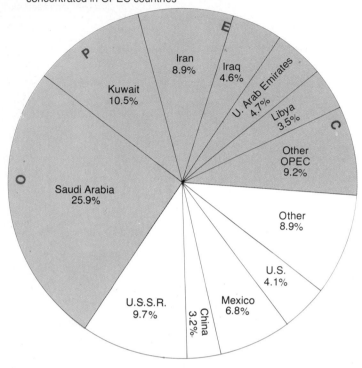

(*b*) . . . there is a serious imbalance
between the world's oil production

(*c*) . . . and consumption

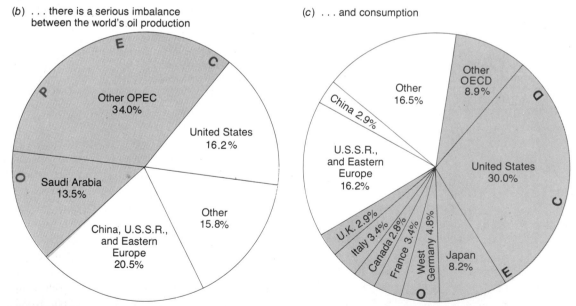

Figure 22-3
World's oil reserves, production and consumption
The OPEC nations produce almost 50 percent of the world's oil. Almost two-thirds is consumed in the countries
of the Organization for Economic Cooperation and Development. (The OECD includes most high-income
industrial countries.) Reserve figures are for 1980; production and consumption figures for 1978.
(*Source:* Energy Information Administration, Department of Energy, *Annual Report to Congress, 1980,* vol. 2, pp. 42, 74.)

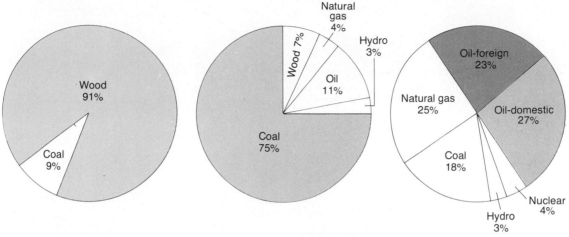

(a) In 1850, we used wood

(b) By 1920, coal was king

(c) By 1977, oil accounted for half the energy used

Figure 22-4
How our energy requirements have historically been satisfied

[*Sources:* S. Schurr and B. Netschert, *Energy and the American Economy,* 1950–1975 (Baltimore: The Johns Hopkins Press, 1960); U.S. Bureau of Mines, *Mineral Yearbook;* and Robert Stobaugh and Daniel Yergin, *Energy Future* (New York, Random House, 1979), pp. 15, 18.]

coming from foreign sources, imported oil was satisfying about one-quarter of the total U.S. energy requirement. Any substantial reduction in foreign supply or further increase in the OPEC price could have serious consequences for the U.S. economy. Another view of our vulnerability to external oil shocks is provided in Figure 22-5, which shows how the $4 billion U.S. oil import bill in 1973 (the area of the first rectangle) had within 8 years grown by about fifteen times to almost $60 billion.

STEPS TO REDUCE OUR DEPENDENCE ON FOREIGN OIL SUPPLIES: SHORT-RUN EMERGENCY MEASURES

It is conceivable that OPEC will go the way of other collusive arrangements, and be split up by competition and disputes among its members. But we can't count on this. In the coming decades, we are likely to face high and quite possibly rising prices for international oil. And periodic disruptions in oil supplies may occur in the event of political upheavals in the Middle East. The question is: What do we do to reduce our vulnerability?

There are a number of long-term measures that may be undertaken, such as subsidizing the development of substitutes for oil. First, consider some short-term emergency measures:

1 Strategic petroleum reserve

By buying and storing up to 1 billion barrels of oil—the equivalent of about half our total imports in 1980—the government plans to acquire a reserve for use in the event of a supply interruption. The program has moved slowly, in fits and starts. By early 1981, only a little more than 100 million barrels (less than a month's normal imports) had been put in storage. However, with the plentiful supplies of oil on the international markets, the rate of purchases for the oil reserve was stepped up during 1981. And the U.S. government negotiated a contract with Pemex (Petroleos Mexicanos, the Mexican state oil company) under which Pemex will supply 110 million barrels for the reserve over the 1981–1986 period.

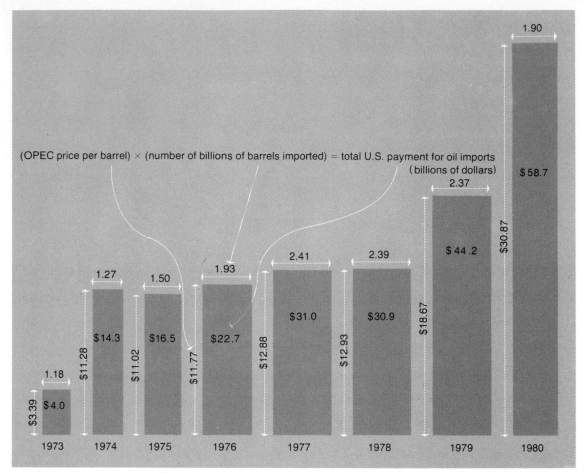

(OPEC price per barrel) × (number of billions of barrels imported) = total U.S. payment for oil imports (billions of dollars)

1973	$3.39	1.18	$4.0
1974	$11.28	1.27	$14.3
1975	$11.02	1.50	$16.5
1976	$11.77	1.93	$22.7
1977	$12.88	2.41	$31.0
1978	$12.93	2.39	$30.9
1979	$18.67	2.37	$44.2
1980	$30.87	1.90	$58.7

Figure 22-5
How U.S. payments for imported oil have increased, 1973–1980

2 Standby rationing

The Energy Policy and Conservation Act of 1975 requested the President to prepare a standby gasoline rationing plan, as a way of dealing with temporary disruptions to supply. It thereby dumped in the President's lap the thorny political problem of how gasoline would be allocated in an emergency. Neither Ford nor Carter showed enthusiasm for this task, and no plan was submitted until March 1979, after our oil supply from Iran had been cut off.

The major problem was, who would get the gas? Would ration coupons be allocated according to the number of cars in a family? (If so, wouldn't people continue to register their old clunkers?). Or according to the number of drivers? (If so, wouldn't the family persuade grandpa to renew his license?) Should more be given to drivers in heavy usage states where travel distances are great, such as California or the Dakotas?

The administration's plan involved the allocation of ration coupons primarily on the basis of car registrations, with special allotments for farmers, police, and other priority activities. Ration coupons could be sold legally in a **white market** (in contrast to the "black market" which arises when such sales are illegal).

The white market proposal would mean that

drivers who have used up their own coupons could get any amount of extra gas they wanted —provided they were willing to pay both the price of the gas *and* the market price for the additional ration coupons they required. Thus, for example, if the price of gasoline were $1.50 and coupons sold for 50 cents, the total cost of gasoline would be $2.00. (This $2.00 would also represent the total cost of gas even for those who used only the coupons allocated to them. Even though they would be out of pocket only $1.50, they would also be giving up a coupon worth 50 cents—the amount they could sell it for.)

In this illustration, a white rationing system is similar to a 50 cent tax on gasoline. (They both increase the price people pay for gasoline by the same amount.) The principal difference is that with a tax the government receives the proceeds (the tax collections). But with rationing, the auto owners receive the "proceeds," in the form of an allocation of ration coupons worth 50 cents each. What, then, was the reason for considering white rationing—with the cumbersome and expensive bureaucracy it would create? Why not simply impose a gasoline tax, and put the money back into the hands of the public by cutting social security or income taxes? The answer is that rationing would ease the shock of high prices on farmers, truckers, and others who have been heavy users of energy in the past. (They could be given a generous share of coupons.) But a gas tax would give them far less protection, since any reduction in other taxes would likely be spread over the whole population rather than being concentrated on them. (It would perhaps be possible to tailor a tax cut so that farmers, truckers, and other heavy gasoline users would benefit most, but this would just replace a complicated rationing system with complications in an already overburdened tax system.)

Disputes over who should get the ration coupons led Congress to reject Carter's standby rationing plan.

3 International Energy Agency

The oil importing nations have an interest in acting cooperatively. When one conserves oil, they all gain from the reduced pressures on the international oil market. In order to promote cooperation in energy policy, 20 noncommunist industrial nations established the International Energy Agency (IEA) in 1974. One of its most important features is an emergency sharing plan, which provides that, if any member country faces a 7 percent shortfall, other members will share their oil. With such assurances, members are less likely to scramble to bid up oil in an emergency. It's not clear how effective the agreement is, since it lacks teeth; it has no tough penalties to deal with countries that won't share their oil. (The plan was not activated during the shortages following the Iranian disturbances of 1979–1980, since no member claimed a 7 percent shortfall.)

LONGER-TERM RESPONSES TO REDUCE OUR DEPENDENCE ON IMPORTED OIL

In the long run, there are four major ways to reduce U.S. dependence on foreign oil:

1 Limit national output; that is, have lower growth than we might otherwise achieve. This would reduce our use of inputs, including oil.
2 Use less energy for each unit of national output; that is, conserve.
3 Increase the quantity of oil produced in the United States.
4 Develop alternative sources of energy. Is it possible to find other sources to supplant oil, just as oil supplanted coal, and coal supplanted wood?

Of these four, a limitation on output is the least satisfactory: Such a broad and costly policy is no more appropriate for dealing with the oil problem than it is for dealing with pollution or any other *specific* problem. (One of the adverse consequences of the oil price increases was that they made the recessions of 1974 and 1980 worse. It is hard to argue that we should go one step further and inflict on ourselves even further reductions in output.)

Therefore, it is to the last three measures that we should look in an effort to reduce our dependence on international oil. For all three measures, the domestic price of oil is significant, since it provides the incentive both for conservation and for increased production of oil and its substitutes. Therefore, before we examine the details of the last three measures, we look first at the U.S. price of oil, and the way in which the government has controlled it.

THE DOMESTIC PRICE OF OIL

In the face of rapid increases in the price of international oil, the government has three options:

1 Hands off—let the price of domestic oil rise to the world price.
2 Control the price of domestic oil to keep it *below* the world price.
3 Take steps to push the domestic price *above* the world price.

Initially, the government chose (2). However, in mid-1979, the Carter administration began a program of decontrol (policy 1) which was scheduled to be completed by October 1981. The Reagan administration moved the timetable forward; price controls were abolished in early 1981. U.S. oil prices now reflect world prices. Because this is the present situation—and is also the simplest—it is considered first. We will then move back in time, to consider the pre-1981 system of controls that kept U.S. price below the world level (option 2). Option 3—involving domestic oil prices *above* the world level—is considered at the end of this section.

Option 1: Allow the domestic price to rise to the world price

In early 1973, the international price of oil was less that $3 a barrel ($P_1$ in Figure 22-6). By 1980 it was above $30 ($P_W$). What happens if the U.S. domestic price is allowed to follow the international price up from P_1 to P_W?

At low price P_1, U.S. domestic demand is P_1F but supply is only P_1A; the difference AF must be imported. As price rises to P_W, imports are reduced to BC. The total payment to OPEC (and other countries selling oil to us) is shown by the red rectangle.[2]

With such a price increase, the market works in two ways to bring about a reduction in imports. First, the higher price induces U.S. producers to move up their supply curve from A to B, thus increasing their output by arrow a. Second, the higher price induces consumers to move up their demand curve from F to C, thus reducing their consumption by "conservation arrow" c. Furthermore, the new equilibrium is efficient (at least as a first approximation that we will qualify later). The marginal cost to the United States of importing a barrel of oil is P_W. The United States should produce any oil whose marginal cost is less than this cost of imported oil. In other words, production efficiency requires domestic oil producers to move up the supply (marginal cost) curve from A to B, and stop there—which is what they do. Similarly, the move by oil users from F to C is also efficient. The reason is that users cut out purchases which would cost more (P_W) than the marginal benefit they would provide (the height of demand curve FC). Since letting the domestic price rise freely with the international price is the efficient outcome—and one which helps to keep imports down by encouraging domestic production and conservation—why was it not allowed to occur until early 1981?

The conflict between efficiency and equity
The answer is, the objective of *efficiency* came into conflict with what was widely considered to be *equitable*. As price rises from P_1 to P_W, there is a large gain in surplus to producers (the gray

[2]To study one thing at a time (the effect of rising price), we assume that "other things remain unchanged" (*ceteris paribus*). In particular, we assume that demand for oil does not shift. (During the period of oil price increases, the U.S. demand for oil did in fact increase. But this is another story. Here we concentrate on the effect of a price rise.)

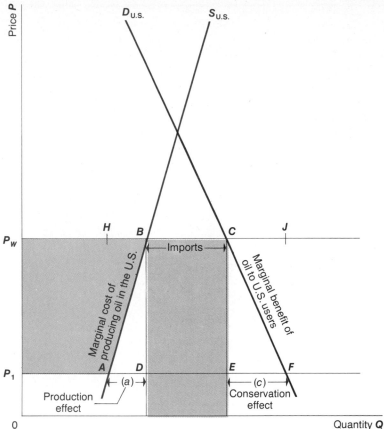

Figure 22-6
Effect of allowing the domestic oil price to rise to the world price

If the domestic price of oil (P_1) is allowed to rise to the world price (P_W), domestic production increases by arrow *a*, and domestic consumption decreases by conservation arrow *c*.

shaded area). And consumers correspondingly pay a higher price. This transfer from consumers to producers was judged unfair.[3] (What is fair is, of course, a matter on which people disagree. Some would argue that it is unfair for people to use cheap gasoline or oil, when the nation has to pay the high price P_W.) One way of reducing this transfer is a windfall profits tax on oil companies.

The windfall profits tax Such a tax was passed in 1980, when a decision was made to decontrol oil prices, and allow them to rise to the world level. (The tax is scheduled to be phased

out over a three-year period beginning in the late 1980s.)

This tax captures much of the gray area for the government, which can then spend these tax receipts in various ways to help the economy adjust to higher oil prices. (Proposed uses included subsidies for research and development on new energy sources.)

A second way to limit the transfer from consumers to U.S. oil producers is to control the domestic price of oil.

[3]This is a *domestic* transfer within the United States. But as the world price of oil rises, there is an *international* transfer as well. (See Box 22-1.)

BOX 22-1

The International Income Transfer as the World Price of Oil Increases

What we are witnessing today in . . . oil and raw material prices is virtually the same as what is going on between trade unions and employers associations on the national level. It is a struggle for the distribution and use of the national product, a struggle for the world product.

Helmut Schmidt, then Minister of Finance and later Chancellor of the Federal German Republic

So far in this book we have concentrated primarily on transfers *within* the United States—like the transfer from American consumers to producers that occurs when the price of oil rises in the United States. One important thing to remember about such a domestic transfer is that it involves gains to one group of Americans and losses to another group that to some degree offset one another. But with rising oil price an *international* transfer also takes place. This is quite different because it involves a loss to one group of Americans (buyers of higher priced imported oil) which is *not* a gain to another group of Americans, but is instead a gain to OPEC. From the U.S. point of view, this transfer (area *BCED* in Figure 22-6) is a dead loss. (Our payment to OPEC increases by this area because we pay *DB* more per barrel on the *BC* barrels we import.) Because it's a dead loss for Americans, color it a very dark red.

The OPEC countries argue that a large price increase was required for efficiency reasons—to force the world to conserve. As noted in Chapter 21, conservation requires that users of a natural resource like oil be charged enough to cover an adequate reservation price. In other words, its price should be high enough now to ensure that it won't be put to trivial use today, rather than much more important uses in the future. Thus, the large price increase was necessary to prevent the wasteful use of oil. (And it's important not to waste it, since the demand for oil will be growing

as the world increasingly industrializes, and other countries put themselves on wheels, American-style.) Since countries such as the United States were not conserving, it was desirable for the price to be raised to a level at which they *would* conserve. So say the OPEC nations.

The oil-importing countries reply: "True, considerations of efficiency—in particular, of conservation—required some increase in the low $3 price that prevailed in 1973—but not the increase of more than ten times that occurred. The world is not rapidly running out of oil 're-serves (Figure 22-2). Oil is not in the future crisis-supply situation that OPEC's exceedingly high price implies. In raising price this much, the OPEC countries are not primarily interested in the *efficient* use of this resource. Instead, their real motive is the same as that of any old-fashioned monopolist: They have raised price in order to transfer income from us to them." ■

Option 2: Keep the U.S. price below the world level

This policy, in a very complicated form, was used by the United States during the 1970s. It became a lesson in how complex things can get when the government balances a number of conflicting objectives—in this case, the objectives of (1) keeping prices low for consumers, (2) preventing large windfall profits from going to oil producers, and (3) encouraging production. (In order to make the discussion manageable, we will skip over many of the fine points.) Before we get into some of the details of the actual controls, consider briefly the problems which would be caused by even the simplest possible form of price control.

(a) A hypothetical, simple form of price control Suppose, in Figure 22-6, that the government sets a price ceiling at P_1. This would involve three problems. As noted earlier:

i) The nation would not get arrow a of additional oil production. [This would involve an efficiency loss of triangle AHB, reflecting the higher cost of importing oil (P_W) rather than producing it domestically (the height of supply curve AB).]

ii) Consumers would not be encouraged to conserve (arrow c). [This would result in an efficiency loss of triangle CJF—reflecting the high cost of importing oil (P_W) compared to the benefit users would get from it (the height of demand curve CF).]

And there would be a third significant problem:

iii) Such a price control would be very expensive for the government: To allow importers to sell oil at the low domestic ceiling price P_1, the government would have to pay them the very large subsidy $HJFA$. [A per-barrel subsidy of AH (the difference between the world price P_W and the controlled domestic price P_1) would have to be paid on AF barrels of imported oil.]

(b) The "blended price" system actually used The system actually used by the government until early 1981 was designed to deal with problems (i) and (iii) listed above.

In this complex system, there were many prices, falling into three basic categories:

1 The world price P_W for imports and "new oil"—that is, oil from newly drilled U.S. wells.

2 A much lower price applicable to "old oil," that is, oil from U.S. wells already in production. (This old oil price wasn't as low as pre-1973 price P_1, but it can be likened to P_1 because it was far below P_W.)

3 The blended price. To simplify a complicated story, this was found by pooling the oil in the first two categories, and taking its average price. This was the price domestic U.S. buyers had to pay.

By allowing the price of new oil to rise to the world level P_W, the government avoided problem (i). Producers responded to the high price by supplying more. Specifically, producers moved to point B in Figure 22-6, and arrow a of production was not lost after all. Because old oil would be produced anyhow—or so it was hoped—keeping its price low would not significantly affect production. Moreover, this low price received by producers achieved the government's objective of reducing the transfer from consumers to producers. Finally, problem (iii) was dealt with: The Treasury didn't have to pay out a large subsidy. (The very low price on old oil made it possible to keep the blended price below the world level.) In theory, it was an ingenious solution. But in practice it involved problems.

A few of the complications in the price control system Because old oil sold for a low price and new oil for a higher price, every refinery obviously wanted to get as much of the old oil as possible. Accordingly, the Department of Energy (DOE) worked out a system of entitlements (allocations) of old oil to each refinery. Refineries getting more than their share were taxed, in order to subsidize refineries getting less (such as coastal refineries that used a lot of expensive imported oil). Small refineries were given a bonus: They were given entitlements to more than their share of the inexpensive oil. Thus, the price control system was used as a way of subsidizing small, inefficient refineries. (It also provided a windfall for illegal operators, who used complex transactions to disguise the source of old oil, so they could sell it as new oil at a higher price.)

Regulation also brought other headaches. When an established old well ran down to less than 10 barrels a day, it was generally no longer economic to operate at the low old oil price. To prevent the loss of this source of supply, the government allowed oil from these "stripper" wells to be sold at the high price. While this did increase production from wells that had already been run down, it reduced production from wells that had been producing somewhat more than 10 barrels a day. (Their output was reduced to below the 10 barrel level so they could be defined as strippers and get the higher price.) Thus, the control program was not as successful in stimulating oil production as had been hoped.

The Department of Energy regulated oil not only as it went into the refineries, but also as it came out; that is, it regulated the price of gasoline and the quantity of gasoline that would go to specific service stations. These allocations were based primarily on how much gasoline had been provided to each service station at an earlier period. Because of this rigid system, oil companies were not allowed to shift gasoline around to meet local needs. One could predict that this arrangement would provide inadequate supplies to high growth areas where demand for gasoline was rising rapidly. And this is exactly what happened. In 1979, after the Iranian revolution interrupted oil supplies, the allocation system contributed to shortages and gas lines in Florida and Southern California.[4]

[4]Other government regulations made the California problem even more acute. A number of California refineries were operating below capacity because environmental regulations prevented them from using the only available oil, namely heavy Alaskan crude. The reason that they could not get their normal supplies of light Indonesian crude was that the Japanese were aggressively buying it to make up for the decline in supplies from Iran. The Japanese would have been willing to leave the Indonesian oil for Californian refineries to buy, if they had been able to get Alaskan oil instead. But this was prevented by U.S. law: In order to protect oil supplies, Congress had forbidden the export of Alaskan oil.

Thus, the complicated three-price system was a headache to administer. Moreover, one of its expected virtues—reducing the equity problem by keeping down the price consumers had to pay—brought with it a serious disadvantage. Keeping the price down meant that consumers were not encouraged to conserve: America was running up an increasingly large oil import bill not only because the price paid to OPEC was rising, but also because the quantity of U.S. oil imports kept increasing: Until 1978, the bars in Figure 22-5 were not only getting higher; they were getting wider as well.

By the late 1970s, the growing oil import bill in Figure 22-5, plus the problems involved in running a complex price control system, led increasingly to the view that this control system should be ended.

Problems of decontrol In announcing the decontrol of oil prices in mid-1979, President Carter also announced that consumers would be protected from a sharp increase in price by having controls phased out over a period of about 2 years.

But even this temporary protection for consumers raised a problem. During 1979, critics of the oil companies charged that they were intentionally withholding supplies in spite of the gas lines. Whether they did so is not entirely clear; the facts are difficult to disentangle because so many things were happening at once. (Most obviously, overseas supplies were disrupted.) However, the critics may have been right. There certainly was an incentive for producers to hold back, and wait for the higher prices that were now guaranteed by phased decontrol. In such circumstances, it is not clear whether the public's anger should be directed toward the oil companies, or toward the government which created the incentive for the companies to hold back their supplies.

Option 3: Push the U.S. price above the world price

In discussing Figure 22-6, we concluded that the efficient U.S. price is the world price because that is the real cost of oil to the United States—

the amount that must be paid to OPEC. However, some economists argue that the U.S. price should be *above* the world price, because the true cost to Americans of imported oil exceeds the world price for three reasons:

1 Because the United States is such a large consumer of oil, the amount we buy affects the OPEC-determined world price. If we had not bought as much oil during the 1970s, the world price would not have risen as far as it did. (The demand for OPEC oil would not have been so strong.) Because those *last* barrels we bought raised the world price, they cost us not only the price we paid for them, but *also* the higher price we had to pay on *all* the barrels we bought. In short, the marginal cost of those last barrels of oil exceeded the price we had to pay for them.[5]

2 Our large imports make us dependent on OPEC, and more vulnerable to an interruption of supply. (For example, a supply disruption could cause a recession.) This risk of a supply cutoff is another reason the cost of imports exceeds their price.

3 In importing so much oil, we pay a heavy political price, as well as the dollar price. Because of the heavy dependence of the United States, Europe, and Japan on Middle East oil, we may at some time feel compelled to become militarily involved in protecting our interests in that volatile part of the globe. The costs of such involvement might be catastrophic.

These then are the reasons why some economists (including James Tobin of Yale) believe that the marginal cost of imported oil exceeds the world price P_W we pay for it. Consequently, they argue that efficiency requires a U.S. price *above* the world price. Only then will we be valuing oil highly enough in our domestic consumption and production decisions. Efficiency requires that the domestic price faced by consumers and producers be equal to all the costs of

a good—in this case, not only the price we pay for oil, but also the three other costs of buying it. Only if the domestic price rises this high will we take strong enough action to reduce our very costly dependence on foreign oil.

(This argument is subject to one reservation. If the increase in domestic price to the world level greatly reduces our dependence on oil imports, the argument for raising domestic price even further is weakened. After all, the three problems cited above exist only because we are very large oil buyers, heavily dependent on imported supplies. If this heavy dependence disappears, so do these problems—and there is little argument left for raising the domestic price above the world price.)

How do we raise oil price above the world level? One method is a tax on oil; another is an import tariff—that is, a tax at the border. Yale's William Nordhaus has suggested a tariff between $25 and $50 a barrel, which could increase the price of gasoline by as much as $1.25 a gallon. Another suggestion is to tax gasoline directly. But such proposals are not very popular. When President Carter imposed a much smaller "gasoline conservation fee" administratively in 1980, Congress overturned his act. Nevertheless, he reiterated his suggestion of a gasoline tax—to start at 10 cents—as he was leaving office in 1981.

[There have been proposals to offset the impact of a gasoline tax on people's incomes by using the revenues to cut income taxes or social security taxes. Critics argue that these proposals make no sense, since people would just use their income tax cuts to buy as much gas as they always had. But that's not so. What this tax would do is to keep people's real incomes from falling, while still leaving them with a strong incentive to buy less gas. (It would now be more expensive compared with other items—such as clothing, food, or TV sets. People would thus have an incentive to switch consumption away from gasoline, and toward other products.)][6]

---

*[5]This idea has already been developed in a different context in Figure 19-3: For a buyer with market power, the marginal cost of a purchase (in that case, the purchase of labor services) is greater than its price (the wage rate).

*[6]In the terms introduced in Appendix 8, only the income *effect* would be offset, while the substitution *effect* would remain.

We have seen how a rising price can result in both conservation and greater domestic production. This leaves two remaining questions: (1) What other non-price measures have been introduced by the government to stimulate conservation? And (2) on the production side, what are the most promising alternative forms of energy?

OTHER CONSERVATION MEASURES

With decontrol and rising domestic oil prices, Americans are beginning to conserve oil. But during the earlier period of control, the price incentive was blunted. Accordingly, the government introduced other measures to promote conservation. To mention a few:

1 Tax incentives were given to businesses and households for insulating buildings and other energy-saving measures such as the installation of solar heating equipment.

2 Speed limits were reduced to 55 miles per hour. (This reduced the gasoline required for any given trip, and reduced the number of trips since they took longer.)

3 In 1975, the government imposed fuel efficiency standards on automobile manufacturers, requiring them to almost double the average number of miles their cars get from a gallon of gas by 1985. (By 1980, the mileage performance of new American cars had already risen by about 50 percent.)

The fuel-efficiency standards provided one of the few bright spots in an otherwise gloomy decade: It forced the American auto companies to design smaller cars before the public was ready to buy them. Paradoxically, an industry that was almost destroyed by one set of regulations (those that kept domestic oil prices down and thus allowed Americans to keep buying big cars long after they had become obsolete) may have been saved by another set of regulations: the fuel efficiency standards that forced the down-sizing of cars in advance of public de-

mand. (In early 1979, the demand for cars with big, gas-guzzling V-8 engines was so great that manufacturers put limits on the number that dealers could order.) Had the government mileage regulations *not* been in force, the effects of the 1979–1980 oil shock on the U.S. auto industry would have been even more severe.

Whether it comes as a result of higher prices or government regulations, conservation is probably the least problematic way of reducing our dependence on foreign oil. The 6-year energy study at the Harvard Business School concluded:

Conservation may well be the cheapest, safest, most productive energy alternative readily available in large amounts. . . . Conservation is a quality energy source. It does not threaten to undermine the international monetary system, nor does it emit carbon dioxide into the atmosphere, nor does it generate problems comparable to nuclear waste. And contrary to the conventional wisdom, conservation can stimulate innovation, employment, and economic growth.[7]

ALTERNATIVE ENERGY SOURCES

The largest currently used alternatives to oil are natural gas and coal, with hydroelectricity and nuclear fission providing small shares. Other minor current sources include solar power, wind, and wood.

There are two major questions in the development of an alternative energy source: (1) What are its costs of production? And (2) what costs does it impose on the environment? The second question has been very important in the case of coal and nuclear energy: Environmental (or external) costs have deterred the development of these otherwise promising sources of energy. But before turning to these other forms of energy, we should recognize that oil *itself* has environmental costs. For example, burning oil in the form of gasoline in cars has serious environmental effects in a large smog-prone city like Los Angeles. Worse yet, the burning of fossil fuels

[7]Daniel Yergin, "Conservation: The Key Energy Source," in Stobaugh and Yergin, *Energy Future,* p. 137.

such as oil or coal may affect the environment in *all* locations. Some scientists fear that the carbon dioxide that is emitted may cause a "greenhouse effect" that may eventually alter the world's climate. If this theory is confirmed, the use of these fuels may have to be reduced long before the world's reserves begin to run out.

Natural gas

Next to oil, this is the largest U.S. source of energy, accounting for about a quarter of consumption. Compared to nuclear power, it involves no waste disposal problem, and less safety risk. Compared to coal, its extraction from the ground does little damage to the environment. And it burns much more cleanly than either coal or oil.

The problem with natural gas is that since 1954 its price has been kept down by controls. (Deregulation was considered in the late 1950s, but failed to get through Congress when a key supporter was so angered by an attempt by the gas industry to bribe him that he switched his vote.) Gas price control may be divided into two broad periods: (1) Before 1978, price controls were applied to gas sent across state lines—that is, **Interstate gas.** But no limits were placed on the price of **intrastate gas** produced within the state. (2) The Natural Gas Policy Act of 1978 extended controls to intrastate gas, but aimed for a phased decontrol of gas prices by 1985.

Intrastate (within-state) natural gas is consumed in the same state in which it is produced. Prior to 1978, its price was determined by supply and demand.

Interstate (out-of-state) gas is consumed in a different state from the one in which it is produced. Traditionally, its price was fixed by the government at a level lower than the price of intrastate gas.

Since within-state natural gas traditionally was allowed to respond to market forces of supply and demand (and since it is a substitute for oil) its price approximately followed the existing U.S. price of oil. This meant that the control system that kept down the U.S. price of oil during the 1970s led to inadequate production and conservation not only of oil, but also of natural gas. But this problem of depressed price was even worse in the case of *interstate* natural gas. The controlled, low price discouraged production from high-cost new wells. Thus, producers had little incentive to search for gas to satisfy out-of-state demand. Between 1967 and 1978, U.S. reserves fell by about a quarter. In the words of an independent gas producer in Kentucky: "Sure, there's gas out there, and there's folks right over the state line in Illinois that will pay . . . whatever price it takes to produce it, but that . . . ain't the price that those fellas back in Washington say you can sell it for. So we don't plan to drill for gas until it's profitable."

Not surprisingly, gas producers fed any existing supplies into the higher priced within-state market first; in the event of any shortage, they cut back their out-of-state sales.[8] The shortage of out-of-state natural gas during the winters of 1976–1977 and 1977–1978 resulted in inconvenience, hardship, and millions of dollars worth of lost industrial production. And it spurred Congress to take action in the form of the Natural Gas Policy Act of 1978 which extended controls to intrastate gas, while providing for gradual price decontrol.

As expected, a higher price for gas has stimulated production; for the first time in years, new gas finds in 1980 were as great as use. Geologists believe that there are substantial enough fields under the United States or its continental shelf to satisfy U.S. requirements into the next century. (Some say not quite; others say almost to the end of that century.) This gas may not be as low-cost as the supply we've enjoyed in the past, but it will be there to tap as price rises.

---

[8]This double price of gas had another strange effect: It gave producers an incentive to encourage their high-paying within-state customers to use more gas. Thus, Texas producers used bumper stickers encouraging Texas consumers to "Turn up the gas and freeze a Yankee." What this really meant was, "Turn up the gas, freeze a Yankee, and increase our profits."

Coal: The conflict between energy and the environment

The United States has an abundance of coal. But coal has an abundance of problems.

Mel Horwich

The United States is the Saudi Arabia of coal, holding about 28 percent of the world's coal reserves (compared to less than 10 percent of the world's gas, and less than 5 percent of its oil reserves). At present rates of consumption there is enough coal in the United States to last for about 600 years. Thus, coal has been regarded by many as our great hope of getting through the present energy scarcity into the next century, when solar energy or nuclear fusion may provide virtually unlimited supplies.

The spiraling price of oil and delays in the development of nuclear power in the 1970s placed coal in a strong position for a comeback from its declining twentieth-century role as an energy source. However, coal's growth has been disappointing, because of the problems encountered both in mining and burning it.

1 Problems in mining Strip-mining in Western states leaves land scarred and unproductive. Therefore coal producers are required, often at substantial cost, to reclaim and reconstruct the landscape. On the other hand, underground mining in the Eastern states involves a different set of problems: acid drainage, and the risk of black lung disease or fatal accidents underground. (Strikes have also been common in the coal industry.)

2 Problems in burning coal in power plants The principal problem is air pollution. To reduce this problem, the government requires that coal burning plants reduce their emissions by installing scrubbers. (Since this creates a sludge, to some degree air pollution is being traded for water pollution.)

Government policy toward coal Because coal raises such environmental problems, government policy toward its development has often been inconsistent. For example, in 1974, the Federal Energy Administration was empowered to order public utilities to convert from oil or gas to coal. But by mid-1977 only 15 out of 74 such orders had been approved by the Environmental Protection Agency. By 1979 the coal conversion policy had been changed: Utilities were being encouraged to convert from oil to natural gas instead. In 1980, in yet another policy shift, the emphasis returned to converting to coal. It was becoming difficult to see how the industry—involving as it does the three interdependent and heavily capital intensive activities of mining, transporting, and burning coal—could get its act together without some clear indication of its future prospects, and in particular, the direction of government policy.

The conflict between energy and the environment has been serious enough for coal; but it has been even more serious for nuclear power.

Nuclear fission

The decade of the 1970s was a decade of disappointed expectations, but nowhere more so than in nuclear energy. As the rapid expansion of nuclear power began in 1965, it was hailed as the cheapest of all sources of energy. By 1974 President Nixon, in Project Independence, called it the response to OPEC—the key to reducing U.S dependence on foreign oil. Yet, we now realize, that was the year in which growth of the industry virtually ceased: Whereas utilities had ordered a total of 100 new nuclear plants in the 1972–1974 period, in no year since have orders exceeded five. The sharp decline reflected unexpectedly high plant costs, slower than expected growth in electrical demand, tough regulations, and public opposition which became much stronger after the Three Mile Island (3MI) accident in 1979. It is now clear that nuclear fission will not be able to "solve" our energy problem as many had hoped. Indeed, by the beginning of the 1980s, there was some doubt whether the industry would even be able to continue to supply the energy it was then providing.

What went wrong? There are two related answers. First, the difficulties of designing and running a safe nuclear plant were underestimated. Second, nuclear power became embroiled in a debate about safety that was fought all the way from state regulatory agencies to the federal courts. The industry claims that, in providing what it views as a realistic means of satisfying our energy needs, it has been subjected to an emotion-charged attack by those who confuse the wartime and peacetime effects of nuclear fission, and who "want to put the genie back in the bottle."

But there is a second, less passionate group of scientific critics of the industry who reply: "You aren't adequately answering the key questions about safety." It is this second group that has been successful in shifting much of the burden of proof onto the industry, which is now being asked to prove that nuclear power is safe. Compare this to the burden of proof in evaluating almost anything else—from an automobile to a tin toy—where the product is allowed unless it is shown to be *unsafe*. Nuclear critics say we should have this different standard because nuclear power involves more unknowns; but advocates assert that this is unfair.

Even with the 3MI experience, the industry feels that it has a strong safety case: Nuclear power has exposed the public to much less radiation than an equivalent use of coal, since coal contains traces of radioactive materials which are released into the atmosphere when it is burned. And while lives have been lost in coal mines, none has been lost in nuclear power plants. The safety issue centers on three questions: What is the chance of a more serious accident in the *future*? Will a worldwide use of nuclear power contribute to the proliferation of nuclear weapons? And what will we do with nuclear wastes?

By 1974, the industry was battle-weary from fighting critics and vocal "not-in-my-backyard" groups opposed to nuclear facilities planned for their communities. These and other delays meant that it was taking from 12 to 14 years to get nuclear power plants into operation; and that meant escalating costs. (Time is money —big money: At a 14 percent interest rate, a

$100,000 cost incurred in day 1 grows over the next 10 years to $400,000—and this investment still hasn't earned a nickel of income. Moreover, with nuclear power, it's far from guaranteed that an investment will *ever* earn income.)

Thus, a debate that began on environmental (safety) issues turned into an equally acrimonious debate on cost as well. In 1978, after weeks of expert testimony, the Public Service Commission of Wisconsin concluded that the variety of views submitted ranged from "nuclear power's being much less costly than coal, to coal's being much less costly than nuclear, and include the view that it is impossible to tell."

Hydro electric power
Although electricity produced by falling water is clean, the construction of large dams does raise environmental objections, in particular by those whose lands are flooded. But it is not clear that the environmental costs of big dams exceed their environmental benefits in the form of (a) flood control that may save property, and (b) recreational benefits such as sailing, swimming, and fishing. In any case, in developing "Big Hydro," environmental concerns are less of a barrier than the scarcity of good undeveloped sites.

However, there is some potential for "Low Hydro"—the installation of power-generating equipment on the 50,000 small dams that already exist in the United States. There are no environmental problems here; the lakes already exist. The Federal Power Commission estimates that U.S. hydroelectric power capacity could be doubled in this way, in a far shorter time than the decade or so it takes to develop Big Hydro, or, for that matter, coal or nuclear power.

UNCONVENTIONAL AND POTENTIAL NEW SOURCES OF ENERGY

Over the coming decades, significant contributions may be made by new sources of energy, such as wind, or biomass—the production of a gas or liquid fuel (gasohol) from vegetation. Synthetic oil or gas may also be produced from coal, tar sands, or shale rock. Although shale has been viewed as highly promising for many years, it has been disappointing commercially. The quip was "Shale is at least 20 percent more expensive than oil, no matter what the price of oil is." Shale also involves environmental problems: It is strip-mined and requires large quantities of water—a serious issue in the Western states where much of the oil-bearing shale lies.

It will be interesting to watch how potential new energy sources develop. We concentrate our attention on two: One that now seems to have good potential—solar energy—and another that is extremely uncertain, yet which may hold out the greatest promise of all: nuclear fusion.

Solar energy
There is a wide variety of ways that we may be able to "plug into the sun" for our energy.

1 Solar buildings designed to capture heat from the sun These need not look like greenhouses, but that's the general idea: for example, glass walls facing south to capture the low winter sun (with shades above to block out the higher, hot summer sun). Much of this technology exists today; in fact, it dates back to the Mesa Verde cliff dwellers in Colorado. Although solar home heating has great potential, it cannot be quickly realized—because it takes time for the existing stock of houses to be replaced.

2 Water heating systems The idea is simple; heat water on the roof, and use it to warm your house or swimming pool.

3 Photovoltaic cells These are produced in waferlike form; when the sun hits them, they produce electricity. (This method of capturing energy from the sun was suggested by Einstein in a classic article in 1905, and one of its first uses was on spacecraft.) This system clearly works, but it has so far been very expensive.

In contrast to these "Small Solar" approaches, the French are now experimenting with a "Big Solar" system.

4 How the French do it with mirrors
This French system involves a set of huge mirrors that track the sun, throwing its rays onto a huge (ten-story high) curved mirror, from which the rays are deflected onto a "giant kettle" where water is boiled to generate steam and thus electricity. Although this system has still not been perfected, it might be used someday in the U.S. Sunbelt to generate electricity at exactly the time when it is needed for air conditioning—when the sun's rays are strongest. Paradoxically, heat from the sun would be used to cool homes.

Nuclear fusion
Existing nuclear plants generate heat by *fission*—that is, by *splitting* (uranium) atoms apart. But research is now underway on nuclear *fusion;* that is, the *joining together* of hydrogen atoms in a controlled, repeated version of what happens in an uncontrolled way when a hydrogen bomb explodes. It is a miniature copy of what is happening all the time in the sun. While fusion releases enormous heat, the problem is that it *requires* enormous heat to accomplish.

While scientists have made great strides toward the creation of enough heat for controlled fusion, they still have a long way to go. The first big milestone to watch for in the future is the *energy break-even point,* where the output of heat energy released by fusion exceeds the input needed to cause the fusion. At this point the process will at least be able, on balance, to create energy. But that energy will at first be extremely expensive. Therefore, the next step to watch for will be the *economic break-even point,* where energy output exceeds energy input by enough to make nuclear fusion economically competitive with other forms of energy.

To achieve this economic break-even point, massive technological problems must be overcome; for example, it's not only a problem of creating enormous heat levels, but also containing the hydrogen when it is being heated, and harnessing the power generated. The most optimistic estimate is that nuclear fusion will not be developed as a commercial source of power until early in the twenty-first century. Nevertheless, research developments in the next decade will have important consequences for the international oil market. Highly successful fusion research would reduce the future price of oil and hence the price OPEC producers could get today. (Since their incentive to keep oil in the ground would be reduced, their reservation price would be lowered.) But if, on the contrary, fusion research hits a dead end, the effects would soon be seen in higher prices in the oil market. (One of the two major research approaches—involving lasers as a way of triggering the fusion—has run into substantial unforeseen problems.)

If and when nuclear fusion does become economically feasible, it will offer great advantages over the nuclear fission that is now being used. The reason is that fission is intrinsically a hazardous process: Radioactive materials are the by-products. If something goes wrong, the uranium core overheats, and it can melt (as happened in an experimental reactor some years ago in the Detroit area, and as was feared might happen during the accident at Three Mile Island.) By comparison, fusion is safe and clean. The problem in nuclear fusion is to keep the process going; if anything goes wrong, the hydrogen escapes, and automatic shutdown occurs. Furthermore, fusion generates very little radioactive waste and uses plentiful hydrogen (rather than the uranium used in fission reactors). Thus, in thirty years, fusion *may* be able to provide us with relatively safe, clean, virtually inexhaustible energy with no risk of nuclear proliferation. If it works, it may heat our buildings and generate our electricity. And, with the improved batteries being developed to increase the range of "plug-in cars," it could allow us to do much of our driving oil-free.

But it's a long and uncertain way down the road. And remember: Thirty years ago there was great optimism about nuclear fission.

Key Points

1 A major problem with oil is that most of the international supply to the world's heavily industrialized oil consuming countries (North America, Europe, and Japan) comes from OPEC (in particular, the countries in the Middle East) and the OPEC nations have used their market power to raise oil price sharply, from less than $3 a barrel in 1973 to more than $30 in 1981.

2 A second problem is that this supply of oil is far from assured, because the Middle East is politically unstable. For example, oil supplies were sharply cut back following the 1979 revolution in Iran and, more recently, the Iran-Iraq war.

3 In 1979 oil satisfied roughly half the U.S. energy requirement, and half of this oil was imported.

4 Short-run measures to deal with an emergency if oil supplies are reduced from the Middle East include (a) government accumulation of an oil reserve, and (b) gasoline rationing. In addition, the world's major oil importing countries have formed an International Energy Agency to share available supplies in the event of an oil shortage.

5 Allowing the domestic U.S. oil price to rise to the world level (the present policy of oil "decontrol") stimulates both domestic production and conservation. But it results in a large transfer within the United States from oil users to the oil companies. (In addition, regardless of what U.S. *domestic* price policy may be, there is a large transfer from the United States and other oil importing countries to the OPEC nations because the *international* price we pay them has risen.)

6 One way of dealing with this transfer to the oil companies is to impose a windfall profits tax,

as the U.S. government did in 1980. Another is to keep the domestic price from rising as much as the world price—for example, by the blended price policy of the 1970s. Under this policy producers were paid the world price for newly discovered oil and a much lower price for old oil—with oil users paying a "blended" price between the two. However, this policy did not encourage conservation, was not as effective in increasing production as was hoped, and was difficult to administer.

7 A case can be made for raising the U.S. domestic price above the world price, as a means of discouraging OPEC price increases and reducing our dependence on uncertain foreign supplies.

8 Non-price measures to encourage conservation include tax incentives for insulating buildings and installing solar heating, a reduction in speed limits, and regulations forcing auto manufacturers to produce cars that go further on a gallon of gasoline.

9 The most important alternative forms of energy are coal and natural gas—and to a lesser degree, nuclear and hydroelectric power. Coal and nuclear development have been deterred by environmental fears, and the production of natural gas has been discouraged by a low, government-controlled price.

10 There are a number of other promising sources of energy that are still in the experimental stage. Some forms of solar energy are already available. On the other hand, nuclear fusion is still a long way off; but if it does develop, it can become a very important source of energy.

Key Concepts

importance of oil imports in U.S. energy picture

insecurity of imported oil supply

strategic petroleum reserve

white rationing

International Energy Agency

decontrol of domestic oil price

conservation effect of higher price

production effect of higher price

transfer to the oil companies

windfall profits tax

blended price policy

new oil vs old oil

non-price measures to induce conservation

intrastate (within-state) natural gas

interstate (out-of-state) natural gas

environmental problems with coal

environmental problems with nuclear fission

nuclear fusion

energy break-even point

economic break-even

Problems

22-1 How did domestic price controls on oil during the 1970s affect the transfer from U.S. oil consumers to U.S. producers?

*22-2 (a) Did holding the U.S. oil price down in the 1970s increase or reduce the international transfer from the United States to oil producing countries? (In your answer, explain the effect of holding the price down on domestic production and consumption, and therefore the effect on the U.S. demand for oil imports.)

(b) In turn, what effect do you think the price ceiling on domestic oil had on the world price of oil?

(c) Which transfer represented the more serious loss for the United States—the one in part (a), or the one in question 1?

(d) Explain why you agree or disagree with the statement: "To reduce a domestic transfer, a U.S. policy was followed that made the international transfer worse."

22-3 The proponents of a tariff to raise the U.S. price of oil above the world price use an argument for protection described in Chapter 29. Which one? Explain why this argument is relevant. Do you think that this makes a valid argument for the imposition of a tariff on oil? Why or why not?

22-4 Suppose that scientists working on nuclear fusion make a major breakthrough, which means that the economic break-even point in fusion energy will be reached by 1990.

(a) What would you expect the effects (if any) to be on the world price of oil (i) now, (ii) in 1990?

(b) What would you expect the effects (if any) to be on the U.S. price of natural gas (i) now, (ii) in 1990?

(c) How would your answers to question (a) change if the discoveries will lead only to the energy break-even point by 1990, rather than the economic break-even point?

CHAPTER 23
Income Inequality

There are many in this old world of ours who hold that things break about even for all of us. I have observed for example that we all get the same amount of ice. The rich get it in the summertime and the poor get it in the winter.

Bat Masterson

Should a disc jockey earn twice as much as a U.S. senator? Should the president of a corporation earn five times as much as the President of the United States? Should a basketball player earn 10 times as much as a violinist with a symphony orchestra? The income distribution is riddled with such glaring differences. In this chapter we shall look at the income of Americans to see whether such examples are the exception or the rule. How unequal are American incomes, overall? And is inequality increasing or decreasing?

Our second task will be to address the question: What is a *fair* distribution of income? Is it the income distribution that results from the free play of market forces? Or, is it an equal income for all? Or, is it some compromise between the two?

The place to begin is with a review of why income differences arise in the first place. Why do some people earn so much more income than others?

REVIEW: WHY DO INCOMES DIFFER?

In earlier chapters, we have seen how market forces result in quite different incomes for different people. For example, the high income of a surgeon is in part a return to *human capital;* it provides compensation for the years of forgone income and hard study in medical school, and further study beyond. It may also be partly a *rent* on greater-than-average *innate talent.* Of course, other individuals are gifted in quite different ways; star athletes and entertainers also earn very large rents.

Income differences also arise because of *wealth:* Those who own stocks, bonds, and other forms of property receive income from them. (In fact, there are even greater differences in wealth than in income. The poorest half of our population holds only about 6 percent of the nation's wealth, and the poorest quarter holds almost none at all.)

Family background explains some income differences. America may be the land of opportunity where someone from a poor low-status family can achieve prominence and success. But coming from the "right family" does help, especially if parents provide not only a silver spoon but also practical advice and inspiration. And an individual in a minority group may have a lower income because of *discrimination.*

In addition, income differences may arise because of the exercise of *market power.* People who find themselves in a monopoly position may be able to profit handsomely in terms of

Don't Phone Red Adair Unless You Are Prepared To Pay

When he answers the phone, there is a $5,000 charge.

If he advises on a problem, there is another $10,000 charge.

But it is only if he goes to work that the cash really starts to flow. For the job of capping the 1977 North Sea oil spill (a job that took his team less than a week), he was paid $6.6 million.

But before you think of competing for his job, ask yourself this: Do you *really* want to handle dynamite as close to burning oil wells as Red Adair does? ■

increased income. (Some of a surgeon's high income may be the result of the restricted supply of medical school graduates.)

Income differences may also arise because some people *work harder* than others. For example, a specific doctor's income may be lower because of a personal decision to sacrifice income for leisure. (The doctor may have chosen to live and practice in a resort area, and to take off every afternoon to fish in the summer and ski in the winter.) On the other hand, many doctors work very hard indeed, and this helps to explain their high incomes.

Some income differences may be the result of differences in *health,* or just plain *luck.* An example is the quarterback who is injured by a vicious tackle and must give up football and the large income that goes with it. And just as bad luck can lower income, good luck can raise it.

Being "the right person at the right time" is a way of earning a windfall income. When there is an oil blowout, it must be capped as soon as possible, and Red Adair commands a very large income because he is known as the "world's best." (See box 23-1.)

Of all the causes of income differences, can we say which is most important? In a surprising study, Jacob Mincer concluded that the answer was: Human capital. He found that *differences in human capital explain roughly 60 percent of the differences in American incomes.*[1]

---

[1]"Education, Experience, Earnings and Employment," in F. Thomas Juster (ed.), *Education, Income and Human Behavior* (New York: McGraw-Hill, 1975), p. 73. This study was based on 1959 data for white urban males.

HOW MUCH INCOME INEQUALITY IS THERE?

It's the rich whot gets the gryvy,
It's the poor whot gets the blime.

English ballad, World War II

Are wide differences in individual incomes the exception or the rule? When we look at the income of all Americans, how much inequality is there?

Table 23-1(*a*) shows the distribution of incomes *before* account is taken of such government policies as taxes, unemployment insurance, and social security. When we exclude these programs aimed at affecting income distribution, we find that the poorest fifth of the population receives less than 1 percent of the nation's income (in fact, only 0.3 percent). At the other extreme, the highest-income fifth receives over half the nation's income.

This unequal distribution is illustrated with a **Lorenz curve.** The first step in drawing such a curve is to rearrange the data in panel *a* of Table 23-1 into *cumulative* form in panel *b*. For example, in the second row, the poorest 40 percent of the population earn 7.5 percent of the nation's income. (To get this figure, we add the first two numbers in panel *a*.) This point, labeled *J*, is then plotted in Figure 23-1, along with other points that are similarly calculated. The result is the Lorenz curve of U.S. income.

To get some feel for how much inequality this curve represents, we ask: What would this Lorenz curve look like if all families received exactly the same income? In that case, we would observe point *F* instead of point *J*: The "lowest" 40 percent of the population would receive 40 percent of the income. And instead of point *K* we would observe point *G* (60 percent of the population would receive 60 percent of the income). When we join all points like *F* and *G*, the result is the "complete equality" line *OFGM*, that is, the 45° straight line drawn from the origin. Thus the degree of income inequality is shown by the amount of bow in the Lorenz curve; that is, by the size of the red slice between the curve and the 45° line.

In fact, inequality is not as serious a problem as this diagram suggests. One reason: Even if each family were earning exactly the same *lifetime* income, the Lorenz curve would still not coincide with that 45° line. We would still observe some "inequality slice." The reason is that, during any single year, we would observe some families that are young (with low incomes), and some families that are in their earning prime (with a higher income). Inequality exists in that year for these families, even though they have exactly the same lifetime income pattern.

Nonetheless, even when such influences are fully taken into account, a substantial degree of inequality exists. Society's response is to reduce this inequality by government taxation that con-

Table 23-1

Income Distribution of United States Families in 1976, before Taxes and Transfers

(a) Income distribution		(b) Cumulative income distribution		
Population	Share of total income	Population	Share of total income	Point in Figure 23-1
Lowest 20%	gets 0.3%	First 20%	gets 0.3%	H
Second 20%	gets 7.2	First 40%	gets 0.3 + 7.2 = 7.5	J
Third 20%	gets 16.3	First 60%	gets 7.5 + 16.3 = 23.8	K
Fourth 20%	gets 26.0	First 80%	gets 23.8 + 26.0 = 49.8	L
Highest 20%	gets 50.2	Total	gets 49.8 + 50.2 = 100.0	M

Source: Congressional Budget Office, *Poverty Status of Families under Alternative Definitions of Income,* Background Paper no. 17, rev. (Washington: Congress of the United States, June 1977), p. 24.

centrates more heavily on the rich, and government expenditure that concentrates more heavily on the poor.

HOW MUCH INEQUALITY DOES THE GOVERNMENT NOW ELIMINATE?

The degree to which government taxes and transfer payments reduce inequality in the nation's income distribution is shown in Figure 23-2. The total red area is exactly the same as in Figure 23-1. But here it is broken down into a

Figure 35-1
Lorenz curve showing before-tax-and-transfer income distribution of U.S. families
If every family had exactly the same income, the American income distribution would follow the 45° "complete equality" line. The actual income distribution is shown by the curve that lies below this—with the red slice between the two showing the amount of income inequality. In Figure 23-2, we show how a substantial part of this inequality is removed by government taxes and transfer payments. (Note that we define income per family and not per person. As noted in Chapter 1, a per-person definition makes no sense. For example, a young child earns no income but that gives no indication of how well off it may be.)

light area that shows how much the government reduces inequality, and a darker area that shows how much still remains.

Whereas curve *a* is a reproduction of the before-taxes-and-transfers curve graphed in Figure 23-1, curve *b* shows the major shift toward equality that occurs as a result of social insurance, including social security and unemployment insurance. (Social security and other government programs that shift this curve are discussed in more detail in the next chapter.) Curve *c* shows the further shift that results from cash transfers (such as Aid to Families with Dependent Children). Curve *d* shows the shift as a result of transfers-in-kind, where the government provides goods (such as food) or services instead of cash. The final shift to curve *e* shows the effect of taxation. When all programs are considered, the overall picture is one of a government that is redistributing income substantially from the rich to the poor, in the process eliminating roughly a third of the income inequality.[2] (Claims that the government is not very effective in changing the nation's income distribution have frequently been based on calculations that do not take some of these programs, such as in-kind transfers, into account.)

One surprise in this diagram is that taxation, often supposed to be a great income redistributor, is relatively ineffective in reducing income inequality. Certainly taxes are a large enough item in our income to make a big difference. But

---

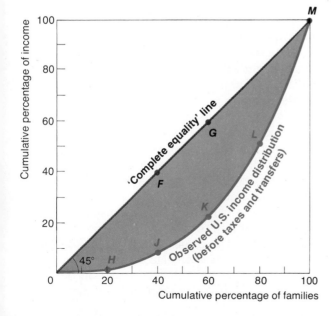

*[2]Perhaps more than this. Remember that if we were to achieve complete equality of lifetime incomes, the Lorenz curve would still have a bow below the 45° line.

Another reason why even more inequality may have been eliminated is that curve *e*, based on government figures, may be on the low side. Edgar Browning (in "How Much More Equality Can We Afford?" *The Public Interest,* Spring 1976, p. 93) has calculated that as early as 1972, the low-income fifth of the population received 11.7 percent of the nation's total after-tax income (rather than the 7.2 percent figure graphed in curve *e*). Moreover, according to Browning's figures, the gap between the Lorenz curve and the 45° line is similarly reduced throughout the rest of its range; in other words, inequality is not as serious as that dark red slice suggests.

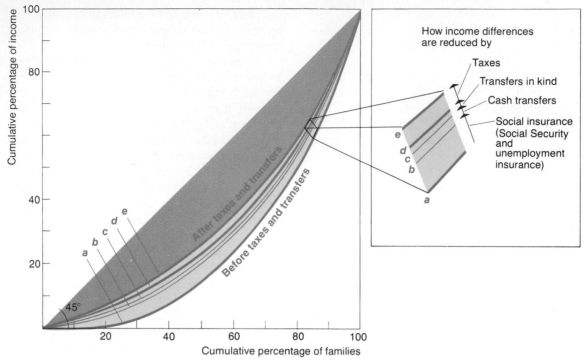

Figure 23-2

How government taxes and transfers reduce U.S. income inequality

Taxes and transfers by all levels of government in 1976 reduced income inequality by about one-third. Taxes, which shifted the curve from *d* to *e*, were a relatively unimportant form of equalization compared to government transfer programs—especially social insurance, which reduced inequality from curve *a* to curve *b*.

Source: Congressional Budget Office, *Poverty Status of Families under Alternative Definitions of Income,* Background Paper no. 17 rev. (Washington, June 1977) p. 24.

they do not redistribute income as much as one might expect because, on balance, they are not highly progressive. (As we have seen in Chapter 5, income taxes are progressive, with the rates rising as incomes rise. But other taxes are regressive. Moreover, loopholes ease the burden of income taxes on the wealthy.)

On the other hand, the more explicit transfer programs such as unemployment insurance, social security, and the various forms of cash transfer seem, when taken together, to be very effective. But we must be cautious about this

conclusion. It is quite true that the payments they provide to the poor *directly* reduce inequality (that is, shift the Lorenz curve up from *a* to *d*). But *indirectly* they *increase* inequality (make the Lorenz curve *a* lower than it would otherwise be) because of their side effects. The income guarantee provided by programs such as unemployment insurance makes unemployed people less desperate to get a job quickly—they can at least survive without one. (In addition, income guarantees reduce the incentive for couples to stay together; welfare may become available in the event of a separation. And when a couple breaks up, one medium-income family may become two poor families.)

These effects reduce the per-family earned income at the low end of the scale and give Lorenz curve *a* a bigger bow than it would otherwise have. In short, income-support programs have two conflicting effects on income inequality. Indirectly they make it worse by giving the "before transfers" curve *a* a bigger bow. But directly they make it better, by shifting the Lorenz curve up from *a* to the "after transfers" curve *d*.

If we want a picture of what's happening to the nation's income distribution over time, we should be looking at what's happening not to curve *a*, but instead to curve *d* (or even better, *e*). When we do this we find that, between the early 1960s and the early 1970s, inequality was reduced at a substantial, but far from spectacular, rate. (During the 1970s, the change was less pronounced.) Most of the change was caused by what happened at the extremes: a rise in the income share of the bottom fifth of the population and a decline in the share of the top fifth.

In deriving policies which affect the distribution of income, what should we set as a target? Is there such a thing as a "fair" or "equitable" distribution?

WHAT IS AN EQUITABLE INCOME DISTRIBUTION?

See how the fates their gifts allot,
For A is happy—B is not.
Yet B is worthy, I dare say,
Of more prosperity than A!

If I were fortune—which I'm not—
B should enjoy A's happy lot,
And A should die in miserie—
That is, assuming I am B.

Gilbert and Sullivan,
The Mikado

A search for an equitable or just distribution of income for society will lead us into treacherous intellectual terrain, from which some of the world's noted philosophers have been unable to escape with reputations intact. Although we cannot expect to arrive at any definitive answer in this elementary treatment, we can at least isolate some of the important issues.

But to begin, we reemphasize two important points made in Chapter 1.

First, *equity and equality are two different concepts.* In our Lorenz curve description of income distribution, we have addressed only the question of equality: How equal *are* incomes? This is an empirical question. We can answer it by looking at the facts—by examining how much each American family earns. On the other hand, the question of equity is not what incomes are, but rather what they *should be.* What income distribution is fair and just? This is an ethical issue on which people are not unanimous. Some believe that equity is equality—that everyone should be paid the same income. On the other hand, some believe that equity is not equality—that, for example, the individual who works harder or more effectively should be paid more.

Equal means "of the same size." *Equitable* means "fair." The two are not necessarily the same.

Second, we reemphasize that government policy cannot be designed to achieve just equity (an appropriate division of the nation's income pie). Instead it must also take into account other, often conflicting goals such as efficiency (increasing the size of that pie). But to sharpen our idea of equity, suppose for now that this is our only concern. *On grounds of equity alone,* what should our target distribution of income be?

Of the many possible answers to this question, we now consider three: first, the distribution that results from the free play of the economic marketplace; second, a completely equal distribution of income; and third, some compromise between the two.

Is the free market's distribution of income equitable?

Whatever is, is right.

Alexander Pope, *Essay on Man*

In economics, few would agree that whatever is, is necessarily right. *The free market does not do an entirely satisfactory job of distributing income.* Consider a monopolist who makes a fortune by successfully cornering the world's supply of a good, selling some at a very high price, and letting the unsold balance rot. In such cases it is very difficult to argue that the free market distributes income in a fair, equitable way.

But our reservations about the free-market distribution are far more fundamental than this, and apply even when markets are perfectly competitive. Such markets will, under certain conditions (no externalities, etc.) allocate factors of production in an efficient way that will maximize the nation's total income. In the process, they determine a set of prices of both goods and factors of production—the wages of labor, rents on land, etc. Thus, they both maximize the nation's income pie and determine how it will be divided. But we make no claim that they divide the pie up in a fair, equitable way. Remember: The size of the pie is maximized for *those who have the income to pay for it.* Output in a competitive market economy may include luxuries for the rich and too few necessities for the poor.

Even the strongest supporters of the free market, while championing its efficiencies, will still vote for aid to the destitute. This point is important enough to repeat: The demonstrable virtues of a free, perfectly competitive market have to do primarily with its efficiency, not its equity.

Perhaps the best illustration is this: In a perfectly competitive economy, rents on land efficiently direct the nation's scarce land into its most productive uses. (If rents are forced below the competitive level, land may be used in wasteful ways.) But the payment of these rents to those who own the land does not necessarily give us a fair and equitable distribution of income. We can see this point by considering an extreme example of land that has been inherited by the idle rich. Why should they earn an income many times that of the able and hard-working people whom they hire to manage and work this land?

Equality as a target

The idea that we should aim for complete equality has an immediate appeal. (See Box 23-2.) Since everyone has certain other rights (the right to vote, freedom of speech, equality before the law, etc.), why should each of us not have the right of equal access to the marketplace—the right of equal economic reward? In other words, since each of us has an equal political vote to cast, why shouldn't everyone have equal dollar votes to spend? In practice, it would be prohibitively costly to give everyone this right: An equal division of the pie would greatly shrink its size.

But even if this cost did not exist, there would still be fundamental philosophical problems. For example, the right to an equal economic reward would come into conflict with the right of equality before the law—in particular, the principle that those who break the law should be punished for their crimes; those who have to pay fines should *not* be left with an equal number of economic votes.

Moreover, there are also practical problems. For example, how is equality to be defined? One way is to define it, most simply, as "equal money incomes." But this answer is not satisfactory, because everyone does not work the same number of hours. Anyone who decides on shorter working hours is taking some of his or her potential income in the form of leisure, rather than cash. Therefore, income should be defined more broadly to include both income taken in the form of cash and "income" taken in the form of leisure. Fairness requires that an individual who takes a lot of income in one form—leisure—should get less in the other form—cash. Similarly, those whose work is dangerous should be paid higher money wages to compensate them for the risk. According to this approach, everyone's *overall* economic position (rather than just money income) should be equalized.

But in turn, this broader approach raises as many problems as it solves. If the overall position of individuals is to be equalized, those who have unpleasant jobs should be paid high enough wages to compensate them, and those whose jobs are fun should accordingly be paid less. But how do we handle the following problem: Some people find a particular job—like teaching—extremely rewarding, while others find it a bore. Should the first set be paid less than the second, in order to make them equal? Quite apart from the practical problem of trying to figure out just how much each person likes teaching, this broad approach leads to an unsatisfactory result: People would be paid for hating their jobs. And, since those who love teaching generally make the best teachers, it would mean that the best teachers would be paid the least. Surely this is not fair.

Worse yet, bored, dissatisfied teachers often don't work so hard; they take "leisure on the job." Is it fair to pay them a premium salary, when those who take a lot of leisure at home receive low pay?

Therefore, we conclude that considerations of *equity alone* have not led us to complete equality as a meaningful objective. We are skeptical of this objective, just as we were skeptical earlier of the free-market determination of income. How about some compromise between the two?

A compromise between the free market and complete equality

It is easy to conclude that both the free-market and complete-equality solutions involve serious problems. What is far more difficult is to say where in the broad range in between we should aim. We will not be able to answer that question. But here are some ideas for you to consider as you grapple with it (and you must, as a voter).

Make it a fair race . . .   Suppose we think of participating in the economy as being in a race in which each runner's income is determined by his or her finish. The egalitarian view that "justice is income equality" implies that the government should equalize all rewards at the end of the race: Give everyone a bronze medal—no golds, and no booby prizes. As the Dodo in *Alice in Wonderland* put it, "Everybody has won, and all must have prizes."

An alternative view is that the responsibility of the government is only to ensure that the race is fair. Disadvantages should be eliminated: No one should start with a 50-yard handicap because of being a woman, or a black, or the child of parents who are not influential. In this race, everyone has a right, but it is the right of equality of *opportunity,* not equality of *reward.* In brief,

everyone should have the right to an equal *start*—but not to an equal *finish.*

While the idea of equal opportunity is appealing, it too is difficult to define. Buried in any definition of a fair race is a judgment on which advantages are unfair and should be removed, and which advantages should not. Advantages of race, color, and ethnic background clearly should be removed. But what should we do about advantages arising from differences in natural ability? Should an individual in the economic race be penalized for natural business talent so that all may start equal? Does it make any more sense to do this than to penalize a marathon runner for strong legs? If we were to embark on such a penalty or handicap system, we would end up in the world of Kurt Vonnegut's Handicapper General, who weighs down naturally talented athletes with scrap metal, and graceful ballerinas with bags of bird-shot (see Box 23-3). In such a world, nobody would even come close to breaking the 4-minute mile; the economy would fall far short of its potential.

. . . but modify the rewards   It is quite possible to have a fair race, yet still have a bad system of rewards. For example, suppose the winner were to be given the Olympic Stadium and the loser were to be thrown, Roman style, to the lions? Believing in a fair economic race does not prevent us from modifying its rewards—in other words, using government taxes and transfer payments to reduce the income differences that result.

To the authors, this idea of a fair race and a modified system of rewards that reduces but does not eliminate income inequality seems to be an appealing principle. But again, the idea is not as simple as it sounds. Is not an individual's economic life less like a standard race than like a relay race? Moreover, a relay race with no beginning or end? The race you run depends on the start you get, in terms of your whole background, including your family wealth. A first reaction is that it should not be like this. To keep the race fair, everyone should be started off equally, without any advantage of inherited

Rawls on Equality

Harvard philosophy professor John Rawls has argued that income equality is a desirable goal—except in special circumstances. His analysis starts in a promising way. A consensus on the fair distribution of income is difficult to achieve because everyone has a special ax to grind: Those with high incomes favor a system in which inequality is allowed, because it lets them keep their higher income. On the other hand, those with low incomes are likely to advocate equality because it will improve their position. Rawls therefore suggests that, to get an objective view, people must be *removed from their present situation* and placed in an **original position** where they decide what the distribution of income should be, without knowing the specific place they themselves will eventually take in this distribution. What income distribution will they choose?

Here are the essentials of Rawls' argument. The typical person in the original position will think along these lines: "Whatever income distribution is chosen, with my luck, chances are that I'll end up at the bottom. So I'll vote for the income distribution that will leave me, the lowest one on the totem pole, as well off as possible." Since everyone is similarly situated in the original position, Rawls argues that all will reason in the same way. He concludes that a consensus will develop in favor of an equal distribution of income—unless there is an unequal distribution that leaves *everyone* better off. This is what Rawls calls the **difference principle.***

While Rawls' approach will generally lead to equality, there are circumstances in which it will not. To illustrate, we use two extreme examples, but the argument applies in less extreme cases as well. For the first example, suppose people in the original position choose between the two income distributions shown in Table 23-2. Option

*In his *Theory of Justice* (Cambridge: Harvard University Press, 1971), p. 63, Rawls was concerned with more than income: "All social values—liberty and opportunity, income and wealth, and the bases of self-respect—are to be distributed equally unless an unequal distribution of any, or all, of these values is to everyone's advantage."

Table 23-2
When Rawls' Theory Leads to Inequality: An Example†

	Income of all individuals but one	Income of last individual
Option A (equality)	$ 5,000	$5,000
Option B (inequality)	$10,000	$5,100*

*Option B chosen because everyone is better off

A represents complete equality, with everyone's annual income at $5,000. Now suppose it is possible to move to Option B, where everyone's income is $10,000 except for the last individual, whose income is $5,100. (Suppose that this move is possible because there was previously a very high tax aimed at equalizing income. When the tax is removed, people respond by working more.) Because everyone benefits, Rawlsian logic leads to a move from A to B—a move *away from equality.*‡ Most people would agree with such a move. So far, Rawls' theory is not controversial: In the circumstances shown in Table 23-2, Rawls, like almost everyone else, would allow inequality.

Table 23-3 illustrates the second, more likely situation, with options A and C. As before, the move away from equality (in this case, from A to C) benefits almost everyone by $5,000. But now we recognize that any such substantial change is likely to leave at least one person worse off. (Note in the last column how the income of the last individual is reduced by $100.) In this case, Rawls argues that people in an original position would choose option A: With their concern about ending up at the bottom of the totem pole, they would focus on the figures in the last column and prefer A with its $5,000 income to C with its

†While we consider the lowest-income individual in our examples, Rawls' focus is on a typical individual in the lowest-income group. But this does not seriously affect his conclusion or our evaluation of it.
‡Envy is not taken into account: It is assumed that nobody's happiness is reduced by the knowledge that someone else has become richer.

Table 23-3
When Rawls' Theory Leads to Equality:
An Example

	Income of all individuals but one	Income of last individual
Option A (equality)	$ 5,000	$5,000*
Option C (inequality)	$10,000	$4,900

*Option A chosen because a move to C would damage the last individual

$4,900 income. Thus, according to Rawls, people would choose equality.

It is here, when he is putting forward a strong argument in favor of equality, that Rawls' theory is open to criticism. Ask yourself: If you were in Rawls' original position, without knowledge of where you would eventually end up, which option would you choose? Would you join the consensus Rawls expects in favor of option A? Most people would find C difficult to resist. The minuscule risk of being $100 worse off seems trivial in comparison with the near certainty of being $5,000 better off. This seems to be a risk well worth taking. Indeed, those who would select Rawls' option A are those who would *avoid risk at almost any cost.* How in the world would you find anyone so risk-averse? (Observe that the risk you would be taking in choosing income distribution C rather than A would be the same as your risk at the racetrack or the stock exchange if you were to bet $100 for a chance to win $5,000, with odds *in your favor* of 220 million to one. Why those odds? There are about 220 million people in the United States. In moving from option A to C, they would all "win" $5,000— except for the one who would lose $100. With such odds, who in the world would turn down such a bet?)

[Try an experiment to see the difficulty with Rawls' argument. Change the $10,000 in Table 23-3 to $100,000. Rawls' argument still leads to the choice of equality (option A). Would this be your choice? If so, would you choose option A or C if the number were even higher, say $1

million? Or $1 billion? Won't you eventually come around to option C and give up voting in a Rawlsian way?]

Because people in an original position would not necessarily vote for equality option A over C, Rawls does not make a convincing case for equality. The difficulty is that his argument is based on the assumption that people's only concern is with what is happening in the last column in those two tables—that is, with that last, poorest individual. Specifically, the choice is based on *maximizing* the *minimum* income; hence, this is often referred to as the **maximin** criterion. But why should we completely ignore the vast majority and be totally preoccupied with that last individual?

In a later reconsideration of the maximin criterion,§ Rawls concluded that although he still viewed it as attractive, "a deeper investigation . . . may show that some other conception of justice is more reasonable. In any case, the idea that economists may find most useful . . . is that of the original position. This perspective . . . may prove illuminating for economic theory." ■

§See "Some Reasons for the Maximin Criterion," *American Economic Review,* May 1974, pp. 141–146.

Advocates of income equality were immediately attracted to Rawls' theory because it seemed to be a more scientific support for equality than the traditional argument. According to the earlier argument, equality is a desirable goal because it would maximize the total utility of all individuals in society. But this conclusion follows only if it can be assumed that all individuals have the same capacity to enjoy income—technically, only if everyone has the same marginal utility of income schedule. (If this assumption does not hold, we can increase total utility by moving away from complete equality, by transferring some income away from those who are less able to enjoy it to those who are more able to enjoy it.) Unfortunately, there is no way we can confirm or deny the assumption that people enjoy income equally; remember, there is no way to meter people's heads to compare the satisfaction they get from $1 of income.

So this traditional marginal utility argument does not provide scientific support for income equality. Nor, as we have seen in this box, does Rawls' theory. Like the older theory, it has a weak link. In Rawls' case, it is the assumption that the only concern is for the lowest person on the totem pole. Moreover, many of those who believe in equality became less enthusiastic about Rawls' theory when they discovered that it allows for a very substantial degree of inequality—as we have seen in Table 23-2 and as Rawls himself has reemphasized. (Rawls, "Some Reasons for the Maximin Criterion," p. 145.)

BOX 23-3

Kurt Vonnegut on Why Only Horses and Golfers Should Be Handicapped†

The year was 2081, and everybody was finally equal. They weren't only equal before God and the law. They were equal every which way. Nobody was smarter than anybody else. Nobody was better looking than anybody else. Nobody was stronger or quicker than anybody else. All this equality was due to the 211th, 212th, and 213th Amendments to the Constitution, and to the unceasing vigilance of agents of the United States Handicapper General. . . .

George [Bergeron, whose] intelligence was way above normal, had a little mental handicap radio in his ear. He was required by law to wear it at all times. It was tuned to a government transmitter. Every twenty seconds or so, the transmitter would send out some sharp noise to keep people like George from taking unfair advantage of their brains. . . .

On the television screen were ballerinas. . . . They weren't really very good—no better than anybody else would have been anyway. They were burdened with sashweights and bags of birdshot and their faces were masked, so that no one, seeing a free and graceful gesture or a pretty face, would feel like something the cat drug in. George was toying with the vague notion that maybe dancers shouldn't be handicapped. But he didn't get very far with it before another noise in his ear radio scattered his thoughts. . . .

George began to think glimmeringly about his abnormal son who was now in jail, about Harrison, but a twenty-one-gun salute in his head stopped that. "Boy!" said Hazel, "that was a doozy, wasn't it?" It was such a doozy that George was white and trembling, and tears stood on the rims of his red eyes. Two of the eight ballerinas had collapsed to the studio floor, were holding their temples. . . .

The television program was suddenly interrupted for a news bulletin. It wasn't clear at first as to what the bulletin was about, since the announcer, like all announcers, had a serious speech impediment. For about half a minute, and in a state of high excitement, the announcer tried to say, "Ladies and gentlemen—"

He finally gave up, handed the bulletin to a ballerina to read. . . ."That's all right—" Hazel said of the announcer, "he tried. That's the big thing. He tried to do the best he could with what God gave him. He should get a nice raise for trying so hard."

"Ladies and gentlemen—" said the ballerina, . . ."Harrison Bergeron, age fourteen . . . has just escaped from jail, where he was held on suspicion of plotting to overthrow the government. He is a genius and an athlete, is under-handicapped, and should be regarded as extremely dangerous."

A police photograph of Harrison Bergeron was flashed on the screen. . . . Harrison's appearance was Halloween and hardware. Nobody had ever borne heavier handicaps. . . . Instead of a little ear radio for a mental handicap, he wore a tremendous pair of earphones, and spectacles with thick wavy lenses. The spectacles were intended to make him not only half blind, but to give him whanging headaches besides.

Scrap metal was hung all over him. Ordinarily, there was a certain symmetry, a military neatness to the handicaps issued to strong people, but Harrison looked like a walking junkyard. ∎

wealth. Should we therefore tax away all inheritances and, for the same reason, gifts?

This is a difficult proposal to defend, even on equity grounds. Consider two men with equal incomes. One spends it all. The other wishes to save in order to pass wealth on to his children. Is it fair to impose a tax that prohibits him from doing so? And is not charity a virtue? What can one say of a society that prevents gifts to family or friends? And isn't it desirable for parents to give their children "in kind" advantages by encouraging them to learn? (Surely we wouldn't want a government to forbid people from encouraging their children, just because not all children are so lucky.)

Conclusions: Can we pin down the idea of equity?

Unfortunately, the answer is no. The important concept of equity is hard to define. The only conclusions we have been able to reach are both negative ones: Equity is not complete equality of income; nor is it the income distribution that the free market generates. We are left somewhere in between. We conclude that, in terms of equity considerations alone, we should move from a free-market distribution some distance, but not the whole way, toward equalizing incomes.

To further complicate matters, any such move tends to involve an efficiency cost in terms of a shrinking national pie. (Guaranteeing people an income regardless of what they do tends to erode their incentive to work, a problem that will be detailed in the next chapter.) Because of this efficiency cost, it is desirable to stop short of the degree of equality which would be chosen if equity were the sole objective.

In practice, we have already moved a considerable distance toward equalizing incomes, as Figure 23-2 illustrates. It is possible that we have not yet moved far enough; and it is also possible that we have moved too far. The question of how the nation's income should be distributed is likely to remain an issue of continuing debate. But it is important that the dispute about how the national income pie should be divided does not become so heated and exhausting that the total size of that pie is substantially reduced. To return to our earlier analogy: If all participants had spent their energies in a squabble about how the race should be run and how the rewards should be divided, no one would have broken the 4-minute mile.

Key Points

1 Large differences exist in the incomes of American families. Some have high incomes because of their human capital, wealth, native talent, family background, market power, or just plain luck. Others have low incomes because they enjoy none of these advantages or for some other reason. For example, they may suffer from discrimination.

2 If we examine the U.S. income distribution *before government taxes and transfers* are taken into account, we observe a great inequality. The poorest 20 percent receive only 0.3 percent of the nation's income, while the highest 20 percent get about half.

3 About a third of this inequality is eliminated by government transfer expenditures that are concentrated heavily on the poor, and by progressive taxes that draw heavily from the rich. (However, our tax system is not as progressive as the income tax alone, and taxes do much less equalizing than government transfer payments.)

4 The most effective government expenditure in equalizing income is social insurance (social security and unemployment insurance). But other government expenditures, both in cash and in kind, also play a role.

5 Equality is a question of fact: How equal *are* incomes? On the other hand, equity is a matter of judgment: What *should* relative incomes be? A strong case can be made that neither a completely equal distribution of incomes nor the unequal free-market distribution is equitable. A desirable target seems to lie somewhere between.

6 While it is very difficult to be more precise than this, two rough guidelines have been suggested. First, keep the economic race as fair as reasonably possible. For example, no one should start at a disadvantage because of race or sex. (However, the appealing principle of equality of opportunity conflicts with the equally appealing principle that parents should be able to help their children.)

7 Equal opportunity need not result in equal reward. Even if everyone could be given an equal start, there is no reason to expect that all will finish in a tie. Some will get greater rewards than others. Thus, the second responsibility of the government is to modify rewards—that is, to reduce income inequality by taxes and transfer payments.

8 Finally, even if we could determine an equitable income distribution, it does not follow that the government should continue to redistribute income up to this point. The reason is that the act of redistributing income (changing the division of the national pie) reduces the incentive to work and hence the level of efficiency (the size of that pie). Therefore, a compromise should be selected between the conflicting objectives of equity and efficiency.

Key Concepts

cumulative income
   distribution (Lorenz
   curve)
social insurance
cash transfers
transfers in kind

difference between equity
   and equality
limitations of the
   free-market distribution
   of income

*Rawls' difference
   principle
*maximin
difference between
   equalizing opportunity
   and equalizing reward

Problems

23-1 Explain to your very bright roommate (who is not studying economics) why some Americans have much higher incomes than others.

23-2 Mark McCormack is, in his own words, an "engineer of careers." His company has grossed $35 million in some years from a 15 to 40 percent agent's fee for managing 250 tennis stars (Bjorn Borg) and golfers (Jack Nicklaus, Arnold Palmer). Others have also tried to set themselves up as agents in this way, but have not succeeded on this handsome a scale, if at all. Do you think McCormack's huge income is the result of (a) only luck; (b) luck and other reasons;

or (c) just other reasons? If you answer (b) or (c), explain what the other reasons might be.

23-3 Explain how the marketplace generates a rental income for those who high reputation (just as for those with great skill).

23-4 Do you agree with the following statement? (Explain why or why not.) "Free market prices of factors of production help to maximize the total national income pie and also divide it in an equitable way."

*23-5 (Based on Box 23-2.) Is this statement true or false? If false, correct it. "Rawls' maximin principle is to *maximize* the *mini*mum possible income. But this is the preference only of people who are unwilling to risk any of their income in the hope of acquiring more. Many people are not like this, including all those individuals who bet a small part of their income (at the races or Monte Carlo) in the hope of winning more.''

*23-6 In 1899, John Bakes Clark wrote (in *Distribution of Wealth*) that ''free competition tends to give to labor what labor creates [that is, the marginal product of labor], to capitalists what capital creates [that is, the marginal product of capital], and to entrepreneurs what the coordinating function creates.'' This sounds as though everyone gets what he or she deserves; that is, free competition distributes income in an equitable way. Do you agree? In your view, what does a free competitive market do well, and what does it do not so well?

CHAPTER 24
Government Policies to Reduce Inequality:
Can We Solve the Poverty Problem?

Welfare has been indicted for encouraging family dissolution, promoting illegitimacy, degrading and alienating recipients, papering over the sins of a society that generates poverty, shielding the dissolute and lazy from their just deserts, failing to support life by providing too little assistance, and fostering sloth by providing too much. Conservatives, liberals, and radicals unite in attacking the welfare system but divide over its specific faults.

Henry J. Aaron

Although Americans may differ on the question of how far we should go in reducing income inequality in general, there is one specific issue on which the overwhelming majority agree: Nobody should starve; nor should children grow up in abject poverty. Yet, in 1980, poverty was still a fact of life for about 1 in 20 American families. You can confirm the effect this has on people by driving from a wealthy suburb of any large American city into a depressed core area. In the United States, overall wealth stands in stark contrast to the poverty faced by those who are insufficiently fed, housed, and clothed. In the mid-1960s this problem was recognized to be so important that the U.S. government declared a "war on poverty," and introduced a number of new measures to improve the lot of the poor.

This chapter is a study of the poor—the individuals who appeared in the bottom left-hand corner of the Lorenz income curve in Fig. 23-1. Who are the poor? Why are they poor?

What programs has the government introduced to fight the war on poverty? Should these programs be viewed as a way of cleaning up an economic mess created by the system, or do they create the mess? And finally, can the faults in these programs be cured—and, if so, how?

POVERTY

The economic definition of poverty is "inadequate income." But this does not mean that poverty is strictly an economic condition. It is often also a state of mind, a condition in which the individual feels helpless and unable to cope. Therefore, poverty is a subject for sociologists and political scientists as well as economists. One of the difficulties encountered in studying poverty is the chicken-or-egg problem: Are people unable to cope because they are poor? Or are they poor because they are unable to cope? Undoubtedly the answer is, "Both."

Poverty exists when people have inadequate income to buy the necessities of life. In 1981 it was defined, for an urban family of four, as an income of $8,500.

How the poverty line is defined

In defining the poverty line—officially known as the "low-income line"—the government starts with the idea that food is the first essential in a poverty budget. Accordingly, the Department of Agriculture calculates the cost of a diet that satisfies the requirements of minimum nutrition. (As in any such definition of subsistence or bare necessity, judgment is very important. To illustrate: About $225 in 1981 prices, spent on just the right combination of things like lard, soybeans, orange juice, and liver, will provide a medically balanced diet for one person for a year. Moreover, this menu will be healthier than the present diet of some well-to-do Americans. But who would you get to eat it? Consequently, the Department of Agriculture does not base its calculation on this, but instead uses a reasonably acceptable, but not luxurious, diet.) Finally, since low-income families typically spend about one-third of their income on food, this food cost is multiplied by 3 to arrive at the official low-income line. This figure is then adjusted, to take account of the size of the family, its location, and so on. Whereas the 1981 poverty line for an urban family of four was about $8,500, for an urban family of six it was roughly $11,200. But if this same six-member family lived on a farm, its poverty line was reduced to $9,500. (For more detail, see Table 1-1.)

Of course, the poverty line has to be adjusted upward periodically to take account of inflation. And historically over the long term it tends to rise for another reason as well: Our concept of poverty keeps shifting up. The poverty income of about $8,500 in 1981 would have been regarded in colonial times as a very handsome income indeed (even after full adjustment is made for inflation). In fact, it would still have been considered a good income as late as the 1930s. When President Roosevelt spoke of one-third of the nation living in poverty at that time, he implied a poverty-line income in the 1930s that was far lower, and that would buy far less, than the poverty income of 1981. So upward adjustments in the definition of poverty do occur. But beware: If the definition of poverty is made too flexible, the concept becomes meaningless. If, for example, poverty is defined as the income of the bottom one-tenth of the population, there is no hope of curing it: By definition, 1 in 10 Americans will *always* be poor, no matter how much we may raise *everyone's* income. And the statement that 1 American family in 10 is living in poverty will tell us absolutely nothing about how serious the problem is, or how successful we have been in curing it.

Who are the poor?

Table 24-1 shows how poverty is related to race and location: A black is more than twice as likely to be living in poverty as a white,[1] and a person living in the South is more than twice as likely to be poor as an individual living in the North. Poverty falls unevenly in other respects as well. For example, the larger the family size, the more likely it will be poor. Someone with less than 8 years of education is about four times as likely to be poor as someone who has finished high school; and going on to complete a university education almost (but not quite) guarantees one against poverty.

People living in the core area of a big city are more likely to be poor than those living in its suburbs. (Part of the reason is that many of those who have been able to afford to move from the core to the suburbs have already done so.) But poverty is not limited to centers of big cities: Many of the poor live on farms, or in small towns or cities. Finally, a fatherless family is about eight times as likely to be poor as a family with a resident father. In fact, about half the nation's poor live in fatherless families.

---

[1] However, there are more poor whites than poor blacks. Without reading further, can you see why? (The answer is: There are more poor whites, because most of the population is white.)

THE WAR ON POVERTY

Following the declaration of the war on poverty, government transfer programs such as unemployment insurance and food stamps grew by about ten times between 1965 and 1981 in dollar terms, and about four times when adjusted for inflation. When the public thinks of antipoverty programs, these are the ones that usually come to mind. But these outlays relieve only the *symptoms* of poverty: They make it more bearable without providing much hope that the problem will be cured (that is, that the poor will be able to increase their earnings). A more promising long-run approach to poverty is to attack its *causes*. For example, expenditures on education or training are designed to cure one of the causes of poverty: inadequate human capital. The objective is to allow people to accumulate this capital in order to provide for their own support in the future. (Although it may be more promising to attack the causes of a problem than its symptoms, this is not always the case. In extreme cases of "clinical" poverty, where individuals have such a low innate capacity or skill that no amount of training will allow them to earn a living, straight support programs may be the more effective form of assistance.)

POLICIES TO REDUCE THE CAUSES OF POVERTY

Before turning to policies dealing with the symptoms of poverty, we consider those that attack its causes.

1 Subsidizing investment in human capital

Federal, state, and local governments subsidize education in various ways. The provision of free elementary and secondary schooling is the most important, but there are also other programs that provide job training. For example, the Comprehensive Employment and Training Act (CETA) provides federal subsidies for training unemployed workers. (The CETA program was cut sharply in 1981.)

Table 24-1
Incidence of Poverty by Race and Region
(Percentage of each group living in poverty, 1976)

By race		By region	
Whites	7.3%	South	12.1%
Blacks	16.1%	West	8.2%
		Northeast	5.7%
		North Central	5.9%

Source: Congressional Budget Office, *Poverty Status of Families under Alternative Definitions of Income*, Background Paper no. 17, rev. (Washington: Congress of the United States, June 1977), pp. 11, 13.

2 Antidiscrimination policies

Another cause of poverty is job discrimination, which reduces the income of blacks, other minorities, and women. The Equal Pay Act (1963) requires that women be paid the same as men for equal work, and the Civil Rights Act (1964) outlaws discrimination in hiring, firing, and other employment practices.

3 Dealing with unemployment and disability

The most promising government policies to cure unemployment are those designed to keep the economy operating at a high level of output. Permanent disability is quite a different problem because it cannot be cured once it has happened. But much of it can be prevented; this is the task of the Occupational Safety and Health Administration. (When unemployment or disability do occur, workers are covered in either case by government insurance programs.)

4 Other policies

The Work Incentive Program (WIN) subsidizes the training and employment of people on welfare. It also enables parents to take jobs by providing day-care facilities for children. This provision is important in reducing poverty in the increasing number of families with only one parent in the home.

POLICIES TO REDUCE THE SYMPTOMS OF POVERTY: GOVERNMENT PROGRAMS TO MAINTAIN INCOMES

Even if it is not possible to cure a disease, it is very important to provide the patient with relief from the symptoms. While we are in the process of developing long-run cures for poverty (such as upgrading human capital and ending discrimination) we also provide public assistance programs that keep many families from falling below the poverty line (Table 24-2).

(a) Social insurance programs

Social insurance programs were not designed specifically to cure poverty; people need not be poor to receive benefits. Nonetheless, they play a key role in keeping many of the population from falling below the poverty line.

1 Social security This is by far the most important income maintenance program. Contributions are made by employees and employers, and self-employed individuals. In turn, these contributions are paid out in retirement, disability, and other benefits.

Table 24-2
Income Transfer Programs

		Public expenditures *(billions of current dollars)*		
	Date enacted	1965	1979	1981 (estimate)
(a) Social insurance				
Cash benefits:				
Social security	1935	$16.5	$102.6	$137.0
Unemployment insurance	1935	2.5	11.2	18.7
Workers' compensation	1908	1.8	9.9	14.8
Veterans' disability compensation	1917	2.2	6.8	7.5
Railroad retirement	1937	1.1	4.3	5.2
Black lung	1969	*	0.6	0.9
In-kind benefits:				
Medicare	1965	*	29.1	38.4
(b) Welfare (public assistance)				
Cash benefits:				
Aid to families with dependent children (AFDC)	1935	1.7	10.8	12.8
Supplemental security income (SSI)[1]	1972	2.7	6.8	8.5
Veterans' pensions	1933	1.9	3.6	4.1
General assistance	**	0.4	1.2	1.5
In-kind benefits:				
Medicaid	1965	0.5	21.8	27.6
Food stamps	1964	0.04	6.8	9.7
Housing assistance	1937	0.3	4.4	6.6
Total expenditures		$31.5	$219.9	$293.2
Total expenditures as a percentage of GNP		4.6%	9.1%	10.0%

*Nonexistent.
**Varied by states.
[1]Prior to 1972, Aid to the Blind, Aid to the Permanently and Totally Disabled, and Old Age Assistance.
Source: Sheldon Danziger, Robert Haveman, and Robert Plotnick, "How Income Transfer Programs Affect Work, Savings and the Income Distribution: A Critical Review," *Journal of Economic Literature,* September 1981, table 1.

BOX 24-1
The Rising Cost of Health Care

It is widely recognized that the quality of medical services in the United States is as good as anywhere in the world—at least for those who can afford it. But it has become very costly: In 1981, Americans spent almost 10 percent of GNP on health care. While the government provides medical services to the elderly (Medicare) and the poor (Medicaid), it still does not provide such services for the rest of the population. Broader government medical programs have been suggested by Senator Kennedy and others. But such proposals have met a cool reception in Congress, largely because they would add to America's medical bill—a bill which is already rising rapidly for several reasons:

1 Rapid advances in medical research have meant that it is becoming possible to save lives in a variety of new ways. But most are very expensive. All available lifesaving opportunities cannot be seized unless a larger and larger percentage of the nation's GNP is directed into this effort. One can argue that, with the opening up of new lifesaving opportunities, more of our GNP *should* be spent in this way. But if we try to capture *all* these opportunities, the cost would become extremely high. (Not all lifesaving procedures are worth the costs. For example, heart transplants are now done only rarely, because they are extremely expensive—particularly in light of the poor prospects for long-term survival.)

Therefore, someone has to decide at what point our lifesaving efforts will be limited—that is, at what point funds that could save lives will be cut off. And someone also has to decide which patients will be the lucky ones who will live because they get access to the limited number of lifesaving machines and treatments that society can afford.

No one likes to make this life-and-death decision. We've seen earlier how difficult it is to put a value on a life. But the task of saying that one *particular* life is worth more than another—and therefore is the one that should be saved—is even more difficult. Doctors on the spot (or administrators or committees allocating funds) have to make this decision. (What's the alternative? To have the decision made by chance in a life-and-death lottery? Then an Einstein may lose out to a suicidal derelict who places no value on his own life.)

Although this life-or-death choice must be made, those who must make it find it exceedingly difficult. Whenever possible, they understandably argue: Instead of choosing between two lives, let's save them both—if there is any *conceivable* way we can get the cost covered. This, then, is one reason there is persistent upward pressure on costs.

2 With medical bills paid for by Medicare, Medicaid, or private insurance schemes, there is inadequate pressure to cut costs: Patients have little incentive to seek out low-cost treatment. (When your health is at stake you don't go bargain hunting, especially when an insurance company is paying the tab.) In turn, this means that doctors and hospitals have little incentive to compete for patients by reducing their fees. (Consequently, Medicare and Medicaid benefit not only patients, but also doctors—in terms of increasing their incomes.)

In the eyes of the critics, a more efficient and less costly system of health care requires that the public be again given a financial incentive to look for low-cost care. One way of providing this is to have insurance schemes with substantial "deductible" clauses that leave part of the cost of treatment for patients to bear. With patients becoming more cost-conscious, competition would be stimulated among doctors and hospitals.

3 There is evidence that some doctors and hospitals are defrauding the plans. A U.S. senate committee investigating the cost of Medicaid

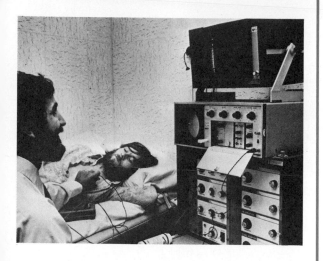

found that some doctors would carry out complete physical examinations—with the whole battery of laboratory tests—on essentially healthy people who came to their offices with a minor complaint. Through referrals, a group of specialist doctors may "ping-pong" patients back and forth among themselves. Medicaid patients getting a doctor's appointment have sometimes been told to bring their children, too: The doctor can then take a brief look at the children and charge Medicaid the fee for an office visit for each. The majority of physicians do not waste time and money this way. But according to the Department of Health and Human Resources, there are enough doctors who do engage in these practices that the cost of Medicare and Medicaid has been raised by a substantial amount. In turn, attempts to fight this problem of "medifraud" have entailed the creation of costly administrative machinery to supervise the payments made under the plans.

Some critics of proposed nationwide insurance schemes concede that an extension of Medicare to the whole population may be desirable on equity grounds. But they are concerned that it could mean an economywide extension of the problems we have just described. It could become extremely costly. ■

2 Unemployment insurance   This provides temporary assistance to people who have lost their jobs.

3 Medicare   This health insurance program provides medical services for the elderly.

(b) Welfare programs
Welfare programs *have* been designed specifically to combat poverty; their benefits are intended exclusively for the poor.

1 Aid to families with dependent children (AFDC)   This program provides cash benefits for poor families with dependent children. Generally, this aid goes to families headed by a single parent. In fact, in some areas a family cannot qualify for AFDC if an able-bodied man is in the home. While this provision has the desirable objective of encouraging able-bodied fathers to go to work, it sometimes drives them out of the home instead. (They may feel that the simplest way for them to support their dependents is to leave, and thus allow their families to qualify for welfare.)

2 Medicaid   This health insurance program is similar to Medicare except that it provides medical services for those with low incomes. (For a discussion of some of the problems the government faces in providing medical care, see Box 36-1.)

3 Food stamps   The federal government provides the poor with food stamps, which they use to buy food at the store.

4 Public housing   This form of assistance, first offered in 1937, has been modified on numerous occasions. The basic idea is this: A local government is subsidized by the federal government to acquire housing and rent it out to low-income tenants who pay 25 percent of their income in rent, with the federal government paying the rest. (For more on housing subsidies, see Box 24-2.)

Whereas AFDC provides *cash benefits*, the

BOX 24-2

Housing Subsidies: Who Benefits?

Many voters believe that better housing is an important social goal—better housing for the poor, and better housing for the average citizen, too. Of the numerous incentives for housing, the most notable is a provision which allows homeowners to reduce the income tax they have to pay. (In calculating their taxable income, they are permitted to deduct property taxes and interest payments on their mortgages.) The idea is to encourage people to own their own homes. As a consequence, more houses are built, and existing houses are kept in better repair. Far from being an antipoverty program, this policy benefits average homeowners more than the poor who own small homes or none at all.

Another government housing policy is urban renewal, which is designed to improve slum housing, revitalize downtown business areas, and attract middle-class residents from the suburbs back into the big cities. This program involves federal subsidies to local governments to tear down central city slums and rebuild these core areas. But this policy has generated heated controversy: Its supporters view it as the last hope of saving the big cities, while its critics point out that, initially at least, it resulted in many more dwellings being torn down than constructed. As a consequence, the central city poor found that their housing supply was shrinking. Another reason for the shrinkage was the success of this

program in its important objective of attracting back the middle class from the suburbs: Thus, much more of the new available space was occupied by the nonpoor. To ensure that the poor will be better accommodated, attempts have been recently made to guarantee that any renewal program includes specified amounts of low-income housing. ■

other three programs (Medicaid, food stamps, and public housing) provide benefits **in kind.** For the 16 years between 1965 and 1981, these in-kind transfers were by far the most rapidly growing welfare programs, with each increasing by more than 20 times in dollar terms, or more than eight times when adjusted for inflation.

ASSESSING THE PRESENT WELFARE PACKAGE

In spending large sums, are we making headway against the poverty problem? Figure 24-1 suggests that the answer is yes. By present poverty

---

***Benefits in kind** are payments, not of cash, but of some good (like food) or service (like medical care).*

standards, one in two Americans was poor in 1929; by 1947, the figure was one in three; by 1965, it was less than one in five; and by 1980, it had fallen to about one in 20.

This result is both impressive and encouraging. However, we should be cautious, because it is not clear how much of this improvement has been due to the antipoverty program, and how much has been due to the fact that, with technological change and the accumulation of capital, our income has been rising and this has automatically reduced poverty.[2] Furthermore, the present system has been subjected to two major criticisms.

Problems with the present welfare system

These criticisms are that the welfare system (1) creates *undesirable incentives,* and (2) is *very complicated.*

Perverse incentives   It is difficult to design a welfare system without creating perverse incentives. In fact, it is so difficult that the problem of incentives will be one of the main themes in this chapter. We have already noted that aid for dependent children may, in certain circumstances, encourage a parent to desert the family. But the problem of incentives is broader than this.

Consider the public housing program. As we have seen, families pay 25 percent of their income in rent. This means that, for every $1 more they earn in income, they must pay 25

cents more in rent, while the government reduces their subsidy. By itself, this effect on the incentive to work may not be very important. But many of the other subsidy programs in Table 24-2 are also reduced as a family's income rises. When the effect of all these subsidies is taken into account, the accumulated impact on the incentive to work may be very substantial. The poor may well wonder: "Why go to work to earn an additional $1,000 of income, if it means that we will have our food subsidy reduced by, say, $200; our housing subsidy by $250; and our AFDC by $450 (for a total reduction of $900)?

Figure 24-1
How the percentage of the population below the poverty line is shrinking over time
By the poverty standard of the mid-1970s, the proportion of people in poverty has declined steadily.
Sources: The 1929 figure is a rough approximation that follows from the fact that the average real income in 1929 was about the same as the poverty level was defined in the mid-1970s. The 1947 figure is from the Council of Economic Advisers, *Annual Report, 1964.* The 1965 figure is from Congressional Budget Office, *Poverty Status of Families under Alternative Definitions of Income* (Washington, June 1977), pp. xiv–xxv. The most recent figures, along with a number of the other estimates quoted in this chapter, are from Sheldon Danziger, Robert Haveman, and Robert Plotnick, "How Income Transfer Programs Affect Work, Savings and the Income Distribution: A Critical Review," *Journal of Economic Literature,* September 1981. The Bureau of the Census estimate for 1978 is also shown (the white dot). It is higher because it takes account only of cash transfers, but not of income received in kind, such as food and medical services.

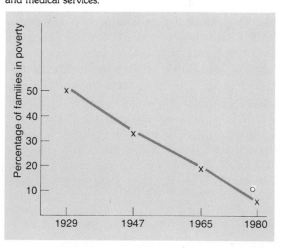

---

[2]If we examine the recent income of U.S. families before taxes and transfers are taken into account, about 20 percent of them are below the poverty line. Taxes and transfers reduce this to only 4–6 percent. This sounds like clear evidence that taxes and transfers drastically reduce poverty. But this conclusion does not follow quite so simply, for the reason already discussed in the previous chapter: If transfer payments did not exist, there would be a greater incentive to work. (Without welfare to fall back on, people would feel under more pressure to get a job. With more people working, there would be *less* than 20 percent initially below the poverty line.) In other words, because taxes and transfers have the indirect effect of reducing incentives to work, they are less effective in reducing poverty than they initially appear.

It's just as though we had to pay a $900 tax on this $1,000 of additional income." Such a family is paying an **implicit tax** of 90 percent on its additional income. But the implicit tax may be even higher than this. If, for example, this family were to lose another $200 of subsidies, the implicit tax in the welfare program would exceed 100 percent; going to work would make them worse off.

The *implicit tax* faced by a family on welfare is the sum of the benefits it loses if it earns another $1 of income. (If its benefits are reduced by 46 cents, the implicit tax is 46 percent.)

Complexity In Table 24-2, two messages stand out clearly: First, a great deal of money is being spent on transfer expenditures. Second, there is a whole set of programs. *Inequity* arises because some families qualify for more of these programs than other equally poor families. By drawing on several of these programs, some poor families are lifted not only to the cutoff poverty level, but above it, while other families are left substantially below it. In some cases, welfare recipients end up with a higher income than some of the workers who pay taxes to support them. (Little wonder that these workers become vocal critics of welfare.) To top it all off, the poor sometimes feel that the welfare workers who administer these programs hold far too much arbitrary power over them; those on welfare are subjected to *hassles* and *humiliation.* In turn, some welfare workers view the programs as a nearly hopeless administrative tangle. On receiving the *Public Assistance Handbook,* former Senator Clifford P. Case declared: "I was appalled to receive a package of regulations weighing almost six pounds, as thick as the Washington, D.C. telephone directory. Leaving the human element aside, this handbook is the best possible evidence that the present welfare program is a bureaucratic nightmare."[3] In view

of these problems, why not replace the whole checkered pattern of policies with a single program that guarantees each family the same minimum income (adjusted, of course, for differences such as family size)?

A GUARANTEED MINIMUM INCOME: A CURE FOR THE POVERTY PROBLEM?

Why not eliminate poverty in one stroke by setting a minimum income at the poverty level? If any family's income were to fall below that level, the government would cover that shortfall with a direct grant. What would this cost? If we add up the shortfall in income of all families below the poverty line, the sum is likely to be substantially less than 1 percent of the U.S. GNP.[4] Considering what we are already spending, why not just commit ourselves to this sort of relatively modest increase in expenditure, and end poverty?

Unfortunately, it is not that easy.

Inefficiencies in a subsidy program

The problem is this: A program that raises the income of the poor by $10 billion costs far more than $10 billion. Waste occurs because such a program has adverse effects on incentives.

Disincentives for those paying for the subsidy The first adverse incentive applies to those who pay the higher taxes necessary to finance this scheme. The heavier the tax rate, the more likely it is that an individual will ask, "Why am I working so hard when the government gets such a large slice of what I earn?" However, studies fail to show as substantial an effect as one might expect. One reason is that although a higher tax makes working less attractive (by reducing the reward), it also makes working more necessary (for anyone trying to maintain previous levels of spending); and these two

---

[3]Quoted in Henry J. Aaron, *Why Is Welfare So Hard to Reform?* (Washington: The Brookings Institution, 1973), p. 11.

[4]In *Equality and Efficiency: The Big Tradeoff* (Washington: The Brookings Institution, 1975), p. 108, Arthur Okun estimated that the shortfall in 1973 amounted to about $9 billion, a figure that was well below 1 percent of GNP.

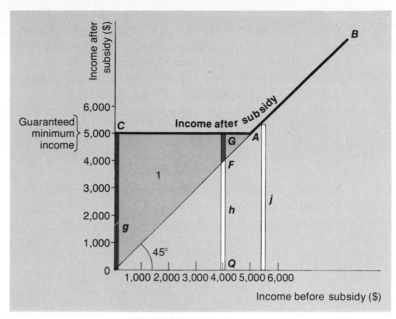

Figure 24-2
Possible disincentive effects of a guaranteed $5,000 minimum income

The 45° line *OAB* is the no-subsidy line. For example, at point *F* on this line, family *h* that earns $4,000 (measured left to right) would end up with $4,000 (measured up). On the other hand, heavy line *CAB* shows income with the subsidy. Family *h* is paid the $1,000 (solid bar) subsidy necessary to raise it to the guaranteed $5,000 level, while family *g* (which earns no income) is paid a full $5,000 subsidy. This program erodes the incentive to work. Why should *h* keep working when he can quit and join *g* and still have his family's income guaranteed at the same $5,000 level? Worse yet, if *j* dislikes his job, why should he keep working? If he quits and also joins *g*, his income will be reduced only slightly (from $5,400 to $5,000).

effects tend to offset each other to some degree. But even though high taxes may not have a large effect on the incentive to work, they do encourage the search for tax loopholes. And as higher-income individuals engage in (or hire lawyers to engage in) socially unproductive efforts to minimize their tax payments, there is a consequent waste imposed on society. As Arthur Okun has described it: "High tax rates are followed by attempts of ingenious men to beat them, as surely as snow is followed by little boys on sleds."[5]

Disincentives for those receiving the subsidy Now let's turn to those at the bottom of the income scale who will receive this subsidy. Here one would expect more substantial incentive effects, for the reasons shown in Figure 24-2. (In this diagram we concentrate on what happens to people at the bottom of the income scale. For simplicity, we disregard any taxes paid now by these people. To simplify further, we use a "round figure" poverty line of $5,000.) Fami-

[5]Okun, *Equality and Efficiency,* p. 97. (This chapter draws heavily on Okun's book.)

lies are plotted along the horizontal axis according to how much income they originally earn. Thus, family *h* with a $4,000 earned income is plotted at point *Q* along the horizontal axis. Income after the implementation of this policy is measured up the vertical axis. If no subsidy were paid to family *h*, its "income after" would also be $4,000, as shown by the white bar. In other words, family *h* would be shown by point *F* on the 45° line, where its before and after incomes are equal. Hence this 45° line may be called the "same-before-and-after" line, or just the "no-subsidy" line.

But, of course, our minimum income program does pay family h a subsidy—specifically, the $1,000 solid bar FG that is necessary to raise its income to the minimum $5,000 poverty level. Since the income of any other family below the poverty line is similarly subsidized up to this $5,000 level, the "income after subsidy" line is the heavy line CAB. Shaded triangle 1 represents the shortfall income gap that the government must fill at an additional cost that we have already noted is likely to run to less than 1 percent of our GNP—*provided people continue to work and earn as much after the subsidy as before.*

The problem is that, because they are being subsidized, some people will *not* work as hard as before. For example, the father of family h may realize: "If I don't work at all, the government will still guarantee us the same $5,000; so why should I work?" And if he stops working, that $4,000 of income he earned disappears. The position of that family on the horizontal axis therefore shifts all the way to the left, from situation h to situation g. At this point, nothing is being earned, that family has become totally unproductive, and it must be subsidized by the full $5,000 solid bar. Therefore, in order to raise this family's income by the original $1,000 shortfall, the government ends up paying out $5,000 (which, of course, it has to raise from the public in taxes). This example illustrates what Arthur Okun referred to as "transferring income with a leaky bucket": Although $5,000 has been spent to increase the income of a poor family, it has increased that income by only $1,000. The other $4,000 has "leaked away" because the family has stopped working. This leakage of the white bar at h also represents the efficiency loss from this policy: The original income this family produced was the $4,000 white bar at h, but this is now lost to society because no one in the family any longer works.

Disincentives that apply to the nonpoor
Disincentive effects may apply not only to poor

families like h with initial incomes below the $5,000 support level; they may also apply to nonpoor families like j with incomes above $5,000. Suppose the breadwinner in family j has been earning the $5,400 shown, in a boring and unpleasant job. The subsidy program will now offer a tempting option: Go fishing, and receive a $5,000 income from the government. If this happens, family j also shifts to the left into position g, where it too qualifies for the full $5,000 subsidy. So the government has to subsidize not only those with initial incomes below the $5,000 poverty level, but *also* some with incomes above the poverty line, for whom this program was never intended.

In short, when the government attempts to fill an income gap by such a simple subsidy, its cost may far exceed the initial income shortfall that it set about to cure. The reason is that the subsidy disturbs incentives, and some people stop working. From the viewpoint of the government paying the subsidy, the problem appears in two forms: On the one hand, some poor families like h may absorb more subsidy than expected; on the other hand, a whole new and unexpected group of families like j may appear on the scene, hat in hand. Moreover, when a family like j goes onto the subsidy program, the overall efficiency loss to society is particularly severe. It is the white bar at j—the $5,400 of income that is no longer produced because someone who used to work is now off fishing.

The reason that this policy is so inefficient is that the portion CA of the "income after subsidy" line is completely horizontal, leaving the poor *no* incentive to work. (The implicit tax they face is 100 percent: They have nothing to show for any additional $1 they earn, because their subsidy is reduced by the same $1.)

Critics charge that, in terms of its antiwork incentives, the present U.S. welfare system is similar to this simple subsidy scheme. In most cases, the present system involves an implicit tax of less than 100 percent, but in some cases it is more. (See Box 24-3.) Thus this guaranteed annual income scheme described in Figure 24-2 can be used (at least in a very rough-and-ready way) to illustrate some of the problems of the current system. But we emphasize: The present system—with its wide variety of programs—cannot be *fully* described by *any* one diagram.

CONFLICTING VIEWS ON WELFARE

Figure 24-2 illustrates why some observers view welfare as the *cure* for society's failure, while others view it as the *cause* of this failure. How can two views be so clearly in conflict?

Economic failure: Is it cured or caused by welfare?

Proponents of welfare programs point to individuals who are disabled or who simply cannot cope. Because they are unable to succeed economically, they are initially left at *g*. The (gray bar) welfare benefits raise them above the poverty line, solving a serious social problem.

On the other hand, welfare critics point to those individuals, initially at *h* or *j*, who respond to welfare by shifting to *g*. According to this view, welfare payments provide potentially productive people with an incentive to stop producing—to stop earning the white bar of income at *h* or *j* and instead go on the dole at *g*. In such cases, welfare creates a social problem.

In practice, a welfare system has *both* effects: It *solves* the poverty problem for people who start at *g*, and it *creates* a problem by inducing some of the people who start at *h* or *j* to move to *g*. In the U.S. system, what is the relative importance of these two effects? In particular, how much does welfare erode the incentive to work? The answer is: apparently not as much as the discussion of Figure 24-2 so far might suggest. Many families at *h* or *j don't* stop working (don't move to the left). Their (white bar) productivity is not lost. Moreover, many people start at *g*. In their case, there is no leak in the bucket at all: Welfare can't reduce their productivity because they don't produce anything in the first place. Thus, the Okun transfer bucket may not be shot through with holes after all. According to a recent "speculative" estimate,

---

BOX 24-3

The Lack of Work Incentives in Our Existing Welfare System

Originally, Aid for Families with Dependent Children (AFDC) involved an implicit tax of 100 percent: If a family earned another $1 of income, its AFDC payment was reduced by $1. Now, however, its AFDC payment is reduced by 40 to 66 cents (depending on the family's income). Although this seems to leave a substantial incentive to work, the poor often qualify for other welfare programs as well. Because most of these are also tied to income, they too involve an implicit tax. Thus, when such programs as Medicaid, food stamps, and housing assistance are also taken into account, the total welfare package involves an implicit tax that frequently exceeds 75 or 80 percent—in some cases even 100 percent.[†] Thus, a poor family that qualifies for several programs may have little or no incentive to work. (Moreover, "reforms" that have been debated by Congress have involved implicit tax rates that sometimes run as high as 120 to 130 percent; families that earn another $1 in income would lose $1.20 or $1.30 in welfare benefits. In this case, they would have a strong economic incentive to stop working.) ■

[†]In practice, these implicit tax rates are very complicated to calculate, and are often sensitive to the income of the recipients. For example, Henry Aaron found that those who received four selected types of assistance in 1972 faced an implicit tax rate that was "high and capricious," running as much as 73 percent in the $4,000 to $8,000 income range, and over 100 percent in the $8,000 to $9,000 range. See Henry J. Aaron, *Why Is Welfare So Hard to Reform?* (Washington: The Brookings Institution, 1973), pp. 33 and 34. In 1977–1978 Aaron was an Assistant Secretary of Health, Education, and Welfare, with responsibility to work on welfare reform.

only about a quarter of welfare payments leak away.[6] But this is still a large leak.

Noneconomic benefits and costs

Not surprisingly, economists focus on the economic consequences of programs such as welfare; for example, how much does the "bucket" leak? But we should recognize that many government programs—such as welfare—also have broader effects on our society.

On the positive side, welfare programs are society's way of stating its commitment to the less fortunate. We would not want to live in a callous nation, which paid no heed to the sick and helpless. By contributing to a humane society, a welfare program can have social gains which go beyond the benefits received by the welfare recipients themselves.

Because of the way in which welfare programs are a symbol of society's values, any flaws in the system can be demoralizing. Critics question whether our welfare system has unintended social costs:

1 One of the many reasons that fathers remain in the home and support their families is the fear of what might happen if they were to leave. If a government welfare program guarantees child support and removes this fear, won't some fathers feel more free to leave? (Worse yet, as we have already seen, some programs like Aid for Families with Dependent Children may provide an incentive for fathers to leave.) Thus, welfare programs may be important in shaping our social structure, and in particular, the family unit.

2 Does welfare encourage a problem it is designed to cure: the "culture of poverty"? Does it encourage dependence and destroy pride and self-respect? Being the breadwinner may be one of the few sources of pride and self-respect left for those with low-paying, no-promise jobs. If welfare provides as adequately for their families as they can, does it make them feel like so much excess baggage and destroy their self-respect?

THE KEY TRADE-OFF: EQUITY VERSUS EFFICIENCY

It all seemed so simple. As we look back over Parts 2 and 3, the following message seemed to be emerging: Where product or factor markets are inefficient, the government should intervene to increase efficiency. (For example, intervene to tax polluters, or to regulate monopoly price.) If this intervention also has favorable equity effects, so much the better; then there are no conflicts, and the appropriate policy choice is a simple one. (For example, it is easy to endorse ending discrimination in the labor market because this increases efficiency and also transfers income equitably to those who have faced disadvantages because of their race or sex.) However, such cases are the exception, rather than the rule; conflicts often do arise. The search for efficiency in product and factor markets does not necessarily lead us to an equitable income distribution. Therefore, to achieve equity, we should rely on direct government transfers rather than inefficient interventions into factor or product markets (like the imposition of an interest rate ceiling).

Unfortunately, it's not so easy after all, because of one weak link in this argument: Direct government transfers may not be very efficient either. In particular, government spending on the poor erodes the incentive to work and reduces national output. So we are still left with the trade-off between the objectives of equity and efficiency: The size of the national pie is reduced if we try to carve it up in a more equitable way.

This is not a recommendation that we go back to transferring income by the inefficient market interventions we have criticized in earlier chapters. Not only are they inefficient. Worse yet, as a means of raising the income of the poor, they are often ineffective. (An interest rate ceiling benefits rich borrowers as well as poor,

[6]Sheldon Danziger, Robert Haveman, and Robert Plotnick, "How Income Transfer Programs Affect Work, Savings and the Income Distribution: A Critical Review," *Journal of Economic Literature,* September 1981.

and in fact, may leave many relatively poor borrowers out in the cold completely. As another example, farm price guarantees benefit the rich farmer without lifting many poor farmers out of poverty.) The message remains: The way to reduce poverty is by direct government policies to aid the poor. But we should be searching for a better way of making these transfers than the simple subsidy programs we have been discussing so far. In particular, we should be seeking a way that is not only *equitable*. We should also be seeking a way that is *efficient*—in other words, that does not destroy the incentive to work.

THE NEGATIVE INCOME TAX: CAN WE COMBINE EQUITY AND EFFICIENCY?

How can we guarantee families a minimum income (for example, $5,000) without destroying their incentive to work? This is an essential question, and it is not an easy one to answer. One proposal is the **negative income tax,** which has been advocated by many of those on both the "left" and "right" of the political spectrum who are critical of the present welfare system. To explain this proposal, let's put our last diagram back on the drawing board in Figure 24-3. This new diagram has the same frame of reference as Figure 24-2, except that it is extended to the right to allow us to take account not only of families that receive a subsidy, but also of higher-income families that pay the government a tax. The 45° "same-before-and-after" line OQB now represents the "no-subsidy, no-tax" line where families would be if the government neither subsidized nor taxed them.

Design of a negative income tax
To see how a negative income tax would work, we begin by assuming, as before, that the minimum income level is set at $5,000. But now, rather than subsidizing incomes just up to the line CA by filling gap 1 as we did in Figure 24-2, the government instead pays subsidies—or "negative taxes"—equal to areas 1 + 2 + 3, thereby bringing incomes up to the heavy line

CQ. (Beyond an income of $10,000, a family pays "positive" taxes to the government, as shown by the red area 4.) By giving the "income-after-tax" line CQH an upward slope, we give people an incentive to work: The more income they earn (the farther they move to the right in this diagram), the more they keep (the higher they rise on line CQ). In this way, we attempt to reduce the leak in the bucket—people quitting work to go on welfare. (Proponents of the negative income tax emphasize that it must replace *all* existing welfare programs, such as food stamps. If some programs remained, their implicit tax in combination with the negative income tax might mean that people were *not* better off by working. They might therefore quit working to draw government benefits.)

The negative income tax should not only improve efficiency. It should also move us toward a greater degree of equity in several ways: (1) It would guarantee a minimum income for all; (2) it would replace the wide variety of existing welfare programs with one consistent policy that would treat all families at the same income level in the same way; and (3) it would also satisfy another equity objective of most Americans —it would leave those who work with a higher income than those who do not.

But this is apparently a very expensive program, since the subsidy is now area 1 *plus* areas 2 and 3. Specifically, the government now provides an even greater subsidy (areas 1 + 2) to poor families earning incomes below the assumed "round figure" poverty line of $5,000. Moreover, it also provides subsidy 3 to nonpoor families with incomes all the way up to $10,000 —roughly one-third of American families in the mid-1970s (the base period of this analysis). Of course, families earning even higher incomes pay a tax. For example, a family earning $12,000 pays the $1,000 tax shown as the red bar *t*. Thus, heavy line CQH shows how the government pays gray subsidies all the way up to point Q, and levies the red tax on incomes above this. (Although this line need not have a constant slope, in our simple example we assume that it does: Any family gets to keep half of

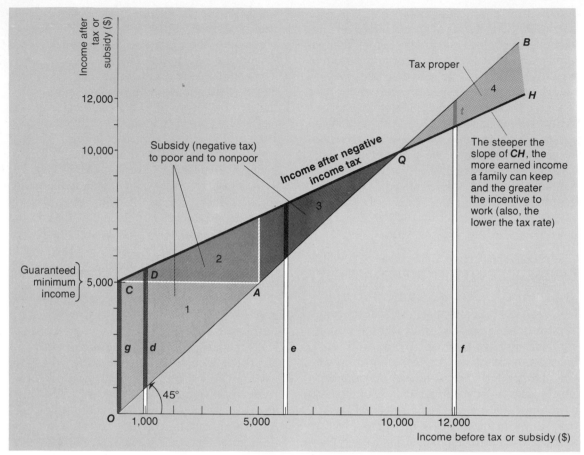

Figure 24-3
How a negative income tax should work
(Compare with Figure 24-2)

Family *g* with a zero earned income is paid the solid bar grant of $5,000. But what do we do with family *d* with $1,000 of earned income? If we make the same mistake we made in Figure 24-2 and raise this income up only to that same $5,000 (by a $4,000 grant), then this will leave that family with no incentive to keep working to earn that $1,000. So to provide an incentive to work, we grant this family $4,500 instead (as shown by the solid bar), thus bringing its total up to $5,500 at point *D*. If we continue in this way, always providing a $500 incentive for families to earn an additional $1,000 of

income, we move up heavy line *CDQ* to cutoff point *Q* where no subsidy is paid. Moreover, if we continue to allow families to keep half of any additional income they earn, we will tax incomes above this level down from *QB* to *QH*. Thus, red area 4 shows us how any income above $10,000 is subject to a tax. (For example, family *f* with a $12,000 income pays the $1,000 tax *t*.) At the same time, gray area 1 + 2 + 3 shows us how any income below $10,000 is subsidized ("taxed in reverse"). Hence the name: negative income tax.

any additional income it earns. In other words, those with earned incomes of less than $10,000 —who are subsidized—face a 50 percent implicit tax; and those with incomes above $10,000 face

a 50 percent regular tax on all income over $10,000.)

Furthermore, the apparent high cost of this program is not limited to just filling new gaps 2 +

3. In addition, the U.S. Treasury loses the taxes previously collected from many nonpoor families in the $5,000 to $10,000 income range. (These families, which are now subsidized, used to pay a tax; the government has now lost this revenue.) And this leads to some extraordinary conclusions. A policy designed to benefit poor families with incomes below $5,000 not only benefits *nonpoor* families in the $5,000 to $10,000 range, but does so for two separate reasons: First, it pays them a subsidy; and second, it relieves them of a previous tax. Moreover, it also reduces taxes of some families in the income range even above $10,000.[7] Benefiting such families was scarcely our objective when we set out to cure poverty incomes below $5,000!

When one takes into account all these considerations, doesn't the negative income tax come out badly in comparison with the simple subsidy scheme in Figure 24-2? Why would anyone recommend it? The answer has already been suggested: It has more favorable built-in incentive effects. The negative income tax should be a far less leaky bucket than a simple subsidy scheme (or our present welfare system). This point is worth considering in detail.

Why the negative income tax should reduce the leaks in the "welfare bucket"

By allowing families to keep half of any additional income they earn, the negative income tax should induce them to get out and earn more, and thus "move to the right" in Figure 24-3. Since this would reduce (and in some cases, perhaps even eliminate) the subsidy some families receive, the cost of this scheme should be less than the gray subsidy area in Figure 24-3 suggests.

Moreover, the cost of this scheme may be reduced even further by modifications. For example, the "after-tax" line *CQH* might be lowered by, say, $1,000. This would maintain the same incentive to work (the same slope of

---

[7] To confirm this statement, consider a family with income just barely over $10,000. In Figure 24-3, it pays a minuscule tax that is less than the tax it used to pay.

CQH), but would substantially reduce the cost (the subsidy areas $1 + 2 + 3$). The one problem is that those at *C* doing no work would now receive less than the $5,000 poverty minimum.

But this problem might be reduced by providing a guaranteed $5,000 income to those who are aged, infirm, or disabled and *cannot* work. If these people can be clearly identified, guaranteeing them a minimum income would result in no inefficiency; it would not affect the amount they work, because they can't work. Such a policy—of identifying specific groups with special needs—is sometimes called *tagging*.[8] The big problem is that, in practice, it is difficult to identify exactly who should be "tagged" as someone who is unable to work. (For example, it is difficult to determine just who is "disabled.") Notice that, if special treatment is given to the disabled in this way, then we have compromised one of the desired objectives of the negative income tax: to treat all families with the same income in exactly the same way. But in this case few would object—especially if we can shift the after-tax line *CQ* down by $1,000, and thus save a lot of taxpayers' money.

The negative income tax does not resolve all conflicts

We can now extend this theoretical discussion of the negative income tax by noting how it gives rise to tension among the following three objectives:

1 Set the minimum income level *(C)* high enough so no one will be left destitute.
2 Give *CQH* enough slope to provide people with a strong incentive to work. (Many would view the slope of *CQH* in Figure 24-3 as being too low and therefore providing inadequate incentive to work. Since people can keep only

---

[8] The advantages of tagging are discussed by George Akerlof in "The Economics of Tagging," *American Economic Review*, March 1978, pp. 8–17. Its major disadvantage is that it provides a perverse incentive for people to get "tagged" and thus qualify for special treatment. (None are likely to blind themselves to get welfare. But some people certainly might falsely argue that they have been disabled because, say, of backaches.)

half of any additional income, they "spend half their time working for the government.")

3 Keep the subsidy areas 1 + 2 + 3 small, in order to keep the cost of the program down and avoid heavily subsidizing the nonpoor.

It is impossible to achieve all these objectives at once, because they are in conflict. For example, the way to achieve the second objective is to make line *CQH* steeper. But a greater slope means that either *C* must be lower or subsidy areas 1 + 2 + 3 must be larger. Thus, objective 2 conflicts with objectives 1 and 3.

While the negative income tax does not resolve all conflicts, it nonetheless does look like a promising approach—at least in theory. Unfortunately, in cases where it has been tested, it has been disappointing in two respects.

The negative income tax in practice: Results of recent experiments

In several recent experiments a number of families have been put on a negative income tax. How have they behaved, compared to families under the present welfare system?

The economic effects The results of the experiments have been disappointing—particularly in Seattle and Denver where the largest, most reliable samples were used. A negative income tax designed to encourage people to work more, in practice seems to make them work less. Instead of reducing the leak in the transfer bucket (estimated at 25 percent for the present welfare programs), the negative income tax increases the leak to an estimated 40 percent to 75 percent.[9] Because recipients work much

less, the negative income tax seems to add as much to their leisure as to their income. The explanation seems to be that the expected positive work incentive is more than offset by three influences that encourage them to work less:

1 Being on a negative income tax eliminates the **hassle** people often encounter when they quit work and go on welfare. Under a negative income tax people feel freer to quit work, and don't search as hard for a new job. If, as seems likely, the Reagan administration tightens welfare regulations, then the current welfare scheme —increased hassle and all—may be even more successful in keeping people on the job.

2 Under a negative income tax system, people can quit their jobs without feeling the social **stigma** faced by those on traditional welfare.

3 When people have participated in the negative income tax experiment, its characteristics have been **clearly explained.** They are told of their rights—in particular, their right to stop working and still continue to receive an income. Consequently, they are more likely to exercise this no-work option simply because they know about it. In contrast, some of those who might draw ordinary welfare stay on the job because they are not so well informed about their options. (Because of the hassle, it may not be clear exactly what their options are.)

Noneconomic effects of the negative income tax Some of these are favorable: For example, there is evidence that a negative income tax may increase the number of adults finishing high school. On the other hand, the 5-year Seattle-Denver experiments indicate that a negative income tax may increase the incidence of marriage breakups by as much as 50 percent. This was another puzzling result because the negative income tax was expected to help keep families together. (For example, it took them off AFDC and its incentive for fathers to leave home.) It isn't entirely clear *why* the negative income tax had this perverse effect; perhaps, once again, it was because participants were fully informed about their options (in this

[9]Using the results of two sets of experiments (one for 3 years, one for 5) in Seattle and Denver, Michael Keeley, Philip Robbins, and others have estimated the leak to be between 38 percent and 58 percent for two-parent families. "Labor Supply Effects and Costs of Alternative Negative Income Tax Programs," *Journal of Human Resources,* Winter 1978, p. 26.

In an unpublished 1981 paper, John Bishop at the University of Wisconsin Institute for Research on Poverty has used only some of the 5-year results, and has estimated that the leak could be as great as 75 percent, or even more.

case, to leave home). If strengthening marriages is viewed as a public policy objective, the negative income tax is a major disappointment, according to evidence now available.[10]

WHERE DO WE GO FROM HERE?

The experimental results so far are not encouraging. Moreover, the longer people stay on this scheme, the worse its effects apparently become: The results from 5-year studies have been worse than for shorter experiments. It has therefore become difficult to argue that this scheme—so promising on the drawing board—is the hoped-for "solution to the welfare problem." Paradoxically, if it is to be introduced, it should probably not be in the hassle-free, stigma-free way that was once viewed as one of its great advantages. Some hassle and stigma seem necessary to ensure that half the world doesn't go fishing.

In the light of these experimental results, economists are now searching for new approaches. One suggestion is a **wage subsidy** that would increase the take-home pay of low-

[10]For more detail on the effect of the negative income tax on marriages, see John H. Bishop, "Jobs, Cash Transfers and Marital Instability: A Review and Synthesis of the Evidence," *Journal of Human Resources*, Summer 1980, pp. 301–323.

income workers. (The subsidy would be higher for workers with more dependents.) Because the government subsidy would come to the family via the worker's paycheck, it might restore the incentive for families to stay together, and increase the worker's pride in having a job and supporting a family. (If a wage subsidy were to replace existing welfare programs, it would also increase the worker's fear of what would happen to the family if he or she were to walk out.) Moreover, it would increase the incentive to work by increasing the take-home wage. [In contrast, under a negative income tax or the present welfare system (with its implicit tax), workers keep only *part* of what they earn.] Finally, by encouraging employment by private firms, a wage subsidy might be used to partially replace present government make-work programs. This in turn should increase productivity, since private employers don't hire people unless there is a productive job to fill; but there is no similar guarantee when the government is hiring as an "employer of last resort."

But this suggestion also is far from being problem-free. A wage subsidy would have to be accompanied by welfare payments to those "tagged" as unable to work because of disability or age. And this in turn means facing one of the most difficult issues in welfare. How do you decide who's in the "tagged" group that doesn't have to work, and how do you keep out others who want to get in?

Key Points

1 Poverty is defined as inadequate income to buy the necessities of life. A specific poverty-line figure is determined by calculating the minimum cost of a nutritious and reasonably edible diet and multiplying that figure by 3. In 1981 the poverty line for a nonfarm family of four was about $8,500. In 1980, 1 in 20 American families were still living in poverty. But this was still a big improvement on the figure of about 1 in 5 in the mid-1960s when the government announced the "War on Poverty."

2 As a result of this war, government income

transfers have increased by almost 10 times when measured in dollars; that is, by about 4 times when adjusted for inflation.

3 Blacks are more likely to be poor than whites, and Southerners more likely than Northerners. The less an individual is educated, the greater the risk of poverty. The problem exists in cities, towns, and farms, with the areas least affected being the suburbs of big cities. Poverty is a serious problem in fatherless families.

4 In the long run, the most promising government antipoverty policies are those that deal with the causes rather than the symptoms of poverty. These policies include subsidizing investment in human capital (both education and on-the-job training), and eliminating discrimination against minorities and women.

5 Government income maintenance programs include social security and unemployment insurance, which are paid to poor and nonpoor alike. But there are also many programs, like Aid to Families with Dependent Children, food stamps, and housing assistance, that are designed specifically for the poor. The problem with these programs is that when the poor earn more income, they face an implicit tax, in the form of a reduction in the subsidies they receive. This implicit tax reduces their incentive to work, thus lowering the nation's output and level of efficiency.

6 The package of present programs is also inequitable. Some of the poor are not lifted up to the poverty line, while others who qualify under several of these programs are lifted above it—indeed, in some cases, even above the income earned by some of the people who pay taxes to support the antipoverty program.

7 Why not, then, replace this present system with a single policy that would lift all the poor up to the same minimum income level? The answer is that the poor, with their incomes thus guaranteed, would have little or no economic incentive left to work. With lost potential output, the economy would operate at a low level of efficiency. Thus, the conflict between greater equality and efficiency persists: As we try to carve up the national pie more equally (by raising the income of the poor), the total size of that pie is reduced.

8 In theory, a negative income is a good method of reducing, but not entirely eliminating, this conflict. Under this policy, families would be allowed to keep part of any additional income they earn. This would leave them with an incentive to work. The program would also guarantee every family a minimum income. Unfortunately, in experiments so far, the negative income tax has been a disappointment. People tend to work less, and their marriages are more likely to break up.

Key Concepts

poverty line
causes of poverty
symptoms of poverty
policies to increase
   human capital
policies to eliminate
   discrimination
Work Incentive Program

Social Security
Unemployment Insurance
Aid to Families with
   Dependent Children
food stamps
public housing
implicit tax
leak in the transfer bucket

guaranteed minimum
   income
noneconomic benefits and
   costs of welfare
tagging
negative income tax
hassle and stigma effects
wage subsidy

Problems

24-1 What is meant by an implicit tax rate of 90 percent? Of 105 percent? What is the effect of such a tax rate?

24-2 Let's review the efficiency losses from our income redistribution policy in Figure 24-2. What is the efficiency loss if this subsidy induces the breadwinner of family *h* to go fishing? The breadwinner of family *j*? What is the efficiency loss if the breadwinner of family *j* takes 1 day off each week to go fishing? What is the efficiency loss from subsidizing a family like *g* that originally earned no income?

If the minimum income level were set at $6,000, rather than $5,000, would the efficiency loss be greater or smaller? Explain.

24-3 Explain to your bright roommate (who is taking economics but hasn't yet reached this chapter) exactly what you mean by a "leaky bucket."

24-4 Let's see if we can't reduce the costs to the government of the negative income tax in Figure 24-3. The incentive to work in that diagram is the $500 a family can keep out of each additional $1,000 it earns. Now suppose that the amount it can keep is reduced from $500 to $300.

(a) Redraw Figure 24-3 to take this into account.

(b) What has happened to the incentive to work?

(c) What has happened to the implicit tax in this welfare proposal?

(d) Are your answers to *b* and *c* related in any way? If so, how?

(e) What has happened to the total amount of subsidy the government pays? (Be careful.)

(f) Has this transfer bucket become more or less leaky?

(g) Now regraph this policy making one further change: Set the poverty level at $4,000, rather than $5,000. Again answer questions *b*, *c*, and *e*. What are the pros and cons of the two policies you have graphed?

24-5 Suppose you are designing a negative income tax. Graph your answers to each of the following questions?

(a) What do you consider a reasonable minimum family income (*OC* in Figure 24-3)?

(b) What do you consider to be the maximum reasonable implicit tax rate? How does the slope of *CQ* in your diagram therefore compare to *CQ* in Figure 24-3?

(c) From your answers to *a* and *b*, calculate the break-even level of income (like the $10,000 at *Q* in Figure 24-3).

(d) Do you think the tax proper (on families to the right of the break-even point *Q*) should be greater or smaller than the implicit tax on families to the left of *Q*?

(e) Explain the possible "public finance problem" in your scheme. In other words, do you think your scheme would make it difficult for the government to collect enough taxes from those to the right of *Q* to cover the costs of subsidizing those to the left of *Q*—and cover other government costs as well? As real incomes rise, would this public finance problem become more serious, or less? Would you agree with the view that we should institute a negative income tax some day, with the only question being how soon we can afford it?

24-6 In economics, experiments (like those on the negative income tax) are seldom possible. Do you think this is a disadvantage? Isn't it possible to establish the effects of a policy using theoretical arguments—rather than experimental evidence? (Use the negative income tax to illustrate your answer.)

CHAPTER 25
Marxism and Marxist Economies

> In proportion as capital accumulates, the lot of the laborer, be his payment high or low, must grow worse.
>
> **Karl Marx, *Das Kapital***

Historically, one of the major criticisms of the free enterprise system has been that it does not distribute income in an equitable way—largely because of the income payments that go to private owners of physical capital ("capitalists"). Moreover, many critics believe that the economic and political power held by capitalists limits the government in its attempts to achieve a more equal and just society. Hence, their solution is to replace our system with one that is fundamentally different—specifically, with a "socialist" system in which capital is owned by the state, and used on behalf of all the people.

This chapter begins with a discussion of the ideas of Karl Marx, whose writings over a century ago have proved to be the most influential and durable criticisms ever leveled against the free enterprise system. This is followed by an examination of the socialist systems of the Soviet Union and Yugoslavia, two illustrations of the many alternative ways in which the philosophy of Karl Marx can be put into practice. Finally, we will have a few brief observations about the Peoples' Republic of China.

KARL MARX

> The capitalist gets rich . . . at the same rate as he squeezes out the labor power of others, and then forces on the laborer abstinence from all life's enjoyments.
>
> **Karl Marx, *Das Kapital***

Today about one-third of the world lives under some form of Marxist-communist economic system. In addition, there are many followers of Marx who do not support any of the existing communist states, but who believe his ideas should be implemented in a different way. Clearly, this means that whether or not Marx was right, he was certainly one of the most influential writers in history.

Marx's criticism of the free market was based on two theories, both accepted by many orthodox economists of his day: (1) the labor theory of value, and (2) the theory that wages tended toward a socially defined subsistence level. According to the labor theory of value, the value of any good is determined by the amount of labor that goes into producing it. (But be careful: As Marx recognized, this value must include both the labor time directly involved in producing the good and the labor time spent on, or "congealed in," the machinery used to produce the good.) Marx then asked: With labor being the source of all value, does it receive the total value of the nation's output in return for its effort? His answer was: No. All that labor receives is a low wage representing only a fraction of what is produced. The rest is **surplus value** that goes to the employer or capitalist (the owner of the capital equipment which labor uses). Marx's conclusion: This surplus value should go to labor. Because it does not, the working class is exploited.

Surplus value and the class struggle

According to Marx, the exploitation of the proletariat (workers) by the bourgeoisie (capitalists) results in a **class struggle.** He urged workers to organize themselves to fight this struggle. In his words, "Let the ruling classes tremble at a Communist revolution. The proletarians have nothing to lose but their chains. They have a world to win. Working men of all countries, unite!"[1] In his view, the capitalist class would continue to accumulate more and more capital and use it to exploit labor more and more. Thus there would be ". . . an accumulation of misery, corresponding to the accumulation of capital." Marx's cure was a revolution (which he viewed as inevitable[2]), in which the workers would seize power and abolish the ownership of capital by private individuals: "By despotic inroads on the rights of property [workers would] centralize all instruments of production in the hands of the State."[3] Finally, after this new **socialist** system has been firmly established, the state will wither away, leaving Marx's ideal **communist society.**

Socialism is an economic system in which the "means of production" (capital equipment, buildings, and land) are owned by the state.[4]

In countries like the Soviet Union, *communism* means an ideal system in which all means of production are owned by the community as a whole, with all members of the community sharing in its work and income. The Soviet Union makes no claim to having achieved communism. Rather, it claims to be working "through socialism towards communism."

In the West, communism has a quite different meaning. It refers to the present economic and political system of countries like the Soviet Union.

How the critic has been criticized

Marx's critics have pointed out that a number of his predictions have proven false. For example, there is little evidence that any existing governments, such as that of the Soviet Union, are withering away, even though the Soviet state has existed for 65 years. The idea that the state

---

[1]Karl Marx and Friedrich Engels, *Manifesto of the Communist Party* (Peking: Foreign Languages Press, 1975), p. 77. Note that Marx went far beyond an analysis of economic forces to prescribe what should be done to change them. (Marx and the Marxists strongly deny the suggestion by some economists that a "value-free" economics is possible.)

*[2]If this revolution is the inevitable result of an historical process governed by unchangeable economic laws—as Marx believed—what's the point of exhorting workers to struggle hard to achieve it? One possible answer: Even an inevitable event may be speeded up.

[3]Marx and Engels, *Communist Manifesto,* p. 59.

[4]"Socialism" has become an emotion-laden word that is now used loosely in a wide variety of meanings. To the campus radical, it is a tool for attacking the shortcomings of American society. To the American millionaire, it is a plot to deprive the wealthy of their hard-earned fortunes. To the Swedish politician, it means a mixed economic system, combining substantially free markets and a large degree of private ownership with a highly developed social welfare system. To Nobel prizewinner Friedrich Hayek, it represents a tragic step along "the road to serfdom." To the British Fabian Socialist, it means the gradual evolution of a more humane economy, with a more equal distribution of income. With such diversity on the meaning of socialism, it is little wonder people have difficulty in debating its virtues and vices.

would "wither away" ranks as one of the most curious in the history of economic and political thought. One need not be as cynical as Lord Acton ("Power corrupts; absolute power corrupts absolutely") to doubt that those who have struggled for power will be prepared to give it up voluntarily.

Indeed, the most significant single weakness of Marxism, in the view of a number of its sympathetic critics,[5] is that it provides enormous political power to individuals without providing adequate ways to control them—such as free elections in which the public can throw them out. (Voting yes or no to a single slate of candidates is obviously not enough.) Thus Marxism provides inadequate restraints against the ruthless exercise of power by a ruler like Joseph Stalin. The majority of Marxists now reject Stalin as an aberration that no better reflects true Marxism than the Holy Wars reflected Christianity. While there may be some truth in this defense, we should be careful with it. Specifically, it is inappropriate to argue, as Marxists sometimes do, that *every* Marxist failure (like Joseph Stalin) is not true Marxism, while *every* capitalist failure proves that this system is corrupt.

And the principal point remains: There were in fact no controls in the Soviet system to prevent Stalin from rising to the top and, worse yet, from staying there. Nor are there safeguards against the accumulation of power by more recent Soviet leaders. Thus, Marxism is paradoxical: While it promises greater political freedom, it delivers less. Although a Marxist society is initially revolutionary, it may tend eventually to become very conservative, with the leaders viewing their prime objective as maintaining their own personal power—that is, maintaining the status quo.

Another criticism of Marxism is that, as capital has accumulated in capitalist economies, there has not been the accumulation of misery that Marx predicted. Quite the contrary: Misery has been reduced. And for good reason: Over the long run, the accumulation of capital has raised the demand for labor, and thus has raised, rather than lowered, the wage rate.[6] (Remember: Workers driving bulldozers are paid more than workers with shovels.)

Still, there is a gap between what the nation produces and what labor is paid. We have referred to it as payments to other factors of production. Marx called it surplus value. In particular, he focused his attack on the payments going to owners of capital. Was he justified in dismissing these payments as simply the exploitation of labor?

How are capital costs to be covered?

Here we must be careful. Part of the cost of capital is the payment for the labor time spent on producing machinery. As Marx recognized, this is an appropriate payment to labor; therefore it is not surplus value. But Marx did regard as surplus value the interest and profit paid to those who provide the funds to finance investment. Remember: Investment requires that someone,

[5]For example, see Robert Heilbroner, *Marxism for and Against* (New York: Norton, 1980).

[6]While many Marxists concede that workers' income has risen in *absolute* terms, they reinterpret Marx's prediction to mean that workers would become poorer, not in any absolute sense, but *relative* to other classes in society. But even this weaker claim is difficult to support from historical data.

Another argument that Marxists make is that although capitalists may have been unable to exploit labor in Europe and North America to the degree that Marx predicted, they have succeeded in exploiting labor in the less developed countries (LDCs), which have become the modern economically subjugated proletariat. While there is not space here to discuss this issue in detail, we cite two reasons why we should be skeptical of any general charge that we exploit the LDCs when we do business with them. First, our investment in the LDCs is not, as sometimes supposed, a "zero-sum game" in which they lose what we gain. Instead, foreign investment often provides both a profit to investors and benefit to the host countries, where foreign investors bid up wages and pay out part of their profits in taxes to host governments. Second, our trade with the LDCs isn't a zero-sum game either. As we saw in the discussion of comparative advantage in Chapter 16, it is quite likely that both parties gain from trade. (In particular, beware of the argument that we exploit the LDCs when we trade more with them, and that we also exploit them when we trade less with them—for example, when we impose high tariffs on their goods.)

somewhere, defers consumption. And in our system, interest is a reward to those who voluntarily defer consumption.

The Marxist contention is that it is precisely the interest and profit payments that make our system inequitable. Moreover, Marxists maintain, it is possible to set up a system without an interest rate incentive: The government simply ensures that people defer consumption by taxing away part of their income, and uses the proceeds for investment. Then the ownership of capital is held by the state on behalf of the people, rather than by capitalists.

While communism may achieve Marx's objective of ending income payments to capitalists, it raises several new problems. First, raising investment funds by such a system of involuntary saving (that is, by taxes) may "hurt" more than our system of voluntary savings. Under our system, people can save during the most convenient periods, and need not save during the periods when it is most difficult. Under a Marxist system, they are forced to save during all periods of their taxpaying lives; taxes must be paid, no matter how much they hurt.

Second, can investment decisions made by government officials in a communist state be as flexible and innovative as decisions made by the owners of capital in a free enterprise system?

Investment decisions

To invest wisely, two of the questions that must be answered are: (1) Should existing types of plant and equipment be expanded? And (2) what *new* products and processes should be developed? Owners of capital have a much greater incentive to ask the second question in our system than they have in the Soviet Union. (In your study of how the two systems compare, ask yourself: Which of our innovations are the Soviets using? And which of their innovations are we using? If you consider that unfair because of the U.S. head start, compare the Soviet Union with Italy or Japan.)

Consider the practical problems communist countries encounter in allocating investment funds across the economy, as they do when drawing up a 5-year plan. To illustrate, first consider what happens in our free enterprise system if there is a major new discovery of, say, copper ore in Montana. To finance its development, the companies involved increase their borrowing (or issue new stock), and the interest rate rises slightly. In response to this, marginal investments elsewhere in the nation are cut back. Thus, funds for this development are raised from all over the country, as a result of a large number of individuals and firms reacting to a market interest rate. In comparison, what occurs in a communist country that, 6 months ago, set its 5-year investment targets for each sector? Do the planners sit down and go through the planning process all over again? For a big enough discovery, they might. But for a less significant one, they might simply say: Let's wait until the next planning period to develop it.

Any society must have some mechanism to determine which investments are undertaken, and which are not. In our economy, the interest rate and expected profits are the mechanism: They are used to direct funds to the high-return investments, not to the low-return ones. While this system is far from perfect, it does provide a framework within which to make choices. Recognizing this, central planners now quietly make their interest-like calculations after all. (Nevertheless, major blunders are still made. A contributing factor in Poland's economic difficulties was the construction of a $5 billion steel mill in a poor location—the home town of party secretary Edward Gierek. True, politicians anywhere may thus "feather their own nest"; but it's potentially a more serious problem in a Marxist economy where most capital is state owned and controlled by government officials.)

The role of profit

Normal profit may be viewed as a return to capital, like the interest rate (the big difference being that one is paid to equity capital while the other is paid to debt capital). But above-normal profit is an additional return. In a free enterprise economy, it goes to entrepreneurs. Is this justified? To cast light on this issue, consider two kinds of above-normal profit—monopoly profit, and profit from a successful innovation.

Above-normal monopoly profit   Many non-Marxist economists would agree that this sort of profit should be reduced or eliminated by "trust-busting" or regulation. But Marxists charge that we are naive if we believe that we can effectively deal with monopoly in our present economic and political system. The reason, Marxists argue, is that in our system, monopolists can translate their economic power (money) into political power (votes) via political campaign contributions. And this power allows them to thwart antimonopoly action. In short, our elected officials are too often committed to the interests of the rich and powerful, rather than to the interests of the public. Thus, Marxists contend, the only effective way to deal with this problem is to change the system and to prevent the accumulation of wealth that makes such political corruption possible.

There is, of course, an element of truth in this criticism—more, perhaps, than we like to admit. But the question is one of alternatives: If a system is to be set up based on the "public interest," how is that elusive concept to be defined? What better way is there to define it than by elections? It is scarcely satisfactory to say that the communist party by definition represents the will of the people. (The Communist Party of the Soviet Union is also known as the Bolshevik Party; literally, the majority party. It has consistently taken the view that it *automatically* represents the majority. This is one reason why the Soviet Union was so unhappy about the Polish government's recognition of the Solidarity union: Such an independent union implies that the communist party does not invariably represent the interests of the workers.) In Western countries, the prevailing view is that it is far better to let voters choose among two or more alternative political parties; it is better to reform our existing political system than to replace it.

Above-normal profit from innovation   In our system, there are various kinds of innovation that may allow a firm to earn an above-normal profit. Perhaps it has developed a new product that better satisfies consumers. True, in the long run, such above-normal profit may disappear as competing firms follow suit. Nonetheless, this profit still provides the incentive that keeps business innovating and responding to changing tastes. In short, the opportunity for profit is what makes our system go; it determines what will be produced and how. We tax away part of profits, but not all; some incentive to innovate is left. However, many Marxists take the view that although this profit system may have worked well enough in our early stages of development,[7] it is no longer satisfactory. The whole incentive system should be changed and the economy directed in some other way. Precisely how, of course, is the big question.

This question is not answered by Marx's recommendation: "From each according to his ability; to each according to his need." This sounds fine in theory, but in practice it is a totally impractical guideline: If individuals define their own needs, the sum will always outrun a nation's ability to produce. Alternatively, if needs are defined by someone else, two questions remain: Who is to decide? And, How does that person decide who needs what? (In the Soviet Union, the guideline was modified to: "From each according to his ability; to each according to his *work*." Work is interpreted not only in terms of time and effort expended, but also in terms of what is accomplished: Musicians and politicians get much higher incomes than equally hardworking bricklayers.)

THE COMMAND ECONOMY OF THE SOVIET UNION

The first country to attempt to put Marx's philosophy into practice was the Soviet Union, and for almost 30 years it was the only communist nation of any significance.

In 1917, the repressive and decaying czarist

---

[7]In the *Communist Manifesto,* Marx and Engels expressed great admiration for the growth capacity of capitalism, which in the preceeding 100 years "created more massive and colossal productive forces than have all preceding generations together."

Table 25-1
How the Soviet System of Public Ownership and Central Planning Differs from Our System

Basic issues	Soviet system	Modified free enterprise
1. Is ownership of productive assets held by the state or by private individuals?	State ownership (with some exceptions; for example, in parts of agriculture and retail trade)	Private ownership (with exceptions like the post office, some utilities, and some transport systems)
2. How are prices and outputs determined?	Largely by central planning agency	Largely in individual markets, in response to profit motive
3. How much freedom of choice do consumers have?	In theory, free choice in spending income; but in practice, items of desired style, size, etc., may be difficult to obtain	Essentially free choice in spending income, with producers more responsive to a wide variety of tastes

regime in Russia was overthrown by a moderate group led by Kerensky; in turn, Kerensky was overthrown by a small, militant group led by Lenin, a Marxist revolutionary. (The Germans, intent on destroying Russia as an enemy in the First World War, had transported Lenin from his exile in Switzerland, across Germany to the Russian border.) Lenin's control was consolidated when the Red Army defeated the White Russians in a bitter civil war, and turned back an invasion by Western countries trying to purge Russia of its new communist regime. It was only then that Lenin and the other communist leaders could start to think about the design of a new kind of economy.

As it has developed, that economy has differed from ours in two major respects: (1) Productive assets are predominantly owned by the state rather than by individuals; and (2) many production decisions are made by a central authority. Our discussion of each of these is summarized for easy reference in Table 25-1.

Public versus private ownership
In the United States, the basic pattern is private ownership—with some exceptions (for example, school buildings, and public works like the Tennessee Valley Authority). In the Soviet Union, in contrast, the basic pattern is public ownership, with some exceptions. For example, some retail businesses are privately owned. In addition, over one-third of the houses in cities and virtually all houses on farms are privately owned. Moreover,

private ownership in agriculture extends beyond housing. For example, each family working on a collective farm can use a small plot of land and the livestock and equipment to go with it. Finally, of course, personal assets like clothing and household tools are privately owned.

But otherwise, assets in the Soviet Union are predominantly owned by the state. These assets include the "means of production" that, in Marx's view, were used to exploit labor: factories and industrial machinery, natural resources, and transport and banking facilities.

Central planning in the Soviet economy
The second big difference in the two systems is that the important decisions on what will be produced in the Soviet Union are made by a central planning agency (Gosplan). In comparison, in our economy most such decisions are made by individual producers responding to a profit incentive. (But not all: A number of our production decisions, such as the number of schools or military aircraft to be built, are made by federal, state, or local governments.)

In a complex planning process, the Soviet government decides on a 5-year plan which establishes the desired rate of growth, including the necessary investment for that growth. Within this broad framework, a more detailed plan is drawn up for each year, specifying output targets throughout the economy. This decision is not made in a completely arbitrary way by government planners: Instead, it is the result of an elaborate set of consultations, in which each firm and industry suggests amendments to its targets. Nonetheless, these targets are eventually set by the planners, and each plant manager is given a specific quota to fulfill. And, as in our system, the manager will face an array of incentives (bonuses, promotions, etc.)[8] to reach or exceed the quota and to make a profit. Profits do exist in the Soviet Union, and can be calculated just as in our economy. But profits tend only to be a piece of accounting information and are often not even a very meaningful one at that, since they are calculated from output and input prices that are set by planners and may not mean too much. The point is that *profits do not provide the same incentive to produce as in our system: Therefore, they do not play the same key role in allocating resources.* To illustrate: The central planners may decide to contract an activity that is profitable in order to expand one that is unprofitable—a pattern exactly the opposite of what normally happens in our system. Thus, the plant manager tends to be a hired official carrying out a directive of what to produce (and occasionally offering advice), rather than an entrepreneur making decisions about what output will be.

The surprising thing about such a highly complicated planning system is not that it sometimes works badly, but that it works at all. Consider the problem that arises if the planners increase the target for steel, to be used in building bridges. Because steel production requires machinery, the machinery target must

also be increased. But machinery production requires steel, so the steel target must be increased again. In turn, this results in a second-round increase in the machinery target, and so on, and on. Because steel is an input for machinery production and machinery is an input for steel production, one target cannot be set without regard to the other. Moreover, this interdependence illustrates only the simplest possible "loop" in the economic system. In reality, a complex economy like that of the Soviet Union is characterized by a myriad set of much more complicated loops, with the output of one industry being used directly or indirectly as an input of almost all the others. Thus, one industry's target cannot be set in isolation.

It is sometimes assumed that if there are economic problems, they can be solved by planning. Some may be solved, but others cannot; moreover, the act of planning introduces a number of problems of its own. In theory, it should be possible to "get the plan right"—that is, to come up with a consistent set of outputs —by having computers solve an appropriate set of equations (like the input-output equations developed by Wassily Leontief at Harvard). But in practice, the economy is too complex and unpredictable to be adequately managed this way, and bottlenecks frequently occur. What happens if the production of steel is inadequate to meet the needs of the machinery industry and other steel-using industries? Such a bottleneck would raise even greater problems for Soviet planners if they did not have the power to impose a very simple solution: In the face of a shortage, let consumers do without. If steel is in short supply, use it to produce industrial machinery rather than home refrigerators. With this set of priorities, it is no surprise that Soviet performance in heavy industry is better than in consumer goods and housing.

Growth in the Soviet economy

The example just given is but one reflection of the Soviet emphasis on industrial growth at the expense of the consumer. In addition, planners impose a high growth rate by diverting a large proportion of income away from consumption

---

[8]There is no shortage of incentives in the Soviet system. In fact, incentives for individual workers in the Soviet Union are similar to (and sometimes exceed) those available to American workers. Russian workers are paid higher wages in some occupations than in others. Moreover, high piecework rates (that is, payments according to the number of units produced) are more common as an incentive in the Soviet Union than in the United States. Often, highly productive workers are granted tangible rewards, such as free, government-financed holidays. And there are other incentives which may seem odd to us but appear to have a certain appeal in the Soviet Union; for example, highly productive workers are decorated and cited as "Heroes of Socialist Labor."

and into investment. Since investment accounts for about 30 percent of GNP in the Soviet Union—or almost twice as high a percentage as in the United States—it is no surprise that Soviet growth has exceeded that of the United States: Between 1960 and 1974, Soviet growth was 4.9 percent per year, compared with 3.8 percent in the United States. However, recent Soviet growth, like that of the West, has been disappointing; and the Soviets do not have an oil problem, which has been a cause of our poor performance.

We therefore conclude that the historically higher growth rate in the Soviet Union must be interpreted with care. It reflects the fact that Soviet leaders have had the political power to divert a large percentage of income from consumption into investment. It does not necessarily prove that the communist system is a relatively efficient way of generating growth. To illustrate this point: Japan is a noncommunist free-market economy that has been investing roughly the same large 30 percent slice of its GNP, and Japanese growth has far exceeded that of the Soviet Union. (One argument used to explain relatively rapid growth in both the Soviet Union and Japan is that it has been "catch-up" growth, which is easier because a country can copy advanced technology developed elsewhere. Growth becomes more difficult to achieve when the country becomes a world leader and has to develop its own technology.)

The principal way Soviet planners divert income away from consumption is by imposing a tax on consumer goods that accounts, on average, for about one-third of their price. The Soviets have found this tax to be a useful device in at least two respects: First, they have at times made the overall tax system more progressive by raising the tax on luxuries and lowering it on necessities. (At other times, they have made the tax system more regressive by doing the opposite.) Second, this tax finances the heavy Soviet level of investment and takes money out of the hands of the public, thus reducing consumer purchasing power. Consequently, the problem of shortages of consumer goods is reduced, though not avoided.

The position of the Soviet consumer

Consumers tend to be the forgotten people in the Soviet system—although their lot has been gradually improving. We have already seen how they are forced—via heavy taxation—to sacrifice current consumption to finance rapid growth; and how they are also forced to shoulder much of the burden of inefficiency when bottlenecks develop. But there is another cost in the Soviet command economy that consumers also have to bear. To understand it, consider again the Soviet plant manager whose major concern is to satisfy a given output target of, say, nails. If planners have set his quota in terms of tons, the manager can most easily satisfy it by producing large nails.[9] On the other hand, if that quota is defined as a certain number of nails, the manager will produce mostly small ones. In neither case will this nail production satisfy the consumer, who wants a selection of various kinds. Of course, the consumer may be able to make a wrong-sized nail do in a pinch. But what does a person with big feet do if shoe producers meet their quota by concentrating on small sizes? By the mid-1970s, the plight of the consumer (detailed in Box 25-1) was still one of the major weaknesses of the Soviet system.

Recently, Soviet leaders have, with mixed success, been paying more attention to consumers. For example, auto production has been raised substantially, in cooperation with the Italian automaker, Fiat. The result is the rugged but technologically backward Lada, which is sold on world markets at bargain prices, but is very expensive for Soviet purchasers.

(However, in comparing Soviet prices with ours, one must beware: Heavy government subsidies provide Soviet citizens with bargain housing and free medical care. Since these subsidies are paid out of taxes on other goods, the prices of other goods tend to be relatively high. Standard-of-living comparisons therefore

---

[9]In a very old cartoon in the Russian periodical *Krokodil*, about 100 men are pulling a cart laden with a huge nail 100 yards long. When a bystander asks: "What is it for?" the reply is, "We don't know, but it fulfills our complete quota of 50 tons of nails."

BOX 25-1
A Shopper's Guide to the Soviet Union†

Shopping in the Soviet Union is often a lottery. The stores seem well stocked, but typically with inferior or out-of-fashion items that nobody wants. When attractive goods arrive they are quickly snapped up. Long lines immediately form as passersby queue up, sometimes without even asking what's on sale. (They find that out later; sometimes nobody in the last 20 or 30 yards of a lineup will yet know.) When you get to the head of the line chances are you may have to deal with rude sales clerks, who know that you will buy anyway and who may be getting even for the frustrations they face in doing their own shopping. But all this you disregard in order to buy for yourself, your friends, your parents and your cousins.

Buying this way involves a lot of luck and a lot of good management. Shoppers know by heart the sizes and color preferences of relatives and friends; they carry a lot of cash, because credit cards and cheques aren't used, and one never knows where lightning will strike next. To be ready, women carry a bag called an *avoska,* which is derived from the Russia word for "maybe." Remember the 1973–1974 and 1979–1980 gasoline lines in some parts of the United

States? It's like this for many goods in the Soviet Union at any time and in any region of the country. Soviet citizens have lined up through a freezing December night just to get on an 18 month long waiting list to buy a car, and viewed themselves as lucky when they succeeded. Thus the efficiency loss in this centrally planned system includes not only the loss because consumers often get inferior products; it also includes the loss because consumers waste time in queues. The Soviet press estimates that the public spends 30 billion hours in line per year—a waste equal to having 15 million unemployed.

When this wasted time in line is taken into account, it means there is "disguised inflation"— goods cost more than the price the public pays for them. ■

†This box draws heavily on Hedrick Smith, *The Russians,* chap. II (New York: Quadrangle–New York Times Book Co., 1976).

depend on how much bargain housing and medical services individuals acquire compared to their purchase of more expensive goods. Unfortunately, because of a housing scarcity, the average Soviet urban dweller doesn't get much housing—only about one-third as much as the typical American, or one-half the Western European average.)

The interplay of economic and political systems

The Soviet system of political dictatorship is quite consistent with Marx's prediction that the overthrow of the capitalist system would be followed by a "dictatorship of the proletariat." One of the interesting questions to consider is whether a centrally planned economy like the Soviet system would work at all with the degree of political freedom that we enjoy. The more economic commands issued by a central authority, the more dictatorial a system generally becomes.

This is an important issue, because a major Soviet criticism of our system—one that contains considerable truth—is that economic power corrupts political institutions. But if the Soviets' alternative economic system leads to an even worse form of government, what sort of cure is that?

Better macroeconomic balance?

The Soviets seem to be able to do a better job of curing unemployment than we do, since they can set their target outputs at a level to closely approximate full employment. But, while they face less overt (obvious) unemployment, they have a greater problem with "disguised" unemployment; that is, workers on the job who seem to be producing something, but who are in fact contributing little or nothing to the national product. An example is the labor used to produce undersize shoes that never get worn. While this may appear to be productive employment, it is, in fact, wasted effort. An oft-cited failure of the U.S. economy was Ford's decision in the 1950s to introduce the Edsel automobile. Its failure represented a loss not only to Ford, but to the nation as a whole in terms of wasted resources. In the Soviet Union, such a failure would not have occurred. Instead, the public would have bought the Edsel. It might not have been quite what people wanted, but they would have not had much choice. In the United States, an incorrect decision results in a loss to producers and short-run unemployment in an industry; both of these can be identified and evaluated. On the other hand, a similarly erroneous deci-

sion in the Soviet Union results in a loss to consumers that may not be so obvious and so easy to measure, but may be just as real.[10] And this suggests another question to keep in mind when comparing the Soviet and American systems: Do Edsel-type goods still exist in the Soviet Union, or are they disappearing?

Which is the worse problem—the Soviets' disguised unemployment, or our overt unemployment? Our problem may be less damaging in the long run, because it is obvious to all. Therefore, a government is brought under pressure to reduce it. (There may be no similarly strong pressure in the Soviet Union to reduce disguised unemployment, precisely because it *is* disguised and therefore may go unrecognized.) However, in another respect, the Soviet problem of disguised unemployment may be less damaging: The individuals involved are at least working, and hence *feel* productive even though they

---

[10]Or is it? After all, what difference does it make whether the public is driving an Edsel or a Mercury? In terms of basic transportation, they were quite similar cars; the main difference was in styling. This brings into focus again a fundamental criticism of our free enterprise system: What is the point of satisfying existing consumer desires when they are the result of advertising and the other methods producers use to manipulate consumers?

As pointed out earlier, this is an argument that sounds good, but in practice raises serious problems. First, who is to say which desires are basic, and which are contrived? (In the last analysis, almost everything, from good music to dill pickles, is an acquired rather than a "basic" taste.) Second, although we may wish to reform advertising and the other means that are used to influence tastes, what is wrong, at any point in time, in satisfying *existing* consumer desires? This approach may not be ideal, but isn't it better than having someone or some group decide on what our desires should be?

Our democratic political system provides an interesting parallel. It is set up to respect the public's existing political preferences, even though they may have been formed by political parties using advertising and other forms of "manipulation." This may not, in theory, be an ideal system, but in practice we judge it better than a system in which "basic" or "ideal" political preferences are determined for the public by some individual or group.

are not. So its psychological and social effects may be less serious.

The other major macroeconomic problem—inflation—is often also disguised in the Soviet Union (Box 25-1).

Are the two systems becoming more similar?

It is frequently suggested that our free enterprise system and the Soviet command economy are converging, for several reasons. First, we have been attempting through our tax and welfare system to reduce income differences. At the same time, the Soviets have been allowing large differences in income to creep back into their system, as they strive to increase production by providing incentives. Thus scientists receive a much higher income than clerks, and skilled workers earn much more than unskilled workers.[11] As a result, human capital is becoming a significant source of income difference in the Soviet Union, as well as in the United States. (Recall Jacob Mincer's evidence, that about 60 percent of American income differences are due to human capital.) Because of the growing importance of *human capital,* a socialist policy that deals only with *physical capital* (by putting it in the hands of the state) can, at best, provide no more than a partial solution to the problem of serious income inequality. This raises the question: Will the appeal of socialism to those who believe in equalizing incomes become less strong than in Marx's day?

A second respect in which the Soviet and American economic systems are becoming more similar is that our government is intervening more in production decisions, while the Soviet government may be intervening less. Why is our government intervening more? With economic growth, there is an increase in spillover costs like pollution and these require government control. Also, with our increased income, we are better

---

[11]In fact, the differences in wages are even more pronounced in the Soviet Union than in the United States. But this is a bit misleading because many Soviet services (like medical care) are free, and many others (like housing) are heavily subsidized. As a result, the real incomes of Soviet citizens are more equal than simple wage comparisons suggest.

able to afford the things governments provide, including not only public goods (like highways and parks), but also welfare payments (like Medicaid and Aid to Families with Dependent Children).

At the same time, the Soviet government seems to be moving at least some distance away from their highly controlled, planned economy to a less centralized system that depends more on the market. Since the mid-1960s, the Soviet government has introduced a number of reforms along the lines suggested by E. Liberman of Kharkov University. These reforms are designed to increase the efficiency of the Soviet system by making producers more concerned with providing the goods that consumers want and less concerned with merely fulfilling production quotas. For example, producers can now take orders from customers specifying the color, size, and style of a product; and managers who produce shoes of an unwanted size or style are penalized if their product cannot be sold. This decentralization of decisions (from planners to individual producers taking orders from the public) has brought production more closely in line with consumer demand (although, as Box 25-1 indicates, the Soviets still have a long way to go). Moreover, they also seem to be turning more to the profit motive as a way of stimulating production, with a firm's management now being given some limited authority to change price. Ironically, in attempting to offset the post-Afghanistan U.S. embargo on grain sales to the Soviet Union, Moscow announced on May Day, 1980, that there would be a new profit incentive provided to those delivering Soviet-grown grain. (May Day—May 1—is a traditional workers' holiday.)

But, despite this evidence of Soviet-American convergence, great differences in philosophy and practice remain. One important question in the future will be: How far will the Soviets go in decentralizing their system and making it more sensitive to the market? (Some clues may be provided in the next section where we consider the case of Yugoslavia, a communist economy that has been designed to respond to pressures of the marketplace.)

Concluding observations on the Soviet system

The ability of Soviet leaders to impose high taxes has provided substantial resources for investment, and Soviet heavy industry has developed rapidly. But the Soviet system has performed poorly in the many areas where decentralized decision-making is the key to success. Nowhere is this more true than in agriculture, into which the Soviets pour more than 25 percent of their investment—about five times as much as in the United States. Yet despite this, Soviet agricultural productivity remains low. The principal problem is the organization of labor into collective farms where individuals have little incentive to work or innovate. (As much as a quarter to a third of the nation's total agricultural output is produced on the minuscule 2 percent of the Soviet farm land that is privately owned, where individuals are rewarded for hard work and initiative.) Soviet leaders have often attributed poor harvests to the weather, but grain was exported from these same lands before the First World War. (Some critics quip that, since 1917, the Soviet Union has announced a poor harvest due to bad weather 64 times.)

The same sort of problems have dogged the Soviets' efforts over the last 50 years to close the technology gap. True, they have made giant strides. As early as 1957 they were graduating 80,000 engineers to America's 29,000. And now they are world leaders in a number of fields, from theoretical mathematics to applied areas such as oceanography and polar research. Moreover, Soviet scientists developed the most promising line of research for the harnessing of nuclear fusion power. But they have not been successful in getting innovation across the board in a society that rewards caution and conformity, rather than risk taking. Soviet technology has lagged in important areas, such as computers and other electronics.

It is not only the political leaders, concerned with maintaining power, who become devoted to the status quo. Plant managers do also, and resist experimenting with promising but risky new techniques because this may make it difficult for them to meet their quotas. Indeed, they may even resist *proven* risk-free innovations or style changes because introducing them will temporarily reduce their production and make their quotas more difficult to achieve. This preoccupation with meeting quotas affects quality: A plant manager with a quota of 20 trucks may decide to produce 20 that won't run well rather than 15 that will. The chemical industry reportedly had problems with corrosion because the firms that made its pipe wouldn't convert from metal to plastics. (During the conversion period they would have been unable to achieve their quota.) In short, the Soviet economy is not a flexible, innovative one. The Soviets are better at building big factories than at running them efficiently.

Problems of quality, preoccupation with quotas and the heavy diversion of resources by the state from consumption into investment all mean that the consumer is the odd man out. And this is one of the reasons why the Soviets have not, after all, achieved their objective of income equality. The elite not only receive a higher income; they also get to spend it on Black Sea resorts and in special stores which stock highly desirable items such as the French perfume and Yugoslavian toothpaste that are unavailable to the general public. So the Soviets, like us, do not have complete equality. But they reply that they are far closer to it than we are, because huge accumulations of wealth cannot be passed on from generation to generation. But there is a kind of wealth that is increasingly important that *can* be passed on: human capital. By arranging the best education and careers for their children, the Soviet elite pass on their privileged status.

However, as we have already noted, many Marxists in the West would argue that the Soviet Union is an example of communism gone wrong, not of any fundamental weaknesses in communism itself. The degree to which you accept this claim is a matter of judgment, on which you will have to decide for yourselves. But before doing so, it is enlightening to consider the case of Yugoslavia, a communist country in which there is less accumulation of power by the central authority.

THE SOCIALIST MARKET ECONOMY OF YUGOSLAVIA

By the end of the Second World War, Soviet armies had swept the Germans out of the countries of Eastern Europe, imposing communist political and economic systems in their wake. Since that time, the history of these countries has been marked by a long and sometimes unrewarding struggle for political and economic reform. The story of Yugoslavia is somewhat different. That country was liberated from the Germans, not by the Soviet army, but instead by a Yugoslavian guerrilla movement. The civil war that followed was won by Marshall Tito, a communist who nonetheless was sufficiently independent to break politically with Moscow in 1948. He was then able to introduce his own kind of communism, which can best be described as "market socialism." As in the Soviet Union or any other Marxist country, most capital is owned by the government. But Yugoslavia has a less centralized economy than the Soviet Union. The decision on what will be produced depends more heavily on market signals from consumers than on decisions by central planners.

Before we consider how the Yugoslavs have introduced a greater degree of freedom in the marketplace, it is important to keep their economy in perspective by noting the respects in which their government still does exercise a high degree of control. First, although many prices vary as a result of market pressures, they typically do so only within specified limits. Moreover, in some sectors, prices are controlled by the government. Second, the government follows a high-growth policy: As in the Soviet Union, about one-third of GNP is directed into investment. Third, the government determines which sectors will grow more rapidly than others by allocating investment funds to each. However, within each sector there is, typically, considerable competition among enterprises for available funds. Finally, the Yugoslavs, like the Soviets, draw up a 5-year plan. But theirs is less in the Soviet style of setting target outputs in each sector than in the French style of simply indicat-

ing what output levels are likely to be. Thus, a steel firm can see the expected level of output in industries (like machinery and home appliances) that use steel. It can then use this information in making its own decision on how much steel to produce.

The greater degree of market freedom in Yugoslavia

In Yugoslavia, a firm may be owned by the state, but it is operated by its workers, who elect a manager to make day-to-day decisions. The manager acquires labor and other factors of production and sells the firm's output in more-or-less free markets, with the objective being to earn profits, which in turn go to the workers. The enterprise may succeed or it may not, depending on its ability to earn profits by responding to changes in consumer tastes and other market pressures. And, within limits, the firm can change its price.

Because production decisions are influenced by the profit motive and are sensitive to consumer wants, the Yugoslav system achieves some of the efficiencies of ours.[12] But (no surprise) it consequently also encounters some of our problems. First, managers who are in a monopoly position soon discover that they can exploit this position: They can increase their workers' profits by restricting supply and raising price.[13] Thus the

---

[12] But there is still evidence that the Yugoslav system falls considerably short of its objective of satisfying consumers. In a celebrated case in 1977, police broke up a ring that was smuggling blue jeans into Yugoslavia, using a wire strung across the Idria River. When this wire was cut, 1,200 pairs of jeans were backed up into the hands of the "Italian connection" on the other side.

*[13] At first, socialist theoreticians were optimistic that the monopoly problem could be solved by setting up a system in which planners would announce prices. This would force producers into the role of price takers. As a consequence, they would produce to the point where their marginal cost would be equal to price. At the same time, consumers would also take market price as given, and would consume to the point where their marginal utility would be equal to price.

But how would a planner decide on the price to announce? If the price that had been previously announced did not equate producers' supply and consumers' demand, the planner would change it until it did. With producers and

efficiency losses of monopoly may arise in such an economy, just as they do in ours.

Second, workers' income depends on earnings from the enterprise, rather than on just a formal wage. And since some enterprises are more successful financially than others, some workers have higher incomes. Thus, workers' ownership introduces incentives to labor to work harder (thereby increasing efficiency); but it also results in an uneven distribution of income that many socialists view as inequitable. Even in this socialist state, *there is still a basic conflict between the objectives of efficiency and equity.*

Third, compared with the Soviets, the Yugoslavs face a greater problem of overt unemployment[14] (though a smaller problem of disguised unemployment). The reason is that, in Yugoslavia, profits determine whether an enterprise will prosper or not, and if it does, it may expand. Hence, regions that have profitable enterprises may have no problem in absorbing a growing labor force and thus maintaining full employment. But regions with unprofitable firms that do not grow may face an unemployment problem. There is no Soviet-type command for production to expand in these areas.

Special problems

In Yugoslavia, there is still a relatively healthy, small-scale, privately owned sector where new firms are set up by private individuals, just as in our system. But, if we concentrate on the rest of the economy where capital is publicly owned, an

important question (common to any socialist economy) is: Who sets up new enterprises? In Yugoslavia, existing firms develop new product lines and open up new branches. But how are *new* firms established?

This is a major issue because the entry (or even just the threat of entry) of new firms into an industry may reduce or prevent monopoly abuse, thus increasing the efficiency of the economy. Moreover, new firms may mean an even greater variety of new products to satisfy consumer demand more effectively, as well as new jobs in regions of severe unemployment. New firms in our system are formed by entrepreneurs who know they will own them and expect to earn profits from them. But where private ownership is not allowed, what then? In Yugoslavia, new firms may be set up by a local community using government-supplied funds. But the problem is that the initiator loses control of the enterprise as soon as it is established and passes into the hands of its workers—so the incentive to exercise such an initiative is reduced.

CHINA: ANOTHER SOCIALIST EXPERIMENT

While the Soviet Union is the oldest of the communist countries, China is by far the largest in terms of population. China has primitive agriculture, and underdeveloped industry. It has recently been undergoing such substantial changes that it is difficult to get a clear reading of where it is going economically. However, its recent leadership has been encouraging some moves toward a more market-oriented economy: Incentive systems for workers have been introduced to get them to produce more, and state-owned enterprises have been encouraged to aim their efforts at increasing efficiency and better satisfying consumer wants. As in the case of Yugoslavia, this move in the direction of a market system has brought both advantages and disadvantages. For example, ending the practice of cramming unnecessary workers into factories has improved productivity, but has also meant

consumers all acting as price takers, wouldn't such a socialist system provide the efficiency of perfect competition—even better than our imperfectly competitive free enterprise system? The answer is: Not necessarily. The profit-seeking manager with monopoly power would still be able to exercise it. As the only producer, the manager would just reduce the supply. The planner would then observe that supply was falling short of demand, and would raise price to the monopoly level the producer was seeking. In other words, a monopolist who figures out how the system works will not take price as given, even if it is announced by a central planner.

[14]See A. Sapir, "Economic Growth and Factor Substitution: What Happened to the Yugoslav Miracle?" *Economic Journal,* June 1980, p. 305.

that unemployment has again become a problem.

Over the years, deep hostilities have developed between the People's Republic of China and two neighboring communist states—the Soviet Union and Viet Nam. Just as a common religion has not prevented conflicts between Christian countries, so a common Marxist ideology is no guarantee of peace among communist countries. And for Marxists, this has perhaps been the most disillusioning development of all. In Marxist doctrine, the cause of war is the greed of capitalists trying to make profits by producing weapons. Workers have nothing to gain from war. Thus, it should be eliminated as communist parties come to power. But the world is not this simple.

CONCLUSIONS

In previous chapters we have seen how, in our system, redistributing income via government transfer payments affects incentives—in particular, the work incentive of those receiving the payments. In this chapter we have seen how a more drastic socialist policy of redistributing income (by giving the ownership of capital to the state) also affects incentives—most notably, the incentives to initiate and innovate. Thus, there is no system that works ideally, solving all problems at once.

Judgment on which economic system is better depends not on what it promises, but on what it delivers. In *practice,* which system does a better job of solving the basic economic problem of transforming resources into the satisfaction of human wants? As you evaluate this issue for yourself in the future, remember that the standard criticism of socialism is that it does not do a particularly good job of satisfying these wants. And also remember the basic criticism of free enterprise: It does a far worse job of satisfying the wants of the poor than of the rich.

Another criticism of free enterprise is that large corporations often exercise too much economic and political power—power that should be exercised by the government on behalf of the people. But if socialists cure this problem by transferring a great deal of economic power (including the ownership of capital) to the government, does too much power then fall into the hands of the state? Lane Kirkland, president of the AFL-CIO, has expressed American labor's reservations about dealing with a powerful state:

We on the whole prefer to negotiate with private companies that have roughly equivalent bargaining power than with [government] corporations that control the courts, the police, the army, the navy, and the hydrogen bomb.

The problem of dealing with a powerful communist state has had to be faced recently by Polish workers when they formed a union. They discovered that a state which has always paid lip service to the interests of the workers could still strongly resist any attempt by workers to pursue those interests.

Finally we must distinguish between the physical capital that a socialist state brings under government ownership and control, and the human capital that cannot be dealt with in this way: the skills, experience, and expertise we carry around in our heads. Labor is no longer the largely unskilled commodity that Marx observed over a hundred years ago; labor now exists at widely varying skill levels. Consequently, our nation's capital today is in the hands not only of those who own physical plant and machinery, but also of those who own human capital. And these people range all the way from semiskilled workers to managers and those who work in scores of professions. As a result, it is now much more difficult to argue that our society is simply divided into two groups: those who exploit (the capitalists) and those who are exploited (the workers). Most workers are also "capitalists"—some because they own physical capital, but most because they own large quantities of human capital.

Key Points

1 Most of the physical capital in our free enterprise system is owned by individuals; under socialism it is owned by the state on behalf of all the people. The theoretical appeal of socialism is that it eliminates one of the major causes of inequality in our system: the power and income enjoyed by those who own capital.

2 The two major economic characteristics of the system that exists in the Soviet Union today are: (a) physical capital is owned publicly rather than privately; and (b) investment and output levels are determined by a central planning authority.

3 One of the advantages of Soviet economywide central planning is that industry output targets can be set at a level that keeps unemployment low. But there are disadvantages. Central planning results in a great accumulation of power in the hands of the central political authorities. And the more that such power is centralized, the greater the risk that this power will be abused. A key question is: Could a Soviet-style command economy be run without political dictatorship?

4 A further problem with economywide planning is that it is extremely difficult to administer and therefore often results in bottlenecks and other inefficiencies. Accordingly, central planning tends to result in higher levels of disguised unemployment, with workers engaged in unproductive activities, such as producing goods that poorly satisfy consumer tastes.

5 In recognition of this problem, the Soviets have recently been attempting to make their system more sensitive to "messages from the marketplace." This approach has brought them closer to Yugoslavia's economic system.

6 Yugoslavia is, like the Soviet Union, a socialist country in which productive capital is owned by the state. But it differs from the Soviet Union because much less economic decision-making is done by a central authority and much more is handled by individual enterprises responding to profits and subject to market pressures.

7 For this reason, the Yugoslavian economy is closer to our system than is the Soviet economy. As a result, the government encounters some of the same problems that we face (such as overt unemployment). And the fact that the Yugoslavs' capital is publicly owned means that they face a problem common to the Soviet Union or any other socialist country: how to attain the levels of innovation and initiative that exist in a free enterprise system, where those who own capital take great risks in order to earn profits.

8 The Chinese economy is difficult to "read" because of recent policy changes. However, it seems to be moving towards a greater reliance on the market.

Key Concepts

capitalist
labor theory of value
subsistence level of wages
surplus value
proletariat
bourgeoisie
socialism

communism
Gosplan
5-year plan
output target
overt vs disguised
   unemployment

Soviet/American
   convergence
Liberman reforms
Yugoslav market socialism
worker management of
   firms

Problems

25-1 What did Marx mean by "surplus value"? Does it include some, all, or none of the costs of capital that must be paid by firms undertaking investment?

25-2 What are the two forms of unemployment? Which is worse in the Soviet system? Which is worse in our system? Explain.

25-3 In your view, what is the most important difference between the Soviet and the Yugoslav systems?

25-4 Consider the following view:

"The interests of labor are in conflict with the interests of the owners of capital. The greater is capital accumulation, the greater will be the forces arrayed against labor. Rapid capital accumulation is thus not in the interest of workers."

Is this so under our system? Explain why or why not. Is this so in the Soviet Union?

25-5 A recent planning failure in Poland resulted in a shortage of batteries. As a result, thousands of tractors and other vehicles could not be used. Explain why such a problem is unlikely in the market economies of Western Europe.

25-6 Discuss why you think the free enterprise and socialist systems will, or will not, eventually converge into an "ideal" system.

25-7 Do we acquire more new technology from the Japanese, British, and Germans, or from the Russians and Czechs? Are there several reasons for your answer?

25-8 "Under unrestricted free enterprise, a stupid, shiftless individual who has inherited a great deal of valuable land can charge a high rent, and through the diligent pursuit of idleness, become very wealthy—indeed, far wealthier than the intelligent, hardworking person who rents the land. Something is wrong." Explain why you agree or disagree.

Now consider three alternative solutions to this problem, carefully criticizing each:

(a) Put a ceiling on rent, to transfer income from landlords to tenants.

(b) Charge the market rent, but have the land owned by the state, with all income going to the state.

(c) Let the shiftless owner continue to own the land and charge an unregulated rent. But place a heavy percentage tax on his income.

Which solution is closest to the socialist blueprint? Which is closest to our modified free enterprise system?

25-9 "Although socialism and communism promise less, they deliver more." Explain why you agree or disagree.

Glossary

(Not all these terms appear in the text; some are included because they occur frequently in readings or lectures. Page numbers provide the primary references for the terms. Numbers in italic refer to pages in the companion volume. For additional references, see the index.)

ability-to-pay principle. The view that taxes should be levied according to the means of the various taxpayers, as measured by their incomes and/or wealth. Compare with *benefit principle.* (p. 86)

absolute advantage. A country (or region or individual) has an absolute advantage in the production of a good or service if it can produce that good or service with fewer resources than other countries (or regions or individuals). See also *comparative advantage.* (p. 38)

accelerationist. One who believes that an attempt to keep the unemployment rate low by expansive demand policies will cause more and more rapid inflation. *(p. 360)*

accelerator. The theory that investment depends on the change in sales. *(p. 329)*

accommodative monetary policy. (1) A monetary policy that increases aggregate demand when wages and other costs increase, in order to prevent an increase in unemployment in the face of cost-push forces. *(p. 278)* (2) A monetary policy that allows the money stock to change in response to changes in the demand for loans; that is, a monetary policy aimed at the stabilization of interest rates. *(p. 346)*

accounts payable. Debts to suppliers of goods or services. (p. 102)

accounts receivable. Amounts due from customers. (p. 102)

action lag. The time interval between the recognition that adjustments in aggregate demand policies are desirable and the time when policies are actually changed. *(p. 339)*

actual investment. *(p. 152)* See *investment demand.*

adjustable peg system. A system where countries peg (fix) exchange rates but retain the right to change them in the event of fundamental disequilibrium. (In the adjustable peg system of 1945–1973, countries generally fixed the prices of their currencies in terms of the U.S. dollar.) *(p. 395)*

ad valorem tax. A tax collected as a percentage of the price or value of a good.

aggregate demand. Total expenditures on consumer goods and services, government goods and services, (desired) investment, and net exports. *(p. 145)*

allocative efficiency. Production of the best combination of goods with the best combination of inputs. (p. 14)

annually balanced budget principle. The view that government expenditures should be limited each year to no more than government receipts during that year. *(p. 182)*

antitrust laws. Laws designed to control monopoly power and practices. Examples: Sherman Act, 1890; Clayton Act, 1914. (p. 261)

appreciation of a currency. In a flexible exchange-rate system, a rise in the price of a currency in terms of another currency or currencies. *(p. 405)*

arbitrage. A set of transactions aimed at making a profit from inconsistent prices.

arbitration. Settlement of differences between a union and management by an impartial third party (the arbitrator) whose decisions are binding. (p. 406)

arc elasticity of demand. The elasticity of demand between two points on a demand curve, calculated by the formula

$$\frac{\Delta Q}{Q_1 + Q_2} \div \frac{\Delta P}{P_1 + P_2} \qquad (p.\ 121n)$$

asset. Something that is owned. (p. 102)

automatic stabilizer. A feature built into the economy which tends to reduce the amplitude of fluctuations. For example, tax collections tend to fall during a recession and rise during a boom, slowing the change in disposable incomes and aggregate demand. (Thus they are an automatic fiscal stabilizer.) Interest rates tend to fall during a recession and rise during a boom because of changes in the demand for funds. These changes in interest rates tend to stabilize investment demand. (Thus they are an automatic monetary stabilizer.) *(p. 178)*

average-cost pricing. Setting the price where the average-cost curve (including normal profit) intersects the demand curve. (p. 228)

average fixed cost. Fixed cost divided by the number of units of output. (p. 165)

average product. Total product divided by the number of units of the variable input used. (p. 164)

average revenue. Total revenue divided by the number of units sold. In perfect competition, where the seller takes the price as given, average revenue equals price. (p. 219)

average total cost. Total cost divided by the number of units of output. (p. 165)

average variable cost. Variable cost divided by the number of units produced. (p. 165)

balanced budget (1) A budget with revenues equal to expenditures. (2) More loosely (but more commonly), a budget with revenues equal to or greater than expenditures. (p. 80)

balanced budget multiplier. The change in equilibrium national product divided by the change in government spending when this spending is financed by an equivalent change in taxes.

balance of payments. The summary figure calculated from balance-of-payments credits less balance-of-payments debits, with certain monetary transactions excluded from the calculation. (There are various ways of defining monetary transactions; thus, there are various balance-of-payments definitions. The most common excludes official reserve transactions.) *(p. 412)*

balance-of-payments accounts. A statement of a country's transactions with other countries. *(p. 409)*

balance-of-payments surplus (deficit). A positive (negative) balance of payments. *(p. 413)*

balance of trade (or balance-on-merchandise account). The value of exports of goods minus the value of imports of goods. *(p. 414)*

balance sheet. The statement of a firm's financial position at a particular time, showing its assets, liabilities, and net worth. (p. 101)

band. The range within which an exchange rate could move without the government's being committed to intervene in exchange markets to prevent further movement. That is, under the adjustable peg system, governments were obliged to keep exchange rates from moving outside a band (of 1 percent either side of parity). *(p. 396)*

bank reserve. See *required reserves.*

bank run. A situation in which many owners of bank deposits attempt to make withdrawals because of their fear that the bank will be unable to meet its obligations. *(p. 203)*

bankruptcy. (1) A situation in which a firm (or individual) has legally been declared unable to pay its debts. (2) Loosely, a situation in which a firm (or individual) is unable to pay its debts. *(p. 342)*

barrier to entry. An impediment that makes it difficult or impossible for a new firm to enter an industry. Examples: patents, economies of scale, accepted brand names. (p. 179)

barter. The exchange of one good or service for another without the use of money. (p. 33)

base year. The reference year, given the value of 100 when constructing a price index or other time series. *(p. 120)*

beggar-my-neighbor policy. A policy aimed at shifting an unemployment problem to another country. Example: an increase in tariffs. (p. 341)

benefit-cost analysis. The calculation and comparison of the benefits and costs of a program or project. (p. 275)

benefit principle. The view that taxes should be levied in proportion to the benefits which the various taxpayers receive from government expenditures. Compare with *ability-to-pay principle.* (p. 86)

benefits in kind. Payments, not of cash, but of some good (like food), or service (like medical care). (p. 488)

bilateral monopoly. A market structure with a single seller (monopolist) and a single buyer (monopsonist). (p. 399)

bill. See *Treasury bill.*

blacklist. A list of workers who are not to be given

jobs because of union activity or other behavior considered objectionable by employers. (p. 386)

black market. A market in which sales take place at a price above the legal maximum. (p. 58)

block grants. Grants that may be used in a broad area (such as education), and need not be spent on specific programs (such as reading programs for the handicapped). (p. 80)

bogus type. Type that is set but not actually used. The setting of bogus type is a way of protecting typesetters' jobs when ready-made type is already available (for example, from a newspaper advertiser). (p. 392)

bond. A written commitment to pay a scheduled series of interest payments plus the face value (principal) at a specified maturity date. (p. 99)

book value. The book value of a stock is its net worth per share. (It is calculated by dividing the net worth of the firm by the number of its shares outstanding.) (p. 103)

bourgeoisie. (1) In Marxist doctrine, capitalists as a class. (2) The middle class. (3) More narrowly, shopkeepers. (p. 503)

boycott. A concerted refusal to buy (buyer's boycott) or sell (sellers' boycott). A campaign to discourage people from doing business with a particular firm.

break-even point. (1) The output to which costs just equal revenues and therefore profits are zero. (p. 170) (2) The level of disposable income at which consumption just equals disposable income and therefore saving is zero. *(p. 149)*

broker. One who acts on behalf of a buyer or seller. (p. 109)

budget deficit. The amount by which budgetary outlays exceed revenues. (p. 80)

budget line (or income line). The line on a diagram which shows the various combinations of commodities which can be bought with a given income at a given set of prices. (p. 157)

budget surplus. The amount by which budgetary revenues exceed outlays. (p. 80)

built-in-stabilizer. See *automatic stabilizer.*

burden of tax. See *incidence of tax* and *excess burden of tax.*

business cycle. The more or less regular upward and downward movement of economic activity over a period of years. A cycle has four phases: recession, trough, expansion, and peak. *(p. 326)*

cap. A limit on the upward adjustment of an indexed wage in response to a rise in the price index. *(p. 320)*

capital. (1) Real capital: buildings, equipment, and other materials used in the production process which have themselves been produced in the past. (p. 21) (2) Financial capital: either funds available for acquiring real capital *or* financial assets such as bonds or common stock. (3) Human capital: the education, training, and experience which make human beings more productive. (p. 21)

capital consumption allowance. See *depreciation.*

capital gain. The increase in the value of an asset over time. (p. 90)

capitalism. A system in which individuals are permitted to own large amounts of capital, and decisions are made primarily in private markets, with relatively little government interference.

capitalized value. The present value of the income stream which an asset is expected to produce. *(p. 226)*

capital market. A market in which financial instruments such as stocks and bonds are bought and sold. (p. 106)

capital-output ratio. The value of capital divided by the value of the annual output produced with this capital. *(p. 332)*

capital stock. The total quantity of capital.

cartel. A group of producers who set price and/or divide the market in order to reap monopolylike profits. (p. 244)

categorical grant. A federal grant to a state or local government for a specific program. Such a grant requires the recipient government to pay part of the cost of the program. (p. 80)

cease-and-desist order. An order from a court or government agency to an individual or company to stop a specified action. (p. 265)

central bank. A banker's bank, whose major responsibility is the control of the money supply. A central bank also generally performs other functions, such as check clearing and the inspection of commercial banks. *(p. 204)*

central planning. Centralized direction of the resources of the economy, with the objective of fulfilling national goals. (p. 507)

certificate of deposit (CD). A marketable time deposit. *(p. 201)*

ceteris paribus. "Other things unchanged." In demand-and-supply analysis, it is common to make the *ceteris paribus* assumption; that is, to assume that none of the determinants of the quality demanded or supplied is allowed to change, with the sole exception of price. (p. 50)

check clearing. The transfer of checks from the

bank in which they were deposited to the bank on which they were written, with the net amounts due to or from each bank being calculated. *(p. 209)*

checking deposit. A bank deposit transferable by check. *(p. 198)*

checkoff. The deduction of union dues from workers' pay by an employer, who then remits the dues to the union. (p. 388)

circular flow of payments. The flow of payments from businesses to households in exchange for labor and other productive services and the return flow of payments from households to businesses in exchange for goods and services. *(p. 156)*

classical economics. (1) In Keynesian economics, the accepted body of macroeconomic doctrine prior to the publication of Keynes' *General Theory*. According to classical economics, a market economy tends toward an equilibrium with full employment; a market economy tends to be stable if monetary conditions are stable; and changes in the quantity of money are the major cause of changes in aggregate demand. *(p. 142)* (2) The accepted view, prior to 1870, that value depends on the cost of production. [In the late nineteenth century, this was replaced with the "neoclassical" view that value depends on both costs of production (supply) and marginal utility (demand).]

class struggle. In Marxist economics, the struggle for control between the proletariat and the bourgeoisie. (p. 503)

clean float. A situation where exchange rates are determined by market forces, without intervention by central banks or governments. *(p. 402)*

closed economy. An economy with no international transactions.

closed shop. A business that hires only workers who are already union members. (p. 389)

cobweb cycle. A switching back and forth between a situation of high production and low price and one of low production and high price. A cobweb cycle can occur if there are long lags in production and if producers erroneously assume that price this year is a good indicator of price next year. (p. 202)

collective bargaining. Negotiations between a union and management over wages and working conditions. (p. 385)

collective goods. Goods which, by their very nature, provide benefits to a large group of people. (See also *public goods*.)

collusion. An agreement among sellers regarding prices and/or market shares. The agreement may be explicit or tacit. (p. 244)

commercial bank. A privately owned, profit-seeking institution that accepts demand and savings deposits, makes loans, and acquires other earning assets (particularly bonds and shorter-term debt instruments). In the United States, a commercial bank may receive its charter from the federal government (in which case it is a *national bank*), or from a state government (a *state bank*). *(p. 204)*

common stock. Each share of common stock represents part ownership in a corporation. (p. 95)

communism. (1) In Marxist theory, the ultimate stage of historical development in which *(a)* all are expected to work and no one lives by owning capital, *(b)* exploitation has been eliminated and there is a classless society, and *(c)* the state has withered away. (2) A common alternative usage: the economic and political systems of China, the Soviet Union, and other countries in which a Communist party is in power. (p. 503)

company union. A union dominated by the employer.

comparative advantage. If two nations (or regions or individuals) have different opportunity costs of producing a good or service, then the nation (or region or individual) with the lower opportunity cost has a comparative advantage in that good or service. (p. 324)

compensating wage differentials. Wage differences that may result if labor views some jobs as less attractive than others. (Employers have to pay a higher wage to fill the unattractive jobs.) (p. 407)

competition. See *perfect competition*.

competitive devaluations. A round of exchange-rate devaluations in which each of a number of countries tries to gain a competitive advantage by devaluing its currency. (Not all can be successful; each must fail to the extent that other countries also devalue.)

complementary goals. Goals such that the achievement of one helps in the achievement of the other. (Contrast with *conflicting goals*.) (p. 17)

complementary goods. Goods such that the rise in the price of one causes a leftward shift in the demand curve for the other. (Contrast with *substitute*.) (p. 51)

concentration ratio. Usually, the fraction of an industry's total sales made by the four largest firms. (Sometimes a different number of firms—such as eight—is chosen in calculating concentration ratios, and sometimes a different measure of size—such as assets—is chosen.) (p. 241)

conflicting goals. Goals such that working toward one makes it more difficult to achieve the other. (p. 17)

conglomerate merger. See *merger*.

consent decree. An agreement whereby a defendant, without admitting guilt, undertakes to desist from certain actions and abide by other conditions laid down in the decree.

conspicuous consumption. Consumption whose purpose is to impress others. A term originated by Thorstein Veblen (1857–1929).

constant dollars. A series is measured in constant dollars if it is measured at the prices existing in a specified base year. Such a series has been adjusted to remove the effects of inflation (or deflation). Contrast with *current dollars. (p. 120)*

constant returns (to scale). This occurs if an increase of x percent in all inputs causes output to increase by the same x percent.

consumer price index (CPI). A weighted average of the prices of goods and services commonly purchased by families in urban areas, as calculated by the U.S. Bureau of Labor Statistics. *(p. 121)*

consumer surplus. The net benefit that consumers get from being able to purchase a good at the prevailing price; the difference between the maximum amounts that consumers would be willing to pay and what they actually do pay. It is approximately the triangular area under the demand curve and above the market price. (p. 147)

consumption. (1) The purchase of consumer goods and services. (2) The act of using goods and services to satisfy wants. (3) The using up of goods (as in capital consumption allowances). *(p. 125)*

consumption function. (1) The relationship between consumer expenditures and disposable income. (p. 147) (2) More broadly, the relationship between consumer expenditures and the factors that determine these expenditures.

convergence hypothesis. The proposition that the differences between communistic and capitalistic societies is decreasing. *(p. 147)*

cornering a market. Buying up enough of the commodity to become the single (or at least dominant) seller, and thus acquire the power to resell at a higher price. (p. 205)

corporation. An association of stockholders with a government charter which grants certain legal powers, privileges, and liabilities separate from those of the individual stockholder-owners. The major advantages of the corporate form of business organization are limited liability for the owners, continuity, and relative ease of raising capital for expansion. (p. 95)

correlation. The tendency of two variables (like income and consumption) to move together.

cost-benefit analysis. See *benefit-cost analysis*.

cost of living allowance. An increase in wages in response to a rise in the price index, as provided in an indexed wage contract. *(p. 320)*

cost-push inflation. Inflation caused principally by increasing costs—in the form of higher prices for labor, materials, and other inputs—rather than by rising demand. Contrast with *demand-pull inflation*. *(p. 277)*

countercyclical policy. Policy which reduces fluctuations in economic activity. *(p. 335)*

countervailing power. Power in one group which has grown as a reaction to power in another group. For example, a big labor union may develop to balance the bargaining power of a big corporation. A term originated by Harvard's John Kenneth Galbraith. (p. 398)

craft union. A labor union whose members have a particular craft (skill or occupation). Examples: an electrician's union, or a plumbers' union. Contrast with *industrial union*. (p. 385)

crawling peg system. An international financial system in which par values would be changed frequently, by small amounts, in order to avoid large changes at a later date. (p. 399)

credit instrument. A written promise to pay.

credit rationing. Allocation of available funds among borrowers when the demand for loans exceeds the supply at the prevailing interest rate. *(p. 254)*

creeping inflation. A slow but persistent upward movement of the average level of prices (not more than 2 or 3 percent per annum).

cross-section data. Observations taken at the same time. For example, the consumption of different income classes in the United States in 1982. *(p. 146)*

crowding out. A reduction in private investment demand caused by an expansive fiscal policy (that is, by an increase in government spending or a cut in tax rates). *(p. 258)*

currency. (1) Coins and paper money (dollar bills). (p. 198) (2) In international economics, a national money, such as the dollar or the yen. *(p. 390)*

current account surplus. The amount by which a country's export of goods and services is greater than the combined sum of its imports of goods and services plus its net unilateral transfers to foreign countries. *(p. 414)*

current dollars. A series (like GNP) is measured in current dollars if each observation is measured at the prices that prevailed at the time. Such a series reflects both real changes in GNP *and* inflation (or deflation). Contrast with *constant dollars. (p. 120)*

current liabilities. Debts that are due for payment within a year.

customs union. An agreement among nations to eliminate trade barriers (tariffs, quotas, etc.) among themselves and to adopt common barriers to imports from nonmember countries. Example: the European Economic Community.

cutthroat competition. Selling at a price below cost, with the objective of driving competitors out of the market (at which time prices may be raised and monopoly profits reaped). (p. 262)

cyclically balanced budget. A budget whose receipts over a whole business cycle are at least equal to its expenditures over the same cycle. Unlike an annually balanced budget, a cyclically balanced budget permits countercyclical fiscal policies. Surpluses during prosperity may be used to cover deficits during recessions. *(p. 184)*

debasement of currency. Reduction of the quantity of precious metals in coins.

debt instrument. A written commitment to repay borrowed funds.

declining industry. An industry whose firms make less than normal profits. (Firms will therefore leave the industry.)

deficiency payment. Government subsidy to farmers for each unit of output to raise the price they receive to a prespecified target level.

deficit. The amount by which expenditures exceed revenues. (p. 80)

deflation. (1) A decline in the average level of prices; the opposite of inflation. (p. 12) (2) The removal of the effects of inflation from a series of observations by dividing each observation with a price index. The derivation of a constant-dollar series from a current-dollar series. *(p. 121)*

deflationary bias. Such a bias exists in a system if, on average, monetary and fiscal authorities are constrained from allowing aggregate demand to increase as rapidly as productive capacity. (The classical gold standard was criticized on the ground that it created a deflationary bias.) *(p. 395)*

deflationary gap. See *recessionary gap.*

demand. A schedule or curve showing, *ceteris paribus,* how much of a good or service would be demanded at various possible prices. (p. 47)

demand deposit. A bank deposit withdrawable on demand and transferable by check. *(p. 198)*

demand mangement policy. A change in monetary or fiscal policy aimed at affecting aggregate demand.

demand-pull inflation. Inflation caused by excess aggregate demand. *(p. 277)*

demand shift. A movement of the demand curve to the right or left as a result of a change in income or any other determinant of the quantity demand (with the sole exception of the price of the good). (p. 50)

demand shifter. Anything except its own price that affects the quantity of a good demanded. (p. 50)

depletion allowance. A deduction, equal to a percentage of sales, which certain extractive industries have been permitted in calculating taxable profits.

deposit multiplier. See *money multiplier.*

depreciation. (1) The loss in the value of physical capital due to wear and obsolescence. (2) The estimate of such loss in business or economic accounts; that is, a capital consumption allowance. *(p. 129)*

depreciation of a currency. A decline in the value of a floating currency measured in terms of another currency or currencies. *(p. 405)*

depression. An extended period of very high unemployment and much excess capacity. (There is no generally accepted, precise numerical definition of a depression. This text suggests that a depression requires unemployment rates of 10 percent or more for 2 years or more.) (p. 10)

derived demand. The demand for an input that depends on the demand for the product or products it is used to make. For example, the demand for flour is derived from the demand for bread. (p. 365)

devaluation. In international economics, a reduction of the par value of a currency. *(p. 397)*

dictatorship of the proletariat. In Marxist economics, this exists after a revolution has eliminated the capitalist class and power has fallen into the hands of the proletariat. (p. 511)

differentiated products. Similar products that retain some distinctive difference(s); close but not perfect substitutes. Examples: Ford and Chevrolet automobiles, different brands of toothpaste. (p. 255)

diminishing returns, law of eventually. If technology is unchanged, then the use of more and more units of a variable input (together with one or more fixed inputs) must eventually lead to a declining marginal product for the variable input. (p. 164)

discounting. (1) The process by which the present value of one or more future payments is calculated, using an interest rate. (See *present value.*) *(p. 226)* (2) In central banking, lending by the central bank to a commercial bank or other financial institution. *(p. 225)*

discount rate. (1) In central banking, the rate of interest charged by the central bank on loans to commercial banks. *(p. 225)* (2) Less commonly, the interest rate used to calculate present value. *(p. 226)*

discretionary policy. Policy which is periodically changed in the light of changing conditions. The term is usually applied to monetary or fiscal policies which are adjusted with the objectives of high employment and stable prices. Contrast with *monetary rule.* (p. 352)

disposable (personal) income. Income that households have left after the payment of taxes. It is divided among consumption expenditures, the payment of interest on consumer debt, and saving. *(p. 133)*

dissaving. Negative saving. *(p. 148)*

dividend. The part of a corporation's profits paid out to its shareholders.

division of labor. The breaking up of a productive process into different tasks, each done by a different worker (for example, on an automobile assembly line). (p. 32)

dollar standard. An international system in which many international transactions take place in dollars and many countries hold sizable factions of their reserves in dollars. Also, other currencies may be pegged to the dollar. *(p. 401)*

double-entry bookkeeping. An accounting system in which each transaction results in equal entries on both sides. When double-entry bookkeeping is used, the two sides of the accounts must balance. *(p. 409)*

double taxation. The taxation of corporate profits first when they are earned and second when they are paid out in dividends. (p. 97)

dumping. The sale of a good at a lower price in a foreign market than in the home market—a form of price discrimination.

duopoly. A market in which there are only two sellers. (p. 244)

dynamic efficiency. A term applied to a system or market which encourages rapid innovation in the form of new products and new cost-cutting techniques. (p. 196)

dynamic wage differential. A wage difference that arises because of changing demand or supply conditions in the labor market. It tends to disappear over time as labor moves out of relatively low wage jobs and into those that pay a relatively high wage. (p. 407)

econometrics. The application of statistical methods to economic problems. *(p. 354)*

economic efficiency. The goal of getting the most out of our productive efforts. (p. 14) See also *allocative efficiency, dynamic efficiency,* and *technical efficiency.*

economic integration. The elimination of tariffs and other barriers between nations. The partial or complete unification of the economies of different countries.

economic rent. The return to a factor of production in excess of its opportunity cost. (p. 424)

economics. (1) The study of how people acquire material necessities and comforts, the problems they encounter in doing so, and how these problems can be reduced. (p. 3) (2) Frequently, a narrower definition is used—the study of the allocation of scarce resources to satisfy human wants.

economies (diseconomies) of scale. See *increasing (decreasing) returns.*

economize. To make the most of limited resources; to be careful in outlay. (p. 20)

efficiency. See *economic efficiency.*

effluent charge. A tax or other levy on a polluting activity based on the quantity of pollution discharged. (p. 288)

elastic demand. Demand with an elasticity of more than one. A fall in price causes an increase in total expenditure on the product in question, because the percentage change in quantity demanded is greater than the percentage change in price. (p. 121)

elasticity of demand. The price elasticity of demand is

$$\frac{\text{Percentage change in quantity demanded}}{\text{Percentage change in price}}$$

Similarly, the income elasticity of demand is

$$\frac{\text{Percentage change in quantity demanded}}{\text{Percentage change in income}}$$

The unmodified term "elasticity" usually applies to price elasticity. (p. 121)

elasticity of supply. The (price) elasticity of supply is

$$\frac{\text{Percentage change in quantity supplied}}{\text{Percentage change in price}}$$

(p. 123)

elastic supply. Supply with an elasticity of more than one. A supply curve which, if extended in a straight line, would meet the vertical axis. (p. 123)

emission fee. See *effluent charge.*

employer of last resort. The government acts as the employer of last resort if it offers jobs to those who are willing and able to work but cannot find jobs in the private sector. *(p. 296)*

employment rate. The percentage of the labor force employed.

endogenous variable. A variable explained within a theory.

Engel's laws. Regularities between income and consumer expenditures observed by nineteenth-century statistician Ernst Engel. Most important is the decrease in the percentage of income spent on food as income rises. *(p. 147)*

entrepreneur. One who organizes and manages production; who innovates and bears risks. (p. 22)

envelope curve. A curve that encloses, by just touching, a series of other curves. For example, the long-run average-cost curve is the envelope of all the short-run average-cost curves (each of which shows costs, given a particular stock of fixed capital). (p. 175)

equation of exchange. MV = PQ. *(p. 255)*

equilibrium. A situation where there is no tendency for change. (p. 48)

equity. (1) Ownership, or amount owned. (2) Fairness. (p. 473)

escalator clause. A provision in a contract or law whereby a price, wage, or other monetary quantity is increased at the same rate as a specified price index (usually the consumer price index). See also *indexation. (p. 320)*

estate tax. A tax on property owned at the time of death.

Eurodollars. Deposits in European banks, that are denominated in U.S. dollars.

excess burden of a tax. The decrease in efficiency that results when people change their behavior to reduce their tax payments. *(p. 187)*

excess demand. The amount by which the quantity demand exceeds the quantity supplied at the existing price (that is, a shortage). (p. 49)

excess reserves. Reserves held by a bank or other financial institution in excess of the legally required amount. *(p. 207)*

excess supply. The amount by which the quantity supplied exceeds the quantity demanded at the existing price (that is, a surplus). (p. 49)

exchange rate. The price of one national currency in terms of another. *(p. 390)*

exchange-rate appreciation (depreciation). See *appreciation (depreciation) of a currency.*

excise tax. A tax on the sale of a particular good. An *ad valorem tax* is collected as a percentage of the price of the good. A *specific tax* is a tax per unit, fixed in dollars or cents.

exclusion principle. The basis for distinguishing between public and nonpublic goods. If those who do not pay for a good can be excluded from enjoying it, then it is not a public good. (p. 306)

exogenous variable. A variable not explained within a theory; its value is taken as given.

external costs. Costs borne by others. Pollution is an example of an external cost (sometimes called a cost spillover or a neighborhood cost). (p. 287)

externality. An adverse (or beneficial) side effect of production or consumption. Also known as a *spillover* or *third-party effect.* (p. 83)

externally held public debt. Government securities held by foreigners.

Fabian socialism. Form of socialism founded in Britain in the late nineteenth century, advocating gradual and evolutionary movement toward socialism within a democratic political system.

factor mobility. Ease with which factors can be moved from one use to another.

factor of production. Resource used to produce a good or service. Land, labor, and capital are the three basic categories of factors. (p. 21)

fallacy of composition. The unwarranted conclusion that a proposition which is true of a single sector or market is necessarily true for the economy as a whole. *(p. 143)*

fair return. Return to which a regulated public utility should be entitled.

featherbedding. Make-work rules designed to increase the number of workers (or the number of hours) on a particular job. (p. 391)

federal funds rate. The interest rate on overnight loans between banks. *(p. 207)*

fiat money. Paper money that is neither backed by nor convertible into precious metals but is nevertheless legal tender.

final product. (1) Products that have been acquired for final use and not for resale or for further processing. (2) The economy's output of goods and services after all double counting has been eliminated. *(p. 124)*

financial intermediary. Institution that issues financial obligations (such as demand deposits) in order to acquire funds from the public. The institution then pools these funds and provides them in larger amounts to businesses, governments, or individuals. Examples: commercial banks, savings and loan associations. (p. 104)

financial market. A market in which financial instruments (stocks, bonds, etc.) are bought and sold. (p. 104)

fine-tuning. An attempt to smooth out mild fluctuations in the economy by frequent adjustments in monetary and/or fiscal policies. *(p. 352)*

firm. The decision-making business unit which organizes and directs the production of goods or services. A firm may direct the activities of one or more plants.

fiscal dividend. A budget surplus, measured at the full-employment national product, that is generated by the growth of the productive capacity of the economy. *(p. 180)*

fiscal drag. The tendency for rising tax collections to impede the healthy growth of aggregate demand that is needed for the achievement and maintenance of full employment. *(p. 179)*

fiscal policy. The adjustment of tax rates or government spending in order to affect aggregate demand. *(p. 168)* (*Pure* fiscal policy involves a change in government spending or tax rates, unaccompanied by any change in the rate of growth of the money stock.)

fiscal year. A 12-month period selected as the year for accounting purposes.

Fisher equation. See *equation of exchange.*

fixed asset. A durable good, expected to last at least a year.

fixed cost. A cost that does not vary with output. (p. 165)

fixed exchange rate. An exchange rate that is held within a narrow band by the monetary authorities. *(p. 396)*

fixed factor. A factor whose quantity cannot be changed in the short run.

floating (or flexible) exchange rate. An exchange rate that is not pegged by monetary authorities but is allowed to change in response to changing demand or supply conditions. If governments and central banks withdraw completely from the exchange markets, the float is *clean.* (That is, the exchange rate is *freely flexible.* A float is *dirty* when governments or central banks intervene in exchange markets by buying or selling foreign currencies in order to affect exchange rates.) *(p. 402)*

focal-point pricing. This occurs when independent firms quote the same price even though they do not explicitly collude. They are led by convention, rules of thumb, or similar thinking to the same price. (For example, $39.95 for a pair of shoes.) (p. 253)

forced saving. A situation where households lose control of some of their income, which is directed into saving even though they would have preferred to consume it. This can occur if the monetary authorities provide financial resources for investment, creating inflation which reduces the purchasing power of households' incomes (and therefore reduces their consumption). Alternatively, forced saving occurs if taxes are used for investment projects (such as dams).

foreign exchange. The currency of another country. *(p. 390)*

foreign exchange market. A market in which one national currency is bought in exchange for another national currency. *(p. 390)*

foreign exchange reserves. Foreign currencies held by the government or central bank. *(p. 392)*

forward price. A price established in a contract to be executed at a specified time in the future (such as 3 months from now). See also *futures market.*

fractional-reserve banking. A banking system in which banks keep reserves (in the form of currency or deposits in the central bank) equal to only a fraction of their deposit liabilities. *(p. 201)*

freedom of entry. The absence of barriers that make it difficult or impossible for a new firm to enter an industry. (p. 196)

free good. A good or service whose price is zero, because at that price the quantity supplied is at least as great as the quantity demanded.

free-market economy. An economy in which the major questions "What?" "How?" and "For whom?" are answered by the actions of individuals and firms in the marketplace rather than by the government. (p. 44)

free rider. Someone who cannot be excluded from enjoying the benefits of a project, but who pays nothing (or pays a disproportionately small amount) to cover its costs. (p. 308)

free trade. A situation where no tariffs or other barriers are imposed on trade between countries.

free-trade area (or free-trade association). A group of countries that agree to eliminate trade barriers (tariffs, quotas, etc.) among themselves, while each retains the right to set its barriers on imports from nonmember countries. Compare with *customs union.*

frictional unemployment. Unemployment that is not due to a lack of aggregate demand but rather occurs because some workers have quit their jobs to look for something better and because entrants and reentrants into the labor force spend a reasonable time looking for jobs. (The term is also sometimes applied to temporary layoffs attributable to other nondemand causes, such as bad weather.) *(p. 145)*

front loaded debt. A debt on which the payments, measured in constant dollars, are greater at the beginning than at the end of the repayment period. *(p. 309)*

full employment. (1) A situation in which there is no unemployment attributable to insufficient aggregate demand; that is, where all unemployment is due to frictional or structural causes. (2) A situation where all who are able and willing to work can find jobs reasonably quickly. (p. 10)

full-employment budget (or high-employment budget). Full-employment government receipts (that is, the receipts which would be obtained with present tax rates if the economy were at full employment) minus full-employment government expenditures (that is, actual expenditures less expenditures directly associated with unemployment in excess of the full-employment level). *(p. 180)*

full-line forcing. See *tying contract.*

fundametal disequilibrium (in international economics). A term used but not defined in the articles of agreement of the International Monetary Fund. The general idea is that a fundamental disequilibrium exists when a long-lasting international payments imbalance cannot be eliminated without increasing trade restrictions or imposing unduly restrictive aggregate demand policies. *(p. 397)*

futures market. A market in which contracts are undertaken today at prices specified today for fulfilment at some specified future time. For example, someone selling a futures contract for wheat undertakes to deliver wheat at a specified future date (say, 3 months from today) at a price set now.

gain from trade. Increase in income that results from specialization and trade. (p. 325)

game theory. Theory dealing with conflict, in which alternative strategies are formally analyzed. Sometimes used in the analysis of oligopoly.

general equilibrium. Situation where all markets are in equilibrium simultaneously.

general equilibrium analysis. Analysis taking into account interactions among markets. (p. 56)

general gut. Occurs when excess supply is a general phenomenon. The quantity of goods and services which producers are willing to supply greatly exceeds the quantity buyers are willing and able to purchase. *(p. 143)*

general price level. Price level as measured by a broad average, such as the consumer price index or the GNP deflator.

Giffen good. A good whose demand curve slopes upward to the right. (The income effect is greater than, and opposite in sign to, the substitution effect.) (p. 161)

Gini coefficient. A measure of inequality derived from the Lorenz curve. It is the "bow" area (in Figure 23-1 on p. 471) between the curve and the diagonal line, divided by the entire area beneath the diagonal line. It can range from zero (if there is no inequality and the Lorenz curve corresponds to the diagonal line) to one (if there is complete inequality and the Lorenz curve runs along the horizontal axis).

GNP deflator. The index used to remove the effects of inflation from GNP data. *(p. 121)*

GNP gap. Amount by which actual GNP falls short of potential GNP. *(p. 353)*

gold certificate. Certificate issued by the U.S. Treasury to the Federal Reserve, backed 100 percent by Treasury gold holdings.

gold exchange standard. International system in which most countries keep their currencies pegged to, and convertible into, another currency which, in turn, is pegged to and convertible into gold. *(p. 401)*

gold point. An exchange rate at which an arbitrager can barely cover the costs of shipping, handling, and insuring gold.

gold standard. System in which the monetary unit is defined in terms of gold, the monetary authorites buy and sell gold freely at that price, and gold may be freely exported or imported. If central banks follow the "rule of the gold standard game," they allow changes in gold to be reflected in changes in the money stock. *(p. 236)*

gold sterilization. A gold flow is sterilized when the central bank takes steps to cancel out the automatic effects of the gold flow on the country's money supply (that is, when the "rule of the gold standard game" is broken). *(p. 395)*

good. Tangible commodity, such as wheat, a shirt, or an automobile. (p. 21)

graduated-payment mortgages. A mortgage on which the money payments rise as time passes. If the money payments rise rapidly enough to keep the real payments constant, then the mortgage is fully graduated. *(p. 309)*

Gresham's law. Crudely, "Bad money drives out good." More precisely: If there are two types of money whose values in exchange are equal while their values in another use (like consumption) are different, the more valuable item will be retained for its other use while the less valuable item will continue to circulate as money. (p. 36)

gross (private domestic) investment. Expenditures for new plant and equipment, plus the change in inventories. *(p. 130)*

gross national product (GNP). Personal consumption expenditures plus government purchases of goods and services plus gross private domestic investment plus net exports of goods and services. The total product of the nation, excluding double counting. *(p. 130)*

holding company. A company that holds a controlling interest in the stock of one or more other companies.

horizontal merger. See *merger*. (p. 266)

human capital. Education and training which make human beings more productive. (p. 417)

hyperinflation. Very rapid inflation. (p. 13)

identification problem. The difficulty of determining the effect of variable *a* alone on variable *b* when *b* can also be affected by variables *c, d,* etc. (p. 139)

impact lag. The time interval between policy changes and the time when the major effects of the policy changes occur. *(p. 339)*

imperfect competition. A market in which some buyer(s) or seller(s) are large enough to have a noticeable effect on price. (p. 241)

implicit (or imputed) cost. The opportunity cost of using an input that is already owned by the producer. (p. 171)

implicit tax In a welfare program, the benefits a family loses when it earns another $1 of income. (If its benefits are reduced by 46 cents, the implicit tax is 46 percent.) (p. 490)

import quota. A restriction on the quantity of a good that may be imported. (p. 345)

incidence of a tax. The amount of the tax ultimately paid by different individuals or groups. (For example, how much does a cigarette tax raise the price paid by buyers, and how much does it lower the net price received by sellers?) (p. 126)

income-consumption line. The line or curve traced out by the points of tangency between an indifference map and a series of parallel budget (income) lines. It shows how a consumer responds to a changing income when relative prices remain constant.

income effect. Change in the quantity of a good demanded as a result of a change in real income with no change in relative prices. (p. 161)

income elasticity of demand. See *elasticity of demand*. (p. 132)

income line. See *budget line*.

income statement. See *profit-and-loss statement*.

incomes policy. A government policy (such as wage-price guideposts or wage and price controls) aimed at restraining the rate of increase in money wages and other money incomes. The purpose is to reduce the rate of inflation. *(p. 275)*

incremental cost. The term which business executives frequently use instead of "marginal cost."

incremental revenue. The term which business executives frequently use instead of "marginal revenue."

index. A series of numbers, showing how an average (of prices, or wages, or some other economic measure) changes through time. Each of these numbers is called an index number. By convention, the index number for the base year is set at 100. *(p. 120)*

indexation. The inclusion in a contract or law of an automatic adjustment for inflation. A wage contract is *indexed (p. 320)* if it contains an *escalator clause* providing for an automatic increase in the wage in the event of a rise in the average level of prices (as measured, usually, by the consumer price index). The income tax is *indexed (p. 312)* if tax brackets, exemptions, and other provisions of the tax code automatically increase by the same proportion as the increase in the average level of prices.

indifference curve. A curve joining all points among which the consumer is indifferent. (p. 154)

indifference map. A series of indifference curves, each representing a different level of satisfaction or utility. (p. 156)

induced investment. Additional investment demand caused by an increase in national product. *(p. 160)*

industrial strategy. An attempt by the government to identify and subsidize the most promising industries for future development. *(p. 382)*

industrial union. A union open to all workers in an industry, regardless of their skill. (p. 385)

industry. The producers of a single good or service (or closely similar goods or services). (p. 46)

inelastic demand. Demand with an elasticity of less than one. See *elasticity of demand*. (p. 121)

infant-industry argument for protection. The proposition that new domestic industries with economies of scale or large requirements of human capital need protection from foreign producers until they can become established. (p. 343)

inferior good. A good for which the quantity demand declines as income rises, *ceteris paribus.* (p. 50)

inflation. A rise in the average level of prices. (p. 12)

inflationary gap. The vertical distance by which the aggregate demand line is above the 45 degree line at the full-employment national product. *(p. 171)*

inheritance tax. Tax imposed on property received from persons who have died.

injection. Spending for a GNP component other than consumption. *(p. 153)*

injunction. Court order to refrain from certain practices or requiring certain action. (p. 387)

innovation. A change in products or in the techniques of production.

inputs. Materials and services used in the process of production.

interest. Payment for the use of money. (p. 411)

interest rate. Interest as a percentage per annum of the amount borrowed.

interlocking directorate. Situation where one or more directors of a company sit on the boards of directors of one or more other companies that are competitors, suppliers, or customers of the first company. (p. 263)

intermediate product. A product which is used as an input in producing another good or service. *(p. 124)*

internal cost. A cost incurred by those who actually produce (or consume) a good. (p. 287)

internalization. A process that results in a firm or individual taking into account an external cost (or benefit) of its actions. (p. 288)

international adjustment mechanism. Any set of forces which tends to reduce surpluses or deficits in the balance of payments. *(p. 394)*

international liquidity. The total amount of international reserves (foreign exchange, SDRs, etc.) held by the various nations. *(p. 400)*

interstate gas. "Out-of-state" gas consumed in a different state from the one in which it is produced. In contrast, *intrastate gas* is consumed in the *same* state in which it is produced. (p. 461)

inventories. Stocks of raw materials, intermediate products, and finished goods held by producers or marketing organizations. *(p. 128)*

investment. Accumulation of capital. (p. 21) See also *gross investment, net investment.*

investment bank. A firm that merchandises common stocks, bonds, and other securities. (p. 106)

investment demand. (Also known as desired investment or planned investment.) This is the amount of new plant and equipment acquired during the year, plus additions to inventories which businesses wanted to acquire. Undesired inventory accumulation is excluded. (If undesired inventory accumulation is included, the result is *actual investment.*) *(p. 151)*

investment good. A capital good. Plant, equipment, or inventory.

invisible. An intangible; a service (as contrasted with a good).

"invisible hand." Adam Smith's phrase expressing the idea that the pursuit of self-interest by individuals will lead a desirable outcome for society as a whole. (p. 8)

iron law of wages. The view (commonly held in the nineteenth century) that the high human birthrate creates a tendency for the supply of labor to outrun the productive capacity of the economy and the demand for labor. As a consequence, it was an iron law of nature that wages would be driven down to the subsistence level. (Any excess population at that wage would die from starvation, pestilence, or war.) (p. 67)

jawbone. Persuade; attempt to persuade, perhaps using threats. *(p. 275)*

joint products. Products produced together. Example: meat and hides. (p. 53)

joint profit maximization. Formal or informal cooperation by oligopolists to pick the price that yields the most profit for the group. (p. 245)

jurisdictional dispute. Dispute between unions over whose workers will be permitted to perform a certain task. (p. 388)

key currency. A national currency commonly used by foreigners in international transactions and by foreign monetary authorites when intervening in exchange markets. Examples: the U.S. dollar, and, historically, the British pound. *(p. 400)*

Keynesian economics. The major macroeconomic propositions put forward by John Maynard Keynes in *The General Theory of Employment, Interest and Money* (1936): A market economy may reach an equilibrium with large-scale unemployment; steps to stimulate aggregate demand can cure a depression; and fiscal policies are the best way to control aggregate demand. Contrast with *classical economics. (p. 142)*

kinked demand curve. A demand curve which an oligopoly firm faces if its competitors follow any price cut it makes but do not follow any of its price increases. The kink in such a demand curve occurs at the existing price. (p. 250)

labor. The physical and mental contributions of people to production.

labor force. The number of people employed plus those actively seeking work. (p. 11)

labor-intensive product: A good whose production uses a relatively large quantity of labor and relatively small quantity of other resources.

labor participation rate. See *participation rate.*

labor productivity. The average amount produced in an hour of work. It is calculated by dividing output by the number of hours of labor input. *(p. 360)*

labor theory of value. Strictly, the proposition that the sole source of value is labor (including labor "congealed" in capital). Very loosely, the proposition that labor is the principal source of value. (p. 502)

labor union. See *union.*

Laffer curve. The curve tracing out the relationship between the tax rate and the total tax revenues of the government. Laffer put forward the proposition that tax rates had become so high that a decline in the rate of taxation would lead to an increase in government revenues. *(p. 383)*

laissez faire. Strictly translated, "let do." More loosely, "leave it alone." An expression used by the French physiocrats and later by Adam Smith, meaning the absence of government intervention in markets. (p. 8)

land. This term is used broadly by economists to include not only arable land but also the other gifts of nature (such as minerals) which come with the land. (p. 21)

law of diminishing marginal utility. As a consumer gets more and more of a good, the marginal utility of that good will (eventually) decrease. (p. 144)

law of diminishing returns. See *diminishing returns, law of eventually.*

leading indicator. A time series that reaches a turning point (peak or trough) before the economy as a whole. *(p. 356)*

leakage. (1) A withdrawal of potential spending from the circular flow of income and expenditures. *(p. 152)* (2) A withdrawal from the banking system that reduces the potential expansion of the money stock. (p. 214)

leakages-injections approach. The determination

of equilibrium national product by finding the size of national product at which leakages are equal to injections. *(p. 152)*

legal tender. An item that, by law, must be accepted in payment of a debt. *(p. 235)*

leverage. The ratio of debt to net worth. (p. 107)

liability. (1) What is owed. (p. 101) (2) The amount that can be lost by the owners of a business if that business goes bankrupt. (p. 94)

life-cycle hypothesis. The proposition that consumption depends on expected lifetime income (as contrasted with the early Keynesian view that consumption depends on current income).

limited liability. The amount an owner-shareholder of a corporation can lose in the event of bankruptcy. This is limited to the amount paid to purchase shares of the corporation. (p. 95)

line of credit. Commitment by a bank or other lender to stand ready to lend up to a specified amount to a customer on request. (p. 108)

liquid asset. An asset that can be sold on short notice, at a predictable price, with little cost or bother. (p. 201)

liquidity. Ease with which an asset can be sold on short notice, at a predictable price, with little cost. (p. 106)

liquidity preference. The demand for money (that is, the willingness to hold money) as a function of the interest rate. *(p. 252)*

liquidity preference theory of the interest rate. The theory put forward by J. M. Keynes that the interest rate is determined by the willingness to hold money (liquidity preference) and the supply of money (that is, the stock of money in existence). Contrast with *loanable funds theory of interest. (p. 251)*

liquidity trap. In Keynesian theory, the situation where individuals and businesses are willing to hold all their additional financial assets in the form of money—rather than bonds or other debt instruments—at the existing interest rate. In such circumstances, the creation of additional money by the central bank cannot depress the interest rate further, and monetary policy cannot be effectively used to stimulate aggregate demand. (All additional money created is caught in the liquidity trap and is held as idle balances.) In geometric terms, the liquidity trap exists where the liquidity preference curve is horizontal. See also *speculative demand for money. (p. 252)*

loanable funds theory of interest. The theory that

the interest rate is determined by the demand for and the supply of funds in the market for bonds and other forms of debt. Contrast with *the liquidity preference theory of interest.*

lockout. Temporary closing of a factory or other place of business in order to deprive workers of their jobs. A bargaining tool sometimes used in labor disputes; the employer's equivalent of a strike.

logarithmic (or log or ratio) scale. A scale in which equal proportional changes are shown as equal distances. For example, the distance from 100 to 200 is equal to the distance from 200 to 400. (Each involves a doubling.) (p. 110)

long run. (1) A period of time long enough for the quantity of capital to be adjusted to the desired level. *(p. 465)* (2) A period long enough for equilibrium to be reached. (3) Any extended period.

long-run Phillips curve. The curve (or line) traced out by the possible points of long-run equilibrium; that is, the points where people have adjusted completely to the prevailing rate of inflation. *(p. 283)*

long-run production function. A table showing various combinations of inputs and the maximum output which can be produced with each combination. For a simple firm with only two inputs (labor and capital), the production function can be shown by a two-dimensional table. (p. 175)

Lorenz curve. A curve showing cumulative percentages of income or wealth. For example, a point on a Lorenz curve might show the percentage of wealth owned by the poorest half of the families. (The percentage of wealth or income is shown on the vertical axis, and the percentage of families on the horizontal axis.) Such a curve can be used to measure inequality; if all families have the same wealth, the Lorenz curve traces out a diagonal line. See also *Gini coefficient.* (p. 482)

lump-sum tax. A tax of a constant amount. The revenues from such a tax do not change when income changes. *(p. 171)*

M-1. The narrowly defined money stock; currency (paper money plus coins) plus demand deposits held by the public (that is, excluding holdings by the federal government, the Federal Reserve, and commercial banks). Prior to 1980, the basic definition of money. Now known as M-1A. *(p. 199)*

M-1A. See *M-1*.

M-1B. Since 1980, the basic definition of money. Currency (paper money plus coins) plus checking deposits held by the public (that is, excluding holdings by the federal government, the Federal Reserve, and commercial banks). *(p. 199)*

M-2. The more broadly defined money stock; M-1B plus noncheckable savings deposits plus small time deposits. *(p. 200)*

M-3. An even more broadly defined money stock; M-2 plus large time deposits. *(p. 201)*

macroeconomics. The study of the overall aggregates of the economy (such as total employment, the unemployment rate, national product, and the rate of inflation). *(p. 117)*

Malthusian problem. The tendency for population to outstrip productive capacity, particularly the capacity to produce food. This is the supposed consequence of a tendency for population to grow geometrically (1, 2, 4, 8, etc.) while the means of subsistence grows arithmetically (1, 2, 3, 4, etc.). The pressure of population will tend to depress the wage rate to the subsistence level and keep it there, with the excess population being eliminated by war, pestilence, or starvation. A problem described by Thomas Malthus in his *Essay on the Principle of Population* (1798). (p. 65)

managed float. A dirty float. See *floating exchange rate.*

marginal. The term commonly used by economists to mean "additional." For example: *marginal cost* is the additional cost when one more unit is produced; *marginal revenue* is the addition to revenue when one more unit is sold.

marginal cost pricing. Setting price at the level where MC intersects the demand curve. (p. 226)

marginal efficiency of investment. The schedule or curve relating desired investment to the rate of interest. *(p. 250)*

marginal physical product. The additional output when one more unit of an input is used (with all other inputs being held constant). For example, the ***marginal physical product of labor*** (often abbreviated to the *marginal product of labor*) is the additional output when one more unit of labor is used. (p. 363)

marginal productivity. The dollar value of the marginal physical product of an input. (p. 363)

marginal propensity to consume (MPC). The change in consumption expenditures divided by the change in disposable income. *(p. 149)*

marginal propensity to import. The change in imports of goods and services divided by the change in GNP.

marginal propensity to save (MPS). The change in saving divided by the change in disposable income. 1 − MPC. *(p. 150)*

marginal rate of substitution. The slope of the indifference curve. The ratio of the marginal utility of one good to the marginal utility of another. (p. 155)

marginal revenue product. The additional revenue when the firm uses one additional unit of an input (with all other inputs being held constant). (p. 364)

marginal tax rate. The fraction of additional income paid in taxes. *(p. 175)*

marginal utility. The satisfaction an individual receives from consuming one additional unit of a good or service. (p. 144)

margin call. The requirement by a lender who holds stocks (or bonds) as security that more money be put up or they will be sold. A margin call may be issued when the price of the stocks (or bonds) declines, making the stocks (or bonds) less adequate as security for the loan. *(p. 230)*

margin requirement. The minimum percentage which purchasers of stocks or bonds must put up in their own money. For example, if the margin requirement on stock is 60 percent, the buyer must put up at least 60 percent of the price in his or her own money and can borrow no more than 40 percent from a bank or stockbroker. *(p. 230)*

market. An institution in which purchases and sales are made. (p. 45)

market economy. See *free-market economy.*

market failure. The failure of market forces to bring about the best allocation of resources. For example, when production of a good generates pollution, too many resources tend to go into the production of that good and not enough into the production of alternative goods and services.

market mechanism. The system whereby prices and the interaction of demand and supply help to answer the major economic questions "What will be produced?" "How?" and "For whom?" (p. 45)

market power. The ability of a single firm or individual to influence the market price of a good or service. (p. 217)

market share. Percentage of an industry's sales accounted for by a single firm.

market structure. Characteristics which affect the behavior of firms in a market, such as the number of firms, the possibility of collusion, the degree of product differentiation, and the ease of entry.

Marxist economy. One in which most of the capital is owned by the government. (Individuals may of course own small capital goods, such as hoes or hammers, but the major forms of capital—factories and heavy machinery—are owned by the state.) Political power is in the hands of a party pledging allegiance to the doctrines of Karl Marx. (p. 44)

measure of economic welfare (MEW). A comprehensive measure of economic well-being. Per capita real national product is adjusted to take into account leisure, pollution, and other such nonmonetary influences on welfare. *(p. 134)*

median. The item in the middle (that is, half of all items are above the median and half are below).

medium of exchange. Money; any item that is generally acceptable in exchange for goods or services; any item that is commonly used in buying goods or services. (p. 35)

member bank. A commercial bank that belongs to the Federal Reserve System. *(p. 206)*

mercantilism. The theory that national prosperity can be promoted by a positive balance of trade and the accumulation of precious metals.

merchandise account surplus. The excess of merchandise exports over merchandise imports. *(p. 414)*

merger. The bringing together of two or more firms under common control through purchase, exchange of common stock, or other means. A *horizontal merger* brings together competing firms. A *vertical merger* brings together firms which are each others' suppliers or customers. A *conglomerate merger* brings together firms which are not related in either of these ways. (p. 266)

merit good. A good or service which the government considers particularly desirable and which it therefore encourages by subsidy or regulation (such as the regulation that children must go to school to get the merit good, education). (p. 84)

microeconomics. The study of individual units within the economy (such as households, firms, and industries) and their interrelationships. The study of the allocation of resources and the distribution of income. *(p. 417)*

military-industrial complex. A loose term referring to the combined political power exerted by military officers and defense industries; those with a vested interest in military spending. (In his farewell address, President Eisenhower warned against the military-industrial complex.)

minimum wage. The lowest wage that an employer may legally pay for an hour's work. (p. 367)

mint parity. The exchange rate calculated from the official prices of gold in two countries under the gold standard.

mixed economy. An economy in which the private market and the government share the decisions as to what shall be produced, how, and for whom. (p. 44)

model. The essential features of an economy or economic problem, explained in terms of diagrams, equations, or words—or some combination of these.

monetarism. A body of thought which has its roots in classical economics and which rejects much of the teaching of Keynes' *General Theory.* According to monetarists, the most important determinant of aggregate demand is the quantity of money; the economy is basically stable if monetary growth is stable; and the authorities should follow a monetary rule, increasing the money stock at a steady rate. Many monetarists also believe that the effects of fiscal policy on aggregate demand are weak (unless accompanied by changes in the quantity of money), that the government plays too active a role in the economy, and that the long-run Phillips curve is vertical. (The most famous monetarist is Milton Friedman, a retired University of Chicago professor.) (p. 256)

monetary base. Currency held by the general public, and commercial banks, and other depository institutions, plus the deposits of financial institutions in the Federal Reserve. (p. 215)

monetary policy. Central bank policies aimed at changing the quantity of money or credit conditions; for example, open market operations or changes in required reserve ratios. (p. 118)

monetary rule. The rule, proposed by monetarists, that the central bank should aim for a steady rate of growth of the money stock. (p. 365)

money. Any item commonly used in buying goods or services. Frequently, M-1 or M-1B. (p. 198)

money illusion. Strictly defined, people have money illusion if their behavior changes in the event of a proportional change in prices, money incomes, and assets and liabilities measured in money terms. More loosely, people have money illusion if their behavior changes when there is a proportional change in prices and money incomes. (p. 283)

money income. Income measured in dollars (or, in another country, income measured in the currency of that country).

money market. The market for short-term debt instruments (such as Treasury bills).

money multiplier. The number of dollars by which the money stock can increase as a result of a $1 increase in the reserves of depository institutions. (p. 213)

money stock (or supply). Narrowly, M-1 or M-1B. More broadly and less commonly, M-2 or M-3. (p. 198)

monopolistic competition. A market structure with many firms selling a differentiated product, with low barriers to entry. (p. 255)

monopoly. (1) A market in which there is only a single seller. (2) The single seller in such a market. A *natural monopoly* occurs when the average total cost of a single firm falls over such an extended range that one firm can produce the total quantity sold at a lower average cost than could two or more firms. (p. 46)

monopsony. A market in which there is only one buyer. (p. 69)

moral suasion. Appeals or pressure by the Federal Reserve intended to influence the behavior of commercial banks or other financial institutions. (p. 231)

most-favored-nation clause. A clause in a trade agreement which commits a country to impose no greater barriers (tariffs, etc.) on imports from the agreement country than it imposes on imports from any other country.

multinational corporation. A corporation that carries on business in more than one country. (p. 347)

multiplier. The change in equilibrium national product divided by the change in investment demand (or in government expenditures, tax collections, or exports). In the simplest economy (with a marginal tax rate of zero and no imports), the multiplier is 1 ÷ the marginal propensity to save. (p. 158)

municipals. Bonds issued by local governments.

national bank. A commercial bank chartered by the national government. (p. 204)

national debt. (1) The outstanding federal government debt. (2) The outstanding federal government debt excluding that held by federal government trust funds. (3) The outstanding federal government debt excluding that held by federal government trust funds and the 12 Federal Reserve Banks. (p. 185)

national income. The return to all factors of production owned by the residents of a nation. (p. 132)

national product. See *gross national product* and *net national product.*

natural monopoly. See *monopoly.*

natural oligopoly. See *oligopoly.*

natural rate of unemployment. The equilibrium rate of unemployment. The rate of unemployment to which the economy tends when those making labor and other contracts correctly anticipate the rate of inflation. The rate of unemployment consistent with a stable rate of inflation. *(p. 283)*

near-money. A highly liquid asset that can be quickly and easily converted into money. Example: a Treasury bill. *(p. 201)*

negative income tax. A reverse income tax, involving government payments to individuals and families with low incomes. (The lower the income, the greater the payment from the government.) (p. 495)

negotiable order of withdrawal (NOW). A check-like order to pay funds from an interest-bearing savings deposit. *(p. 199)*

neocolonialism. The domination of the economy of a nation by the business firms or government of another nation or nations.

net exports. Exports minus imports. *(p. 129)*

net (private domestic) investment. Gross (private domestic) investment minus depreciation. *(p. 130)*

net national product (NNP). Personal consumption expenditures plus government purchases of goods and services plus net private domestic investment plus net exports of goods and services. GNP minus depreciation. *(p. 130)*

net worth. Total assets less total liabilities. (p. 102)

neutrality of money. Money is neutral if a change in the quantity of money affects only the price level without affecting relative prices or the distribution of income.

neutrality of taxes. See *tax neutrality.*

New Left. Radical economists; Marxists of the past two decades.

nominal. Measured in money terms. Current dollar as contrasted to constant-dollar or real. *(p. 120)*

noncompeting groups. Groups of workers that do not compete with each other for jobs because their training or skills are different.

nonprice competition. Competition by means other than price; for example, advertising or product differentiation. (p. 252)

nontariff barrier. Impediment to trade other than tariffs. Example: import quota. (p. 345)

normal good. A good for which the quantity demanded rises as income rises, *ceteris paribus.* Contrast with an *inferior good.* (p. 161)

normal profit. The opportunity cost of capital and/or entrepreneurship. (Normal profit is considered a cost by economists but not by business accountants.) (p. 173)

normative statement. A statement about what should be. Contrast with a positive statement. (p. 29)

NOW account. A savings account against which a negotiable order of withdrawal may be written. *(p. 199)*

official settlements surplus. The net acquisition of international reserves. (A country has such a surplus if its international reserves are increasing more rapidly than foreign countries' reserve claims on it.) *(p. 413)*

Okun's law. The observation that a 3 percent change in real GNP (compared with its long-run trend) has been associated with a 1 percent change in the opposite direction in the unemployment rate. (Named after Arthur M. Okun.)

old age, survivors, and disability insurance. Social security.

oligopoly. A market in which there are only a few sellers who sell either a standarized or differentiated product. A *natural oligopoly* occurs when the average total costs of individual firms fall over a large enough range that a few firms can produce the total quantity sold at the lowest average cost. (Compare with *natural monopoly.*) (p. 241)

oligopsony. A market in which there are only a few buyers.

open economy. An economy which has transactions with foreign nations.

open-market operation. The purchase (or sale) of government (or other) securities by the central bank on the open market (that is, not directly from the issuer of the security). *(p. 222)*

open shop. A business that may hire workers who are not (and need not become) union members. Contrast with *closed shop* and *union shop.* (p. 389)

opportunity cost. The amount that an input could earn in its best alternative use. The alternative that must be foregone when something is produced. (pp. 23, 172)

output gap. The amount by which output falls short of the potential or full-employment level. The recessionary gap times the multiplier. The GNP gap. *(p. 169)*

panic. A rush for safety, historically marked by a switch out of bank deposits into currency and out of paper currency into gold. *(p. 203)* A *stock-market panic* occurs when there is a rush to sell and stock prices collapse. (p. 110)

paradox of thrift. The paradoxical situation, pointed

out by Keynes, where an increase in the desire to save can result in a decrease in the equilibrium quantity of saving. *(p. 160)*

paradox of value. The apparent contradiction, pointed out by Adam Smith, when an essential (such as water) has a low price while a nonessential (such as a diamond) has a high price. (p. 200)

Pareto improvement. Making one person better off without making anyone else worse off. (Named after Vilfredo Pareto, 1848–1923.) (p. 198)

Pareto optimum. A situation where it is impossible to make any Pareto improvement. That is, it is impossible to make any individual better off without making someone else worse off. (p. 198)

parity price. The price of a farm product (such as wheat) that would allow a farmer to exchange it for the same quantity of nonfarm goods as in the 1910–1914 base period. (A concept of fair price used in American agricultural policy since the Agricultural Adjustment Act of 1933.) (p. 134)

partial equilibrium analysis. Analysis of a particular market or set of markets, ignoring feedbacks from other markets.

participation rate. Number of people in the civilian labor force as a percentage of the civilian population of working age. (p. 382)

partnership. An unincorporated business owned by two or more people. (p. 94)

par value of a currency. Up to 1971, under the IMF adjustable peg system, the par value was the official price of a currency specified in terms of the U.S. dollar or gold. *(p. 396)*

patent. Exclusive right, granted by the government to an inventor, to use an invention for a specified time period. (Such a right can be licensed or sold by the patent holder.) (p. 214)

payroll tax. A tax levied on wages and salaries, or on wages and salaries up to a specified limit. Example: social security tax.

peak. The month of greatest economic activity prior to the onset of a recession; one of the four phases of the business cycle. *(p. 326)*

peak-load pricing. Setting the price for a good or service higher during periods of heavy demand than at other times. The purpose is to encourage buyers to choose nonpeak periods and/or to raise more revenue. Examples: electricity, weekend ski tow.

pegged. Fixed by the authorities, at least temporarily. Examples: pegged interest rates (1941–1951), pegged exchange rates (1945–1973).

perfect competition. A market for a standardized product, in which there are many buyers and many sellers, with no single buyer or seller having any (noticeable) influence over price. That is, every buyer and every seller is a *price taker*. There are no impediments to entry (such as government licensing). (p. 179)

permanent income. Normal income; income that is thought to be normal. *(p. 196)*

permanent-income hypothesis. The proposition that the principal determinant of consumption is permanent income (rather than current income). *(p. 196)*

perpetuity (or "perp"). A bond with no maturity date that pays interest forever. *(p. 226)*

personal consumption expenditures. See *consumption.*

personal income. Income received by households in return for productive services and from transfers, prior to the payment of personal taxes. *(p. 132)*

personal saving. Loosely but commonly, disposable personal income less consumption expenditures. More strictly, disposable personal income less consumption expenditures less payment of interest on consumer debt. *(p. 131)*

petrodollars. Liquid U.S. dollar assets resulting from payments for oil received by the members of the Organization for Petroleum Exporting Countries (OPEC).

Phillips curve. The curve tracing out the relationship between the unemployment rate (on the horizontal axis) and the inflation rate or the rate of change of money wages (on the vertical axis). *(p. 270)* **Long-run Phillips curve.** The curve (or line) tracing out the relationship between the unemployment rate and the inflation rate when the inflation rate is correctly anticipated. *(p. 283)*

planned investment. Desired investment; investment demand; ex ante investment. *(p. 152)*

plant. A physical establishment where production takes place.

policy dilemma. This occurs when a policy that helps to solve one problem makes another worse. *(p. 272)*

political business cycle. A business cycle caused by actions taken to increase politicians' chances of reelection. *(p. 341)*

positive statement. A statement about what is (or was) or about how something works. Contrast with a *normative statement.* (p. 29)

poverty. Exists when people have inadequate income to buy the necessities of life. (p. 15)

poverty level (or poverty standard). An estimate of the income needed to avoid poverty. In

1981 it was $8,500 for an urban family of four. (p. 15)

precautionary demand for money. The amount of money that households and businesses want to hold to protect themselves against unforeseen events.

preferred stock. A stock that is given preference over common stock when dividends are paid. That is, specified dividends must be paid on preferred stock before any dividend is paid on common stock. (p. 100)

present value. The value now of a future receipt or receipts, calculated using the interest rate, i. The present value (PV) of $X to be received n years hence is $X \div (1 + i)^n$. *(p. 226)*

price ceiling. The legally established maximum price.

price discrimination. The sale of the same good or service at different prices to different customers or in different markets, provided the price differences are not justified by cost differences, such as differences in transportation costs. (p. 231)

price-earnings ratio. The ratio of the price of a stock to the annual (after-tax) earnings per share of the stock.

price elasticity of demand (supply). See *elasticity of demand (supply)*.

price floor. (1) The price at which the government undertakes to buy all surpluses, thus preventing any further decline in price. (p. 207) (2) The legally established minimum price.

price index. A weighted average of prices, as a percentage of prices existing in a base year. *(p. 122)*

price leadership. A method by which oligopolistic firms establish similar prices without overt collusion. One firm (the price leader) announces a new price, expecting that the other firms will quickly follow. (p. 252)

price line. See *budget line*.

price maker. A monopolist (or monopsonist) who is able to set price because there are no competitors. (p. 244)

price mechanism. See *market mechanism*.

price parity. See *parity price*.

price searcher. A seller (or buyer) who is able to influence price, but who also has competitors. An oligopolist. (p. 244)

price support. A commitment by the government to buy surpluses at a given price (the support price) in order to prevent the price from falling below that figure. (p. 207)

price system. See *market mechanism*.

price taker. A seller or buyer who is unable to affect the price and whose market decision is limited to the quantity to be sold or bought at the existing market price. A seller or buyer in perfect competition. (p. 244)

price-wage flexibility. The ease with which prices and wages rise or fall (especially fall) in the event of changing demand and supply. *(p. 142)*

prime rate of interest. (1) A bank's publicly announced interest rate for short-term loans. (2) Traditionally, the interest rate charged by banks on loans to their most credit-worthy customers. *(p. 225)*

procyclical policy. A policy that increases the amplitude of business fluctuations. ("Procyclical" refers to results, not intentions.) *(p. 335)*

producer surplus. Net benefit that producers get from being able to sell a good at the existing price. Returns to capital and entrepreneurship in excess of their opportunity costs. Rents on capital and entrepreneurship. Approximated by the area left of the supply curve between the breakeven price and the existing price. (p. 182)

product differentiation. See *differentiated products*.

production function. The relationship showing the maximum output that can be produced with various combinations of inputs. (p. 175)

production possibilities curve. A curve showing the alternative combinations of outputs that can be produced if all productive resources are used. The boundary of attainable combinations of outputs. (p. 23)

productivity. Output per unit of input.

profit. In economics, return to capital and/or entrepreneurship over and above normal profit. (p. 174) In business accounting, revenues minus costs. (Also sometimes used to mean profit after the payment of corporate income taxes.)

profit-and-loss statement. An accounting statement that summarizes a firm's revenues, costs, and income taxes over a given period of time (usually a year). An income statement. (p. 101)

progressive tax. A tax that takes a larger percentage of income as income rises. (p. 77)

proletariat. Karl Marx' term for the working class, especially the industrial working class.

proportional tax. A tax that takes the same percentage of income regardless of the level of income. (p. 77)

proprietors' income. The income of unincorporated firms. *(p. 132n)*

prospectus. A statement of the financial condition and prospects of a corporation, presented when new securities are about to be issued. (p. 111)

protective tariff. A tariff intended to protect domestic producers from foreign competition (as contrasted with a revenue tariff, intended as a source of revenue for the government).

protectionism. The advocacy or use of high or higher tariffs to protect domestic producers from foreign competition.

proxy. A temporary written transfer of voting rights at a shareholders' meeting. (p. 98)

proxy fight. A struggle between competing groups in a corporation to obtain a majority vote (and therefore control of the corporation) by collecting proxies of shareholders.

public debt. See *national debt.*

public good. A good (or service) with benefits that people cannot be excluded from enjoying, regardless of who pays for the good. (p. 306)

public utility. A firm that is the sole supplier of an essential good or service in an area and is regulated by the government. (p. 239)

pump priming. Short-term increases in government expenditures aimed at generating an upward momentum of the economy toward full employment.

purchasing power of money. The value of money in buying goods and services; 1 ÷ the price index.

purchasing power parity theory. The theory that changes in exchange rates reflect and compensate for differences in the rate of inflation in different countries.

qualitative controls. In monetary policy, controls that affect the supply of funds to specific markets, or the credit conditions in specific markets. *(p. 229)*

quantitative controls. In monetary policy, controls that affect the total supply of funds and the total quantity of money in an economy. *(p. 229)*

quantity theory (of money). The proposition that velocity is reasonably stable and that total spending therefore will be strongly influenced by changes in the quantity of money. *(p. 256)*

quota. A numerical limit. For example, a limit on the amount of a good that may be imported. *(p. 391)*

random sample. A sample chosen from a larger group in such a way that every member of the group has an equal chance of being chosen.

rate base. Allowable capital of a public utility, to which the regulatory agency applies the allowable rate of return. (p. 239)

rate of exchange. The price of one national currency in terms of another. *(p. 390)*

rate of interest. Interest as a percentage per annum of the amount borrowed.

rate of return. (1) Annual profit as a percent of net worth. (2) Additional annual revenue from the sale of goods or services produced by plant or equipment, less depreciation and operating costs such as labor and materials, expressed as a percent of the depreciated value of the plant or equipment. *(p. 249)*

rational expectations. Expectations based on available information, including information about the policies being pursued by the authorities. Expectations are rational if they are unbiased, given available information. (In simple terms, people do not consistently make the same mistake.) *(p. 362)*

rationing. (1) A method for allocating the right to acquire a good (or service) when the quantity demanded exceeds the quantity supplied at the existing price. (2) More loosely, any method for allocating a scarce resource or good. In this sense, we may speak of the market *rationing by price.*

ratio scale See *logarithmic scale.*

real. Measured in quantity terms; adjusted to remove the effects of inflation. *(p. 120)*

real capital. Buildings, equipment, and other materials used in production, which have themselves been produced in the past. Plant, equipment, and inventories.

real rate of interest. (1) The rate of interest less the expected rate of inflation. *(p. 305)* (2) The rate of interest less the rate of inflation.

real wage. The quantity of goods and services that a money wage will buy; the money wage adjusted for inflation. *(pp. 274, 363)*

real wage insurance. A government guarantee of a real wage, which may be given (for example) in return for labor's agreement to a wage guidepost. If inflation erodes the real wage below the guaranteed level, the goverment compensates workers (for example, by reducing their taxes). *(p. 291)*

recession. A cyclical downward movement in the economy, as identified by the National Bureau of Economic Research. *(p. 326)*

recessionary gap. The vertical distance by which the aggregate demand line is below the 45 degree line at the full-employment national product. *(p. 169)*

recognition lag. The time interval between the beginning of a problem and the time when the problem is recognized. *(p. 339)*

regression analysis. A statistical calculation of the relationship between two or more variables.

regressive tax. A tax that takes a smaller percentage of income as income rises. (p. 77)

regulation Q. A limit on interest rates that commercial banks may pay on deposits.

rent. (1) in economics, any payment to a factor of production in excess of its opportunity cost. (p. 424) Other common definitions: (2) The return to the owners of land. (3) Payments by users to the owners of land, buildings, or equipment.

replacement-cost depreciation. Depreciation based on the current replacement costs of buildings and equipment rather than their original actual acquisition costs. *(p. 317)*

required reserves. The reserves that a bank or other financial institution legally must keep. Reserves are held in the form of currency or deposits with a Federal Reserve Bank. *(p. 204)*

required reserve ratio. The fraction of deposit liabilities that a bank must keep in reserves. *(p. 204)*

reservation price of a resource. The cost of harvesting the resource today plus the amount necessary to compensate for the reduction in the quantity of the resource available in the future. (p. 434)

restrictive agreement. Agreement among companies to restrain competition through practices such as price fixing or market sharing.

retail price maintenance. Practice whereby a manufacturer sets the minimum retail price of a product, thereby eliminating price competition among retailers of that product. (p. 265)

return to capital. See *rate of return.*

revaluation of a currency. An increase in the par value of the currency. *(p. 397)*

revenue sharing. Grant by the federal government to a state or local government. *General revenue sharing* involves grants whose use is (practically) unrestricted. (p. 80)

revenue tariff. See *protective tariff.*

right-to-work law. State law making it illegal to require union membership as a condition of employment. State prohibition of closed shops and union shops. (p. 389)

risk premium. The additional interest or yield to compensate the holder of bonds (or other securities) for risk. (p. 108)

roundabout production. The production of capital goods and the use of these capital goods in the production of consumer goods. The production of goods in more than one stage. (p. 413)

rule of the gold standard game. The understanding that each country would permit its money stock to change in the same direction as the change in its gold stock. That is, if a country's gold stock were to rise, it should allow its money supply to increase, and vice versa. *(p. 394)*

rule of 70. A rule that tells approximately how many years it will take for something to double in size if it is growing at a compound rate. For example, a deposit earning 2 percent interest approximately doubles in $70 \div 2 = 35$ years. In general, a deposit earning x percent interest will double in about $70 \div x$ years.

satisficing theory. The theory that firms do not try to maximize profits but rather aim for reasonable target levels of profits, sales, and other measures of performance.

saving. See *personal saving.*

saving function. (1) The relationship between personal saving and disposable income. (2) More broadly, the relationship between personal saving and the factors (like disposable income and family size) that determine saving. *(p. 149)*

Say's law. The discredited view that supply in the aggregate creates its own demand (regardless of the general price level). *(p. 167)*

SDRs. See *special drawing rights.*

seasonal adjustment. The removal of regular seasonal movements from a time series. *(p. 327)*

secondary boycott. Boycott against a firm to discourage it from doing business with a second firm, in order to exert pressure on the second firm (which may be in a strong position to withstand other forms of pressure).

secondary reserves. Bank holdings of liquid assets (Treasury bills, etc.) that can readily be converted into primary reserves (currency or reserve deposits).

second best, theory of the. The theory of how to get the best results in remaining markets when one or more markets have defects about which nothing can be done. (p. 225)

secular stagnation. A situation of inadequate aggregate demand extending over many years. Consequently, large-scale unemployment persists, and it may even become increasingly severe. *(p. 191)*

secular trend. The trend in economic activity over an extended period of many years.

selective controls. See *qualitative controls.*

sell short. See *short sale.*

seniority rules. Rules giving preference to those who have been longest on the job. Individuals with seniority are typically the last to be discharged or laid off, and the first to be rehired. (p. 385)

shared-appreciation mortgage. A mortgage on which the borrower is committed to pay the lender a fraction of the appreciation of the property on which the loan is made. *(p. 319)*

shortage. (1) The amount by which quantity supplied is less than quantity demanded at the existing price; the opposite of a surplus. (p. 49) (2) Any deficiency.

short run. (1) The period in which the quantity of plant and equipment cannot change. (2) The period in which the quantity of plant cannot change. (3) The time period taken to move to equilibrium. (4) Any brief time period.

short-run production function. The relationship between the amount of variable factors used and the amount of output that can be produced, in a situation where the quantity of capital is constant. For the simple case of a firm with just two inputs—capital and one variable factor—the short-run production function is one row in the long-run production function. (p. 164)

short sale. A contract to sell something at a later date for a price specified now.

single-tax proposal. The proposal of Henry George (1839–1897) that all taxes be eliminated except one on land. (George argued that all returns to land represent an unearned surplus.) (p. 430)

snake. An agreement among some Western European countries to keep their currencies within a narrow band of fluctuation (the snake). Prior to 1973, they restrained their currencies jointly within in a wider band with respect to the dollar. (This was called the *snake in the tunnel.*)

socialism. An economic system in which the means of production (capital equipment, buildings, and land) are owned by the state. (p. 503)

soil bank program. A government program under which the government pays farmers to take land out of production in order to reduce crop surpluses.

South. See *third world.*

special drawing rights (SDRs). Bookkeeping accounts created by the International Monetary Fund to increase the quantity of international reserves held by national governments. SDRs can be used to cover balance-of-payments deficits. *(p. 401)*

speculation. The purchase (or sale) of an asset in the hope of making a profit from a rise (fall) in its price. (p. 203)

speculative demand for money. The schedule or curve showing how the rate of interest affects the amount of assets that firms and households are willing to hold in the form of money (rather than in bonds or other interest-bearing securities). A key concept in the Keynesian theory of unemployment equilibrium. See also *liquidity trap. (p. 248)*

speculator. Anyone who buys or sells an asset in the hope of profiting from a change in its price. *(p. 398)*

spillover. See *externality.*

stagflation. The coexistence of a high rate of unemployment (stagnation) and inflation. *(p. 271)*

standard of value. The item (money) in which the prices of goods and services are measured. *(p. 198)*

state bank. A commercial bank chartered by a state government. *(p. 206)*

sterilization of gold. See *gold sterilization. (p. 395)*

store of value. An asset that may be used to store wealth through time; an asset that may be used to finance future purchases. *(p. 198)*

structural unemployment. Unemployment due to a mismatch between the skills or location of the labor force and the skills or location required by employers. Unemployment due to a changing location or composition of jobs. *(p. 268)*

subsidy. A negative tax.

subsistence wage. Minimum living wage. A wage below which population will decline because of starvation or disease. (p. 67)

substitute. A good or service that satisfies similar needs. Two commodities are substitutes if a rise in the price of one causes a rightward shift in the demand curve for the other. (p. 51)

substitution effect. The change in the quantity of a good demanded because of a change in its price when the real income *effect* of the change in price has been eliminated. That is, a change in the quantity demanded as a result of a movement along a single indifference curve. See also *income effect.* (p. 161)

sunspot theory. The theory put forward in the late nineteenth century that cycles in sunspot activity cause cycles in agricultural production and hence cycles in business activity.

superior good. A good whose quantity demanded rises when incomes rise. A *normal good.* (p. 50)

supply. The schedule or curve showing how the price of a good or service influences the quantity supplied, *ceteris paribus.* (p. 48)

supply of money. See *money stock.*

supply shift. A movement of the supply curve of a good (or service) to the right or left as a result of a change in the price of inputs or any other determinant of the quantity supplied (except the price of the good or service itself). (p. 52)

supply shifter. Anything that affects the quantity of a good or service supplied except its own price. (p. 52)

supply-side economics. The view that supply factors—such as the quantity of capital and the willingness to work—are the principal constraints to growth. (According to this view, a lack of aggregate demand is not the main constraint.) *(p. 381)*

surplus. (1) The amount by which quantity supplied exceeds quantity demanded at the existing price. (2) Any excess or amount left over. Contrast with *shortage.* (p. 49)

surplus value. In Marxist economics, the amount by which the value of a worker's output exceeds the wage; the share of output appropriated by capitalists. (p. 503)

sustainable yield. The amount of a renewable resource (like fish) that can be harvested while still leaving the population constant. (p. 439)

sympathy strike. A strike by a union that does not have a dispute with its own employer but rather is trying to strengthen the bargaining position of another striking union.

syndicate. An association of investment bankers to market a large block of securities. (p. 106)

tacit collusion. The adoption of a common policy by sellers without explicit agreement. (p. 253)

target price. Agricultural price guaranteed to farmers by the government. (If the market price falls short of the target price, the government pays farmers the difference.) (p. 206)

tariff. A tax on an imported good. (p. 8)

tax-based incomes policy (TIP). An incomes policy reinforced by tax penalties on violators or tax incentives for those who cooperate. *(p. 291)*

tax incidence. See *incidence of a tax.*

tax neutrality. (1) A situation where taxes do not affect relative prices. (2) A situation where the excess burden of taxes is zero.

tax shifting. This occurs when the initial taxpayer transfers all or part of a tax to others. (For example, a firm that is taxed may charge a higher price.) (p. 126)

technical efficiency. Providing the maximum output with the available resources and technology, while working at a reasonable pace. The avoidance of wasted motion and sloppy management. (p. 196)

terms of trade. The average price of goods sold divided by the average price of goods bought.

theory of games. See *game theory.*

theory of public choice. Theory of how government spending decisions are made and how they should be made.

third world. Countries that are neither in the "first" world (the high-income countries of Western Europe and North America, plus a few others such as Japan) nor in the "second" world (China and the countries of Eastern Europe). Low and middle-income countries other than those run by Communist parties. Also sometimes known as the *South* (in contrast to the industrial *North.*)

time preference. The desire to have goods now rather than in the future. The amount by which goods now are preferred over goods in the future.

time series. A set of observations taken in successive time periods. For example, GNP in 1979, in 1980, in 1981, etc.

TIP. See *tax-based incomes policy.*

total cost. The sum of fixed costs and variable costs. (p. 165)

total revenue. Total receipts from the sale of a product. Price times the quantity sold. (p. 168)

transactions demand for money. The amount of money that firms and individuals want to cover the time between the receipt of income and the making of expenditures. *(p. 247)*

transfer payment. A payment, usually made by the government to private individuals, that is not a payment for current productive activity. (p. 75)

Treasury bill. A short-term (less than a year, often for 3 months) debt obligation of the U.S. Treasury. It carries no explicit interest payment; a purchaser gains by buying a bill for less than its face value. *(p. 224)*

trough. The month of lowest economic activity prior to the beginning of a recovery; one of the four phases of the business cycle. *(p. 326)*

turnover tax. A tax on goods or services (whether they are intermediate or final products) whenever they are sold.

tying contract. Contract which requires the purchaser to buy another item or items in a seller's line of products in order to get the one that is really wanted. (p. 263)

underwrite. Guarantee by an investment banker that the whole new issue of stock will be sold. (An investment banker unable to sell all the underwritten stock must buy the remainder.) (p. 106)

undistributed corporate profits. After-tax corporate profits less dividends paid. *(p. 132)*

unemployment. The inability of people who are willing and able to work to find jobs. More generally, the underuse of any resource. (p. 10)

unemployment rate. The percentage of the labor force unemployed. (p. 11)

union. An association of workers, formed to negotiate over wages, fringe benefits, and working conditions. (p. 384)

union shop. A business where all nonunion workers must join the union within a brief period of their employment. Compare with *closed shop* and *right-to-work law.* (p. 389)

unit elasticity. Elasticity of one. If a demand curve has unit elasticity, total revenue remains unchanged as price changes. (p. 122) A straight-line supply curve with unit elasticity will, if extended, go through the origin. (p. 123)

unlimited liability. Responsibility for debts without limit. (p. 94)

value added. Value of the product sold less the cost of intermediate inputs bought from other firms. *(p. 126)*

variable-rate mortgage. A mortgage whose interest rate is periodically adjusted in response to changes in the market interest rate. *(p. 319)*

variable costs. Any costs that increase as output increases. (p. 165)

velocity of money. The average number of times per year that the average dollar in the money stock is spent. There are two principal ways of calculating velocity. (1) *Income velocity* is the number of times the average dollar is spent on final products (that is,

GNP ÷ M). (2) *Transaction velocity* is the number of times the average dollar is spent on *any* transaction (including those for intermediate goods and financial assets). That is, total spending ÷ M. *(p. 255)*

vertical merger. See *merger.*

workable competitition. A compromise that limits monopoly power while allowing firms to become big enough to reap the economies of scale. A practical alternative to the often unattainable goal of perfect competition. (p. 266)

yellow-dog contract. Contract in which an employee agrees not to become a member of a union. (p. 386)

yield. Of a bond, the discount rate at which the present value of coupon payments plus the repayment of principal equals the current price of the bond. *(p. 226)* Of real capital, see *rate of return.*

zero-base budgeting. A budgeting technique that requires items to be justified anew "from the ground up," without regard to how much has been spent on them in the past.

Photo Credits

Index